# THE CORIOLIS GROUP'S
# ZEN
## OF
# WINDOWS 95
### PROGRAMMING

# THE CORIOLIS GROUP'S ZEN OF WINDOWS 95 PROGRAMMING

## Lou Grinzo

CORIOLIS GROUP BOOKS

| | |
|---|---|
| **Publisher** | Keith Weiskamp |
| **Interior Design** | Bradley Grannis |
| **Cover Design** | Anthony Stock |
| **Layout Production** | Rob Mauhar and Jenni Aloi |
| **Editor** | Ron Pronk |
| **Proofreader** | Elizabeth Friedel |

Distributed to the book trade by IDG Books Worldwide, Inc.

**Library of Congress Cataloging-in-Publication Data**

Grinzo, Lou
    Zen of Windows 95 Programming / by Lou Grinzo
        p.  cm.
    Includes Index
    ISBN 1-883577-58-6

Printed in the United States of America

10 9 8 7 6 5 4 3 2 1

### Who Is This Book For?

This book is for intermediate to advanced Windows programmers who are making the move from Windows 3.1 to 32-bit Windows—Windows 95 and Windows NT. If you're new to 32-bit Windows development, you'll find the techniques and insight for moving applications to the 32-bit world to be a great asset.

### What Do I Need to Use It?

You need some background in Windows programming with C++. A PC running Windows 95 is required to run most of the code. To compile and make changes to the code, you'll need Microsoft's Visual C++ or MSC.

### What Sort of Code Is Present on the Companion CD-ROM?

The CD-ROM contains numerous example programs and resources to help developers create great 32-bit Windows applications. The programs have been tested with the latest version of Microsoft's Visual C++ (Version 2.2 at the time this book first went to press) and MFC. A few examples are 16-bit code that can be compiled with Visual C++ 1.52. All files created by the compilers and their IDEs are provided.

# *Acknowledgments*

I would like to thank: Phil Jurgenson, the cyberbrother I never had and whom I've *still* never met face-to-face, for offering copious advice and reading most of this book (which means any mistakes you find are his); Jim Kyle, a.k.a. Dr. CRC; Pete Davis; Matt Pietrek; Richard Alverson; the Coriolis Gang: Ron, editor dude, Shannon, P.R. doobie extraordinaire and ad hoc counselor, and, of course, Keith and Jeff; Maria Vallone and David Winkler; Paul and Adele Everett; Virg Meredith, Wes Ernsberger, Gary Hine, Jack Hooper, Daryl Kahl, and everyone else from the gone but not forgotten Building 9; the entire Denning clan, particularly Michael and Marianne, my programming students, for reminding me of the wonder and sheer electric fun that computers can be, especially after I've spent an endless (and endlessly frustrating) day bending the Windows API to my will.

Last and certainly most of all, thanks to Liz: wife, partner, best friend, business advisor, personal counselor, and relentless proofreader, without whom this book literally would not exist. Nor, for that matter, would I.

*This book is dedicated with love to the memory of Irene May Kirby Grinzo and Louis Anthony Grinzo, Senior.*

Dear Reader:

Time and again, I'll bet you've looked at some three-inch-thick software manual and wondered, *How do I make sense of all this?* All the facts may be there, but something important is usually missing: that not-quite-definable right-brain sense of orientation that comes of knowing what the big picture is and how to impose its order on that impenetrable ocean of details.

To help you move in the direction of that necessary big-picture understanding of the software tools you use, The Coriolis Group has created the Zen series of books for software developers. Early books in the series will focus on code optimization, high-performance graphics, component-oriented programming, and arcade game development. Mastering these subjects requires more than just a list of API calls and a haphazard description of how things work.

No. Mastering topics like these requires that you study the experience of the Zen masters in each area, people like Michael Abrash, Peter Aitken, and Diana Gruber—people who have spent years of study, experimentation, and thought becoming what they are. Bringing this experience to you in readable, accessible, *enjoyable* form is what we're doing with our Zen titles.

We don't think there's ever been anything quite like these books, and we invite your comments and suggestions. In what areas have you encountered the sorts of walls that only a Zen master can truly climb? Let us know. We'll do our best to bring the wisdom down the mountain and place it on your bookshelf.

—Jeff Duntemann KG7JF

# Contents

# Chapter 3    A Philosophy of Software Engineering: Micro Issues     63

# Chapter 4    Tools     99

## Chapter 7   Minimized Windows Programs, a World in an Icon   177

## Chapter 8   Tamper Proofing Your Programs   199

## Chapter 9   Smart Data Files   219

# Chapter 10  Abstraction in Action: Creating Your Own Virtual Machines                                            249

# Chapter 11  Give Your Program a Locked Persona         281

# Part 3  Crossing the Great Divide         297

# Chapter 12  From Win16 to Win32           299

## Chapter 16    Mixed Media Guide      433

# Appendices      443

## Appendix A    MegaZero, The World's Most Complete Do-Nothing Windows Program      445

## Appendix B    A Compendium of Programmer's Fables    489

# Introduction

*"You use your creative talents to transform a business environment."*

> Fortune cookie fortune I
> got the day I signed the
> contract to write this book.

*Forward, forward let us range,*
*Let the world spin for ever down the ringing grooves*
*    of change.*

> Alfred, Lord Tennyson

I don't believe in fortune cookies or anything even remotely New Age, but the above fortune nicely summarizes my goals in writing this book: To change how most of you think about your users and Windows 95 programming, and improve the way you practice your craft. Right there I've already made a sweeping assumption (several, actually, but let's limit ourselves to the most obvious and pertinent one for now): Programming is neither an art nor a science, but it clearly has elements of both, as well as other characteristics that make it a craft. I think this fact has significant, even profound, implications for all programmers, particularly at this time in the evolution of the Windows world.

Thanks to the arrival of Windows 95, the explosion of the home computer market, the dismal quality of commercial software as a whole, and the increased popularity of Windows NT and OS/2 Warp, the computing world has literally changed shape around us within the last year. When that happens, you have two choices: Stay the course and play extinction roulette, or get on with the job of adapting and growing. I prefer the latter strategy, and if you've survived in this game for any length of time, I suspect you do, too.

## What Is Programming?

As you'll see in this book, I argue repeatedly (and, I hope, persuasively) that to be the best programmer possible, you must take a long and inclusive view of issues whenever possible and strive for a balance.

Few professions are as susceptible to missing the forest for the trees as is programming, so it is vitally important that you get used to taking the "30,000-foot view" of your task (even if it requires you to Cuisinart a few metaphors in the process).

OK, enough dodging. What's programming? Programming is the craft of using various tools (hardware, software, research materials, your own experience, etc.) to create and employ levels of abstraction to achieve a logical task. These levels of abstraction allow you to construct a layered hierarchy of architectures or virtual machines, which ultimately work together to perform the needed task.

Hmm. Sounds like we're already in the deep end of the pool, and we're not even through the bloody introduction. As an example of this layering of virtual machines, consider how you deal with mathematical operations in your programs. When you write statements in C++ that perform simple arithmetic on floating point values, you have a level of expectation about how these routines in your compiler's runtime library will work, how they'll handle overflow, divide-by-zero, and other common error conditions. But what if the computer your program runs on doesn't have a math coprocessor? Programmers have long ago become so used to the idea of reliable emulated floating point support that they hardly ever give it a thought; this capability is simply another given, part of the landscape, and it works as it should, period.

Please don't dash past this familiar assumption as we're all wont to do. Stop and think about it for a second. If the computer doesn't have a math coprocessor, then there's literally no such thing as floating point math as far as that particular system is concerned; within that computer's universe, floating point math is a pure artifice. The emulation support provides a layer of abstraction—a virtual machine—on top of the existing hardware. This virtual machine gives you a higher, stronger platform on which to build your software.

To extend the example, let's say you need to use complex numbers in your program, so you use a commercial library that provides you with a complex number type and all the needed operations. You're now using a second abstraction, another virtual machine, built on the foundation of the first. Even more interesting, the people who wrote the complex number library neither know nor care about whether your floating point math is emulated or not. They know how it is supposed to work, so they coded to that documented interface. If your computer meets their expectations (which is highly likely, to say the least), and their work meets your expectations, then the layers of abstraction melt away and everything works as planned. Just like magic, your computer that can't even add 1.0 and 1.0 by itself will apparently manipulate complex numbers with perfect ease.

If you want another example, think about sitting down at a Windows system and running an SQL query against a relational database. Between "SELECT * FROM CUSTOMERS" down to the level of ones and zeros encoded on a spinning disk platter, there's quite a lot going on. Again, levels of abstraction and virtual machines. (I'd love to teach a computer architecture class some day and put only one problem on the final exam: Detail all the levels of architecture and interface in this example. I suspect the students wouldn't enjoy the experience quite as much as I would.)

Clearly, working with layers of abstraction and constructing your own virtual machines means that everything you do as a programmer is shot-through with assumptions. Burrow far enough below those assumptions, and you reach a bedrock layer, your programming philosophy. This influences and interacts with everything you do as a programmer, whether you realize it or not. Your philosophy is shaped by your experience and education, and often by things that have nothing to do with programming, such as your age. (If you think your hair and clothes look funny in 15- or 20-year-old photographs, try looking at some of your own code that's even close to that old. It's like watching a hexadecimal version of *The Brady Bunch*.)

Much of what you do as a programmer is selecting and using tools (particularly in the larger sense of the word, as I argue later on), not just slinging lines of code, swilling Jolt Cola, and ignoring directives from those wacky but pathetically misguided funsters in management. Again, changes in the desktop computing field, thanks in no small part to the arrival of Windows 95, have made this task much more interesting and important, and in some ways, precarious. Tool selection is a topic that I'll talk about in great detail later on.

# My Approach

In the interest of truth in advertising and attempting not to scare you off (something my publisher and I would strongly prefer I not do), I should tell you how I'll approach all this.

- This book is as much about what you shouldn't do as what you should. For example, I'll talk about the "programmer fables" that we all tell ourselves to justify shortcuts and our particular style. Please note that I don't claim to have a blinding level of purity on this count; in fact, I'll say here and now that I've committed every sin I mention in this book multiple times, and my programs and I have the scars to prove it. I've been lucky, and more than once I've done the programming equivalent of waking up in the morning with a ferocious hangover and no memory of how I got home the previous night, only to discover my car parked on the front lawn with the door still open. (And if you think for a nanosecond that that analogy is in any way an endorsement of such behavior, you missed the scathing sarcasm.)

- I've often had to rely on you to use your judgment about applying particular pieces of advice. As much as we all wish it were otherwise, modern programming very seldom presents binary issues; nearly every decision you'll face, and certainly all the interesting ones, happen in the vast, murky gray zone between the black and the white. When I say "be reasonable," those are not just weasel words substituting for a more concrete recommendation; they're an indication that the right answer is highly dependent on your situation, and that I would be irresponsible if I made a more definitive suggestion. Many decisions simply come down to context. Which tools are you using? What constraints are imposed by time, your management, and your users? What is your background? Even more interesting, what's right for you today might be terribly wrong for someone else or for you a few months from now. The trick is to see through your own prejudices (and everyone in this profession has plenty!) and select the optimal course of action for your project. Every time I hear a programmer say, "I had to use tool X, management made me/it was the only one available/I didn't have time to learn the right one," an alarm goes off in my head. Sometimes the programmer is right and there was no other choice but an obviously sub-optimal one, but all too often the programmer is making an excuse for having used a favorite tool or a shiny new toy.

- In places, I've walked you through a solution, including discussion of potential solutions that turned out to be dead ends. I think this is a useful way to present programming material, particularly where Windows is concerned, since it mimics the process we all go through in struggling to find solutions to our programming problems.

- There are a few places where I also give you the best solution I've found to some problem, and ask you to tell me if there's a better one I've missed. I don't claim to possess perfect knowledge about the issues in this book; almost no technical writer could honestly do that (although many will still make the claim, however implicitly). Similarly, please don't expect my opinions to be cast in stone. If you run into me at a conference or we exchange e-mail six months or a year after this book hits the shelves, I might very well tell you that I've had some interesting experiences that changed my mind on one or more issues. As I say below, this book is really a snapshot taken during one point in my personal odyssey through programming. Things change, and so do I.

# My Assumptions about You

Fiction writers often talk about a mythical "average" or "typical" reader they keep in mind as they write a given work. Similarly, technical writers have a mental model of our readers. Since my perception of you colors practically every word in this book, let me pry open my box of assumptions and give you a peek inside:

- You like programming and you do it either professionally or as a dedicated hobbyist. I consider everyone who programs for money a professional, even if their job title is not "programmer." One of the disturbing aspects of today's Windows world is that more and more non-programmers are writing programs that other people rely on for real work, a situation that I address throughout the book.

- You're a "quality bigot." While I normally detest those jokes and excessively cute observations that divide all of humanity into two camps, I find that computer users by and large do fall into two groups regarding bugs in software. One group shrugs off such flaws, says "bugs happen," and gets on with life and the task at hand. I have a grudging respect for these people, mostly because I'm in the second category, the group of people who go ballistic when we hit a bug. My swearing has been known to reach Wagnerian proportions when I stub my toe on what I call "a real howler."

  You've no doubt noticed that this is not a happy time in our industry to be a quality bigot. The quality of commercially available software has been traveling down the slippery slope at breakneck speed for some time. Even more disturbing, the vendors are moving to a different model of customer support (and I use the term *very* loosely and charitably), one that makes at best a lukewarm effort to provide bug fixes, and often winds up charging customers for the singular experience of reporting a bug. (You've probably heard the definition of chutzpah as a boy who kills his parents and then throws himself on the mercy of the court because he's an orphan. It seems to me the software industry is getting perilously close to one-upping that definition. But I digress.)

- You're interested in serious, long-term development projects, not just thrown together, use-and-nuke quickies. This is a critical dichotomy I talk about in Chapter 1, "An Introduction to the Real World," the difference between public and private programs.

- Related to the previous point, but not quite the same thing, you often have to wrestle with the most distasteful aspect of programming: "old code." Nearly all programming books today assume that you're starting every project with a clean screen, the world is your binary oyster, you're a colossus astride your hard disk, etc. In the real world of professional programming, it just doesn't happen that way, at least not nearly as often as we'd like. In my consulting and contract programming work I routinely have to enhance or rewrite programs that were written by one or more programmers who no longer work for the client, and obviously were not very experienced at the time they committed the source code. My experiences in this regard are far from unique; programmers at companies of all sizes face similar challenges on a daily basis.

- You're interested in source portability as well as application compatibility across the various Windows incarnations. I'll tell you right now that if you think you're not interested in this, then you're probably kidding yourself. I expect that our users will be running a hodge podge of Windows versions, everything from Windows 3.0 up to and including Windows NT 4.0 not long after this book is published. The age of innocence is over; the time when we can ignore this complexity is a fond but quickly dimming memory.

- You have some significant experience with Windows programming in C/C++ and/or Pascal and/or Basic. By "significant" I mean roughly 3,000 lines of code in the last year, or 20,000 lines in the last five years.

# What's in the Book

This book is arranged in four major sections: Foundation, Practice, Crossing the Great Divides, and Resources, plus several appendices.

*Foundation* is where I'll take a long look at the craft of programming, and many parts of it that we all get wrong from time to time. This section covers many issues that experienced programmers are familiar with, but I urge those of you who have been around the edit/compile/test cycle a few billion times to read this section anyway, since many of the issues covered there are more important than ever in light of the new rules in our changing world.

In *Practice* I'll demonstrate some of the tropes, techniques, and idioms that I invented, discovered, or picked up (read: stole) from friends. Nearly all of the code in this section is most definitely *not* rocket science, which is precisely the point. Nothing in the section depends on arcane, bleeding-edge tricks such as undocumented Windows features or APIs. Rather, these chapters are meant to demonstrate how, with just a little planning, you can combine simple and highly maintainable coding techniques to make your Windows 95 programs more usable and useful.

*Crossing the Great Divides* covers the increasingly important topic of porting code from one Windows implementation to another, as well as the binary compatibility of the three Win32 platforms (Win32s, Windows 95, and Windows NT). Before Windows 95 and Windows NT 3.51 (and ensuing releases) came along, this wasn't an issue for the overwhelming majority of Windows programmers. We wrote for 16-bit Windows and went about our merry way, blithely ignoring Windows NT and its school-bus-load of users (relatively speaking).

Finally, in *Resources* I'll talk about tools and resources that I think are worthwhile for the Windows programmer. As I said above, programming is a craft, which means its practice is intimately intertwined with its tools to a degree not seen in many other professional fields. Because of this, I feel that any book-length discussion of programming is sterile and incomplete unless it at least touches on the topics of tool selection and specific tools. Put another way, theory and philosophy are clearly necessary components of your mental tool kit as a programmer, but they're not sufficient.

Actually, I lied, and there is a fifth section, which consists of three appendices:

- **Appendix A:** MegaZero, the world's most complete, 32-bit, do-nothing application (which just happens to demonstrate several of the techniques from the Practice section).

- **Appendix B:** A Compendium of Programmer Fables, where I catalog and attack many of the lines we all use to delude ourselves from time to time.
- **Appendix C:** The Win32u Library, the first, primordial version of a wrapper library that you can use to overcome some of the compatibility problems between Win32s, Windows 95, and Windows NT.

# What's the Code?

The code samples in this book are included on the CD ROM. Obviously, I had to pick one language, compiler, and framework for the samples, or risk losing my mind and never delivering this book to Coriolis. (Selecting a compiler was remarkably similar to selecting the tools for a conventional development project, in fact.) I chose Microsoft's Visual C++ 2.2 and MFC, the most recent versions available as I was writing this book.(There are a few examples of 16-bit code, which were created with Visual C++ 1.52, plus one (gasp!) Pascal module.

Thanks to the vastness of the CD-ROM format, I included all files created by the compilers and their IDEs. This should allow you to install the samples and use them with all the facilities of Visual C++. In the interest of saving time, I didn't bother to delete unnecessary resources from the programs or create custom icons, so I hope you don't hate the default "AFX" icon that Visual C++ uses as much as I do, because you'll see it a lot in these samples.

Please note that the decision to use Microsoft's compilers is more a reflection of market realities than an endorsement of Visual C++ and MFC. As I started writing this book in March of 1995, OWL's future (as well as Borland's) was very uncertain, and MFC had nearly become the *lingua franca* of Windows programming.

# What's Not in the Book

Truth in advertising time, again. This is most definitely not a survey book that exhaustively covers C++ or OOP or OLE 2.0 or the Win95 API or WinG or any other single topic. If you want a topic-specific book, Coriolis and other publishers will gladly sell you one that addresses almost any nook, cranny, corner, crevice, or back alley of programming that you find compelling or amusing. This book's mission is to address Windows 95 programming at a foundational and philosophical level; as such, I'll be talking about concepts and issues that are common to all programming but have a special relevance to Windows 95 coders.

# Time for a Shameless Plug

One of the more educational and entertaining things I've done over the last few years is produce and market a shareware program for Windows called Stickies!.

Stickies! provides the user with an electronic form of 3M's Post-It notes, plus a file cabinet-like database, alarms, and numerous other features. Throughout this book I'll mention things I learned about programming and dealing with unknown users while marketing Stickies!, as well as some surprising porting issues I ran into courtesy of Windows 95.

For the pathologically curious, Stickies! was first released on October 2, 1992, and the next version (4.0) will be released shortly after this book is finished and I sleep for a week. An evaluation copy of Stickies! 3.1 is on the CD ROM, in ZEN\STICKIES. (And we've included a coupon worth a one-third discount on Stickies! licenses in the back of this book.)

# The Shape of the World

We all make jokes about how the only constant in the computer business is change, and how today's hot new gizmo is tomorrow's door stop. Well, just to provide a few cheap laughs for people who will stumble across this book on a dusty shelf 20 years from now, let me tell you what the state of the industry was when I started writing it:

- Windows 95 was still in beta test, with hot debates everywhere about whether Microsoft would make its then-current ship date, the end of August.

- Cairo was the shining city on the hill, expected to go into beta in Feb. 1996, although no one outside of Microsoft seemed to know much about it, aside from the fact that it was the next generation of NT and no one had reported a single bug in it yet.

- OS/2 Warp was selling briskly, thanks in large part to the infamous Generation X-er and nun television ads, and people were talking about "The New IBM" with less and less irony every day.

- Microsoft had announced that they would release a version of NT with the Windows 95 UI that would sell for the same price as Windows 95, and that it would go into beta shortly after Windows 95 shipped. This version of NT still didn't have a version number outside of Microsoft, so people routinely referred to it as version 3.52, 3.6, or 4.0.

- Borland had recently launched Delphi to strong reviews and reportedly strong sales. But Borland was also still under the cloud of the Lotus look-and-feel lawsuit, and just about everyone in the business expected Novell to buy Borland at any time.

- Intel's 120MHz Pentium was about to debut in desktop computers, and everyone was just beginning to learn about the next chip in the Intel family, the P6. IBM was a few months away from launching its PowerPC desktop computers, which would reportedly include a native version of Windows NT, but not OS/2.

# Stay in Touch

A career in programming, like life itself, is a journey. In one sense this book is a checkpoint in my personal programming odyssey, a selective summary of my adventures, including both successes and failures, plus some observations and recommendations, all viewed through Windows 95-tinted lenses. But with your help, this book can be much more than that. Early in this project I talked with Keith Weiskamp, my publisher, and Ron Pronk, my editor, and we agreed that this book should have a relaxed feel, like a gathering of friends. So I hope you'll forgive me if I tell you that as I wrote this book in the summer of 1995 I often imagined a dozen of us on my patio on a cool summer night after a great cookout and a day of water balloon fights and tossing Frisbees, talking about programming, sharing anecdotes and jokes and management horror stories, and even lapsing into the occasional "religious" programming argument.

Whatever you do, don't be a stranger. Tell me where you think I'm right and wrong, tell me your programming anecdotes (the wilder the better, but they're all welcome), and tell me what should (and shouldn't) be in the next edition of this book. I'll spring for the food, you bring the refreshments, and this time, when the Frisbee lands in my neighbor's yard, we'll send Ron or Keith over the fence to retrieve it.

Lou Grinzo
P. O. Box 8636
Endwell, NY 13762-8636

CompuServe: 71055,1240

Endwell, NY
October, 1995

# Part 1

# *Foundation*

Chapter

1

# An Introduction to the Real World

# An Introduction to the Real World

**Chapter 1**

*The universe is not hostile, nor yet is it friendly. It is simply indifferent.*

Rev. John H. Holmes

*All suffering is caused by ignorance of the nature of reality and the craving, attachment, and grasping that result from such ignorance.*

Buddha's Second Noble Truth

*Suffering can be ended by overcoming ignorance and attachment.*

Buddha's Third Noble Truth

As cold as Rev. Holmes' words seem, I think that in the compound world our programs inhabit, made up as it is of millions of users' screens, he would still be considered a shade optimistic. This is not idle pessimism; heck, if I were pessimistic about programming, I never would have considered writing this book, and would have long ago moved into another profession. But I do know from experience that there's a stunning number of ways in which programs can fail when tossed into the roiling cauldron of the general user population. And, as I'll detail in this chapter, the less "power" your programs use, the more precarious the situation can be.

## Windows 95 and the Big Picture

Let's heed Buddha's observations and try to improve our lot in life by understanding what Windows 95 really is and isn't. Long before it was actually available,

5

many people criticized Windows 95 for not being a 100 percent 32-bit, multi-everything, TURBO (The Ultimate Really Better Overall) operating system. These critics were right on the facts, and I would not argue with anyone who says that the hype surrounding Windows 95's launch was astounding. But the product is here now, and without letting any of the spinmeisters off the hook (and you all know who you are), I consider such issues ancient history. What matters is what is in the box, how well it works, and, for my purposes in this book, what it means to programmers.

Another, larger group was initially disappointed in Windows 95, and I was one of them. The product has many small oddities and outright bugs that I find very annoying, especially because it's the first major upgrade to Windows in years. Luckily, most of the bothersome problems, from an end user's viewpoint, are in Explorer, which means we can avoid them by simply replacing that part of the product. (And no, I'm not going to burden this discussion with my list of gripes with Explorer. I assume that anyone technically savvy enough to read this book can assemble quite an impressive list of Explorer's flaws without my help.)

Yet there's clearly much to like about Windows 95. Most notably for power users, the immensely better resource management is almost reason enough to upgrade. The day I got my copy of the shipping version of Windows 95 (as opposed to yet another beta copy), I installed it on the computer I use to keep my business records and other critical data. I instantly got a significant benefit: I was able to keep Stickies!, Lotus Organizer, Word for Windows, Access, and Visual C++ running at the same time and still have 76 percent of my system resources free. In fact, one of my biggest problems in using Windows 95 in a work environment is breaking my habit of shutting down and restarting the same program several times in one session. Like most of you, I've operated that way for years out of necessity. There's no longer a need for such mouse gymnastics; it's now much more efficient to simply start programs as they're needed, or even before they're needed, and leave them lounging on the task bar.

The point is that Windows 95 is a different animal than Windows 3.1, one that encourages users to do different things. As I write this, no one knows how quickly home users and businesses will adopt Windows 95, but we can all be sure it will be a very important presence in the desktop computer market, and is likely to be the dominant OS, in terms of sheer numbers, for years to come.

# Public and Private Programs

Another concept that is key to this book is the difference between public and private programs.

*Private programs* are those that you or a *very* limited number of people with known skills, requirements, and computers will use. By "very limited number," I don't mean a few dozen of your closest friends, but at most six, and even then only under rigidly controlled circumstances. And by "known," I mean literally that; known to you personally, with a virtual certainty that what you know about them and how they will use your program applies to every person in the user audience, not just to users in the aggregate. It's not enough to say that your program is to be distributed to hydraulic engineers who use computers "a lot" and are therefore highly computer literate. Such sweeping generalizations are too often used as excuses to cut corners in programs.

Never forget that even when you're confident that you have effective control over distribution, you don't. Your program is very likely to get wide, unofficial distribution without your knowledge unless it is so incredibly specialized that very few people would even know what it does, let alone find it useful. I've seen numerous cases of this unintended distribution in the past, and now that users everywhere are networked and modemed together like never before, it's even more likely.

Some people take the extreme viewpoint that as soon as you let even one other person use your program, it crosses the line and becomes public. I understand this viewpoint, but I think it's extreme. For example, my wife, Liz, has been a systems analyst and programmer for 16 years, and she most definitely knows her way around a computer. I could easily give her or some computer consultants I know a private-quality program, say that it's not ready for prime time, and not have to worry. But these situations are by far the exception.

*Public programs*, by contrast, are those that are distributed to other people or for use in unknown situations. This includes distribution either to more than six people, or to people whom you don't know, or for use on computers with wildly differing or unknown traits. Public programs include everything from a simple printing utility that you write and put on the networked utilities disk at work to mass-distribution titles like WordPerfect or Windows 95 itself. In the former case, you might not intend your little utility to be used outside of your company, and you might even add some sort of disclaimer to the program's interface to that effect. But rest assured, if it has any general applicability to Windows users whatsoever, it will get out. Someone from work will take a copy home as an aid in doing take-home work, that person's child will see the program and start handing out copies to friends, one of the friends will upload it to a few BBSes in the interest of gaining peer acknowledgment for not only supplying a cool program, but one that clearly was not meant to be distributed (the sweetness of purloined fruit, and all that). In no time, the utility you cranked out in an hour of casual coding is in use by thousands of people.

(I should say that Frederick Brooks mentions private and public programs on page 164 of his classic work, *The Mythical Man-Month*. He seems to be using these terms in the same sense as I use them here, although he only touches on the concept in passing. For the record, I didn't steal the terms from Brooks; I was using them before I read his book for the first time, making this coincidence just another of life's little unexpected entertainments.)

## How Public Is Public?

Even when you intend a program for public distribution, you can be in for some surprises. I intended Stickies!, my shareware note manager program, to be used as a simple, handy reminder program, with enough database-like features that users could keep track of past appointments, ideas, or whatever. I've talked to numerous customers about how they use Stickies!, and typically I hear that they're employing it pretty much as I intended, with the occasional genealogy hobbyist using it to track ancestors.

Then one day I got a fax that really caught my attention. It had a pair of large military insignia and was from a Lieutenant Colonel in the U.S. military who wanted me to call him about Stickies!. I called and had a great conversation with this gentleman, who wanted to license a copy of the program. He told me that he uses it to track location and minor personnel information on 30 generals and 600 colonels. This is a far more "serious" application of Stickies! than I had ever anticipated. As you can imagine, I was pleased and relieved when this customer told me that he tried to "wring the devil" out of my program before he used it for this purpose, and that it had passed his tests. You can argue that all public programs should be robust enough that it doesn't matter how users employ them; the programs either work properly or refuse in a graceful manner without loss of data. In fact, that's exactly my view. Still, a phone call like this one focuses the mind wonderfully on quality issues.

There are no inherent differences between private and public programs; the differences are all external to the programs and are dictated by their distribution, how they are used, and by whom they are used. It would be nice if there were a compiler or linker switch we could use to force a program to remain private, but I don't expect to see that feature anytime soon.

## Ethics and Metaphors

Private programs are not very interesting as far as this book is concerned. If you're writing a program for your own use, do it however you want. Write it in some arcane language, possibly even one for which you invented and wrote your own interpreter or compiler, if that sort of thing interests you. Don't burden your program with so much as a single line of code that performs error checking; don't even consider making it bother to prompt you before formatting your hard disk in response to the /TERMINATOR:YES command line option. Knock yourself out. It's your microkingdom and you're the ruler, so what you do is your business. Just don't come crying to me when your program turns out to be a foot-seeking missile with uncanny accuracy.

Public programs, on the other hand, are a whole different sphere of bee stuff, ethically speaking. Once one of your programs "goes public," it is literally an encapsulated version of your personal philosophy, a script of your personal actions that will be run on other peoples' computers, with access to no end of vital information that represents a great deal of your users' money, time, and effort. This difference between private and public programs alone should be enough to require us all to rethink how we approach programming, although, once again, judging by the quality of commercial software, this doesn't seem to be the case.

Another point worth keeping in mind as you write a public program, and one that is traditionally hard for many programmers to remember, is that when you're finished, your program is only beginning life. You might be done with it once it's released, but the myriad of assumptions you made along the way about Windows, your users, their systems, performance and usability tradeoffs, and how these factors will all interact, are just coming into play. No matter how many hours of designing, coding, and testing went into your program's creation, it's just a string of lifeless ones and zeroes until human beings run it and derive utility from it; that's when the magic happens. In this sense, good software is like an example of good fiction or any other fine art; it's the closest thing we have to genuine magic in this world because it transforms the lives of distant, unknown people.

If I can be allowed one more analogy, I often think of software as a violin. A violin in the abstract is nothing exciting. Some varnish and carved wood, bits of metal and some string. Inert, boring, and even a little funny looking. But hand the violin to Itzhak Perlman and it seems almost to come alive, suddenly able to wring emotion from an audience and tell a story nearly as well as the spoken word. Not bad for such a silly contraption (or a string of ones and zeroes).

# Meet Your Users

But enough metaphors; let's return to the real world and the people who will be using your programs. As I've pointed out above and elsewhere (for instance, my "Dialog Box" column in the July, 1995 *Windows Magazine*), the Windows world changed forever in 1994, long before the arrival of Windows 95, thanks to the sudden explosion in the sales of PCs to home users. Various analysts and companies had optimistically predicted for years that this segment was about to take off. In the end, it wasn't the warm and fuzzy usability of Apple's Macintosh or Windows or any of the other intentional efforts to lure the non-computer jocks into our fold. It was simple, cold-blooded economics: Sell decent computer systems cheap enough, and people will flock to buy them for home use, largely for their children. And that's exactly what happened. Bang-per-buck ratio finally got high enough, with a low enough entry price, that home computer sales took off, and the profile of most vendors' customer base changed dramatically. (Never forget Lou's First Law of Computers: A good economic incentive beats a royal flush.)

In the bad old days, computers were the province of lab-coated experts who dedicated themselves to mastering their intricacies. Now, PCs have gone mainstream with a vengeance, and millions of home computer owners are learning about DOS and Windows (and, in particular, Windows 95) and computer hardware and application software and games and the whole mess, all in one gigantic gulp. And that means that you can no longer assume a relatively high level of computer literacy among the users of your public programs. For example, your public programs can no longer blissfully ignore certain situations under the assumption that "the users will know not to do that." Such assumptions were always suspect, in my opinion; now they're flat out wrong.

## Games People Play

I'm not about to launch into a fit of "dumb-user bashing," in this forum or any other, as I've heard many programmers do, since users deserve our respect. Heck, without users, our programs are merely ones and zeroes, and we're a bunch of geeks who should get out more. But I do think that it's worth pointing out some of the things I've seen computer tyros (and not-so-tyros) do over the last few years, since these incidents really opened my eyes....

- The debacle that the Pentium floating-point bug turned into should be seen as a huge, neon billboard announcing to the entire industry that Things Have Changed. Every major release of every microprocessor has at least some bugs. This is not news. Given the incredible complexity of microprocessors, it's not a surprise, either. Yet when the Pentium bug surfaced, it made mainstream news. Jim Louderback (then of *PC Week*, now Editor-in-Chief of *Windows Sources*) was interviewed on CNN, and the whole world seemed to sit up and take notice. Intel initially fumbled the matter badly, saying that they would decide if the type of work you do on your computer meant you really needed a fixed chip. (This was yet another of life's little impromptu IQ tests. Most people would agree that Intel flunked.) Their response would have been acceptable (but still arrogant) in the mid-80s, but in the mid-90s, after the transformation of the PC industry into something akin to the stereo component market, it was a laughable blunder. Intel, to their credit, eventually figured this out and offered a free replacement Pentium to everyone who asked for one.

- I've encountered users who think DLLs are some kind of plain text configuration file, and change them with a text editor. The appearance on screen of all that binary garbage in the text editor doesn't dissuade these people in the least. They ignore the unreadable stuff, scroll around until they find some bit of plain text that seems to be relevant to the change they have in mind, edit it, save the file, and run the program again. Then they call technical support.

- At a consulting client's location, I once saw the head of their marketing department start up Windows, start a word processor, write something in the document with a stylus, fumble around with various screen controls for a few seconds, and then switch off the computer. The person did this several times as I watched. I finally realized what was going on: This person didn't know how to erase the text and start over with a fresh copy of the document, so turning the computer off and on was the next best thing. (And yes, this client was a computer company.)

• As I talk to Stickies! customers, I see one problem on a weekly basis: Some new users have a hard time with the concept that the Windows desktop is really three-dimensional. Time and time again I hear from new computer users that "Stickies! displays my notes and then they disappear! Where did they go?" The answer, of course, is that they didn't go anywhere. The user clicked on some other program which got the Windows focus and rose to the top of their session's z-order, obscuring all other windows, including the Stickies! notes. Some users have even argued with me and claimed that Windows can't possibly work this way, since it makes no sense.

• The Save As common dialog is a familiar part of Windows for even new computer users. But it can lead to a subtle misunderstanding regarding file formats. Users become accustomed to the idea that if you want to save a graphic as a .PCX file instead of a .BMP, for example, you merely use the File|Save As feature, select .PCX files in the dialog box's drop-down, and the file is saved properly. Unfortunately, some users don't realize that there's such a thing as different file formats, not just different naming conventions, so they think the Save As dialog box is merely a convenient way to save a file with a different name. Depending on the program they're using, they're likely to open the Save As dialog box, check the formats drop-down, and not seeing "PCX files" in the list, simply type into the filename field "FRED.PCX," and click on OK. Of course, they don't get a PCX file, but a BMP or TIFF, or whatever format was selected on the dialog. This is why it's more critical than ever that your custom file formats are all self-identifying, a topic I'll take up in greater detail in Chapter 9.

• Watch new computer users save files, and you'll quickly see that many of them ignore those parts of the common dialogs that have to do with directories. They do a File|Save or File|Save As, type in the filename they want, and click on the OK button, unwittingly letting the program place the file wherever the dialog happens to be pointing. If that happens to be some obscure directory on their system, then that's where the file ends up, and the next time the user goes looking for the file, it seems to have disappeared. Even if the file lands in the right place, if the File|Open dialog doesn't start at the right directory the next time, the file will still seem to be missing. This example points out how simple it can be to make life easier for your users; make sure your common dialogs display an appropriate directory when they come up.

• I saw an employee at one of my clients "upgrade" DOS 5.0 to 6.0 by copying the contents of the C:\DOS directory from one system to another. (He thought that running the upgrade program would be too much trouble.) This resulted in a barbarism (in the original sense of an alien intruder); DOS was version

5.0, but the external commands in C:\DOS, such as FORMAT.COM, were all from version 6.0 and refused to work with the down-level DOS.

I can't stress this enough: New computer users are neither good nor evil; they're merely different from what you expect. This is particularly true if you're surrounded by programmers and other power users all day.

Even when they're not exploring the back alleys of event space, users do all sorts of things that appear perfectly reasonable to them but can wreak havoc with your program. They'll routinely do things like install your program according to your directions on one computer and then try to do a second installation by copying the files that obviously belong to the application and then trying it out. Similarly, concepts that programmers take for granted, like closing down a program before doing anything with a data file it has loaded, just don't compute for many users. In some cases, Windows will save you from these problems, but it's often up to the programmer.

I want to stress one last time that I'm not relating these anecdotes to embarrass or beat up new computer users; I'm telling these stories because collectively they tell a cautionary tale about programming in the mid-90s and beyond.

## Love Is Fleeting, but Software Is Forever

One of the more insidious side effects of this influx of new users is that they hate to upgrade software. They buy a computer at Montgomery Ward's or Sam's Club, and they'll use the same copy of DOS, Windows, and most bundled programs that come with the computer until they replace the entire system, years down the road. After all, it works okay, so why bother spending money to change it?

This upgrade issue reminds me of one of the most interesting quotes I've ever seen attributed to a Microsoft employee. The October 1994 issue of *Windows Magazine* said:

> *[Steve] Ballmer said 5.5 to 7 percent of MS-DOS users upgraded to version 6.0, and only 24 percent of registered users ever upgraded from Windows 3.0 to 3.1. Application upgrades, such as revisions to Word and Excel, average between 20 and 30 percent.*

Even assuming that there's at least some piracy taking place (for example, a company with 100 computers buys one upgrade and uses it on all systems), and that Microsoft is probably calculating the Windows figure using confirmed upgrades divided by total Windows licenses shipped (which includes preloads and therefore some licenses that aren't actually used and will never be upgraded), I still find this 24 percent surprisingly low. Remember how dreadful Windows 3.0. was compared to 3.1? That was the mother of all no-brainer upgrades, yet even before the home market got into the act in a big way, the percentage was still just under a quarter.

I often think of new computer owners in terms of home owners. They might have plans for some major renovation some day, like adding a bathroom or nuking and reworking a kitchen, but until then, they won't make any changes. For many new computer users, changing a major program or (shudder!) the operating system on their computer is something just as unpleasant (on its own scale) as enduring a major construction project in their home.

This reluctance to upgrade has a very serious ramification for programmers, since the one part of their system new users are most reluctant to upgrade is the operating system. This means that any bugs in the initial version of Windows 95 or any ensuing release will become permanent potholes in cyberspace that we'll all have to drive around. To some extent this has always been true, and programs have always had to be aware of earlier versions of the operating system, or at least they should have been. But things have changed, and this is a more important factor that it would have been just a few years ago.

## How Not to Deal with New Users

I can hear the "it's not my fault/you can't do everything/users have to be responsible for their own systems" crowd warming up their word processors now. If you're in that category, let me save you the effort: I'm *not* about to suggest that you should strive to make your programs completely idiot-proof. I know that can't be done, since there are always people who will do bizarre things like turn off the computer while your Windows 95 program is writing to a disk file and then expect your program to recover magically the next time they run it.

And no, I definitely don't think you should festoon your programs with prompts and "nannyisms" in an effort to keep the user from making the slightest error. Even deciding what is and isn't a nannyism can be difficult; I certainly expect word processors and other document-based programs to warn me if I try to quit without saving my changes. But even this simple level of protection can be mishandled and turned into an annoyance. Borland's Resource Workshop will erroneously tell you that a RES file you've looked at has been changed, when it hasn't, a fact that drives me crazy. Even more annoying is a development tool I used that included a complex editor for a custom, structured file. The editor would let you hop from screen to screen and change fields, and never so much as peep if you tried to exit without saving your work. When I asked the developer why it worked this way, I was told that it was too much work to do what I wanted. Even for a developer tool, that's unacceptable.

The user does have to take responsibility for the computer and what happens on it; my point is that the dividing line between what is your responsibility and what is the user's has shifted with the change in overall computer literacy. Put another way, lawyers often refer to the "reasonable person test," meaning they examine a situation and ask themselves, "what would a reasonable person expect or do in this situation." (Insert gratuitous lawyer joke here.) In our field, the definition of a "reasonable user" has changed considerably in the last 12 to 18 months (at this writing), and it will continue to change at a rapid pace for at least the next few years. And this, in turn, changes the definition of reasonable program. In one sense, I find this terribly ironic, since I've always believed that on average programs should be much more usable and accommodating than they were. Many programmers rejected such notions with the fable that their users all do (or should) know what they're doing, and if they don't, well, it's the users' fault for being ignorant—it's not up to the exalted programmers to save the users from their own ignorance. Now, with a compelling economic incentive forcing programs to be more accommodating, the power users and the beginners alike are finally getting the increased usability we should have had all along.

# How Should We Deal with Users, New and Otherwise?

In a sense, the answer to this question is found throughout this book. There isn't a single silver bullet I can give you, although I will present in Chapters 2 and 3 a set of Windows 95 software engineering guidelines that I think will help a great deal.

One thing we all can and should do is adjust our mental model of our average or typical user. Fiction authors often talk about having a mental image of their typical reader. I'm convinced, having once been a writer of fiction, that all authors have such a mental guide for their work, even if they don't think of it in such explicit terms. The presence of a mythical average user brings with it all sorts of assumptions about what is and isn't appropriate in the finished work, whether it's a novel or a word processor used to write novels.

A far more important influence on our work is our philosophy of design and program implementation, which is the topic of the next two chapters.

## The Amazing Case of CON.TXT and Other Devices of Destruction

I discovered one of the oddest things about Windows 3.1 and Windows 95 wholly by accident. I was copying and moving files about one day under Windows for Workgroups 3.11 using Central Point's File Manager. I like this File Manager replacement because it does a nice job of handling ZIP archives as directories, allowing me to dodge the incredibly wasteful cluster size mess in the FAT file system. (See Chapter 2 for more details on the cluster size debacle.)

I wanted to copy a plain text file to a new file with the name CON.TXT in the same directory. So, I pressed F8, which caused Central Point's File Manager to open a prompt for the target file name. I typed in CON.TXT, and hit enter. Instead of copying the file to the new file name, as I expected, Windows copied it directly to my screen, in text mode, right on top of my Windows session. This was not in a DOS box or anything of the sort; the text of the file was literally overlaid on top of the graphics of my Windows desktop. See Figure 1.1 for a sample of what a program on this book's CD ROM, HOLYCOW.EXE, will do to a Windows 95 session.

The answer, of course, is that CON.TXT or plain old CON or CON.anything is a device name under DOS, and attempting to open and write to a disk file with such a name results in opening and writing to the console device, not a disk file. (Why Windows/DOS isn't smart enough to see that CON.TXT isn't the same as CON is of only academic value. The point in this and many other examples in this book is that right or wrong, smart or dumb as dirt, this is the way it is, and it's up to us programmers to find a path through the pitfalls.)

Once I saw this problem in action, I found that our trusty friends, the common dialogs are smart enough to check for and reject standard device names. This is only a partial safety net, of course, since not all prompts for an output filename are done via the common dialogs. Central Point's File Manager, for example, simply prompts the user for the target name with a vanilla dialog box, and then, I assume, based on the program's observable behavior, does the typical check to see if the file already exists. If everything looks okay, they do the copy.

As another test, I connected to CompuServe with Procomm Plus for Windows 2.0 and selected a file for download. I told CompuServe and Procomm that I wanted to download the unsuspecting file to CON.ZIP. Instead of coloring my screen with all manner of binary garbage, as I expected, Procomm and Windows locked up tight as a drum, requiring a power off/on to regain control.

Not content to stop at CON.TXT, I next tried PRN.TXT, which resulted in a system modal dialog box that said:

```
System Error
Cannot write to the device PRN.
Make sure the network is working. If it is a local drive,
check the disk and the device driver.
```

Attempting to write to COM1.TXT was even more enlightening. I got another system modal dialog, with the same text as above, except the strangely formatted device name was COM1. This time, the system locked up tight as a drum and required a power off/on cycle to regain control. Writing to NUL.TXT apparently sent the text strings to the big bit bucket in the sky.

If you want to see these pyrotechnics in action, run the HOLYCOW.EXE program that's in ZEN\CHAP01\HOLYCOW under Windows 95 or Windows 3.1. The provided version uses CON.TXT as the file name. But before doing anything with this program, *please* take appropriate precautions to safeguard your data and other programs. I've yet to see the CON.TXT variation do anything nasty to a computer, but there's no sense in taking unnecessary risks.

A friend of mine, Phil Jurgenson, says that on his Windows 3.1 system, all HOLYCOW.EXE did was change the color of his mouse cursor. If you see anything except the text on the screen, please let me know.

The immediate, nuts and bolts, lesson, of course, is to be careful about file names you attempt to use. CON and some of its friends should be screened for, either with the common dialogs or your own code. (This applies only to 16-bit Windows and Windows 95. Run HOLYCOW.EXE under Windows NT, and your screen won't be overwritten text. On the other hand, tell the Windows NT 3.51 File Manager to search your C: drive for a file name of "con.txt," and it claims to find a matching file named "con" in every directory.)

The larger lesson, of course, is that you can never be sure you've covered all the bases in your public Windows programs. Surprises will always come up, and you'll just have to make sure you and your programs are flexible enough to react.

**Figure 1.1  Using CON as a file name.**

Chapter

2

# A Philosophy of Software Engineering: Macro Issues

# A Philosophy of Windows Software Engineering: Macro Issues

Chapter 2

> *Axioms in philosophy are not axioms until they are proved upon our pulses: we read fine things but never feel them to the full until we have gone the same steps as the author.*

John Keats

As in the more important things in life, everything we do as programmers is directly or indirectly traceable to our philosophy. Our coding styles, our selections of datatypes for variables, literally every one of the dozens of decisions we make in creating even minimal programs all boil down to judgment calls that depend less on hard facts and more on craftsmanship than we often realize. In this chapter and the next, I'll take a long look at the main philosophical issues of Windows programming and present a series of guidelines that should help you avoid some of the short- and long-term pitfalls. This chapter focuses on the macro, or long-range issues, while Chapter 3 will cover the micro issues.

## Style

Before getting into the details of what makes a good program and how to create one, I want to spend a little time on a related concept: style.

Style is perhaps the one characteristic that programmers talk about even more than philosophy (even though they might not know they're talking about either at the time). You often hear people talk about a particular programmer's style of formatting code, using or not using Hungarian notation, how aggressively the person uses (or abuses) the features of C++, etc. In some cases, style is nothing more than the habits we've fallen into and haven't had reason to abandon. Do things a certain way long enough and it just seems right; as long as the practice doesn't cause you problems, you stick with it, and next thing you know, it's become part of your style and it influences the rest of your work.

But not all programming style is the residue of chance and inertia. Often style is an emergent property of personal philosophy and assumption. For example, Windows programmers often treat local storage in functions as nearly free, at least for relatively small amounts. For example, should you use a four-byte integer or a two-byte integer for a small number that will fit easily into either datatype? One camp says you should make the variable's size match its intended use as closely as possible, in an effort to make it "self-documenting." The other camp says not to worry about this detail, and besides, it's more efficient in the long run to use an integer that's the machine's natural word size. It's one of those arguments that can go in circles forever, dragging in more and more detail about the characteristics of the target machine, the compiler, etc.

In fact, most of us don't even think about this issue (unless we need to pass the variable to an API or another function, and it's actually more convenient to declare it one way or the other to avoid a cast). Whatever an individual's approach, a programmer will simply code it one way or another and get on with the task at hand, without giving it much thought. Yet which way we lean on this minor question is really as much a philosophical issue as it is a concern for performance rooted in hard fact. (It's an interesting sign of the times that almost no one talks about this issue any more. When I started programming professionally, during the Carter Administration, mainframers still discussed such things. What do you want, we didn't have mice or GUIs to play with (and you can only play the mainframe version of Adventure so many times), so we had to fill our idle moments somehow.)

# Mathematicians and Cabinetmakers

I've known a lot of programmers over the years, and I find that most, but certainly not all, fall into one of two categories: mathematicians and cabinetmakers. (Despite the way I've qualified this statement, I'm sure that I'll get a few pieces of angry e-mail from programmers, mathematicians, and cabinetmakers. If you feel you've somehow been slighted, I apologize.)

The mathematicians are the abstract scientists, the ones who place a very heavy emphasis on the provable correctness (or otherwise) of a piece of code, sometimes to the exclusion of other factors. Their overriding concern is that a piece of code does what it claims to do when provided with proper input. If the answer is yes, then that's the end of the discussion as far as they're concerned. Next question.

From a purely logical, flinty hearted, specification-driven standpoint (which surely must be the starting point when evaluating any piece of code), it's pretty hard to argue with this group, at least as far as their position goes. The specification says that a function is supposed to produce A when presented with inputs X, Y, and Z. Does it or doesn't it? If it does, then it's obviously correct. So what's your problem? (That last part is usually added only by New York programmers.)

As hard as it can be to argue with the mathematicians, I find that professionally I often must, since they tend to ignore ancillary issues that can be just as important as the hard-and-fast correctness of a program or function. Let's say that the function Barney() clearly does exactly what it's supposed to, but it's an unmaintainable mess that takes 18 parameters of interchangeable types, which leads to frequent errors in code that calls it. Clearly this is a bad design and the function can, and should, be improved. Yet in such cases (and this fabricated example is less fabricated than I wish) the more extreme mathematicians can be very adamant about not "opening up" working code and risking the introduction of new bugs into a part of the system that currently has no known errors. (I've done maintenance programming on an operating system written in assembly language, so I have more than a little sympathy for this viewpoint.)

The cabinetmakers, on the other hand, present a different problem. They're the ones who often talk about the elegance of algorithms and finding ways to do the job that are just the slightest, albeit unmeasurable, bit better. This is normally a good attitude, whether we're talking about programming, gardening, or any other endeavor. But too much is too much, and the habits of the more extreme cabinetmakers often turn into endless tinkering, causing problems throughout a large project. To return to the mythical case of the Barney() function again, the cabinetmakers typically want to move all or part of those 18 parameters into a new record structure that is then passed to the function, or to otherwise alter its interface in an effort to reduce errors, which then triggers changes for other programmers throughout a project. And it does indeed run the risk of introducing a new error into the system, something they were trying to avoid in the first place.

I've been in numerous arguments with mathematicians and cabinetmakers over the years, and the "religious wars" between the camps almost always boils down to the following judgment call: Is it better to live with the shortcomings and drop-by-drop expense of the status quo, or is it better to spend more of your scarce development and testing resources to try to fix the situation once and for all, but risk triggering an even larger problem? It's almost never a cut-and-dry situation (except for the arguments about which I have a strong opinion; those are *always* painfully clear), which once again means we're right back to philosophy, and how it guides our judgment, decisions, and ultimately, our work.

You've probably figured out by now that I tend to be more of a cabinetmaker than a mathematician. This is true, but I've also been known to go ballistic over APIs that don't behave exactly in accordance with their documentation. See my discussion in Chapter 14 about some of the adventures we'll all have working with the Win32 API, for example.

This is even more of a generalization, but it's interesting to watch how the two camps view each other. The cabinetmakers tend to see the mathematicians as two-dimensional, overly rigid, simple folk who don't grasp the big picture and long-term consequences. They think the subtleties of most designs are lost on them. Mathematicians, on the other hand, lose patience with the cabinetmakers and see them as too wishy washy and insufficiently concerned with the hard and fast requirements of a program. I bring this up not to play pop psychologist, but to make the point that both groups are right, in a way. Their pet concerns really are important, and callously ignoring them can lead to disaster. The problem, as always, is finding the right balance for your project.

My desire is to see programmers take a different approach, one in which we all broaden our viewpoints so that we can encompass both camps, and at the same time think far enough ahead that many of the situations, like the case of the mythical Barney() function, never come up in the first place. (After all, we can't waste time arguing over how to fix something that never breaks. Well, we can, programmers being programmers, but you get my point.) Much more on this later. First, I want to talk about what makes for good software.

# Degrees of Goodness

Your primary goal for any software you write, whether it's a major application program that many end users will employ, or a function in a library that only a few other programmers will see, is to make it empowering. (Don't bolt for the exits, folks, I'm not about to get new age here.) "Empowering," as far as software is concerned, is nothing more than a fancy, trendy word for that old phrase "genuinely useful." If a piece of software is genuinely useful, meaning the benefits of using it far outweigh the costs, people will recognize that fact and they will use it, because it extends their capabilities and saves them time. In some cases, such as the one ancient DOS program that I still use on a daily basis, this can be true even when the whole world seems to have passed it by.

Your more immediate goal for any widely distributed piece of code or finished program should be to make it correct, intelligent, and accommodating. Do that, and the empowering part will happen automatically, since it's an emergent property of those three characteristics. If this is sounding too cozy and touchy-feely, you can also think in terms of tactics and strategy. The strategy is to make your program empowering; your tactics are to make it correct, intelligent, and accommodating.

One administrative detail: When I refer to a "program" in the rest of this chapter, I'm using the term more loosely than normal, and I mean any piece of software that an outsider will interact with, whether it's a complete application program or an individual function in a shared library. Likewise, I'll talk about "users" in a more general way, and not just limit that term to people running application programs.

## Correct

Correct programs have only two possible responses to any user input:

- Perform the expected processing exactly as requested, taking the full program and system context into account, as appropriate.
- Gracefully refuse the request because of invalid input data, unavailable resources, etc. Needless to say, "gracefully" is not a euphemism for "by formatting the user's hard disk and then causing a GPF" or anything similar.

You should consider correctness to be the bare minimum level of acceptable functionality. Judging correctness is another one of those surprisingly knotty problems. As far as I'm concerned, the API definition, user's manual, etc., is the software's contract with the world. If the documentation and the software disagree, then the entire package is flawed. Whether the flaw lies in the documentation or the program is another, deeper issue, and one that causes its own endless cycle of arguments. I've seen numerous cases where a function was intended to work one way, and documented as such. Later, it was discovered that in some oddball case the implementation didn't match the specification, so the code was left unchanged and the documentation was updated to cover this anomaly. Sometimes this is merely the belated discovery that there is some pathological case that the function can't possibly handle as originally documented (meaning the error was in the original design, since it promised a result it couldn't possibly deliver), and sometimes this is just laziness on the part of a programmer or company that doesn't want to fix its software, so they resolve the disagreement in the cheapest way possible, by changing the documentation to match the code.

*One of the great sins of programming is writing a functional specification that includes the infamous "undefined behavior" clause. This is usually some disclaimer along the lines of "if the lpFlapDoodle parameter is NULL, then this function's behavior is undefined." Translation: "The programmer was too shortsighted to realize that you might accidentally pass a NULL in the lpFlapDoodle parameter (or too lazy to do anything about it), so this function doesn't bother to check for this case. Pass a NULL in that parameter, and*

*your entire program (and possibly the operating system) will hit the pavement like a ton of bricks dropped from low Earth orbit."*

*It's important to distinguish between blatant programmer laziness and conditions that can't be detected. Take the common C run-time function memset(), which sets all the bytes in a given range of memory to a specified value. If you use this function to zero-out a structure before using it, as is often done in Windows programming, the memset routine must rely on you to pass it a valid length parameter, since there's no way for it to know how long your data structure is. (Although the implementation in Visual C++ 2.2 (and, likely, most others) will accept and use a NULL pointer.)*

*A more extreme example is new computer users turning off their systems without shutting down Windows, and losing data in the process. I don't know anyone who would blame Microsoft for not preventing this common problem.*

## Intelligent

As important as correctness is, it's far from "good enough." Intelligent programs don't merely accept proper input and provide correct output, they anticipate caller or user errors and react accordingly. In this case, I'm using "anticipate" in the narrow sense of not only foreseeing an action, but taking a counteraction before the original action happens. The counteraction can take many forms, including the extra diligence on the part of the program to validate the provided parameters, or making the user confirm that a changed document should be discarded without first saving it to disk.

Given all the places in Windows programming that pointers are used as parameters, it's not surprising that one of the easiest ways to break software is by passing NULL pointers. Which inevitably starts instance 1,372 of the philosophical war over whose job it is to ensure that NULL pointers don't make it into the core of a function's code, the caller's or the function's. The answer, of course, should be found in the specification for the function, since that's the function's contract with the world.

Unfortunately, trying to find explicit documentation of how this and other common pathological cases (CPCs) are handled is almost impossible. Many Win32 APIs, for example, are documented in the SDK as accepting certain parameters, and returning a TRUE for success or FALSE for failure (or vice versa), with additional error code values available to the caller via the GetLastError() API. But the API "definition" (to use the term in a conspicuously loose and charitable way) doesn't explicitly say for the vast majority of APIs what Windows does about bad input, nor does it even give you a hint by defining which error codes you might get from GetLastError(). (See Chapter 14 for much more on the GetLastError() debacle.)

There's far more to intelligent software than merely doing a "check and bail out" on provided parameters, of course. In some cases, a function is merely looking for an inconvenient condition that it can safely correct, and not one that prevents it from performing its job. In this, less virulent, strain of bad data we run into one of my favorites: unwanted leading and trailing blanks on string data. I've seen numerous programs over the years that lost their minds (or your data) when presented with nothing more heinous than a name typed in by a user with a leading or trailing blank. Depending on the circumstances, it's often trivially easy for a program to correct such situations, although many don't. I'll take up this point in more detail in Chapter 3, when I talk about defensive programming.

Users aren't the only source of slight irregularities (to borrow a term from the clothing industry). Programs are often handed surprises by third-party library functions, Windows itself, or even a more passive (but far from static) entity, the state of the user's system, if, for example, a "gotta be there" DLL isn't, or it is, but it's the wrong version, or it's a completely unrelated DLL that just happens to have the same name.

I'll have a lot more to say about DLLs in Chapter 6, but I want to stress now that whenever using a non-system DLL, the intelligent approach is to load it explicitly (via the LoadLibrary() API), and give the user some sort of meaningful dialog box with an option for custom help, if the DLL isn't found or is an unusable version. There's also the issue of what to do if a non-vital DLL isn't found. Many programs will refuse to run if they can't find such a DLL (actually, they implicitly load the DLL and let Windows reject the attempt to run the program, which never even gets control).

As with many other issues I mention in this book, this is a matter of balance. If you're writing one of the incredibly few functions that literally can't afford the few instructions needed to do this:

```
if(lpSomeData == NULL)
  return ERROR_BAD_PARAMETER;
```

then document in a clear and unmistakable way that your function will go berserk if it's passed a NULL pointer, and in the code itself document just as clearly why the pointer check wasn't done, so that some well meaning cabinetmaker won't come along, while you're on vacation next year, and insert the above code snippet.

## *Accommodating*

Accommodating programs take that extra step to make life easier for the user, particularly the rookies. Were you wondering when I would get around to human factors? If so, you can stop wondering, the time has come.

For example, *every* dialog box in your public programs should have a Help button. This includes not just the "worker" dialogs that actually present information to the user and collect input, but the diagnostic dialogs that "merely" display a piece of text, whether it's an "operation done" message or something more serious, like news that some file or other needed resource doesn't exist.

I'm amazed at how often Windows itself or some program presents a dialog box that will no doubt trigger questions in the user's mind ("Why???" typically being number one with a bullet), and then doesn't provide any further explanation or help. One of the silliest examples of this I've seen is the way Windows NT 3.51 responds to an attempt to run a program which has an "expected Windows version" greater than 4.0. (The "expected Windows version" is a set of major and minor version codes stored in the executable's header that tells Windows which version of the operating system the program requires.) Instead of telling the user to get a new version of Windows, as Windows 95 does (albeit with less then optimal wording), Windows NT displays a dialog box with a caption and text that both say, "Cannot run program." I'd say this is one time when the exclamation point icon in a dialog box is quite an understatement. (This example might not seem like much of a problem now, but once Win32 programs with expected Windows versions greater than 4.0 start appearing, as we all know they will, eventually, users will start seeing this behavior and asking the authors of the unrunnable programs what the heck is going on. In this way, Windows NT's choice of an unnecessarily cryptic diagnostic message becomes the application programmer's problem.)

Even when programs do provide help, it's sometimes in a decidedly less than helpful way. In my opinion, PageMaker 5.0 wins the "Secret Handshake Award" for its approach to providing help. Instead of doing something as mundane and pandering as displaying a Help button, it requires the user to hold down the Shift key and click on the dialog's background with the right mouse button.

This isn't merely a user interface issue. Libraries of functions should always be designed with the caller's most pressing question or goal in mind. For example, many APIs or functions take a series of parameters and return a result value that indicates if the call was successful. If the call was a success, the data it returned, if any, is placed into a buffer pointed to by one of the parameters. This is a simple, obvious, highly usable model that allows the caller to do things like:

```
if(SomeAPIFunction(/* parameters */))
  {
  /* Function succeeded, process its output */
  }
else
  {
  /* Function failed, complain to the user, shut down, etc. */
  }
```

But there are exceptions. One that drives me crazy is:

```
UINT GetDlgItemInt(
    HWND  hDlg,          // handle to dialog box
```

```
int  nIDDlgItem,    // control identifier
BOOL* lpTranslated, // points to variable to receive success/failure
                    // indicator
BOOL bSigned        // specifies whether value is signed or unsigned
);
```

This API retrieves the value from a dialog box's control, such as an edit box, and converts it into an unsigned integer. GetDlgItemInt() is designed "inside out," in my opinion, since its return value is the converted value, which could very well be zero on a successful call, making it impossible to test it in an if statement, the form that Windows programmers normally employ. I would much prefer to have seen this API prototyped as:

```
BOOL GetDlgItemInt(
   HWND  hDlg,         // handle to dialog box
   int  nIDDlgItem,    // control identifier
   UINT* lpValue,      // points to variable to receive converted value
   BOOL bSigned        // specifies whether value is signed or unsigned
);
```

where it would return FALSE for failure and TRUE for success, setting the buffer pointed to by lpValue as needed.

## Examples: Good, Bad, and Nagging

Nearly every Windows computer is packed with instances of both good and bad design decisions. I think the following examples are good role models (or cautionary tales), and that they show how fine the line is between intelligent, accommodating software and software that just misses the mark.

* Windows 95 autoloads CD ROMs . This struck me as one of those "why didn't someone think of this years ago" ideas when I first saw it. In case you haven't seen it, and you don't know what I'm talking about, it works like this: Insert a CD ROM into your computer, and Windows 95 will automagically check the root of the CD for a plain text file called AUTORUN.INF. If it finds the file, it reads it and follows the commands it contains. The Windows 95 distribution CD ROM contains an AUTORUN.INF file with the following lines:

```
[autorun]
OPEN=AUTORUN\AUTORUN.EXE
ICON=AUTORUN\WIN95CD.ICO
```

which obviously makes it run AUTORUN.EXE and use the specified icon. This might seem like pretty tame, even techno-weenie level stuff, which is exactly my point—intelligent, accommodating features don't have to be rocket science that require tens of thousands of lines of bleeding edge code. If Explorer didn't twitch like Kramer from *Seinfeld* when you inserted the disk, I'd give Microsoft a solid A+ for Windows 95's handling of CD ROMs.

- One of the most noticeable things you see when you convert to Windows 95 is the two full-screen shutdown bitmaps (which are stored in the files LOGOW.SYS and LOGOS.SYS in your Windows directory, by the way). One of the persistent problems with Windows 95 is users shutting off the computer without shutting down Windows, or doing so before Windows has finished closing down. These bitmaps won't perform magic in solving this problem, but they do nicely reinforce the idea that users are supposed to shut down the system before hitting the power switch. Given the number of computers I see with file systems mangled by premature power off operations, I'm glad to see even minimal help in this area.

- Transfer a file to or from America Online, and the access program does something interesting. It shows you the obligatory "gas gauge" graphic with your remaining time for the file transfer, no surprise there. But the text it uses to tell you the remaining time is not the typical hyper-precise minutes and seconds readout you see in most communications packages. Instead, it rounds the time. For example, it says "about 5 minutes remaining," then changes it to "under 5 minutes remaining," "about 4 minutes remaining", etc. I much prefer this approach, because frankly, I don't need to know exactly how many minutes and seconds are left in the transfer. If it's going to take more than a minute or so, I'm probably off doing something else and not watching the silly gas gauge. (Zen question: Do the numbers really change on a gas gauge if no one is looking?) And if for some reason I am watching it, the information the rounded value provides is sufficient for the purpose. By approximating the value, America Online also gives the interface an ever so slightly less artificial or forced feeling, and a more human touch.

- I've seen at least two installation programs recently that do their thing in copying files from floppies to your hard disk, and then prepare to do the inevitable system restart so that the configuration changes can take effect. But at this point, the programs show a glimmer of intelligence: They check to see if there's still a floppy in the A: drive, and if there is, they pop up a dialog box telling you to remove it. This is another "not rocket science" issue that I think is an excellent addition to a program. In this case, it nicely anticipates a common user error, and at very little expense to the installation program.

- The Windows 95 task bar is an innovative solution to a problem that Microsoft supposedly found many new Windows users were having: Losing their open windows. (And I know for a fact that some new Windows users do indeed have a problem in this area.) This was another Windows 95 feature that seemed a bit gimmicky the first time I saw it, but I quickly grew to like it. Notice that another Windows 95 feature, its much better handling of the dreaded free system resources, would have effectively made the "lost windows" problem even worse in Windows 95: If you make it easier for people to run more programs at once, even the beginners will, which only increases the probability that they'll start losing them. In my opinion, Microsoft came very close to getting the task bar wrong, though. If they hadn't included the "autohide" option, which makes the task bar disappear when another program gets the focus, it would have been far too intrusive. (I don't know when in the design cycle the autohide feature was added to the task bar, but it still serves as a good example of how close you can get to a good solution without getting it quite right, and how small a change it can take to score a direct hit.) I wish they had also given us an option to make the task bar automatically resize itself, so that buttons always stayed full-size. Maybe next release.

- Have you noticed what happens under Windows 95 if you try to print something and your printer (like my stone age HP Laser Jet Series II) isn't done warming up yet? Windows 95 displays a dialog box telling you that the printer wasn't responding. But the nice detail is that if you just ignore the dialog box, or if you're not in the room (hopefully indistinguishable events from the computer's perspective, but we can never be sure), Windows 95 keeps trying to send data to the printer. When the printer responds, Windows closes the dialog box and prints the file without further ado.

- Here's one I discovered by accident: Load a file into Visual SlickEdit for Windows, then load the same file into another editor, change the file, and save it to disk. Now give Visual SlickEdit the focus and it will display a dialog telling you that the file has changed, and ask you if you want to reload it. I don't know about you, but I tend to have a lot of windows open in my Windows sessions, and this feature removes one small way for me to mess up and lose editing changes. (There's a lesson-within-an-example here, since it's still possible that the user has forgotten about changes made to the copy of the file loaded in Visual SlickEdit. When the file is reloaded from the copy on disk, these changes will be lost (unless the same changes were made via the other program used to edit the file). There's no good way for Visual SlickEdit or any other program to catch this case. Probably the only viable solution would be to check and see if the user has ever changed the file in the current editing session (not just changed it since the last save operation), and remind the user that work could be lost unless the file is saved to disk under another name before it is reloaded.)

- Spell check a document with Word for Windows 6.0, and it will remember corrections you make for that session, even if you don't add them to a custom dictionary. For example, if your document contains the word "WinWord," the spell checker will flag it as a misspelled word. Change this word to "Word for Windows" via the spell checker, and it will suggest "Word for Windows" as a replacement for all ensuing occurrences of "WinWord" in that checking session. (Unfortunately, Word 6.0 doesn't remember these corrections in other spell checker runs in the same or other editing sessions.)

- Unlike the America Online file transfer item I mentioned above, Explorer uses the same approach with different data and only manages to frustrate me to no end. In this case, the rounded values are file sizes. I can't imagine whatever possessed Microsoft to round file sizes to the nearest kilobyte, and then not even give the user the option of seeing the exact size for the files a directory at a time. Whatever the rationale, I sure don't agree with the decision. When I was beta testing Windows 95 and first saw this, I thought the option was buried somewhere in the menu structure and I couldn't find it, or that it would be added at a later date. The option never showed up, which is one of several reasons why I use Explorer only for testing purposes. (I've researched this some more, and I still can't find a solution. If you know of a super secret registry switch or other mechanism that controls this behavior, please tell me.)

- Version 4.0 of Windows help added some welcome features and characteristics, but one that I most definitely could do without, at least in its current form, is the "Creating Word List..." dialog with the pen that fills page after page in its little book. Notice that this feature breaks several human factors rules: It's a sometimes (very) long-running operation, yet it doesn't give you a way to cancel (if there is one I sure haven't found it; it should have a Cancel button right under the little book on the dialog), and it doesn't even give you a progress indicator or an estimate of how long the operation will take. I found out just how annoying this can be when I created a word index for the 39,750,389-byte API32.HLP file that came with Visual C++ 2.2, and watched that goofy pen scribble for at least 15 minutes. (When I re-ran this test for this example, I told WinHelp to create the full-feature version of the word index for API32.HLP on a 75MHz Pentium with 24MB of RAM. It ran for exactly 12 minutes, then popped up a dialog that said, "Please free memory by closing applications or by removing unnecessary files." This system had 24MB of RAM and two hard drives that had 50MB and 700MB of free space, respectively. The dual-purpose dialog box left me wondering which type of storage it ran out of, RAM or hard drive space, and thinking that someone at Microsoft should have taken the time to use a single-purpose dialog.)

- My all-time "favorite" quirk in Windows 95 (the Explorer, actually), is this silliness of how it handles left-mouse-button file drags. Left-button drag a non-program file, say FRED.TXT, from one directory to another, and the file is moved, as expected. But left-button drag FRED.EXE, and Windows 95 takes it upon itself to leave the original file in place and shortcut it in the destination directory. (By the way, I hereby claim coinage rights to the use of "shortcut" as a transitive verb meaning "to create a shortcut for." Every time you use it, you owe me a penny. You can forward the money to me at my local BMW dealership.)

It's pretty obvious that Microsoft did this to keep us poor, dumb users from accidentally moving executables all over the place and breaking file associations. I find this amazing, because there was a much better way to accomplish the same thing without annoying all us old Windows hands. All they had to do was make the current right-mouse-button drag function (the popup menu with the "Move Here," "Copy Here," and "Create Shortcut(s) Here" options) work with the left mouse button, the one that we were all used to, and leave the right-button-drag function out of the product completely. Then they should have given us a "guru switch" for the left-button operation that would have made it work just like a left button drag in File Manager and the bazillion-and-one File Manager (and soon, Explorer) replacements out there. That way, the Power Users could have configured things to our liking, the new/casual users would have had the added protection of the new feature, and none of us would have accidentally littered our hard disks with unwanted shortcuts.

- We keep hearing about how object technology and even lowly DLLs will transport us to a magical realm in which we can customize our systems, use only the components we really want, etc. I don't know about you, but I haven't seen much evidence of this emerging utopia. In many cases, the solution is obvious: Need to save some disk space on your notebook computer, and you never use the drawing or equation editing components of your word processor? Just delete the external programs that implement those features. Such ham-fisted customizations are almost never documented, even when they're safe and they'll have the desired effect. That's why I gave the user the option of turning off several ancillary features in Stickies! (the tip of the day, today in history, and quote of the day notes), so that the databases for these features can be deleted. And yes, I documented this fact clearly in the help file. (Some larger application programs will give you installation options not to install some components in the first place or even to uninstall them later. Unfortunately, not enough programs today are that flexible in helping the user manage a computer's resources.)

*Please try to remember that in software, the magic is behind the scenes and not in the user interface. I can't stress this enough, particularly at a time when Windows development is deluged with interface gizmos from Microsoft and countless VBX (and soon, OCX) vendors. Don't misunderstand, I welcome these user interface advancements with open arms, and I'm delighted to see a thriving, competitive market of vendors in a knock-down, drag-out fight for our dollars. But no matter how much these tree views and richedit controls and animated thing-a-ma-jiggies improve the usability of a given program (and in some cases they're quite a help), it's still the core functionality, the "real programming," if you will, that decides whether that program is something we want to live with day in and day out. One of my favorite authors, Joyce Carol Oates, once said, "Technique holds a reader from sentence to sentence, but only content will stay in his mind." I couldn't agree more.*

# Ten Macro-Level Guidelines

Let's get specific. This section is where I'll present the first ten guidelines for writing better Windows programs. It could be argued that nearly everything here is really general software engineering advice, and that it's not specific to Windows work. In one sense this is true, but it's equally true that the shifting sands of the Windows world make many of these guidelines particularly important to Windows developers, sometimes for not so obvious reasons.

All the guidelines in this chapter are on what I consider the macro level; Chapter 3 will present the micro-level guidelines. This dichotomy does not mean that I think the macro issues are more important than the micro issues. Rather, this division is meant to indicate how these guidelines affect your work. The macro items are more design and long-range oriented, while the micro issues tend to come into play when you're in the trenches, i.e. when your fingers are on the keycaps and you're cruising along at 1AM with Thomas Dolby on the headphones (and not always thinking about anything beyond getting the next clean compile).

## 0. Take the Big View and Plan for the Future

> He [the poet] must write as the interpreter of nature,
> and the legislator of mankind, and consider himself as
> presiding over the thoughts and manners of future gen-
> erations; as a being superior to time and place.
>
> Samuel Johnson

I wish that all programmers, like Johnson's poet, were far more conscious of their place in time, and their obligations to the future (and the past, for that matter). In fact, if I could wave a magic wand and do one, and only one, thing to reshape programmers' heads this would be it, without hesitation. Programmers today, as a group, are far too interested in "getting it to work," and far less interested than they should be in creating something that will not be, effectively, disposable code come the next version of the operating system, their tool, or the program itself.

To a large extent, I don't blame programmers for this situation. Virtually all professional programmers are under extreme schedule pressures today, which means that much of the code that goes into public programs isn't as well designed or thought out as it should be, because there simply isn't time. The person who coined the old one-liner that there's never time to do something right, but there's always time to do it over, must have been a maintenance programmer fixing other people's mistakes. For Windows programmers, things are much worse, since we spend so much time just trying to figure out how the latest version of our frameworks, compilers, linkers, resource editors, DLLs, third party libraries, and, last but certainly most of all, the Windows API, all work, that it's a minor miracle we get *anything* written, let alone concern ourselves with the future adaptability of our code.

Still, there are some minor things we can all do to make our code more "future friendly," to coin a phrase, and most of them take very little time:

- Always, always, always try to think through *all* the ramifications of your design decisions and make sure that you understand to the best of your ability all the costs and benefits of your choices. The best example of this that I can find in Windows 95 is the decision to implement its GDI and USER components in 16-bit code, and then to clip (read: mangle) GDI coordinates and listbox index values. (See Chapter 14 for much more on these issues.)

  Obviously, you can't see far into the future, and even if you could, the software you'd design with such knowledge would often be a very poor match for the hardware and other software of the present day. [See the sidebars "Pathological Case: FAT Cluster Size" and "The End of the (Computing) World is Near" for more thoughts on prognostication.] But there are easily foreseeable changes that you should (or should have) evaluate(d) and plan(ned) for appropriately: Windows' move to 32 bits, the addition of new, standard C++ features, as widely discussed in various magazines long before the ANSI/ISO standard was even finished, etc.

- Decide as early as possible in the development cycle of your public Win32 program whether it's the inaugural version, a port from Win16, or simply a minor revision of an existing 32-bit program, which of the three Win32 platforms (Win32s, Windows 95, and Windows NT) you will officially support. Much to my dismay, this is far from a simple, "let's run everywhere" question, as there are numerous small differences (and a few large ones) that could easily persuade you to shun one or two of the platforms. In fact, I strongly recommend against even allowing your program to run under Win32s. (See Chapter 14 for much more on Win32 issues and how to deal with them.)

- Worry about localization now, not at release time. (By "localization," I mean producing versions of your program that use various national languages to communicate with the user.) Certainly not all programs need to be localized, not even all public programs. But some do, and you're far better off if you make a serious effort to find out as soon as possible if yours is one of them. This is one of those issues that can turn into endless arguments between management and the techies, so the techies often shy away from it, and avoid bringing it to management's attention. Management sees the issue as a no brainer—plan for the future, put in the capability now, even though we have no immediate plans to support anything but the single language version, etc. The techies see this as potentially wasted effort, so they try to ignore the issue. Sometimes this is the right thing to do, sometimes it isn't. It depends on several issues, mostly the probability that other languages will need to be supported and the availability of resources to do it right the first time.

- I often see public programs written with no provisions at all for obvious future enhancements, which means that when a client, management, or paying customers request the inevitable change (or you realize that it was a good idea all along), you find that it takes a lot of work to implement the change, often involving throwing out and changing a considerable amount of old code. And that leads to more bugs and a greater testing burden over the life of the program, since you had to test the old code to make sure it was right, and then test it again after you changed or replaced it.

You can sometimes reduce your testing and coding work significantly by using one of my favorite tricks, which I unceremoniously call "hanging a feature off a boolean." In English, this means that you identify a new user-customization that you think you will or may want to add to your program in a future release. Perhaps you want to give the user a choice of "short" or "long" menus, as some Windows programs do, or you'll want to make the creation of backup files (for example, *.BAK) for saved documents optional. Once you've identified this type of likely future enhancement, do the following:

1. Add a global variable that specifies the setting of that feature. In my experience this variable usually turns out to be a boolean, hence my name for this technique. Set the variable to the value that will be the default setting once it is configurable in the future release.

2. Make sure you *clearly* document via comments what you've done! This is one of those rare cases where you're writing code that is decidedly self-undocumenting, so you must take a minute to clarify the situation. You don't have to write *War and Peace*, just insert a line that says something like, "The UseShortMenus flag controls how the program displays its menus. This value doesn't change in the current implementation, but it might in the future as part of a new configurable option."

3. Write all your code in a way that modifies its behavior according to the setting of the variable, even though it never changes in the current version of the program.

4. Make sure your program saves and restores the variable from whatever persistent storage (for example, .INI or custom format file) your program uses to preserve the user's configuration settings between sessions.

5. Test your program with the variable set to all pertinent legal values that you will eventually allow once it is configurable. Once you're convinced that your program is correct, you're done with this feature for this release. (Obviously, if the variable can take on a large range of possible values, you won't test every single one. Instead, test with a few extreme-but-legal values that are most likely to trigger a problem.)

6. When the future release rolls around, and you decide to make this feature configurable, all the hard work is already done and tested. You merely have to add a control to the appropriate configuration dialog and hook it up to the global variable. Your old code is unchanged, which means your testing burden is relatively small, and consists of making sure that changing the setting during a session won't cause problems, and that the configuration dialog works properly. All your old code is unchanged, and still known to be good, and you just got a new program feature for little work and very little risk of introducing a new bug.

I've used this approach in programs I've written for clients, as well as in Stickies! several times during its early releases. In some cases, I wanted a program to do something a particular way, but I simply wasn't sure if this behavior should be user configurable or not. In others, I was anticipating a client's future request and ensuring that there would be no trouble when they called and wanted the change made ASAP, if not sooner. In all these cases I "hung the feature off a boolean," which gave me (or my client) great flexibility to decide later on if I would surface this variable as a configuration option. In most cases I eventually did make the change, and the required work was minimal—on average the development literally took less than 10 minutes, as it was entirely confined to the configuration dialog's class.

This approach can also bail you out in an emergency, if you find out that your new whiz-bang feature has some subtle interaction with the system or a weird bug that you somehow missed in design and testing. You can simply flip the switch in the source and recompile to turn it off, or you can even give your users a way to change the configuration setting in the stored options (.INI file, custom data file, whatever). None of us likes making a knee-jerk fix, but it can save the day in a crisis.

*Am I really telling you to guess which features you'll have to implement in a future release and spend scarce development resources on them now? Am I crazy? Yes, I'm telling you to do this, and no, I'm not crazy. I'm not suggesting that you sit down with your program's listing and look for every conceivable future change that your boss or you yourself might want to make, and festoon your program with support for every one before it's needed. That would be an absurd, irresponsible waste of your time. But I am saying that there are times when you're working on a program or talking to a client or your boss or your users and you get an unmistakable gut-level feeling about what they'll ask for next, even when you aren't looking for such issues. It doesn't happen often, but I've found that when it does, it's more often right than not.*

- Never forget that it's easy to get carried away when building flexibility into your programs, and only burden your users. For example, the RegQueryValueEx() Win32 API defines its third parameter as

```
lpdwReserved
    Reserved; must be NULL.
```

A reserved, must-be-NULL pointer to a DWORD? This is absurd, and the people responsible for this should have their hands slapped. Please don't confuse this example with the many places in the Windows API where a message that doesn't need a wParam and/or an lParam says that these values must be zero. In these cases, Microsoft has no choice but to include these parameters, since they're built into the basic messaging architecture of Windows. It also makes perfect sense to specify that they must be zero, since that gives Microsoft maximum flexibility for future API enhancements without breaking existing applications. In this case, a very minor interface requirement benefits everyone.

## Pathological Case: FAT Cluster Size

All file systems (or at least all that I'm aware of) allocate disk space in "chunks," which means that the amount of free disk space consumed by the addition of a new file is always some multiple of that chunk size. Create a one-byte file, and the system will allocate a lot more than that one byte, even above the administrative overhead of a directory entry.

In the FAT file system, this "chunk size" is also known as the cluster size. With the coincident arrival of incredibly cheap hard disks and Windows 95, this situation is quickly becoming known as the "cluster size problem." I won't go into all the technical detail, but the problem boils down to the fact that the FAT file system is limited to 64K clusters for a logical volume. This means that as your disk gets larger, the FAT file system must allocate more storage per cluster so that it can still address the entire volume, which in turn results in more storage wasted per file. How much gets wasted? The Microsoft PSS article #Q67321 (which is on the *Microsoft Developer Network* CD ROM) gives the following summary:

| Drive Size | FAT Type | Sectors Per Cluster | Cluster Size |
|---|---|---|---|
| 0 MB - 15 MB | 12-bit | 8 | 4K |
| 16 MB - 127 MB | 16-bit | 4 | 2K |
| 128 MB - 255 MB | 16-bit | 8 | 4K |
| 256 MB - 511 MB | 16-bit | 16 | 8K |
| 512 MB - 1023 MB | 16-bit | 32 | 16K |
| 1024 MB - 2048 MB | 16-bit | 64 | 32K |

In other words, every file wastes, on average, 16KB (half of 32KB) on a FAT file system when the volume size is over 1GB, a common disk size today. Very small files, such as the numerous small headers and OBJ files developers often live with, waste nearly the entire 32KB each.

Back in the early stone age, when these limitations were cast in, well, stone, the very thought of someone having a hard drive larger than a gigabyte in their PC must have seemed like it was so far off in the misty future that it wasn't worth thinking about. Guess what? It's past time to start thinking about it.

The first serious problem I encountered regarding this cluster size situation in the real world involved my accountant, Charlie. I had just helped him upgrade the PCs in his business to larger, faster systems with more hard disk space. We had analyzed his needs in detail and jointly decided on how much speed and space he needed, so that he could avoid having to do more upgrades in a year. A few months after we installed his shiny new hardware, he called and wanted to know why he was running out of disk space. I was sure there must be some simple answer, like a TEMP directory loaded with garbage files that we could erase and free up a hundred megs or so.

When I examined the system, I found no such hidden cache of junk files. I did find a directory with 3,434 client files, all created by the income tax preparation package he used. The average size of the files was almost exactly 500 bytes. On Charlie's 540MB hard disk, that meant he was losing about 16KB - 500 bytes = 15884 bytes per file, or 54,545,656 bytes, or 96.9 percent of the occupied disk space for those files. That's a lot of gas, by anyone's reckoning.

While I was writing this book, I added a new computer to my holdings. It arrived with an 850 MB hard disk and the usual virtual plethora of preinstalled software. The hard disk included a directory C:\MSINPUT\MOUSE\EFFECT that contained 457 cursor files, each exactly 326 bytes long. This meant I was using 7,487,488 bytes (457 * 16KB) to store 148,982 bytes (457 * 326) of actual data, for a stunning 98 percent gas rating. (I'll give you 457 guesses which files I zipped into an archive first on this system, and the first 456 guesses don't count.)

My point is not to beat up the original FAT file system design for not planning for the future (although this situation does serve as an interesting cautionary tale about planning). But notice that Windows 95 doesn't give us a general solution to this problem. I expected that it would provide, at least as an added-cost option, an installable component to make it use NT's file system, NTFS, which is much better at managing disk space. Unfortunately, this isn't an option, although I suspect one enterprising vendor or another will step up to the plate on this issue eventually. Whatever the case, we have Windows 95 coming to market at a time of astonishingly cheap hard disk space (a situation that Microsoft surely was aware of), and yet that's the one system resource it can't manage in anywhere near a reasonable fashion.

In fact, less than two weeks before Windows 95 became generally available, I purchased a 1.2GB hard disk at my local Sam's Club for a mere $298 (which is, incredibly, under 25 cents a MB, and will no doubt sound expensive very soon after this book is published). The mouse cursor files I mentioned above would have taken up a whopping 14,974,976 bytes on this drive, or almost exactly 100 times their actual data content.

If this example seems artificial, let me tell you what happened when I installed a real product onto this new hard disk. I installed a C++ compiler, but not the full package—just the tools, headers, and libraries. I didn't install the samples (which are notoriously large and include hundreds of very small files) or the RTL source. The result was 1,767 files with a total data size of 89,759,861 bytes, consuming 146,538,496 bytes of disk space, wasting 56,778,635 bytes of disk space, or about 39 percent. This is actually a charitable example, since C++ compilers installed this way include some very large files which tend to minimize the amount of storage lost to the cluster size problem. Still, extrapolating this meager percentage to a full disk, I'd lose about 468MB, or $116, of disk space.

So, how do we get around this problem? One solution is to use disk compression, which allocates storage via its own scheme and avoids the cluster debacle. This isn't a viable solution for some people, like me, who have to share the disk space on a given computer between Windows 3.1, Windows 95, Windows NT, and OS/2. There isn't a common disk compression solution between 16- and 32-bit Windows; don't even ask about that alien artifact, OS/2.

Historical note: I have a copy of *PC* magazine (as opposed to *PC Magazine*), Volume 1 Number 1, February-March 1982, which has an ad on page 22 from a company named VR Data. The ad offers several hard drives, including a 6.3 MB unit that came in a housing about the size of most modern desktop computers' system units, for a paltry $2,895 ($459.52 per megabyte [cough, cough]), not counting the $249 adapter and driver software. Imagine what the good folks at VR Data would have said had they seen my 3.5"x1", 1.2GB drive in 1982.

## 1. Strive for Balance in All Decisions

*Then at the balance let's be mute,*
*We never can adjust it;*
*What's done we partly may compute,*
*But know not what's resisted.*

Robert Burns

One point I'll come back to repeatedly throughout this book is one that we all fail to remember from time to time: There are almost no absolutes in programming.

Almost every decision you make, whether it's choosing a programming language and development environment for a new project or the datatype for a local variable, has tradeoffs that you should weigh. These tradeoffs can be very subtle at times, and they almost always have very long memories, meaning they can come back to haunt you a surprisingly long time down the road (see the sidebar "The End of the (Computing) World is Near" for a disturbing example).

One way to avoid problems is simply to remember that these tradeoffs are everywhere, and that almost all your decisions have two sides. It's not simply a matter of making something work as well as you can; that's a fanatical stance that leads to disaster as surely as does not caring at all about quality. You've probably heard the old aphorism that perfection is the enemy of the good. This is particularly appropriate in our field, since programmers will often strive for perfection

## The End of the (Computing) World Is Near

By now I'm sure you've heard that many of the business application programs in the world will lose their minds when the year changes to 2000. The problem, of course, is that these programs store the year as only two digits, and when they start to calculate elapsed time for interest or retirement benefits or whatever in January 2000, the "00" in the year will cause no end of havoc.

As far as I can tell, this is one time when the doom sayers are right. It's widely known that many companies today are running quite old software, and in some cases, they don't even have the source to the code, so they couldn't fix the problem even if they were aware of it. And in many cases the two digit year is so ingrained in their company databases and other programs that making the change will be hideously expensive, and will surely introduce bugs and trigger reports on CNN for months to come, as people get bills or benefit checks for millions of dollars. Aside from the CNN hilarity, I expect there to be at least one or two major incidents traceable to this problem, for example, a bank's overly aggressive account management software starts locking people out of their own accounts, or something with graver human cost. I honestly hope I'm wrong, but it doesn't feel like it.

I find this situation professionally quite embarrassing, and I think it shows just how shortsighted many programmers can be. To be fair, many of the people who wrote these programs had no choice—they were writing a new program that used the company's existing database, and they simply had to employ the data in the available format, no matter how obvious it was that they were only making the coming train wreck worse.

You can see what a cautionary tale this is for all programmers about the value of looking forward, so I won't belabor the point. But please, be careful out there.

and shun the sufficient, and end up delivering nothing of value. That blade does have two edges, though, in that programmers will also use this observation as an excuse and claim that since perfection can't be achieved, there's no sense in making some proposed set of changes to enhance the quality of a program.

Put another way, you should be an economist. (Bet you didn't see that one coming.) You should always think in terms of cost-benefit ratios as a way of avoiding the pitfalls of extremism. For example, programmers often say that there's no sense in adding minimal security features to a program, because they can be easily defeated by someone who knows what they're doing. How much do you want to bet these same people lock their cars when they leave them in a shopping center parking lot for even a few minutes during the middle of the day? They do this (as do I), because they know that there's a benefit to this type of security, and that it does keep at least some people at bay, even if a skilled and determined thief can get into and away with a car in a matter of seconds. In other words, locking your car in such cases makes sense because it provides at least some security for almost zero cost. That's a good ratio, so we do it.

When I talk about calculating the "cost" of a design decision, I'm not talking about merely the time to implement it, or the impact on your program's size or execution speed. I use the term in the largest possible sense and include things like the long-term maintainability of the code, the usability of the resulting program, and the overall "system friendliness" of the final program (for example, how easily it can be installed or uninstalled, whether it requires changes to the user's SYSTEM.INI file, etc.). Of course, balancing the user's cost, in this sense, against your own quickly turns into its own endless, philosophical argument. Speaking as a user of many commercial software packages, I firmly believe that programmers, are much less considerate of their users than they should be, something I'll take up in guideline 4.

In his classic work, *The Mythical Man Month*, Frederick Brooks says, "Because ease of use is the purpose, this ratio of function to conceptual complexity is the ultimate test of system design. Neither function alone nor simplicity alone defines a good design." He doesn't call it a cost-benefit ratio, but I'm sure he's talking about this same concept, and I think he's absolutely right. As I said above, however, I think all programmers need to take a much more expansive and inclusive view of both parts of that calculation, particularly the cost side.

In particular, when you're assessing the cost of some contemplated design, remember to include:

- Total development cost, including documentation. No one likes to think about documentation in this business (at least that's the unmistakable impression I get from how dreadful and wildly inaccurate most of it is). But it's a significant part of the big picture, even if you're "merely" creating a function library for in-house use by one or two other people and not a public program that will be sold as shrinkware to millions.

- Maintenance cost. Again, think big, and remember that the source code you write for a public program could have a very long lifetime. If you create your program using some oddball language or technique, and other people (which includes yourself, months from now) have to maintain it, you could be taking on a long-term cost that far outweighs the benefits. Also, be cautious about adopting operating system features. Don't load up your program with complex items like OLE support if your program doesn't really need them. (This is what I call "tick mark inflation," and it afflicts many commercially available software titles. In order to get all the "tick marks" in the reviewers' summary tables in magazine articles, companies pile on features that users might not really want or need. The result is huge programs that are filled with features almost no one uses, yet consume development and support resources that can no longer be used for other purposes. If you think I'm kidding, talk to people who use the current crop of Windows word processors, and see how many of the whiz-bang features they disable or ignore.)

- Potential enhancement cost. If you're going to reduce your development time by using some third-party product, such as a library or framework, what are the chances that you'll get good support from that third party, or that they'll still be in business, two or three years from now? What if you want to port your program to OS/2 for its next release, and the company doesn't have a version of its product for that platform? You can wind up using a third-party package to get the current release out the door on schedule, only to create a huge problem down the road, one that is very expensive to fix. For many projects, this won't be an issue. But make sure you know as early as possible if yours is one of them, and then plan appropriately.

- Your user's cost, which includes the learning curve needed to master the new feature, the speed and actual desirability of the feature, the resources it consumes, etc. Again, I'll talk about this in much more detail in guideline 4.

In one sense, the issue of balance really boils down to the question: "Is X a good deal for everyone involved?" Unfortunately, many technical decisions are made in the writing of public programs that have nothing to do with this question. Managers, for example, often push their pet projects or techniques because they're more interested in "empire building" (increasing the size of their staff and extending their influence within the company) than in producing the best possible product. We programmers have a far from pristine record in this regard, as we often indulge ourselves by using tools and techniques that we shouldn't, often to the long term detriment of the finished program. The only advice I can give you on that front is to guard against such tendencies in yourself, as well as others on your team, and be ready to fight the good fight.

## *2. Make KISS Your Religion*

*Give me a look, give me a face,*
*That makes simplicity a grace;*
*Robes loosely flowing, hair as free:*
*Such sweet neglect more taketh me,*
*Than all the adulteries of art;*
*They strike mine eyes, but not my heart.*

Ben Jonson

*Our life is frittered away by detail... Simplfy, simplify.*

Henry David Thoreau

Ah, the KISS ("keep it simple, stupid") principle. If ever there was something that nearly all programmers recited, almost mantra-like, but roundly ignored, this is it. I sometimes think that every computer used by a programmer should have a sign on the monitor that says, "KISS: It's not just a good idea, it should be the law." (In practice, this would do little good. Programmers, being the wacky funsters that they are, would likely use the signs as ice scrapers, doorstops, or shims to balance tables.)

Let me be clear: In this context, "simple" refers to how understandable and maintainable the source code is. For some bizarre reason I have yet to discover, many programmers misinterpret KISS to mean "write it in as few lines of code as possible." As a result, they turn some programming efforts into contests ("I can implement that function in 47 keystrokes! Top that!"). (I detest generalizations based on gender, but in my experience this phenomenon is almost exclusively a "guy thing." Even more amusing, most men who are guilty of this deny it, and most women are not the least bit surprised that men do it.)

Nowhere is this problem more acute than in C programs. Some of the production C code I run into (get run over by?) looks like it was written by someone under the influence of recreational chemistry. I'm not arguing against all idiomatic C; well written C has a characteristic and minimalist grace that can be quite esthetically pleasing, and can also make it easier to understand. I do object, however, to pointless constructs like the conditional operator. Examine the generated assembler for a statement like:

```
x = a > 100 ? y : z;
```

and you're likely to find that it generates the exact same code as if you had written:

```
if(a > 100)
  x = y;
else
  x = z;
```

In fact, some time back I experimented with several compilers and found that the conditional statement did indeed generate the same code as the more mundane if-then-else, and in some cases it actually produced slightly more code. I tried to find a case where it was actually more efficient, but couldn't. In other words, we have a cost to using this operator, its lower readability and its sometimes slightly greater pathlength, but no benefit. (I often refer to code that's been manually tweaked in this way in the interest of performance, but ends up actually running slower, as "hand sloptimized.") In particular, many programmers fall into the trap of assuming that fewer keystrokes or lines of code equates to fewer instructions. This is a dangerous and quite often invalid assumption that can lead to performance problems.

Even when you're not indulging in extreme C-isms and you're writing genuinely good code, you can accidentally violate the KISS principle. Perhaps the best way to accomplish some task is via a slightly odd algorithm. The solution is mindlessly simple—use the algorithm and add a few lines of commentary that explain what the code is doing. I know how mundane and obvious this point seems, but I mention it anyway, because I keep running into code where the author hasn't thought of this or was so busy "getting the code to work" (there's that phrase again), that no thought was given to commenting it.

Of course, there are competing goals involved in the effort to simplify. I mentioned above that when I'm reasonably sure that I'll need to make some feature user configurable in the future, I'll use my "hang the feature off a boolean" trick. In the short run that technique clearly violates the KISS principle, since the implementation is slightly more complex, and the testing burden greater than it needs to be for the current release. But in the long run this practice makes sense, since the benefits typically far outweigh the minor additional costs.

## 3. You(Now) != You(Later)

> *Time present and time past*
> *Are both perhaps present in time future,*
> *And time future contained in time past.*
>
> T. S. Eliot

The title of this guideline is really just C-like shorthand for the observation that all professional programmers have to work on a variety of projects and code modules over time, and that during that time, we change. Our programming philosophies and styles change, our world views on nearly all issues change, and we slowly become literally different people. This navel-staring point has some non-trivial, real world consequences for programmers. Most important, it says that even if you're the only person who will ever see the source code for a particular program (and quite often even that judgment is wrong in the long run), over enough time even such a project will, in effect, become a team effort. Normally, a programming team is several to several hundred people working in parallel on the project, meaning that the team is primarily spatially dispersed. A team can also be temporally dispersed, as in you(now) plus someone else (or you(later)) months or years from now working on the same project. Notice that temporal dispersion can be a greater problem than the spatial variety, simply because it can't be overcome by walking into someone's office, plunking down a listing, and asking what the heck some code does. (There's probably an idea in there for a truly dreadful science fiction story about time traveling maintenance programmers, but I'll resist the urge to pursue it if you will.)

And don't think for a moment that it takes years for this phenomenon to happen. A few months working on another project will often make you an outsider to your own code. Programmers are particularly susceptible to this problem, because we tend to be very good at loading an entire design into short-term memory, marinating ourselves in it, implementing it, and then unloading it and going on to the next task. In my nine years at IBM, I worked on numerous different projects, as a programmer, designer, and tester. There were a few times when I ran into this situation, when someone else was given the job of fixing a bug or changing some code I had written months or years ago, and the person came to me with a question. I remember looking at the code, which I knew was mine, barely recognizing it, and struggling to remember why I had done something in a particular way.

This issue is at the heart of one of the most dangerous of all programmer fables, "I'll know what this means when I see it again." If the "next time" is only a few weeks down the road, then the programmer probably will understand the code with little trouble. But if it's six months or more, and another project and its endless details and concerns have taken possession of the programmer's head in the meantime, I'm not so confident. The problem, of course, is that programmers tell themselves this fable as an excuse for not documenting their code properly.

The you(now) != you(later) phenomenon is dangerous because it's a slippery slope that leads directly to quality problems and inefficiency. When the time comes for someone else (including you) to interpret your "old" code, it's often to fix a bug or make some last-second change under extreme schedule pressure. And you know what that means—a quick look at a listing, a few minutes in furrowed brow mode while you try to decipher what the code "is really doing," some quickly written code that often ignores some undocumented detail of the overall design or implementation, and, if the program isn't sufficiently well tested, a bug shipped to your users. If the testing process does catch your bug before it goes to the field, the code winds up back in your lap and you have to fix it, probably under even more schedule pressure the second time around.

The solution to all this is, of course, documentation. You've no doubt seen the practice of including the entire change history for a module in its initial block comment. All programmers should be required to follow this practice, since it implicitly recognizes the fact that nearly all code has its own life span, and that it can change dramatically over that time period. This is particularly true if different people work on it or if the services the code provides to its callers change significantly.

Just as important as documenting what is there, is documenting what isn't. Almost no one removes old history-of-changes (nor should they), but few people document the "road not taken," either. This is a critical use of commentary, particularly in Windows where we so often find ourselves experimenting with various techniques until we find the right magic incantation (read: combination of API parameters or calls) that does what we want. It's even more important to guard against the inevitable time later on when you'll look at the code again and try to "clean it up." That's when you'll be looking for the minor optimizations, and it's all too easy to free a bitmap or some piece of memory prematurely if you haven't documented that it's still needed sometime later. This sort of optimization can be particularly insidious, since well meaning people will look at the code, spot what appears to be a good potential performance or general algorithm improvement, and they won't see anything in the code that tells them not to do it, so they start making changes.

For example, in my Windows code I'm constantly inserting short comments that say things like, "The following line has to go here and not in the constructor, since we need a valid hWnd for the API call," or "We can't use the FredEx() API since it appears to break in this case, so we do it the long way via Fred() and get the same result."

At the routine level, you should take great pains to document all non-parameter dependencies (for example, the program's main window is not minimized, or the character string passed to it is in the format that the GetOpenFileName() API uses to return a sequence of files selected by the user). Even more important, you should both document and respect the prior documentation of a routine's error checking. It's very easy to look at a routine and say, "This is silly. Why bother checking if the pointer is NULL? That's never going to happen." If the routine is documented as rejecting a call with a NULL parameter, then it's extremely risky to change this behavior, particularly in a very large program or if the routine is in a general library used by several people, since there's a very good chance that some other code depends upon this behavior, possibly without documenting the fact.

For example, in Chapter 3 I include a function called FileExists() which returns a BOOL that indicates if a specified file exists. FileExists() checks for a NULL pointer to the file name, and it also checks for a file name of zero length; in either case, it returns FALSE. I also call this function from the Win32u wrapper for the GetShortPathName() API, uGetShortPathName(), and that function counts on FileExists() to do this pointer validation, so it doesn't bother to check the parameter before passing it on to FileExists(). Remove this parameter validation from FileExists(), and a change ripples though to the uGetShortPathName(). This is why I consider commentary a macro issue and not a micro issue; its use and misuse can often solve or create problems that go far beyond the boundaries of an individual source file or subroutine.

Let me give you another real world example: Some time back a business partner and I had done some custom programming for a client. Over a year after we'd last touched the code, the client called and wanted a minor change to the program. I had written a 100-line block comment at the beginning of the program's main source file that detailed the history of changes, things we had tried and rejected, exactly which version and implementation we had provided to the client, as well as a couple of my "features hung off booleans." The change the client wanted was simple, but it turned out to be one of those things that we could have chased around in circles for days, thanks to how long it had been since we'd worked with the code. Because everything was closely documented, we were able to pick up the project in about a half hour and add and test the feature in just a couple more. In this case, we made the change without introducing any bugs, and the time we saved was easily more than the time it took me to write the commentary.

One of the more interesting programmer fables that I hear all the time is that a given piece of code is "self-documenting." Is there such a thing as self-documenting code? Of course there is! I'm the last person who would tell you to write a comment for every line of code. That's not the issue. (In fact, my own code is loaded with subroutines that don't have a single line of commentary (aside from the block comment that describes what the routine does and its input and output values), since none is needed. These are typically single-purpose routines that do a simple table lookup, for example, and contain only a dozen or so lines of code.) The issue is that, like other programmer fables, this one either has some genuine truth to it or is plausibly true, but programmers misapply it to create an excuse not to do what they should. (I know, I know—I'm about to start sounding like Wilford Brimley in his oatmeal commercials again, but it's true.) In fact, many programmers turn it into a macho thing—"Why should I comment this? Can't you understand what this does? It's clear to me." Even when they aren't blatant enough to say it that way (and yes, I've heard it put that bluntly and transparently), many programmers make it quite clear that they consider it a test of skills and wills to see how little commentary they can add to code.

Another problem is the flip side to this, the programmers who have the bizarre idea that if they capriciously employ some incredibly bad coding practice, it somehow becomes acceptable if they comment it. Of course that isn't true, and they should know better.

I see such nonsense all the time in production code, and it makes my head swim. The only advice I can give you on these issues is not to give in and follow the bad practices, and to try to keep other programmers you work with from doing it. There is no tool or technique that can help you in this area, just your own diligence and judgment. Most important of all, remember the person you eventually help out down the road might be a friend of yours, or it might even be you.

## Mighty Tom and the Mystery Loop

When I was at IBM, working on the VM mainframe operating system, I once had to incorporate some 370 assembly code that had been written at a research site into the system. The code was very well written, but poorly documented. Its overall function was to create a shared segment, which is roughly a combination DLL and memory mapped file in Windows.

At one point, I hit a snippet of code, just a few lines, that didn't seem to make any sense. The code looped through the memory range that was to be used for the shared segment, and loaded a register from the first four-byte area of each 4KB page of memory. The code never did anything with the values it read, so it was clearly "touching" all the pages in the memory range, and it was obviously doing so for a good reason. I had no idea why, though, so I was not about to remove the code. I checked with several of the local VM gurus, and none of them knew what the code was doing. Finally, I found the grand guru of this part of the operating system, Tom, who looked at the code and pretty quickly figured it out. The code needed to make sure that all the pages in memory and in the paging pool were synchronized. As it turned out, there was a pathological case in which the in-core pages and the copies in the paging pool wouldn't be the same, which would cause the shared segment to be built incorrectly, and this paltry loop was all that was needed to close the, well, loophole. (There was a lot more technical detail than this to this issue, but you get the idea.)

Once I understood what was going on, I wrote an extensive block comment that explained the pathological case and what the code was doing. (I must have set some kind of record for the ratio of commentary to lines, probably better than 10:1.)

I took some kidding from one of the reviewers at the code inspection for that work, who thought that the commentary was gratuitous. I disagreed, since I knew how much legwork it had taken to track down the meaning of those few lines of code. I felt vindicated a few months later when someone else who didn't realize I had worked on this code casually mentioned to me that she would have to modify the code for a new release of the operating system, and that she was grateful that whoever had originally implemented it had taken the time to comment it so heavily.

## 4. Respect Your User's Resources

*Is there no respect of place, persons, nor time, in you?*

William Shakespeare,
*Twelfth Night*

How's this for an obvious point: You're writing software that will run on a machine, but your users are people. Sound trivial? If so, then why is it that so much of today's software ignores this point and treats your computer like a cheap motel full of fraternities during spring break?

Whether you're writing commercial software that you'd like to sell a few million copies of, or simply some minor program that's only intended for in-house use at your place of employment, it makes sense to respect your users and all their resources. This takes place on several levels:

- Not mangling the user's installation. This is the big one, the one that has made me reject more software than I can count. Between programs that replace DLLs and VBXs without first getting your permission (and no, telling the user this in the README.TXT file is not sufficient), programs that alter your AUTOEXEC.BAT, CONFIG.SYS, WIN.INI, or SYSTEM.INI files without even telling you until the deed is done, programs that hijack your file associations, and programs that simply must have their files installed in certain directories, there's a lot to hate about some software and their installation programs. In particular, I'll talk a lot more about DLL-related issues in Chapter 6.

  A related issue is making it easy for your users to run your program on more than one Windows installation on the same system. If you perused the installation programs for most of the commercial software available today, you'd think that this capability was a completely alien concept. I can't tell you how many times I've had to install the same program several times just to get it to work on Windows 3.1, Windows 95, and Windows NT on the same computer. Of course, this becomes an issue because so many programs burrow so deeply into the user's installation that running them from different Windows versions is far more complicated than simply running the main executable. This is of even greater interest thanks to Windows 95, since the installed base of tens of millions of Windows 3.1 users will migrate slowly to the new version (the installed base of an operating system always moves slowly), and many people, particularly in business settings, will no doubt run both Windows 3.1 and Windows 95 on the same computers for months. (And the greater importance of the registry in Windows 95 will cause new headaches of its own as users try to run the same Win32 applications under Windows 95 and Windows NT 3.51.)

- Allowing your users to work as they prefer. It's always important to remember that users' resources are not limited to the computers and other software sitting on their desk (or lap), but include things like their knowledge, background, and even personal experience. For example, I consider myself pretty fast with a keyboard and mouse. I can zip through most Windows programs that I've used before, or Windows itself, at a respectable clip. But a friend of mine, Maria, has been a graphic designer for about eight years, and when I watch her use PageMaker on her Mac, I feel like I should sign up for Remedial Mousing Class. Watching Maria tearing through a DTP job at about Mach 3 reminds me how deeply entrenched procedures become for users, and how important it can be when bringing out a new release of a program to keep this in mind. I got another, less dramatic, reminder of this fact when I first started using Windows 95 and Explorer; I kept hitting F8 to initiate a file copy operation, which, of course, doesn't work.

- Not wasting your user's time. I'm not talking about programs that run slowly (I'll get to that sin shortly), but programs that do silly things like force the user to watch an animated splash panel every time they're started, with no documented way to turn it off.

  In general, whenever your program is going to "put on a show," meaning do something animated, play a WAV file, etc., the behavior should be easily configurable. (Merely providing a way to cancel it is not enough; the user should have a way of avoiding the show that requires zero marginal effort once the program is configured.) Traditionally, people have said that you should allow users to turn off all sound, since it's often bothersome in a work environment. This is excellent advice, but I would extend it to include all such non-essential demonstrations. Your users are often in a hurry, and making them watch that stupid (in their opinion) animated sequence for the 7,325th time, no matter how endearing you and your beta testers thought it was, can be enough to drive them away.

  Which, of course, brings us indirectly to Easter Eggs, those little doodads programmers just love to hide in programs that show the user the names of the developers once the user performs some "secret" combination of keystrokes or mouse actions. See the sidebar "The Windows 95 Easter Egg" for an extravagant example. I admit that I have mixed feelings about these things. They're fun once or twice, but then you're stuck with them on your system forever. I'm also not exactly thrilled when I see an Easter Egg in a product that also has some truly awful bugs, or is lacking some functionality that I miss. (Perhaps I'm becoming a curmudgeon in my late thirtysomethings, but in Windows 95 I can't help but look at the fancy Easter Egg and wonder why they didn't ditch it and use those developer hours to make the Explorer optionally display the attribute bits for files a directory at a time, ala File Manager, or support F8 as a way to initiate a file copy operation.) I'm also bothered by the fact that the Easter Egg in Windows 95 obviously required a change to a basic part of the operating system, shell object (re)naming, and is not confined to an "About" box, as are most goodies. Do we really want the shell support in an operating system altered, in even the slightest way, for this purpose? (Think about it: The way this is implemented, Windows has to check for the Easter Egg sequence of events on every folder rename or open operation.) It's not a big deal, but if I'd had a voice in the matter, I certainly would have voted against doing it this way.

- Not wasting your user's disk space, RAM, or processor. Part of this issue is simply writing better installation programs, and letting the user decide not to install certain features, and thereby giving the user more control over disk space usage. The key, of course, is that you should then obey the user's wishes and not actually install the unwanted components. I've seen this problem numerous times—and users wind up with installed components they specifically tried to exclude.

In the larger sense, this is just a plea for efficiency, which I admit sounds almost comical (or pathetic, depending on your level of cynicism) in an age of 30MB+ word processors and 100MB+ C++ development environments that, thanks in large part to their frameworks, create nearly 200KB "hello, world" programs.

• Simple politeness. I'm sure this is will raise some eyebrows, but I'm often surprised at how rude some messages are. For example, try to run a program with an "expected Windows version" greater than 4.0, and Windows 95 will display a dialog box that says, "The <name> file expects a newer version of Windows. Upgrade your Windows version." The first time I saw that, I wanted to ask Microsoft if they'll upgrade my system to the polite version of Windows 95 for a few additional dollars (or what the difference is between upgrading my Windows installation and upgrading its version). What would it have cost them to change this message to, "The <name> file expects a newer version of Windows than your current version. Sorry, but you'll have to upgrade to a newer version

## The Windows 95 Easter Egg

Whenever a major Windows program or release of Windows itself ships, there's always a scramble to find the infamous Easter Egg, the "hidden" show that the developers put into the product. Here, thanks to several corespondents, are the directions for displaying the Windows 95 Easter Egg. (Type carefully. You have to get the folder names exactly right for this to work.)

1. Click on the desktop with the right mouse button and then select the New | Folder option from the context menu.

2. Name the new folder "and now, the moment you've all been waiting for" (without the quotes).

3. Rename the folder you've just created to: "we proudly present for your viewing pleasure" (again, no quotes).

4. Rename the same folder again, this time to: "The Microsoft Windows 95 Product Team!".

5. Open the folder and watch (and listen to) the show. (On one of my computers, canceling the egg before the show completes sometimes leaves my Sound Blaster card emitting a low, annoying hum until I shut down Windows. I wonder if Microsoft will accept bug reports for the Easter Egg?)

of Windows to run this program." I don't mean to beat up Microsoft; this example just happened to be the one nearest to hand and most pertinent for this book. In fact, I think that overall Microsoft does a slightly better job than most companies in this area.

Let me let you in on a little secret that I've discovered via the shareware market: If people like your program and they find it useful, it will sell better than if they merely find it useful. And if your program is polite and friendly (without being sickening about it, of course), then people will like it more. So you can make your program's diagnostic messages more polite because you think, as I do, that it's the right way to talk to your users (without whom we'd be a bunch of unemployed people will remarkably little fashion sense and nothing to do), or you can do it out of simple greed. This is one time when doing the right thing for the wrong reason is just as good as doing it for the right reason; your program's users won't care about your motivation, they'll just be happier with your program if you do it.

## 5. DLL with Care

DLLs are easily the best example of a "hothouse feature" in Windows. (A hothouse feature is one that works beautifully in the tightly controlled environment of a hothouse, which typically means in the hands of experts or even the feature's creator, but doesn't work nearly as well when left to fend for itself in the hostile, unpredictable environment of the real world.)

I'll talk about DLLs in much greater detail in Chapter 6, but for now, let me stress that DLLs are often grossly overused (read: misused) and misplaced in Windows application programming, which only results in problems for everyone involved, particularly users.

## 6. Take the Big View on Tools

> *Man is a tool-using animal...Without tools he is nothing, with tools he is all.*
>
> Thomas Carlyle

As I discuss at length in Chapter 4, nearly all programmers just love to play with their tools; yet, as a group we're conspicuously bad at selecting them. This has significant and negative ramifications for our programs.

I feel that one aspect of this situation is important enough that I included it here as a guideline as well as discussed it in Chapter 4: Programmers define the concept of "tool" much too narrowly. They tend to think of "tools" as compilers, linkers, debuggers, text editors, third party libraries, etc., and little else. This is shortsighted because of the kind of behavior it so often leads to: Programmers will often spend considerable money to put the latest and greatest upgrade of a tool on their hard disks, but they'll neglect a tool that's just as important as all their software combined, their own education.

It's critical, especially at a time when Windows programming is such an incredibly tall and narrow layering of tools, interfaces, and architectures, that we all try as best we can to be full-time students of programming and remain as open as we can to new sources of information.

For example, years ago, back in the bad old, early days of DOS programming, you bought a compiler package, perhaps C or Turbo Pascal, and maybe a couple of books, and you were armed for quite a bit of real work. SDK's? Developer Network subscriptions? Third party libraries? CD ROMs of source code? These were all either unheard of (literally, because they didn't exist), or high-end/specialized tools that few mainstream programmers really needed.

Another side effect of programmers loving their tools as they do, and being so continually pressed for time, is that many of us never take the time to really get to know our tools adequately. (I often imagine Calvin, from the comic strip *Calvin and Hobbes*, hands on hips, surrounded by the reference cards, manuals, CD, and other paraphernalia for the latest C/C++ compiler, saying, "What? I still have to learn to use all of this stuff?") Of course, just owning the tool isn't enough; no one would suggest that. But time pressure often leads us to act that way—we'll install the new version of a compiler, ignore 95 percent of its new features, and remain content to get whatever better optimization, linking, or bug fixes the new release automatically delivers. (Follow the compiler discussions on CompuServe, and you'll often see comments from top-flight professionals who still do all their development with the command-line version of the tools. These people aren't neo-Luddites, afraid of the brave new world of visual development; they merely know what does and doesn't work for them, so they stick with what works.) The problem is that by not knowing our tools as well as we should (and I'm just as guilty of this as most other programmers), we don't know what they can or can't do. It's all too common to hear two programmers talk about a compiler, say Visual C++, and hear one of them complain that "Visual C++ 2.2 still doesn't support creating or editing version resources." The other programmer (hopefully) jumps in quickly and points out that the 32-bit version of VC++ has had this ability for a while (although it's still missing from the 16-bit version).

As I said above, this problem is made all the more acute by the current state of Windows programming. A close friend of mine who has considerable experience in programming, but not for Windows, commented on this situation sometime back in an interesting way: He asked me how someone who knew the basics of DOS/C programming would go about learning the needed skills to do professional quality Windows development. I realized he was asking this question on two levels. He wanted a straight answer, but he also was making a point. When I started listing the educational areas that I would recommend to this hypothetical Windows tyro (C++, a framework (likely MFC), the basic Windows architecture, event-driven programming, etc.), we were both surprised and dismayed by the number of major items and the formidability of their combined learning curves.

In this same vein, another friend of mine has observed that it's nearly impossible for one programmer to write a large Windows application today, thanks to sheer size and complexity of the tools and architectures that must be mastered. I think the profession was going in that direction, but recent developments, such as the mainstreaming of RAD (rapid application development) packages, including Delphi, are counteracting the trend. I have to stress that I'm not saying that Delphi or any other product can substitute for programmer knowledge of the system. These products are very good at helping you leverage existing code through their facilities for reuse, and they can protect you from many of the pitfalls of the Windows API, but they can't protect you from everything. Once you get much beyond "hello, world," you're back in the deep, cold water and once again your only hope is to rely on your most important and basic tool, your own knowledge.

## 7. Keep a Perspective on Performance

*You can't be too rich, too thin, or have a too fast computer.*

Old Programmer Aphorism

*Dost thou love life? Then do not squander time, for that's the stuff life is made of.*

Benjamin Franklin

Time for a little truth in advertising: I'm a bit-head from way back. I've always been one of those people others accused of wanting the biggest, fastest, mostest computer on the block, whether I needed it or not. In some cases, that was true; I'm also a gizmonaut from way back. But I'm also convinced that some people underestimate the importance of performance. I just love, for example, hearing the old line that you don't need much computing power to do word processing. If you define "word processing" as "typing," then I agree. If you include many of the other operations that most writers perform, like generating indexes and tables of contents, spell-checking large documents, running macros, etc., then you start hankering for the latest BelchFire 5000 Wunderbox in no time. (I mention all this to make the point that when I recommend against changing code to improve its performance, I do so with more than a little careful thought and hesitation, since, by nature, I want *everything* to work with sub-second response time.)

The point of this guideline is not just that program performance is important; most (but not all) programmers have that concept down cold and really don't need to be reminded that faster is better. I'm most concerned about what happens when programmers "get religion" about performance issues, and what it often leads them to do. There are several separate manifestations of this problem, including:

- Fewer lines == fewer instructions == better performance. This myth is very subtle, and it can lead to some incredible arguments. I've seen even very experienced programmers forget that when they write in a HLL (high level language) they're by definition working with an abstraction, a virtual machine, and that they're giving up quite a bit of control over code generation. The fact that C or Pascal is often translated into something that closely follows their original work is not guaranteed, as anyone who has looked at the highly optimized output of a compiler can attest. Optimizers routinely move code around, change it, or delete it altogether, depending on how aggressively it is trying to optimize your source, and how well written your original source is.

  This misunderstanding surfaces most often with C/C++ programmers, as I mentioned in guideline 2, when they start trying to cram a function into as few keystrokes as possible. The result, of course, is wholly counterproductive and creates "hand sloptimized" code.

- By far the biggest mistake, and the one that most often harms the quality of public software, is what I call the "unweighted average syndrome." Let me explain via a simple problem: If you buy six items at the store, priced $2, $2, $2, $2, $2, and $10, what's the average price of an item? Is it $3.33 ($20/6), or $6 ($12/2)? The answer, of course, depends on whether you're calculating a weighted or an unweighted average. (And whether it's in your interest to report a higher or a lower number; indeed, statistics don't lie, but statisticians are a whole other issue.) Similarly, programmers who are concerned about performance, particularly those who have just joined the cause, tend to look at everything in an unweighted fashion, which leads them to spend a great deal of time optimizing things that they shouldn't. Is faster better than slower? Of course it is. But that doesn't mean that every possible avenue for saving a few clock cycles is worth pursuing. Balance is the key. If you find that you can cut the printing time of your program by about 2 percent, but the change requires you to scrap and rewrite 20,000 lines of code, is it worth it? Unless you're developing your program under extremely unusual circumstances, I suspect the answer is no.

  By focusing on the wrong issues, development teams often squander their most precious resource, programmer hours, and they neglect more important but less sexy things like improving the commentary of the source code and performing more extensive testing. These less glamorous items are precisely the ones that improve the quality of the product, particularly in the long run, when extensive changes have to be made for future releases.

- There's another side effect of the "unweighted average syndrome" that's even worse than wasted programmer time. (I bet the MIS managers of the world would disagree with that statement.) It can cause programmers to make tradeoffs in a way that creates unnecessarily hollow and weak code. As I point out in the next chapter when I discuss defensive programming, it's very important that you take a skeptical view of any data your code is using that it does not create itself, on the spot. (Data that comes from other code you've written, even in the same program, is nearly as suspect as something that the user types in.) The best way to handle this situation is to create fire walls that will either correct or detect and reject errant data. And when a programmer is looking to squeeze every last clock cycle out of a routine, one of the first things that gets tossed overboard is error checking.

Even small things, like checking for a NULL pointer or an integer value out of range, often get deleted when people start cutting corners. It's tempting, too, because the programmer feels so much better afterward—the routine just shrank from 23 to 17 lines of code. That's a savings of over 25 percent! Of course, the performance benefit isn't anywhere near that, since the deleted lines are things like:

```
if(lpStuff == NULL)
  return ERROR_BAD_PARAMETER;
```

which take very few instructions to implement. Plus, the meat of the routine often includes a loop that does considerable "heavy lifting," which means that the actual savings in instruction pathlength can be far less than one percent. (I don't mean to sound like I'm implying that programmers are stupid, but I've been there and I know what happens: You're pressed to make some code execute faster, so you start cutting corners, and it feels ever so good to the right side of your brain to see that routine shrink by 25 percent on your screen, even though the left side of your brain knows that it's only a one percent savings. But you're in a hurry, and you need to speed up this code *now*, so you delete the lines anyway, get a quick buzz of satisfaction, and move on to the next function.)

Casting this tendency in terms of cost-benefit ratio, what do we get? In many cases, an insignificant performance benefit and a sizable but non-obvious cost—the lines you deleted might have been quietly correcting a bad data problem in some obscure stress condition, and no one on your programming team even realized it was happening. Maybe the problem doesn't even get caught in the ensuing regression testing, and you wind up shipping a bug. In highly technical terms, you just shot yourself and your product in the foot for the sake of a performance improvement too small to measure, let alone notice.

As with so many other general programming issues, this one is magnified by the realities of the Windows environment. Between endless driver quirks, users running several programs at once (something they'll be doing much more often thanks to Windows 95's greatly improved resource handling), and some programs that don't know enough to leave other programs alone (see Chapter 12 for the discussion of how Symantec's Norton Navigator can break other programs), your code should be downright paranoid.

My recommendation, aside from carefully evaluating what is to be gained from squeezing code, is to concentrate on the algorithmic issues first: Which sort should we use in this spot; do we really have to use a linked list, or should we allocate large blocks of fixed-size elements and avoid all that pointer traversal? The problem, of course, is that it often isn't "discovered" until very late in the development cycle that a program has a "performance problem." (The quotes are meant to convey the idea that the development team knows all along that the product is a pig, but it takes a while for this information to filter up the chain of command to the point where an edict can be issued to do something about it.) By the time fixing the performance becomes a hot issue, it's often so late in the cycle that there isn't time to do this kind of algorithmic analysis and make the needed changes to the code. Facing the dual guns of the schedule and performance pressure, programmers go on a rampage and start ripping out whatever they can, and error checking that's "not really needed since it doesn't do anything" is often the first victim.

As for knowing when you'll have to really squeeze the performance out of your code, in many, possibly even most, cases you'll know before you even write the program. Another writer I know, Pete Davis, wrote a bitmap cruncher for a client. The program's main purpose was to scale down a bitmap, but it had to do it intelligently, so that the bitmap would look good in its smaller form. This is a highly processor-intensive task, so he knew from the start that he could write the user interface to the program in C/C++ and MFC, but the crunching engine would have to be hand-tuned assembly language.

There are exceptions to this observation, but mostly they're traceable to an oversight (and perhaps a lack of non-linear thinking) on the part of one or more programmers. I worked on one project that nicely illustrated this—the (very large) program used its own custom memory allocation and management services. An early alpha of the code showed horrible performance, which surprised everyone on the project. Some investigation turned up the fact that deep in the heart of the custom memory management code was a loop, written in a high level language, no less, that cleared out the memory for every allocation request one byte at a time. This was changed to a bit of inline assembly that used the equivalent of an Intel 80x86 string instruction to blast hex zeroes into the allocated memory, and the performance of the entire system increased dramatically.

One last thing to keep in mind is that code reuse can be an important ally in improving your program's performance. Sometimes you know that there's a better performing way to do some task in your program, but you just don't have the time to implement it. Instead of keeping the part descriptions in several sorted lists and using a binary search for lookups, you just stuff them into a linked list and burn a lot of cycles and memory references running up and down the chain. In such a case, it can often make sense to take the larger view and recognize that you'll have to use this same function in other programs, so it makes sense to take a little more time now, code it the right way, and make sure that it's a separate component that can be dropped into other programs. By spreading the cost over more than one project, you can often convince management to give you the time to do things the right way, and everyone wins. (See guideline 9 for more about code reuse.)

## 8. Keep a Perspective on Testing

> *It is amazing how complete is the delusion that beauty is goodness.*
>
> Leo Tolstoy
>
> *Computers don't make mistakes. They do, however, execute yours very carefully.*
>
> Jack Hooper

Do you hate testing? I sure do. As far as I'm concerned, there's no task in the development cycle less interesting or less fun than testing. Even meetings and code inspections are usually more enjoyable, since you get to talk with other people on the project, and someone usually brings doughnuts or some other consumer non-durables. But I digress.

The irony, of course, is that no one likes testing, so it's often looked down upon as grunt work in many development shops, yet it's incredibly important. My wife, Liz, has been a programmer and system analyst for 16 years, and she and I often comment on how easily we can find an error in a commercial Windows application. Typically it takes less than ten minutes of casual use. I'm not talking about showstoppers, like crashed systems or lost data (although I've hit far more than my share of those in the first ten minutes), but senseless, minor problems, like edit controls that run off the edge of a dialog box, bitmaps that are obviously misplaced on the screen, conflicting accelerator keystrokes, and, my all-time favorite, typos in the help file and on dialogs.

There are two interesting aspects to how testing is (and isn't) done in Windows application development:

• Testing is your program's safety net, your last, best hope for catching bugs and generally improving the quality of your product before it ships. It's the bright line that divides your program's life cycle into the "private, we can do anything we want" stage and the "public, we're affecting real people" stage. Yet all too often, testing is the part of the development cycle that has to "eat" a schedule slip by the design and development groups (sometimes the same people).

I find this dismaying and surprising, since testing is really one of the great bargains of development. Most programmers have seen one version or another of the infamous graph that relates the cost to fix a bug as a function of when it is discovered. The cost during design is minimal; during development it's greater but still quite small. During test, it's already getting expensive, and after the product ships we see the "knee in the curve," as the line goes from nearly horizontal to nearly vertical, and the fix requires not just design, development, and testing, but distribution of the fixed version to customers. (Of course, via the now-common practice of slipstreaming bug fixes (that is, quietly rolling them into the next release without providing them to current customers), some Windows software vendors have found a way to radically reduce the cost of fixing bugs. Incredibly, they've even found a way to turn their bugs into a new revenue source. Want all the latest versions and bug fixes? Just subscribe to our yearly update service. Hmm. Where's that pesky Department of Justice when you *really* need them?)

Of course, Windows applications can be hideously difficult to test thoroughly, and I'm willing to bet that nearly every commercially available Windows application can be made to fail if the proper system resource is low enough. (I'm drawing a distinction here between programs that detect a low resource situation and gracefully shutdown and those that keep plowing ahead, oblivious to the problem, and operate incorrectly.)

- Developers, solely interested in pleasing management by getting their code done and shipped on schedule, can use cursory testing as a crutch. They perform some minimal testing on a function, and say, "See? It works." This is the cardinal sin of cowboy coding, because programmers use these little demonstrations as proof, to themselves or to others, that the code in question is finished, and that there's literally nothing else to be done with it. This is not an issue of mathematicians versus cabinetmakers; it's a matter of performing a reasonable amount and type of testing. These minor demonstrations almost never do that— the programmer hands the code in question a few relatively tame sets of input, which almost never include all relevant CPCs (common pathological cases), and pronounces the code ready for prime time.

The solution to the first problem is conceptually very simple but very difficult to implement, since it's really more of a management culture issue (at least for large projects). Simple proscriptions, like saying that code must be completely tested on every supported Windows variation (all the more relevant thanks to the numerous odd differences between the three Win32 platforms), or insisting that late code changes are thoroughly re-tested, are often ignored thanks to lack of time or other resource. Given a choice of releasing a product into a competitive environment in a timely fashion, albeit with a not completely known quality risk, or releasing it in better shape but so late that it loses its edge against the competition, most companies will roll the dice and choose the first alternative. When push comes to shove, money talks in the software business, and it usually says, "Ship it!" It's up to us to fight the good fight and make sure that what gets shipped is of good quality.

## 9. Think in Terms of Code Reuse

*If men could learn from history, what lessons it might teach us! But passion and party blind our eyes, and the light which experience gives is a lantern on the stern, which shines only on the waves behind us!*

Samuel Taylor Coleridge

Call it software components, software ICs (integrated circuits), objects, templates, or whatever, I believe that programming is finally, at long last, about to embrace code reuse in a serious way, because we're just now getting the tools we need to convince people that it's a mainstream issue. We're finally about to start standing on other programmers' shoulders, and not their feet. It's about bloody time.

Notice that I didn't say we're finally getting the tools (such as Delphi) to reuse code. That would be silly. Everyone in the DOS and Windows programming game has been reusing code in one form or another for over a decade, and mainframe programmers did this for decades before PCs were invented. Adding an "include" directive for a header to your C program, and then linking with the proper .LIB file isn't nearly as sexy or even buzzword compliant as Dragging and Dropping Components from a Gallery in your Visual IDE onto your Program Object, but it does get you at least 95 percent of the same benefit: You're leveraging well tested and (typically) well understood code instead of re-inventing the binary wheel. And that's what matters.

You should always have another process running in the back of your head, filtering your work. In this case, that process should be looking for code that can and should be made into a reusable component. In the majority of cases the code you write is so application specific that it would be silly and a poor use of your time to convert it into a reusable component. (After all, what's the sense of having a reusable component that's only ever used in one program?) But there are some good candidates floating about your work, and they usually have the following characteristics:

- They're either general purpose, or they can be generalized easily enough. Things like container classes, and even entire Windows programming frameworks, such as MFC, are general enough in their design and provide enough hooks and backdoors for customization that you can do just about anything needed with them.

- They're single purpose. I have quite a toolbox of code that I carry from one project to the next, including single purpose routines that do little chores like reset the read-only bit on a file, append a backslash to a string if it doesn't already have one, count the number of file identifiers in a string as defined by the format of the GetOpenFileName() API, etc.

- They do some really nasty job that you don't want to code and test more than once (or even once, if you can find a usable third-party example). Windows frameworks are a perfect example of this. As I point out in Chapter 4, there might be cases today when you would rationally choose not to use MFC or OWL or whatever other framework, but you'd have to have a pretty good reason. By turning the nasty chore into a reusable component, you can significantly improve the quality of your programs.

- They lend themselves to a robust implementation. You should always give preference to those would-be components that will result in what I call "naively reusable" software, meaning code that you can make as close to 100 percent bullet-proof as possible. This is important, because once you write a component and add it to a shared library, people tend to treat it as they would a function in the compiler's run-time library: They assume it's infallible, and they don't always read the documentation as carefully as they should before using it. (Always remember the big picture; your goal is to improve your productivity and your program's quality, not win arguments at the coffee machine over who misused whose code.)

In Chapter 10 I talk a lot more about using abstraction and creating your own libraries to enhance your Windows programming. Unfortunately, the Win32 API has just enough quirks and differences between its three platforms that you might also want or need to write some of your own API wrappers. Again, see Chapter 10 for much more on this aspect of code reuse.

How to test reusable code your team developed can be a touchy issue. One of the supposed benefits of reusing code, after all, is supposed to be shortened test cycles. You're using known-good code, so why are you wasting your time hammering it with test cases all over again? There are actually a couple of good reasons. First, the boundary lines between reused and new code seldom match up with the boundary lines of your test cases. For example, let's say you write a class that manages a list of customer names and numbers, you test it with sample programs, and deem it worthy of duty in your reusable component arsenal. Later on, you use this class in your invoice program, and everything appears to be running fine. But when you test the invoice program, you won't see any significant savings thanks to your use of the customer tracker class. Many of your test cases will indirectly exercise the class, of course, but the only real savings you'll see is when you're tracking down bugs, since you will likely be able to ignore the reusable components and concentrate first on the new code.

Second, even when you can isolate the reusable components, you'll find that you're often using them in a way that's at least somewhat different from their intended use. Maybe this difference is merely one of quantity and not kind; your customer tracker class was intended to be used for at most a few hundred customers, and it was rigorously tested for that usage. But in your new program you need it to track many thousands of customers, which means you should test it further, since there might be a surprise lurking in the component, such as a design or coding bug that makes the class lose its mind (and some of your data) if you ask it to manage over 32K names and numbers.

The right answer to this testing dilemma is to test the components in isolation to make sure they're reliable before they're subsumed into the application. This is the type of testing (or re-testing) that most often is tossed overboard when schedules get tight; people rationalize the situation and say that if they test the finished application well enough, they'll catch the bugs, which really is all that matters. I find this argument fascinating, since it amounts to saying that you can drastically cut corners on some testing, or eliminate it entirely, as long as your remaining testing is extraordinarily good.

As important as code reuse can be in any type of programming, it's even more valuable, potentially, in Windows work. As I mentioned in guideline 6, it's quite a struggle today keeping up with everything a Windows programmer needs to know. Whether your programming team is several people (spatially dispersed) or just yourself working on different parts of a program at various times (temporally dispersed), you can, in effect, parcel out various jobs and then leverage the components you create as part of each one. When you're working alone, it's tempting to forgo the extra work needed to make some snippet of code a real component or even a .LIB file, but it's often worth it. By the time you get around to viewing the component as a customer, and not as its author, you may well have forgotten some crucial details of its use. Whenever possible, take the extra time to create and document the component as if it will be used by someone you've never met and won't be able to assist; you'll be amazed at how much more usable the component will be when it's your turn to decipher its documentation and interface.

# 3

# A Philosophy of Software Engineering: Micro Issues

# A Philosophy of Windows Software Engineering: Micro Issues

Chapter 3

> 'Yes, I have a pair of eyes,' replied Sam, 'and that's just it. If they wos a pair o' patent double million magnifyin' gas microscopes of hextra power, p'raps I might be able to see through a flight o' stairs and a deal door; but bein' only eyes, you see my wision's limited.'
>
> Charles Dickens,
> *Pickwick Papers*

Like Sam, all programmers have limited vision, but sometimes that can be plenty. In particular, if we make a determined effort to "think globally and act locally," to borrow a phrase from another venue, the payback can be considerable.

In Chapter 2 I talked about what makes a good Windows program, the part programming philosophy plays in our work, and some macro-level guidelines. Now it's time to turn inward and examine the micro-level guidelines.

## Six Micro-Level Guidelines

As I mentioned in Chapter 2, the difference between the macro and micro issues is not one of importance, but one of how they are applied. Macro issues are more design and planning oriented, while the micro issues exist in the realm of the coding trenches, the line-by-line construction of programs. As difficult as it can be to deal correctly with the macro issues in a large programming project, the micro issues can be even more of a challenge in some ways. Because the decision to follow these guidelines is often the province of individual programmers, there is often no overriding control, and the same programming team will create code with wildly different styles and philosophies. This is far from just a matter of esthetics (that is, making everyone's code look like it was written by the same person, a dubious accomplishment, even if feasible), since differences in the degree to which someone practices defensive programming, for example, can ripple through an entire project, sometimes with hideous consequences.

Some of the guidelines in the micro list look like good candidates for the macro list. After all, aren't decisions about how to store persistent data, and how completely to separate your program's user interface and implementation code design issues? Yes, they are, or at least they should be. The way Windows development is often performed today pushes them from the macro realm to the micro. The problem is lack of time, ever the monkey on programmers' backs, and how it shortens or even eliminates design cycles. This tendency greatly increases the ratio of "keyboard time" to "whiteboard time," which means that critical decisions that should be made during the cool, clear-headed time allotted for design are increasingly made instead in the frenzied heat of battle as the actual program is being written.

Whatever the specifics of your program development situation, I hope you'll try to keep all these guidelines in mind, including the micro-level ones that follow.

As valuable and exciting as I find our profession's new emphasis on RAD (rapid application development), I have to say that it's only magnifying the problem of projects being ruled by knee-jerk decisions. Programmers (and in many cases non-programmers) are pointing and clicking, dragging and dropping like crazy, and creating disposable programs that are sometimes deployed with minimal testing, and more often with little or no knowledge of the Windows architecture. The result is programs that work an acceptable percentage of the time, even though their creators have almost no idea how or why the Windows-specific parts function as they do.

Lest anyone misunderstand, let me say that I get as misty eyed as any other cyberpopulist at the thought of bringing computing power to the masses. The problem with RAD tools is not that they can take power out of the hands of experts, but that they can put it into the hands of non-experts who then create public programs. If the neophytes want to write programs for their own use, that's great, and I'm more than willing to help them learn the ropes. But when their programs cross the line into public distribution, even within a single company, that's when I get nervous, because suddenly other peoples' computers and data are at risk.

*Put another way, RAD tools do two very different things that are often conflated:*

1. *They allow experts to create programs much more efficiently, with far less mucking about with the "plumbing" of Windows programming. Speaking as someone who has done more than his share of mucking about, I can say without hesitation that this is a very good thing.*

2. *They allow non-experts to create programs and "get them to work." Depending on the nature of the programs, where they wind up, how they are used, who uses them, and who maintains them, this can be a very bad thing. In fact, I've heard numerous stories already about people approaching the MIS department in their company with a request for some new program, and coming away with an (accurate) explanation of how huge their backlog of programming work is, and a copy of Visual Basic or Delphi. That's right, in some cases companies are telling the accountants, engineers, etc., to do their own minor programming.*

## 10. Abstract, Abstract, Abstract (And don't worry about the cost of a function call until the program tells you otherwise)

In my opinion, the craft of programming consists of creating and employing layers of abstraction to bridge the gap between the system's physical capabilities and the logical desired result. These wickedly fast, but dumb as dirt, computers need to be shown the way at every step, which places an enormous burden on everyone who uses them, particularly programmers. Abstraction is the key to managing this mind-bending complexity.

One of your primary goals in programming should be to work at the highest logical level you can. Very few programmers work in assembly language today, largely because there's little need for them to do so. C/C++, Pascal, BASIC, and other high level languages are far more productive tools for most types of programming. By working at the higher logical level of one of these compiled languages, a programmer is really working with an abstraction or virtual machine, stacked atop other virtual machines, including the runtime library provided with the language, third-party libraries, and DOS and Windows.

My point in this guideline is that programmers habitually accept this ready-made stack of abstractions and virtual machines and use them, but then fail to think in terms of creating their own virtual machines. They consider the existing abstractions part of the programming landscape, but they fail to make sufficient use of abstraction as a tool. (See Chapter 10 for much more on abstraction and the related topic of writing Win32 API wrappers.)

## 11. Practice Defensive Programming

*Things without all remedy*
*Should be without regard; what's done is done*

William Shakespeare

*Never check for an error condition you don't know how*
*to handle.*

Programmer aphorism

*This error should never happen.*

Far too many dialog boxes

Defensive programming is like defensive driving: If everyone supposedly knows what a good idea it is, as we all claim is the case, then why are there still so many people driving up telephone poles, the wrong way on one-way streets, or worst of all, under the influence of one foreign substance or another, and why are so many commercially available programs even buggier than an early beta test version should be? My theory is that in both cases it's largely a cultural issue. Neither defensive driving nor defensive programming is cool enough or sexy enough. Especially among Americans, it's far hipper to live on the edge and take a few chances, to be a cowboy, and leave the worrying to the boring people on the sidelines.

Well, I hate to bring your party down, but the plain fact is that boring old defensive programming is the single most important micro-level issue you'll face. Even though it's practiced in the microcosm, it can easily affect the reliability of your entire program.

## What Is Defensive Programming?

At its core, defensive programming is minimizing the dangerous assumptions your code makes. In this usage, "dangerous" means that if the assumption is wrong it could lead to your program running incorrectly, and it's the bright line between those incorrect assumptions that do and don't matter. (In my opinion, if an error harms a program's appearance but still allows it to run properly and without loss of function or data, it's still seriously flawed. Many programmers I've spoken to disagree with me on this, and I've even had support people tell me that it's only a cosmetic problem, the implication clearly being that as long as I didn't lose any data and the program still did its job, then I shouldn't care. It was also clear that they weren't going to worry about it, either. Sometimes when I get into one of my two cars, both Hondas, I marvel at how solid and well designed they are, and I fear what will happen if the Japanese ever decide that mainstream application development is a strategic industry worthy of their undivided attention.)

Assumptions are bad for a simple but often overlooked reason: Every assumption in your code is a dependency, and every dependency is a potential exposure to a future change. This could be a change to your tools, Windows, or some other code in your program.

## The Nature of Assumptions

Obviously, you can't avoid making dozens of assumptions in even the most trivial of programs. Every line of code you write assumes that your compiler will properly translate it into machine language, that your variables won't have been corrupted by the system or another agent since the previous line of code executed, etc. Your code is literally afloat on a sea of assumptions. There's nothing you can or should do about those baseline assumptions, except realize that they're part of the continuum, and then concentrate on the assumptions you should be concerned with.

Those interesting assumptions, the dangerous ones I mentioned above, fall into two broad categories:

1. Data based. Data is your program's blood stream. Without it, all the logic in the world has nothing to work on. A trivial point, perhaps, but one that points to a disturbing fact: Just like a real blood stream, your program's blood stream can become infected. I'm not talking about computer viruses, but bad data. Bad data (meaning data that is not correct or is not in the documented or reasonably expected format) can come from a user's typo, other code in your program (including third-party code that you might be using), and even Windows itself.

   Remember that not all sources of bad data under Windows are obvious. *Windows/DOS Developer's Journal*, in their ongoing series of Windows SDK annotations, has documented several cases where an API call will modify some piece of the caller's data that the API definition explicitly says it won't modify. This can lead to some nasty surprises and long debugging sessions.

2. Procedure based. The other half of your program's yin-yang existence is algorithms. Whenever you yield control to another piece of code (always a more interesting way to think of it than "calling" or "invoking" a "subroutine"), you're inevitably making assumptions about what the range of valid outcomes are from that act. These assumptions are based on two sources: Documentation and observation. (I'm discounting here things like idle conversations with other programmers at the coffee machines, or under-the-table deals programmers cut with each other to change ever so slightly the behavior of their code as a mutual convenience.)

Why should you care about anything except the documentation? Sadly, it's often flat out wrong or wildly underspecified, leaving you no other choice. The great grand daddy of examples of such flaws is the Win32 API documentation. There are numerous APIs that react to the same input and conditions differently, depending on whether your program is running under Win32s, Windows 95, or Windows NT, and the documentation for things like extended error codes (retrieved by the GetLastError() API) is truly abysmal. So in many cases you're forced into guessing and performing experiments to see how things really work. (For an example of how much a single API's behavior can vary between Win32 platform's, see the discussion in Chapter 14 of GetShortPathName().) Since none of us has the time to test literally every single API, we're forced to make yet more dangerous assumptions.

## *"Trust but Verify"*

Paranoia is good for two reasons: Sometimes they really are out to get you, and even if they're not, a random error can be just as dangerous as malicious intent, and often far more subtle.

Taking a different slice through the issue of trust and assumptions, defensive programming takes place on three fronts:

1. How you treat data your code receives from unreliable sources. This is the traditional, narrow sense in which this topic is typically addressed. Just as you should always think of programs in two tiers, private and public, you should also think of data integrity in two tiers: complete and all bets are off. Claiming that data from a given source is "mostly reliable" makes exactly as much sense as saying a woman is "a little bit pregnant." Either the data is reliable enough that you can simply use it without validating it, or it isn't. Period.

   Programmers sometimes talk about "trusted interfaces," and the near-mythical reliability of the sources of data they will rely upon. This is another fable and another slippery slope argument. There are indeed many cases where you should not perform data validation, but it's very easy to get lazy and use such arguments to avoid doing it when you should. And whenever you write a routine that does no verification of its parameters, this should be explicitly stated in the routine's initial block comment. This declaration doesn't have to be a warning boxed off with neon asterisks, just a one liner like: "Validates parameters: No" is fine. If your code is also documented in a HLP file or other means, for in-house use, then its parameter validation (or lack thereof) should be clearly detailed there, as well.

   When you make the decision about how much data verification is appropriate in your routines, you should always think in terms of fire walls: Look for ways to enforce the correctness of data, or at least make sure that bad data doesn't get to the core of your algorithm by rejecting the call, as needed. You should also guard against passing unverified data on to other routines unless you're sure that they'll handle the situation properly.

When your code does validate data, it often makes sense to think of it as passing through stages of certainty about data of unknown pedigree. For example, in the function:

```
void DoStuff(int x, char *y)
{
    if((x > max_x) || (x < min_x) || (y == NULL) || (strlen(y) == 0))
      return BAD_PARAMETER;

    /* Now do real work */
}
```

the statement that validates the parameters carries the program from a state of very low certainty about the parameters to one that is sufficiently high that they can be trusted and used without further validation. This "range of uncertainty" exists at the beginning of every function, and also at any point in your program where data enters it from another source. The range persists until your code or some function it calls validates the data. The range therefore extends into all routines your code calls, which is how your program's blood stream becomes infected—bad data gets passed around, and sometimes is saved in persistent storage and only causes a serious problem days later. (If you've ever had to track down a problem that was traceable to bad persistent data, and you ultimately had to find the place in a program where the corruption was happening, you know what a challenge this can be.)

Your most entertaining source of syntactically or semantically challenged data will always be your users, of course. Ask them for their name, and they'll type in their phone number, ask them for their phone number and they'll enter their address, ask them for their address and they'll accidentally hit enter and give you a blank string. They'll also give you data that mixes zeroes and O's, and places extraneous blanks in the darndest places. It's your program's job to detect these exercises in gonzo data entry and do one of two things: Force the data to a usable format (such as stripping leading blanks from a string), or reject it with an appropriate error indicator (either a return value to a program or a diagnostic message to the user).

Of course, there are times when a routine is buried so deep in a program's logic, or the chances of it having to use a "bad data" return value are so slim that it's probably not worth even doing the "check and bail out" two-step. In such cases, you should carefully examine the code to see if it makes sense to validate the parameters or other data and simply do nothing if it's unusable. I know how crazy that sounds, but I've found cases where this is true. You have to make this decision carefully, though, since you're looking for instances where the program will surely crash itself (and possibly Windows) if it continues with bad data (typically a pointer), and where the program would not crash if it simply did nothing. Code that truly satisfies both of these conditions is rare, but it happens. And you also have to decide exactly how the function should return to its caller. Make your code employ a "maximally safe" set of output values.

If you do find one of these safe-to-do-nothing cases, make sure you document it very clearly, both at the point where you do the return (and, presumably, an OutputDebugString() call, in the debug variation of your program), and also in the block comment at the head of the function. (I suspect that these situations lead overly zealous programmers to display those infamous "this should never happen" dialog boxes. If you catch yourself about to do that, don't.)

2. How you exercise code that you call. This can be a precarious situation, particularly in regards to the Win32 API, a virtual open hydrant of surprises. The difficulty, of course, is that you can't exhaustively test every single API. About all you can do is watch the documentation (including all of Microsoft's bug reports in their *Developer Network* CD) and test those APIs that are critical to your program. A critical API is one for which you might possibly be creating a common pathological case by passing it unvalidated data (you're extending a range of uncertainty into its execution), or for which you examine the GetLastError() value, which Microsoft says varies between the Win32 platforms for the same API and conditions (and it does, too).

Everyone tells you not to count on or use undocumented side effects of other routines. That's great advice, even though it's sometimes very hard to follow, since it seems that those pesky side effects are so often just the thing you need to do some job (or even the only way to do it). Still, resist using anything undocumented unless you have an overwhelming reason to do so. Then document what you're doing and include an explanation why you're doing it. And make the explanation so clear that no one likely to see the code could mistake what's going on.

Adopt the philosophy that any code other than the routine under your fingertips is probably buggy and was quite likely written by a lunatic. This applies to your own code, Windows API calls, etc. This is in dramatic contrast to the assumption most programmers make, however implicitly, that they and their code are at the center of a kind and loving universe that will shield them from deranged users, gamma rays, and stale Doritos. It ain't so, and never will be. You should look at every exposed routine you write and try to anticipate the creative ways that it can be misused, and then try to prevent as many of those as you can at reasonable cost. The key word, again, is reasonable. You're not trying to achieve some mythical degree of perfection; you're merely trying to anticipate (which means to foresee and prepare for) how things can go wrong.

I remember one team project I was on, and how we had persistent crashes when we were trying to perform a function with a disk file that didn't really exist. This seemed like such a simple situation that we couldn't understand why the code wasn't handling it properly. Another person on the project and I did some investigating and found that a routine written by a third programmer had a piece of code that did roughly the following, in pseudocode:

```
file_handle = OpenFile(file_name);
rc = ReadFile(file_handle,buffer);
while(rc == OK)
    {
      ProcessBuffer(buffer);
    rc = ReadFile(file_handle,buffer);
    }

CloseFile(file_handle);
```

The problem, of course, was that the programmer assumed that the file always existed. The first attempt to read the file returned an error code, which this code assumed was an end-of-file condition, and it then attempted to close the file and dropped into more code that assumed the file's contents had been loaded into memory and processed, resulting in all sorts of mayhem.

3.  The design of your own code, and what it implies about how others will use it. A lot of programmers will contend that this is not a defensive programming issue at all, but I disagree. How you design your functions that other code will call is very important, and you should strive to anticipate errors on the part of code that calls your functions, just as you should anticipate common errors in data your code receives from other sources. (I'll have a lot more to say about the design of API wrappers and functions in Chapter 10, but here I'll concentrate on the defensive programming aspects.)

Your first line of defense against someone misusing your code is documentation. Make it complete and accurate, and you'll leave other programmers (possibly including yourself, of course), very little room for "creative interpretation." As much as I hate to say it, it's also true that the better your documentation, the greater your chances of winning an argument if some other programmer tries to blame a bug on your code. I'd like to think that most programmers are above such concerns, but office politics sure do have a way of creeping into technical matters.

You should always consider what will happen if the caller ignores or misinterprets the success-failure indicator your function returns. It happens, and in some cases it makes sense to burn a few instructions by setting your returned output to a safe value if your function can't complete its task, for whatever reason. This is another case that requires careful judgment on your part, but such cases do pop up from time to time.

*You can get into trouble with your functions' return values without even realizing it. Don't rely on "what everyone does" or "what everyone knows." I see this kind of minor violation in code all the time, typically when a function defined to return a BOOL returns the return value from another function. This is particularly dangerous when dealing with the Win32 API, since some of the calls will return some apparently random non-zero value instead of TRUE (which is defined as one). This seems like a minor issue, but it isn't; if your function is declared as returning a BOOL, and it returns anything except TRUE or FALSE, it's a bug. Period. (The fact that you can try to blame it on the Win32 API is meaningless; Microsoft's sins should not be your accepted behavior.)*

## Defensive Programming and Code Reuse

One of the oft-cited benefits of code reuse is that not only aren't you expending resources to reinvent the wheel, but you're getting to use an exceptionally well designed and implemented wheel. Presumably this is battle-hardened code that uses appropriate defensive programming techniques.

But there's another, subtler connection between code reuse and defensive programming. In my experience, one of the prime reasons programmers don't practice defensive programming is that they're lazy (and I'm just as guilty of this as anyone). By assembling a toolbox of small routines that you can use to verify or correct data, you can make it much easier to do the right thing. As I mentioned above, think in terms of fire walls and limiting the spread of bad data. The key issue, as always, is balance, and you should strive to take all reasonable precautions.

As I mentioned in the introduction, much of the code I present in this book is not rocket science, and that it wasn't my intention to shoot for the moon. Well, the toolbox code here is about as non-rocket-science-like as it gets, and yet it just might be the kind of code that saves you and your programs' users the most grief in the long run. The trick is to make sure you have the right things in your toolbox and then diligently use them. To paraphrase a line from a wildly different arena, it's not what you have, but how you use it. (I talk a lot more about abstraction and wrapping the Win32 API, related but slightly different topics, in Chapter 10.)

The best candidates for your toolbox are routines that examine a piece of provided data for conformance to some format or state and return a BOOL indicating what they found. Good examples from the Win32 API are IsIconic(), IsChild(), and IsWindow(). And note the naming convention, which not only concisely describes the function's purpose, but also leads to more natural-language-like statements:

```
if(IsIconic(fred_hWnd))
  ::SendMessage(fred_hWnd,WM_SYSCOMMAND,SC_RESTORE,0);
```

Don't become too enamored with building your toolbox, though. It's very easy to start looking for any and all defensible opportunities to create yet another small routine, and wind up spending all your time writing a programming kit instead of programs. (This is one of the chronic problems with C++, in general, since programmers can spend a lot of time crafting classes and not using them.) Don't worry if your toolbox isn't orthogonal, or if it doesn't seem elegant enough. You should let your toolbox grow organically; when you find that you could really use a new routine in the toolbox, say, LooksLikeCISID() (to validate a string as a potential CompuServe ID), then take the time to write, test, and document it, and add it to your toolbox. If you go looking for toolbox additions, you'll wind up burning endless hours hassling with tiny problems that you might never need.

And don't worry about writing routines that are less than 100 percent certain of their opinions about data. As long as you document and use them appropriately, they can still be useful. The example I mentioned above, LooksLikeCISID(), which I also talk about below in a sidebar, is a good example. An isolated piece of code can't possibly tell if a character string is actually a valid CompuServe ID, at least not without calling CompuServe and trying to send e-mail to the account, for example. The most a program can do is see if the string appears to be in the proper format. If your program needs to ask the user for a CompuServe ID, then you can call this function, and if the function returns false, prompt the user with a dialog box that says something like, "The CompuServe ID you've entered doesn't appear to be in a valid format. Do you want to use it anyway?" This gives the user a chance to override the program, always a good idea in a changing world that can generate "false negatives." Also, the dialog box should include a Help button that will display a topic that explains what a "normal" CompuServe ID looks like and why the program was complaining.

Whenever I write a function that performs a less than certain check, I always use the naming convention LooksLike<something>, since this reinforces the idea that it's not performing a hard and fast validation, as would a function named Is<something>.

The general point is that you want to exploit domain-specific knowledge to improve the usability and robustness of your program. The best way to do this and make sure everyone on your programming team does it, is via a shared toolbox.

Let me give you some examples of routines I use, well, routinely, in my work. These are all included in the sample program for this chapter, TEST_TB, which includes the toolbox and a simple Win32 console application that exercises the toolbox routines a bit.

## Building the Samples: TEST_TB

**CD Location:** ZEN\CHAP03\TOOLBOX

**Platform:** Win32

**Build instructions:** Use the provided .MAK file with Visual C++ 2.2, and compile normally.

- AppendTrailingSlash(). There are many times in working with directory and file names that you're not 100 percent sure if the string you're working with (or possibly building one component at a time), has a trailing backslash. That's where this routine comes in. All it does is check, and if the string doesn't include a trailing backslash and there's room for one, it appends one:

```
//////////////////////////////////////////////////////////////////////
// AppendSlash: Append a backslash to the provided string only if there is
// room for one and the string does not already end in a backslash.
//
// dest: string to be modified
// max_len: Maximum allowable length of dest, including a term. NULL
//
// Parameters are validated:
//   NULL or zero-length dest parameter is rejected
//   max_len less than 3 is rejected
//////////////////////////////////////////////////////////////////////

void AppendSlash(char *dest, size_t max_len)
{
#ifdef _DEBUG
  if((dest == NULL) || (*dest == '\0') || (max_len < 3))
    OutputDebugString("AppendSlash: Invalid parameter detected!\n");
#endif

  if((dest == NULL) || (*dest == '\0')|| (max_len < 3))
    return;

  if((strlen(dest) + 1 < max_len) &&
    (dest[strlen(dest) - 1] != '\\'))
      strlcat(dest,"\\",max_len);
}
```

This is a good example of a small, high performing routine that could save your neck (or other body parts) without your even knowing it. (And don't worry about the mysterious strlcat() function it calls; I'll get to it shortly.)

- stripLeading(), stripTrailing(), stripLT(). As I've mentioned already, leading and trailing blanks in string data can cause no end of headaches. Luckily, this is one case where you can almost always modify the data in question to fit your needs with no danger of losing information or causing more problems. I use these three routines for this chore, and I call them constantly, even when I'm reasonably sure they're not needed.

```
///////////////////////////////////////////////////////////////////////////
// stripLeading: Strip the leading blanks and tabs from a character string.
//
// Parameter is validated:
//   NULL or zero-length string is rejected
///////////////////////////////////////////////////////////////////////////

void stripLeading(char *s)
{
#ifdef _DEBUG
  if((s == NULL) || (*s == '\0'))
    OutputDebugString("stripLeading: Invalid parameter detected!\n");
#endif

  if((s == NULL) || (*s == '\0'))
    return;

  char *z = s;

  while(*z && ((*z == ' ') || (*z == '\t')))
    z++;

  if(s != z)
    memmove(s,z,strlen(z) + 1); // Safe-- can't possibly overflow
}

///////////////////////////////////////////////////////////////////////////
// stripLT: Strip leading and trailing blanks and tabs from a char. string.
//
// Parameter is validated:
//   NULL or zero-length string is rejected
///////////////////////////////////////////////////////////////////////////

void stripLT(char *s)
{
#ifdef _DEBUG
  if((s == NULL) || (*s == '\0'))
    OutputDebugString("stripLT: Invalid parameter detected!\n");
#endif

  if((s == NULL) || (*s == '\0'))
    return;

  stripLeading(s);
  stripTrailing(s);
}

///////////////////////////////////////////////////////////////////////////
// stripTrailing: Strip trailing blanks and tabs from a character string.
//
// Parameter is validated:
//   NULL or zero-length string is rejected
///////////////////////////////////////////////////////////////////////////

void stripTrailing(char *s)
{
#ifdef _DEBUG
  if((s == NULL) || (*s == '\0'))
    OutputDebugString("stripTrailing: Invalid parameter detected!\n");
#endif
```

```
    if((s == NULL) || (*s == '\0'))
      return;

    int z = strlen(s);

    while((z >= 0) && ((s[z] == ' ') || (s[z] == '\t') || (s[z] == '\0')))
      z--;

    s[z + 1] = 0;
  }
```

- Clipping functions. There are times when you can safely force data into a required range of values. When you can (and this is obviously a judgment that
has to be made carefully), it makes sense to do so, especially when "there's
absolutely no way Z can be greater than X or less than Y," since Z so often finds
a way to do just that, causing no end of havoc in the process.

```
///////////////////////////////////////////////////////////////////////////
// ClipInt: Forces an integer to be within the specified limits
//
// x: value to be limited
// limit1, limit2: the limits used for x
// Note: limit1 and limit2 do not have to be supplied in ascending order.
//
// Parameters are not validated, since all values are legal
///////////////////////////////////////////////////////////////////////////
long int ClipInt(int x, int limit1, int limit2)
{
  long int min_x, max_x;

  // Set up min and max values appropriately.  Caller can pass 'em in
  // incorrectly and we'll still get it right.
  if(limit1 < limit2)
    {
      min_x = limit1;
      max_x = limit2;
    }
  else
    {
      min_x = limit2;
      max_x = limit1;
    }

  if(x <= min_x)
    return min_x;
  else
    if(x >= max_x)
      return max_x;
    else
      return x;
}
```

Note in ClipInt() how the limits are handled, and that the caller can provide
them in ascending or descending order. This is not just frippery. This type of
routine is often used in circumstances where the limits are not manifest constants,

but calculated from variable, possibly even suspect, data. Making the routine smart enough to accept the limits in any order can prevent some nasty, hard to reproduce problems in the future.

• Length- and termination-safe string routines. The standard C routines for manipulating strings (strcpy(), strcat(), etc.) present almost endless opportunities for problems, since they either make no attempt at safety, or they only do so in ways that are inconvenient. (I won't give you the *sturm und drang* routine on the C string routines here; see Chapter 10.)

My solution is a set of string functions that all take the maximum length of the destination string that is being copied to, appended, or whatever. These routines will never overrun the target buffer, and will never leave a string in an unterminated state (as strncpy() can, in some cases). Of course, you have to have the willpower to use these routines when appropriate, which leads to some interesting conversations. I've heard people say that you can't always use such routines, because you don't always know the maximum allowable length for a string. Which begs the question: If you don't know how long the destination string can be without overrunning its allocated space and stomping on other data, then why in the world are you copying data into it or appending another string to it, and what makes you think this is a safe thing to do? (This question usually results in a classic blank stare.) In all seriousness, I see this all the time in production code—a routine receives a pointer to a string and not the maximum length, and it goes about changing the string in ways that can or could make it longer. This is obviously horrible practice, and should be banned.

I want to stress that I'm not saying you should use these routines in all cases. There are clearly times when you can use the standard C runtime routines with perfect safety, since you know that your destination string can't possibly be overrun. I normally use these routines (or similar variations) all the time, since there's no telling when some other change in a program will violate an assumption, and create an overrun exposure.

One of the issues you face with such routines is what to do when there isn't room in the destination string to complete the operation, but there's still room to copy or concatenate some characters. Should the function handle what will fit, or should it refuse to do anything? The answer, of course, is that it depends on the caller's specific situation. You can easily imagine conditions when either answer is the right one. To that end, I've provided both varieties of the routines. The ones with the "Atomic" suffix on their names will only work if they have completed the entire operation as specified. (This naming convention is meant to indicate that the operations are performed on an "all or nothing" basis, not how severely the functions will blow up when faced with bad parameters.)

```
///////////////////////////////////////////////////////////////////////////
// strlcat: Concatenate characters from src onto dest, with a maximum length
// for dest of max_len, and always ensure proper termination.  This function
// will concatenate as many characters from src onto dest as will fit.
//
// max_len includes the term. null
//
// Returns TRUE if concatenation was performed, FALSE if it wasn't.
//
// Parameters are validated:
//   NULL or zero-length strings are rejected
//   max_len of 0 or smaller than dest's initial length is rejected
//
///////////////////////////////////////////////////////////////////////////

BOOL strlcat(char *dest, const char *src, size_t max_len)
{
#ifdef _DEBUG
  if((dest == NULL) || (src == NULL) || (max_len == 0) || (strlen(dest) >=
      max_len - 1))
    OutputDebugString("strlcat: Invalid parameter detected!\n");
#endif

  if((dest == NULL) || (src == NULL) || (max_len == 0))
    return FALSE;

  UINT d_len = strlen(dest);

  if(d_len >= max_len - 1)
    return FALSE;

  strncat(dest,src,max_len - d_len - 1);
  return TRUE;
}

///////////////////////////////////////////////////////////////////////////
// strlcatAtomic: Concatenate characters from src onto dest, with a maximum
// length for dest of max_len, and always ensure proper termination.  This
// function will only concatenate characters from src onto dest if all the
// characters in src will fit.
//
// max_len includes the term. null
//
// Returns TRUE if concatenation was performed, FALSE if it wasn't.
//
// Parameters are validated:
//   NULL or zero-length strings are rejected
//   max_len of 0 or smaller than dest's initial length is rejected
//
///////////////////////////////////////////////////////////////////////////

BOOL strlcatAtomic(char *dest, const char *src, size_t max_len)
{
#ifdef _DEBUG
  if((dest == NULL) || (src == NULL) || (max_len == 0) || (strlen(dest) >=
      max_len - 1))
    OutputDebugString("strlcatAtomic: Invalid parameter detected!\n");
#endif

  if((dest == NULL) ||
     (src == NULL) ||
```

```
    (max_len == 0))
    return FALSE;

 UINT d_len = strlen(dest);

 if(d_len + strlen(src) >= max_len - 1)   // Ensure all chars will fit
    return FALSE;

 strncat(dest,src,max_len - d_len - 1);
 return TRUE;
}

//////////////////////////////////////////////////////////////////////
// strlcpy: Copy characters from src to dest, with a maximum length for dest
// of max_len, and always ensure proper termination.  This function will
// copy as many characters from src to dest as will fit.
//
// max_len includes the term. null
//
// Returns TRUE if copy was performed, FALSE if it wasn't.
//
// Parameters are validated:
//    NULL or zero-length strings are rejected
//    max_len of 0 is rejected
//
//////////////////////////////////////////////////////////////////////
BOOL strlcpy(char *dest, const char *src, size_t max_len)
{
#ifdef _DEBUG
  if((dest == NULL) || (src == NULL) || (max_len == 0))
    OutputDebugString("strlcpy: Invalid parameter detected!\n");
#endif

  if((dest == NULL) || (src == NULL) || (max_len == 0))
    return FALSE;

  *dest = '\0';
  return strlcat(dest,src,max_len);
}

//////////////////////////////////////////////////////////////////////
// strlcpyAtomic: Copy characters from src onto dest, with a maximum length
// for dest of max_len, and always ensure proper termination.  This function
// will only copy characters from src onto dest if all the characters in src
// will fit.
//
// max_len includes the term. null
//
// Returns TRUE if copy was performed, FALSE if it wasn't.
//
// Parameters are validated:
//    NULL or zero-length strings are rejected
//    0 max_len is rejected
//
//////////////////////////////////////////////////////////////////////

BOOL strlcpyAtomic(char *dest, const char *src, size_t max_len)
{
#ifdef _DEBUG
```

```
      if((dest == NULL) || (src == NULL) || (max_len == 0))
        OutputDebugString("strlcpyAtomic: Invalid parameter detected!\n");
#endif

    if((dest == NULL) || (src == NULL) || (max_len == 0))
      return FALSE;

    *dest = '\0';
    return strlcatAtomic(dest,src,max_len);
  }


//////////////////////////////////////////////////////////////////////////
// strlncat: Concatenate up to n characters from src onto dest, with a maximum
// length for dest of max_len, and always ensure proper termination.  This
// function will concatenate as many characters from src onto dest as will fit
// (up to n).
//
// max_len includes the term. null
//
// Returns TRUE if concatenation was performed, FALSE if it wasn't.
//
// Parameters are validated:
//   NULL or zero-length strings are rejected
//   max_len of 0 or smaller than dest's initial length is rejected
//
//////////////////////////////////////////////////////////////////////////

BOOL strlncat(char *dest, const char *src, size_t max_len, size_t n)
{
#ifdef _DEBUG
  if((dest == NULL) || (src == NULL) || (max_len == 0) || (strlen(dest) >=
      max_len - 1))
    OutputDebugString("strlncat: Invalid parameter detected!\n");
#endif

  if((dest == NULL) || (src == NULL) || (max_len == 0))
    return FALSE;

  UINT d_len = strlen(dest);

  if(d_len >= max_len - 1)
    return FALSE;

  // Does the dest. have room for at least n data characters?
  if(max_len - d_len - 1 >= n)
    strncat(dest,src,n);     // Yes: Copy all n
  else
    strncat(dest,src,max_len - d_len - 1);  // No: Just do what will fit.

  return TRUE;
}


//////////////////////////////////////////////////////////////////////////
// strlncatAtomic: Concatenate characters from src onto dest, with a maximum
// length for dest of max_len, and always ensure proper termination.  This
// function will only concatenate characters from src onto dest if all the
// characters in src will fit.
//
// max_len includes the term. null
//
// Returns TRUE if concatenation was performed, FALSE if it wasn't.
```

```
//
// Parameters are validated:
//   NULL or zero-length strings are rejected
//   max_len of 0 or smaller than dest's initial length is rejected
//
////////////////////////////////////////////////////////////////////////

BOOL strlncatAtomic(char *dest, const char *src, size_t max_len, size_t n)
{
#ifdef _DEBUG
  if((dest == NULL) || (src == NULL) || (max_len == 0) || (strlen(dest) >=
      max_len - 1))
    OutputDebugString("strlncatAtomic: Invalid parameter detected!\n");
#endif

  if((dest == NULL) ||
     (src == NULL) ||
     (max_len == 0))
    return FALSE;

  if(max_len - strlen(dest) - 1 < n)  // Ensure all chars will fit
    return FALSE;

  strncat(dest,src,n);      // Yes: Copy all n
  return TRUE;
}


////////////////////////////////////////////////////////////////////////
// strlncpy: Copy up to n characters from src to dest, with a maximum length
// for dest of max_len, and always ensure proper termination.  This function
// will copy as many characters from src onto dest as will fit (up to n).
//
// max_len includes the term. null
//
// Returns TRUE if copy was performed, FALSE if it wasn't.
//
// Parameters are validated:
//   NULL or zero-length strings are rejected
//   max_len of 0 is rejected
//
////////////////////////////////////////////////////////////////////////

BOOL strlncpy(char *dest, const char *src, size_t max_len, size_t n)
{
#ifdef _DEBUG
  if((dest == NULL) || (src == NULL) || (max_len == 0))
    OutputDebugString("strlncpy: Invalid parameter detected!\n");
#endif

  if((dest == NULL) || (src == NULL) || (max_len == 0))
    return FALSE;

  *dest = '\0';
  return strlncat(dest,src,max_len,n);
}


////////////////////////////////////////////////////////////////////////
// strlncpyAtomic: Copy characters from src onto dest, with a maximum length
// for dest of max_len, and always ensure proper termination.  This function
// will only concatenate characters from src onto dest if all the characters
// in src will fit.
```

```
//
// max_len includes the term. null
//
// Returns TRUE if copy was performed, FALSE if it wasn't.
//
// Parameters are validated:
//   NULL or zero-length strings are rejected
//   max_len of 0 is rejected
//
/////////////////////////////////////////////////////////////////////

BOOL strlncpyAtomic(char *dest, const char *src, size_t max_len, size_t n)
{
#ifdef _DEBUG
  if((dest == NULL) || (src == NULL) || (max_len == 0))
    OutputDebugString("strlncpyAtomic: Invalid parameter detected!\n");
#endif

  if((dest == NULL) || (src == NULL) || (max_len == 0))
    return FALSE;

  *dest = '\0';
  return strlncatAtomic(dest,src,max_len,n);
}
```

- CopyFileForceRW(). This one is really simple, yet your users will thank you for using it. This function is merely a slight functional enhancement of the CopyFile() Win32 API. All it does is call CopyFile() with the requested parameters, and then forces the destination file to be read/write. Without this last step, a file copied from a CD ROM will preserve all the original file's attributes, including the read/only bit. This can lead to minor annoyances for your users, and even your own programs, if you forget to account for the fact that the file can still be read/only.

```
/////////////////////////////////////////////////////////////////////
// CopyFileForceRW: Use the CopyFile API to copy a file, but then force
// the file to be R/W.
//
// Returns TRUE if the copy is performed and the destination file's attribute
// is successfully set to R/W.  Returns FALSE otherwise.
//
// Parameters are validated:
//   NULL or zero-length strings are rejected
//
/////////////////////////////////////////////////////////////////////

BOOL CopyFileForceRW(char *src, char *dest, BOOL copy_flag)
{
#ifdef _DEBUG
  if((dest == NULL) || (src == NULL) || (*dest == '\0') || (*src == '\0'))
    OutputDebugString("CopyFileForceRW: Invalid parameter detected!\n");
#endif

  if((dest == NULL) || (src == NULL) || (*dest == '\0') || (*src == '\0'))
    {
    SetLastError(ERROR_INVALID_PARAMETER);
```

```
      return FALSE;
    }

// All remaining API calls use SetLastError(), so we allow them to
// dictate the setting.

  if(!CopyFile(src,dest,copy_flag))
    return FALSE;

  DWORD fa = GetFileAttributes(dest);
  if(fa != 0xffffffff)
    {
      fa &= ~FILE_ATTRIBUTE_READONLY;
      return (SetFileAttributes(dest,fa) != 0);
    }
  return FALSE;
}
```

- FileExists() and DirExists(). Two more simple ones that can save your program's neck (the neck being in an undocumented part of the PE-format executable header, by the way). All they do is return a BOOL that indicates if the file you passed in is the name of an existing file or directory.

  As simple as these functions are, they still contain a few subtleties. FileExists() will return FALSE, if the item does exist but is a directory. This behavior reflects how these functions are normally used: You would call FileExists() with a string just before you were about to use that string as a file name, and not a directory name. Similarly, DirExists() returns TRUE only if the existing file is a directory. Also, notice that the final return statement in DirExists() takes pains not to simply return the non-zero value of the logical AND operation; only TRUE or FALSE values should be returned in a BOOL.

```
///////////////////////////////////////////////////////////////////////
// FileExists: Checks to see if the specified file exists and is NOT a
// directory.
//
// Returns TRUE if the file exists, FALSE if it doesn't or is a directory.
//
// Parameter is validated:
//   NULL or zero-length string is rejected
//
///////////////////////////////////////////////////////////////////////

BOOL FileExists(const char *fn)
{
#ifdef _DEBUG
  if(fn == NULL || (strlen(fn)) == 0)
    OutputDebugString("FileExists: Invalid parameter detected!\n");
#endif

  if(fn == NULL || (strlen(fn)) == 0)
    return FALSE;

  DWORD dwFA = GetFileAttributes(fn);
```

```
  if(dwFA == 0xFFFFFFFF)
    return FALSE;
  else
    return ((dwFA & FILE_ATTRIBUTE_DIRECTORY) != FILE_ATTRIBUTE_DIRECTORY);
}


///////////////////////////////////////////////////////////////////////////
// DirExists: Checks to see if the specified file exists and is a
// directory.
//
// Returns TRUE if the file exists and is a directory, FALSE otherwise
//
// Parameter is validated:
//   NULL or zero-length string is rejected
//
///////////////////////////////////////////////////////////////////////////

BOOL DirExists(const char *dn)
{
#ifdef _DEBUG
  if((dn == NULL) || (*dn == '\0'))
    OutputDebugString("DirExists: Invalid parameter detected!\n");
#endif

  if((dn == NULL) || (*dn == '\0'))
    return FALSE;

  DWORD dwFA = GetFileAttributes(dn);

  if(dwFA == 0xFFFFFFFF)
    return FALSE;
  else
    return ((dwFA & FILE_ATTRIBUTE_DIRECTORY) == FILE_ATTRIBUTE_DIRECTORY);
}
```

- AliasToLFN() and LFNToAlias(). These two are admittedly not related to defensive programming, but they are first cousins to other routines in this section, since they can help your program look a bit more intelligent. These routines merely translate a file's alias (possibly fully qualified) to its long file name or back. Both routines return just the file name portion of the translated name, and not the drive or path components. This is most useful when you want to translate a file name that's in an unknown state into a particular format for long term storage or for viewing by the user.

Both functions return a FALSE value if the file name you provide doesn't exist. This makes perfect sense, since by definition, they're not performing some algorithmic transformation on the provided file name, but looking up the other, already existing name for the same file. If the file doesn't exist, then the entire operation makes no sense.

```
///////////////////////////////////////////////////////////////////////////
// AliasToLFN: Translate an 8.3 filename to its long file name.  The returne    d
// value is just the name portion of the file's name, i.e. NOT including the
// path.  This function can ONLY work if the file exists.
//
```

```
// lfn_length includes the term. null
//
// Returns the length of the returned long file name if successful, -1 otherwise.
//
// Parameters are validated:
//   NULL strings are rejected
//   lfn_length less than MAX_PATH is rejected
//
///////////////////////////////////////////////////////////////////////

int AliasToLFN(const char *alias, char *lfn, UINT lfn_length)
{
#ifdef _DEBUG
  if((lfn == NULL) || (alias == NULL) || (lfn_length < MAX_PATH))
    OutputDebugString("AliasToLFN: Invalid parameter detected!\n");
#endif

  if((lfn == NULL) || (alias == NULL) || (lfn_length < MAX_PATH))
    return -1;

  WIN32_FIND_DATA temp;
  HANDLE search_handle = FindFirstFile(alias,&temp);

  if(search_handle == INVALID_HANDLE_VALUE)
    {
      lfn[0] = 0x0;
      return -1;
    }
  else
    {
      strlcpy(lfn,temp.cFileName,lfn_length - 1);
      FindClose(search_handle);
      return strlen(lfn);
    }
}


///////////////////////////////////////////////////////////////////////
// LFNToAlias: Translate a long file name to its 8.3 form.  The returned
// value is just the name portion of the file's name, i.e. NOT including the
// path.  This function can ONLY work if the file exists.
//
// alias_length includes the term. null
//
// Returns the length of the returned alias if successful, -1 otherwise.
//
// Parameters are validated:
//   NULL strings are rejected
//   alias_length less than MAX_PATH is rejected
//
///////////////////////////////////////////////////////////////////////

int LFNToAlias(const char *lfn, char *alias, UINT alias_length)
{
#ifdef _DEBUG
  if((lfn == NULL) || (alias == NULL) || (alias_length < 13))
    OutputDebugString("LFNToAlias: Invalid parameter detected!\n");
#endif

  if((lfn == NULL) || (alias == NULL) || (alias_length < 13))
    return -1;
```

```
    WIN32_FIND_DATA temp;

    HANDLE search_handle = FindFirstFile(lfn,&temp);

    if(search_handle == INVALID_HANDLE_VALUE)
      {
        alias[0] = 0x0;
        return -1;
      }
    else
      {
        strlcpy(alias,temp.cAlternateFileName,alias_length - 1);
        FindClose(search_handle);
        return strlen(alias);
      }
}
```

*Perhaps it's just me, but I find it curious and bothersome that an API as rich and complex as Win32 doesn't provide functions that perform these simple operations. There are some that seem to come close, like GetShortPathName(), which is unfortunately riddled with its own quirks, and which returns the fully qualified file name if one is provided. Another near-miss is GetFullPathName(), which merely takes your file name and uses it to build a fully qualified path with the current drive and directory. (I would have given that API a different name, like PrependCurrentDir(), that more closely describes what it does.)*

## LooksLikeCISID(): Traversing the Layers of Uncertainty

As I mentioned earlier in this chapter, there are often times when you can, and should, validate data. There are also times when, for the convenience of your user, you should "sanity check" data, as well, and toss out a "do you really want to use this" message if data doesn't appear to be in quite the right format. Examining a string to see if it could possibly be a valid CompuServe ID is a good example of such validation, and how domain-specific knowledge can be used to your program's advantage. It also shows how you can cross the range of uncertainty I talked about earlier in stages.

What do we know about CompuServe IDs? They're of the form <some numbers><comma><some numbers>, with no letters, blanks, or other punctuation, and the comma is never the first or last character. How long are the ID's? The longest CompuServe ID I've seen to date was eleven characters (six digits, a comma, and four more digits), and the shortest was seven (five digits, a comma, and one digit). If we reject anything with more than twelve digits or less than five, that should be safe. (By the definition of the problem, we can't be

100 percent sure, since we're merely syntax checking the string, not verifying that the string is in fact an active CompuServe ID.)

The code for LooksLikeCISID() follows a very simple pattern that is useful for such validation: Start with the assumption that the string is valid, and immediately reject it (by returning with a value of FALSE) whenever you find something that disqualifies it from consideration. If you get to the end of the routine, then it must have passed all your tests, so you can return TRUE.

```
/////////////////////////////////////////////////////////////////////////////
// LooksLikeCISID: Syntax check the provided string to see if it could
// possibly be a legal CompuServe ID.  Tests include:
//
// 1. Length of 5 to 12 characters, inclusive.
// 2. Exactly one embedded comma, not in the first or last position
// 3. All non-comma characters are digits (0-9)
//
// Returns TRUE if the string passes the above examination, FALSE otherwise.
//
// Parameter is validated, and is rejected if it is NULL or zero-length
//
/////////////////////////////////////////////////////////////////////////////
BOOL LooksLikeCISID(const char *id)
{
#ifdef _DEBUG
  if((id == NULL) || (*id == '\0'))
    OutputDebugString("LooksLikeCISID: Invalid parameter detected!\n");
#endif

  // First, validation:
  if((id == NULL) || (*id == '\0'))
    return FALSE;

  char local_id[MAX_PATH];

  // Grab a local copy and clean it up:
  strlcpy(local_id,id,sizeof(local_id));
  stripLT(local_id);

  // Gross check for appropriate length:
  if((strlen(local_id) < 5) || (strlen(local_id) > 12))
    return FALSE;

  int commas = 0;

  // Scan once, looking for anything non-numeric or more than one comma
  for(UINT i = 0; i < strlen(local_id); i++)
    {
      if(local_id[i] == ',')
        {
          // Comma can't be first or last
          if((i == 0) || (i == strlen(local_id) - 1))
            return FALSE;

          commas++;
```

```
        // Wrong number of commas?
        if(commas != 1)
            return FALSE;
        }
    else
      if(!isdigit(local_id[i]))
          return FALSE;
    }

    // It passed all our tests, so it looks like a CIS ID
    return TRUE;
}
```

## 12. Separate Your Program's User Interface from Its Implementation

This is another one of those guidelines that seems to be nothing but common sense. After all, with our profession's current emphasis in object technology and reusability, isn't it only natural to separate the user interface code and the code that does your program's "real work?" It is, but sometimes it takes just a bit more work, and that can result in cut corners, code being in places where it shouldn't, and maintenance problems down the road.

I find that this breakdown in practice happens most commonly in Windows development at the ends of the technology spectrum:

• C (not C++) programs that do things the old fashioned way, without frameworks, and do hand-to-hand combat with the API for all services. Such programs are often organizational nightmares, with all manner of functions and logical services piled into too few source files. When it comes time to maintain this code, the programmer often has to spend a lot of time figuring out the true relationship between all those items in those few namespaces (functions, constants, variables). Sometimes simple maintenance tasks can turn into exercises in "breaking out" code from other functions into new functions or adding new parameters to existing functions, either of which can greatly increase the chance that one or more new bugs will be created in the process of fixing one or adding some minor feature.

• C++ programs that use the IDE's helpers (wizards, experts, and the whole friendly, if limited, lot) to do what I call the plumbing of Windows programs. Face it, just connecting events to the desired code in Windows can be quite a chore, thanks to callbacks, various message formats and conventions, etc. (I often say that the biggest frustration in Windows programming is how often you add some code that appears to be 100 percent correct, and when you test your program it quietly does nothing, because you got the plumbing wrong and the new code never gets called.) Frameworks and IDE's help a great deal in this area, since you can drop a button onto a dialog and then quickly tell the IDE to create a function that will get control when the user clicks the button. Just like that, you have your cursor in the body of the new function, and you're ready to rock and roll. This is precisely the problem, since that ease of use also makes it ever so easy to write your code right there in that event function, and not mess around with new source files or functions in other source files, etc.

In both cases, this is a micro-level issue thanks to the lack of design work behind many Windows programming projects; the programmer is making the decision about how to implement some detail of the program with fingers on the keycaps, always a dangerous state for a programmer.

Whenever possible, you should stick to one rule: All implementation details needed for the program's "real work" should be in different compilation units than the user interface. When the user interface code needs to trigger some feature or refer to some variable, it should be through the smallest possible aperture in the wall between user interface and implementation. For example, some programmers will bristle at code that looks like this:

```
// Handle a click on the Reset button on our dialog
void CLoadDlg::OnReset()
{
  ResetAllData();      // In main implementation
  EndDlg(ID_OK);       // We're outta here
}
```

because they think it's silly to have an entire routine that does nothing but make a subroutine call and then close a dialog. I couldn't disagree more, and I'm always happy to see things like this in code I have to modify, because it makes my job easier, and it also makes for a higher quality program in the long run.

## 13. Use Smart Data Files

If you want to start a religious war between programmers, you could do worse than start with this topic. Some people just don't see the value in going through all the effort to define and use a custom, self-identifying data file format. If their program is storing configuration information, they place it in an .INI file, and data in a more traditional, document-centric sense is casually dumped into a binary format file. Other programmers, myself included, think it's worth the effort. I call these self-identifying files smart data files.

The implementation of smart data files that programmers are most familiar with, even if they don't think of it as such, are executable files. In particular, the new PE-format executables used for Win32 programs contain a lot of information, in addition to the program's code and data segments. Lest anyone suggest that I'm painting with a too-broad brush to call executables data files, remember that at the very beginning of a program's life cycle in your system, it is nothing more than a data file. The user double clicks on your program or a file that is associated with it, which causes Windows to load and execute your program. But in order to do that, it must verify that the file is indeed an executable and that its "expected Windows version" is compatible with the system (unless you're running Win32s, which doesn't bother with this mundane detail). Windows also must resolve all implicit DLL references and perform numerous other minor tasks before your "Hello, world" program can think about opening its mouth or even begins life.

In more traditional usage, smart data files are equally indispensable for major applications. They allow word processors, spread sheets, and databases to use and create files in the custom formats used by competing products, and not rely on something as undependable as naming conventions to identify files.

A related issue is how you use your persistent data. Some programs store their configuration data in plain-text .INI files, and can be tripped up very easily once an adventuresome user starts looking for fun in all the wrong places with a text editor. (Storing your data in the Windows registry is even riskier, in a way, since Windows comes with a special program for editing the registry. What message do you think that sends to users?) This is yet another reason why I'm still a big fan of binary configuration files, even though they seem quite retro at times. Handled properly, they can be more efficient, and slightly safer than .INI files or registry entries, if only because your users won't have a convenient way to edit them. (I've seen people edit DLLs with a text file, oblivious to the fact that their screen is filled with all sorts of binary garbage surrounding a few bits of readable text. There's simply no way you can dissuade some people from doing things like this; but most users who load a binary file into Notepad will immediately realize they've strayed into forbidden territory, and will retreat.)

In short, all data files, whether they store a user's document or configuration information, should be self-identifying or verifiable with a high degree of certainty, and they should always be used intelligently. All binary data files should be designed so that they're prepared for new, not necessarily foreseeable changes. This second requirement is much simpler than it sounds, as I'll detail when I talk about smart data files at length in Chapter 9.

## 14. Handle Configuration Surprises Gracefully

We're all used to performing certain minor ritual checks in our code, things like verifying that requests for dynamic memory are satisfied before we try to use the returned point, making sure that files we're about to use are really open before we start reading or writing, etc. In the Windows realm, these rituals include things like making sure that window and other object handles are valid before using them for the first time, or as needed. (At least I hope we're all used to this idea!)

I see these little programming riffs we all code on automatic pilot as lying at one end of a spectrum of program behavior that runs from simple, obvious validations to more involved steps that might have a great deal of thought behind them (such as how you handle DLLs or which Win32 platforms your program should run under). The items at the simpler end of this spectrum are nothing more than basic defensive programming. But when you stretch the general concept to include more complicated issues, it becomes its own topic (and guideline) and slightly different cut at the development process. It quickly becomes a matter of a program looking out for problems that aren't strictly of its own making, which brings us right back to intelligent and accommodating software once again.

Among the more important things you should be aware of and do in this area:

- Whenever possible, try to verify the availability of all resources outside the control of your program before they're needed. Notice the qualification—I am not suggesting that your program should validate every one of its internal resources upon start up. This would be a waste of time, and it would make your program an unmaintainable mess. (Having said that, I almost expect to hear from some reader with news of a new Department of Defense Software Contracting guideline for Windows programs that requires just such extreme steps.)

- Restrict your Win32 program to running under those versions of Windows that you are willing to support fully. As I detail in Chapter 14, the Win32 API contains more surprises than a pre-K class on a gang sugar high. As a result, you have to choose between trying to support or pave over these differences, or restricting your program to running under only one or two of the three WIN32 platforms. (I confess. Because of the long-term planning that goes into this decision, often involving marketing and technical support issues, this one is clearly a macro-level issue within a micro-level one. Even under the warping influence of time constraints that I mentioned at the start of this chapter, I can't see many development teams deciding on the fly not to support Win32s, for example. At least I hope that's not how they're making their decisions.)

- Intelligently load DLLs. At the very least, your users deserve to have some application- and DLL-specific help available when your program can't find one of its DLLs. Just as important, your program should be able to degrade its feature set gracefully if some DLL can't be located or loaded. (The classic example is that your program should disable all e-mail related features if it can't successfully hook up with MAPI.DLL.) (See Chapter 6 for much more on DLLs.)

- Intelligently handle missing or corrupt persistent data. As I say in guideline 13 and Chapter 9, this can be more of a chore than programmers sometimes recognize when dealing with .INI files and registry-based data.

## 15. Be Wary of Unnatural Acts

When programming in Windows, it's not like the bad old days when it was you and your compiler against all comers. Now, you're perched atop a tall, narrow architecture of virtual machines and abstractions, and you have so many tools in your toolbox that it can present a learning challenge all its own.

With all that architecture and help from Microsoft and third parties, there should be a clean, efficient, and robust way to do virtually anything you care to do, right? (I'll wait a few seconds while the more experienced Windows programmers stop laughing and get up off the floor.) Of course, the world isn't that simple, and we all wind up using or at least being tempted by, an undocumented Windows call from time to time. If your Win32 program wants to call the GetFreeSystemResources() API, for example, you can't do it directly, at least not according to Microsoft. You have to resort to using the thunking support, a truly ugly solution. Again, that's the official solution. In fact, you can directly call a 16-bit DLL from a Win32 program sans thunks, if you're willing to resort to using undocumented APIs. (See Chapter 12 for the gruesome details.)

Are you waiting for the moment where I hop up on my soapbox and tell you how using undocumented APIs will (in the words of George Carlin) "infect your soul, curve your spine, and keep the country from winning the war?" Well, I'll spare you the full-court press on that subject, since I suspect it's probably pretty obvious to all assembled why undocumented APIs are really dangerous, particularly in public programs. After all, Microsoft has committed some serious violence to programmers with the documented parts of the Win32 API (see Chapters 12 and 14 for details); what makes you think they'll be any more careful with the undocumented ones? (I know the running joke—the undocumented APIs are the ones Microsoft's own products *really* need, so they're probably the safest. I'm not willing to bet my program on that reading of the situation.)

The truly nasty detail about undocumented APIs, of course, is that they force you to make some very tough decisions. As in the GetFreeSystemResources() example above, you have to choose between a simple and straightforward (if undocumented) way of doing something, and the officially blessed route, which is a pain in the neck, to be politically, if not necessarily anatomically, correct.

The choice can be even more extreme, and come down to using an undocumented API or detail, or not implementing some feature at all. I faced this choice in Stickies!, where I wanted to report USER and GDI free resources on the About box, and had to resort to using an undocumented API. I didn't like doing it this way, but I reasoned that if the code broke it wouldn't disable the program, and I could very quickly change the About box and remove that feature. As of Windows 95, it still works, and I'm still keeping my fingers crossed.

But using undocumented APIs and structures is merely the most obvious (and, some would say, most extreme) example of unnatural acts. The genre as a whole includes any instance when a programmer is clearly misusing a feature of any tool or architecture in a way that creates either short- or long-term problems. The programmers who commit such acts inevitably have a good reason (in their judgment) to do so, which only makes the issue thornier. The heart of the matter is, once again, balance. The programmer has identified a benefit to the unnatural act and minimally "proved" that it's safe (see guideline 8 for the "See? It works!" programmer fable). That's not in dispute. The question is whether it's a good idea, in the long run, to do things this way.

My business partner and I were involved in a consulting situation some time back that I think provided an excellent example of an unnatural act that likely seemed perfectly natural to the programmer. The company needed a significant amount of rework done on a large amount of custom C code. This code was written over a period of years by several people, most of whom were not programmers by profession. As a result, the code was what I would call "a bloody mess," to use a technical term.

For all its rough-hewn charm, however, one thing about the code really stood out: Nearly every C source file included a header file called PASCAL.H. As you've probably already guessed, this file contained things like:

```
#define begin {
#define end }
#define integer int
#define then
```

which allowed the programmers to commit no end of barbarisms:

```
integer fred = 0;

if(fred > 0) then
  begin
    printf("fred was > 0\n\n");
  end
else
  begin
    printf("fred was <= 0\n\n");
  end;          // Note the gratuitous semicolon!
```

And they did, too. Nearly the entire body of source code was written in this style. I don't know about you, but this kind of thing makes my skin crawl. To be clear: I think that well written Pascal is significantly more readable than well-written C, but this mixed mode syntax is the worst possible approach. My partner and I quickly dubbed this practice "faux Pascal" and told the client in no uncertain terms that this would be the first thing we'd change.

*If this is the first time you've ever seen this "faux Pascal" trick, and you think it's "A Neat Thing," please don't use it in production code, and if you simply can't help yourself, please don't tell anyone that you learned it here. I think this is one of the worst things you can do in C (which is saying quite a lot, considering how I feel about most of the production C code I encounter), and I would hate to think that someone, years from now, will have to wrestle with code that's loaded with "faux Pascal" and credits my book as the source.*

A similar, if less hair-raising, example that programmers sometimes face is the decision about whether to modify the source for an application framework. As large and complex as frameworks are today, you'd think there's little or no reason to do this, but every once in a while an instance pops up. I had to do this with OWL in Stickies!, since I needed to change how a multi-line edit control was created, all the way up the hierarchy at the CreateWindow level. Since I wanted to preserve all the other convenient support for edit controls that OWL provided, I had to modify OWL at several levels of its hierarchy to get exactly the desired effect. This is generally a risky approach since you might introduce a subtle bug into the framework, which could literally take you days to track down. The more likely problem is that you'll get it right, and then have to port your customizations to new versions of the framework as they appear. With MFC, that happens more often than you'd like once you've put yourself into this situation. And there's always the chance that the framework vendor will add the same (or nearly the same) support, which makes you choose between converting your program to use the official version of the feature or continuing to use your home-grown solution.

There's a particularly nasty programmer fable at the root of some unnatural acts (at least those involving programming): "I had to do it that way." This one really folds my floppy, because I know that often this is nothing more than a flimsy attempt to dodge responsibility. A programmer is presented with a tough choice of ways to implement some feature, as mentioned above, and this fable becomes an excuse for taking the easy way out. (Notice that when someone uses this as an excuse (as opposed to an accurate description of the situation) and they didn't take the easiest route, there was invariably some overriding value to the programmer in the chosen implementation, such as a chance to play with the programmer's favorite tool.)

Certainly, there are times when you really don't have a choice but to commit some sin against all of programmerhood. Often enough, such cases are non-technical in nature, and programmers are doing things at their management's direction that they'd rather not. This can include the use of the "wrong" language or framework, third-party library or other tools, or even an in-company, strategic product instead of another in-company product. In such cases, the programmers literally had to do it that way.

And there are also times when a programmer is rushed for time and doesn't have a chance to fully investigate alternatives, and makes a bad choice out of partial ignorance. I don't condemn programmers for such situations (although the managers responsible for creating the situation should stay out of my way).

*As with so many other issues in programming, avoiding unnatural acts comes down to your judgment and diligence against the forces of evil. Often the best solution for an experienced programmer is to listen to your feelings. When you or someone on your team is about to commit an unnatural act, you'll know it (whether you'd like to admit it or not), and that's precisely the time to slam on the brakes and look for a better way.*

# Chapter 4

# Tools

# Tools

*gizmonaut, n. 1. a person willing to embrace any new tool simply because it is new, with no regard for how well it does the intended job or fits into the person's work environment, or the cost of adopting the technology. 2. anyone on your project who wants to use a new tool instead of the old one which you've been using for years because it's clearly superior.*

*neo-Luddite, n. 1. a person who refuses to switch from old, inefficient tools and techniques to new, better ones, and attempts to justify this action with specious arguments about tangential issues. 2. anyone on your project who wants to stick with an old tool instead of the new one you just discovered that's clearly superior.*

Compilers and editors, debuggers and libraries.

Widgets, gizmos, things, toys.

Stuff.

*Tools.*

Few topics are as near and dear to a programmer's heart as tools. And why shouldn't they be? That first whiff of polycarbonate-suffused air from a freshly opened CD-ROM jewel case. The thrill of paging through the latest Programmer's Extravaganza Catalog, knowing that this time, at long last, you might find the silver bullet that enhances your productivity, reduces your error rate to a barely measurable level, and improves your looks. Who could ask for anything more?

If tools are so important to us (and they surely are, as they collectively form the primary link or "cerebral interface" between our minds and our development projects), then why are so many programmers so incredibly bad at selecting them? In my experience in development projects ranging from new releases of a mainframe operating system to minor changes to small shareware programs, the majority of programmers are either gizmonauts or neo-Luddites. In other words, a lot of people out there are selecting tools for the wrong reasons. In my experience the middle ground is quite sparse, to be kind.

In this chapter, I'll address the topic of tools, what they are, how to select them, and most important of all, how to use them.

# What Is a Programming Tool, and Why Is This a Big Deal?

More than just nouns/things/products, a programming tool includes verbs/processes/techniques. Tool selection therefore happens on a macro level ("Use Delphi/32 instead of VC++"), as well as on a micro level ("Turn off optimization for this product"). It includes all hardware, software, and information you use directly or indirectly, for example, the server down the hall counts although it's not on your desktop, and even half-remembered snippets of conversations with other programmers contribute in their own way.

In fact, your knowledge, which in this context includes all your designing, coding, and testing experience, is your most important single tool, although programmers often don't think of it that way, if at all. Once you're much beyond the "Hello, world!" stage, you're in the deep, cold water, where it's your wits against the sharks. Vendors all tout their IDE-a-matics and love to put together white papers and little trade show demonstrations: "Look! In only six mouse clicks you too can create an application with print preview, an about box, and common dialogs, all without writing a single line of code!" I'm waiting for them to start including a set of Ginsu knives, a salad spinner, and a magic car duster with every order.

As for more conventional, tangible tools, why is it so important that programmers are good at selecting their tools?

- Your set of tools directly affects what can be done in your program. Try to field certain Windows messages in Visual Basic 3.0, and you'll find that you can't. (At least not without a third-party add-on package.) For many programmers this isn't a problem, and they create excellent programs with Visual Basic, but for others it's a showstopper.

- In large development shops, management often issues decrees about which programming languages and other tools will be used for a project. These pronouncements are all too often based on no information or incorrect information culled from "technical" people who are as clueless as the managers. It's your job to fight for the right to use the proper tools for the job at hand, and the only way you can win these battles is with facts.

- Choice of tools can directly affect your coding and testing schedule. This is probably the most traditional and obvious form of cost-benefit analysis that I'll talk about in this book, but it bears repeating, as so many programmers seem to ignore the point: If a $400 tool can provide a net time savings (meaning the total number of hours it saves minus the time needed to learn it) of just a few hours during a single development cycle, then it's probably worth buying. (There are exceptions to such a cut-and-dried analysis, as I'll explain shortly.)

- Windows greatly amplifies tools issues. Windows programmers are balanced atop a very tall, very narrow, and none-too-solid tower of architectures, APIs, and tools. The tower is shot through with bugs, undocumented side effects, and lousy documentation. Some days I think it's a miracle that anything more complicated than "Hello, world!" *ever* works.

# Tool Selection and Usage Guidelines

Theory is wonderful, but it doesn't feed the bulldog. Put another way, when you're flipping through the pages of a development tools catalog, and you're faced with what seems like endless choices and even meta-choices, you need a way to make concrete buying decisions and recommendations.

Sorry, but I can't help you make all your decisions. Heck, I can't even keep myself from making the occasional-yet-amazing tool selection blunder. But there are some guidelines I can give you that should help you navigate the rapids.

## 0. Explore and Exploit

*Exploration* means that you should always be open-minded about new tools and techniques. Look at *everything* that comes along, every widget and library that you can find the time for. This can take the form of getting your employer to buy an evaluation copy (or getting a free copy from the vendor; some will provide those under the right circumstances), or simply reading all the reviews of development tools you can find. Exploration should be the wild, unbound, promiscuous part of the tools selection process, which never ends because there are always more tools coming out on the market.

*Exploitation,* in contrast, is the conservative, steely-eyed accountant side of the equation. This is where you very selectively choose which tools you will use, and exploit them as fully as you can. At this stage, no tool is worth adopting until it proves itself in your analysis.

Pay attention to how well tools work together. Your goal is to assemble the best overall toolbox you can, not just pick out neat gizmos. Does your third-party debugger work with the executables your compiler produces? Will your compiler accept the source code for the library or framework without undue modification?

Look for "kill shots," single-purpose tools that are dedicated to solving a particular, relatively separable problem. For example, if you need to include a full-featured editor in your program, don't write your own. If you don't need Windows 3.1 or pre-Windows NT 4.0 compatibility, use the new Windows 95 rich edit control. If you do need such compatibility, there are several third-party rich edit components available. In either case, it's often best to adopt a new tool if you can find one that does just one thing, but does it so well that it makes one part of your application a non-issue. (My use of "kill shot" here is not a military reference; it's a term used in some sports, such as racquetball, for a shot that your opponent can't possibly return.)

There is always cost to consider, and not just in terms of money. What about hardware requirements? If a compiler vendor claims you need 16MB of RAM for their product, will you really be comfortable working with 16, or will you find yourself budgeting for an additional 8 or 16MB the day after you compile something larger than "Hello, world?"

At this point you're still working on the macro level, and examining the universe of available tools. Your decisions at this level all relate to *which* tools to select.

Once you make your selections—this compiler, those libraries, that third party debugger—the exploration and exploitation cycle enters a new phase on a micro level. Here, you're exploring the features of individual products and deciding *how* to exploit them. Just as on the macro level, on the micro level you should be willing to look at, play with, and evaluate everything a product can do (or claims to do). But when it comes time to decide exactly how a tool will be used, you should put on your virtual green eye shade and become a hard sell. Make every feature prove itself to you, and then make the necessary commitment to using it in an intelligent fashion.

Remember that just because you've decided to use a particular compiler or framework, that doesn't mean you've implicitly decided to use all of its features. There very well might be some that are not very interesting, or are even completely wrong for your project. Crossing the product boundary and making a selection doesn't end your selection process, it merely moves it to another level.

*Sign every programmer should have near the computer: "OOP is good, OOP is our friend, but OOP is not a panacea."*

*Larry Constantine once observed that OOP is primarily better packaging. It is. And the plain truth is that sometimes the extra effort to construct that packaging simply doesn't pay for itself. Despite what at least one vendor has claimed, there can be a downside to using objects: Unneeded complexity. Sometimes the optimal approach is to place the code and data needed to perform some logical task into a separate compilation unit and then expose a single function that other parts of the hosting program can call. The sample program in Chapter 8 follows this approach, in that all the code and data in the CHECKER compilation unit could have easily been objectified, but to what gain? In my opinion, none. All the hosting program ever needs or wants to do with that code is call the GoodCRC() function and examine the return value, so there's no need to fiddle with classes and constructors and destructors and such.*

*Isolating the code and data in a separate compilation unit like this really amounts to following some of the principles of OO, but without using all the plumbing. Perhaps we should call it OSC, for "OOP sans classes."*

*Don't get me wrong, I'm a big believer in the concepts of OO design, but I also know overkill when I see it, and many programmers see OOP as their shiny new hammer, and the world as a forest of nails stretching out before them.*

It's hard to overstress this point. I've seen this mistake many times. A development shop agonizes over their tool selections and then leaves it to the individual programmers to decide which features will and won't be used. Often enough, the carefully chosen tools aren't used at all, and end up in the back of a storage cabinet, dust covered, in the original shrink wrap, next to the boxes of dried-up red felt-tip pens.

Take into account the short run/long run issues, and look at the cost of undoing this decision, as well. This can be a very tough decision to make. Perhaps some new interface standard within Windows (MAPI, TAPI, etc.) seems like a great help. But what if you adopt it, get locked in, and then find out you can't easily get to a new destination from there?

Make sure a product really does what it promises, and that it provides a good cost/benefit ratio. I'm not saying that there are software vendors who would consider lying, but best to be on the lookout, just in case.

Examine a product's documentation whenever possible. Documentation is the great multiplier for many tools. If a product is otherwise an excellent match for your needs, see if there is third-party documentation available. It seems silly to have to buy a book at Barnes & Noble or B. Dalton so you can effectively use a brand new piece of software, but who cares? The whole tool selection process is about results, not logic.

Also remember that he who dies with the most toys *doesn't* win. Knowing how to use 10 percent of 50 tools is not effective or economical. What's your goal? To have the spiffiest, fullest hard drive full of goodies, or to be the best, most effective programmer you can?

## 1. Look for Synergy between Tools

When selecting tools, look for how they work together. This is more than just a reminder about source and object compatibility, as mentioned above. For example, you should always keep a hard copy of your source code around (once it's stabilized), even if it's a large printout. Why? Not only is it often a handy reference, but it can serve as an emergency backup. In an age of cheap flatbed scanners and good OCR (optical character recognition) software, that printout might save your neck when your hard disk crashes and you suddenly discover that your backup tape is unreadable, or someone forgot to back up that volume for the last four months.

Another example is using indexing and retrieval software, such as Isys from Odyssey Development Corporation, to index source code on CD ROMs. You can buy many CDs of source code today for less than $50 each, but finding something on these disks, which include no searching facilities of their own or custom programs that differ from disk to disk, can be such a chore that it's hardly worth it. By building indexes of these files, you can search for individual words in seconds and jump right to the files. This is also a very handy way to access the copious samples that come with most Windows compilers. You could grep the source files every time you wanted to look for something, but that forces you to choose between installing the samples on your hard disk and grepping directly from the CD. Some choice.

Yet another use for indexing software is managing your own hoard of source code. I suspect that I'm like most programmers in that I'm a source code pack rat. I'll download source, save it from floppies that come with magazines, etc. Indexing it makes sense, especially if you use a package that will work directly with ZIP archives. That means you can sacrifice minimal disk space for your files, and still have instant access. (It also neatly gets around the infamous DOS cluster size problem with larger hard disks. See guideline 0 in Chapter 2 for more details on the cluster size debacle.)

Another source of synergy is tools that will accept or produce plain-text versions of their input or output. The flowcharting package allCLEAR will accept a plain text description of a flow chart. This makes it very easy for you to write your own program that has much of the charting power of allCLEAR. For example, you might want to write a program that reads your company's internal phone directory and builds an organization chart. Writing a program to do all that drawing would be a lot of work; writing one that simply created a plain-ASCII listing of the people with markup tags would be a snap in most cases. In general, think of plain text as an intermediate language that sits between your custom front end and the engine that produces the actual output.

## 2. Don't Spread Your Wetware Too Thin

Whether your development team is just yourself or 1,000 people, be careful to honestly evaluate the needed skills base for your tools and project. For example, if you plan to use Visual Basic 3.0 and create a gaggle of custom VBX controls, you can't get by with just Visual Basic expertise; you'll also need C/C++ or Pascal skills and tools, since you can't write VBX's in Visual Basic. This means multiple sets of tools and, more important, tool skills.

It can be very difficult to assess your installed skills base accurately. Programmers are notorious for claiming to "know" a language or development tool that they spent a few idle hours with a year ago and would like to know more about, or they see as a way to get out of their current, unpleasant assignment. This leads to disaster, of course; the team is assembled, schedules are carved into stone, and only months later it comes to light that the lead programmer responsible for the critical, C++ part of the project has never actually used that language, although it looked interesting in books and magazine articles.

## 3. Don't Be Too Trusting of Your Vendors

Some programmers think they should look at only the technical merits of tools and ignore things like the financial health of the vendors or their support policies. This is a huge mistake, especially for public programs. If some company has a track record of abandoning products, or if you have reason to believe they will do this in a particular case, you have a problem. See the sidebar, "Whither OWL?" for details on some of my personal experience in this area.

How do you know which vendors to trust? This is where you have to use your own horsesense and talk to other programmers. But beware, it's not enough simply to listen in on some public conversations on CompuServe or the Internet. Spend enough time in the various discussions there and you'll hear glowing praise for and scathing condemnation of every vendor in the business. About all you can do on this count is keep your ear to the ground and decide which complaints are relevant to your situation and which are just hot air.

Just as in guideline 0, there's also a micro level to be concerned with. Even though your general inclination should be to minimize the number of discrete tools and vendors you rely on, you also shouldn't become too reliant on the features of a single product. Sometimes you're better off using one vendor's compiler, but another's framework or container classes, if that results in a set of tools that does a better overall job of meeting the needs of your project.

Another aspect of this is being as skeptical as you can about the gee-whiz features in products. Lily Tomlin once said that no matter how cynical you get, it's impossible to keep up. Sounds to me like she's been programming in her spare time.

Whenever you examine the features of a tool, there should be a concurrent process running in the back of your head that constantly checks what you're reading to see if it looks suspiciously like a free lunch. As the saying goes, "if it looks too good to be true, it probably is." The feature of C++ compilers that I think best passes (fails?) the free-lunch test is optimization. See the Compilers section below for more detail on this, and how the conventional wisdom about how to employ optimization is wrong.

Finally, don't be too trusting of your vendor's design decisions. One product I examined while writing this book did an excellent job of knocking a specific programming problem flat. The product was a classic "kill shot." Unfortunately, the problem this tool solved is typically a very small part of the hosting application (at least as I would use it), and the tool required you to ship external data files, with no way to embed the files into your program's resources.

This design is not acceptable in a public program, because a minor part of the application places a significant configuration burden on the entire finished product. These external data files require care and feeding at installation time, plus care on the part of the application programmer to make sure they were present at startup. After all, users wouldn't find it acceptable to get deep into a work session with a program, only to find that it suddenly refused to continue working because it only then discovered it couldn't find some obscure file. And then, there's always the problem of the files being lost, or deleted, or accidentally replaced or changed. As I've stressed elsewhere in this book, you can't assume anything about what will happen to your exposed data when your program isn't looking.

The moral is that you shouldn't let your tools make bad design decisions in your product.

## 4. Intelligently Exploit Published Source Code

There's a veritable tidal wave of free source code out there—books, magazines, CD ROMs, CompuServe forums, Internet discussion groups, ftp sites, etc. The world is awash in a sea of C, ablaze in Pascal, and listing under the weight of LISP. Heck, look in enough places and you'll probably find a COBOL version of Pong.

The question then becomes, should you use it?

The answer is a heavily qualified yes. The qualification being that you should do so "intelligently." In this context, that means judging the source code on its merits (or lack thereof). You should neither accept nor reject an instance of something simply because of the arbitrary category, such as freeware, to which you've assigned it. It doesn't work with people, and it doesn't work with software.

"Intelligently" also means you should have a well thought out adoption procedure for bringing outside source code into your project. In most cases, you don't even know who wrote the code, let alone know them personally, so you have no idea if they're a guru or a Neanderthal. Clearly you should exercise an appropriate degree of caution. For example, don't even think about using this kind of material in a public program unless you have *all* the source. Desk-check and test all the source before using it in a production environment; don't just assume that because it compiles with little effort that it's correct.

Some programmers will balk at using someone else's source code, programmers being the unchallenged champions of the NIH (not invented here) syndrome. Do you know everything there is to know about programming? Can you write production-quality functions that will do Huffman encoding, perform FFTs, do a digital dissolve with a Windows BMP file, and find the exact date of Easter Sunday for a given year? I can't, at least not without a fair amount of research or using freely available code.

Of course, there's no rule that says you actually have to use such source code directly in your product. Maybe you'll simply learn from it and pick up an algorithm or technique that you can use in a code you write from scratch. However, if you decide to use a published source, you should consider it a valuable resource, and something to be handled carefully.

## 5. Don't Fall in Love with Your Shiny New Hammer

And it's so darn easy to do, too. You decide to make a commitment to a tool, and you descend to the next lower level of the explore and exploit cycle where you find all manner of Truly Cool Things in the product. Before you know it you're smitten, and you're sending friends copious, gushing e-mail about this new WunderGizmo you've discovered, and boring them to tears at the coffee machine and over lunch. That's fine, if a little embarrassing.

The danger is what all too often comes next: Your sweet infatuation ferments into a state of zealotry that warps your judgment. Suddenly every problem is a nail just aching to be driven flat with your shiny new hammer.

Your best defense against this problem is a concurrent process, as I mentioned above. You should always be on the lookout for this kind of devotion to a tool or technique, whether it's in yourself or someone on your programming team. How you handle the situation, especially when you detect this problem in someone else, is an issue of office dynamics that's well beyond the scope of this chapter.

*I have to confess, I'm quite prone to this problem, so I know first hand about the dangers. I remember quite clearly and with some embarrassment a period early in my programming career when I first encountered finite state machines, a table-driven processing method that can be used to write extremely processing-cycle efficient parsers. I was smitten bad, and I wanted to use FSMs on practically every programming problem that came along. My IBM manager and my wife (different people, mind you), almost had to have me restrained before the fever passed.*

A particularly nasty variation of this theme emphasizes the "new" part of the shiny hammer metaphor. All too often projects are forced to use or incorporate bleeding edge technologies and/or tools for the wrong reasons: programmer infatuation, well meaning but ill-informed management decree, too much trust in a vendor, or some combination of these. Whenever possible, you should resist the pressure to adopt new tools and technologies before they're ready. After all, this *is* the industry in which people have joked for years about how insane it is to buy version 1.0 of anything. More recently, this wisdom has evolved to don't buy version x.0 of anything, a pretty sad, albeit accurate, commentary on the state of commercial software development. Unfortunately, this guideline is all too true of development tools and technology, as well.

For example, remember when OLE first came on the scene, and magazines talked about minimal demonstration OLE programs that required thousands of lines of code just for the OLE support? Now that we have framework support for OLE, it would take quite an extreme set of circumstances (or a fit of insanity) for anyone to code OLE support manually and accept that huge risk of introducing errors into a project.

In my opinion, architectural features such as OLE, or even less daunting ones, like the new Windows 95 controls, are very seldom worth exploiting until genuinely good infrastructure (read: framework) support is available. If nothing else, you know that there will soon be a framework or other support, and your original implementation will either live on as an artifact of a bygone era in your code, or it will have to be redone with the new support.

# Types of Tools

Obviously, you can't naively apply one set of guidelines to all tool decisions, especially when you define "tool" as broadly as I (and, I hope, you) do. In this section, I'll talk about various categories of tools a little, and bring up some special issues for each one.

## Reference Material

It's hard to have too much programming reference material handy. In other words, when you're talking about this particular type of tool, the answer to "how much?" is almost always "more."

The real issue is how you use the reference material. This is the second level of tools exploration and exploitation as I mentioned above; if you approach it correctly you can save yourself considerable time.

For example, whenever you find yourself wandering into a new part of Windows programming for the first time, or delving deeper into it than you ever had, you should take a few minutes to look up the APIs (or methods in your framework or functions in your library) that you'll be using for the first time or exercising more thoroughly. Check them out in the standard online documentation, plus the Microsoft Developer Network CD. Sounds like I just told you to have a wild time reading the dictionary, doesn't it? Well, in a way I did, and there's a lot of cool stuff in the reference material that you'll find useful. (And if you've never read a dictionary or part of one, I suggest that, too. Tell people you're doing a frequency analysis of Latin vs Greek word roots, under a really big contract from the U.S. Government.)

Once you think you have the API's nailed down, it's often worth the time and effort to write some very simple test programs to exercise them and make sure they really work as you think they do. Why on earth should you spend precious developer time doing this? Simple: Virtually all programming documentation you work with, particularly that for Windows itself, is abysmal. It's inaccurate, it omits critical details, it's sorely lacking in hotlinks to other topics, and it never gives you the big picture. (This is another area where *Windows/DOS Developer's Journal* helps. Every month they publish several annotations for the SDK help file that fill in gaps and correct errors. This is highly recommended, even if W/DDJ's efforts are humbled by the size of the task.)

In case you think I'm being silly or overly cautious with this API stuff, think about this:

- One of the biggest Windows 95 (*not* Win32s) surprises is that all coordinates passed to a GDI call, whether from a direct API invocation or via a framework, have their coordinates clipped from 32 bits to 16. Whatever the clipped value yields is what GDI uses (which means that coordinates can change sign, not just magnitude), and the program is never notified via return code or any other mechanism of the problem. See Chapter 14 for much more on this issue, including some workarounds.

- Some Win32 API's under Windows 95 don't really return TRUE; they return an unpredictable non-zero value. This can lead to some bizarre problems, like the test:

```
if(GetClientRect(hWnd,lpRect) == TRUE)
  { /* ... */ }
```

failing even when the call is successful. You could spend hours figuring out that even though you're testing the return value of the API in a way that is completely legal according to the documentation, your program is still failing. While C/C++ programmers typically follow the convention of treating all non-zero BOOLs as TRUE (which is defined in the Win32 headers as 1, by the way), you certainly can't criticize this code for being incorrect, as it follows the letter of the law (always the ultimate test of program correctness). Yet this problem could be a very costly error, especially if your users find it before you do.

This could also lead to other, more subtle problems. What if you write a function that is supposed to return a BOOL and after some custom processing it returns the value from GetClientRect() or some other API that uses this imprecise interpretation of TRUE. I've stressed repeatedly in this book that you should be skeptical about the validity of any data you don't create or verify. Here's a good, if minor, example of how bad data can enter your program and then get propagated.

The most reliable solution, albeit one that looks a little odd, is to replace:

```
return SomeWIN32API(/* parameters */);
```

with

```
return (SomeWIN32API(/* parameters */) != FALSE);
```

This will force the returned value from the API call to meet your function's definition. See Chapter 10 for much more on wrappers and API definitions.

- The Win32 API FindFirstFile (which is used to translate aliases to long file names, and back, as well as to find files) won't accept a trailing backslash on a directory name, but it will accept forward slashes in place of backslashes. Neither fact is documented. Also, there's a documented bug in how FindFirstFile() handles wild cards, in that it treats "?" as any character, not any one or zero characters. (See Microsoft's problem report Q130860 on the Developer Network CD for details.) This is another problem, like the non-TRUE TRUE return value, that could result in a long debugging session.

- Similarly, Get Long Path Name (the new int 21h/7160h service introduced in Windows 95, which doesn't have a Win32 API equivalent) will accept a trailing backslash on a path name. If you worked with this service first, you might reasonably assume that all of the new file system functions accepted and ignored an extraneous trailing slash on a directory. You'd be wrong.

- Our old friend, _lopen(), will accept and correctly handle a long file name, even when called from a Win16 program that has an "expected Windows version" stamp of 3.1. Yet this possibly very convenient fact isn't documented in the help for this API, or anywhere else, as far as I know. (I discovered this by accident, while experimenting with the LFNCD sample program in Chapter 12. See the sidebar "Using LFNs from Win16 Programs: Better Living through Alchemy" for more detail.)

- GetShortPathName() works differently under Windows 95 and Windows NT in some cases. See Chapter 14 for more details and a way to wrap this API to unify its behavior across platforms.

These are specifics; in a larger sense, it's critical for you to remain a student of programming. This is more important for Windows coders than ever before. With the onslaught of new APIs and features, we all feel like George Jetson on his treadmill, running 100 miles per hour just to stay in place. (I could speculate on who gets to be Astro, George's dog, sitting nearby and enjoying George's predicament, but that wouldn't be prudent.) It's tiring, but we really don't have a choice. Once you fall behind, it's very difficult for a professional programmer to find the time to catch up.

As limited as your educational time is, you should read about areas of programming other than the one you normally work in. I've long been convinced that all coders should read about game programming, both in the conventional AI-sense, as in chess and checkers programs, as well as in the graphics-intensive meaning of Doom. Why? Game programming is often as difficult as this stuff gets, and you might learn some optimization techniques that apply to your work.

*I think of Windows programmers, collectively, as a group of runners in a steeplechase event. Here comes a tiny hazard to jump over (a new version of DOS); then there's a fairly high wall to get over (the conversion from DOS to event-driven Windows); now here comes a huge wall (OLE, Win32, network programming, and all the other important changes of the mid-90's and beyond). At almost every hazard, some runners drop out of the race through exhaustion (sometimes more mental than physical), or go on to specialize in some niche, while others surge to the front of the pack. But most of us keep on running, lap after lap, and marvel that on every lap the obstacles are different yet somehow the same.*

## Compilers and Languages

Okay, time for a good, old fashioned religious war. To be honest, I wasn't sure when I started this book if I wanted to get into the C/C++ vs. Pascal issue; it was oh so tempting to ignore it completely. Given the sorry state of the Windows Pascal market in early 1995, there seemed little reason even to mention Pascal. After all, the language war was all but over, the one-two punch of C/C++ and Visual Basic had pretty clearly won, and Pascal was quietly sliding into the sunset just off the coast of Scotts Valley. The fact that Borland was widely known to be in deep financial trouble sure didn't help matters either.

Then a funny thing happened on the way to the funeral: Borland released Delphi.

Perhaps it wasn't so funny if you were Microsoft happily selling Visual Basic, or any of the C/C++ vendors, because Delphi sold 125,000 copies in its first full quarter of availability. These sales contributed significantly to Borland's strong showing for the quarter ending June 30th, in which they surprised analysts and just about everyone else on planet earth by showing a profit.

What happened?

I think that Delphi met a desperate need not for a Pascal product per se, but for a non-C++ product. Based on my conversations with numerous programmers, I'm convinced that many of them are sick of the bizarre intricacies of C/C++ and its attendant frameworks and IDEs, and they simply want a rational alternative. It was a classic case of a product meeting a pent-up demand.

I published an article in the April, 1995 issue of *Software Development* about the code reuse features in Delphi, one of its strongest points. That article drew numerous pieces of e-mail that were eerily similar. They were almost all from people in corporate development environments who were getting ready to start new, sometimes large, projects, and they wanted my advice on whether they should abandon C/C++ for Delphi. I gave them what advice I could, based on what they had told me about their projects, and I suggested that they buy a copy of Delphi and evaluate it for themselves. (I find it deeply ironic that Delphi was touted as a "Visual Basic killer" before its release, yet not one person who contacted me was even considering Visual Basic for a large project. The choice was always between C/C++ and Delphi, with one person asking about PowerBuilder. I suspect that Delphi is indeed taking a bite out of Visual Basic, but it seems that a much larger game is afoot, too.)

Long-time veterans of the language wars often point out that you have to distinguish between a language and the compiler. While this is true when you're having a good-natured, theoretical argument about tools, when you're selecting a product for use in the real world it's a distinction without a difference; in that context you don't pick a language, you pick a product that happens to include a language. This leads to some difficulty, of course, because in the Windows world, Borland's Delphi, including the VCL framework, effectively has 100 percent of the market, while there are different C++ compilers and various frameworks, including some from third parties, that allow quite a degree of mixing and matching.

Enough dodging. I'll come right out and say that I strongly prefer Pascal over C++ for virtually any programming task. In fact, whenever I can, I use it in my contract programming and consulting work. I can create robust, high quality, easily maintained programs with it in far less time than I can with any C++ product. I've used Visual C++ for the examples in this book purely out of recognition that it's currently the dominant package for Windows development, and it therefore makes the code the most accessible.

# C/C++: A Systems Language Being Used for Applications

C/C++ began life in the early 70's and was intended to be a systems programming language. Not surprisingly, C, and to the large extent that C++ is built on top of C, exhibits a philosophy appropriate for that time and role. Today, we're using them for applications and burdening them in ways their designers never imagined. The basic header model of separating code into compilation units is a classic example. Back in the bad old days, headers were small, a reasonable approach, at least from a performance viewpoint. Today, it isn't. Visual C++ 2.2 provides the following headers:

\MSVC20\INCLUDE: 247 header files, 4.4MB
\MSVC20\INCLUDE\SYS: 5 header files, 6KB
\MSVC20\INCLUDE\GL: 3 header files, 84KB
\MSVC20\MFC\INCLUDE: 44 header files, 604KB

Of course you won't use all these headers on any single project, but the mandatory headers for any Windows development are still several hundred KB of text, which causes significant performance problems at compile time.

In a valiant effort to avoid this problem, vendors have resorted to precompiled headers, which do work surprisingly well, but they're far from perfect. Even small C++ projects result in several megs of precompiled header sitting around on your hard disk for the duration of your project, and almost any change to your project settings will cause the compiler to regenerate the precompiled header (often when it's not actually necessary), adding about a minute to the next compile.

*Pop quiz: What's the difference between "const char \*x" and "char const \*x"? The first is a pointer to a constant character, the second is a constant pointer to a character. Many programmers who use C++ will get this wrong when the question is not asked in the context of a source listing from a real project, or they'll have to think about it long enough that they might as well get it wrong.*

C/C++ compilers don't provide a reasonable level of assistance to the programmer. As one small example, Visual C++ 2.2 won't even issue a warning for the following line, even at the highest warning level:

```
int fred[100] = { 10, 10 };
```

Some C/C++ aficionados claim this is a good thing ("It's not a bug, it's a feature!"); the behavior of the compiler is well defined in this case, and it gives the programmer a nice shorthand way of initializing the first few elements of an array, and then leaving the rest automatically set to a known and useful value, zero. Think about what a maintenance nightmare this can turn into: You have several arrays in a large project whose size is determined by a constant:

```
int fred[fred_size] = { 10, 10 };
```

Now you find that you have to change the size of these arrays, so you change the definition of fred_size from two to four. You have to make sure that every place where you use fred_size to define an array has the proper initialization, and you get no help from the compiler. In Delphi, if the number of initializers doesn't match the array size, it's an error, and you can't get it wrong.

And while I'm on the topic of arrays, I'm amazed that C/C++ still doesn't support arrays that aren't zero-based. Do you need an array with indexes from -37 to 104? Declare it that way in Delphi and away you go. In C/C++ you have to resort to doing index arithmetic by hand. And amazingly enough, Delphi is the development environment that gives you the option of making your code automatically bounds check all array references, even though C/C++ needs it more than Pascal does.

C++ does give you another option regarding arrays: Write your own array class and make it do whatever you want: Bounds check references, use arbitrary bounds, etc. This is laughable, and it only supports my long-held contention that for application programming C++ is closer to being a very complete language kit than it is a fully functional language.

*What's the difference between a language that's essentially a "language kit" and one that supports the creation of reusable components? Simple: It's a matter of whether programmers are frequently using the reuse facilities of the language to "program down," meaning to add features like bounds-checking arrays and decent strings that arguably should be in the base language, or to "program up" and create application-specific components like a particular style of "About box" that they can then incorporate easily into several programs.*

These are just a few minor examples (see Chapter 3 for more discussion of the bizarre world of C strings and terminating nulls); sadly for those who use it C/C++ is loaded with such gotchas that make all implementations I've seen programmer-hostile. As one last example in this area, have you ever noticed how C/C++ loses its mind when you forget a semicolon? If you leave one off a function prototype that happens to be the last non-commentary statement in a header file, you can get a set of wildly misleading error messages reported in the source file that includes the header. Drop a semicolon in Delphi, and the compiler almost always puts the cursor right on the spot and tells you that a semicolon was expected.

Some people argue that this behavior is a by-product of the basic language, and that the C/C++ vendors are doing the best they can to make these packages more usable. That's precisely the problem: The underlying language is so outdated and squirrely that, when used for Windows application development, even these Herculean efforts on the part of the vendors aren't enough. I couldn't care less about assigning blame to one party or another for these problems, and neither should you. All that matters are the short- and long-term characteristics of the tools we use.

## The Myth of Portability

For years, people have claimed that one of C's (and later, C++'s) strengths is portability. This is laughable, particularly in the Windows arena. Take the WordPad example, written for Visual C++ 2.2 with the MFC framework, and try porting it to Borland's C++, which doesn't support MFC. Think that's a loaded example? Try dealing with differences in implementations of templates, exception handling, and minor language features. Thanks to frameworks and the fact that C++ is still a language without a standard, all the existing C/C++ Windows development packages are really different dialects of the same language, and in some cases, effectively different languages.

Borland's Object Pascal, on the other hand, is wildly non-standard and it will always be so. But it does have one overwhelming benefit: There's only one of it, so porting Object Pascal code from one person's computer to another is never a problem. The purpose of a standard is to make sure that all implementations of a language are sufficiently similar so that porting code from one system to another can be done efficiently and yield predictable, useful results. Ironically, it's the non-standard language, Delphi, that has the ultimate answer to the porting issue: There's only one implementation, so by definition all installations are identical, not just acceptably (or unacceptably) close.

## C/C++ and User Defined Types

In my opinion, the strangest single feature of C++ is its obsession with letting you make your own classes look like intrinsic datatypes. This one design decision required a host of other features that make the language more complicated and slower to learn and compile, and often results in bugs: implicit constructor and destructor invocation, copy constructors, operator overloading, and references.

Object Pascal, by contrast, is so much simpler in its OOP facilities that people coming to it from C++ are shocked. No multiple inheritance? No function or operator overloading? No references as function return values? How can this be a serious OOP language? Isn't it really OOP-lite? As it turns out, you don't need these things as language features, even if you have to provide an equivalent logical function via other means. For example, C++ programmers often provide a canonical copy constructor to provide a way to make a "deep" copy of an object. Without one, C++ will perform a bit-by-bit copy of an object, which will cause all manner of problems if the object contains a pointer member. You'll now have two (or more) objects with pointers to the same physical piece of memory, and one of them is going to wreak havoc when it tries to free this memory after another already has. Object Pascal has this same problem: Perform a simple assignment with objects and you get a shallow copy. In both languages you have to know enough to write your own deep copy function and use it. In Object Pascal this might look like:

```
DeepCopyFred(destFred,sourceFred);
```

In C++:

```
destFred = sourceFred;
```

C++ does not provide extra language features merely to make this one-liner a bit more elegant. The C++ support for objects is undeniably deeper and more complete than is Object Pascal's. This is clearly a benefit, as it enables a more general and seamless use of objects in programs. But at what cost? Is the added complexity of the language a reasonable price to enable this fuller exploitation of objects, or is this merely a hothouse feature that isn't worth the trouble in the real world? In my experience, based on many thousands of lines of Windows code, it's the latter.

## Benchmarks, There Are Always Benchmarks

Pascal's units are the equivalent of precompiled headers plus .OBJ files in a fraction of the space, but without the nasty overhead of long initial compiles to build them. This is one reason why Delphi compiles so much faster than C/C++ compilers. How fast is it? On my 486DX4-100 system with 32MB of RAM and Windows 95, I ran some benchmarks using Stickies!, Delphi, WordPad (the source came with Visual C++ 2.2), and Visual C++ 2.2. I adjusted options in the WordPad project to make the comparison as close as possible. I turned off all optimizations, since Delphi is a non-optimizing compiler, as well as the creation of a browser database and a map file, and used static MFC libraries, since the Pascal version of OWL can only be statically linked into the application. Here's the tale of the tape:

### Stickies!
43,696 lines of application source code, 16-bit Borland Pascal/OWL
48 compilation units

32 RES files, totaling 146KB
Time to build all source code and link: 16 seconds

### WordPad

14,392 lines of application source code (11,421 lines of C++, plus 2,971 lines of application header), 32-bit C++/MFC
36 compilation units
24 resource files compiled into one RES file of 54KB
Time to build all source code and link: 5 minutes 7 seconds
    Compile resources: 10 seconds
    Compile STDAFX.H: 53 seconds
    Compile source: 3 minutes 28 seconds
    Link: 36 seconds

Performance purists will howl at comparing a 16-bit compiler to a 32-bit compiler, mixing languages, benchmarks, and just about everything else in the same test. This would be a valid argument if I were trying to isolate the performance impact of a feature, such as the language or framework. But I'm not. My goal here is to provide a feeling for how fast these development environments are relative to each other with real projects. As you can see from these numbers, it's not even close. WordPad is just under a third of the line count of Stickies!, and it takes over *19 times longer* to do a complete build.

But you more often do a partial rebuild in a project. So I found a compilation unit in each project that was about 250 lines long, made a trivial change to that file, and then timed a "make". The results: Delphi/Stickies! 5 seconds, Visual C++/WordPad 35 seconds. Well, the ratio is at least down to single digits. Notice that Visual C++ 2.2's make (35 seconds) time is still over twice the complete build time for Delphi (16 seconds).

Some people will tell you that this kind of performance difference is immaterial in the real world, because on large, serious development projects most of your time is spent in design and testing, not watching your cursor blink while the compiler and linker run. This is a valid point, to a certain extent. Anyone who has used C++ for a large project will tell you how onerous compilations can become, and how the process warps your work habits. You'll quickly find yourself batching numerous small changes together, in the interest of trying to avoid unnecessary compilations. I do this all the time. By comparison, when I work with Delphi, I compile much more often simply because it's so fast and there's very little cost to the operation. In effect I use the compilation step as a quick syntax check.

I don't mean to flog a dead equine, but take the WordPad numbers from above and extrapolate them, even with the generous assumptions that the resource compilation, linking, and header compilation steps will take the same amount of time, and that the compilation of the main source code will be a linear function of the source size. This gives us a build time of nearly 14 minutes for a 50,000 line program, and nearly 26 minutes for a 100,000 line program. I've seen build times much longer than this on fast computers with all the RAM and HD speed and space you could ask for.

Another example of how tool speed affects development: Have you ever had to change the name of a widely used constant or variable in a project? What a chore, finding all those references with a browser or grepping the source. In Delphi, I simply change the name where the item is defined and then keep running compilations at a few seconds a pop. At every reference, Delphi stops and puts the cursor right on the now-unknown symbol, a trick that Visual C++ still can't manage.

## And Lest We Forget...

These problems are just some of the obstacles C/C++ and the current generation of compilers place in programmers' paths. These are the same tools, after all, that give us:

- Case sensitivity, which engenders a whole class of Stupid Syntax Errors, plus countless semantics-free variable declarations like:

```
HWND hwnd;
```

- The conditional or "?" statement, which normally generates exactly the same code as a normal if/then/else construct, yet reduces the source code's readability. In other words, you get negative benefit (loss of readability) for zero gain (no performance improvement). That's the wrong ratio in anyone's book.

- Array reference/pointer conflation. If there's a single feature of C/C++ that reveals its inherent systems programming orientation, and therefore its inherent awkwardness as an application programming language, this is it. Have you ever tried to teach a new programmer about this part of the language? I have, and it would take only one such session to convince anyone how counter-intuitive this part of the language is.

- Null-terminated strings. A close second behind the array/pointer issue. This implementation, plus the questionable design of the standard string library functions (see Chapter 3 for a discussion and some more robust solutions), is no doubt at the root of countless errors in existing programs.

- Integers that change size as the target executable changes from 16 to 32 bits. Could you come up with an architected characteristic more insane than this? (But Borland committed the same error with the 32-bit version of Delphi. See the sidebar "Delphi32: Borland's Pascal Comes of Age" for more details.)

- Endless compiler and linker options. I still shake my head in disbelief at how easy it was to create a project with Borland's C++ 3.1 that compiled and linked without trouble, and immediately GPF'd when run. The problem, and the solution, in these cases was solely with the build options; on several occasions I caused such problems with Borland's samples by changing options.

- Lack of local functions, a subject I take up in Chapter 5.

- Compilers that issue a profusion of incorrect or irrelevant error diagnostics. If C/C++ development packages didn't take so long to compile and link a sizable project, I'd tell the compiler to stop after it encountered the first error. But makes and builds take so long that I need to catch all the errors I can on each pass. This means we choose between spending a lot of time compiling or staring at error diagnostics trying to filter out the bogus ones. (I considered having a contest for the greatest number of unique error diagnostics generated by a one-character problem in a C/C++. I decided against it, since although the entries would indeed make my point in this regard, they would be too depressing to look at.)

Before the C/C++ faithful form a lynch mob and storm Endwell, I should say that none of this is meant to suggest that you can't write first-rate applications in C/C++. That would be an absurd viewpoint, simply because the market has hundreds of counter examples. My point is that C/C++ places a far greater burden on programmers and requires us to be far more diligent to avoid whole classes of errors that either aren't possible or are clearly much harder to make with other tools. Based on the quality of commercially available Windows programs, it seems diligence (or time for adequate testing, or both) is in short supply.

Put another way, you could write entire, first-rate Windows applications (as opposed to device drivers) in assembly language, if you really wanted to. But almost no one would consider that a reasonable course, except under quite extreme situations. It's all a matter of where you place the dividing line between "reasonable" and "unreasonable" programming tools for a given set of circumstances and task. In my opinion and experience, C/C++ and its attendant tools are almost always on the same side of the line as assembly language.

# If Pascal Is so Bloody Wonderful…

…and C++ is dreadful, why isn't everyone using Pascal? That's a fair question. There are numerous reasons for this, but the one that sticks out in my mind is that Borland's Pascal products have long had a severe image problem. I mean, how seriously can you take any compiler that had "Turbo" in its name and didn't cost hundreds of dollars? Too many developers made the mistake long ago of rejecting Borland's Pascal as a "toy" based on such irrelevant issues, and this reputation has stayed with it.

Borland's Pascal products did and do have real limitations, however, such as the lack of support for various memory models (although I've almost never found this to be a hindrance in real work), and more serious, the inability to produce standard format .OBJ files. Also, there still isn't a 32-bit version of Delphi available at this time. Borland is expected to release Delphi32 about the time this book hits the shelves, and I expect it to make things quite interesting in the tools market. (See the sidebar "Delphi32: Borland's Pascal Comes of Age" for more details.)

But back to Object Pascal's flaws. The canonical criticism of all flavors of Pascal is that it's a "straight jacket," and that it doesn't allow the programmer the freedom to code normally. I would love to find out how this one got started (it's probably related to sightings of Elvis and Jimmy Hoffa creating crop circles from a UFO), because it just ain't so. If you run afoul of type checking in Object Pascal, you do the same thing you have to do all the time in that other popular, strongly-typed language, C++: You use a cast. In fact, for all development I find that I use far fewer casts in C++ than I do in Pascal. There are only about a dozen casts in the 43,000+ lines of Pascal that make up Stickies!, and only one variant (read: deviant) record structure. Given all the hand-to-hand combat with the Window API and OWL that Stickies! does. That doesn't sound much like a straight jacket to me.

Another genuine problem is that Borland's Pascal products have always been weak on project management features. Borland Pascal and Delphi let you set all compilation switches from the IDE, as you would expect, but they don't let you save named sets of options within a project, similar to the "Release" and "Debug" sets of options all C/C++ programmers have used for years. In Delphi, you have to resort to separate projects that use the same source files. This is a silly and needless hassle.

Finally, my single biggest gripe with Borland's Pascal products has always been that they flag errors, but not warnings. I realize that this is one reason why they can compile so incredibly fast, but it seems there should be a middle ground where the compiler will optionally flag some of the nastier problems, for example returning a pointer to a local variable, terminating a function without setting the return value, local variables that aren't used, etc. For a language that was designed as a teaching tool and is now in widespread use for creating applications, these are pretty serious limitations. (See the sidebar on Delphi32 for a description of how Borland has addressed this issue.)

## Living with C++

C/C++ will not go away overnight, or ever, for that matter. It's already so deeply entrenched that we'll all surely live and work with it for decades, in one form or another. How to best do this?

I mentioned above that when you select a tool, your exploration and exploitation task isn't over, you then continue it on a new, micro level, within the boundaries of that tool. This is probably more true of C/C++ compilers than it is of most development tools. (See the sidebar, Optimization: Get Your Free Lunch Here!" for a discourse on one of the most misused features of C/C++ compilers.)

First, you should make sure that you truly understand what C/C++ and your compiler package can and cannot do for your project. There are numerous good books on C++ available, and I've recommended some in Chapter 16. Browse through your local bookstore and find two or three that seem right tfor you, buy them, and then read them cover to cover, don't just use them as references. You'll be amazed at all the interesting things you'll pick up.

Second, decide how deep into C++ you should delve. Bjarne Stroustoup, the father of C++, says in his excellent book, *The Design and Evolution of C++*:

> In my experience, the safest bet is to learn C++ bottom-up, that is, first learn the features C++ provides for traditional proce-dural programming, the better-C subset, then learn to use and appreciate the data abstraction features, and then learn to use class hierarchies to organize sets of related classes.

I agree completely, but I would add that you should not be the least bit con-cerned if you find that you explore much more of C++ than you exploit. In fact, I call this the "C++ minus strategy," and I use it all the time in my commercial work. When I'm writing C++ Windows code—I write a lot of C++-as-a-better-C, my own dialect of the language—I use MFC as a set of pigeonholes into which my code is slotted. By contrast, some of my older Object Pascal code looks like an explosion in an object factory, solely because I'm more comfortable with its object model, which doesn't hold near as many surprises for developers as does C++'s. In Stickies!, for example, I use dozens of objects to good effect.

This C++ minus strategy is what works for me and my projects. You have to decide what's right for you. Just remember going into the decision process that there's no rule that says you must employ all the features of a language or tool.

*Stickies! is a good example of the You(now) != You(later) guideline from Chapter 2. I began writing the initial version in early 1992, at a time when I was interested in pushing the OOP envelope. As a result, the source in Stickies! is more OO than it would be if I wrote it now, and code added for ensuing releases was less OO, resulting in a conspicuous mix of design and coding styles, even though I'm the sole author. Like you, I never get a chance to rewrite debugged, ship-ping, production code solely for the purpose of unifying its style, so Stickies! will stay in its somewhat confused state until I rewrite the entire program for another reason.*

## Frameworks

Your choice of a framework, or even if you should use one, is just as important as your choice of language. It will largely define what you can do, or at least what you can do easily.

I'm sure some of you reacted to the suggestion above that not using a framework is a valid option. That's becoming less true, thanks to things like OLE and concern for porting code to other platforms. But it's still an option, and depending on all the usual circumstances that influence any tool selection, it might be the right choice. The key point is not to reject options out of hand; make your selections within the context of your project. For example, if you're writing a simple utility that must fit into the remaining sliver of free floppy disk space in a set of distribution disks, then a non-framework application might be the solution. Given a choice between using a framework, thereby adding a disk to a set that will be sent to tens or hundreds of thousands of people, and not using a framework but keeping your job, the decision is pretty easy.

If you're going to use a framework, particularly when cross-platform porting is important, you should evaluate your alternatives very carefully, to make sure they really provide the features you need and in a way that's reasonable to both you and your users. Do they support the creation of minimized programs? What about drag and drop, DDE, and OLE support? What about the new Windows 95 controls? If you think you'll need to do owner-draw listboxes, will they let you do this, or do they provide a facility that lets you perform the same logical task using nothing but features of the framework? How much coverage of the Windows API does the framework supply? More coverage isn't always better; if you and your team won't be doing much GDI work, then extensive coverage of that part of the API doesn't matter, and it isn't a benefit, no matter how good it sounds in the four-color brochures.

## Add-Ons and Accessories

Just as no person is an island, no compiler is a complete development suite (despite what the vendors would like you to believe). You can and should augment your main tool selection with smaller add-ons. In this section I'll talk about some of the more common ones.

## Third-Party Libraries and Components

The programming tools catalogs are packed with these. You can hardly turn a page in a tools catalog without being assaulted by an ad or a product description for VBX controls. This will soon be the case for Delphi components, as well as OCX controls that work with Visual Basic 4.0. Should you use them? As always, the answer is: It depends. It depends on what you need to do, your skills base, the libraries available, your budget, and your schedule.

And you have to tread carefully. I've seen numerous comments from professional programmers complaining about the terrible quality of licensed components and the non-existent support. If you're writing a public program, make sure you research the vendor and the product thoroughly before you make a commitment to either. Also make sure that the product either comes with full source code or that the source is readily available. With the rapid proliferation of components on the market, there will certainly be some turnover among vendors and more than a few orphaned products, which means you're in deep trouble if you find a bug or hit a hard limitation.

## Debugging Aids

All major Windows development tools come with their own debuggers, so why should you buy a third-party debugging product when that money could be better spent replenishing the Jolt Cola and Doritos supplies? Simple: There's one product I've seen that's worth it for C/C++ developers: Bounds Checker from Nu-Mega Technologies. Bounds Checker works with the debugging information in your program, and it alerts you to a whole host of problems, such as API calls with invalid parameters, resource leaks, and various memory allocation and deallocation issues. Best of all, when it detects the problem it takes you to the exact line in the source where the problem occurs.

This is exactly the kind of high-leverage tool you should be looking to add to your tool kit. In fact, whenever possible you should make it a point to run all your tests under Bounds Checker.

## Version Managers

You're not a corporate animal, you're a lone wolf, independent and free, coding your way across the cyberplain as you see fit. So why would you need or want to use a version manager? Isn't that, well, kind of stuffy? No, it isn't.

Even if you're doing most of your development work as a one-person team, you can use a version manager to great benefit. How many times do you find that you have to experiment with some new feature in a program, or cut a special version for just one or even a few users? These situations pop up a lot, I find, and a version manager can make them much easier to handle. Sure, you can manually create a new directory tree and copy all project files to it, but how do you collect and merge changes from different variations of a common project into a new version? Or how do you partially back out one feature change that affects a dozen files?

Of course, the larger your development team, the more critical such issues become. If you've ever been in a team programming environment where someone's important changes somehow got lost, or worse, were only partially carried over to a new version of the project, you already know how much of a quality risk and a hassle this can become.

One word of caution: Version managers are not just like other tools and utilities. I've worked with several, and they all have their own terminology, rules, and quirks, much more so than most tools you'll use. Don't assume that you can buy your first version manager, slap it on your system(s), ignore the manual, and merrily start versioning by the seat of your pants. It won't happen, and you'll risk losing file updates. If nothing else, you'll waste time and end up frustrated by the time you figure out how the package really works. (As a group, I found the documentation for version managers even worse than average among development tools, which is saying quite a bit.) My suggestion is to get an early start, create a dummy project, and then exercise all the features of the version manager that you expect to use, most notably the branching and merging facilities. This won't take long, perhaps only one afternoon, but it will be time well spent.

## Installation Programs

Many of you will be tempted to ignore this category if you don't commercially distribute your software. After all, if your program is going to be used only within your company, by a few dozen people, why bother with an installation program?

As it turns out, a small and simple installation program (not one of the several-hundred-KB behemoths you see advertised in all the programming magazines) can be a great time saver in the long run. Even if your program merely requires that its files are copied to the right directories, this can be worth the effort, since it gives your program's users a simple, automated way of performing the installation, and you won't have to worry about users getting creative with file placement, overlaying or not properly installing DLL's, etc., and then calling you for help.

The more complicated your program's installation is, the more important it is that you automate it. With the arrival of Windows 95 and its obsession with the registry, this has become a critical area. Even if you'll be supporting a mix of Windows 95 and Windows 3.1 users for a while (which I'm sure will be the case for many of us), one of the smaller installation packages, such as Eshcalon Development's Install Pro, could easily pay for itself in short order.

## Optimization: Get Your Free Lunch Here!

Create a new project with Visual C++ or any other Windows C++ development package and then check the project settings. You'll see something quite interesting: The "Debug" options include debug information in the executable, and turn off all optimization. The "Release" options disable the generation of debug information, as expected, but by default specify some fairly aggressive optimization setting (typically either "Maximize speed" or "Minimize size").

How the heck did this happen? When did we collectively agree that shipping products should include a high degree of code optimization? And when did we decide that the current (or any, for that matter) generation of C/C++ compilers was reliable enough to be trusted with this delicate and arcane task? As far as I know, the answer to both questions is we didn't, because nobody asked.

Well, I think it's time we take a minute to examine the assumptions behind these compiler settings, and what they mean for real world projects.

The conventional wisdom says that during development and test, you want to use the debug settings for the following reasons:

1. Compiler features such as TRACE() and ASSERT() rely on the debug preprocessor symbol (_DEBUG) to work properly.

2. You need the debug information in the executable.

3. You want the fastest possible compiles and links, since you'll likely spend a lot of time in the edit/compile/link/test loop. If the executable isn't the smallest or fastest possible, it's not a concern, since real users won't see it.

By contrast, once you're ready for release, you want to neuter TRACE() and ASSERT(), remove the debug information from the executable, and squeeze the most performance possible out of the finished application.

This all makes perfect sense, and it agrees completely with the default project settings we find in our C/C++ environments. The biggest problem with this rosy scenario is that optimizers aren't perfect, and they sometimes introduce bugs into your otherwise correct code as they attempt to perform their black magic. (If you're not convinced that compiler optimization borders on black magic, see the March, 1995 issue of *Microsoft Systems Journal* for an article about Visual C++ 2.0's features in this area. Optimizers routinely move code around, delete it, and rewrite it. Considering the quality of large Windows programs in general, including compilers, if you're not concerned about this I respectfully suggest that you haven't been paying attention.)

Check Microsoft's Developer Network CD, and you'll find several acknowledged bugs and problems whose recommended solution is to disable optimization, either completely or just a particular setting. Look at the sidebar in this chapter, "C++: It Isn't Soup Yet, and Neither are Its Compilers", and you'll see that in the short time *Windows/DOS Developer's Journal* has been running their "Bug++ of the Month" column, they've reported two optimizer bugs, one in Borland's compiler, one in Microsoft's.

By developing and testing with one optimizer setting and then shipping with another, you're playing compiler roulette. Eventually your program will hit a chamber that isn't empty.

This is a subtlety worth stressing: By linking the presence of debugging information in the produced executables with optimization, compiler vendors are effectively guaranteeing that many projects will only have optimization turned on *after* all testing has been completed. Programmers need to have debugging information in the program during the test cycle, so they use the "Debug" settings, but they often trust the vendor's predefined settings for the release version.

Another interesting assumption about optimization is that you don't want to turn it on early because it slows down compiles and links too much. For real world projects, this is a specious argument. I ran some tests with the WordPad example that comes with Visual C++ 2.2 and that compiler, using the same project settings mentioned in the chapter. Here's what I found:

| Optimization setting | Time to build all components |
|---|---|
| None | 5:07 |
| Minimize size | 5:42 |
| Maximize speed | 5:48 |

| Optimization setting | Time to recompile one unit and relink WORDPAD.EXE |
|---|---|
| None | 35 seconds |
| Minimize size | 36 seconds |
| Maximize speed | 38 seconds |

For the complete builds, I consider these differences irrelevant. Once a build takes more than about two minutes, a change of only 13% (the difference between 5:07 and 5:48) doesn't matter; run that build more than a few times in a day and you're already spending far too much time on your juggling or practicing your guitar chords instead of writing code. For the partial builds, the time is so swamped by the linker step that it doesn't matter whether the compile has optimization turned on or not; you can barely measure the savings.

As always, the pertinent question is what to do about this in the real world? For public programs, my recommendations are:

1. Be *extremely* skeptical of any compiler optimization. You should research your compiler's track record in this area; ask in the appropriate forum on CompuServe, check the vendor's published bug information, if any exists, etc.

2. Do not accept the vendor's predefined settings without evaluating how well they meet your needs for the current project. As I've said elsewhere in this chapter, it's critical that you continue to evaluate a tool once you've chosen to use it. You must remain a hard sell for individual features, particularly those that have a chance of causing you and your users considerable grief if they're buggy.

3. Decide as early in the project as you can what your optimization settings will be for the released version, and then make sure all testing is done with those exact settings. You can perform early development with different settings, but all testing must be done with the final settings. In general, you should only use optimizations if you're convinced that the tangible benefits to your project will outweigh the risk. In my experience, optimizations are seldom worth using in the real world, but you have to decide what's right for your situation. If nothing else, remember that if you choose to dance with the devil, be sure you know the steps.

## Whither OWL?

The recent (as of this writing) history of Borland is an interesting cautionary tale about selecting tools, and indirectly, vendors. In late 1994 and early 1995, Borland went through an extremely bad financial period: takeover rumors were rife, and virtually every "low friend in a high place" I talked to in the industry expected one company or another to buy out Borland at any time (Novell was considered the most likely suitor).

Delphi shipped in March of 1995, and was a big hit right out of the chute, despite documentation that was roundly (and fairly, in my opinion) criticized. As Delphi sales zoomed, Borland's picture brightened considerably, which unfortunately is more than can be said for the installed base of Borland Pascal programmers. Delphi has outstanding facilities for code reuse, some welcome extensions to Object Pascal, and a new, more modern framework, VCL (Visual Component Library) that will provide a migration path to 32-bits. The problem is that VCL is incompatible with OWL, and there's no easy way to port BPW/OWL source code to Delphi/VCL. Anyone with a sizable body of source code in BPW/OWL was marooned.

I spoke in e-mail with two high-ranking employees at Borland about this situation and was told that there was no plan to port the Pascal version of OWL to 32-bits (there already was a 32-bit version of OWL in their C++ product, of course). They even said Borland was looking for a third party to do the port for them, and that they would consider allowing the other company to market the ported version. So not only had Borland marooned BPW/OWL code in the old framework, they marooned it in 16-bits.

This left developers with precious few options:

1. Port the code to Delphi/VCL, and do all the necessary rewriting.
2. Port the code to Borland's C++ 4.5 (the current version at the time of Delphi's release). This would allow the code to stay in OWL, albeit a very different dialect, but it would require a line-by-line translation from Pascal to C++, an unpleasant proposition for any program more than a few hundred lines long.

3. Abandon the source code and rewrite it from scratch with a new package.

4. Don't port it and live with the 16-bit version of the product.

For a small program, up to two or three thousand lines, this isn't that big a problem; you allocate a couple of weeks, study up on the new framework, and you can accomplish the port via option 1, which leaves you in fine shape for the jump to 32-bits once Delphi for Windows 95 shipped (still a future event as I write this).

And for many, probably most, of the vocal Borland faithful, this wasn't an issue. I hardly saw it discussed on Borland's DELPHI forum on CompuServe. (Perhaps Delphi programmers were only creating new programs, and throwing all their old code away? Or maybe there really is something about that "barbarians at the gate" attitude that Philippe Kahn, founder of Borland, used to preach, and they're just a tougher lot than the average programmer.)

But what about those people who had large bodies of BPW/OWL of source code? I had one client with over 200,000 lines of such code in various programs, who was suddenly faced with no economical path to 32-bits. I personally have well over 100,000 lines of BPW/OWL code that can only be converted at great expense. I keep hoping that someone will pick up OWL from Borland and do the port to 32-bits; however, so far no one has stepped up to the task.

My point here is not to bash Borland; heck, for years I was one of their more faithful supporters. But when their technical support started to go downhill in the early 90's, and they abandoned their customer's base of BPW/OWL code, I became as skeptical of them as I am of other companies. (And the fact that I gave them the benefit of the doubt over other companies clearly shows that I was guilty of being too trusting, a mistake you shouldn't make.) And to be perfectly clear, Borland's track record is certainly no worse than that of other companies in terms of abandoning their own standards and products. They're merely an example.

Will the magic be back at Borland? I hope so, as it would be a good thing for us all to see more vigorous competition and more genuine choices in the compiler market. I expect to see Borland's situation continue to improve dramatically, thanks to their new focus on development tools, and I wouldn't be the least bit surprised if the barbarians are once again giving the competition fits in 1996.

## C++: It Isn't Soup Yet, and Neither Are Its Compilers

As I write this, in August of 1995, there still isn't an ANSI standard for C++, and compilers differ considerably in how much of the emerging standard they support. Visual C++ 1.5, for example, does not support templates and never will. No compiler that I know of supports the new boolean type (yes, after all these years of typedef-ing our own BOOLs, C++ is finally getting a real honest-to-Pete boolean), the new casts, and name spaces. Yet how long have we been creating public programs with C++, apparently with proto-compilers?

Even though the answer is that C++, in effect a beta language, has already been in use an uncomfortably long time, the current crop of C++ compilers for Windows development is surprisingly immature. I checked my back issues of *Windows/DOS Developer's Journal* and Mark Nelson's excellent "Bug++ of the Month" column, and here's what I found:

- October 1994: Watcom C++ 10.0 fails to call destructors for an automatic object when the code executes a return from within a switch statement.
- November 1994: Borland C++ 4.02 generates destructor calls for non-existent automatic objects.
- December 1994: Visual C++ 1.5 creates hundreds of spurious calls to a constructor when optimization is enabled (/Ox option switch).
- January 1995: Visual C++ 1.5 fails to issue a warning about code that attempts to return a reference to a local variable, even at the highest warning level.
- February 1995: Borland C++ 4.5 fails to clean up the stack when generating 386 code with optimization.
- March 1995: Visual C++ 2.0 uses the wrong default value on a constructor.
- April 1995: Borland C++ 4.5 incorrectly handles 16- and 32-bit iostream calls, resulting in corrupt output.
- May 1995: Visual C++ 2.0 would not handle friend functions and templates correctly.
- June 1995: Borland C++ 4.5 won't allow run-time type information to be disabled unless exception handling is also disabled.
- July 1995: Visual C++ 1.5 generates incorrect code for a 386 (/G3 option switch).
- August 1995: Borland C++ 4.5 converts an enum to an unrelated class in order to test its value.

(Of course, if you're interested in any of these bugs, *don't* rely on my terse summaries to decide if they impact your work. Dig up the issue of W/DDJ or download the file for that month's issue from library 7 of the SDFORUM on CompuServe.)

Most, if not all, of these bugs will have been fixed by the time this book is on the shelves, and it's not my goal to provide you with a list of bugs in C++ compilers. This list, as well as problem reports on Microsoft's Developer Network CD and third-party compilations of bugs, does illustrate that C++ compilers are not yet mature products. Given the rapid rate of change in the industry, thanks to the scramble to make compilers 100 percent ANSI compliant once the standard is carved in granite, and the endless upgrades needed to support new Windows features in frameworks and IDEs, I don't expect to see this situation change in the foreseeable future. (In this business, "foreseeable future" is anywhere from five minutes to a year, but for compilers I think it's safe to say that they won't get a chance to catch their breath and mature for at least a year. Then it will be time for the carousel ride to start all over again with Windows 96 and Cairo.)

What should we do about this? We can't go hide in caves and make believe this problem doesn't exist. That would be irresponsible, and it would do nothing to improve the quality of our public programs. Our only recourse is always to remember that C++ compiler packages as a group are an evolving, sometimes buggy lot. That means that sometimes the bug in our program really isn't really in our program, and that we have to be prepared for that eventuality. (C++ compiler bugs are like hard disk crashes and other massive-lost-data disasters; it's not a matter of if, it's a matter of when.)

We should be diligent about reporting bugs in compilers and all other software to vendors. All too often this amounts to begging for abuse, but you should still do it. As Wilford Brimley says on the oatmeal commercials, "It's the right thing to do." After all, there's a chance you're wrong and it's not a bug but your own error that you can fix in a few seconds. There's even the chance that a vendor will fix the problem in an upcoming release, or even provide a fix or usable workaround in the short run. Stranger things have happened.

## Delphi32: Borland's Pascal Comes of Age

Borland has been marketing Pascal compilers since the first Reagan Administration. As mentioned elsewhere in this chapter, these compilers have long had a reputation for being fast, and highly usable, but somehow "toy" compilers not fit for real work. While these products have certainly had their limitations and quirks, as do all development tools, I think the "toy" tag was largely unwarranted, based on my use of them.

Delphi is quickly erasing that image problem, and Delphi32 should obliterate what's left when it hits the shelves. As I write this Delphi32 is still in beta, but it should ship about the time this book does. In the context of this chapter and the issues that I bring up throughout this book, let me highlight some of the more interesting features of Delphi32:

- Full 32-bit compiler, with no 64K boundaries. I'll take a minute while you declare this Pascal Programmer Liberation Day and celebrate.

- Full Delphi16-like compatibility and operation, including VCL support.

- Full support for the new Windows 95 controls.

- A much better linker. I can't and shouldn't give benchmark results for a beta version of a product, but in my limited testing Delphi32 compiles and links very quickly, and it produces smaller executables than the 16-bit version did.

- The ability to create 32-bit OBJ files that can be linked with C/C++ projects. Pascal purists will sneer at this feature, but I'm convinced that it will be the biggest single factor in ensuring Delphi32's long-term success. Before Delphi32 came along, there was no practical way to mix Borland's Pascal and C/C++ on the same project. (Yes, there was the primitive ability to link OBJ files into Pascal, and there are always DLLs as a way of making compilation units in different languages peacefully coexist, but these are little use on many real-world projects.) Now you can write a Pascal unit, compile it into an OBJ file, and then use it with a C/C++ project just as you would any object code that began life as C/C++. This feature will allow large development shops to test Delphi32 incrementally on their real projects, without making an all-or-nothing commitment to it. Corporate shops typically have such an enormous backlog of programming work that they can't afford the luxury of evaluating a new tool in isolation; they often have to test it in battle. The OBJ support in Delphi32 will let them do just that, and I predict many will, and then will adopt Delphi as their main development tool for many projects.

- On the downside, Delphi32 followed C/C++'s lead and redefined the integer type to be 32 bits, and introduced a new 16-bit integer type, smallint. Given that they already had a 32-bit integer type, longint, I think this is silly, since it needlessly breaks existing code and changes the size of many user-defined records.

(Of course, some of what I've described above could change by the time Delphi32 is a real product. There's not a lot I can do about that, except to encourage Coriolis to develop books that can be updated after they're purchased.)

Making predictions in the software business is a job for lunatics and egomaniacs. Still, I'll creep out onto a limb and predict that Delphi16's early success will be a springboard for Delphi32, and that Delphi32 will start to turn the tide against C/C++, possibly not until late in 1996. As I mentioned earlier in this chapter, I'm convinced there's a significant pent-up demand for a serious alternative to C/C++. Now, for 32-bit Windows application development, there is one.

# Part 2

# Practice

Chapter

# 5

# *A Local Function Idiom*

# A Local Function Idiom

Chapter 5

> *The last thing one knows in constructing a work is what to put first.*
>
> Blaise Pascal

> *All politics is local.*
>
> American aphorism

> *Render therefore unto Caesar the things which are Caesar's; and unto God the things that are God's.*
>
> Matthew 22:21

> *...and unto local functions the things which belong there, too.*
>
> Lou Grinzo

Local routines are like David Lynch movies: either you like them, understand their appeal right down to your DNA, and think it's silly that anyone should have to defend them, or you just don't get them. If, like me, you work in various programming languages, you probably miss local routines when you work in C/C++, particularly when translating code from a language that supports them. In fact, translating Pascal code with local routines into C++ is awkward enough that I developed the local function idiom.

In this chapter, I'll look at local functions as Pascal implements them, why they're a small but very useful tool that belongs in all of our toolboxes, and how you can easily create them using C++, although the language doesn't natively support the construct.

# Local Routines: Pascal Gets It Right

My zeal for local routines, as implemented in Pascal, is founded in pure, flinty-hearted, self-centered pragmatism. If properly used, they support abstraction, data hiding, and encapsulation, and make it easier for me to package code to more closely mimic its logical flow. This means my programs are easier to write, and more importantly, easier to read six months later when a completely different person (including myself) needs to add a new feature or fix a bug.

Listing 5.1 shows a very simple Object Pascal program that demonstrates how local routines and variable scoping interact. In my real programming, I find this to be a very powerful, flexible, and intuitive model. (PASCAL.PAS merely calculates and displays twice the sum of the integers to a given number, using an intentionally strange approach. This is hardly a stunning display of algorithmic expertise, but then it isn't meant to be.)

## Listing 5.1 PASCAL.PAS

```
program Pascal;

uses
  WinCRT;

var
  pre_Rtn1: longint;   { Visible everywhere }

{ -------------------------------------------------- }

function Rtn1(R1Parm: longint): longint;

var
  pre_Fn1: longint;     { Visible to Rtn1 and Fn1 only }

  { -------------------------------------------------- }

  function Fn1(F1Parm: longint): longint;

  var
    in_Fn1: longint;         { Visible to Fn1 only }

  begin
    if F1Parm > 1 then
      Fn1 := F1Parm + Fn1(F1Parm - 1)
    else
      Fn1 := 1;
  end;

  { -------------------------------------------------- }

var
  post_Fn1: longint;    { Visible to Rtn1 only }

begin
  Rtn1 := 2 * Fn1(R1Parm);
end;
```

```
{ ------------------------------------------------- }

var
  post_Rtn1: longint;  { Not visible to Rtn1 and Fn1 }

begin
  WriteLn('Rtn1(10) = ',Rtn1(10));
end.
```

## Building the Samples: PASCAL.PAS

**CD Location:** ZEN\CHAP05\PASCAL

**Platform:** Win16

**Build instructions:** Load PASCAL.PAS into Borland Pascal for Windows or Delphi and compile. (Although it's not clear why you would actually want to build and execute this program or the other examples in this chapter.)

There are five variables in PASCAL.PAS that are interesting from a scoping perspective, even though they're not actually used in the program:

- pre_Rtn1 is visible throughout the entire program, including all routines, and is "maximally global."
- post_Rtn1 is still at global scope, but because of its placement, it is not visible to Rtn1 or Rtn1's local routine, Fn1.
- pre_Fn1 is local to Rtn1, and is therefore visible only to Rtn1 and Fn1.
- post_Fn1 is also local to Rtn1, but because of its placement after Fn1, it's only visible to Rtn1, not Fn1. This is the classic placement in Object Pascal for the declaration of a variable that is to be visible only to the program's main routine.
- in_Fn1 is a classic local variable, and is only visible to Fn1.

If you look at this program and its variables in the abstract, you'll see that the programmer has quite a lot of control over which entities in the program are accessible from which other entities. In particular:

- Variables can be global to the entire program, or just those routines beyond a certain point (pre_Rtn1 vs. post_Rtn1).
- Variables can be local to a routine, local to a local routine (in_Fn1), and even local to a routine, but not accessible from a local routine with that routine (post_Fn1). (Try to say *that* three times fast with a mouth full of ice cubes.)
- Routines can be globally accessible (Rtn1) or local to an enclosing routine, and inaccessible from any other entity (Fn1).

This capability is really an extension of the basic concept of parameters and local variables; with minimal effort you can create variables and routines whose accessibility very closely match the logical structure and flow of your program. This allows you to control scoping well enough that you can nearly eliminate an entire class of errors, for example, code "stepping on" data it shouldn't even have access to. After all, no one disputes that excessive use of global data can be a bad thing and should be minimized. The capability demonstrated in PASCAL.PAS is simply a more complete implementation of that philosophy than C/C++ programmers normally have available.

*Trying to achieve ultimate control of scoping can require convoluted packaging, whether you're using Pascal or C/C++. For example, you can try to cluster groups of routines in their own compilation units because they're the only ones that need access to certain common data. This is a bad idea and not worth the effort. In the general case, you can't accommodate all such requirements, for example, routines A and B are the only ones that need access to variable X, but routines B and C are the only ones that need access to Y. So there's no way to package them at the compilation unit level to enforce optimal (i.e. both sufficient and minimal) accessibility. Even if you could manage this, it would pervert your program's highest level of packaging, compilation units, since it would be dictated by low-level implementation details. This would also result in a profusion of compilation units. I examined one program I wrote that was about 32,000 lines and 35 compilation units in Pascal, and found that restructuring it to isolate routines and their subroutines to simulate local functions (but not to modify variable scoping) would have resulted in over 150 compilation units, and a case of premature insanity for yours truly. Adding variable scoping into the packaging considerations would have been a nightmare.*

# Step 1: Brute Force Conversion to C

Sadly, C does not support local functions. This means that if we were to translate PASCAL.PAS into C.C, and attempt to mimic its variable scoping as closely as possible, we would wind up with something akin to Listing 5.2.

## Listing 5.2   C.C

```
#include <windows.h>
#include <stdio.h>

int pre_Rtn1;  // Visible everywhere

int pre_Fn1;  // Visible everywhere, unless this variable, Fn1, and
              // Rtn1 are all moved to the end of the file.
```

```
int Fn1(int Fn1Parm)
{
  int in_Fn1;   // Visible to Fn1 only

  if(Fn1Parm > 1)
    return(Fn1Parm + Fn1(Fn1Parm - 1));
  else
    return 1;
}

int Rtn1(int Rtn1Parm)
{
  int post_Fn1;  // Visible to Rtn1 only

  return 2 * Fn1(Rtn1Parm);
}

int main()
{
  int post_Rtn1;  // Not visible to Rtn1 or Fn1

  printf("Rtn1(10) = %d\n\n",Rtn1(10));

  getchar();
  return 0;
}
```

## Building the Samples: C.C

**CD Location:** ZEN\CHAP05\C

**Platform:** Win32 console application

**Build instructions:** Load C.MAK into Visual C++ 2.2 and compile normally.

C.C is a Win32 console program that performs the same pointless calculation as PASCAL.PAS. I've used all the same routine and variable names. As for scoping, notice that:

- in_Fn1 is still local to Fn1, post_Fn1 is still visible to only Rtn1, and pre_Rtn1 is still maximally global, just as they are in PASCAL.PAS. Similarly, post_Rtn1 is still visible only to the main routine, although it now has the traditional C placement for such a variable, just inside main()'s opening brace.

- pre_Fn1, which was local to Rtn1, but still accessible to Fn1 in PASCAL.PAS, is now global from the point at which it appears onward in this compilation unit. This can easily create a problem in a real program, since you will often add new functions after this point. These functions will have access to this variable, when in many cases they shouldn't. (This problem is reminiscent of the bad old days of DOS when we had to juggle the loading order of TSR's to accommodate the ones that had to be first or last, or at least think they were first or last. As with the compilation-unit-level packaging discussed above, this is another losing battle, and you very quickly hit a combination of requirements that you can't satisfy.)

- Fn1 has now been "promoted" to the same level of visibility as Rtn1. This means that not only can Rtn1 still call Fn1, but so can any other function. In the case of C.C, this is a trivial detail, thanks to the simplicity of the program and the purely algorithmic nature of Fn1. However, often in the real world a local routine will use both its parameters and variables which are local to its enclosing routine (for example, pre_Fn1 in PASCAL.PAS) to perform some task that only makes sense in the context of the parent routine. Placing such a routine in the general name space is poor practice because it's very misleading. We've all heard the term self-documenting code, meaning source code that is so clearly written and is so self-evident in its intent and usage that no commentary is needed. (See guideline 3 in Chapter 2 for my take on commentary, in general, and my annoyance at the term "self-documenting code.") Exposing a function that shouldn't be is just the opposite, and is therefore decidedly self-*un*documenting code, requiring commentary simply to dispel the incorrect inference that a reasonable programmer could draw from its placement.

Clearly, the physical implementation of C.C does not fully support the logical intent of the program, thanks to C's lack of support for local functions, although this program clearly will execute properly and return the correct (if boring) result. As I've stressed throughout this book, the point here is not merely a matter of whether a tool or technique allows you to create a correct program, but a question of how well it supports the creation of correct, robust, and maintainable programs. This seems like an abstract, purely theoretical point when the example is as simple as the one in this chapter: when you have to fix a bug in or add a new feature to a 100,000 line C/C++ program you're not familiar with, you must spend hours figuring out data and function scoping issues, and the problem springs to life in a decidedly fixating way.

# Step 2: C++ and the Local Function Idiom

So much for C; let's fast-forward a decade to C++. Unfortunately, C++ still doesn't support local functions, but it does support something tantalizingly close from a scoping perspective: classes. After all, what have we been talking about all along, but packaging and controlling access to code and data. Isn't that what classes are all about? It is, and that leads us to the local function idiom.

Listing 5.3 shows CPP.CPP, the C++/local function idiom version of PASCAL.PAS.

## Listing 5.3    CPP.CPP

```cpp
#include <windows.h>
#include <stdio.h>

class cPackageRtn1
  {
    public:
      cPackageRtn1(void);
      int Rtn1(int Rtn1Parm);

    private:
      int pre_Fn1;  // Visible to Rtn1 and Fn1 only
      int Fn1(int Fn1Parm); // Visible only to Rtn1

    private:
      // Why define these without implementing them?  See Chapter 5.
      cPackageRtn1& operator=(const cPackageRtn1& x);
      cPackageRtn1(const cPackageRtn1& x);
  };

int pre_Rtn1;  // Visible everywhere

cPackageRtn1::cPackageRtn1(void) { }

int cPackageRtn1::Fn1(int Fn1Parm)
{
  int x;   // Visible to Fn1 only

  if(Fn1Parm > 1)
    return(Fn1Parm + Fn1(Fn1Parm - 1));
  else
    return 1;
}

int cPackageRtn1::Rtn1(int Rtn1Parm)
{
  int post_Fn1;   // Visible to Rtn1 only

  pre_Fn1 = 0;

  return 2 * Fn1(Rtn1Parm);
}

int post_Rtn1;  // Not visible to Rtn1 or Fn1

int main()
{
  cPackageRtn1 fred;

  printf("fred.Rtn1(10) = %d\n\n",fred.Rtn1(10));

  printf("Press Enter... ");
  getchar();
  return 0;
}
```

## Building the Samples: CPP.CPP

**CD Location:** ZEN\CHAP05\CPP
**Platform:** Win32 console application
**Build instructions:** Load CPP.MAK into Visual C++ 2.2 and compile normally.

*Did you notice that in CPP.CPP I defined a private copy constructor and a private assignment operator for the class cPackageRtn1, but didn't implement them? Why? Simple: In doing so, I prevent anyone using this class from passing it as a parameter to a function or making a copy via assignment. (The missing assignment operator generates a compiler error if someone tries to use it, and the missing copy constructor generates a linker error.) I seldom have to resort to such tricks in C++, but since this idiom amounts to warping the class mechanism and making it serve another purpose, I think it's an appropriate precaution. After all, in this usage the class does not represent an object in the classic OOP sense (its data members aren't meant to be persistent between invocations, for example), but merely a function with some interesting, non-OOP traits, so there's no reason why anyone would need or want to copy it or pass it around. This is one of the few "stupid C/C++ tricks" that I find genuinely useful, although it makes me cringe every time I use it, since I'm declaring methods that are never implemented, and the compiler and linker never utter a peep.*

CPP.CPP includes a class, cPackageRtn1, which is an example of what I call a packaging class. This class contains both the enclosing and the local functions as members, and the definition of the variables that will be accessible to both functions (for example, pre_Fn1).

To use the local function idiom:

- Create a packaging class for each function that will have one or more local functions.

- Make the enclosing function and the local functions members of the packaging class, with only the enclosing function being public. This placement means that the local functions can be called from only the enclosing function, and the enclosing function is the class's only public, non-constructor member. This example uses only one local function, but you're certainly not limited to one per packaging class.

- Place variables that are to be local to the enclosing routine, but not accessible to the local function, in the enclosing routine. See the placement of post_Fn1 in cPackageRtn1::Rtn1, for example. This regains the scoping for this variable that we had in the Pascal version and lost in the translation to C.

- Place global variables and those local to any given routine exactly as they would be in Pascal, C, or C++.

- Make sure that all relevant initialization is performed in the method you call to do the actual work, for example Rtn1, and not in the constructor. Class members persist for the life of the object instance, which means you can easily get into trouble if you call the same instance of your package more than once and assume the constructor has done its job. Using a class in this way is subtly different from the normal OOP practice, so you have to be aware of such issues.

- Define an instance of the packaging class at the same scope as that of the most global function in your program that will have to use it. For example, if your enclosing function is a general utility routine that will be called from many compilation units in your program, you should place it in your toolbox compilation unit, at global scope. If it will be used in only one compilation unit by a few functions, then it should be local to that compilation unit.

With this idiom, you have the same degree of control over your program's scoping as you do in Pascal, without resorting to changing your program's packaging at the level of compilation units. As you use this technique in your own programs, you have to guard against getting too cute for your own good. Just as with local routines in Pascal, or even non-local ones in good old C/C++, you still have to worry about all the normal data accessibility issues, such as improper use of globals.

Notice, however, that because some data is persistent for the lifetime of an instance of your packaging class (pre_Fn1), you have to ensure that your program won't overlap calls to the same instance. For example, if function A in your program calls fred, an instance of Rtn1, and then function B from a separate thread calls the same instance, fred, you can get wildly unpredictable results if you use variables at the package level. This situation can be easily avoided by giving each thread that uses the enclosing routine a local instance.

*C++ does support nested or local classes, which would seem to be ideal for our purposes in this chapter but suffer from a serious limitation: Members of a nested or local class cannot reference automatic variables in the enclosing scope. It even appears this limitation has a quite specific intent; The Annotated C++ Reference Manual, in discussing local class declarations, says on page 189, "Allowing reference to the enclosing function's automatic variables would imply the introduction of nested functions." This restriction becomes even more curious when one realizes that local classes can reference types, enums, and statics from the enclosing scope. Worse yet, local classes cannot have static members.*

> *I'm sure there's a valid reason for such limitations, but I don't know what it is. And speaking as a programmer who views Pascal, C++, etc., as mere tools to get my job done, I don't care what the reason is. The only interesting issue is what are the characteristics of the tools. (Actually, I lied; I'm not sure that there's a good reason for these odd limitations, but not having looked into the matter in any detail, I'm willing to give the C++ architects the benefit of the doubt.)*

Let's talk about recursion for a minute. In PASCAL.PAS, C.C, and CPP.CPP, Rtn1 and Fn1 could call themselves or each other, as needed. No surprise there. But there's a subtlety involving variables and recursion: Variables in the package, but not local to the enclosing routine (Rtn1), are not regenerated when it recurses. This makes sense, since these variables (such as pre_Fn1) are in the name space that encloses both Rtn1 and Fn1, so when Rtn1 recurses and then calls Fn1, Fn1 will see the pre-recursion generation of pre_Fn1. In Pascal and languages that support true local functions, the automatics at this level of scoping are regenerated. The solution is simple: If your local function must see a new generation of variables at this scope, then declare these variables local to the enclosing routine (Rtn1) and pass them to the local function as parameters. When the enclosing routine recurses, the variables will be regenerated, and the local function will see the appropriate versions.

The biggest single drawback to the local function idiom is that it's literally shallow— it only goes one level deep (although you can include several local functions in the same class, for example siblings to Fn1). If you try to go a second level of function enclosure, you quickly run into variable accessibility problems. Nested classes aren't able to address automatic variables in the enclosing scope, and creating a hierarchy of classes results in even more arcane convolutions, and is clearly too much trouble and too much of a maintenance burden. Still, as useful as local routines are, I find that I almost never go to a second level in real code. In fact, I can't remember the last time I had to do this in production code.

# The Idiom in the Real World

If you want to see the local function idiom in action and not just as a contrived example, check the WIN32VER component that's presented in Chapter 14. The parts of WIN32VER.CPP that are relevant to the local function idiom are shown here in Listing 5.4, but Chapter 14 gives more detail on this component's use and operation.

In WIN32VER, I could have implemented the code in the DoIt() method of pckComplainIfNot as a simple, standalone function. But that would have caused a problem with the AddPlatform() function. If AddPlatform() is a separate function, then I have to choose between making the data, which it shares with its one caller, global, or passing this data as additional parameters. I also could have placed these functions in their own compilation unit, which is both silly and ugly for such a small amount of code. In other words, none of these solutions were a good fit for the code's functionality. (I'd say that the code "wanted" to do things with a local function, but that would be painfully New Age-y, so I won't say it. (Even though it felt that way.))

By using the local function idiom and a wrapper function in WIN32VER, I get exactly the level of scoping that all parts of the program require, including the caller, which simply sees the ComplainIfNot() function, and is blissfully and properly ignorant of the implementation details.

## Listing 5.4   Abbreviated Version of WIN32VER.CPP

```
#include "stdafx.h"
#include "win32ver.h"

// Note: Numerous material removed from this copy for the sake of clarity

// Local Function Idiom.  See book for explanation.
class pckComplainIfNot
  {
    public:
     pckComplainIfNot(void);
     BOOL DoIt(DWORD Aneeded_OS, char *Atitle);

    private:
     int platforms_needed, platforms_remaining;
      char *title;
     char msg_text[500];
     DWORD needed_OS;

     int  CountOneBits(DWORD x);
     void AddPlatform(DWORD platform, char *platform_name);
     pckComplainIfNot& operator=(const pckComplainIfNot& x);
     pckComplainIfNot(const pckComplainIfNot& x);
  };

pckComplainIfNot::pckComplainIfNot(void) { }

pckComplainIfNot::DoIt(DWORD Aneeded_OS, char *Atitle)
{
  if(!have_version_info)
   GetVersionInfo();

  // We have what the caller says is needed, so bail out
  if(Aneeded_OS & Windows_version)
   return FALSE;

  // Modify the following as needed if more platforms are defined.  This
  // merely restricts needed_OS to valid bit flags.
  needed_OS = Aneeded_OS & (WV_WIN32S | WV_W95 | WV_AnyNT);

  platforms_remaining = platforms_needed = CountOneBits(needed_OS);
```

```
      title = Atitle;

      strcpy(msg_text,"Sorry, this program requires ");

      AddPlatform(WV_WIN32S,"Win32s");
      AddPlatform(WV_W95,"Windows 95");
      AddPlatform(WV_NTWS,"Windows NT Workstation");
      AddPlatform(WV_NTSERVER,"Windows NT Server");
      AddPlatform(WV_NTAS,"Windows NT Advanced Server");

      MessageBox(0,msg_text,title,MB_OK | MB_ICONEXCLAMATION);

      return TRUE;
    }

  int pckComplainIfNot::CountOneBits(DWORD x)
  {
    int count = 0;

    for(int i = 0; i < sizeof(x) * 8; i++)
      {
        if(x & (DWORD)1)
          count++;

        x = x >> 1;
      }

    return count;
  }

  void pckComplainIfNot::AddPlatform(DWORD platform, char *platform_name)
  {
   if(needed_OS & platform)
      {
        strcat(msg_text,platform_name);

        platforms_remaining--;

        switch(platforms_remaining)
          {
            case 0:
             strcat(msg_text,".");
              break;

            case 1:
             if(platforms_needed > 2)
               strcat(msg_text,", or ");
             else
               strcat(msg_text," or ");
             break;

            default:
             strcat(msg_text,", ");
          }
      }
  }

  // Simple wrapper/gateway function
  BOOL ComplainIfNot(DWORD needed_OS, char *title)
  {
```

```
    pckComplainIfNot worker;

    return worker.DoIt(needed_OS,title);
}
```

# Alternatives and Hope

When I published an earlier version of this chapter as an article in *Software Development*, I got an unsolicited e-mail from someone who wanted to know why I didn't just use Watcom's compiler, since it supports local functions. As I replied to that person, I don't consider that an acceptable solution. I assumed that this person was right, and that Watcom does indeed support local functions; I never checked because I don't care if it does. It's wildly non-standard, and it ties your code to one vendor's compiler in a way that can be particularly difficult to unsnarl. I don't need such porting nightmares, and I suspect you don't, either.

Whether to use such compiler features is yet another tool exploitation issue that can only be examined in the context of your project. In a private program, go ahead and use non-standard, vendor-specific extensions. It's your program, so you and you alone will reap the benefits of and pay the consequences for your decisions. But when you're writing a public program, especially one that involves other programmers and a raft of maintenance and portability issues, then it's a much different matter, and using such extensions is almost always a bad idea.

As for hoping that the C++ architects will relent and add local functions, I'm not optimistic or even sure we should be wishing for such a change. As I write this, the ANSI/ISO C++ standard is coming down the home stretch, and the result is that C++ will be an even larger and more complex language than it is today. (For example, none of the commercially available Windows-based C++ compilers I know of support name spaces, but you can bet your mouse ball that they will as soon as the standard is carved in granite, if not before.) As useful and powerful as local routines are, I think it would be a mistake to add them to the language at this point, especially since there are alternatives.

Chapter

# 6

# *Living with DLLs*

# Living with DLLs

Chapter 6

*Though we travel the world over to find the beautiful we must carry it with us or we find it not.*

Ralph Waldo Emerson

*If we do not find anything pleasant, at least we shall find something new.*

Voltaire

Pop Quiz: When a Win16 program calls the LoadLibrary() API, where does 16-bit Windows look for the requested DLL? I won't be coy and make you wait for the answer. The complete search order is:

1. the current directory,
2. the main Windows directory (e.g. C:\WINDOWS),
3. the Windows system directory (C:\WINDOWS\SYSTEM),
4. the directory containing the program's executable,
5. the directories in the PATH environment variable, and
6. the directories mapped in a network.

Notice that I specified a Win16 program and 16-bit Windows. For a Win32 program and 32-bit Windows, the answer is subtly different:

1. the directory containing the application's executable,
2. the current directory,
3. the 32-bit Windows system directory,
4. the 16-bit Windows system directory,

5. the Windows directory, and

6. the directories in the PATH environment variable.

Windows being Windows, there are other variations, too: When Windows NT searches for a Win16 DLL, it checks the 32-bit system directory (e.g. C:\WINNT\SYSTEM32) immediately after the 16-bit system directory; Win32s looks for Win32 DLLs, first in the Win32s home directory, before using the Win32 search order; and Windows 95 provides a new registry key that allows individual Win32 apps to specify a custom search path that is used just before the PATH environment variable.

Do I have your attention now? Are you suddenly wondering how your programs are finding their DLLs in the real world, and what happens when they load the wrong ones? Good. That's exactly why I wrote this chapter, to address these issues.

# Desperately Seeking DLLs

The fact that different DLL search orders are used in the same operating system installation for programs that differ only in an incredibly minute way (from a user's viewpoint) is interesting, to say the least (and it makes one wonder if our pal Voltaire was running a r*eally* early alpha of Windows when he was writing *Candide*, which is the source of his quote). But as the answers to the pop quiz show, a Win16 or Win32 program can't count on seeing the same DLL search order on all Windows incarnations, or even the same search order from one invocation to the next, depending on the current directory and PATH statement setting.

I'm stressing this Windows arcana to make a point: The overwhelming majority of Windows programmers would fail this quiz, including myself (at least until I researched this chapter). Yet how Windows locates and uses DLLs can make a significant difference in the usability of our public programs, especially in a time when vast numbers of people are buying their first computers, nearly all of which, at least in the U.S., come preloaded with Windows.

For example, in the dim and distant past, just before Windows 3.1 was released, I bought a new computer which included Windows 3.0 and several software titles. Months later I installed Windows 3.1 and some of the software that came with my computer, and I immediately noticed an annoying bug in the font selection common dialog. After talking with several support people and checking file dates and sizes on my system, I realized that I had two copies of the Windows 3.1 common dialogs, in the form of our old friend COMMDLG.DLL. The release version was in C:\WINDOWS\SYSTEM, while a buggy, pre-release version had been installed into C:\WINDOWS by one of the free software packages. Thanks to the Win16 DLL search order, the correct version was never loaded. I deleted the pre-release COMMDLG.DLL, and just like magic my font selection dialog was fixed.

While I was writing this chapter, a friend encountered two situations that make excellent examples. In the first, a program replaced the copy of CTL3DV2.DLL in his Windows system directory with an older one that made Procomm Plus for Windows 2.0 refuse to run. Apparently writing installation programs is still a black art, even after countless warnings from tools vendors and authors to check the date on system files before replacing them. This is a perfect example of a software package not respecting the user's resources, something I talked about in guideline 5, Chapter 2.

The other example, which surely wins some sort of award for perversity, involves two document management programs that include DLLs of the same name, but different versions. Product X places its DLLs in its own directory, including an older version of what I'll call FRED.DLL, and product Y places its newer version of FRED.DLL in the user's Windows system directory. Run program X and it loads FRED.DLL from its own directory (presumably because that was the current directory when the program started). At this point, everything is working fine, and the program has loaded exactly the version of FRED.DLL that it intended to use. Unfortunately, upon termination, X erroneously leaves FRED.DLL loaded. This means the user is unable to run Y, since that program can't load the newer version of FRED.DLL from disk. Windows sees that a DLL of the requested name is already in memory and forces the program to try to use that copy, which is older and incompatible with Y. (The authors of program Y don't get any bonus points for gracefully declining to run in the absence of the correct version of FRED.DLL, however. Windows itself stopped Y from running since it needed a routine that was not in the older, already loaded version of FRED.DLL, and the dynamic linkage failed.)

DLLs can lead to interesting times even when properly installed and segregated. Stickies! uses a DLL, STKB.DLL, to hook the keyboard so it can provide the user with global hotkeys. I've seen customers try to edit this (and other) DLLs with text editors, delete them, rename them, and hide them in other directories. In fact, many, probably most, Windows users today don't even realize that DLLs are executables, even though Explorer tags them as "Application extensions," until they misplace or mangle one, and an application suddenly refuses to work, typically with the "Cannot find BARNEY.DLL. Windows needs this file to run C:\TEMP\FRED.EXE." dialog box we all know so well. Even worse, these users seldom see the connection between that file they deleted days ago and the program they want to run now. After all, what the heck is BWCC.DLL, and why should they care?

Even the most experienced users misplace DLLs, simply because these files are often stored separately from their associated executables, and when they try to move a program from one system to another there's no obvious link between this EXE and that DLL file. They probably don't even know the DLL exists. Consulting clients of mine have lost DLLs at extremely inopportune times, leading to all manner of hysteria.

Before I forget—keep in mind that DLLs are not limited to files with the .DLL extension. Windows and third-party products just love DLLs. For example, font files (.FON), AfterDark screen saver modules (.SCR), and Visual Basic controls (.VBX) are all special purpose files, but implemented as plain old DLLs under the covers.

# Who's Loaded First?

Another subtle problem with DLLs is name collisions. Win16 support, whether under Windows 3.11, Windows 95, or Windows NT 3.51, is almost laughably perverse in how it tracks the names of loaded modules, whether they're EXEs or DLLs. (For a mind-blowing description of how Windows 3.1 handles all this, see Chapter 3 of Matt Pietrek's excellent book, *Windows Internals*.) I'm not about to get into all the gory details, but the bottom line is that EXEs and DLLs can block each other and cause all sorts of havoc in the process (not to mention in the task). (Hey, I allotted myself one intentional pun for the entire book, and that was it. Just be glad no one was hurt.)

For example, if you run FRED.EXE which loads BARNEY.DLL, and then, while FRED.EXE is still active, try to run BARNEY.EXE, Windows will refuse, and not even issue an error message. It simply does nothing, leaving the user to wonder why the heck BARNEY.EXE won't run, when in fact there's nothing wrong with the program. Even worse, every time the user tries to run BARNEY.EXE and is blocked by the already loaded BARNEY.DLL, Windows will increment the usage count for BARNEY.DLL, ensuring that when FRED.EXE terminates and frees BARNEY.DLL, the DLL will remain in memory and will continue to block the execution of BARNEY.EXE. This condition will persist until the user restarts Windows or runs a program that performs enough FreeLibrary() calls on BARNEY.DLL to decrement its usage count to zero and cause Windows to remove it from memory.

Similarly, FRED.EXE will be unable to load BARNEY.DLL if BARNEY.EXE is already active, but FRED.EXE is still loaded and running, which can cause major pyrotechnics.

If you want to experiment with this DLL loading and unloading and name collision stuff, I've included a set of Win16 executables on the CD you can use. The directory \ZEN\CHAP06\WIN16 contains:

- BARNEY.DLL, a DLL that exports a single routine, SayHello(), that merely says hello via MessageBox

- FRED.EXE, a program that executes the SayHello routine in BARNEY.DLL

- BARNEY.EXE, a program that happens to have the same module name (BARNEY) as BARNEY.DLL

- BARNEY2.EXE, a copy of BARNEY.EXE, still with the same module name, BARNEY
- UNBARNEY.EXE, a program that merely does a FreeLibrary() call

*Be extremely careful with these programs!* If you run BARNEY.EXE, and then start FRED.EXE while BARNEY is still active, you'll see the blocked DLL load that I mentioned above. You'll also likely see FRED.EXE lock up tight when you try to shut it down, and then mangle your entire Windows session to the point where you have to resort to a power off/on to regain control. I've seen this behavior under Windows 95 and Windows 3.1. Under Windows NT 3.51, FRED.EXE doesn't hang, but the still-running BARNEY.EXE disappears, and the area covered by its window turns into a ghost on the screen that never gets redrawn. Even worse, the system becomes unstable, screen savers won't write to the screen properly, etc. (In my experience NT really does deserve its "solid as a vault" reputation, but even it isn't 100 percent immune to such problems, as these minimal tests prove. Perhaps I should have called the files TBOLT.EXE and LITEFOOT.DLL.) The bottom line is: If you're going to play with these programs, it's up to you to take all appropriate precautions to safeguard your data and other programs, because they WILL crash your system. (The scary part of this situation, of course, is that you can accidentally run into such a problem, and spend hours or days figuring out what's going on.)

This blocked execution issue is quite the condemnation of the basic 16-bit Windows architecture. After all, there's nothing wrong with any of the sample executables; they're perfectly legal EXEs and DLLs that don't go near undocumented features or anything of the sort. Two of them (BARNEY.DLL and BARNEY.EXE) just happen to share the same internal module name, yet that's enough to give 16-bit Windows (or the 16-bit Windows support in the form of the WOW layer) fits. Which reminds me—you can't dodge this problem by renaming BARNEY.EXE. The name collision involves the module name of BARNEY.EXE, which is stored inside the program, not the file name of its executable. You can see this for yourself by using BARNEY2.EXE instead of BARNEY.EXE in your experiments, and also by using Heap Walker, the utility that comes with Visual C++, to check for memory allocations when BARNEY2.EXE is active. Again, if you're at all interested in this, go read Matt's *Windows Internals*, just don't come crying to me if it gives you nightmares.

# Win32 to the Rescue?

This is all interesting, in a voyeuristic, "driving past the accident scene" sort of way, but I'm sure at least some readers are wondering: Isn't this book primarily about Windows 95 programming, and therefore Win32, not decrepit old Win16 issues? Of course not. As I've said many times throughout this book, the big issue that I'm concerned about, and I hope you are, too, is how well your Windows 95 programs work in the real world. That means worrying about how your programs will use and interact with various versions of Windows and their facilities, including DLLs. And to no one's surprise, as the Windows community makes the transition from 16- to 32-bit programs, DLLs will provide even more excitement than we've seen to date.

To be clear, the blocked execution problems mentioned above with Win16 programs do not happen with Win32 programs under Windows 95 and Windows NT. You can run all manner of EXEs and DLLs with colliding module names, and Windows NT and Windows 95 will keep them straight and everything will run just fine. The reason that Windows 95 and Windows NT are so much more intelligent when dealing with Win32 executables than in their own Win16 support is an involved architectural issue that's not really relevant to this chapter (even though its ramifications certainly are). In particular, see some of the articles in *Microsoft Systems Journal* about Win32 architecture, and Helen Custer's book, *Inside Windows NT.*

Microsoft's most heart-felt wishes to the contrary, the installed base of Windows will not embrace Win32 and embark on an unprecedented buying spree on August 25th, and upgrade every piece of software they own to shiny new 32-bit applications. I can't imagine more than a minuscule percentage of Windows users thinking this would be an economical thing to do, even if the programs were available. In my case, I know that I won't replace at least a dozen of my Win16 programs with Win32 variations for several years (not to mention a few DOS programs), simply because the companies that made them are no longer in business or supporting them, and these programs work just fine under 32-bit Windows. Why should I go through the expense and the upgrade hassle to replace something that isn't broken?

The point is that virtually all Windows 95 and Windows NT systems will be a stew of 16- and 32-bit EXE's and DLLs for years to come, and it's up to us programmers to recognize that fact, and its ramifications, and adapt to them. Many people will be upgrading at least some of their programs to 32-bit versions, which means they'll be fiddling with their systems and relying on those stunningly arrogant, brain damaged installation programs that have already caused more problems than you can count. And with the arrival of OCX controls, we'll have yet another category of external files to be misplaced and overlaid, all of which just amplifies our situation.

*Don't get me wrong. My complaint is not with the companies that make installation programs (some of which are excellent), but the people who underutilize and misuse them. Based on my experience with installing numerous Windows programs, I'm sure that many vendors view the installation process as a mere afterthought, or overhead. The real work is in the creation and marketing of the product;*

*the installation stuff isn't "sexy" enough to be of much interest, and is nothing more than a boring packaging concern, on the same level as selecting the cardboard for the dividers inside the box.*

*I'd start an Installation Hall of Shame, but it would be pointless, given the percentage of the commercially available products that would qualify.*

Of course, mixing bitness between EXEs and DLLs isn't allowed, except when explicitly using Windows' thunking support. But you know that programs will, in effect, try this, thanks to the mess that DLL search orders have become. As you would guess, the results aren't exactly what we would hope for.

For example, if a Win16 program tries to use a Win32 DLL under Windows 3.11, the user gets a DOS box and the familiar "This program requires Microsoft Windows" message, even though all executables involved are indeed Windows programs. When I ran this same test under Windows NT 3.5, I got a persistent "application starting" mouse cursor, the application never started, and I never got a message from NT or File Manager. I tried numerous times to shut down the system, and it only did so after several minutes. (Another chink in the vault's armor, it would seem.) This can be a serious problem with a public program. Imagine trying to explain to a paying customer (or someone your employer is paying you to support, like other people in your company) that this strange behavior is not your program's fault, but a side effect of the user's having a 32-bit DLL that happens to have the same module name as your 16-bit DLL, squirreled away in some other directory that doesn't seem relevant to your application. I think we all know how that conversation ends.

*Know of any verifiable DLL Horror Stories? If so, let me know (my CompuServe address is in the Introduction). I'll want as much specific detail as you can provide, for example FredCalc 2.0 doesn't unload its DLLs, or WordOpolis 3.0 replaces MFC30.DLL with an older version without telling the user or getting permission, etc. If I get enough verifiable cases (and I find it very hard to imagine that I won't), maybe I'll start a DLL Hall of Shame.*

# The Intelligent DLL Protocol

Despite everything I've said so far, I don't hate DLLs. They're clearly a very useful tool, and a boon to developers and users alike under the right circumstances. As a developer and Windows user, I would hate to forego their benefits, such as having MFC in a DLL on all Windows 95 systems. Unfortunately, when you're talking about your own applications and their custom DLLs, "under the right circumstances" too often means "in the hands of experts," an assumption that makes DLLs a classic hothouse feature, and one that is increasingly difficult to defend given the tsunami of new Windows users who will be running our public programs.

In light of all this, I believe developers and users can benefit from a new model of DLL usage in public programs, which I call the Intelligent DLL Protocol. The protocol's primary goal is to increase the usability of Windows programs. It seeks to do this by avoiding the DLL search order mysteries whenever possible, and making applications take a more intelligent approach to DLL usage. The Intelligent DLL Protocol has three guidelines:

- DLL Only When You Must
- Place DLLs Properly
- Explicitly Load All DLLs

## DLL Only when You Must

There are times when you either must or should place code into a DLL for overwhelming reasons, such as when you need to share a large body of code (e.g. the MFC run time library) between several programs. Evaluate your program's (or even your suite of programs') situation carefully, and if you're convinced that it makes sense to use a DLL on your project, then do so with a clear conscience.

Such judgments are a classic slippery slope, if there ever was one. I've seen more cases of code unnecessarily stuffed into DLLs than I can throw a dried-up whiteboard marker at. In short, you should presume that all code belongs in a monolithic EXE unless and until proven otherwise. Not only does placing code in the EXE avoid the pathological cases described above, but it also simplifies product distribution and installation.

*I don't know what it is about DLLs, but they seem to make programmers who have just discovered them envision themselves as a combination of Superman and Nicklaus Wirth, able to leap tall buildings and poorly written functional specifications in a single DLL. If there's one feature of the Windows architecture that is susceptible to the shiny hammer syndrome (see Chapter 4), this is it.*

*The key point is that you shouldn't take advice from me or from anyone else to use DLLs as you see fit as some sort of official permission to go on a DLL binge. That's bad for your program and, more important, it's terrible for your users.*

*And don't think it's not a temptation. Once you start using DLLs, it's very easy to convince yourself that you should put your "tricky" code into a DLL so that if (read: when) it needs to be updated you can "simply" distribute one DLL and not the whole package. Likewise, it's easy to convince yourself that your first program could blossom into a whole suite of related applications, and that you should therefore plan ahead and put every routine that could possibly be shared between two or more programs in your suite into a DLL. This last scenario is a particularly tricky judgment call: Is there a genuine need for you to plan ahead and start packaging your routines this way now, or are you just looking for an excuse to swing your shiny new hammer? Only you can answer that one.*

## Place DLLs Properly

Like so many other, relatively simple topics in Windows programming, where to place your DLLs got a lot more interesting with the arrival of Windows 95. No doubt Microsoft was painfully aware of the kinds of horror stories and situations I mentioned earlier in this chapter, and they decided to do something about it. As you'll see, they made quite a change to the basic model of DLL placement, but it should help straighten out matters, assuming we all follow it. (Why are you rolling your eyes? Did I just say something wrong?)

To start with, we have to distinguish between Win16 and Win32 programs, and whether a program is running under a version of Windows that supports the new DLL management facilities. Note that I didn't just say Windows 95, since it's highly likely that Windows NT 4.0 will also support these features, and it's due on the market not too many months after this book arrives. (If Windows NT 4.0 doesn't have these features, the hue and cry from developers will be something to behold, and I'll be leading the chorus.) For now, Win32 programs under Windows 95 get the special treatment I'll describe shortly, while Win16 programs running anywhere, plus Win32 programs under Windows NT, don't. For the rest of this discussion, I'll call the combination of program and environment that results in the special treatment the AppPaths case. (There is a way to make an exception for Win16 programs, however, which I'll cover below in Explicitly Load DLLs.)

We also need to distinguish between the types of DLLs your program uses, in terms of how visible or widely accessible they need to be in your system. There are three levels of visibility we should be concerned about:

• Application-specific, which is exactly what you think it is. Your program package includes a DLL that your program and only your program will ever use, and no other program will ever have to worry about.

• Suite-specific. These DLLs are the ones that are used by several programs from the same company. Packages such as Norton Utilities and some Aldus/Adobe programs have used these, as well as the actual suites of office applications that are so wildly popular today. Here, the critical issue is making sure that all the programs in the suite, possibly installed at different times, can find the DLLs.

• Global. These DLLs are typically used by a wide variety of programs that the creator of the DLLs doesn't even know exist. For example, VBRUN300.DLL, the Visual Basic 3.0 runtime library, is used by numerous programs Microsoft knows nothing about. These DLLs must be easily found from anywhere on your system, by any program, with no special setup required.

## *The Old Days*

Since we'll all be worrying about non-Windows 95 and pre-Windows NT 4.0 installations for quite some time (the non-AppPaths case), and this is the environment that has spawned the DLL Horror Stories du Jour, let me start there. (See Table 6.1 for a summary of all the cases I'll discuss.)

In this combination of environment and program, application-specific DLLs belong in the application's home directory. Not locating these files properly is probably one of the most common mistakes Windows developers make, and is one of the surest signs that a product is a company's first major Windows offering—they dump all their application-specific DLLs into the user's Windows or Windows System directory. Hey, it works fine on the test systems, so what's the problem, I can almost hear them saying in their own defense. As we all know by now, there's plenty wrong with this sort of "DLL dumping," and I'm not going to rehash the problems. Files in the application's home directory will be found as part of the Win16 or Win32 search order, and this directory is even the first one searched under Win32, making it slightly faster, a small but welcome performance bonus.

Placing application-specific DLLs in the program's directory also makes it easier for users to uninstall your program or run it from multiple operating systems, something that many experienced users will be doing with greater frequency as they make the slow transition from Windows 3.1 to Windows 95. (See the sidebar "Managing Your DLLs" for another strategy you, as a user, can employ in this kind of environment.)

---

**Table 6.1   Placing DLLs**

| Type of DLL | AppPaths Case | Non-App Paths Case |
|---|---|---|
| Application-specific | Application's SYSTEM directory, plus App Paths registry setting | Application's home directory, no other setup needed |
| Suite-specific | Common Files directory, plus App Paths registry settings | Either suite-specific directory with PATH or other environment variable to locate the DLLs, or central directory. |
| Global | Windows or Windows System directory, plus SharedDLLs registry settings | Windows or Windows System directory |

---

Suite-specific DLLs are a problem. Basically, you have two options, neither of which is entirely pleasant. First, you can place all suite-specific DLLs in a special location, such as the MSAPPS directory that Microsoft creates under your Windows directory for some of Word's external components. If you use this method, then you have to provide some mechanism for your programs to find these DLLs, which can be an application-specific configuration setting, adding the DLLs location to the user's PATH statement, or creating and setting a new environment variable, such as the ones C compilers have used for years to specify the include and library search orders. This is a messy solution, since it makes it harder for your users to change their configuration, and in practice it gives users little or no choice about where these directories are placed. It also puts a greater burden on the installation process and creates yet more subtle things that can go wrong in the real world.

The other option is much simpler and cleaner, but potentially much deadlier: You can place the DLLs into the user's Windows directory. This approach is fraught with danger and often leads to the kind of overlaid-DLL horror stories I mentioned earlier in this chapter.

This leads us to global DLLs, the ones that must go into the user's Windows or Windows System directory. As with so many other issues in Windows programming, you should be a very hard sell when it comes to placing DLLs here; you're fooling with a basic component of your users' system configurations, and you should tread lightly. It's always important to take care in replacing existing DLLs. Make sure the file you're replacing is not just newer, but whenever possible, make sure that it's also still compatible. I've seen DLLs change in newer releases and become incompatible with older versions of their calling programs. This is even more important with global DLLs, since you are, by definition, changing a resource that's freely accessible to the entire system.

 It's almost as bad to place global DLLs into the application's home directory as it is to dump application-specific files into the Windows directory. For some odd reason, Visual Basic's runtime library, VBRUN300.DLL, seems to wind up in the strangest places. I often find several copies of this file strewn about the system of a client or friend, consuming nearly 400KB of disk space each.

## The New Days

Windows 95 introduces some interesting details into this picture. For starters, there is a new registry key, App Paths, that you can use to specify one or more additions to your program's PATH statement, which is perfect for locating application-specific DLLs. If your program is named FRED.EXE, the registry key might look like the one I set up for testing purposes, shown in Figure 6.1. Notice that

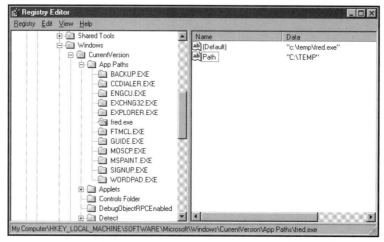

**Figure 6.1  App Paths setting with one directory.**

the default value of the key specifies the fully qualified name of the application. (Windows 95 will change this entry as needed if you move or rename the application.)

Now, what all this means is that when Windows 95 starts FRED.EXE, it looks in the registry, finds this entry, and adds the component "c:\temp" to the beginning of the current PATH environment variable. This allows your program to find its DLLs, even if they're in a special place, not in the Windows or Windows System directories, or in another directory that's on your system's standard PATH setting.

Microsoft suggests that you place your program's DLLs in a directory under the Program Files directory, and that you give your program its own System directory under that. The final step, of course, is updating the registry so Windows 95 knows what you just did and can keep its end of the bargain.

As for suite-specific DLLs, things got somewhat simpler, and you can piggy-back on the App Paths feature. Microsoft suggests that you create a directory under the Common Files directory for your suite:

```
C:\Program Files
    Common Files
        Fred Files
```

and then add this directory to your program's App Paths registry key, as shown in Figure 6.2.

*Notice how the App Paths feature works. Windows 95 appends your program's App Paths value to the front of the system's PATH setting for your program's copy of the environment. Remember where the PATH statement fell in the answer to the pop quiz? For Win32*

*programs it was fifth, sixth if the system has a 32-bit Windows System directory. In other words, for Win32 programs the App Paths directories are searched only if Windows 95 comes up empty after checking the application's home directory, the current directory, the Windows System directory, and the Windows directory. This means that App Paths solves one part of the DLL problem, making sure your program can find its DLLs (I call this the "false negative" problem), but it does almost nothing about the other major DLL problem, your program finding DLLs it shouldn't ("false positive").*

*I think it would have made far more sense to place the App Paths setting right at the head of the search order, in position zero. Then, your application could override all DLL resolution simply by putting its own DLLs in that directory. This would have neatly solved both the false positive as well as the false negative DLL search problems. Oh well. Maybe in Windows 98 (which I hear will be code named Endwell).*

Global files also get their own special treatment in the registry. Whenever you really and truly need to install a DLL that is to be globally accessible by a wide variety of programs, the preferred Windows 95 method, according to Microsoft, is to install the file into the Windows System directory, and then add an entry for the DLL as shown in Figure 6.3. The value of the entry for the shared file is its "usage count index," and should be incremented if your program is using a shared file that is already on the user's system and it already has a registry entry.

This all seems like a great idea, and in practice, it appears to work well, at least for Win32 programs. If this sounds like I'm being evasive, well, I am. As I've said before, DLLs are a classic hothouse feature, which means they're more susceptible

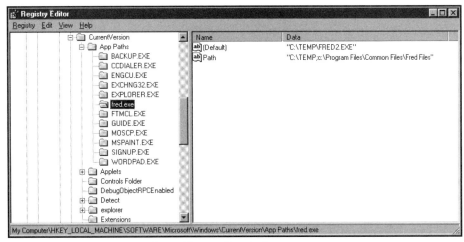

**Figure 6.2   App Paths setting with two directories.**

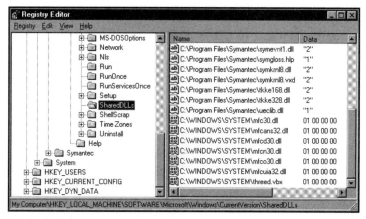

**Figure 6.3    Strings as Counters?**

to being misunderstood and misused than most other Windows features. As I write this paragraph (on the very day that Windows 95 is being launched, in fact), I've only seen one software title that uses this new feature. Will this new facility in Windows 95 suddenly make the people who create installation procedures more diligent and less prone to stomping all over other programs' DLLs? Speaking as a Windows user, and one who installed and uninstalled several dozen new products over the last couple of months, thereby mauling the configuration of four computers, I sure hope so. But until I get a chance to install a few dozen fully Windows 95-aware packages on my systems, I'll reserve judgment (and keep my fingers crossed). (See the sidebar "Standards are for Wimps" for some news on installation woes that surfaced after I had nearly finished this chapter. It seems my pessimism was well founded.)

There's also a problem with using the App Paths feature with 16-bit Windows programs. In fact, when I experimented with this I uncovered what appears to be a bug, or at least a truly inconvenient anomaly. I set up FRED.EXE's App Paths statement to include just c:\temp, and I then placed BARNEY.DLL into c:\temp. (You can use the provided files with these same names to duplicate this test.) When I ran FRED.EXE, Windows 95 complained that it couldn't find BARNEY.DLL. I then modified FRED.EXE to display its PATH environment variable, thinking that perhaps Windows 95 didn't use the App Paths setting for Win16 programs, but to my surprise it clearly did, and c:\temp was the first directory in the PATH variable. On a hunch, I changed FRED.EXE to load BARNEY.DLL explicitly via the LoadLibrary API, and suddenly everything worked like a charm, and FRED found BARNEY. It seems clear that for Win16 programs, Windows 95 is resolving DLL references before it modifies the PATH variable with the App Paths setting.

I haven't investigated the code Windows 95 uses to load Win16 executables, but based on Matt Pietrek's hair-raising description in *Windows Internals* of

LoadModule, the code that performs this job in Windows 3.0 and 3.1, I sure hope that Microsoft has replaced it entirely, or at least reworked it significantly.

*What to make of the fact that the App Paths feature works for Win32 programs, but isn't quite right for Win16 programs? Now that the Soviet Union is a quickly dimming memory, most of the Kremlinologists now seem intent on reading Microsoft's and IBM's minds based on the slimmest of evidence. I think this is wasted time (albeit fair game for programmer arguments while consuming cheap white wine and Doritos). This App Paths/Win16 situation will no doubt send some people into spasms of indignation, claiming that it's yet further proof that Microsoft is trying to "force" software vendors to abandon all 16-bit development. This is possible, but not very likely in my opinion. I strongly suspect that this situation is nothing but a side effect of Microsoft's priorities: Win32 support was far more important than Win16 support, so the interaction between some new features and Win16 support probably got less attention at test and debug time. As a result, this detail slipped between the cracks and created yet another interesting detail for programmers to worry about.*

## Explicitly Load Application DLLs

The standard, implicit way of linking to a DLL causes Windows to search for and load your DLL as part of the process of starting your application. When the DLL can't be found, the user gets a sparse dialog box with no information besides the name of the file that couldn't be located. For many new Windows users, this is a harsh introduction to the complexities of configuration management, and it certainly won't endear them to the program they were trying to run. It's far better to have your application present its own dialog box in this case and offer the user a button that will display a topic in your application's help file.

This approach will give your users immediate answers to the most obvious questions, and it also allows your program to degrade its feature set gracefully if the DLL isn't present. This degradation could be as simple as not enabling e-mail functions if MAPI.DLL couldn't be loaded, or running without hotkey support if a keyboard hooking DLL isn't available (as Stickies! does if it can't make a connection with STKB.DLL). If your program can run in a meaningful way without the DLL, it could even give the user the option of continuing to run with reduced functionality or shutting down. With implicit loading, it's all or nothing, and missing even a minor DLL will prevent your entire application from running.

Even if all your program's DLLs are necessary for it to run, you should still load them explicitly. If nothing else, display a standard MessageBox with Yes and No buttons that says "Sorry, FredCalc can't run without BIGNUMS.DLL. Do you want help?" If the user clicks the Yes button, display a one-page topic in your help file that explains what BIGNUMS.DLL is and why it's required.

Since your program has complete control over an explicit load operation, it can check the version of the DLL that is available, and either refuse to run (after giving the user appropriate notice), or adjust its processing accordingly to the back-level DLL.

*Remember that checking your own DLLs version doesn't have to be an exercise in using version resources or checking file dates and sizes. Simply add a GetVersion routine to the DLL that returns its major and minor version numbers. When your program links to the DLL, it should get the address of this routine first, call it, and then proceed with its processing based on the returned values.*

*You can make this process even simpler, if you like: Create do-nothing routines in your DLL with names like IsVer1, IsVer2, etc., and have your program first try to link to just the IsVer routine that indicates which level of DLL support it needs. If the routine isn't there, then the DLL can't be used. If it is there, then the program can conditionally link to the other routines in the DLL. The point is that by taking control of the DLL load process, you can make your program much more flexible, and it can even adjust to and use a down-level DLL, if that's all that's available.*

Obviously, you can't always load a DLL explicitly. Visual Basic programs, for example, load their run-time support DLL before your code ever gets control, as do C++ programs that use the DLL-based version of MFC. Still, whenever you utilize custom DLLs, from whatever language, you should follow the spirit of this guideline and provide your users with meaningful help and options if the DLL isn't available.

As with most pieces of advice, you have to apply this one with some intelligence. First of all, I would (and do) explicitly load only application-specific DLLs, not system components that you know must be there for Windows to run at all. But depending on where your program might run, it's possible that some normally present DLLs won't be, such as MAPI.DLL, and it only makes sense to have your program react intelligently to that situation.

Also, please do all DLL loads very early in your program's execution. I've seen both commercial and non-commercial programs that let the user get far into a process before they dynamically checked for the existence of a DLL that was necessary to complete the operation. If the DLL wasn't available, the programs refused to continue (they had no choice at that point). This is abysmal form, and any programmer who commits such an act should have to work without an Enter key for a week. The right approach is simple: Make your application explicitly load all the DLLs it might possibly need for the current session when it starts, and handle all the user notification/prompting-to-continue business up front, then the rest of your code doesn't have to worry about it.

# Hello, Sample

The included source code is a mindlessly simple DLL, HELLO.DLL, and a Win32 console application, RUNHELLO.EXE, which loads it explicitly and calls a couple of its routines. In order to implement the DLL protocol outlined in this chapter, I've found that the best approach is to use an interface compilation unit that acts as an abstraction layer between your program and the DLL. In the sample, this abstraction is provided by the file HELLOINT.C, which is shown in Listing 6.1. Notice that:

- LoadHello() returns a single BOOL that answers what is most likely the caller's most pressing question, "Is the DLL loaded?" Notice that the question is not "Did you just load the DLL?" There's a subtle difference here, in that LoadHello() will check the DLL anchor variable HelloAnchor and return TRUE if it's not null. This gives the calling program an intelligent answer, even if it accidentally calls LoadHello() several times in succession. (As always, defensive programming includes looking for the most likely errors and eliminating all chance that someone can make them.)

  LoadHello() is where you can localize the code to handle older versions of your DLL. For example, you might have changed the names of some routines in your DLL when you updated it. By mapping the new names to the old routine anchors in LoadHello(), you shield the hosting program from this change. More important, you can use the anchors and the gateway routines to call a series of DLL routines in response to a single call from the main application, or do some other processing. The key point is that the interface module (HELLOINT.C) is not merely a level of indirection; it's another point of control where you can create another level of abstraction to your program's benefit.

- UnloadHello() checks the DLL anchor variable and only frees it if it's actually loaded, but it always resets all anchor variables to NULL, ensuring that they're in a known state.

- The GotHello() function provides a simple way to check on the presence of the DLL at any time during the application's execution. This function's result can be used conditionally to add or delete entries from program menus, modify processing, etc.

- All access to the DLLs' functions are provided through gateway functions (SayHello, GoBeep), which always check that the DLL is loaded. By keeping the function anchor variables (HelloAnchor and BeepAnchor) local to the IntHello compilation unit, the programmer is forced to use the gateways in the calling program, making this linkage method about as safe as possible.

- You should always ensure that a Win16 program unloads the DLL (it calls UnloadHello) before termination, to ensure that the DLL's usage count is decremented. Windows will clean up after a Win32 program that terminates and leaves a DLL loaded, although it's obviously bad practice to rely on the system to pick up your dirty laundry like this, except in extreme circumstances.

## Building the Samples: RUNHELLO and HELLO

**CD Location:** ZEN\CHAP06\HELLO

**Platform:** Win32 EXE (RUNHELLO) and Win32 DLL (HELLO)

**Build instructions:** Use the provided .MAK files with Visual C++ 2.2. Build HELLO first, then RUNHELLO.

## Listing 6.1   HELLOINT.C

```c
/* Copyright Lou Grinzo 1995
   Zen of WIndows 95 Programming */

#include <windows.h>
#include "helloint.h"

typedef int  (*pfnHello)(LPCSTR lpszText, LPCSTR lpszTitle, UINT fuStyle);
typedef void (*pfnBeep)(void);
typedef int  (*pfnVersion)(void);

// Anchors for the DLL-resident rtns.
static pfnHello   HelloAnchor = NULL;
static pfnBeep    BeepAnchor  = NULL;
static pfnVersion VersionAnchor  = NULL;

// Anchor for the DLL itself
static HINSTANCE hHello = NULL;

// Load the DLL and establish links to the needed rtns.
BOOL LoadHello(void)
  {
  if(hHello != NULL)
    return FALSE;

  if((hHello = LoadLibrary("hello.dll")) != NULL)
      {
          if (((HelloAnchor = (pfnHello) GetProcAddress(hHello,"SayHello"))
                  == NULL) ||
```

```
                   ((BeepAnchor  = (pfnBeep)  GetProcAddress(hHello,"GoBeep"))
                       == NULL) ||
                   ((VersionAnchor  =
                 (pfnVersion) GetProcAddress(hHello,"Version")) == NULL))
          {
               UnloadHello();
           return FALSE;
          }


         }
      else
      {
       UnloadHello();
        return FALSE;
      }

    return TRUE;
  }

// Unload the DLL and set all anchors accordingly.
void UnloadHello(void)
  {
    if(GotHello())
        FreeLibrary(hHello);

      hHello = NULL;
      HelloAnchor = NULL;
      BeepAnchor = NULL;
      VersionAnchor = NULL;
  }

// Is the DLL and its required fns loaded?
BOOL GotHello(void)
  {
    return (HelloAnchor != NULL);
  }

// Gateway for our MessageBox impostor
int SayHello(LPCSTR lpszText, LPCSTR lpszTitle, UINT fuStyle)
  {
    if(GotHello())
        {
        HelloAnchor(lpszText,lpszTitle,fuStyle);
         return 1;
         }
      else
        return 0;
  }

// Gateway for our MessageBeep impostor
void GoBeep(void)
  {
    if(GotHello())
      BeepAnchor();
  }

// Gateway for version retriever
int HelloVersion(void)
  {
    if(GotHello())
```

```
    return VersionAnchor();
  else
    return -1;
}
```

None of what I've presented in this example is rocket science, as the saying goes, and I can imagine some readers saying, "Big deal. Nothing new here." And that's precisely my point. The Intelligent DLL Protocol takes little effort to implement, and it doesn't require an operating system upgrade, new development tools, or (horrors!) the use of additional, redistributable DLLs. Yet it can make a significant difference in both the usability and the usefulness of your Windows programs, especially for new Windows users.

## Managing Your DLLs

If you run multiple versions of Windows on the same computer, something many of us are and will be doing, you can simplify your life somewhat by exploiting the fact that the directories in your PATH environment variable are always part of the DLL search order. In effect, you can mimic the LIBPATH environment variable in OS/2, which specifies a DLL search path.

First, add a new directory to your system, C:\DLLS, and move as many DLLs from your Windows and Windows system directories into it as you can. My C:\DLLS directory contains numerous DLLs from various applications, plus commonly shared DLLs, such as BWCC.DLL and three versions of the Visual Basic run time support. About the only thing I don't move are the DLLs that are part of Windows itself.

Next, make sure that your DLLs directory is in the PATH environment variable for all versions of Windows on your system.

This isn't a complete solution for cross-platform nirvana, since you'll still have to worry about .INI files and registry entries, and you'll have to be diligent about moving DLLs to your dedicated directory as you install new programs; however, this approach can reduce the hassle of running multiple versions of Windows.

## Standards Are for Wimps

As I mentioned in this chapter, when you install your program, you're supposed to increment the SharedDLLs registry entry for any global DLLs that it uses. This seems like a wholly trivial matter, until you find out that there seems to be some confusion as to what datatype these counter entries should be.

I discovered this when I installed the shipping version of Symantec's Norton Navigator, and then found that it set up its SharedDLLs entries as strings, an odd choice, I thought, for a counter. I also noticed that the entries Windows

95 creates for some of its shared files were in a binary numeric format. See Figure 6.3 for a screen shot that shows this rather interesting mixture.

I asked Microsoft about this, and was told by someone in their Windows Development Support group that I should create new entries as REG_DWORDs (as opposed to REG_BINARYs). He also said that when I need to increment a counter I should be prepared to convert it from and to a string value.

The bottom line? On the very day that Windows 95 shipped (August 24, 1995), we already have new, senseless installation hassles to worry about. And we all know what will happen: As soon as enough people are running Norton Navigator or other programs that do unusual or creative things with these counters, installation programs that expect a particular datatype will either fail to increment them, or replace the old value with a new entry, with a count of 1, thereby losing whatever information content and utility the old value had. As a result, these counters will very quickly be seen to be useless, and developers will ignore them. But as we'll see shortly, that wouldn't be such a bad thing, after all. (See Chapter 14 for more on reading registry values and getting surprised by their data types.)

Based on the response I got from someone at Microsoft on this issue, it wasn't even clear to him what the right datatype should be. I checked all the standard references available to me when I was writing this chapter, and I couldn't find anything that specified a datatype (although I'm fairly sure that string shouldn't be our first choice).

In looking for an answer to my datatype question, I found the following in the Win32 SDK, in a topic titled "Adding Entries to the Registry" (search on the text "shareddlls"), which answered another question I had, namely what are these counters for, anyway:

> Your installation program should keep track of shared DLLs. When installing an application that uses shared DLLs, it should increment the usage counter for the DLL in the registry. When removing an application, it should decrement the usage counter. If the result is zero, the user should be given the option of deleting the DLL. The user should be warned that other applications may actually need the DLL and will not work if it is missing.

In other words, Microsoft is telling us that our applications are supposed to police the shared DLLs in the Windows System directory, and that our de-installation programs are responsible for giving the user the choice of deleting the files when the count reaches zero. The mind reels.

Once a few million people are using Windows 95, how often do you think programs will use shared DLLs that have wildly low usage count entries in the registry? Hint: Compile a few programs that use MFC in a shared DLL and see if the count changes automatically. Now generalize from this example. What do you think will happen if some company that is creating their very first Windows product naively follows the letter of the law on this point, as I quoted it above, and gives users the option to delete MFC30.DLL at uninstall time? (After all, their program used MFC30.DLL, they're uninstalling their program, so they decremented the count, and it's now zero. They're supposed to give the user the option of deleting the file, right? And if the user says it's OK, away it goes.) Does any of this sound even remotely like a half-baked design, or a disaster just waiting to happen? It sure sounds that way to me, especially in light of the fact that MFC30.DLL starts off with a SharedDLLs count of only one, putting it right on the ragged edge, merely one installation program error away from peril.

It's almost enough to make me trade in my office of PCs for a herd of Macs, or almost as drastic, move to northern Greenland with Liz, even before the calendar changes to the year 2000 and every COBOL program in the known universe loses its mind. But that's an issue for another time and place.

# Chapter 7

# *Minimized Windows Programs, a World in an Icon*

# Minimized Windows Programs, a World in an Icon

> To see a World in a Grain of Sand,
> And Heaven in a Wild Flower,
> Hold Infinity in the palm of your hand,
> And Eternity in an hour.
>
> William Blake

Peruse programming tools and books, and you would hardly think that Windows programs can be minimized, or that there might be a valid, useful reason to do so. Similarly, many Windows users think that minimizing a program is merely a handy way to push it aside so they can use another program, as a de facto way of juggling the Windows z-order.

I find this very puzzling, since I think minimized programs are quite flexible and useful. A minimized program teamed with Windows' native drag-and-drop functionality creates a powerful combination that I think of as the Windows analog of DOS filter programs. (In case you're not familiar with the genre, a filter program is typically a simple-to-use command-line program that uses the redirection capabilities of the operating system to read input from a file or the keyboard, and then send its output to another file or to the screen. Filters have been around for a long time, and are ideal for things like translating all linefeed characters to carriage return/linefeed pairs, folding text to uppercase, translating all occurrences in legal documents of the name of your ex-spouse to that of your new significant other, and so on. Any task that can be accomplished on a file via single-pass processing is an excellent candidate for a filter. Minimized programs aren't that limited in the types of jobs they can do, but thanks to their utility orientation, they're philosophically similar.)

179

As you'll see, minimized programs are yet another of those interesting cul de sacs in Windows that are worth exploring and exploiting. Each one really is a world in an icon.

# Flavors of Minimized Programs

Much to the surprise of many users, numerous applications shipping today can accept dragged-and-dropped files when minimized. For example, start Microsoft Word, minimize it, and then drag a Word document from Explorer (or File Manager in Windows 3.1) and drop it on the Word icon. (Under Windows 95 this requires you to perform the "hovering mouse maneuver," which I'll get into later.) Word will load the file and restore itself so you can work with the just-loaded document. Note that under Windows 95, if you drop a dragged file onto the document area of Word for Windows, the dropped file is embedded in the document that was already loaded into Word. Under Windows 3.1, you could simply drop the file on Word to load it; now you have to be careful to drop it on Word's caption bar.

Some programs are more subtle than this—too subtle, in my opinion. They'll accept and load the dropped document, but won't restore themselves or otherwise indicate that they did anything in response to the dropped files. This is terrible form. The program should at least give the user a configuration option that acknowledges that it accepted the dropped files.

I call programs that are normally used "open" but that accept dropped files when minimized, Type I programs. It's very easy to create a Type I minimized program— merely create a program that will accept dropped files on its main window, which you do by calling the DragAcceptFiles() API with a parameter of TRUE, and when it's minimized, it will still accept them. This functionality makes such programs more useful, but they're not the focus of this chapter.

Type II minimized programs are the ones near and dear to my heart, the ones that accept dropped files and live their entire life as an icon. Stickies! is one such program, even though it displays many different diagnostic and user input dialog boxes, and it also creates numerous child windows (all those sticky notes).

## *The Mechanics of Minimized Programs...*

How does a program wind up minimized, anyway? This is not a trick question, but a leading one. At the API level, your program is merrily running along, fielding a stream of messages from Windows and the world in general, when it receives a WM_SYSCOMMAND message with a wParam of SC_MINIMIZE. Unless your program "swallows" this message (for example, it looks for the message and intentionally ignores it without passing it on to Windows for processing), the default action causes your program to be turned into an icon on the user's task bar (or on the desktop, before Windows 95). Your program is still active; it's merely showing the world a different face. (See the sidebar "Stupid MFC Tricks" for information on checking for system command codes in your OnSysCommand() method in your MFC programs.)

The user normally sees two ways to minimize a program: the "Minimize" item on the program's system menu, and the minimize button in the program's upper-right corner (assuming your program has both of these standard interface features). But these are really just different front ends for the same interface, the delivery to your program of an SC_MINIMIZE system command. This is an important distinction. If for some reason you don't want your program to be ever minimized (if, for example, you're a maximalist at heart), then it's *not* enough simply to remove your program's minimize button and the minimize command from its system menu.

If any part of your program assumes or depends on the fact that it is never minimized, then you must take pains to swallow SC_MINIMIZE system commands and make sure that your program doesn't start minimized (more on this below). And for the sake of usability, please don't merely neuter the SC_MINIMIZE command and leave the minimize button and system menu item present. This will surely mislead your users—the interface clearly says this functionality is present, but the program won't respond as they expect. There's a special place in Programmer Hell for people who do such things, and it's deep in the heart of the COBOL Country.

When Windows starts your program, it provides the command line plus another parameter that indicates how your program should start: minimized, maximized, or normal. Windows programs typically use this parameter as provided, but they don't have to. For a Type II minimized program, this is the first difference from other programs: Overriding this parameter and always using a value of SW_SHOWMINIMIZE. Depending on which framework, if any, you're using, this code, which is just a one-liner, is placed just before your program calls Windows to initialize your main application. In MFC, you set the m_nCmdShow member of your application's object to SW_SHOWMINIMIZE in its InitApplication() method just before starting the window or dialog that serves as your application's main interface.

As for becoming unminimized, the picture is a bit more complicated. A minimized program can be restored (returned to its last non-minimized, non-maximized size and position) or maximized (zoomed to fill the user's screen). When the user clicks on your program's icon on the Windows 95 task bar (or double clicks on its icon in Windows 3.1), Windows sends your program a WM_SYSCOMMAND message with a wParam of SC_RESTORE. If the user picks "Restore" or "Maximize" from the system menu, then your program receives either SC_RESTORE or SC_MAXIMIZE in the wParam of the WM_SYSCOMMAND message. The user can also send your program an SC_MAXIMIZE system command by double clicking on your program's caption bar.

So, if you want your program to remain minimized, the obvious answer is to intercept those SC_RESTORE and SC_MAXIMIZE commands and not let Windows process them, right? That would work, but there's another technique you should be aware of. After your program gets these messages but before your program is actually restored or maximized, Windows sends another message, WM_QUERYOPEN. This message is Windows' way of asking for permission to open your program. If your program replies TRUE in response to this message, then the operation continues; FALSE is your program's way of saying "thanks, but no thanks." To keep your program minimized, all you have to do is return FALSE from a WM_QUERYOPEN message. It appears that you don't even have to worry about SC_MAXIMIZE and SC_RESTORE, but this is one time when appearances are deceiving, as we'll see shortly. Listings 7.1 and 7.2 show the changes to a standard MFC program, needed to make it a Type II minimized program.

## Listing 7.1   DROP1.CPP

```cpp
// DROP1.cpp : Defines the class behaviors for the application.
//

#include "stdafx.h"
#include "DROP1.h"

#include "mainfrm.h"
#include "DROP1doc.h"
#include "DROP1vw.h"

#ifdef _DEBUG
#undef THIS_FILE
static char BASED_CODE THIS_FILE[] = __FILE__;
#endif

/////////////////////////////////////////////////////////////////////////
// CDROP1App

BEGIN_MESSAGE_MAP(CDROP1App, CWinApp)
    //{{AFX_MSG_MAP(CDROP1App)
    ON_COMMAND(ID_APP_ABOUT, OnAppAbout)
        // NOTE - the ClassWizard will add and remove mapping macros here.
        //   DO NOT EDIT what you see in these blocks of generated code!
    //}}AFX_MSG_MAP
    // Standard file based document commands
    ON_COMMAND(ID_FILE_NEW, CWinApp::OnFileNew)
    ON_COMMAND(ID_FILE_OPEN, CWinApp::OnFileOpen)
END_MESSAGE_MAP()

/////////////////////////////////////////////////////////////////////////
// CDROP1App construction

CDROP1App::CDROP1App()
{
```

```
        // TODO: add construction code here,
        // Place all significant initialization in InitInstance
}

/////////////////////////////////////////////////////////////////////////
// The one and only CDROP1App object

CDROP1App theApp;

/////////////////////////////////////////////////////////////////////////
// CDROP1App initialization

BOOL CDROP1App::InitInstance()
{
        // Make sure we always start minimized
    m_nCmdShow = SW_MINIMIZE;

        // Standard initialization
        // If you are not using these features and wish to reduce the size
        // of your final executable, you should remove from the following
        // the specific initialization routines you do not need.

        LoadStdProfileSettings(); // Load standard INI file options (including MRU)

        // Register the application's document templates. Document templates
        // serve as the connection between documents, frame windows, and views.

        CSingleDocTemplate* pDocTemplate;
        pDocTemplate = new CSingleDocTemplate(
                IDR_MAINFRAME,
                RUNTIME_CLASS(CDROP1Doc),
                RUNTIME_CLASS(CMainFrame),    // main SDI frame window
                RUNTIME_CLASS(CDROP1View));
        AddDocTemplate(pDocTemplate);

        // create a new (empty) document
        OnFileNew();

        if (m_lpCmdLine[0] != '\0')
        {
                // TODO: add command line processing here
        }

        return TRUE;
}

/////////////////////////////////////////////////////////////////////////
// CAboutDlg dialog used for App About

class CAboutDlg : public CDialog
{
public:
        CAboutDlg();

// Dialog Data
        //{{AFX_DATA(CAboutDlg)
        enum { IDD = IDD_ABOUTBOX };
        //}}AFX_DATA

// Implementation
protected:
```

```
        virtual void DoDataExchange(CDataExchange* pDX);  // DDX/DDV support
        //{{AFX_MSG(CAboutDlg)
              // No message handlers
        //}}AFX_MSG
        DECLARE_MESSAGE_MAP()
};

CAboutDlg::CAboutDlg() : CDialog(CAboutDlg::IDD)
{
        //{{AFX_DATA_INIT(CAboutDlg)
        //}}AFX_DATA_INIT
}

void CAboutDlg::DoDataExchange(CDataExchange* pDX)
{
        CDialog::DoDataExchange(pDX);
        //{{AFX_DATA_MAP(CAboutDlg)
        //}}AFX_DATA_MAP
}

BEGIN_MESSAGE_MAP(CAboutDlg, CDialog)
        //{{AFX_MSG_MAP(CAboutDlg)
              // No message handlers
        //}}AFX_MSG_MAP
END_MESSAGE_MAP()

// App command to run the dialog
void CDROP1App::OnAppAbout()
{
        CAboutDlg aboutDlg;
        aboutDlg.DoModal();
}


/////////////////////////////////////////////////////////////////////////
// CDROP1App commands
```

## Listing 7.2   MAINFRM.CPP

```
// mainfrm.cpp : implementation of the CMainFrame class
//

#include "stdafx.h"
#include "DROP1.h"

#include "mainfrm.h"

#ifdef _DEBUG
#undef THIS_FILE
static char BASED_CODE THIS_FILE[] = __FILE__;
#endif


/////////////////////////////////////////////////////////////////////////
// CMainFrame

IMPLEMENT_DYNCREATE(CMainFrame, CFrameWnd)

BEGIN_MESSAGE_MAP(CMainFrame, CFrameWnd)
        //{{AFX_MSG_MAP(CMainFrame)
        ON_WM_CREATE()
        ON_WM_DROPFILES()
```

```
        ON_WM_QUERYOPEN()
        ON_WM_SYSCOMMAND()
        //}}AFX_MSG_MAP
END_MESSAGE_MAP()

///////////////////////////////////////////////////////////////////////
// CMainFrame construction/destruction

CMainFrame::CMainFrame()
{
        // TODO: add member initialization code here

}

CMainFrame::~CMainFrame()
{
}

///////////////////////////////////////////////////////////////////////
// CMainFrame diagnostics

#ifdef _DEBUG
void CMainFrame::AssertValid() const
{
        CFrameWnd::AssertValid();
}

void CMainFrame::Dump(CDumpContext& dc) const
{
        CFrameWnd::Dump(dc);
}

#endif //_DEBUG

///////////////////////////////////////////////////////////////////////
// CMainFrame message handlers

int CMainFrame::OnCreate(LPCREATESTRUCT lpCreateStruct)
{
        if (CFrameWnd::OnCreate(lpCreateStruct) == -1)
                return -1;

        // Grab a handle to our system menu and delete "Restore" and "Maximize"
        CMenu *sysmenu = GetSystemMenu(FALSE);
        sysmenu->DeleteMenu(SC_RESTORE,MF_BYCOMMAND);
        sysmenu->DeleteMenu(SC_MAXIMIZE,MF_BYCOMMAND);

        // Tell Windows that we're open for DND business
        DragAcceptFiles(TRUE);

        return 0;
}

void CMainFrame::OnDropFiles(HDROP hDropInfo)
{
  char file_buffer[MAX_PATH];
        UINT num_files, i;

  // Get the number of dropped files from Windows
        num_files = DragQueryFile(hDropInfo,0xffffffff,
        file_buffer,sizeof(file_buffer));
```

```
// Now retrieve names and process each one
    for(i = 0; i < num_files; i++)
      {
      DragQueryFile(hDropInfo,i,file_buffer,sizeof(file_buffer));
          ProcessDroppedFile(file_buffer);
      }

  // Tell Windows we're done with the DND operation
  DragFinish(hDropInfo);
}

BOOL CMainFrame::OnQueryOpen()
{
    // We always refuse to run as anything but a minimized program
    return FALSE;
}

// Do something visible with a filename. Note the advanced AI algorithm.
void CMainFrame::ProcessDroppedFile(char * fn)
{
MessageBox(fn,"Dropped file:",MB_OK);
}

void CMainFrame::OnSysCommand(UINT nID, LPARAM lParam)
{
  UINT the_real_nID = nID & 0xFFF0;

  // Swallow these system commands, even though we respond FALSE to a
  // WM_QUERYOPEN message.
  if((the_real_nID == SC_RESTORE) || (the_real_nID == SC_MAXIMIZE))
   return;

    CFrameWnd::OnSysCommand(nID, lParam);
}
```

Let's talk about usability for a second. I mentioned earlier that if you delete the minimize or maximize buttons from your program, you should delete the corresponding options from the system menu, as well. Your program should always present a unified, coherent face to the user. When neutering SC_RESTORE and SC_MAXIMIZE, you should also delete those options from the system menu. But this begs the question: Why bother with all that message swallowing hugger-mugger when you can simply delete the menu items and buttons? Isn't that enough? No, it isn't. This is one of those pathological cases that you have to worry about in Windows, albeit one of the less virulent ones.

Even if you change the interface of your program so that the user can't directly trigger these messages, all the user has to do is click on your program's icon on the task bar, and the SC_RESTORE command is sent anyway. Even less obvious, there's also the chance that another program will get your program's window handle from Windows and then post a WM_SYSCOMMAND to it with one of the forbidden wParam values. And don't kid yourself, there are indeed such programs floating around, including some shareware goodies that let you move, minimize, restore, and otherwise manipulate other programs—and they're popular. The point is that your program, which was never supposed to be anything but an icon and has no provisions for running as a normal, open window, can end up doing just that, which means it will probably look pretty silly in the process.

## ...and How Windows 95 Changed the Rules

Minimized programs, whether Type I, II, or MCMLVII, should have no trouble in moving from Windows 3.1 to Windows 95, right? Surprise, they do. Type II programs, the ones that rely on drag and drop to receive the names of files to process, are hit the hardest. The reason is simple but perplexing: Before Windows 95, you could drop files onto a minimized program as easily as you could an open window. But beginning with Windows 95, you have to perform what I call the "hovering mouse maneuver." If you grab some files in Explorer, drag them to the task bar, and immediately drop them on the waiting program icon, you get the dialog box in Figure 7.1 telling you that you can't do that. You're supposed to drag the files to the task bar, hold the mouse cursor perfectly still over the minimized program's button for a moment, and wait for Windows to restore the program so you can move the mouse back up the screen to the program's now-open window and then drop the files on it.

The bottom line is that since Type II minimized programs refuse to be restored, they're precluded from accepting dropped files under Windows 95, which means you have to change your code.

*The first time I saw this new mode of drag and drop operation in Windows 95, I thought it was a bad joke. (In fact, it made me do my Joe Pesci impersonation based on his My Cousin Vinny role: "You was serious about dat???") I'm sure this will be a huge annoyance for people just learning to use a mouse, as well as the coordinationally challenged. I honestly can't figure out why Microsoft changed a very simple, useful interface into a dexterity test. If you have a theory, or better yet, an official explanation, I'd love to hear it.*

Another minor, but strange, issue has to do with z-ordering. As you probably know, the z-order tracks the stacking of windows in your Windows session; the window at the top of the z-order is the one that appears to be on top of the others and nearest to you, while your desktop's wallpaper is at the bottom of the z-order—

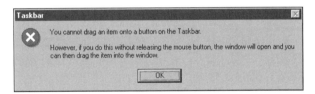

**Figure 7.1    The Windows 95 Taskbar is a no-dropping zone.**

the farthest away, since all other windows appear on top of it. In Windows 3.1, when you dragged and dropped files from File Manager onto a program whose window was partially covered by File Manager, the target program got the focus and automatically popped to the top of your z-order. This is a small but crucial detail from a usability standpoint, and one that Windows handled nicely. Unfortunately, the Windows 95 developers seem to have forgotten this detail, or they made a *very* strange design decision.

Drag files from the Explorer and drop them on a program that is partially obscured by the Explorer, and the operation proceeds properly, but the application remains beneath Explorer in the z-order. This is why the second example program in this chapter, DROP2, issues a SetForegroundWindow() API call as soon as it starts to process dropped files in its OnDropFiles method in the file DROP2DLG.CPP; without this call, the program and the dialog box it immediately displays would remain behind Explorer. This behavior can leave your program's users wondering why your program didn't accept the dropped files, when, in fact, it did. Worst of all, this afflicts Win32 programs, not just evil Win16 artifacts of a bygone era. (You know, the ones we'll all be running for decades because they still get the job done?) Caveat coder.

## Tiny Elvis Lives!

Windows 95 also introduced another change for minimized programs: They can no longer draw to their icons. In practice, this isn't much of a restriction, since very few programs do this anyway. Even some that appeared to do so, such as the popular public domain program Tiny Elvis, actually changed icons to perform simple animation, so they continue to work under Windows 95. This is another trick that Stickies! uses; Stickies! includes 16 icons that each portray a sticky note with a different background color. When you change the background color of a note, Stickies! does the following:

```
DestroyIcon(GetClassWord(hwnd,GCW_HICON));
SetClassWord(hwnd,GCW_HICON,LoadIcon(hInstance,<new_icon>));
```

Where <new_icon> is the resource identifier for the icon that matches the note's new color. This way, the Taskbar or desktop icon for each note matches the general look of the note.

And for those of you who might have led a deprived and shallow existence and not seen Tiny Elvis, it's on the CD in ZEN\CHAP07\T_ELVIS. When Tiny Elvis is run, it draws a miniature Elvis in an icon and then waits. Every so many seconds, the Micro-King springs to life, performs some typical gestures, and comments on some aspect of your desktop. The program works fine under Windows 95, but the small icons on the task bar buttons make it less of a show. Under Windows 3.1 it's a blast.

Tiny Elvis is a public domain program, written by Matthew T. Smith.

This SetForegroundWindow() trick turned out to be one of those frustrating Windows idiocies that we all know and detest. Before I discovered the magic incantation, I experimented with RedrawWindow(), SetFocus(), BringWindowToTop(), SetWindowPos(), and InvalidateRect() and UpdateWindow(). I did find that a pair of SetWindowPos() calls, one that sets the window to be "always on top" (using the parameter HWND_TOPMOST) immediately followed by a second one that undoes that setting (with HWND_NOTOPMOST), works. But that was too ugly for words. I was quite surprised to find that CWnd::BringWindowToTop() didn't work; its description in the Visual C++ online help reads:

> Brings CWnd to the top of a stack of overlapping windows. In addition, BringWindowToTop activates pop-up, top-level, and MDI child windows. The BringWindowToTop member function should be used to uncover any window that is partially or completely obscured by any overlapping windows.

> Calling this function is similar to calling the SetWindowPos function to change a window's position in the z order. The BringWindowToTop function does not change the window style to make it a top-level window of the desktop.

I'm sure there's a reason why BringWindowToTop() doesn't do what I wanted, but it sure isn't clear from this text, and once I discovered SetForegroundWindow(), I had a good solution so I stopped looking into the matter.

Since SetForegroundWindow() is a Win32 API and therefore isn't readily available to Win16 programs, and this Explorer oddity does affect those programs, you have to hold your nose and resort to the SetWindowPos() trick. Simply replace the SetForegroundWindow() call with:

```
::SetWindowPos(m_hWnd,SWP_TOPMOST,0,0,0,0,SWP_NOSIZE | SWP_NOMOVE);
::SetWindowPos(m_hWnd,SWP_NOTOPMOST,0,0,0,0,SWP_NOSIZE | SWP_NOMOVE);
```

and promise you won't tell anyone I told you to do this. If you find a better solution, please tell me about it; this loathsome hack is the best solution I could find.

An even stranger detail is that minimized programs don't always get a task bar icon under Windows 95. Create a standard AppWizard program that uses a dialog box for its main interface, and its task bar button shows the program's name, but not its icon. The day I was finalizing this chapter, I received my subscription copy of Visual C++ 2.2 from Microsoft, and it hadn't even completely implemented support for the WM_GETICON and WM_SETICON messages, which are new for Windows 95 and are used to specify the icons for a program's task bar button and caption bar. To see this effect in non-action, run the DROP2 sample program from this chapter under Windows NT 3.51; it has the standard MFC icon when minimized, just as you would expect. But run it under Windows 95 and its task bar button shows just the program's name. Under Windows 95, for some reason unknown to me, a program only gets an icon on its task bar button if its main window or dialog has both the WS_CAPTION and WS_SYSMENU styles. This is yet another of those odd little compatibility quirks in Windows 95 that we'll all be fixing in upcoming releases of our programs. See Part III of this book, *Crossing the Great Divides*, for many more such items.

Let me walk you through the process of finding a solution, since I think it nicely illustrates some of the design issues that we all have to deal with, particularly with public software. Let's assume that you have a Type II minimized program, and you want to make the minimum changes necessary for it to continue to work in a reasonable fashion with Windows 95. The ultimate version of my solution is included as the sample program DROP2. The native version that exhibits the new Windows 95 behavior is included as DROP1.

As you've probably guessed, the core gimmick in the solution is detecting the SC_RESTORE command and doing something in response to it, since that's the message your program gets from Windows 95 when the user does the hovering mouse maneuver. The easiest and most obvious thing we can do is have the program display a dialog box that will accept the dropped file names, store them in memory, and allow the main program to process them. In an MFC program, the code in your main window's OnSysCommand() method would look something like this:

```
if(nID == SC_RESTORE)
{
if (DoDropDlg())              // Dlg to retrieve dropped files
   ProcessDroppedFiles();     // Process
}
```

The user won't be able to tell that the main program is doing the real work and the dialog is merely a messenger, which is just as well. All the user will know is that after performing the hovering mouse maneuver, your program intelligently displays a user-friendly dialog (with a big bull's eye bitmap or something equally inviting and obvious) that will accept the dropped files, and your program then responds accordingly.

Sounds like a simple, workable solution, right? Not really. This will work as described, but it also has an unwanted and potentially very messy side effect. When the user clicks on your program's icon on the task bar, in an attempt to restore your program, it will display the drop target dialog, which is not what the user expected. Remember, your program is detecting a physical event, the SC_RESTORE command, and interpreting it as a logical event, an attempt by the user to drop files on your program for processing. This is a classic identification problem, and as far as I know, there's no reliable way to tell whether Windows 95 is trying to restore your program in response to a single mouse click or the hovering mouse maneuver. Remember my discussion early in the book about the difference between physical and logical events, and how programming consists of transforming the former into the latter? Here's a prime example.

Sure, you can put some text on the dialog box telling the user that the program doesn't normally open, and that the dialog is only intended as a drop target. That would explain why the user is seeing that dialog after clicking on your program's icon. But it's also likely to trigger a "stupid program!" reaction in many users, something you should avoid like the plague.

## When Windows 95 Tries To Be Too Helpful

If you want to customize the look of your Windows 95 program as described in this chapter, you can be in for some surprises. For example, suppose you tell Windows 95 that your program shouldn't have a minimize button in its upper-right hand corner. You'd expect it not to have one, right? After all, that's how things work under Windows 3.1. Think again. If you delete just the minimize button (by turning off the WS_MINIMIZEBOX bit in the window's style flags), then the button is still there, but grayed out (disabled), as is the "Minimize" option on the window's system menu, leaving the user to wonder when, if ever, this part of the interface is active.

Similarly, disable the maximize button and it will also still be there, in grayed form. Delete both the minimize and the maximize buttons and they'll both finally disappear, but the "Minimize" and "Maximize" options on the system menu are merely grayed, leaving it up to you to delete them. (Given that menu manipulations can be done in terms of the relative position of items, this is really a blessing in disguise. Imagine what would happen if your code that changed your system menu suddenly broke because you deleted the minimize and maximize buttons. Still, the way it works can be a surprise.)

I haven't discussed this issue with anyone at Microsoft, but it appears to be a clear case of a philosophical issue. Microsoft took extraordinary pains to cater to the new computer user in Windows 95, often at the expense of the more experienced user. In this case, I suspect they wanted to make sure the maximize and minimize buttons were always in the same place on a window's frame, even at the expense of having a button there that could never be enabled. I think that this is much more confusing for all users, particularly new ones, since it implies that under some circumstances the grayed button will be active, when in fact, it won't. I think it makes for better usability to allow the buttons to change places (as when a minimize button is desired, but not a maximize button, so the minimize button is placed where the maximize button normally would be), and only show those buttons that are active.

Wherever you stand on this issue, it's another example of how Windows 95 is full of little surprises, and no amount of reading Microsoft's documentation or third-party books or articles will prepare you for them all. The best you can do is maintain a user-centric viewpoint and adapt to the surprises as they appear.

Another complication, as if this first one weren't enough, is that you're now stuck with a modal dialog box on the user's desktop. You don't want a modal dialog monopolizing your program's input until the user remembers to shut it down, because some users will forget about it when the dialog gets covered by other windows, and next thing you know you'll hear that your program "freezes" and won't respond when the user clicks on its icon. Recall my discussion in Chapter 1 of new Windows users and how the first hurdle many struggle to get over is the fact that the Windows desktop is really three dimensional. Even though the Windows 95 taskbar gives new users considerable help in climbing this learning curve, people still lose windows. Best not to give them a chance.

You could use a modeless dialog, of course, but that still is more hassle than it should be, since you have to make sure you don't accidentally run multiple copies, leak memory, or experience any other unforseen problem.

Perhaps there's an even simpler solution, one that is closer to how Windows "wants" to work. In fact, there is. Since your program is a Type II minimized program, that means you have a valuable, unused resource that you can dedicate to solving this problem: your program's main interface. You can easily have your program open in response to a SC_RESTORE command and present a main interface that is merely a dialog that acts as your drop target. That way, if the user forgets that your program is already open, clicking on its task bar icon will simply move the focus to your program and short circuit the confusion. The user can then access the system menu of your program.

In other words, the strategy is to concede the issue and convert your application from a Type II minimized program to what I call a Type III, one that does have a main window (or dialog) interface, but an interface that is dedicated to the chore of receiving dropped files. Some programmers will rebel against this solution, since they don't like to be forced into changing the basic character of a program (and, therefore, the documentation and technical support). I sympathize with that viewpoint, especially since I don't see any value to the user in requiring the silly hovering mouse maneuver, which is what started us down this road in the first place. But making such compromises is often the optimal approach for both you and your users, not to mention your programs.

See Listing 7.3 for the modifications to convert an MFC program that uses a dialog as its main interface into a Type III minimized program.

## Listing 7.3   DROP2DLG.CPP

```
// DROP2dlg.cpp : implementation file
//

#include "stdafx.h"
#include "DROP2.h"
#include "DROP2dlg.h"
```

```
#ifdef _DEBUG
#undef THIS_FILE
static char BASED_CODE THIS_FILE[] = __FILE__;
#endif

#define id_timer 0

/////////////////////////////////////////////////////////////////////////
// CDROP2Dlg dialog

CDROP2Dlg::CDROP2Dlg(CWnd* pParent /*=NULL*/)
      : CDialog(CDROP2Dlg::IDD, pParent)
{
      //{{AFX_DATA_INIT(CDROP2Dlg)
            // NOTE: the ClassWizard will add member initialization here
      //}}AFX_DATA_INIT
      // Note that LoadIcon does not require a subsequent DestroyIcon in Win32
      m_hIcon = AfxGetApp()->LoadIcon(IDR_MAINFRAME);
}

void CDROP2Dlg::DoDataExchange(CDataExchange* pDX)
{
      CDialog::DoDataExchange(pDX);
      //{{AFX_DATA_MAP(CDROP2Dlg)
            // NOTE: the ClassWizard will add DDX and DDV calls here
      //}}AFX_DATA_MAP
}

BEGIN_MESSAGE_MAP(CDROP2Dlg, CDialog)
      //{{AFX_MSG_MAP(CDROP2Dlg)
      ON_WM_PAINT()
      ON_WM_QUERYDRAGICON()
      ON_WM_TIMER()
      ON_WM_DROPFILES()
      //}}AFX_MSG_MAP
END_MESSAGE_MAP()

/////////////////////////////////////////////////////////////////////////
// CDROP2Dlg message handlers

BOOL CDROP2Dlg::OnInitDialog()
{
      CDialog::OnInitDialog();
      CenterWindow();

      SetTimer(id_timer,1500,NULL);

      DragAcceptFiles(TRUE);

      return TRUE; // return TRUE unless you set the focus to a control
}

// If you add a minimize button to your dialog, you will need the code below
// to draw the icon. For MFC applications using the document/view model,
// this is automatically done for you by the framework.

void CDROP2Dlg::OnPaint()
{
      if (IsIconic())
      {
            CPaintDC dc(this); // device context for painting
```

```
                    SendMessage(WM_ICONERASEBKGND, (WPARAM) dc.GetSafeHdc(), 0);

                    // Center icon in client rectangle
                    int cxIcon = GetSystemMetrics(SM_CXICON);
                    int cyIcon = GetSystemMetrics(SM_CYICON);
                    CRect rect;
                    GetClientRect(&rect);
                    int x = (rect.Width() - cxIcon + 1) / 2;
                    int y = (rect.Height() - cyIcon + 1) / 2;

                    // Draw the icon
                    dc.DrawIcon(x, y, m_hIcon);
            }
            else
            {
                    CDialog::OnPaint();
            }
    }


    // The system calls this to obtain the cursor to display while the user drags
    // the minimized window.
    HCURSOR CDROP2Dlg::OnQueryDragIcon()
    {
            return (HCURSOR) m_hIcon;
    }


    void CDROP2Dlg::OnTimer(UINT nIDEvent)
    {
      KillTimer(id_timer);

            PostMessage(WM_SYSCOMMAND,SC_MINIMIZE,0);

            CDialog::OnTimer(nIDEvent);
    }


    void CDROP2Dlg::OnDropFiles(HDROP hDropInfo)
    {
      char file_buffer[MAX_PATH];
            UINT num_files, i;

      // See chapter 7 for the amazing story behind the following line....
      SetForegroundWindow();

      // Get the number of dropped files from Windows
            num_files =
    DragQueryFile(hDropInfo,0xffffffff,file_buffer,sizeof(file_buffer));

      // Now retrieve names and process each one file
            for(i = 0; i < num_files; i++)
              {
               DragQueryFile(hDropInfo,i,file_buffer,sizeof(file_buffer));
                    ProcessDroppedFile(file_buffer);
              }

      // Tell Windows we're done with the DND operation
      DragFinish(hDropInfo);

      // Move our drop target dlg out of the way
            PostMessage(WM_SYSCOMMAND,SC_MINIMIZE,0);
    }
```

```
// Do something visible with a filename. Note the advanced AI algorithm.
void CDROP2Dlg::ProcessDroppedFile(char * fn)
{
 MessageBox(fn,"Dropped file:",MB_OK);
}
```

Converting an existing application from a Type II to a Type III minimized program is relatively simple:

1. Make your program ignore the ShowWindow() constant it receives at startup (the application member m_nCmdShow in MFC). Your program overrides this value with SW_SHOWMINIMIZED to start minimized, as before.

2. Allow it to return TRUE to WM_QUERYOPEN, which is the default Windows behavior. This tells Windows that your program is ready, willing, and able to be de-iconized.

3. Make sure it does not swallow SC_RESTORE commands.

4. Make it swallow SC_MAXIMIZE commands. Remember, since you're now responding true to WM_QUERYOPEN, your program has to handle this case, or it will display a full-screen version of its dialog interface, which looks *really* stupid.

5. Change your program to use a dialog as its main interface, define the dialog, and write whatever handling is necessary to display it properly, such as painting the bull's eye bitmap in response to a paint request from Windows. As part of this support, your program has the option to reminimize itself after it finishes processing dropped files.

Step 5 above requires a little explanation. If you want your program to start up minimized, using a dialog for your main interface can be tricky, depending on which compiler and framework you're using. For example, some old code I'd written with Borland Pascal for Windows converted very easily to a Type III program, thanks to the fact that OWL has a special class for dialogs that are main windows (TDlgWindow), and this class obeys the CmdShow setting (equivalent to MFC's m_nCmdShow) and will start minimized. MFC is more stubborn, though. In that framework, a dialog is just another dialog, and it ignores m_nCmdShow when it's used as the program's main interface. This forces you to choose between mimicking a dialog with a window, or starting with the main interface open. One trick I like to employ in such situations is sending yourself a message based on a timer. In DROP2, for example, I use a dialog for the main interface, but it sets a timer and then posts an SC_MINIMIZE system command to itself after a second or so. This creates a basic splash screen effect to show your user that the program is indeed running, which can be a nice addition if you design the dialog properly.

Notice that when you convert your Type II program to a Type III, the code that processes dropped files does not change. If you separated your user interface and core processing code (guideline 12), your work is confined to interface changes.

Depending on how fancy you want to get, you can make a program adapt its behavior to the flavor of Windows it's running under. It can check the Windows version, and if it sees a version that doesn't have the Windows 95 user interface (there's that physical-to-logical mapping stuff again), it can work like a classic Type II minimized program, and your users who are still running Windows 3.1 won't see anything different in this regard from the previous version of your program. But users running Windows 95 (or Windows NT 4.0, when it's available) will now see a functional and more accommodating Type III minimized program.

Once you've converted your program to Type III, all you have to do is make your program return TRUE in response to a WM_QUERYOPEN message for the Windows 95 interface and process SC_MAXIMIZE and SC_RESTORE system commands. For a version of Windows without the Windows 95 user interface, you return FALSE for WM_QUERYOPEN and swallow the SC_MAXIMIZE and SC_RESTORE system commands. The fact that the additional support and the dialog box or window as the main interface are dormant inside your program when it runs under Windows 3.1 is of no concern to your user, and it adds negligible overhead to your program. (Again, think in terms of cost–to–benefit ratios. Here's a moderate gain for barely measurable pain.) Keep in mind that version checking under various flavors of Windows has become its own can of worms. See Part III, *Crossing the Great Divides*, particularly Chapter 12, for more detail.

# DROP1 and DROP2

As mentioned above, the sample programs for this chapter, DROP1 and DROP2, are Type II and Type III programs, respectively, that simply display the names of dropped files.

## Building the Samples: DROP1 and DROP2

**CD Location:** ZEN\CHAP07\DROP1 and ZEN\CHAP07\DROP2

**Platform:** Win32

**Build instructions:** Use the provided .MAK files with Visual C++ 2.2, and compile normally.

Run DROP1 under Windows 95, and you'll see how utterly underwhelming and unimpressive—not to mention unusable—it is, as it does nothing but sit there like a task bar potato and refuse to open. It works as a classic, if still underwhelming Type II minimized program under Windows NT, though, and will at least accept dropped files. DROP2 works better and retains all the original functionality in a way that won't confuse users. It also uses the timer and post-drop self-minimizing tricks mentioned above, which make its operation just a bit slicker.

# Go Forth and Minimize

Minimized programs are a great example of something you should be itching to explore and exploit in Windows. Be creative. You can add system menu commands to open various configuration and option dialogs, or open such a dialog only after the user drops files. As long as you don't get non-standard enough to confuse your users, minimized programs can be a useful, if somewhat specialized, addition to your toolbox.

## Stupid MFC Tricks

In any product as large and as complex as Visual C++, there are bound to be some documentation errors, as well as a few design gaffes. It's to be expected. But the one that I find the most surprising is the combination of odd design and documentation of the OnSysCommand() method in MFC's CWnd class. The prototype of this method is:

```
afx_msg void OnSysCommand(UINT nID, LPARAM lParam);
```

The Visual C++ 2.2 online help describes the nID parameter by saying: "Specifies the type of system command requested. This parameter can be any one of the following values:", and then lists the SC_* constants with a brief description of each one, including SC_MINIMIZE, SC_PREVWINDOW, and SC_SCREENSAVE. Sounds great, right? Well, this isn't the whole story. If you click on the icon at the bottom of the help topic, the one next to the text "To jump to Books Online, and click the icon or press F2", then Visual C++ will show you a slightly more complete version of this help topic that adds the following to the nID description:

> In WM_SYSCOMMAND messages, the four low-order bits of the *nID* parameter are used internally by Windows. When an application tests the value of *nID*, it must combine the value 0xFFF0 with the nID value using the bitwise-AND operator to obtain the correct result.

So, we have to remember always to mask off those low-order bits. That's a pain in the neck, but it's not *too* bad. Think again. Say you've used the Visual C++ IDE to add a new command identifier to your program, and you've used that command with a custom entry on your program's system menu. You'll very likely wind up with a command value that's not a multiple of 16, and therefore will have significant bits in the four low-order positions. Then, masking off these bits will mean your program won't see these custom system commands. And you really do have to mask them off, despite what some people will tell you. In the sample program for Chapter 11, LOCKER, selecting the "Maximize" system menu entry sends the program a system command code of 0xF030. Double clicking on the program's caption bar, which also maximizes the program, sends a command code of 0xF032. Clearly the masking is needed, but should only be used for standard system commands.

How many mysterious bugs in public programs to you think this design is responsible for? My guess: More than a few. I don't know which is worse, the fact that MFC fails to "crack" these four bits out into their own parameter for a standard command, for example:

```
afx_msg void OnSysCommand(UINT nID, BYTE bMagicBits, LPARAM lParam);
```

documenting their significance only in the Books Online version of the help, thereby guaranteeing that many programmers will miss that detail and make the obvious mistake, or not mentioning at all how easily you can mask out your own command codes. My solution is to add the following line to the beginning of an OnSysCommand() method:

```
UINT the_real_nID = nID & 0xFFF0;
```

You'll see this one-liner throughout the sample programs for this book. If nothing else, the variable name should make it much harder to forget what's going on. I use the_real_nID when checking for standard system commands, and the original nID for my own commands and when handing off to the default processing.

Chapter

# 8

# *Tamper Proofing Your Programs*

# Tamper Proofing Your Programs

Chapter 8

*Trust me, there are evil doobies out there.*

Maria Vallone

Sadly, my good friend Maria is right. And not only do the evil doobies exist, but they're armed with resource and hex editors, with which they can (and will) tear your program asunder and cause all manner of mayhem for you and your users. Think I'm kidding? See Figure 8.1 for an example of what I did to the File Open common dialog box from Windows 3.1 in just a few minutes. Worst of all, this version of the dialog still works. If someone did something not quite so flamboyant to one of your programs, would your users necessarily know that it wasn't your handiwork?

## Welcome to Our Nightmare

Before I get into protecting your programs from such vandalism, let me remind you what the miscreants of the world can do to your program, even when they don't have access to your source code. They can:

1. Delete or replace dialogs.
2. Change dialogs, which includes making them display icons you never intended, deleting, changing, moving or resizing controls, or resizing the entire dialog.
3. Change the text in string resources, including your copyright statements, company name, message strings, and other important information. If this one doesn't sound like a big deal, imagine a couple of unsupervised 12-year-old boys (or even Weird Ed from Accounting) changing your program's string resources to something they find amusing, and then having your users see this text appear in your program's dialog boxes.

201

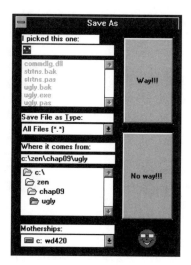

**Figure 8.1   A transmogrified Common Dialog.**

4. Change or delete your version resource. This includes copyright notices, your company's name, as well as the program's version codes.

*In the spirit of full disclosure, I must confess to being a long-time resource mangler. I detest the keyhole-size list boxes and edit controls many programmers foist upon users, so I routinely enlarge dialogs and certain controls. I mean, is there anyone out there who actually likes editing and scrolling around in these itty bitty postage-stamps? Why is Explorer's file open dialog so cramped that it can't display its details view without horizontal scrolling?*

Even beyond the issue of intentional destruction, there's the question of transmission errors. If your program will be widely copied and sent via modem—perhaps it is a freely distributable demo or a shareware version—then there's a small but non-zero chance that it will get mauled in transmission. Or it might be corrupted by a user's third-party archiver utility that wasn't quite ready for prime time. (If you troll the online services for shareware and demos, you've probably seen freely downloadable beta releases of archiving programs. These are usually popular programs that have huge download counts, even in beta form. Think about it.)

The bottom line is that even if you could somehow rule out malicious mischief (and trust me, you can't, except in the rarest of circumstances), there are completely innocent reasons why the program your user runs will not be exactly the same program you released. And lest anyone tell you that it won't happen, let me tell you that it will; I've seen more mangled binaries than I can shake a scratched CD at.

Notice that I haven't brought up the dreaded v-word: virus. I'm sure there are ways to piggyback a virus onto an existing Windows program without access to the source or resorting to hideous amounts of reverse engineering. Perhaps I've led a sheltered life here in scenic Endwell, but I honestly don't think this is a significant threat to your public programs or your users. In fact, I've never heard of someone doing this. If you know of a verifiable instance, let me know. (See the sidebar "A Short Primer on CRC's" for some more v-talk.)

Now that I've introduced a whole new element of paranoia into your life, let's talk about what you can do to protect your programs and users.

## What You Can and Can't Do

No matter how you approach this problem, it quickly becomes clear that you can't do the most desirable things, such as preventing everyone from modifying your program or making sure that your wondrous creation is never mangled by a stray scratch of static on a phone line. This brings us to a classic critical mass design decision: If we can't achieve 100 percent protection, is there a lesser level of functionality that's still worth the cost to everyone involved? What if you could make your program reliably detect that it had been changed, and then alert the user in an intelligent fashion? That's clearly not as good as making your program 100 percent mangle-proof, but it's a useful level of function. The question is whether we can get there at acceptable cost.

The easiest way to check for modifications, of course, would be to do a brute-force comparison between the suspect copy and a known-good copy. But since you can't get a known-good copy to the user's desktop, this doesn't help matters much. (After all, if you could get the known-good copy there intact, you'd do that for the original and make the whole blasted problem go away.)

## CRCs to the Rescue

The next best thing is to use a CRC (cyclical redundancy checking) code. This will tell you with an acceptable degree of certainty if your program was modified, but it won't tell you how many bytes or which ones were changed, nor will it let you repair the damage. Still, for our purpose, it works quite well. The sidebar, "A *Really* Short Primer on CRCs," provides a brief overview of what CRCs are and aren't.

So, the answer is simple—you make your program open its main executable file read/only and calculate a CRC check on itself to see if it gets the expected answer: yes, all is peaches and cream; no, evil is afoot. What could be simpler? Nothing, except for one minor detail: Where does your program store the CRC value for the unmodified version of the program, the one it expects to find when it does its self-check? It can easily calculate the CRC for its own executable, but it must know the right answer to compare it to. You can't simply store the value as a constant in the program itself, since doing so would change the CRC value of the entire program, making whatever result you calculated and stored incorrect.

Storing the CRC value outside the program is too risky, since it exposes the data to manipulation. (I often imagine someone storing the CRC result in an .INI file in plain text, for all the world to see. I haven't seen anyone actually do this, but I'm sure it's been tried.) External storage also creates the possibility that the data simply won't be there when needed, neutering the feature. As I've pointed out elsewhere in this book, there's no telling what will happen to your program's data when it isn't looking.

The trick is to make the program perform the CRC calculation on itself for the entire file, except those few bytes that contain the stored CRC result. If we can pull this off, the part of the file your program will examine will never change, giving us a constant CRC value. This approach requires your program to know where in its executable the CRC result is after the program is built, no matter how it is compiled and linked. This sounds like we just traded one problem (knowing the CRC value at execution time) for another of equal size (knowing where the CRC value is stored). Not quite; all this really means is that we have to store two pieces of data: the CRC value and the location of the CRC in the executable.

## Finding a Place to Stand

Time for a perspective adjustment. Programmers are used to looking at their programs and storage in logical terms: This array of records, that linked list, a floating point number, and so on. You're used to having named variables and constants that you refer to without caring where they reside in memory; your program loads and there they are, ready to rock and roll. When the constants with the CRC value and location are loaded at program initialization time, they work just like any others in this regard, of course. But the location data is not the address of the CRC result in memory; it's the offset of the CRC data in the executable file on disk. Knowing this and the size of the CRC data, your program can easily step over those few bytes and accurately calculate a CRC that should match the stored value.

Notice that this technique is completely independent of changes in the executable file format, the layout of code and data segments within your program, the language used to create your program, etc. When your program is calculating the CRC for its own executable, that file on disk is nothing more than a long stream of bytes, with one tiny section that is to be excluded from the calculation. The fact that the file is the executable for the running program is pure coincidence—albeit a very convenient one.

So far, we've solved half the puzzle: figuring out what data and algorithm is needed in the program to perform the self-check, and how the program will know which bytes in the executable to skip in the CRC calculation. The other half is figuring out how to get the CRC value and location data into the finished executable in the first place. For this, we need a second program, a patching utility that will calculate the CRC for the entire program except your little patch of data, and plug in both pieces of information. Your application can't patch itself, since Windows won't allow you to write to the executable of a currently running program. You probably wouldn't want to do that, anyway, since you'd then have to lock out that function to keep someone from using it to make a modified version of your program look legitimate.

But we're still not home free. How does the patching utility know where the CRC data is in the application? This is where I resort to one of my favorite observations on programming: "At the heart of every artificial intelligence program is a brute force algorithm." In this case, the brute force algorithm is a simple linear search for the data, which you facilitate by making the data more "visible" to the patching utility with an "eye catcher" series of bytes. By attaching this oddball byte sequence to our CRC data, we can also guarantee that the patcher utility won't accidentally change some other area in the application; all it has to do is look for the one, unique copy of the eye catcher.

With the addition of the eye catcher, we've finally covered all our bases: The patching utility can calculate the CRC for all of your application except the few bytes that hold the CRC data, and the application has the information it needs to perform the CRC calculation. Time to put all this theory to work in a sample program.

## Building the Samples: SELFCHCK and PATCHER

**CD Location:** ZEN\CHAP08\SELFCHCK and ZEN\CHAP08\PATCHER

**Platform:** Win32

**Build instructions:** Use the provided .MAK files with Visual C++ 2.2, and compile normally. Then move one of the freshly built executables to the other's directory. (SELFCHCK.EXE and PATCHER.EXE must be in the same directory so that PATCHER can find SELFCHCK.)

# SELFCHCK and PATCHER

The programs for this chapter, SELFCHCKand PATCHER, show how all this comes together in a real, if not exactly feature-rich, program. Both programs use a third compilation unit, CHECKER, to perform the actual CRC calculation, the result of which is stored in a constant in our CRC data. (Calling the CRC data a constant is interesting in its own right, since it's anything but, thanks to the patcher utility—but let's not get into metaphysics.) By storing the CRC data in CHECKER (in the form of a record instance named crc_data), and having both the application and PATCHER use this same compilation unit, we reduce the

chance essentially to zero that the two programs will try to use different eye catch-
ers. (Yes, there's still a chance that you'll change the eye catcher in CHECKER,
rebuild PATCHER, and then use it on the application, which still has the old eye
catcher, only to have it accidentally match and patch some innocent stream of
bytes in the application. The chances of this happening are less than epsilon, as
the mathematicians say. If you're worried about this, or if you're using this technique on a program that has zero tolerance for errors, you can always make
PATCHER check that the application's last modified date is more recent than its
own. To be honest, I'm pretty paranoid, but even I'm not *that* paranoid.) PATCHER
and CHECKER are shown in Listings 9.1 and 9.2, respectively.

## Listing 8.1   PATCHER.CPP

```
//////////////////////////////////////////////////////////////////////////////
// PATCHER.CPP: File patching utility in the form of a WIN32 console app
//
// Copyright 1995 (c) Lou Grinzo

#include "stdafx.h"
#include <stdio.h>
#include <io.h>
#include "checker.h"

FILE* f;
const buffer_size = 16384;
unsigned long i, crc_start, file_pos;
eye_catcher_type pattern;
unsigned short the_crc;
BYTE the_byte;
char buffer[buffer_size];
long buffer_pos, data_size;
char NextByte(void);
void ReadNextCatcher(eye_catcher_type & c);

int main()
 {
 // Change the following to match the name of the file to be patched!
 char * file_name = "selfchck.exe";  // !!!!!!!!!!!!!!!!!!!!!!!!!!!!!!!!!!!!!

 printf("About to patch file \"%s\"...\n\n",file_name);

 if(!(f = fopen(file_name,"rb")))
  printf("Unable to open file.\n\n\n");
 else
   {
   buffer_pos = buffer_size;
   data_size = 0;
   file_pos = 0;

  printf("Searching for the start of the CRC data...\n");

  // Seed the pattern with the initial bytes of the file

  for(i = 0; i < sizeof(pattern); i++)
```

```
  pattern[i] = NextByte();

crc_start = 0;  // Init to "not found" value

// Scan through the rest of the file, looking for the eye catcher.
// Note that we DON'T stop at the first occurrence! We must scan
// the entire file, so that we're completely sure there isn't a
// second copy of the eye catcher floating about.

unsigned long limit = _filelength(fileno(f)) - sizeof(pattern);

for(i = 0; i < limit; i++)
  {
 if(!memcmp(crc_data.eye_catcher,pattern,sizeof(pattern)))
   if(crc_start > 0)
     {
     printf("File contains more than one instance of the eye catcher!\n\n");
     fclose(f);
     getchar();
     return 0;
     }
   else
   crc_start = file_pos - sizeof(pattern);

  ReadNextCatcher(pattern);
  }

fclose(f);

if(crc_start == 0)
  {
  printf("Couldn't find the eye catcher!\n\n");
  getchar();
  return 0;
  }

// Could check here to see if the file is already patched, and bail
// out with a msg if it is. But patching is non-destructive and
// resonably quick, so it's probably not worth the effort in a
// development tool.

printf("Found eye catcher. Doing CRC calculation...\n\n");

// CalcCRC trusts us to supply the one, true offset of the crc_data

if(!FindCRC(file_name,crc_start,&the_crc))
  {
  printf("Couldn't calculate the file's CRC!\n\n");
  getchar();
  return 0;
  }

if(!(f = fopen(file_name,"rb+")))
  {
  printf("Couldn't re-open file!\n\n");
  getchar();
  return 0;
  }

// We have our data, so it's time to patch the crc_data struct in
// the file.
```

```
     // Position to the start of the data we're about to write, which is
     // NOT the beginning of crc-data, but the crc_start field within it.
     //
     // This assumes a specific layout of the crc_data_type structure!
     fseek(f,crc_start + sizeof(pattern),SEEK_SET);

     // Write out our data
     fwrite(&crc_start,1,sizeof(crc_start),f);
     fwrite(&the_crc,1,sizeof(the_crc),f);

     // Take 'er home
     fclose(f);

     printf("\"%s\" has been updated with the following values:\n",file_name);
     printf("  CRC offset: %d\n",crc_start);
     printf("  CRC value: %d\n",the_crc);

     printf("\nDone!!!\n\n");
     }

  printf("(Press ENTER) ");
  getchar();

  return 0;
 }


/////////////////////////////////////////////////////////////////////////////
// NextByte(): Return the next buffered byte of the input file

char NextByte(void)
 {
 if(buffer_pos >= data_size)
   {
   data_size = fread(buffer,1,buffer_size,f);
   buffer_pos = 0;
   }

 buffer_pos++;
 file_pos++;
 return buffer[buffer_pos - 1];
 }


/////////////////////////////////////////////////////////////////////////////
// ReadNextCatcher(): Read a new character, and roll it into our current eye-
// catcher candidate.

void ReadNextCatcher(eye_catcher_type & c)
 {
 memmove(&c[0],&c[1],sizeof(c) - 1);
 c[sizeof(c) - 1] = NextByte();
 }
```

## Listing 8.2   CHECKER.CPP

```
/////////////////////////////////////////////////////////////////////////////
// CHECKER.CPP: Core CRC calculation code and data
//
// Copyright 1995 (c) Lou Grinzo
```

```
#include "stdafx.h"
#include "checker.h"
#include <stdlib.h>
#include <stdio.h>
#include <io.h>
#include <malloc.h>
#include <assert.h>

static long buffer_pos, data_size;
static BYTE *buffer;
static const alloc_buffer_size = 4096;
static FILE *f;

// Local functions
static unsigned short UpdateCRC(BYTE new_byte, unsigned short crc);
static char NextByte(void);

// This instance of a crc_data_type must be here. This is the one that
// will ultimately wind up in the application and contain its calculated
// CRC value.
crc_data_type crc_data =
 {
  'c', 'a', 't', 'c', 'h', 'e', 'r', '!',  // eye_catcher
  0,                       // start
  0                       // crc_value
 };

//////////////////////////////////////////////////////////////////////////////
// The data table used by the UpdateCRC() function to calculate a CRC
static unsigned short crctab[256] =
 {
  0x0000, 0x1021, 0x2042, 0x3063, 0x4084, 0x50a5, 0x60c6, 0x70e7,
  0x8108, 0x9129, 0xa14a, 0xb16b, 0xc18c, 0xd1ad, 0xe1ce, 0xf1ef,
  0x1231, 0x0210, 0x3273, 0x2252, 0x52b5, 0x4294, 0x72f7, 0x62d6,
  0x9339, 0x8318, 0xb37b, 0xa35a, 0xd3bd, 0xc39c, 0xf3ff, 0xe3de,
  0x2462, 0x3443, 0x0420, 0x1401, 0x64e6, 0x74c7, 0x44a4, 0x5485,
  0xa56a, 0xb54b, 0x8528, 0x9509, 0xe5ee, 0xf5cf, 0xc5ac, 0xd58d,
  0x3653, 0x2672, 0x1611, 0x0630, 0x76d7, 0x66f6, 0x5695, 0x46b4,
  0xb75b, 0xa77a, 0x9719, 0x8738, 0xf7df, 0xe7fe, 0xd79d, 0xc7bc,
  0x48c4, 0x58e5, 0x6886, 0x78a7, 0x0840, 0x1861, 0x2802, 0x3823,
  0xc9cc, 0xd9ed, 0xe98e, 0xf9af, 0x8948, 0x9969, 0xa90a, 0xb92b,
  0x5af5, 0x4ad4, 0x7ab7, 0x6a96, 0x1a71, 0x0a50, 0x3a33, 0x2a12,
  0xdbfd, 0xcbdc, 0xfbbf, 0xeb9e, 0x9b79, 0x8b58, 0xbb3b, 0xab1a,
  0x6ca6, 0x7c87, 0x4ce4, 0x5cc5, 0x2c22, 0x3c03, 0x0c60, 0x1c41,
  0xedae, 0xfd8f, 0xcdec, 0xddcd, 0xad2a, 0xbd0b, 0x8d68, 0x9d49,
  0x7e97, 0x6eb6, 0x5ed5, 0x4ef4, 0x3e13, 0x2e32, 0x1e51, 0x0e70,
  0xff9f, 0xefbe, 0xdfdd, 0xcffc, 0xbf1b, 0xaf3a, 0x9f59, 0x8f78,
  0x9188, 0x81a9, 0xb1ca, 0xa1eb, 0xd10c, 0xc12d, 0xf14e, 0xe16f,
  0x1080, 0x00a1, 0x30c2, 0x20e3, 0x5004, 0x4025, 0x7046, 0x6067,
  0x83b9, 0x9398, 0xa3fb, 0xb3da, 0xc33d, 0xd31c, 0xe37f, 0xf35e,
  0x02b1, 0x1290, 0x22f3, 0x32d2, 0x4235, 0x5214, 0x6277, 0x7256,
  0xb5ea, 0xa5cb, 0x95a8, 0x8589, 0xf56e, 0xe54f, 0xd52c, 0xc50d,
  0x34e2, 0x24c3, 0x14a0, 0x0481, 0x7466, 0x6447, 0x5424, 0x4405,
  0xa7db, 0xb7fa, 0x8799, 0x97b8, 0xe75f, 0xf77e, 0xc71d, 0xd73c,
  0x26d3, 0x36f2, 0x0691, 0x16b0, 0x6657, 0x7676, 0x4615, 0x5634,
  0xd94c, 0xc96d, 0xf90e, 0xe92f, 0x99c8, 0x89e9, 0xb98a, 0xa9ab,
  0x5844, 0x4865, 0x7806, 0x6827, 0x18c0, 0x08e1, 0x3882, 0x28a3,
  0xcb7d, 0xdb5c, 0xeb3f, 0xfb1e, 0x8bf9, 0x9bd8, 0xabbb, 0xbb9a,
  0x4a75, 0x5a54, 0x6a37, 0x7a16, 0x0af1, 0x1ad0, 0x2ab3, 0x3a92,
  0xfd2e, 0xed0f, 0xdd6c, 0xcd4d, 0xbdaa, 0xad8b, 0x9de8, 0x8dc9,
  0x7c26, 0x6c07, 0x5c64, 0x4c45, 0x3ca2, 0x2c83, 0x1ce0, 0x0cc1,
```

```
0xef1f, 0xff3e, 0xcf5d, 0xdf7c, 0xaf9b, 0xbfba, 0x8fd9, 0x9ff8,
0x6e17, 0x7e36, 0x4e55, 0x5e74, 0x2e93, 0x3eb2, 0x0ed1, 0x1ef0
};

////////////////////////////////////////////////////////////////////////////////
// UpdateCRC(): Update the current CRC for the data stream by taking into
// account the next byte in the stream, new_byte.

static unsigned short UpdateCRC(BYTE new_byte, unsigned short crc)
 { return crctab[(crc & 0x00ff) ^ new_byte] ^ (crc >> 8); }

////////////////////////////////////////////////////////////////////////////////

BOOL FindCRC(char *fn, unsigned long crc_start, unsigned short * the_crc)
 {
 assert(fn != NULL);
 assert(fn[0] != '\0');
 assert(crc_start != 0);

 if(fn == NULL)
  return FALSE;

 if(fn[0] == '\0')
  return FALSE;

 *the_crc = 0;
 unsigned long i;

 if((buffer = (BYTE *)malloc(alloc_buffer_size)) == NULL)
  return FALSE;

 if(!(f = fopen(fn,"rb")))
  return FALSE;

 // Grab the file size here, and not in a loop!
 unsigned long limit = _filelength(fileno(f));

 // Make sure crc_start points to a valid position in the file
 if(limit - sizeof(crc_data_type) < crc_start)
   {
   fclose(f);
   return FALSE;
   }

 buffer_pos = alloc_buffer_size;
 data_size = 0;

 // Calculate the CRC for the file before the CRC data structure...
 for(i = 0; i < crc_start; i++)
  *the_crc = UpdateCRC(NextByte(),*the_crc);

 // ...then step over the entire structure...
 for(i = 0; i < sizeof(crc_data_type); i++)
  NextByte();

 // ...and finish up with what follows the structure.
 for(i = crc_start + sizeof(crc_data_type); i < limit; i++)
  *the_crc = UpdateCRC(NextByte(),*the_crc);

 free(buffer);
```

```
  fclose(f);

  return TRUE;
 }

///////////////////////////////////////////////////////////////////////

BOOL GoodCRC(void)
 {
 char fn[MAX_PATH];
 unsigned short the_crc;

 if(crc_data.start != 0)
   {
   GetModuleFileName(NULL,fn,sizeof(fn));

   // If something was amiss, we return false
   if(!FindCRC(fn,crc_data.start,&the_crc))
    return FALSE;
    else
    return the_crc == crc_data.crc_value;
   }
  else
   return FALSE;    // No data, no sense in performing calculation
 }

///////////////////////////////////////////////////////////////////////
// NextByte(): Return the next buffered byte of the input file.

char NextByte(void)
 {
 if(buffer_pos >= data_size)
   {
   data_size = fread(buffer,1,alloc_buffer_size,f);
   buffer_pos = 0;
   }

 buffer_pos++;
 return buffer[buffer_pos - 1];
 }
```

PATCHER's search for the eye catcher is indeed brute force, as you can see. I probably could have made this search smarter by using another approach, but this program isn't shipped to my users, and it's run so seldom that I haven't bothered to optimize it. Notice also that when PATCHER scans for the eye catcher, it doesn't stop when it finds it. It always scans to the end of the file. *This is a crucial detail.* If PATCHER didn't do this you'd be exposed to the slight chance that it would stumble across another string of bytes that just happens to match the eye catcher. This would result in the patched data going into the wrong location and likely overlaying something that you'd prefer wasn't overlaid. If PATCHER finds exactly one copy of the eye catcher, it proceeds; if it finds zero or more than one occurrence, it doesn't change the application; it tells you what happened, and ends.

SELFCHCK does very little in response to a user's request to do the self check. (The user's interface for this feature is the "Perform Self-Check..." item on the

"Help" menu.) In the message handler, OnSelfCheck(), it simply does the check via the GoodCRC() function in CHECKER, and then reports the result to the user, albeit in a minimal way:

```
//////////////////////////////////////////////////////////////////////////
// CMainFrame message handlers

void CMainFrame::OnSelfcheck()
{
 if(GoodCRC())
  ::MessageBox(0,"Self-Check Passes!","",MB_OK);
 else
  ::MessageBox(0,"Self-Check Fails!","",MB_OK);
}
```

GoodCRC() returns true if everything checks out okay, and false if crc_data was never patched, the file failed the check, or the check couldn't be completed for whatever reason. (For longer-running self-checks, you should make your application display a modeless dialog box while the self-check runs, saying something like "Performing self-check. This will take a few moments.") Notice the extreme level of abstraction the CHECKER compilation unit makes possible. All code and data reside in CHECKER's domain, which means the host application merely calls the GoodCRC() function, without parameters, and gets a yes or no answer to its implicit question.

CHECKER does the actual CRC calculation work for both SELFCHCK and PATCHER. Its two functions are FindCRC() and GoodCRC(). FindCRC() is used by PATCHER after it has scanned for and found the unique crc_data structure. This function calculates the CRC for a specified disk file that has a crc_data structure at an offset specified by the caller.

GoodCRC() is called by your application program to perform a self check. This function uses the Windows API GetModuleFileName() to find the executable's own, fully qualified file name, and it picks up the location field in the crc_data structure. It calls FindCRC() with these values, and simply reports whether the calculated CRC matches the stored one. GoodCRC() doesn't bother calling FindCRC() if it sees that the location data is still 0; in that case it simply returns false. This heuristic is bullet-proof, since there's no way that the CRC data structure can be at offset 0 in a legal executable.

This use of GetModuleFileName() is interesting for a couple of reasons. First, if you hard-wire the name of the application's executable into a constant, you create a potential exposure. It's unlikely that your users will rename the executable and make the program unable to find itself on disk. (Although I'm sure that if your program sees wide enough distribution, someone, somewhere will do this for a perfectly valid reason that none of us foresaw.)

Also, you have to make sure that the program uses a fully qualified name for the file. A fully qualified name (one that includes drive and the full path to the executable, not just the file name and extension) frees you from worrying about what the current directory and drive are when your program does the self-check. You're not guaranteed that your program will start with its home directory as the current directory—and even our old, trusty friends, the common dialogs, can change the current directory if you don't tell them not to.

# Adding Self-Checking to Your Program

Let's assume you have an existing program that you'd like to make perform self-checks. This is very simple, and consists of the following steps:

1. Add some sort of gizmo to the user interface that allows the user to request a self-check. This can be as simple as an entry on the program's system menu.

2. Add the self-check handler to your program and make your program call it in response to a request from the user. This step also requires that you include the CHECKER.H header in the compilation unit that contains this code, and include CHECKER.CPP in your project.

3. Pick an eye catcher byte sequence and modify the copy in CHECKER.CPP. Remember, you're looking for something that will be unique in the linked executable and won't be easily spotted by the human eye. The example in CHECKER.CPP, "catcher!", is a decidedly bad one, chosen for demonstration purposes. When you select your eye catcher, make it whatever you want—the license plate of your first car, your sweetheart's birthday encoded one hex digit per byte, and so on.

4. Update the program name in PATCHER to match your application's name.

5. Compile your program and PATCHER. Run PATCHER. If PATCHER said it finished successfully, run the program and perform the self-check. The program should report that it passed the check. As an additional verification, write down the offset of the CRC data that PATCHER said it used, and examine your application with a hex editor to make sure that the eye catcher is indeed at the reported offset. (I always do this check the first time I use PATCHER on an application that's been significantly changed. Hey, I said I was paranoid, didn't I? I don't even trust my own code.) Obviously, you'll have to run PATCHER before you distribute any changed version of the application; this is another small step that gets added to your product packaging checklist.

6. Decide when your program should perform the self-check. Only when the user requests it? Also at installation? Every time it is run? This decision will be heavily influenced by several issues, and is taken up in more detail below.

At this point, you have a functional, albeit minimal, implementation of the self-checking feature. But why stop here? You can give your program a nice air of professionalism and boost the user's confidence in your skills by making it perform the self-check the first time it is run after installation. My preferred way to make this happen is simple: Have your program look for an undocumented command-line switch of your choosing (e.g. "/CRC"), and perform the check on startup if it's found. Then, make your installation program run your application with the secret command-line option. This is the approach I use with Stickies!. It works very well and avoids the nonsense of trying to determine with 100 percent accuracy when a program is running for the first time on a given system.

7. Decide what other files in your project you want to include in the self-check feature. If your application includes DLLs and critical data files that will not change over the lifetime of your program's installation, you might want to include them in the checking feature. For each additional file that you want to check, you'll have to extend the crc_data structure by one member, the calculated CRC value. (The location isn't needed, since there won't be a crc_data structure in the other files, so there's nothing FindCRC() will have to step over in performing the calculation.) This approach stores all the CRC data in the main executable, allowing your other files to remain unchanged yet protected. You'd also have to extend PATCHER to process the entire set of files, CHECKER to calculate CRCs for files that don't have an embedded crc_data structure, and the main application, to do several checks. But these are simple extensions to the sample programs in this chapter; making a program check itself is the trickiest variation, and that one's already done.

Yet another decision involves handling files that are distributed with your program but will change once your program is run. Perhaps your application includes some sample documents or other data files that the user is expected to experiment with, edit, or eventually delete. You could make your application interpret the undocumented command line switch as a request to check the main executable and all the data files that it finds. (And don't forget to quietly skip files that can't be found, instead of reporting them as failing the check!) You could then make your installation program use the switch to verify that all important files in the package had been installed intact. The control you give the user to trigger a manual self-check would only examine the application's main executable, since at least some of the data files would likely have changed.

As I said above, there's the question of making the application perform the self-check every time it is run. This sounds like overkill and a sure way to annoy your users, but not necessarily. As I keep saying in this book, you should reject canned answers to such questions. How large will your application be? What do you know about the hardware your users are running? (If your program is to be widely distributed, then your users will be running on everything from ancient 386-16s that should have been relegated to doorstop duty during the Bush administration, up to the latest BelchFire 5000 Multiprocessor Wunderbox. So you can't make any useful assumptions on this point. But if your program will be used only within your company, say, then you probably know something about the hardware base.) Also, is there any benefit to doing the check that often? In most cases, the answer clearly is no; checking the executable at installation time and in response to an explicit user request is sufficient. But once again, not always. Perhaps your application will run in an environment that exposes it to many users, some of whom you can't trust farther than you can throw the entire editorial staff of *PC Magazine*. Depending on the nature of your application and users, and how long it takes your program to do the self-check, it might make sense to do it every time, and tell the user what's happening only if it fails.

Similarly, you can also make your program store a CRC in its data file, and then check the CRC before it loads a file. Normally this would be overkill; disk drives are so reliable that it makes sense to assume they're perfect. But sufficiently critical data, in an environment populated with sufficiently questionable characters, might make even this a reasonable approach; it's a judgment call that you can make only in the full context of your program's expected environment.

# Go Forth and Calculate

As you can see, this basic technique is flexible, and with a little thought, it can be a nice addition to your toolbox that provides your programs and your users with some cheap, effective insurance. But don't get cocky. Like all tools, this one is only as useful as its wielder (read: you) makes it. And never forget Maria's admonition about the evil doobies; they're still out there, and they're still gunning for all of us.

## A *Really* Short Primer on CRCs

It seems that everyone in the software business knows in general terms what CRCs are, but no one can tell you exactly where they come from, what kinds of errors they will and won't detect, and other relatively crucial information. This was one of the more interesting oddities I discovered while researching and writing this book; another was how little *I* knew about CRCs. Don't get your hopes up; I won't even try to provide a complete treatment of CRCs, since I think it makes more sense to talk about them in logical, general terms, and how useful they are in making self-checking programs.

In short, a CRC reduces a data stream to a "checkword," a conveniently short code that is very "twitchy," in that it will react to small changes in the data. The two most common variations of CRCs are CRC-16 and CRC-32, which produce 16- and 32-bit checkwords. The implementation used in this chapter and the MegaZero sample use CRC-16.

In theory, a CRC treats the entire data stream as one immense number and divides it by another, carefully chosen, immense number called the "generator polynomial." The quotient from this division is ignored, and the remainder is our prized checkword. When you're calculating a CRC for an entire file, "immense" can take on whole new meanings. The copy of EXCEL.EXE (version 5.0) on my system at this writing is 4,185,600 bytes long. Treating that data stream as a single unsigned integer gives you a data type with a maximum value of $2^{(8 * 4,185,600)} - 1$, a number so large that I'll gladly leave its expression as an exercise for the reader.

Luckily, this division operation really is theoretical, and you never have to wrestle with such outrageously large numbers. CRCs are commonly calculated with a table-driven method, such as the one used in this chapter's sample code, that is very easy to implement and reasonably fast. The method is really just a variation on the "casting out nines" method of division that was taught in grade school years ago. The casting out method allows you to process an arbitrarily large number from most- to least-significant digit, and calculate the remainder of the entire number divided by nine. All you do is start with the first digit of the number and at each step, add the next digit in the number to your result and subtract nine if the new result is nine or larger. When you're out of digits in the input, you're done.

For example, to use this method on my CompuServe ID, 71055,1240, you start with the seven, add the one, the zero and the first five, and we finally have a number greater than or equal to nine, 13. Subtract nine, add the next five to our result so far, then the four, finally the zero. When you finish, you have seven, which is the remainder of 710551240 divided by nine.

Similarly, the standard method that I use for calculating CRC-16 accepts the current checkword and the next byte of data from the stream, then uses a simple algorithm and a data table of 256 16-bit entries to produce the new checkword. This approach treats the data stream as one large number and processes it using the most significant digit first. Calculating the checksum for a file or any other data stream is as simple as initializing the CRC value to zero and then feeding the data one byte at a time to this core routine (UpdateCRC() in the file CHECKER.CPP). After UpdateCRC() has processed the last byte, the current CRC checkword is the checkword for the entire data stream.

## How Much Protection Is This, Anyway?

Another way to look at CRCs is that they reduce a data stream of any size into a single value that's about as likely to produce one legal value as another. In other words, the CRC-16 checkword for a file is just about equally likely to be any one of the 65,536 values in the range 0 to 0xFFFF. (CRC-32 produces values in the range 0 to 0xFFFFFFFF.) This is a valuable characteristic, since it makes CRCs completely unpredictable. The checkword value itself is meaningless; it's merely a value that either matches or doesn't match when it is calculated again for the same data stream after you do something potentially hazardous to the data, like send it over a phone line. This means you can't derive any meaning from the fact that a CRC-16 checkword is within a certain range, the way Social Security numbers give away what state the holder lived in when the number was assigned.

A CRC-16 checkword will detect all single-bit errors, all errors of 16 or fewer consecutive bits, and all double bit errors that are less than 65,536 bits apart. (See John Kodis' article "Fletcher's Checksum" in the May, 1992 *Dr. Dobb's Journal* for these and other details on CRCs.) While this sounds great, these facts also subtly point out that it's quite possible for two completely different files, even of wildly different sizes, to produce the same CRC checkword. This makes sense, since a 16-bit checkword can only take on 65,536 unique values, and there are certainly more than that many unique data streams in the universe; somewhere along the line, somebody has to share. (This is also why some people like to say that CRC is nothing more than a fancy hashing algorithm with "only" 2^16 or 2^32 buckets; perform the calculation on enough data streams, and hashing collisions are inevitable.)

## More on Viruses

CRCs are good at detecting innocent, random changes to a file. But what about malicious, intentional changes? As it turns out, some people claim that if you know the CRC of a file, you can change the file at will and then add some spurious bytes whose value will force the entire file to have the original CRC. This would be much faster than trying random values for the additional bytes until you stumble upon a set that works. (And no, I didn't bother tracking this down; you'll see why in a second.)

The technique demonstrated in this chapter doesn't prevent this type of attack, but it does make it quite a bit harder. Remember all the hugger-mugger we went through to make sure your program knew where the CRC value was in its disk image? Someone who wants to reverse-engineer your calculated CRC will have to find your data first. If you select a good eye catcher that looks like binary garbage in a hex editor, you'll make a would-be intruder's life that much more difficult.

# Chapter 9

# Smart Data Files

# Smart Data Files

**Chapter 9**

*And the best and the worst of this is*
  *That neither is most to blame,*
*If you have forgotten my kisses*
  *And I have forgotten your name.*

Algernon Charles Swinburne

*Action is transitory,—a step, a blow,*
*The motion of a muscle, this way or that—*
*Tis done, and in the after-vacancy*
*We wonder at ourselves like men betrayed:*
*Suffering is permanent, obscure and dark,*
*And shares the nature of infinity.*

William Wordsworth

With all due respect to Mr. Wordsworth, if he thought suffering was permanent (a viewpoint I most certainly reject), he should have seen some of the files and the file formats on our computers. And as for "obscure," I would refer him to the nearest Windows 95 system and its registration database. Top that one, Billy Boy.

In all seriousness, designing and implementing the persistent disk storage techniques for your Windows programs is a task loaded with pitfalls and tradeoffs. It's also yet another important factor in creating intelligent, accommodating programs. In this chapter I'll talk about some of the options and one technique, smart data files, that's quite flexible and powerful.

# Uses of Persistence

Application programmers normally don't even think about why they need data files or how they use them—they need "a place for their stuff," as George Carlin once said, so they "stick the data in a disk file" and go about their merry way. In reality, the situation usually isn't quite that simple, of course.

The two most interesting things you can ask about persistent data is what will it be used for, and how and where will it be stored. Since the "what" issue is so often overlooked by programmers who are in a rush to find the latest magic incantation to make something work under Windows (and I'm no different from anyone else when it comes to falling into that particular trap), let's cover that one first, and we can come back to the "how and where" issue in the next section.

For our purposes, there are three main uses of persistent data: system configuration data, application configuration data, and application document data.

## System Data

I'm sure everyone reading this book is familiar with Apple's TV ads in which two people are struggling to get a Windows system working. In most of the ads, one person holding an open manual dictates SYSTEM.INI or WIN.INI changes that the other person laboriously types in. All questions of this campaign's effectiveness aside, it does illustrate the simple point that any modern operating system needs a vast array of configuration information if it's to have any chance at all of running on the mind-boggling installed base of PC hardware. (If you've done any significant amount of computer setup and configuration management for co-workers, friends, or relatives, you probably know that just the multimedia part of the PC universe can make you spend an absurd amount of time unintentionally mimicking those Apple ads. Universal support for Plug and Play can't possibly get here too soon, in my opinion.) All that critical configuration data has to go somewhere, and it has to be readily accessible to the operating system, particularly at startup.

There's an interesting requirement for system data that doesn't normally apply to the other two categories: Often you must access or change it when the system is in less than perfect health. (This is why, in fact, some consultants are hesitant to use Windows NT's native file system, NTFS—they know that if something goes wildly wrong with a FAT-based system, they can always boot from a DOS floppy and edit or copy files.) In fact, this is one reason why Windows and Mac users disagree so vehemently over those TV ads—many Windows experts say that it's a good thing that the configuration of the system can be changed so simply and without even running Windows, while the Mac users claim that if PCs had a more cohesive hardware and software design all that .INI file noodling wouldn't be needed in the first place. In this case, both sides have valid points. I'll have much more to say about .INI files in the section "Forms of Persistence."

## Application Configuration Data

Like Windows itself, or any other operating system, application programs need to store configuration data between runs or sessions. I'm distinguishing here between document-specific settings, such as the font(s) used in a particular word processing document, and more global configuration settings, such as the default font you want your word processor to use when you create a new document. I include suite-level and multiple-application configuration data in this group as well as data for a single application.

Some application programs, particularly simpler ones, don't even bother to store this type of application-level configuration data; they store all their configuration settings in their documents. Other programs store it in more subtle ways, such as Word for Windows' use of NORMAL.DOT for many formatting settings. An interesting side effect of storing this type of data off in a special place like this is that users often literally don't think about or even realize that their application has a "back pocket" which it uses for such purposes. They just know that when they tell Word to use Arial 12-point for their "Normal" style in new documents, the program remembers and obeys.

## Application Document Data

In contrast to the often overlooked data in the previous category, application document data is what users normally refer to when they talk about "my data"—their letters, budget reports, scanned Dilbert cartoons, customer databases, etc. This category includes not just the few thousand files that physically reside on the user's desktop system, but distant client-server databases, as well.

This category doesn't provide a clean distinction from the previous one, since nearly all document files include at least some application configuration information. Word for Windows, for example, stores the "view" setting ("normal", "page", "outline", or "master document") in the document, so that when you reopen a document, Word will restore your setting for this option.

One interesting detail that makes application document data very different from the other two categories is how users employ these files. You almost never hear of users moving their WIN.INI files, for example, many Windows users don't even know they have such beasts inhabiting their systems. But when it comes to "their data," users are quite comfortable with moving the files around, storing them where they want, renaming them, sharing them with other people, etc. From the system's perspective these are all nothing but disk files, of course, yet the expectations people place on what they can and should be able to do with them can differ radically depending on which of these three categories a file falls into.

# Forms of Persistence

The other axis of the persistence two-space, if you will, is the question that normally first comes to programmers' minds—the physical implementation of the storage. This is in stark contrast to users, who are concerned with the features and characteristics of their programs, and normally don't much care about such issues. Nor should they.

In choosing a physical implementation of persistent data, we have to make tradeoffs, as always. There are two tightly interwoven issues we have to be concerned with:

- Performance and type of access. No matter how you look at it, all the variables such as the size of the application data, the way it's used, whether it's accessed sequentially or randomly, all come down to performance. After all, if you need to perform random access on some large body of data, you certainly could serially read the data stream for every access, beginning at byte 0. For any body of data larger than a few kilobytes, this would be silly, of course, but it would work, and the only reason programmers spend so much time fiddling with indexes and other means of storing data is to improve performance. (Sometimes the goal is to improve overall application performance by allowing the program to retrieve records in the desired order and avoid a sorting step, but performance is still the core issue.)

  In this vein, I think the worst case scenario among commercially available products are those sets of CDs you can buy that contain a phone directory for the entire United States. Obviously, such products would be completely useless without some serious work on indexing and data format optimization. Some of these products have nearly 100 million names, addresses, and phone numbers; there's no such thing as a fast enough CD ROM drive or CPU to search that much data in a brute force manner.

  Luckily, performance is only a major factor in selecting a form of persistent data storage in extreme cases. Normally we can blissfully ignore this factor, store our data in the simplest, most convenient form on a hard disk, and get on with other matters.

- Security. I'm not talking about security in the typical sense, such as using a password to prevent a user from obtaining access to a disk volume, but security at a much lower level. As I've said elsewhere in this book, some users are quite creative and adventuresome when you turn them loose on a Windows system with a text editor. But most users will respect the unknown, so to speak, and will not edit a file that is clearly in some indecipherable binary format. Depending on the type of data being stored, keeping it in an obscure format can be an effective guard against some (but certainly not all) casual tinkering.

## .INI Files

This is the form of persistent data storage that Windows programmers (and, sadly, users) are most familiar with. Unfortunately, .INI files are another Windows hothouse feature. In theory, they're a convenient and simple way of storing and retrieving limited amounts of system and application configuration data. (Theoretically, you could use them for storing document data, I suppose, but I'd hate to see anyone do that for more than a few bytes.)

I consider .INI files hothouse features because of how they're used and misused in the real world. For starters, almost no one bothers to check or correctly interpret the return codes from API calls that write or read .INI files. This is particularly true when reading .INI files, and programmers seem to be almost religiously averse to ensuring that these calls complete properly. (Given the strange way that GetPrivateProfileString() defines its return code, perhaps this isn't so surprising. See Chapter 10 for more on this.)

In fact, if you're in the mood to commit some relatively harmless vandalism, .INI files can be the perfect vehicle. Just edit the .INI file for some application, and you can often make a program lose its mind. For example, if you change the [Microsoft Excel]/Font setting in EXCEL5.INI to "Fred" (obviously not a valid setting, since this entry is supposed to be a font name followed by a comma and a point size, for example, "Arial,10"), you get the results shown in Figure 9.1. Clearly, Excel is reading the setting from the .INI file and then using it without sanity checking the returned font to see if it got something usable. Also note that the one-point font it is attempting to use has thrown some of Excel's screen drawing logic for a loop—examine Figure 9.1 carefully, and you'll see a short, wide rectangular area in the screen's upper-right section (between the button bar and the spreadsheet grid) where the underlying screen contents still show through. In this figure, you're seeing a snippet of Explorer's screen. This is a charming effect, but probably not what Microsoft had in mind. (I think this is an interesting example, simply because it could have been avoided so easily. Excel simply had to check for the point size and revert to 10-point Arial, for example, if it was missing. I would even consider putting in a safety check for a font size below 4 points and above 36 points, say. Anything not in that range would get the user a prompt that explained the condition and asked to continue or revert to a more typical font size. (And yes, the prompt would include a checkbox so the user could permanently disable that warning.) But I digress.)

Another subtle problem with .INI files is that the entire file isn't re-created when a single value is changed. This means that if you manually change some setting to a wildly wrong value, and then run the associated program, the bad data could persist across numerous sessions. Using Excel again, if you change the [Microsoft Excel]/Options setting in EXCEL5.INI to "Hello, world!" (the old setting in my EXCEL5.INI was 339), then this friendly but distinctly unusable value will persist until you change and save the options settings from within Excel.

I don't mean to sound like I'm beating up Microsoft or Excel with these examples. Microsoft is no worse than the overwhelming majority of software vendors and programmers in this regard. I use Excel as an example simply because it was the first program I experimented with, and it served my purposes quite nicely.

Some people protest that this application behavior really isn't a problem, since .INI files are so clearly the domain of the programs, users should realize this and leave them alone. I disagree. This theory fails in the real world for two reasons: First, users all too often must edit .INI files, AUTOEXEC.BAT, CONFIG.SYS, and even MSDOS.SYS to make their systems work as expected, so they're already quite accustomed to the idea that if you want to tune or tweak your system, you fire up your handy dandy text editor and go .INI file spelunking; and second, the simple fact that .INI files are plain ASCII text is an open invitation for people to experiment.

Another problem with .INI files, as we all know only too well, is that there's no good way to clean them up. I've seen systems with a truly amazing amount of irrelevant text in their WIN.INI files, artifacts from various programs the user installed and de-installed months or even years ago. In fact, one of the best selling categories of Windows programs are uninstallers, those programs that clean out unneeded DLL and INI files and entries. I don't mean to make a big deal of this, but I do think it's quite the telling detail.

Did you flinch when I said that users will now be editing MSDOS.SYS? It's true. One of the strangest details of Windows 95 is that C:\MSDOS.SYS is just another plain text configuration file. I think this is a very bad naming convention, and I would have called it something like WIN95.CFG. I suppose that Microsoft's reasoning was that they needed something there called MSDOS.SYS (see their comments below in my MSDOS.SYS file), and they assumed that the naming

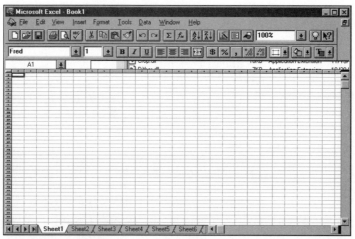

**Figure 9.1　Result of fiddling with EXCEL5.INI.**

convention, and installing the file with the hidden, read-only, and system attribute bits would keep at least some people from playing with the file.

```
[Paths]
WinDir=C:\W95
WinBootDir=C:\W95
HostWinBootDrv=C

[Options]
BootMulti=1
BootGUI=1
Network=1
;
;The following lines are required for compatibility with other programs.
;Do not remove them (MSDOS.SYS needs to be >1024 bytes).
;xxxxxxxxxxxxxxxxxxxxxxxxxxxxxxxxxxxxxxxxxxxxxxxxxxxxxxxxxxxxxa
;xxxxxxxxxxxxxxxxxxxxxxxxxxxxxxxxxxxxxxxxxxxxxxxxxxxxxxxxxxxxxb
;xxxxxxxxxxxxxxxxxxxxxxxxxxxxxxxxxxxxxxxxxxxxxxxxxxxxxxxxxxxxxc
;xxxxxxxxxxxxxxxxxxxxxxxxxxxxxxxxxxxxxxxxxxxxxxxxxxxxxxxxxxxxxd
;xxxxxxxxxxxxxxxxxxxxxxxxxxxxxxxxxxxxxxxxxxxxxxxxxxxxxxxxxxxxxe
;xxxxxxxxxxxxxxxxxxxxxxxxxxxxxxxxxxxxxxxxxxxxxxxxxxxxxxxxxxxxxf
;xxxxxxxxxxxxxxxxxxxxxxxxxxxxxxxxxxxxxxxxxxxxxxxxxxxxxxxxxxxxxg
;xxxxxxxxxxxxxxxxxxxxxxxxxxxxxxxxxxxxxxxxxxxxxxxxxxxxxxxxxxxxxh
;xxxxxxxxxxxxxxxxxxxxxxxxxxxxxxxxxxxxxxxxxxxxxxxxxxxxxxxxxxxxxi
;xxxxxxxxxxxxxxxxxxxxxxxxxxxxxxxxxxxxxxxxxxxxxxxxxxxxxxxxxxxxxj
;xxxxxxxxxxxxxxxxxxxxxxxxxxxxxxxxxxxxxxxxxxxxxxxxxxxxxxxxxxxxxk
;xxxxxxxxxxxxxxxxxxxxxxxxxxxxxxxxxxxxxxxxxxxxxxxxxxxxxxxxxxxxxl
;xxxxxxxxxxxxxxxxxxxxxxxxxxxxxxxxxxxxxxxxxxxxxxxxxxxxxxxxxxxxxm
;xxxxxxxxxxxxxxxxxxxxxxxxxxxxxxxxxxxxxxxxxxxxxxxxxxxxxxxxxxxxxn
;xxxxxxxxxxxxxxxxxxxxxxxxxxxxxxxxxxxxxxxxxxxxxxxxxxxxxxxxxxxxxo
;xxxxxxxxxxxxxxxxxxxxxxxxxxxxxxxxxxxxxxxxxxxxxxxxxxxxxxxxxxxxxp
;xxxxxxxxxxxxxxxxxxxxxxxxxxxxxxxxxxxxxxxxxxxxxxxxxxxxxxxxxxxxxq
;xxxxxxxxxxxxxxxxxxxxxxxxxxxxxxxxxxxxxxxxxxxxxxxxxxxxxxxxxxxxxr
;xxxxxxxxxxxxxxxxxxxxxxxxxxxxxxxxxxxxxxxxxxxxxxxxxxxxxxxxxxxxxs
```

## The Windows Registry

The Windows registry wasn't invented for Windows 95, of course, but the emphasis on using it certainly is new with this release (Windows NT almost doesn't count in this regard, thanks to the low number of people running it on their desktops). I admit that I have mixed feelings about this turn of events. On one hand, the registry is a "cleaner," more centralized repository for system and application configuration information, as compared to .INI files. On the other hand, it's yet another "vertical," architected solution, which unfortunately means it can only be accessed from within Windows, and our options for using it are limited.

At one level this is a moot point, since the registry is indeed an important part of Windows 95 and Windows NT, now and in future releases, and we all have little choice but to accept it as a fact of life (at least in our roles as computer users and programmers). But that doesn't mean we should naively embrace the registry and rush to store any and all application configuration data in it.

And yes, the registry is yet another hothouse feature, simply because it suffers from the same problems as .INI files: There's no way to police its usage, which places every user's configuration at the mercy of every software vendor whose products are on the user's system. Actively use Windows 95 for a year, install and uninstall a fair amount of software, and I'm sure that you'll wind up with a mind-blowing amount of incorrect and obsolete entries in your registry. (To its credit, Microsoft is encouraging other vendors to provide uninstall programs that clean up such things. But based on the track record vendors have with mauling our DLLs, changing our configuration files without getting our permission or even telling us what they did, and all the other various and sundry installation sins they commit, I hope you'll forgive me if I remain skeptical. In fact, see Chapter 6 for a description of how Symantec's Norton Navigator product uses a string registry entry for a counter value, when Microsoft says that a REG_DWORD type should be used.)

Clearly, you must use the registry for some types of application configuration data, such as application-specific DLL directories, if you want to use the associated Windows 95 features. But this is only a viable solution if your program will be running under Windows 95. Under any other variation of Windows (as of this writing), application-specific paths don't exist, so you must choose between abandoning this feature entirely or supporting more than one standard configuration.

On the security front, the Windows registry is also vulnerable to user fiddling, since Microsoft provides that handy program, REGEDIT.EXE, which takes all that incomprehensible binary stuff and presents it in a quite usable and inviting hierarchy. Don't misunderstand—I'm quite happy to have REGEDIT.EXE available when I must make a change to the registry; I'd be one of the first and loudest protesters if Microsoft forced us to write a custom program just to modify a registry entry. But I'm also a little uneasy about people traipsing through their registries, given its importance in Windows 95. (As I write this, I've only seen a few Windows 95-specific programs, yet I've already encountered one, Symantec's Norton Navigator, that tells the user to fiddle with a binary registry entry to turn off the splash screen. I guess that the more things change, the more they really do stay the same.)

## Custom Binary Files

The third, and oldest, approach to storing persistent data is the custom format binary file. This is the approach I tend to use for most application document and configuration data, since it's slightly more secure than .INI files, and it's more portable from one Windows installation to another (including on the same system) than registry entries.

Binary files used for configuration data suffer from one of the same problems as .INI files: Windows directory pollution. Install, run, and then uninstall enough programs, and it matters little whether they used their own .INI files or their own binary files; if the configuration files wind up being cyberdetritus in your Windows directory, they're still a pain to clean up. For programs that are not run from a shared drive, a cleaner solution, and one that I use in Stickies!, is to place binary configuration files into the application's home directory (the one that contains the application's main .EXE file).

Aside from reducing Windows-directory pollution, this has a couple of more important real world benefits. First, users can run the program from different Windows configurations on the same computer without having to endure the idiocy of reinstalling an already installed program merely to effect the needed configuration changes. I run into this all the time, as all my computers have multiple versions of Windows (and even the occasional copy of OS/2 here and there). Installing a program onto a single computer can sometimes require three or four trips through the installation program, which is never quite as much fun as I hope it will be. Second, uninstalling your program can be a trivial matter. If your program uses a binary configuration file, it typically has no need for .INI files, so the user can often delete the entire installation simply by deleting the application's home directory, and not have any .INI or registry "residue" left over. (This will still leave the application's document files in other directories, of course, but short of providing a *very* aggressive uninstall program (one that I would be quite hesitant to use, in fact), there's nothing you can do about that.)

A more common use of custom binary files is for application data. The overwhelming majority of application programs we use rely on one or more such file formats, whether they're word processing files, precompiled headers, or any other of the (seemingly) billion-and-one different types of graphics file. For most applications, custom binary files are about the only viable solution (with the exception of some of the seven-bit ASCII formats, such as RTF for word processors, but those are so cryptic that they might as well be binary formats).

I also want to mention canned database functionality, via libraries that support ODBC or a specific database format. This is another good theory that doesn't quite measure up in the real world for some applications. The main problem with such libraries is their size and additional installation burden. In many cases such libraries add well over a megabyte to your program's total size, and even worse, you now have new installation worries to deal with. Minimally, you have to install the library properly, and hope that if you install a newer version onto a user's system, you're not going to break some other critical application that will work with only the older version of the library.

Still, in some cases the benefits of these libraries far outweigh the costs, since you can access databases in a third-party format or use extensive indexing facilities without having to spend weeks coding your own sufficiently reliable library of routines. This is a generalization, but in my experience the decision of whether to use such a library usually boils down to whether your program will have to access pre-existing data in a standard format, or create data in a standard format so that it can then be manipulated by another program. Unless your program faces these requirements, you're likely better off avoiding the overhead and configuration hassles of standard database libraries.

This is another area where RAD (rapid application development) can be disappointing in a real world project. You can quickly create an application that uses dBase or Paradox or Access files, for example, and you didn't even have to touch the code that understands the database formats. What a great idea! But suddenly it's time to distribute your program, and you're faced with numerous packaging, distribution, and installation problems. As I've said so many times in this book, this is a decision that only you can make, and it must be made in the context of an individual project.

# Smart Data Files

All smart data files are binary files, but not all binary files are smart. This is a critical distinction because there's a huge difference to you and your users between simply dumping some binary data into a file (a practice I see all too often) and employing smart data files. As I'll show below, smart data files are not merely files with certain characteristics; the term also implies a lot about how the application program uses them. You could argue that how a file (or any data) is used is beyond the scope of the file itself, but in this case the two issues are intertwined more so than normal.

Enough theory. Time to get down to brass bits. Smart data files and the programs that use them have the following characteristics:

- They can be used for any type of data (system configuration, application configuration, or application document).

- They are completely self-identifying. By "self-identifying" I mean that any program that examines the file can tell unambiguously and with trivial effort what kind of file it is and which version of the custom format is used. The file's name, extension, and location in the file system can not participate in this identification process; all information must come from the file's contents. (This is a critical detail, since users love to rename files, and, as I pointed out in Chapter 1, many beginning Windows users confuse a file's format and naming convention.) You only need a trivial amount of information in the file to accomplish this—a short "fingerprint" sequence of bytes, plus a major and minor version number—and the foresight to do it.

This characteristic does not say that a program can determine with equal ease the exact contents of the file, such as the number of pages in a word processing document. In many cases, a program can only do that by a more laborious process involving reading most or all of the file. Obviously, you should make your files as easy to interpret as possible, and there might be times when you want to make more information readily available. For example, you create a custom database format for customer records, and you can easily read the file one record at a time to allow the user to view or edit the data. So you don't bother to store the number of records in the file's header, since it isn't needed. But soon enough you start getting requests from Windows 95 users for a file viewer they can access with the right mouse button that will show them a snapshot of the file. Suddenly you wish you had stored the number of customer records in the file's header, so that your viewer doesn't have to laboriously read the entire file counting records, or calculate the number of records based on the file's size (assuming all the records are known to be the same length). This is a perfect example of how "version triggered format extensions" can come into play, another characteristic of smart data files that I'll get to shortly.

It's worth pointing out that not all efforts to identify files, whether binary format or not, work exactly as expected. When I first started working with Visual C++ 2.x and Windows 95, I was reminded of this numerous times. Every once in a while I would accidentally double click on a .MAK file for a Visual C++ 1.5 project. Since I had .MAK extensions associated with Visual C++ 2.x, the wrong program would be executed. Visual C++ 2.x did detect that the .MAK file was the wrong version, but the overall effect wasn't very pleasing. When I clicked on the file, here's what happened:

1. Visual C++ 2.x displayed its splash panel.

2. Visual C++ displayed its main window and a dialog box appeared for just a moment, not nearly enough time for me to read it. (I would later see that this dialog was telling me that the older file format was detected and asking if I wanted to convert it.)

3. Explorer got the focus and covered up Visual C++ and the dialog box.

4. I saw a system modal dialog box telling me that the .MAK file (or one of its components) could not be found. See Figure 9.2 for this dialog box and the one from step 2.

Perhaps I'm missing something obvious, but the modal dialog box really surprised me, since it was clear that Windows had followed the letter of the law, and associated a .MAK file with Visual C++ 2.x, exactly as I'd told it. Visual C++ 2.x was running, so I knew that there was, in fact, no trouble in starting it. I didn't bother to investigate this further, but it is clearly an oddity.

Try to open a Visual C++ 2.x .MAK file with version 1.5 and the results are even less impressive. Visual C++ 1.5 fails to recognize the version 2.x format and displays two dialog boxes. The first one asks if the .MAK file is an external one, and if you say no, the second one reports a syntax error in line one. My point is not that I expect an older version of a program to use a data file from a future version; that would be absurd. But I am saying that a file format should be constructed with enough foresight that the older version of the program can still identify the file (for example, some sort of Visual C++ MAKE file), and see that it's a newer version that it can't handle. Then, even an older version of the

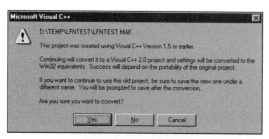

**Figure 9.2  Version detection with a twist.**

program can say something intelligent, like, "FRED.MAK can only be used with a later version of Visual C++," and not resort to this silliness of asking the user what kind of file it is and reporting bogus syntax errors.

The most prevalent form of this type of version checking is in Windows itself, in that executables are all stamped with an "expected Windows version." Unfortunately, Microsoft corrupted this mechanism, and Win32s 1.30 even allows the user to run programs that contain a version number greater than 4.0. (See Chapter 14 for much more on Windows and version checking.)

One of the primary benefits of smart data files is that using them can make it easier to create intelligent, accommodating programs. We're all used to seeing this effect in action, in the form of applications that gracefully detect and convert between various custom data formats for their documents. Save a file in Word for Windows 6.0, and you normally get a Word 6.0 file, but you can easily save it as a Word 2.0 file, rich text format, WordPerfect, MS Write, etc. This is such common practice with modern application programs that we seldom think about it.

A subtler variation of this convenience involves application configuration data. When you upgrade to a new version of an application program, you never have to run a conversion program that re-does your .INI settings for that program. But not that long ago, it was common practice when upgrading some programs, such as many communications applications, to have to run a special utility to convert the program's data (for example, dialing directory) to the new version's format. Unfortunately, some programs still require this extra step, a fact I find astonishing. Separate file conversion utilities are almost always a sign of programmer laziness, and I know from experience that they tend to be even less pristine code than the main application, since the programmer knows from day one that they're "throw away" utilities.

In my opinion, no program should require a user to do more than reply to a prompt in order to convert data to a new format. A good example, albeit with document data and not configuration data, is how Word for Windows 6.0 handles Word 2.0 files. Load the file and edit to your heart's content, and you won't even know you're using a Word 2.0 file. When you try to save the file, though, Word will tell you that it's a version 2.0 file and will give you the option of saving in the same format or converting it to version 6.0. In fact, this is probably one of the best examples I can cite of intelligent, accommodating software, since it's useful and as unobtrusive as possible.

- They use reserved/must-be-zero fields to minimize file format changes. This is one of those techniques that's amazingly easy to employ, yet surprisingly few programmers take the time. When you're creating a custom format for a smart data file, you almost always wind up with at least two logically distinct sections: A header, which contains the fingerprint and version fields, and sometimes other administrative data; and the actual data and configuration portion(s). Once you define what goes where, you can stare at your shiny new data structures and conjure up all sorts of contingencies and still not be able to think of a single extra byte you could need or want to add. Yet almost without fail, within a week of distributing the program to users, something pops up, and you're suddenly annoyed that you have to resort to a format extension (see next item) because you didn't include enough (or any) reserved fields. Things like this long ago convinced me that Murphy (of "Murphy's Law" fame) was a programmer.

The main trick is not just adding a few bytes to the header and making sure they're always zero; that's trivial stuff. You have to be careful when the time comes to use some of those precious reserved bytes for a new purpose. I did this several times in Stickies! over the years, and it was a great convenience. The key is to remember that those fields are always all binary zeroes, and what that translates to in various data types (FALSE, zero-length string, 0, etc.). As long as all-zeroes results in an unambiguous, usable, and safe value, you can allocate some previously reserved fields and preserve your old data format. In some cases, you might have to make your code jump through hoops, though. Say you want to allocate a BOOL for a new configuration option that will normally be on or TRUE, with FALSE being the more risky setting for the advanced users (perhaps you want to give your users an option not to be prompted for some error condition). It's not pretty, but in such cases the best option is to use inverted logic; instead of calling the BOOL warn_about_files, which might be the most natural approach, you'd call it something like dont_warn_about_files, and have the default be FALSE. In this way, you and your users get the new feature, and you don't have to change your file format or spend time writing a converter.

As for how many bytes you should reserve, I typically use from 20 to 50. That gives me enough room for a good number of small fields, but doesn't bloat the data file significantly. If you're reasonably sure that you'll have to add some fields for a new feature, don't rely on reserved fields. Instead, use the "hanging a function off a boolean" trick I described in Chapter 2, and allocate the required fields now, even if they won't be used until the next version. And even then, be sure to include some reserved fields.

When you switch some bytes from reserved to active duty, please take the time to examine the data structures carefully, to make sure that you haven't accidentally changed the size of the structure or the offset of any of the old fields within it. One easy way to guard against this is with a file dumper utility, which I'll talk about a little later.

*When you start fiddling with reserved fields, it's very easy to get carried away and start playing the programming version of "name that tune," or rather, "I can encode that customer number in three bytes!" Pretty soon, you find yourself doing all sorts of bizarre things in an effort to shoehorn just a little more information into the few remaining bytes. If at all possible, resist the urge. In the long run these unnatural acts are never worth it, and you only wind up making your program harder to maintain. Besides, format extensions aren't that bad. Trust me.*

- They use version-triggered format extensions, when needed. Face it, sometimes, no matter how crafty you are with your reserved/must-be-zero fields, you'll still run into situations where you need to extend your custom file format. These new fields typically fall in a new structure that's stored at the end of the header, sandwiched between the old header (or the most recent format extension) and the data portion of the file. All you have to do is:

  1. Make sure you really need the extension. You have to examine your data file and your application's needs carefully—do you need room for new document-level settings, in which case an extension is in order, or does it make more sense to change the format of the data? If the latter is the right path, then you should still change the version number, so that there's no possibility of an older version of the program trying to read the new format and becoming terminally confused. (And don't forget that sometimes you have to change both the header and the data format. Perhaps you're adding a new field to a custom database, which obviously requires a change to the data. But your application lets the user specify default values for all the fields on a per-database basis, which means you have to change the header format or add an extension, as well, to make room for the default value for the new field.)

2. Define a new structure for the format extension, and make sure to add some reserved fields, so you can avoid this in the future. This might not be a format extension, but an entirely new configuration data format. That's fine, but make sure that the file's fingerprint and version codes are still at the same offset in the file, so that all versions of the program can still identify it. The best way to isolate the fingerprint and version codes is to place them in their own structure, and then never change that structure over the life span of the program.

I strongly prefer to use extensions instead of entirely new formats, simply because it makes things easier in the long run. If you redefine the file format, then your program must do a lot of bucket-brigading of data from the old format to the new when it encounters a data file in the old format. It's almost always easier just to leave the old structures as they are and add new ones as needed.

3. Add an instance of the new or changed configuration data structure to your program's data, initialized with default values, and at the proper level of visibility in the program, typically global. (By this point in this book, you're probably surprised that someone as paranoid as I am would tell you to place anything at global scope in a program. As it turns out, for many pieces of data, particularly configuration settings, it makes a great deal of sense to make them global, since you often wind up reading and writing them from many different places in the program.)

4. Select a new version number for this variation of the file format. The format changes must be monotonic: If version 2.1 of the data file still uses just the original version of the format, and you add an extension for version 3.0, then all versions after 3.0 must also use that extension, plus, possibly, some new ones.

5. Modify your program so that it will examine the version number and then read the extension only if it is present. If the file happens to be an old format, this isn't a problem, since your program will use the pre-initialized version of the new structure defined in step 3. If the file is in the new format, you'll simply overlay the initialized version with the values from the file.

6. Decide how to handle saving the file. If your program will automatically update the file to the new format, then it must make sure to use both the new version number and the new file format extension. Depending on the application and the nature of the data, you might want to give the user an option at save time, as Word for Windows does.

7. Update your file dumper utility to handle the new format extension. See the next page for more on this.

- They use the "detect and rename" idiom for files with fixed locations. When you're saving a configuration file to the user's Windows directory or any other specific location, there's always a chance that you'll have a file naming collision, no matter how close to "unique" you think your chosen file name is. It happens.

I'm not saying that there's a significant risk some other programmer will name a configuration file BAZOOKA.DAT; you're pretty safe on that front. The most likely source of trouble is your program's user, who might delete, move, rename or replace your data file when your program isn't looking. That's why I always make programs that use smart data files check that the file is what it should be, both when it reads from the file and when it's about to write to it. If the user has accidentally (or even intentionally, without realizing the consequences) placed another file into the Windows directory with the name your program is about to use, you can't just overwrite that file and destroy the user's data. (I'm taking liberties here with the word "can't", of course, since I've seen programs do exactly this. But you get the point.)

My solution is the "detect and rename" idiom. Whenever your program is about to read from or write to the configuration file, it should check the file's fingerprint and version code. If it's really the program's file, then it can go ahead and read it or replace it with a clear conscience. However, if it isn't, then the program should rename the file to preserve its contents and tell the user what just happened.

Another internal detail of using smart data files is overlaying the default configuration settings. I don't consider this a requirement of smart data files, but in almost all cases it works so well that I don't even consider not using it. As I mentioned above, you simply create an instance of each file structure, initialized to the default values. When you read the structure from the file, you overlay the initialized structure, and when you save the data to the file, you simply write out whatever is in the structures. The benefit of this approach comes when your program can't find the configuration file (possibly because this is the first time the user has run it). Then, your program still refers to these same in-memory structures throughout its execution, which just happen to contain all the carefully chosen default values for option settings. As your program runs, it makes changes directly into these structures, and then writes them to disk as needed.

I mentioned above that you should maintain a file dumper utility. Well, you should. This doesn't have to be anything fancy, since it's a private program, just a simple little utility that reads your custom data file and displays all its fields in a nicely formatted way. If your file will contain any significant amount of data, you'll want to make your dumper program write its results to a plain-text file; for small amounts of data, such as the example in this chapter, you can get by with a simple Win32 console application. You'll find that the dumper utility is useful as a way to sanity check the files your program is creating during testing.

You'll also want to use the dumper utility to make sure you don't run into data alignment problems. (Alignment refers to how your compiler will lay out the fields in your data structures. With one-byte alignment, there is never any padding between fields, since they're all on a one-byte boundary. Any other alignment means that all fields are on a boundary that's at an address divisible by two, four, or eight (the other alignment options for most C compilers), which opens the possibility for some padding between fields, and therefore changes in the size of your structures. If the file on disk and your program disagree on the exact layout of your structures, disaster will ensue.) There's nothing difficult about slaying this particular dragon—pick an alignment and then make sure that it can't change. In this chapter's sample, I did this by using the Win32 SDK's packing headers, PSHPACK1.H and POPPACK.H in the header that defines the structures. This ensures that I get the desired data alignment setting (one byte), without changing the setting for any other source file that includes this header.

One last thing about writing a dumper utility: Make sure that it dumps all the fields from the file in a way that allows you to tell unambiguously what's going on. For example, if you include a buffer for text and a second field that indicates the length of the text, then don't just dump the beginning of the text buffer—dump it all, and dump the length indicator as a separate piece of information, if it's critical. Similarly, it often makes sense to have your dumper utility provide both a physical and logical view of data, such as showing the reserved fields and then displaying a more conspicuous warning message if any of them are not zero. This kind of programming can be quite tedious, but the resulting utility can often help you catch some subtle errors before your program sees prime time.

# Configuration Data Sample

Rather than create a new sample just for this chapter, I thought it would be better to examine the smart data file usage in the MegaZero sample from Appendix A. MegaZero is a simple program that remembers the names of the last ten files that were dragged and dropped onto it, as well as the date it was last run. It stores this information in a disk file called MEGAZERO.DAT in the user's Windows directory (typically C:\WINDOWS).

Listings 9.1 and 9.2 show CONFIG.H and CONFIG.CPP, the parts of MegaZero that are most pertinent to this chapter.

In particular, notice:

- The use of the PSHPACK1.H and POPPACK.H alignment headers in CONFIG.H. This sets the desired alignment (one byte), and ensures that the alignment is not propagated to any other source file that includes this header.

- Each component of the file's two component structures (config_header and config) is only read or written once anywhere in the source. By centralizing the reading and writing tasks, the code is easier to maintain without introducing errors. This is always a concern with any program, of course, but when you're maintaining code that does binary file manipulation, it's even more important because of all the subtle errors that can creep in when you're making "just one little change."

- The way this support is packaged, the hosting program can do nothing more than call LoadConfigData() at startup, and SaveConfigData() at shutdown. But notice that LoadConfigData() doesn't provide the caller with an indication of whether there's a valid configuration file on disk (either pre-existing or newly created). Your program will still operate acceptably, since it has its in-memory data structures loaded with default values. But depending on the nature of your program, that might not be good enough. You might want to modify LoadConfigData() to return a BOOL that indicates everything is OK with the data file, and then make the main program refuse to run if it receives a value of FALSE from LoadConfigData().

- The extensive use of OutputDebugString(). I've found that this can save you considerable grief when you're dealing with binary file access, and you're trying to track down some persistent mystery, like exactly why the new version of your program refuses to recognize an old copy of your data file. In such cases, the WINDBG utility that comes with the Win32 SDK and OutputDebugString() can be your best friends.

- The code uses a local routine, GetBaseDirectory(), to provide the directory for the file. This might seem like frippery, since it does nothing in this implementation but front-end the GetWindowsDirectory() API. I've found that this use of abstraction can be a real life saver when you need or want to make a change to the program's behavior in this area. For example, you might want to make your 16-bit program store its configuration file in the Windows directory when it's running under Windows 3.1 or from a networked drive, but in its application's home or custom data directory under Windows 95. If your code uses a special routine to fetch the file's directory, this change is localized, and there's no chance you'll accidentally miss one or more places where the code must be changed.

*Please make sure that whenever you access any file under Windows that you never accidentally use an unqualified name, meaning a file name without the drive and path components. If you do use a "bare" filename, Windows assumes you meant to use the current drive and directory, which isn't always what you had in mind. This is another of those odd little errors that can drive you crazy for days while you try to find out why your program can't seem to find a file that you know is there, or sometimes creates one in the strangest places. If you make a habit of using a routine like BuildFN() in CONFIG.CPP, your chances of avoiding this problem will be much better.*

- IsOurFile() is a critical routine, since it has the task of looking at an open file and determining if it's really what it's supposed to be. If the file is too short or it doesn't have the proper fingerprint, then this routine simply returns FALSE. If your program uses one or more format extensions, then it reads them according to the version stamp it finds and returns TRUE. Less obvious is what to do about a file with the proper fingerprint, but with a version number it doesn't know how to handle. Clearly the program can't accept this as a valid file, but you must decide if the function should notify the user via a MessageBox() call or other means, or if it should merely communicate this situation to its caller. As always, the answer depends on the nature of your program and users.

## Listing 9.1    CONFIG.H from MegaZero

```
#ifndef __CONFIG_H__
#define __CONFIG_H__

#include <pshpack1.h>        // Byte packing, please

void LoadConfigData(void);
void SaveConfigData(void);

struct config_type
   {
    char fn1[MAX_PATH];
    char fn2[MAX_PATH];
    char fn3[MAX_PATH];
    char fn4[MAX_PATH];
    char fn5[MAX_PATH];
    char fn6[MAX_PATH];
    char fn7[MAX_PATH];
    char fn8[MAX_PATH];
    char fn9[MAX_PATH];
    char fn10[MAX_PATH];

    int last_run_month;
    int last_run_day;
    int last_run_year;

    BOOL locked;
    char password[MAX_PW_LEN + 1];

    int  reserved[10];
};

// Our globally accessible array of configuration data

extern config_type config;

// Our header, which normally isn't referred to by code outside of this
// compilation unit.

#define eye_catcher_len 9

struct config_header_type
   {
```

```
      char eye_catcher[eye_catcher_len];
      WORD major_version;
      WORD minor_version;
    };

#include <poppack.h>        // Back to whatever was in effect

#endif
```

## Listing 9.2    CONFIG.CPP from MegaZero

```
/* Copyright Lou Grinzo 1995
   Zen of Windows 95 Programming */

#include "stdafx.h"
#include "config.h"
#include "io.h"
#include "tb_int.h"
#include "toolbox.h"

// Our global configuration data array, which will be overlaid with
// data from the file, assuming it exists.

config_type config =
  {
    "[no setting]",   // fn1
    "[no setting]",   // fn2
    "[no setting]",   // fn3
    "[no setting]",   // fn4
    "[no setting]",   // fn5
    "[no setting]",   // fn6
    "[no setting]",   // fn7
    "[no setting]",   // fn8
    "[no setting]",   // fn9
    "[no setting]",   // fn10

    0,                // last_run_month
    0,                // last_run_day
    0                 // last_run_year

    FALSE,        // locked
    "",               // password

    { 0, 0, 0, 0, 0,  // reserved
      0, 0, 0, 0, 0 }
  };

static char data_fn[] = "megazero.dat";

config_header_type config_header =
  {
    "megazero",   // eyecatcher (9 chars, incl. term. null)
    1,            // major_version
    0             // minor_version
  };


///////////////////////////////////////////////////////////////////////
// Headers for Local Routines
///////////////////////////////////////////////////////////////////////
```

```
static BOOL BuildFN(char *fn, size_t max_len);
static BOOL CreateNewFile(void);
static UINT GetBaseDirectory(LPTSTR lpBuffer,UINT uSize);
static BOOL IsOurFile(FILE *f);
static BOOL RenameImpostor(void);
static void SetUpData(void);
static BOOL StoreData(FILE *f);

static BOOL strlcat(char *dest, const char *src, size_t max_len);
static BOOL strlcatAtomic(char *dest, const char *src, size_t max_len);

//////////////////////////////////////////////////////////////////////
// Exported routines
//////////////////////////////////////////////////////////////////////

//////////////////////////////////////////////////////////////////////
// LoadConfigData(): Load the in-memory copy of the config array from our
// custom format file.  This function handles all the pathological cases:
// File not found, file found but not really our file, etc.  If a usable data
// file doesn't exist, then the default settings in config_header and config
// are not changed, and they can be used as-is.
//////////////////////////////////////////////////////////////////////

void LoadConfigData(void)
{
  char fn[MAX_PATH];
  FILE *f;

  if(!BuildFN(fn,sizeof(fn)))
      {
#ifdef _DEBUG
      OutputDebugString("*** LoadConfigData: Unable to build data fn.\n");
#endif
        return;
      }

  // Handle the special case and get it out of the way.

  if(!FileExists(fn))
      {
#ifdef _DEBUG
      OutputDebugString("*** LoadConfigData: Data file didn't exist; \n");
        OutputDebugString("creating    new one.\n");
#endif
      CreateNewFile();
        return;
      }

  if((f = fopen(fn,"rb")) == NULL)
      {
#ifdef _DEBUG
      OutputDebugString("*** LoadConfigData: Unable to open data file\n");
#endif
        return;
      }

  if(IsOurFile(f))
      {
#ifdef _DEBUG
      OutputDebugString("*** LoadConfigData: IsOurFile() == TRUE\n");
#endif
```

```
        // Step over the header, which has already been read in
        fseek(f,sizeof(config_header),SEEK_SET);

        if(fread(&config,sizeof(config),1,f) == 0)
            {
#ifdef _DEBUG
            OutputDebugString("*** LoadConfigData: Unable to read data file\n");
#endif
            }

        // If we were handling more than one version of the data file, then this
        // is where we'd conditionally read the extensions to the data format,
        // based on the version number

        fclose(f);
      }
    else
      {
#ifdef _DEBUG
      OutputDebugString("*** LoadConfigData: IsOurFile() == FALSE\n");
#endif
        fclose(f);

        if(RenameImpostor())
          CreateNewFile();
      }
}


///////////////////////////////////////////////////////////////////////////
// SaveConfigData(): Save the in-memory copy of the config array in a file
// that has our custom header.  This function handles all the pathological
// cases: File not found, file found but not really our file, etc.
///////////////////////////////////////////////////////////////////////////

void SaveConfigData(void)
{
  char fn[MAX_PATH];
  FILE *f;

  if(!BuildFN(fn,sizeof(fn)))
      {
#ifdef _DEBUG
      OutputDebugString("*** SaveConfigData: Unable to build data fn.\n");
#endif
        return;
      }

  // How could this happen?  Perhaps the user or some other program deleted
  // our data file while we were running?  Whatever the case, it's easily
  // covered.
  if(!FileExists(fn))
      {
#ifdef _DEBUG
      OutputDebugString("*** SaveConfigData: Data file didn't exist;\n");
        OutputDebugString("creating new one.\n");
#endif
      CreateNewFile();
        return;
      }
```

```
  // Open the file...
  if((f = fopen(fn,"rb+")) == NULL)
    {
#ifdef _DEBUG
    OutputDebugString("*** SaveConfigData: Unable to open data file.\n");
#endif
    return;
    }

  // ..if it's ours...
  if(IsOurFile(f))
    {
#ifdef _DEBUG
    OutputDebugString("*** SaveConfigData: IsOurFile() == TRUE\n");
#endif
    // ...write the header and data...
    StoreData(f);

    // ...and we're done.
    fclose(f);
    }
  else
    {
#ifdef _DEBUG
    OutputDebugString("*** SaveConfigData: IsOurFile() == FALSE\n");
#endif
    // ...if it's not ours, then we close the old file, whatever it was,
    // rename it, and then create a new file with our in-memory data.
    fclose(f);

    if(RenameImpostor())
      CreateNewFile();
    }
}


///////////////////////////////////////////////////////////////////////////
// Local routines
///////////////////////////////////////////////////////////////////////////


///////////////////////////////////////////////////////////////////////////
// BuildFN(): Build a fully-qualified file name for our data file.  The
// string is built right into the caller's provided buffer.
//
// Return TRUE if the string was built properly, FALSE otherwise.
//
// max_len includes the term. null
///////////////////////////////////////////////////////////////////////////

static BOOL BuildFN(char *fn, size_t max_len)
{
  UINT rc = GetBaseDirectory(fn,max_len);

  if((rc == 0) || (rc > max_len))
    {
#ifdef _DEBUG
    OutputDebugString("*** BuildFN: Unable to retrieve base dir\n");
#endif
    return FALSE;
    }
```

```
        // We don't have to verify that AppendSlash did anything or had room for
        // a slash, if one is needed.  strlcatAtomic() will handle the out-of-
        // space problem for us.

        AppendSlash(fn,max_len - 1);

        return strlcatAtomic(fn,data_fn,max_len);
    }


///////////////////////////////////////////////////////////////////////////
// CreateNewFile(): Create a new copy of our custom data file from the in-
// memory data structures.  Notice that we DON'T check to see if the file
// exists-- we just hammer whatever is there.  Any and all steps to preserve
// the contents of a file with the same name as the one we're about to create
// must be taken before we're called!
//
// Return TRUE if the file was successfully created, FALSE otherwise.
//
///////////////////////////////////////////////////////////////////////////

static BOOL CreateNewFile(void)
{
    char fn[MAX_PATH];
    FILE *f;

    if(!BuildFN(fn,sizeof(fn)))
        {
#ifdef _DEBUG
        OutputDebugString("*** CreateNewFile: Unable to build data file\n");
#endif
        return FALSE;
        }

    if((f = fopen(fn,"wb")) != NULL)
        {
        BOOL rc = StoreData(f);

        fclose(f);

        return rc;
        }
    else
        {
#ifdef _DEBUG
        OutputDebugString("*** CreateNewFile: Unable to open data file\n");
#endif
        return FALSE;
        }
}


///////////////////////////////////////////////////////////////////////////
// GetBaseDirectory(): Retrieve the directory used for our data file.
// Currently, this is always the user's Windows directory, which is why
// this function mimics the GetWindowsDirectory() interface.
///////////////////////////////////////////////////////////////////////////

UINT GetBaseDirectory(LPTSTR lpBuffer,UINT uSize)
{
    if(lpBuffer == NULL)
        {
```

```
#ifdef _DEBUG
    OutputDebugString("*** GetBaseDirectory: Null pointer detected\n");
#endif
    return 0;
    }

 return GetWindowsDirectory(lpBuffer,uSize);
}

///////////////////////////////////////////////////////////////////////
// IsOurFile(): Examine the specified open file, and determine if
// it is our custom data file format.
//
// If the file is our custom format, then we return TRUE, FALSE otherwise.
// The file is always left positioned at its beginning (offset 0), when we
// exit, regardless of its contents.
///////////////////////////////////////////////////////////////////////

static BOOL IsOurFile(FILE *f)
{
  // Check the file length.  Anything but this length and it isn't our file

  if(_filelength(_fileno(f)) != sizeof(config_header_type) + sizeof(config_type))
    return FALSE;

  // Check the header contents

  config_header_type test_header;

  if(fread(&test_header,sizeof(test_header),1,f) < 1)
    return FALSE;

  // Back to the beginning of the file we go.
  fseek(f,0,SEEK_SET);

  // If it's not our eye-catcher, then it's not our file.
  if(memcmp(&test_header.eye_catcher,&config_header.eye_catcher,
    sizeof(test_header.eye_catcher)) != 0)
    return FALSE;

  // We'll only accept version 1.0 for now
  if((test_header.major_version > 1) || (test_header.minor_version > 0))
    {
     // Possibly issue a version-specific warning to the user here
     return FALSE;
    }

  // Do this copy so that other parts of the program can correctly
  // refer to the header information, including the version codes.
  memcpy(&config_header,&test_header,sizeof(test_header));
  return TRUE;
}

///////////////////////////////////////////////////////////////////////
// RenameImpostor(): Someone else has determined that there is a file with
// the exact same fully qualified name as the one we want to use, but it
// isn't our file.  Since we don't know what it is, we can't very well
// delete it.  But we need to save our data, so we must first rename the
// the blocking file to something else.
//
```

```
    // We do NOT verify that the blocking file exists, nor do we check its format!
    //
    // Return TRUE if the rename operation succeeded, FALSE otherwise.
    /////////////////////////////////////////////////////////////////////////////
    static BOOL RenameImpostor(void)
    {
      char blocking_fn[MAX_PATH], new_fn[MAX_PATH], win_dir[MAX_PATH];

      if(!BuildFN(blocking_fn,sizeof(blocking_fn)))
        {
#ifdef _DEBUG
        OutputDebugString("*** RenameImpostor: Unable to build blocking_fn\n");
#endif
          return FALSE;
        }

      UINT rc = GetBaseDirectory(win_dir,sizeof(win_dir));

      if((rc == 0) || (rc > sizeof(win_dir)))
        {
#ifdef _DEBUG
        OutputDebugString("*** RenameImpostor: Unable to retrieve base dir\n");
#endif
          return FALSE;
        }

      if(GetTempFileName(win_dir,"OLD",0,new_fn) == 0)
        {
#ifdef _DEBUG
        OutputDebugString("*** RenameImpostor: Unable to retrieve");
          OutputDebugString("temp file name.\n");
#endif
          return FALSE;
        }

#ifdef _DEBUG
        OutputDebugString("*** RenameImpostor: blocking_fn: ");
        OutputDebugString(blocking_fn);
        OutputDebugString("\n*** RenameImpostor: new_fn: ");
        OutputDebugString(new_fn);
        OutputDebugString("\n");
#endif

      if(CopyFile(blocking_fn,new_fn,FALSE))
        {
        char buffer[1024];

        wsprintf(buffer,"Your existing file: \n  \"%s\"\nhas been renamed:\n
              \"%s\".  \n\nDo you want help?", blocking_fn,new_fn);

        if(MessageBox(0,buffer,"Please note!",MB_YESNO | MB_ICONEXCLAMATION |
          MB_TASKMODAL) == IDYES)
          MessageBox(0,
          "Imagine brilliant, insightful, context sensitive help here."
          "Help",MB_OK | MB_ICONINFORMATION | MB_TASKMODAL);
        return TRUE;
        }
      else
        {
#ifdef _DEBUG
        OutputDebugString("*** RenameImpostor: FAILED.\n");
```

```
#endif
        return FALSE;
    }
}

//////////////////////////////////////////////////////////////////////////////
// SetUpData(): Set our date fields in the config array for the current
// date, and make sure that all filename strings are terminated.
//////////////////////////////////////////////////////////////////////////////

static void SetUpData(void)
{
  // Set our header fields with today's date

  time_t now;
  tm now2;

  time(&now);
  now2 = *localtime(&now);

  config.last_run_month = now2.tm_mon + 1;  // month is zero-based(!?)
  config.last_run_day   = now2.tm_mday;
  config.last_run_year  = now2.tm_year;

  // If we're going to convert the data file to a newer version, this is the place
  // update the major and minor version numbers, as needed.

  // This is probably the height of paranoia, but at least it ensures that
  // no matter what is in the filename variables, they're still terminated.

  config.fn1[sizeof(config.fn1) - 1]  = '\0';
  config.fn2[sizeof(config.fn2) - 1]  = '\0';
  config.fn3[sizeof(config.fn3) - 1]  = '\0';
  config.fn4[sizeof(config.fn4) - 1]  = '\0';
  config.fn5[sizeof(config.fn5) - 1]  = '\0';
  config.fn6[sizeof(config.fn6) - 1]  = '\0';
  config.fn7[sizeof(config.fn7) - 1]  = '\0';
  config.fn8[sizeof(config.fn8) - 1]  = '\0';
  config.fn9[sizeof(config.fn9) - 1]  = '\0';
  config.fn10[sizeof(config.fn10) - 1] = '\0';

  return;
}

//////////////////////////////////////////////////////////////////////////////
// StoreDataFile(): Save the header and data for the file using the open
// file handle provided by our caller, which we assume is opened for binary
// writes.
//
// Return TRUE if the writes are successful, FALSE otherwise.
//////////////////////////////////////////////////////////////////////////////

static BOOL StoreData(FILE *f)
{
  // Clean up data, update the version number, etc. as needed
  SetUpData();

  if(fwrite(&config_header,sizeof(config_header),1,f) < 1)
    {
#ifdef _DEBUG
      OutputDebugString("*** StoreData: Unable to write data file\n");
```

```
#endif
     return FALSE;
   }

  // If there are version-specific extensions to the file's header, they
  // would be written to the file here.

  if(fwrite(&config,sizeof(config),1,f) < 1)
     {
#ifdef _DEBUG
     OutputDebugString("*** StoreData: Unable to write data file\n");
#endif
     return FALSE;
   }

  // If there are version-specific extensions to the file's data, they
  // would be written to the file here.

  fclose(f);

  // If we got here, everything went according to plan...
  return TRUE;
}
```

# 10

# *Abstraction in Action: Creating Your Own Virtual Machines*

# Abstraction in Action: Creating Your Own Virtual Machines

Chapter 10

As I've said elsewhere in this book, I believe that functional abstraction, whether in the form of local subroutines or carefully architected libraries, is a programmer's single most powerful tool for the creation of usable, robust, and portable programs. In this chapter, I'll talk about how you can employ abstraction in your own programs, and some of the problems and techniques unique to this type of programming.

## Why Bother?

You already do employ abstraction as a tool, of course, although you might not think of what you're doing in exactly this way. (After all, even the most basic use of subroutines falls into this category, albeit at the low end of the spectrum.) The most immediate and pragmatic answer to the above question is that thinking in

251

terms of abstraction, and making a conscious decision to use (or not use) it in individual projects will influence your work for the better.

To illustrate what I mean by using abstraction as a tool, let's start with a more traditional view of software design. A common strategy for solving some problems is "divide and conquer," in which you take some unmanageable task, such as sorting an extremely long list of customer records, and physically divide it into ever smaller subtasks, until each one is of a manageable or more convenient size. Similarly, programmers can employ abstraction to divide the distance between levels of abstraction, and thereby bridge the gap in several smaller, manageable steps, instead of a single huge one.

Bridging a conceptual gap is also like the sorting example in another way: They each behave non-linearly. In other words, with a simple, in-memory sort, you might be able to handle 1,000, 10,000, or even 100,000 records with the same very straightforward piece of code. (Your sorting time would increase dramatically as the number of items increased to these levels, but the point is that the same routine would handle the task.) Perhaps you then have to sort ten or twenty million items, and suddenly you find that your sorting routine can no longer handle the task, no matter how much time you can give it, since it runs into architectural limits and must be replaced with a disk-based sorting algorithm. In effect, the original algorithm's response time becomes infinite, because it can never do the job. (This is admittedly a forced example, since very few people sort that many pieces of data; for the obvious performance reasons they find ways to maintain the data in order and avoid the sort step entirely.)

When trying to bridge a conceptual gap, or manage sufficient complexity, we see the same non-linearity. Add a few functions or constants to an existing API and programmers, plucky bunch that we are, take it in stride. But add hundreds of new details, and soon we'll be lost in the fog and unable to get anything done without Herculean effort. That's when we stop working, and start looking around for solutions in the form of application frameworks or third-party libraries, i.e. new virtual machines that provide a higher, more usable (and sometimes more stable) platform for us to build on. By creating a middle layer (or, as my mother used to say, "splitting the difference"), you can create that new virtual machine, and be much more efficient in the long run.

As with so many other issues in programming, it's easy to get carried away and spend all your time writing a bigger, fancier programming kit instead of finished programs. (If nothing else, this is a danger because writing a tool kit is often a lot more fun than writing a complete program.) But short of that excess, your goal should be to make your finished program's code look more like pseudocode and less like a demonstration of the facilities of your programming language. I've seen this curious phenomenon many times: A programmer writes beautiful, very easily understood pseudocode at the design stage, then translates it into Medusa code (looking directly at it will turn you to stone). Even if you have to perform the calculation of the arithmetic mean only once, the code:

```
void IssueWarning(DATA *d, int num_obs)
{
  float mean = CalcMean(d,num_obs);
  if(mean < min_mean)
    MessageBox(0,"Data isn't mean enough!","Silly Example",MB_OK);
  else
    if(mean > max_mean)
      MessageBox(0,"Data is too mean!","Silly Example",MB_OK);
}

float CalcMean(DATA *d, int num_obs)
{
  float total = 0;
  for(int i = 0; i < num_obs; i++)
    total += d[i];
  return total / num_obs;
}
```

is easier to read than:

```
void IssueWarning(DATA *d, int num_obs)
{
  for(int i = 0; I < num_obs; I++)
    total += d[i];
  float mean = total / num_obs;

  if(mean < min_mean)
    MessageBox(0,"Data isn't mean enough!","Silly Example",MB_OK);
  else
    if(mean > max_mean)
      MessageBox(0,"Data is too mean!","Silly Example",MB_OK);
}
```

If C/C++ supported local functions, the first example could be packaged even better, by making CalcMean() a local function within IssueWarning(), but that's a topic for another time and place (in this case, Chapter 5). The point is that whenever possible any block of code that accomplishes a discrete (and possibly even discreet) logical function should be isolated unless there's an overriding reason not to do so.

In rare cases, this approach to programming can have performance implications, because subroutine calls and all that pushing and popping of parameters isn't free, and extra levels of indirection and parameter validation can add up. But the cost, at least in conventional performance terms, is almost never as high as programmers claim. This is especially true when you're already using some gargantuan framework that adds 200KB to your program (or requires a runtime DLL of over 300KB). In such a case, an additional hundred or so bytes of code in your entire program and the few extra clock cycles isn't much to get excited about. The minor performance impact of employing your home-grown abstraction is overwhelmed by the cost of using the framework in the first place. As I said in guideline 7, the key is to keep a perspective on performance.

I've also noticed another interesting, beneficial side effect when applications are written with a heavy reliance on abstraction: They're more usable. I know this sounds silly, since the usability of a program has nothing to do with the low-level details of its implementation; there's nothing to stop you from writing a beautiful, highly usable Windows program in "spaghetti assembly," for example. But in the real world there's often a positive connection once a program starts evolving over several releases, especially for Windows programs written under extreme time pressure: Highly abstracted code tends to be much easier to modify, so when a development team gets a request from their program's users (or from management) for some new usability enhancement, they're much more likely to add it, since it's so much easier. (In a way, this phenomenon is really just a generalization of the "hanging a function off a boolean" trick that I mentioned in guideline 0, in that you're constructing your entire program in a way that supports the notion of quick, high quality changes.)

The most immediate benefits of creating and using a middleware layer or platform are those of any code reuse: You're leveraging a body of known, presumably robust, code, which allows you to write higher quality programs more efficiently. Another issue, particular when creating Windows programs, is that you literally must choose between playing "API roulette," or taking action to insulate your code from the API's legions of problems. You can't merely decide to use MFC and assume that it will protect you and your programs; as I point out later, many of the MFC methods are merely paper-thin wrappers over API function calls and messages, with no effort at all in the framework to resolve these differences. (In fact, this is one of the more subtle dangers of using any Windows framework: A programmer can be lulled into a false sense of security, and assume that a framework delivers much more than it does. As with any tool, it pays to know a framework's limitations.)

As for what form your own abstractions take, it doesn't have to be anything fancy; a simple library of routines is sufficient. The magic is in the design of the individual functions, not the number of lines of code you write or how many OOP features you can cram into the package.

In short, my point is that programmers tend to lose sight of the doublewords for the bits; they forget that they can indeed create their own platforms on which they can build new code, not just use the architectures (such as the Windows API and their framework) presented to them.

*Paul, a close friend of mine, commented to me while I was writing this chapter that some programmers have an interesting reaction to any talk of creating a middle layer of software. He pointed out that some programmers will scoff at this, and dismiss it as frippery or an excuse for programmers not to do the real work at hand; yet, these are usually the same programmers who are the first to ask you for a copy of your library or class that implements some functionality they suddenly need. I've also seen this phenomenon, and I*

*think it's attributable to the difference between what software, tools, or techniques often promise and what they deliver in the real world. I'm sure everyone reading this book has been disappointed by over-blown marketing hype from software vendors more times than they can count. Some promised function either isn't in the product at all, or it works so poorly or so slowly that it's not worth using. This creates a significant amount of cynicism in all computer users, including programmers. As a result, when they hear about some new tool or technique, they discount the claims made on its behalf by more than half. Once they see the specific code (such as Paul's networking objects), though, they often recognize the immediate, pragmatic benefits, and want a copy.*

*I bring all this up because I think it's relevant to any attempt to introduce the creation of a large library or wrapping layer into a multi-person programming project. You have to sell two distinct groups on the idea: Management, which is often wary of anything that even remotely looks like programmers playing and not doing real work (I wonder where they get such ideas), and other programmers, who can be an even tougher sell, since they're the ones who will have to implement and use the library. This is really a matter of office politics, something I detest as much as the next code slinger, but it's something we all have to recognize and deal with from time to time.*

## "Trust but Verify" vs. "Steamrolling"

In a just and proper world (and, for all I know, in a parallel universe that lies a scant nanometer away in a direction we can't quite perceive), using the Windows API would not be a source of concern (no pun intended). We would simply refer to the documentation, use it directly (or indirectly via a framework), and go about our merry way, concerned only with things that happened "above the deck" in our program and safe in the knowledge that our Win32 code would run everywhere.

Sad to say, this isn't the case.

The Win32 API is far from the "consistent and uniform API for all of Microsoft's 32-bit platforms" that Microsoft claims it is. (See the beginning of Chapter 14 for the full quotation and source.) There are numerous minor, and some not so minor, differences between the three Win32 platforms (Win32s, Windows 95, Windows NT), including some very subtle ones that can cause you no end of grief (not to mention bugs) in a public program. (I won't go into examples here; see Chapter 14 for much more on Win32 issues.)

This situation, which is only aggravated by poor documentation, forces all Win32 developers to ask themselves constantly "should I test this?" when dealing with the API. As one example, I show in Chapter 14 that the API GetShortPathName() uses different extended error codes (retrieved via the GetLastError() API), and even succeeds or fails depending on which Win32 platform the program is running, even with the same input and system context. If you want to write solid, reliable code that actually takes the radical step of examining error codes and behaving appropriately, you have two choices:

1. Spend a lot of time testing the critical APIs in question in an effort to fully explore their behavior, including success and failure conditions and which error codes they return. This "trust, but verify" approach can be time consuming, and you run the risk of not sufficiently exploring the API's behavior when it's faced with common pathological cases. You might not think that there's a reasonable possibility that some API will be called with the name of a disk file that doesn't exist, for example, but a later release of your program might allow the user to enter some file name, resulting in a dependency on the API to detect this situation and respond gracefully (with one of the error codes your program is already checking for). When your program is distributed, it might be run under Win32s, say, which implements this now-critical detail of the API differently. Perhaps Win32s returns an error code you didn't expect, or it succeeds where Windows 95 and Windows NT fail (or vice versa), and you now have a bug and angry users to contend with.

   The "trust but verify" gambit (and don't kid yourself, it truly is a gambit) is particularly risky, because it's so easy to look at a snippet of code in isolation and say, "X will never happen. Why worry about it?" In many cases the speaker is absolutely correct, and X literally cannot happen. At least until the next release, or some maintenance is performed on the program, and new dependencies and assumptions are created, which not all parts of the code can sustain.

2. Wrap the critical and known troublesome APIs and unify their behavior. This is the "steamroller" approach, and if properly employed it can save you a great deal of time and grief in the long run. The key is to become aware of the problem APIs, which is much more difficult thanks to the state of the Win32 documentation. To allow programmers to use this API effectively, the documentation needs to be much more complete than it is, and to include more information on things like platform differences and error codes. Maybe next release.

   The first step of the solution is to identify those APIs which are critical to your program and might be "twitchy" on different platforms. In practice, this includes any Win32 API for which your program examines the extended error code (via GetLastError()), or to which it passes data of suspect pedigree. Once you identify a potential candidate, run a few minor tests under all the Win32 platforms that your code will support. If you find any differences between platforms, or even some surprising and/or inconvenient behavior on a single platform, don't rush to your code and start trying to accommodate these new-found quirks. Instead, determine if there's a simple way to wrap the API and "pave over" or "steamroll" the problem.

I mentioned GetShortPathName() above. It turned out to be an excellent example of an API that was easily unified via steamrolling. All the oddities I've found in this API to date (and I'm not the least bit convinced I've found them all) relate to how the API responds when the long file name you provide does not map to an existing file. Sometimes the function succeeds, sometimes it fails, and when it fails, it has different modes of failure. The solution was the wrapper uGetShortPathName(), which is in the Win32u library in Appendix C.

```
//////////////////////////////////////////////////////////////////////////////
// Unifying wrapper for the GetShortPathName() API.  Returns 0 with an
// appropriate extended error if the provided string does not name an
// existing file or directory.  Otherwise, the result from calling
// GetShortPathName() is returned to the caller.
//
// Pointer parameters are validated
//////////////////////////////////////////////////////////////////////////////

DWORD uGetShortPathName(LPCTSTR long_path,LPTSTR buffer,DWORD buffer_len)
{
#ifdef _DEBUG
  if((long_path == NULL) || (buffer == NULL))
    OutputDebugString("\nuGetShortPathName: Detected bad parameter!\n\n");
#endif

  // This also catches the zero-length and NULL ptr cases
  if(FileExists(long_path) || DirExists(long_path))
    {
     SetLastError(0);
     return GetShortPathName(long_path,buffer,buffer_len);
    }
  else
    {
     if((long_path == NULL) || (strlen(long_path) == 0))
      SetLastError(ERROR_BAD_PATHNAME);
     else
      SetLastError(ERROR_PATH_NOT_FOUND);

     return 0;
    }
}
```

This function checks to see if the provided file name is an existing file or directory. If it is, then the underlying API is called. If it isn't, then the wrapper returns with an appropriate, predictable error code and indicates failure. This provides uniform behavior with minimal exposure to platform quirks and future changes.

*In testing various techniques for this book and my other work, I found a couple of surprises in how the debugging version of Windows 95 handles two of its biggest problems: Listbox index and GDI coordinate clipping. (The Win32 API accepts 32-bit values for these numbers on all three platforms, but since the USER and GDI components are still 16 bit under Windows 95 and Win32s, these values are truncated to 16 bits and used as-is. See Chapter 14 for more on this.) Run a program that passes a GDI coordinate that gets clipped by Windows 95, and the debugging version of the operating system doesn't issue a message, which I find puzzling. After all, if there's one time when you're willing to burn cycles and bytes to flag everything that a developer might want to know about, running this version of Windows 95 should be it. The other surprise involved listbox indexes. When one of those is clipped, the debugging version of Windows 95 does issue a message, but it gets it wrong—instead of reporting the entire 32-bit value that the program attempted to pass, it reports only the high-order word as the invalid value. (For example, a value of 983040, which is 0x000f0000 is reported as 15, not 983040.)*

# Three Degrees of Abstraction

Before we get to the "how to" part of abstraction in the, well, abstract, let's spend a little time on the "what" aspect. It's very easy for programmers to fall into a simple, mechanical mode of thought where code is concerned, and to categorize it into code that's "here," meaning directly inline in the function the programmer is looking at, and code that's "not here," and has to be called. (Notice that I'm sidestepping the issue of C++ inline functions, which are physically the former (assuming your compiler deigns to make them truly inline) and logically the latter.) Programmers also, in the heat of battle, take a similarly narrow and mechanical view of using routines; they want to know the simplest possible incantation they can use to get the routine to do something for them. This is a non-trivial point that I'll return to later.

You could turn this discussion into its own endlessly detailed exercise in programming taxonomy, of course, but I don't see much value in that. (Unless you're looking for a topic for your master's thesis, of course.) As I see it, there are primarily three degrees of functional abstraction:

1. Wrapper. This is an extremely "tight" layer around an API (whether Windows, C run-time library, or whatever) that is constructed for the benefit of the caller. In fact, the defining characteristic for a wrapper is the fact that it changes in some way the interaction between the caller and the function being wrapped, but it does not change how the wrapper or wrappee interacts with the rest of

the system. The uGetShortPathName() function I mentioned above is a wrapper, in that it doesn't make any changes to the system; it unifies the interaction between the caller and its core API across platforms. Notice that a wrapper is not restricted to being very small or to calling just the wrapped function; it often works out that way, but a function is a wrapper because of how it interacts with the caller and the system, not how it performs its task.

In general, a wrapper should very closely follow the wrapped function's interface definition. When the wrapped function is a Win32 API, it's even more important that the wrapper's interface be identical to the API's. (I make an exception for an API wrapper whose sole purpose is to rework the interface into a more usable form. See the uGetDlgItemInt() example in the Win32u library.) Keeping the interfaces identical ensures that it's much easier for you and others on your team to use the wrappers without having to make needless changes to existing code; it also makes it easier to switch between wrapped and unwrapped APIs in different parts of the same program. See Appendix C for the Win32u library, which uses this approach for the coordinate-safe GDI wrappers.

Another key characteristic of Win32 API wrappers is the use of SetLastError() for setting extended error codes. This is one of those areas where reasonable people can disagree. My approach is to use SetLastError() in a wrapper only when the API documentation says the wrapped API uses it. My reasoning is simple: As code is maintained over a period of months or years, it's possible that programmers with different opinions of wrapper usage will modify the code. When someone changes code from using a wrapped API to the bare API, it's possible that the old application code called GetLastError() and performed some conditional processing based on the returned error code. If the code now uses the bare API, and that API doesn't use SetLastError(), the code could wind up processing a bogus, leftover error code value. (This assumes, of course, that the programmer doesn't realize that the bare API doesn't use SetLastError(), which is a natural enough mistake.) It's just as important to make sure that your wrapper uses SetLastError() in all paths if the wrapped API does. The last thing you want to do is accidentally leave the extended error code unchanged, and then have your caller check it. (Incredibly, the GetShortPathName() API does this in one case; there's no need to mimic it.)

Similarly, if someone is converting a given call from a bare API to a wrapped one, it doesn't makes sense to add extended error code processing (unless absolutely needed), since that will only act as a slight deterrent, and an excuse for programmers who don't want to make the change in the first place.

The most precarious issue in wrapping the Windows API is what to do about version checking. On a simple level, you can make your wrapper code check to see if it's running under Windows 95 before it does a Windows 95-specific parameter validation, for example. But that raises the question: Which version(s) of Windows 95? For example, many of the wrappers I present in the Win32u library in Appendix C are needed because the current version of Windows 95 still implements USER and GDI in 16-bit code. This is why listbox string indexes and GDI coordinates are restricted to 16 bits on that platform. (It's most definitely *not* why those values accept 32-bit values and then truncate them to 16 bits and naively use whatever is left. That behavior reflects either a conscious design decision by Microsoft not to warn the calling program that its data was being mangled by the system, or the single biggest design error I've ever seen.) What happens if you guard against this coordinate and index clipping, you ship your code, and then you discover that Nashville or Memphis, the next two versions of Windows 95, will move USER and/or GDI to 32 bits? Now what? This isn't as bad as it sounds, since the worst case should be that your program gracefully refuses to handle some task, when it could actually manage it. (I assume that if you're going to all the trouble of using an API wrapper that you'll actually check its return value and make your program react intelligently.)

Still, it doesn't hurt to be prepared, and you might want to include a fail-safe switch: Make all your API wrappers check a flag before they do something different from the basic API. Normally this flag would be on (thereby enabling the wrapper functionality), but you could give your program an undocumented command line switch (for example, "/BAREAPI=YES") that would make it turn off this flag at program startup. Then, if you run into a serious problem, you can have your users employ the formerly secret command line switch as a stopgap until you can fix the program and redistribute it. I'm not at all fond of such tactics, but depending on the nature of your users and exactly what you're doing in your wrappers and your program, this might be worth considering.

2. Minor Functional Abstraction. The next rung up the ladder from a pure wrapper, minor functional abstractions might or might not change how the caller and the function interact, but they normally change how the function and the system interact. For example, in Chapter 3, I presented CopyFileForceRW(), a function that calls the CopyFile() API, and then uses GetFileAttributes() and SetFileAttributes() APIs to make sure the copied file's read-only attribute bit is off. This function technically isn't a wrapper, simply because it makes a change to the system in addition to whatever the basic CopyFile() API does.

As with wrappers, it's important to keep the interface definition of this type of function as close to the original as possible, particularly when a Win32 API is at the core of your function. This is because programmers will often want to do some task, like copy a file, and they will want to get some added assurance of how it's done (for example, leaving the file in a read/write state), so they'll want to convert the old, bare API call to the wrapped one with a minimum of effort. In some cases, this sort of conversion to a wrapper is done as a quick and easy way of fixing a bug. Whatever the programmer's motive, if you can make the conversion as easy as changing the name of the called function, people will be more inclined to use it.

Similarly, minor functional abstractions should exactly follow the extended error code behavior of the APIs they use. In CopyFileForceRW(), for example, SetLastError() is used since CopyFile() uses it. But it's only used when bad parameters are rejected; the error codes set by CopyFile(), GetFileAttributes(), and SetFileAttributes() are allowed to flow through to the caller unchanged. The point is that making your function behave properly with respect to extended error codes is not difficult and it does not require a lot of intricate code, just an awareness of the issue. (In this example, had the attribute-manipulation APIs not used SetLastError(), I would have made CopyFileForceRW() call SetLastError() when they failed.)

There's also the issue of what to do about some of the odd SetLastError() choices the Win32 API makes. For example, when I call CopyFile() with a source file name on the F: drive, which is a CD ROM on my test system, and there is no disk in the drive, the call fails with an error code of five, ERROR_ACCESS_DENIED. I would prefer to see that case lumped together with error code three, ERROR_PATH_NOT_FOUND, even at the slight loss of information, since both cases will likely be handled the same way, by the calling program. Obviously, you can re-map extended error codes in your wrappers and minor functional abstractions, but I advise against it. I think it amounts to making a highly non-standard change in the system's behavior, for what is normally very little gain.

*I honestly wish that I could drag out my soap box at this point, climb up on it, and start bellowing about how you shouldn't change the error code usage because it's part of the system's defined behavior. But I can't do that, since Microsoft hasn't defined which APIs set which error codes, and they've even said that the same API uses different error codes on different Win32 platforms. Notice that I distinguish between re-mapping error codes and unifying their usage across platforms. This is admittedly a fine point, but one that I think is important: Changing error codes purely out of whim or to gain a minor convenience is very bad practice, but making them usable across all the platforms your program will allow itself to be run under is a worthwhile, some would say necessary, endeavor.*

3. Major Functional Abstraction. This is the level at which we're all the most familiar with abstraction: the subroutine. In this guise, functional abstractions are synthesizing new and significantly different behavior from one or more

other system resources. These system resources can be APIs, functions, files, your program's bound-in resources, etc.

In Chapter 6, I talked about explicitly loading DLLs. The sample program in that chapter includes the file HELLOINT.C that loads the required DLL and provides safe gateway functions for accessing the DLL's routines. I consider that implementation of LoadHello() a minor abstraction, almost a wrapper for the LoadLibrary() API, since it doesn't do much besides load the DLL and hook up the anchor variables to the DLL's functions. But if you consider the entire HELLOINT.C translation unit, including the intelligent gateway functions, then I think it's clearly a minor functional abstraction, possibly a major one. (You could also enhance the LoadHello() function even further by making it version check the loaded DLL, unload it, and return to its caller with an appropriate return code, as needed. If you were ambitious (or desperate) enough, you could even make it smart enough to check the DLL before loading it to ensure that it was a 32-bit DLL. Such changes would clearly make this function a major functional abstraction, since the code would then be adding significant new and logical function to the purely physical task of loading the DLL and hooking up the plumbing so that its routines can be called.)

A natural question is how application frameworks fit into all this. The most interesting aspect of frameworks is the new architecture they impose on a program, not to mention the learning curve that this architecture imposes on programmers. As I've said elsewhere, I think frameworks are an undeniably good thing, but they're not something you'll pick up in an afternoon. Still, most Windows frameworks are largely wrappers and very minor functional abstractions. As an example, take a few minutes to peruse the files AFXWIN1.INL and AFXWIN2.INL that are part of MFC. You'll see numerous methods and functions that are nothing but the thinnest possible wrappers for messages and API calls, and provide no additional functionality at all. In most cases, the interface definition is the same as that of the underlying Windows facility being called (except for the removal of the object's handle from the parameter list, since the object already knows that), so there's very little immediate benefit to calling these functions instead of the bare API. The main benefit comes in porting, and in the hope of insulation from future changes to the bare API.

Another issue that comes up when programmers start talking about building libraries is the proper role of OOP. This is one area where programmers can get more than a little carried away, as I said above, particularly when they write in C++. (What is it about C++ that encourages this sort of thing? Is it the challenge of mastering all that OOP machinery and using it to create your own Baroque masterpiece? Or does it just appeal to the would-be compiler writer/"language lawyer" that lurks in most programmers?) My advice is to be very wary of such tendencies, since they can lead to significant loss of programmer hours if one or more people go hide in a corner, and work on a library that no one on your project really needs. In fact, one way to minimize this problem is to use what I call the "inheritance rule": If you're creating a library that will likely not require inheritance, then you're not allowed to write it with objects.

This rule sounds quite neo-Luddite at first blush, but hear me out. The primary value of writing a library is to gain leverage from code reuse. As such, unless your code actually requires inheritance, you can normally get all the benefits of data hiding, abstraction, and encapsulation by simply packaging your code properly in one or more separate compilation units. Make your library's state variables local to the translation unit, provide "set" and "get" functions to access them, as necessary, and expose the fewest possible other functions to provide the needed services, and you'll likely be in fine shape.

I think this approach has considerable merit for two reasons:

1. It minimizes the risk that you or someone else on your team will go wild with objects. It's ever so tempting, once you've begun such a project, to keep adding just one more level to an object hierarchy, or just one more data conversion method, etc., until your library's class diagram looks like an organization chart for the entire U.S. Pentagon. Besides creating an unnecessarily large learning curve for other programmers, such bloated class libraries often add a lot of code to the programs that use them. (This is another often overlooked point: OOP is such a powerful tool in part because it lets you leverage a hierarchy of code. But leveraging code means using it, which means it all goes into the calling program, and in many cases code that isn't strictly needed is pulled in by an object hierarchy, and then left in place by linkers that aren't quite as good as we all wish they were. For example, Visual C++ creates a 195KB standalone "hello, world" program, even without debugging information in the .EXE file.)

2. It minimizes the chances of people not using the library, even when the library's authors aren't runaway OOPers. Face it, many programmers today are less than enthralled with OOP, and they're still using C++ as a "better C." (I'm not passing judgment on this viewpoint, merely stating a fact.) If you provide a set of features via plain old functions, then anyone who uses C++ can use them, regardless of their stance on OOP. I've found that forcing people to use objects, in even a very minor and wholly pleasant way, is one of the surest ways to encourage programmers to find excuses not to do something. This is another case where it doesn't matter one iota (an ANSI iota being 1/256th of a bit, while an ISO iota is 1/128th of a bit) who's right, and who's wrong. If you write a library that other programmers won't use, then your time was wasted. Whether your overall task is writing "just a few little utilities" for use in your department (and you want to share some code between them), or you're writing a combined desktop publishing, spreadsheet, database, and really nifty phone dialer program which will be marketed around the world, you probably can't afford that lost time.

# The Art of Abstraction

Time to get down to brass bits. Whether you're creating Virtual Machines and Employing Abstracting as a Tool, or "just stickin' some code into a library so everyone can get to it," or something in between, there are some design issues that are particularly appropriate. (But please note that block-copying a bunch of source code from one or more other files into a new one and then mashing it all together into a new LIB file is not practicing abstraction or library creation; it's nothing more than repackaging some source code.) In this section, I'll take a look at the most important issues in the form of a series of abstraction guidelines.

- Always strive to address the caller's most pressing need. This is a trivial detail when you're writing something as simple as the "get" and "set" functions or methods that we're all familiar with that provide controlled access to private library or object data. But when you move on to more complicated functions, it's surprisingly easy to lose your bearings and forget that you're writing a function or method for exactly one reason: To provide a specific service to the caller. Because of this fact, it's imperative that you try to keep in mind what the calling code's circumstance is likely to be, and what its intention is in calling your routine.

  This is why I find the behavior of the Win32 API GetShortPathName() so puzzling. Why would this API ever succeed if the long file name passed to it doesn't name an existing file or directory? Since a long name can only be mapped to a short name (or vice versa) if the file exists, it doesn't make sense for it to accept what can only be a long file name (for example, "c:\temp dir2"), and copy the input string to the output buffer and report success, when no directory or file of that name exists. After all, what is the caller likely to do with the returned alias of the provided long file name, but attempt to use it to access a file? True, the documentation for GetShortPathName() doesn't explicitly say that the file must exist, but since that's the only condition under which such a translation makes sense, it's understood. (Also note that in some cases GetShortPathName() will fail when the long file name provided by the user doesn't indicate an existing file, so in a sense it gets it half right. This type of inconsistency is often worse than getting a detail completely wrong, since it can lead programmers to make the wrong assumption about the API's overall behavior.)

- Always strive to create an interface that accommodates the caller's likely usage. This guideline relates to the first as syntax relates to semantics. As I say elsewhere in this chapter, the Win32 API GetDlgItemInt() is oddly formed, in that it doesn't support the most natural, idiomatic way for a Windows programmer to call it, since it does not return its success/failure indicator directly from the function, but via another means.

By contrast, the standard C run-time library routine strcmp() (and its related comparison functions), provides a lot of information in a very simple and usable form. This function takes two pointers to character strings and returns a value less than zero if the first string is lexicographically less than the second, zero of they're equal, and something greater than zero if the first string is greater than the second. This convention supports very natural usage, such as:

```
if(strcmp(string1,string2))
  printf("Strings weren't equal.\n");
else
  printf("Strings were equal.\n");
```

and

```
int rc = strcmp(string1,string2)
if(rc > 0)
    printf("string2 was greater\n");
else
    if(rc == 0)
      printf("Strings were equal\n");
    else
      printf("string1 was greater\n");
```

In fact, many C programmers are so comfortable with such formations when using the string routines that they probably don't even think about them in this light. (By comparison, imagine how much less useful strcmp() would be if it merely returned TRUE if the strings were equal, and FALSE if they weren't, with no indication of their lexicographic ordering.)

I'm convinced that this aspect of API design has subtle ramifications for program quality. Returning to GetDlgItemInt(), it's ever so tempting to cut corners and call it, and then use the returned value without checking the success indicator. Yes, programmers shouldn't be lazy, and they shouldn't do things like this, but if you can design your function's interface in a way that makes it even slightly less possible that programmers will ignore things they shouldn't, and at no additional cost to anyone involved, do it.

- Keep common pathological cases in mind. One of the fundamental rules of programming is that computers can't think and programmers can't count. It's a good thing they have each other. This observation is relevant because it suggests that your programs will only act intelligently if you take pains to make them do so, and that you can assume that sooner or later every routine will get called with an incorrect parameter, whether it's a NULL pointer, a numeric value outside of a valid range, an unterminated C-style string, or whatever. As I pointed out in guideline 11, bad data happens, and you should take reasonable steps to defuse it. Please practice defensive programming in the shared libraries you create; nowhere else will your code be more susceptible to common (and sometimes not so common) pathological cases.

I mentioned above that strcmp() was a good example of concise interface design. Unfortunately, the other C run-time library string routines aren't nearly as well thought out. It's astonishing that several of them accept a pointer to a destination string they will modify, without knowledge of the string's maximum allocated size. The fact that programmers routinely use these functions and pass them pointers to strings that have been passed to them as parameters, with no validation and no clue as to the string's actual buffer size, is positively fixating. As I said in guideline 11, I see this all the time in production code, as well as other errors that result in unterminated strings and buffer overruns. Have you ever seen a program display a dialog box with a message that had numerous "garbage characters" at its end? I've seen this more times than I can count (being a programmer, that's not too surprising). I can't vouch for every instance of such interface problems, but I'm willing to bet that most are traceable to string routine misuse.

• Use a good, consistent naming convention. This doesn't have to be anything special or fancy; use your common sense and avoid misleading names. After all, we give routines names like IsIconic() and CreateWindowEx() solely for the benefit of programmers. As you name your functions, messages, constants, and structures, remember that good names have predictive value, in that they allow a user just learning about your library to predict successfully what some functions do, solely based on their names. And that predictive quality greatly lowers the learning curve.

As for using Hungarian notation, that's a decision for you and your programming team to make. Personally, I dislike it, since I think that on balance it does more harm than good to the human factors of the interface.

• Don't be afraid to mix control and data semantics. Here's another one that Windows programmers use all the time but seldom think about in exactly this way: Many Windows APIs have dual-mode return values. They will return a handle to an icon, say, or a 0, indicating that the operation failed. Zero isn't a valid icon handle, of course, which makes it perfect for overloading the return value and indicating failure. Similarly, some listbox messages will return a value of LB_ERR (which is defined in WINUSER.H as -1) if an error occurs or if you ask Windows to perform a task on a listbox string that doesn't exist.

This mixing of semantics can be a very useful and concise way of reporting information to the caller, although it should be used with care. For example, the LB_GETITEMDATA messages lets you retrieve the 32-bit value associated with a specified string in a listbox (presumably a value your program set earlier with the LB_SETITEMDATA message). If an error occurs, the message returns LB_ERR. But what if the string has never had a value explicitly associated with it? In my tests, this returns a 0, but the API definition is moot on this point. And what if an error does occur, such as your program asking for the data for string number 37 when the listbox contains only 21 strings? How can you distinguish between the returned value of -1 and a -1 that you might have associated with the string, or a "real" 0 and a "not set" 0? Using the bare API, you can't easily make these distinctions. (If you can live with 31 or fewer bits for the stored data, you can, of course, allocate one bit as a "used" indicator, and write some simple wrapper functions to do the bit manipulation necessary. Of course, this isn't completely reliable unless you guarantee that the stored value will never have all bits on. An approach this colorful is probably verging on an unnatural act, something you should always avoid if possible. Still, in an extreme situation this technique might come in handy.)

Another example from the Windows API is the FormatMessage() function, which mixes flags and a buffer size in the same parameter, one of the oddest practices I've seen. I discuss this one in the sidebar "The Win32 API: Binary Calvinball?"

- Always make sure the caller can unambiguously determine if the function succeeded or failed. This sounds silly and trivially obvious, but as I pointed out in the previous item and below in my discussion of GetSysColor(), it's still not universal practice.

  As a guideline-within-a-guideline, whenever possible you should use the same technique for indicating success or failure for all functions in a library. Skim through the Win32 API and you'll find just about every imaginable method for doing this. This sort of minor inconsistency only increases the learning curve other programmers must scale to use your code. (But notice that when you're writing a set of wrappers, as I've defined it in this chapter, then you have little practical choice but to violate this guideline and propagate the behavior of the wrapped functions in indicating their success or failure.)

- Don't be afraid of a high API count in your library. I have to be careful how I state this, since I don't want people to think I'm encouraging runaway API creation. There is clearly such a thing as too many APIs for a given library's purpose in life, and exceeding that limit creates usability and maintenance problems that will reduce the library's overall utility, and therefore its use. That's never a good thing. But most programmers are more cautious in this area than they need to be. They realize that they need to strike a balance, but they think the balance point is farther toward the low end of the "number of APIs" scale than it really is. As long as the entire library is well designed, meaning every API serves a genuine need and is in itself usable, then it doesn't much matter if your library has five APIs or 500.

  This guideline is also a plea for programmers to stop jamming what should be two or more APIs into one. Later on I talk about the LB_SELITEMRANGEEX message, which clearly should have been two separate messages. Instead of using two messages, Microsoft used the convention that the order of the listbox indexes passed in the message's wParam and lParam indicate whether the range of strings they indicate is to be added to or removed from the current selection—ascending means add and descending means subtract. I've provided two wrappers for this message, uLBSelItemRange() and uLBDeselItemRange(), in the Win32u library.

- Always document clearly how null-terminated strings are used. I admit it, I hate null-terminated strings for a number of reasons. The biggest single reason is how often I see off-by-one errors in their use (including in my own code, I'm embarrassed to admit), unterminated strings, and all manner of unneeded pointer manipulation. Thanks to how deeply C-style strings are embedded in the Windows API and common C usage, we're all stuck with them at least until the sun burns out. Maybe longer.

  As a result, you should take great pains to document exactly how your functions use null-terminated strings, and when lengths refer to the string sizes with or without the terminating null. This doesn't have to be wordy; the occasional well placed "incl. TN" or "not incl. TN" is all that's needed, as long as it's unambiguous.

  A related issue is consistency—whether you think that functions should accept the maximum size of a target buffer as the number of characters including the terminating null (which I call the "sizeof()" case, since this parameter is often passed by coding "sizeof(<string variable>)"), or just the number of actual data characters (the "sizeof() minus one" case), pick one and stick with it! Nothing will confuse your code's users and lead to errors quicker than mixing conventions needlessly. If you find that for some reason you simply must mix conventions, make it painfully clear in the documentation which functions follow which ones.

- Make sure your functions follow the letter of the law regarding their returned value and behavior. This is really a two-part guideline: Make sure your functions are clearly documented, and then make sure they fulfill their contracts. It's ever so tempting when you're writing the documentation to intentionally gloss over some detail, either because you're not sure what happens in some oddball case, or because you aren't completely sure how some other function, or Windows API that your code relies on, works. In such cases, don't guess, but still try to be as complete and clear as you can. If nothing else, say that your function returns with whatever extended error code is set by a particular Windows API, and that it's therefore not guaranteed to be consistent across Win32 platforms. This isn't the best possible answer you can give your code's users, but at least it's honest, and it points them in the right direction for further investigation, as needed. (Of course, if you find yourself in this situation, a better solution often is to write a wrapper that unifies the API's use of extended error codes, and then call the wrapper instead of the bare API from your function.)

## *The Win32 API: Binary Calvinball?*

You've no doubt noticed that I'm not exactly the Win32 API's biggest fan. You're right, I'm not. That's why I thought it was important to present some of the silliness in the Win32 API here, both to make it clear why I'm less than enthralled with it, and to present some useful examples of practices you should avoid when constructing your own libraries.

*   GetPrivateProfileString(). I find this one interesting because it's so subtle, and because it could have been fixed so easily. The problem is determining if the function succeeded. This API's interface is:

```
DWORD GetPrivateProfileString(

    LPCTSTR  lpAppName,          // points to section name
    LPCTSTR  lpKeyName,          // points to key name
    LPCTSTR  lpDefault,          // points to default string
    LPTSTR   lpReturnedString,   // points to destination buffer
    DWORD    nSize,              // size of destination buffer
    LPCTSTR  lpFileName          // points to initialization filename
    );
```

The API definition describes the return value as follows:

> If the function succeeds, the return value is the number of characters copied to the buffer, not including the terminating null character.

> If neither lpAppName nor lpKeyName is NULL and the supplied destination buffer is too small to hold the requested string, the string is truncated and followed by a null character, and the return value is equal to nSize minus one.

> If either lpAppName or lpKeyName is NULL and the supplied destination buffer is too small to hold all the strings, the last string is truncated and followed by two null characters. In this case, the return value is equal to nSize minus two.

Think about this for a moment and you'll see that you can't tell in all cases if the API returns all of the string from the .INI file. For example, if you pass a 1,000-byte buffer, and the string is only five characters long, this API puts the string plus a terminating NULL into the buffer and returns a value of five. But if the string is five or more characters long, and you provide a six-byte buffer, you get the first five characters plus the NULL, and a return value of five. How can you tell if you got the entire string? You can't, because the API has given you five characters of data plus a NULL, and returned the length of the provided data (not counting the NULL), which is five—or nSize minus one—which just happens to be the return value that is used to indicate that your six-byte buffer isn't large enough. In other words, when your buffer is exactly the size needed for the requested data, this API will return all of the string, properly terminated, plus a value that is indistinguishable from an error condition, even though the API completed successfully.

This situation could have been avoided quite easily, by defining the API as:

```
BOOL fantasyGetPrivateProfileString(

    LPCTSTR  lpAppName,            // points to section name
    LPCTSTR  lpKeyName,            // points to key name
    LPCTSTR  lpDefault,            // points to default string
    LPTSTR   lpReturnedString,     // points to destination buffer
    DWORD    nSize,                // size of destination buffer
    LPCTSTR  lpFileName,           // points to initialization filename
    LPINT lpNeededSize             // size of needed buffer
    );
```

In this alternate definition, all the old parameters have their current meaning. The new parameter, lpNeededSize, is a pointer to an integer that would be used to indicate how large a buffer is needed, including the terminating NULL, if the provided one wasn't large enough, or set to 0 if it was large enough or the function couldn't complete for another reason. The return value of the API would be TRUE if the function succeeded in retrieving the entire string without truncation, FALSE if otherwise. This fantasy variation of the API wouldn't change the buffer for the returned string unless it could return the entire string.

Why you would ever want the actual GetPrivateProfileString() API to return a truncated version of the string is another issue. If your program could somehow be completely certain of the exact format of the string in the file (something it can't very well do, given how easy it is for users to edit .INI files), I suppose that it could exploit this API's behavior to retrieve only the first part of a string. In the real world that's a far too risky way to code something that simple.

You could, of course, remedy this problem of an ambiguous return value with a wrapper, such as uGetPrivateProfileString():

```
BOOL uGetPrivateProfileString(LPCTSTR lpAppName,LPCTSTR lpKeyName,
  LPCTSTR lpDefault,LPTSTR lpReturnedString,DWORD nSize,LPCTSTR lpFileName)
{
  // First, try the underlying API with the caller's parameters...
  DWORD result1 = GetPrivateProfileString(lpAppName,lpKeyName,lpDefault,
    lpReturnedString,nSize,lpFileName);

  // If we hit one of the ambiguous conditions, then we have to try again
  // with a local buffer to see if we really got the whole result.  See the
  // API documentation for details on the nSize -1 and nSize - 2 conditions.
  if((((lpAppName == NULL) || (lpKeyName == NULL)) &&
    (result1 == nSize - 2)) ||
    (((lpAppName != NULL) && (lpKeyName != NULL)) &&
```

```
    (result1 == nSize - 1)))
    {
    char *local_buffer = (char *)malloc(nSize + 1);
    if(local_buffer == NULL)
      return FALSE;

    // Retry, using our own buffer but the caller's other parameters.
    DWORD result2 = GetPrivateProfileString(lpAppName,lpKeyName,lpDefault,
      local_buffer,nSize + 1,lpFileName);

    free(local_buffer);  // Whatever happened, we're done with this

    // If we got the same result both times it was a false alarm
    if(result2 == result1)
      return TRUE;
    else
      // If we didn't, then the caller's buffer was too small
      return FALSE;
    }
  else
    // The caller got lucky on the first try, so we just return TRUE
    return TRUE;
}
```

As you can see, this wrapper is very simple. It first tries to score a hit by calling GetPrivateProfileString() with the caller's original parameters. If this results in an unambiguous result, then it immediately returns. If the result is ambiguous (meaning that the caller's buffer was either the exact size needed or too small), then it allocates a buffer that is one byte larger than the caller's buffer and re-executes the call. If it gets the same return value on the second call, that means both calls succeeded; a different result means the caller is out of luck, since the provided buffer wasn't large enough.

- The LB_SELITEMRANGEEX message is sent to a list box to add or remove a range of consecutive strings from those currently selected. The definition of the message parameters is:

```
wParam = (WPARAM) wFirst;    // first item
lParam = (LPARAM) wLast);    // last item
```

The interesting detail is that there's no way for a program to indicate if it wants to select or deselect the range of items; all you get to work with in any message is the message code, the wParam, and the lParam, and they're all spoken for in this definition. Instead of using lParam as a pointer to a structure with the required field, or even using two different messages (one for selection, one for deselection), Microsoft chose an interesting route. The API definition for LB_SELITEMRANGEEX includes the note:

> If the wFirst parameter is less than the wLast parameter, the specified range of items is selected. If wFirst is greater than wLast, the selection is removed from the specified range of items.

This is poor practice, since not only is it too tricky by half, but it can lead to subtle errors if the program calculates the index ranges (and it might therefore accidentally swap them). Microsoft could have defined a new structure that included the string indexes and a BOOL indicating if the range of strings should be selected or deselected, and made the message pass a pointer to the structure. Then the API could have intelligently handled the indexes, and accommodated the case where the program accidentally got them reversed. (See the clipping functions in Chapter 3 for a sample of this behavior.) Better yet is to give in and break these two functions out in separate messages, a solution I mimic with the two wrappers in the Win32u library.

- A listbox will accept a -1 as the string index of the LB_SETCURSEL message, and interpret it to mean remove the selection. By itself this practice is fine, and is a good example of mixing control and data semantics in the same parameter. The problem is that in this case the API still returns LB_ERR, even though no error occurred.

  This situation is also a good example of a phenomenon I mentioned in guideline 3, blessing some bad practice by documenting it, and this one is clearly bad practice. I haven't seen the code that implements this (or any other) part of Windows, but it's not hard to imagine what's happening here—the support likely employs some shared validation code, which sees the -1 parameter, which is never a valid listbox index, sets the return value to LB_ERR, and then the code specific to this message checks for the special value of -1 and handles it appropriately, but never bothers to reset the return value. (Even if I'm wildly off-base on what Windows is doing behind the scenes in this case, this still serves as a useful lesson in how not to do something.)

- GetSysColor() is an oddity—an API that doesn't even try to define a failure condition. It accepts one of a couple of dozen manifest constants, each of which specifies some part of the Windows user interface, and it returns the color definition of the specified interface element. Simple stuff. The first problem is that if you pass it a constant that's not in its range, it returns a zero, which is indistinguishable from the RGB setting for black. OK, some people will say, don't make a silly mistake and pass this API anything except a valid parameter, and you're safe. Well, not exactly. As it turns out, the issue of what's a valid parameter got a lot more complicated with the arrival of Windows 95. (Are you surprised? I'm not.)

  The problem is the new, Windows 95-only parameters for GetSysColor(). WINUSER.H contains the following definitions for this parameter:

```
#define COLOR_SCROLLBAR        0
#define COLOR_BACKGROUND       1
#define COLOR_ACTIVECAPTION    2
#define COLOR_INACTIVECAPTION  3
```

```
#define COLOR_MENU                   4
#define COLOR_WINDOW                 5
#define COLOR_WINDOWFRAME            6
#define COLOR_MENUTEXT               7
#define COLOR_WINDOWTEXT             8
#define COLOR_CAPTIONTEXT            9
#define COLOR_ACTIVEBORDER           10
#define COLOR_INACTIVEBORDER         11
#define COLOR_APPWORKSPACE           12
#define COLOR_HIGHLIGHT              13
#define COLOR_HIGHLIGHTTEXT          14
#define COLOR_BTNFACE                15
#define COLOR_BTNSHADOW              16
#define COLOR_GRAYTEXT               17
#define COLOR_BTNTEXT                18
#define COLOR_INACTIVECAPTIONTEXT    19
#define COLOR_BTNHIGHLIGHT           20

#if(WINVER >= 0x0400)
#define COLOR_3DDKSHADOW             21
#define COLOR_3DLIGHT                22
#define COLOR_INFOTEXT               23
#define COLOR_INFOBK                 24

#define COLOR_DESKTOP                COLOR_BACKGROUND
#define COLOR_3DFACE                 COLOR_BTNFACE
#define COLOR_3DSHADOW               COLOR_BTNSHADOW
#define COLOR_3DHIGHLIGHT            COLOR_BTNHIGHLIGHT
#define COLOR_3DHILIGHT             COLOR_BTNHIGHLIGHT
#define COLOR_BTNHILIGHT            COLOR_BTNHIGHLIGHT
#endif /* WINVER >= 0x0400 */
```

Ignoring the last six definitions, which merely duplicate pre-Windows 95 values, we have four that are unique to Windows 95. (The header says they're unique to version 4.0, but the API definition says they're unique to Windows 95. Presumably when NT 4.0 arrives with the Windows 95 shell interface, this will become a moot point.)

What happens when your Win32 program runs under Windows NT 3.51 and tries to use one of these four Windows 95-only constants? Here's a pleasant surprise—it knows about them and provides the correct answers. But run the same program under Win32s 1.30a (build 166), and you get a return value of zero (black) for all the Windows 95-specific values. This is a perfect example of how not to mix control and data semantics—in this approach, the control value used for "I have no idea how to interpret the value you passed to me" is indistinguishable from a valid data value.

Wrapping this API is not as straightforward as it seems. You could easily write a wrapper along the lines of:

```
BOOL uGetSysColor(
    int  nIndex,        // display element
    LPDWORD lpColor     // returned color value
    );
```

that returns FALSE for an invalid parameter (based on the Win32 platform it was running on), and TRUE plus the correct answer for a valid parameter. The trick, of course, is determining with an acceptably high degree of reliablility (read: 100%) what is and isn't a valid parameter. It seems unlikely that Win32s will ever support these new color indexes. But what about new color values that Windows 96 or 97 or whatever, or Cairo, might add to the API? If your wrapper rejects any value less than 0 or greater than 24, then it could suddenly fail when the user upgrades to a new version of Windows. As a fallback position, you could make your wrapper not only check the platform, but the version as well, and if it sees a version number greater than 4.0, it could simply bucket-brigade the parameter to the API and return its value to the caller.

- The message EM_GETLINECOUNT retrieves the number of lines of text in a multi-line edit control. The API definition also includes the description: *The return value is an integer specifying the number of lines in the multiline edit control. If no text is in the edit control, the return value is 1.*

This one makes me shake my head, since it requires any program that wants to get the actual count of lines in the control to do something like:

```
DWORD uEMGetLineCount(HWND edit_handle)
{
  if((lines = SendMessage(edit_handle,EM_GETLINECOUNT,
    0,0)) > 1)
    return lines;
  else
    {
    int start_char = SendMessage)edit_handle,
      EM_LINEINDEX,0,0);
    if(SendMessage(edit_handle,EM_LINELENGTH,
      start_char,0) == 0)
      return 0;
    else
      return 1;
    }
}
```

(This wrapper is in the Win32u library, shown in Appendix C.) This wrapper still leaves you with the problem of exactly how EM_GETLINECOUNT counts lines that are blank and don't even have a carriage return. For example, if you type a few characters into a multi-line edit control and then hit Ctrl-Enter to force a hard line break, EM_GETLINECOUNT will still report that the control has two lines of text. In this case, the control is reporting this number based on its view of the situation (how many lines it might have to position the cursor on), and not what the caller might expect (how many lines have text or a hard return). In this case, it counts a "phantom line" as being in the control.

- RegQueryValueEx() surely wins the "Always Prepared" award for its third parameter, lpdwReserved, which must be NULL. Why would you ever design a function's interface with a reserved/must-be-zero parameter? I honestly can't think of a good reason to do this. (Although reserved/must-be-zero fields can be very useful in the design of custom data file formats and data structures, something I talk about in Chapter 9.)

- FormatMessage() is a very useful API: It can be used to translate an extended error code to some descriptive text. This is your key to turning values returned by GetLastError() into something that makes sense to human beings. My gripe with this API is its first formal parameter, a doubleword of flags, which can be specified with the usual virtual plethora of manifest constants (nothing new there), but also takes a line length for the formatted message. Specifically, the API definition describes this parameter as follows:

  **dwFlags**

  Contains a set of bit flags that specify aspects of the formatting process and how to interpret the lpSource parameter. The low-order byte of dwFlags specifies how the function handles line breaks in the output buffer. The low-order byte can also specify the maximum width of a formatted output line.

  One trivial program I wrote that uses this API to display the meaning of GetLastError() codes contains the line:

```
cMsgLen = FormatMessage(FORMAT_MESSAGE_FROM_SYSTEM |
              FORMAT_MESSAGE_ALLOCATE_BUFFER | 64, NULL, err_code,
              MAKELANGID(0, SUBLANG_ENGLISH_US), (LPTSTR) &msgBuf,
                 512, NULL);
```

  Notice the first parameter is passed as two flag constants (FORMAT_MESSAGE_FROM_SYSTEM and FORMAT_MESSAGE_ALLOCATE_BUFFER) ORed together with 64, the line length I wanted the API to use in formatting the message. This is terrible form, since the API is mixing semantics within the same usage of the same piece of data (for example, it's using the same parameter for flags and a piece of data). Even though this API already has seven parameters, which is more than I like to see passed like this (as opposed to in a structure), Microsoft should have broken this length out as one more parameter.

- Non-TRUE TRUEs. As I've mentioned elsewhere in this book, some of the Windows 95 APIs which are defined to return a BOOL will return 0 for FALSE, which is fine, of course, but they'll return something besides TRUE (which is defined as 1) for TRUE. This can lead to some fascinating errors, such as:

```
if(GetClientRect(the_handle,&the_rect) == TRUE)
  {
```

```
      /* Do stuff with returned rect */
    }
  else
    {
    /* Refuse to continue execution--can't display our data */
    /* Under Windows 95 we ALWAYS wind up here! */
  }
```

Some programmers will contend this isn't a problem, since "everyone" knows that the convention is really FALSE == 0 and TRUE != 0. I disagree, since that's not what the API definition says. This brings me back to my earlier point about the documentation being an API's contract with the world. In this case, the API violates its contract in a way that would make perfectly legal, if slightly unusual, code like the snippet above break.

There are a few places in the API documentation where Microsoft says that a given API will return a non-zero value for TRUE, but from what I can see these APIs are not new to Windows 95, and they've always worked this way. The new cases of non-TRUE TRUE return values are not documented, which means no one outside of Microsoft knows which APIs are involved. (And I would venture a guess that no one inside Microsoft has a complete list of the offenders, either.)

There are two lessons here for Windows programmers: First, take the loosest possible interpretation of values returned from the Win32 API. Second, be careful not to propagate non-TRUE TRUEs throughout our programs. That's why in some of the sample code you'll see where I ended a function that returns a BOOL with:

```
return (SomeWin32API(/* parms */) != FALSE);
```

This looks silly, but it forces the value returned by SomeWin32API() to an acceptable and strictly correct value, which guarantees that your code will meet its contract with the world (even if some of the code it calls doesn't).

- The EM_LINELENGTH message wins the "Say what?" award for its documentation and use of its wParam:

> Specifies the character index of a character in the line whose length is to be retrieved when EM_LINELENGTH is sent to a multiline edit control. If this parameter is -1, the message returns the number of unselected characters on lines containing selected characters. For example, if the selection extended from the fourth character of one line through the eighth character from the end of the next line, the return value would be 10 (three characters on the first line and seven on the next).

I see. Obviously, you shouldn't overload a user interface like this. Please don't.

- For an example of how important a good naming convention can be, I don't think you can top GetDlgItem() and GetDlgItemInt(). The first API returns the handle to a control with a given resource ID. (For example, the code associated with a dialog box might use the call GetDlgItem(my_handle,IDC_EDIT1) to retrieve the handle to the edit control on the dialog with the resource ID of IDC_EDIT1.) The second API, GetDlgItemInt(), is used to read the text associated with a given control, such as an edit box, and convert it to an integer.

  Obviously these APIs do wildly different things, yet their names are so similar that someone new to Windows programming might very well overlook the second one. (In fact, I know of a case where exactly this happened. A friend of mine was just starting to program in Windows, and he looked for a function to retrieve the handle of a child control, and couldn't find it. When he asked me if there was such an animal and I told him about GetDlgItem(), he said that wasn't at all what he was talking about, and that he wanted the handle, not the contents of the control. We went around in circles for a minute or so on this before he saw that we were talking about two different APIs, and that the one I was talking about did what he wanted. I strongly suspect that my friend isn't the only person who's stumbled over this problem.) Why Microsoft didn't call GetDlgItem() something more descriptive like GetChildHandle() is a mystery.

  And I'm not even going to discuss seriously the possibility of wrapping one or the other of these APIs merely to change its name, or using a preprocessor directive to rename it. We all have better things to do than waste our time like that. You can do it, if you want, but don't tell me about it, and please don't tell anyone you got the idea here, because you didn't, OK?

- GetDlgItemInt() is also noteworthy because its design violates one of the basic points I mentioned earlier: It ignores how callers are most likely to use it, and in a way that invites errors. As I mentioned in Chapter 2, this API is written "inside out," in that it returns its converted value instead of its success/failure indicator. This prevents callers from using the obvious and very familiar construct:

```
if(SomeAPIFunction(/* parameters */))
  {
    /* Function succeeded, process its output */
  }
else
  {
    /* Function failed, complain to the user, shut down, etc. */
  }
```

Instead, GetDlgItemInt() passes its success/failure indicator back via a pointer parameter, and the API's return value is the converted value. But since this API is returning an integer, by definition, it could contain any pattern of bits in the returned value, which means the above coding style can't be used.

As I also mentioned in Chapter 2, it would make more sense for this API to have an interface like:

```
BOOL uGetDlgItemInt(
    HWND  hDlg,              // handle to dialog box
    int   nIDDlgItem,        // control identifier
    UINT* lpValue,           // points to variable to receive converted value
    BOOL  bSigned            // specifies whether value is signed or unsigned
    );
```

and return TRUE or FALSE to indicate whether the retrieval and conversion was successful. In fact, I've included this wrapper in the Win32u library, even though it's merely a reformulation of the user interface. (In this case, the wrapped version is so much easier to use that I think it (just barely) justifies its existence.)

- The biggest problem of all with the Win32 API, of course, is the documentation. Between undocumented uses of extended error codes (every API that uses them should have a list of all values the caller might get from GetLastError() after calling the API, and when each is used), no version-specific information (For example, which Win32 APIs were added in Windows NT 3.5 or 3.51? Your guess is as good as mine.), precious little documentation on platform differences (such as varying GetLastError() results and non-TRUE TRUE values), and numerous outright errors, you can't possibly know what to trust. (Note that I'm talking about the Visual C++ 2.2 documentation, the official 7/11/95 Win32 SDK, and the July, 1995 *Microsoft Developer Network* CD ROM, all the latest versions available as I wrote this book. I sincerely hope that by the time this book is on the shelves, Microsoft has cleaned up and enhanced the documentation significantly, but I'm not holding my breath.)

We all should consider the state of the Win32 API documentation a cautionary tale, in effect. Throughout this book I talk about the numerous problems with developing for Windows, and many of these problems could be alleviated or eliminated entirely with better documentation. When you're writing your own library, whether you're the only one who will call it, or it will be used by many thousands of other programmers, it's always worth the extra few minutes to document details, such as those I've mentioned here, as thoroughly as possible.

*On the off chance that you're not conversant with Calvinball, let me explain: In the brilliant comic strip Calvin and Hobbes, which is about a wickedly inventive little boy named Calvin and his imaginary playmate, Hobbes the tiger, we often see them playing Calvinball. The most interesting (and pertinent) detail of Calvinball is that the players literally make up the rules as the game progresses. This leads to*

*all sorts of silliness, like "zones of reversal," instant requirements to walk backwards, or sing a song praising the opposing player, etc.*

*I admit, it's an exaggeration to compare the Win32 API to Calvinball, even in jest. Still, I have to admit that almost every time I open the online help for a given API, particularly one I've never used before, I get the feeling that I'm about to be pounced on by Hobbes, or forced by Calvin to do something really silly.*

# E Pluribus Unum

No, this isn't Programmer Latin for "#include <windows.h>". But it does nicely indicate the overall philosophy that you should be striving for when you build a library: Your goal is to create a new, coherent entity out of simpler parts. If you do that, you can both raise and level the platform on which your programs are built, and gain the greatest possible benefit from code reuse. Put another way, with surprisingly little planning you can make your code stand on its own shoulders (surely a recursive image that only programmers will appreciate), and reach higher than it could before.

# Chapter 11

# Give Your Program a Locked Persona

# Give Your Program a Locked Persona

Chapter **11**

*Opportunity makes a thief.*

Francis Bacon

Computer security is a classic "Mandelbrot set" topic; no matter how closely and deeply you look, there's always another level of complexity that you can barely see in outline form. But don't worry, I'm not about to plunge into the murky depths of encryption algorithms and U.S. Department of Defense security classifications. I'll gladly skim the surface and leave such arcana for the experts in the field. Instead, I'll use this chapter to present an example of "minor" or "little brother" security, one that includes an interesting and not entirely obvious way of approaching Windows programs. I call this technique the locked persona.

A program's locked persona is a mode, or personality. When your program is in this state, it presents an icon on the user's task bar (or desktop, in the pre-Windows 95 user interface), and no other windows or dialogs, but doesn't let the user do anything with the program except shut it down or unlock it with the password. The program will recall its locked state the next time it is run and every time after that, until the user supplies the password. When the program is in its unlocked persona, it operates normally.

And yes, this is yet another use for minimized programs. I told you in Chapter 7 that there are all sorts of ways to exploit them. Read on for another example.

## The Value of Minimal Security

By "little brother" security, I mean exactly that: security that is intended to do nothing more than stop a casual would-be snooper, like your little brother, who happens upon your running computer while you're out of the room for a few minutes.

283

Why bother with such flimsy security? For the same reason that the companies that make aluminum storm doors still insist on putting locks on them. Ever try to "force" open such a door when it's locked? Many that I've seen can be popped open with a single, moderately strong pull on the handle. Saying that these cheesy locks can be easily broken misses the point; they're not intended to deter a skilled and determined thief, but to present an unmistakable, if unwritten "Keep Out" sign, and to keep your neighbor's inquisitive six-year old at bay.

Similarly, anyone who uses a PC in a busy office (or displays PCs in a store) knows the value of a Windows screen saver with a password. Again, it's not much real security; anyone with knowledge of Windows can defeat a screen saver in a few minutes. But it does serve a purpose.

## To Lock or Not To Lock

So, why not add such a feature to your public Windows programs? It's simple, it adds very little to your program's size, and, based on my experience with my customers, some of your users will love it. In other words, your program gets a moderate benefit for very little cost, always an intriguing ratio. I added this feature to Stickies! some time back, and I know from talking to my customers that many of them who work in an office environment use it on a regular basis.

Why isn't it better simply to shut down the program and then restart it when you return to your computer? Depending on the nature of the program, it might make sense to do just that; some programs are obviously bad candidates for this feature. For example, it would be pointless to add a locked persona to Windows 95's Notepad applet. Notepad loads a file so quickly that it's a minor inconvenience to have to reload it when you get back from lunch or the coffee machine. But have you loaded a large RTF file into Word for Windows lately? Have you tried loading a *really* big RTF file? Or how about several very large ones all at once? That little gas gauge at the bottom of the screen loses what little charm it had—in a hurry. I would love to see Word add a locked persona that allowed users to keep such files securely in memory and avoid a long reload process.

Now, I can imagine some of the more performance-conscious readers (and rest assured, I'm one of you) reaching low Earth orbit at the thought of holding a meg or more of RTF file in memory like that. In fact, it shouldn't be a problem; it's all virtual memory, so assuming that you have enough swap file and real memory available, the loaded files in this example would quickly get swapped out to disk, and you should be able to keep running normally with no real performance hit.

There's also the issue of those precious free system resources that we've all learned to be paranoid about over the years. Windows 95 improves that situation radically, so much so, in fact, that now you'd really practically have to try to exhaust or significantly reduce system resources. In fact, even with all its user interface changes and other more obvious new features, I'm convinced that the improved resource utilization will be the most compelling single reason for users to upgrade to Windows 95 from Windows 3.1.

In summary, a locked persona can provide your users with minimal security without the hassles of lengthy document reloads.

# The Basic Model, Take I

When I first implemented a locked persona, I did it in a Borland Pascal for Windows program, using the OWL framework. Pascal OWL users are familiar with the following code sequence that appears in nearly every program's main routine:

```
begin
        MyApp.Init(AppName);
        MyApp.Run;
        MyApp.Done;
end.
```

It occurred to me that there was no reason why a program could have only one application object, or why it couldn't switch between them:

```
begin
        repeat
        MyApp1.Init(AppName);
        MyApp1.Run;
        MyApp1.Done;
        if not finished then
        begin
                MyApp2.Init(AppName);
                MyApp2.Run;
                MyApp2.Done;
                end;
        until finished;
end.
```

Here, *finished* is a global Boolean variable that is set by the main window of each of the application objects, as needed, to indicate whether the program is really done, or if it was merely locked or unlocked and should switch to the other persona. (I've eliminated a lot of detail from this example, but you get the general idea.) In this approach, when the user tells the program to lock or unlock itself, the application that corresponds to that persona sets global variables as needed, and then ends, allowing the other application to take over.

Notice that this approach makes it a bit trickier to keep the program's data intact. As I had originally written the program in question, the data files were closed when it ended, of course. When I added the locked persona, I was concerned about the program consuming too much of the user's free system resources while it was locked, so I simply made the unlocked persona unload the files. This solution greatly limits the applicability of a locked persona, since it only makes sense to use it when the program's data file can be unloaded and reloaded quickly. And if document loading is quick, then there's little need for the locked persona. (This is not universally applicable. If your program stores its data in a custom, human unreadable format and allows only one instance of itself to run, then a locked persona can provide minimal security for a program's data files. The files can't be easily opened or changed, since the one program that knows how to interpret them is already running, and it refuses to do the would-be intruder's bidding, since it's password locked.)

When I tried to port this technique to Visual C++, I got a rude surprise. As a test, I wrote a simple program that used a custom WinMain() function and simply tried to run the same application twice in a row. Not a very exhaustive test of the technology, to be sure, but it was more enlightening than I expected. When I ran my program, I got only one execution of the application object. After much fiddling, I figured out that the problem was somewhere in the application's Run method.

This left me at a crossroads that I'm sure is familiar to many Windows programmers. I had to choose between diving into the MFC source code and finding the magic variables or code to twiddle to make this work, or finding another physical implementation of the same logical feature.

I'm sure I could find a way to make MFC bend to my will, if I were willing to spend enough time framework spelunking, and if I were willing to go that far out on a limb. I wasn't, so I didn't.

Fiddling with a framework's DNA is seldom a good idea and should be considered a Minor League Unnatural Act. I did this with Stickies!, and it meant that every time I got an update to OWL I had to go into its source and reimplement a few dozen lines of modifications. This is a very risky proposition, even if you're sure you know the framework inside-out.

But again, it's a judgment call and there are no absolutes. If changing the framework's source really is the best alternative, then do it with a clear conscience, but keep in mind all the costs and risks, and document the changes as if your life depends on it.

## The Basic Model, Take II

As is so often the case in programming, it was valuable to think of this problem purely in terms of what the user sees. When the user locks the program with a password, it closes its main window, but still appears on the task bar (or the user's desktop) as an icon. When the user unlocks the program, it restores itself and still has the same documents loaded as when it was locked, assuming it was locked in the same session.

Obviously, all I had to do was set up a global flag that indicates the app's locked status, and use some of the minimized program tricks from Chapter 7. The accompanying program, LOCKER, shows a minimal implementation of a locked persona in an MFC program. I didn't bother with the mundane details of really prompting the user for a password and verifying it, since the purpose of this example is to illustrate the core technique. The password dialogs in LOCKER merely let the user click on a button to simulate entering a proper or improper password. MegaZero, the sample application in Appendix A, includes a fuller implementation of password handling.

## Building the Samples: LOCKER

**CD Location:** ZEN\CHAP11\LOCKER

**Platform:** Win32

**Build instructions:** Use the provided .MAK file with Visual C++, and compile normally.

## Listing 11.1    LOCK.CPP

```
////////////////////////////////////////////////////////////////////////////
// LOCK.CPP: Demonstration version of app. locking/unlocking support
//
// Copyright (c) 1995 Lou Grinzo

#include "stdafx.h"
#include "locker.h"
#include "lock.h"

static BOOL locked = FALSE;
static char password[MAX_PW] = "";


////////////////////////////////////////////////////////////////////////////

BOOL RetrieveLockedStatus(void)
{
 // The implementation of this function is highly dependent on external
 // factors, such as how secure the programmer needs/wants to make the
 // locking facility, etc. The password can be stored in an .INI file,
 // the Windows registry, or a custom data file.

 // Whatever storage/retrieval method you use, make sure that this function
 // leaves the program UNLOCKED if the actual state cannot be read! E.g.
 //
 // if(can't read locked state from persistent storage for any reason)
 //   return (locked = FALSE);
 //

 locked = FALSE;
 return locked;
}


////////////////////////////////////////////////////////////////////////////
```

```
BOOL SaveLockedState(void)
{
// The implementation of this function is highly dependent on external
// factors, such as how secure the programmer needs/wants to make the
// locking facility, etc. The password can be stored in an .INI file,
// the Windows registry, or a custom data file.

return TRUE;
}

////////////////////////////////////////////////////////////////////////////

BOOL LockPWDlg(void)
{
// If we're already locked, then we should never be called. Rather than
// display the wrong dialog and confuse the user, we just return and tell
// our caller that everything is fine. This should help the calling code
// synchronize its perceived state with actual state of affairs.

if(locked)
 return locked;

CDialog the_prompt(IDD_LOCKPW);

if(the_prompt.DoModal() == IDOK)
 locked = TRUE;

return locked;
}

////////////////////////////////////////////////////////////////////////////

BOOL UnlockPWDlg(void)
{
// If we're already unlocked, then we should never be called. Rather than
// display the wrong dialog and confuse the user, we just return and tell
// our caller that everything is fine. This should help the calling code
// synchronize its perceived state with actual state of affairs.

if(!locked)
 return locked;

CDialog the_prompt(IDD_UNLOCKPW);

if(the_prompt.DoModal() == IDOK)
  {
  locked = FALSE;
  password[0] = '\0';
  }

return locked;
}

////////////////////////////////////////////////////////////////////////////

BOOL IsLocked(void)
{
 return locked;
}
```

## Listing 11.2   MAINFRM.CPP from LOCK Sample

```cpp
// mainfrm.cpp : implementation of the CMainFrame class
//

#include "stdafx.h"
#include "locker.h"
#include "lock.h"

#include "mainfrm.h"

#ifdef _DEBUG
#undef THIS_FILE
static char BASED_CODE THIS_FILE[] = __FILE__;
#endif

/////////////////////////////////////////////////////////////////////////
// CMainFrame

IMPLEMENT_DYNCREATE(CMainFrame, CFrameWnd)

BEGIN_MESSAGE_MAP(CMainFrame, CFrameWnd)
     //{{AFX_MSG_MAP(CMainFrame)
     ON_WM_SYSCOMMAND()
     ON_WM_CREATE()
     //}}AFX_MSG_MAP
END_MESSAGE_MAP()

/////////////////////////////////////////////////////////////////////////
// CMainFrame construction/destruction

CMainFrame::CMainFrame()
{
     // TODO: add member initialization code here

}

CMainFrame::~CMainFrame()
{
}

/////////////////////////////////////////////////////////////////////////
// CMainFrame diagnostics

#ifdef _DEBUG
void CMainFrame::AssertValid() const
{
     CFrameWnd::AssertValid();
}

void CMainFrame::Dump(CDumpContext& dc) const
{
     CFrameWnd::Dump(dc);
}

#endif //_DEBUG

/////////////////////////////////////////////////////////////////////////
// CMainFrame message handlers

void CMainFrame::OnSysCommand(UINT nID, LPARAM lParam)
```

```
    {
    UINT the_real_nID = nID & 0xFFF0;

    if(nID == CM_LOCKUNLOCK)
      {
      OnLockUnlock();
      return;
      }

    switch (the_real_nID)
      {
      case SC_RESTORE:    // If we're unlocked, we process these normally
      case SC_MAXIMIZE:   // If locked, we display the unlock PW prompt
       if(IsLocked())
        OnLockUnlock();
       else
          CFrameWnd::OnSysCommand(nID, lParam);
       break;

      default:
          CFrameWnd::OnSysCommand(nID, lParam);
      }
    }

    int CMainFrame::OnCreate(LPCREATESTRUCT lpCreateStruct)
    {
        if (CFrameWnd::OnCreate(lpCreateStruct) == -1)
            return -1;

        CMenu *sysmenu = GetSystemMenu(FALSE);
        sysmenu->AppendMenu(MF_STRING,CM_LOCKUNLOCK,"Lock/Unlock...");

     if(RetrieveLockedStatus())    // Only call DoLockUnlock() if we are locked
      DoLockUnlock();

        return 0;
    }


    ///////////////////////////////////////////////////////////////////////////
    // CMainFrame locking/unlocking: Dialog invocation
    //
    // We only call DoLockUnlock() on a verified state change.

    void CMainFrame::OnLockUnlock(void)
    {
     if(IsLocked())
         {
       TRACE("OnLockUnlock: IsLocked() == TRUE\n");
       if(!UnlockPWDlg())   // FALSE: We're now unlocked
        DoLockUnlock();
         }
     else
         {
       TRACE("OnLockUnlock: IsLocked() == TRUE\n");
       if(LockPWDlg())      // TRUE: We're now locked
        DoLockUnlock();
         }
    }
```

```
///////////////////////////////////////////////////////////////////////
// CMainFrame locking/unlocking: State changes
//
// This code assumes that it is only called when actually needed, i.e. when
// the program's locked status has actually changed.

void CMainFrame::DoLockUnlock(void)
{
 if(IsLocked())
  {
    // Change to the locked icon
    DestroyIcon((HICON)GetClassLong(AfxGetApp()->m_pMainWnd->m_hWnd,GCL_HICON));

    SetClassLong(AfxGetApp()->m_pMainWnd->m_hWnd,
     GCL_HICON,
     (long)AfxGetApp()->LoadIcon(IDR_LOCKEDMAINFRAME));

    // Is DND normally enabled? If so, disable it.
    // DragAcceptFiles(FALSE);

    // Minimize ourself
    PostMessage(WM_SYSCOMMAND,SC_MINIMIZE,0);
  }
 else
  {
    // Change to the normal icon
    DestroyIcon((HICON)GetClassLong(AfxGetApp()->m_pMainWnd->m_hWnd,GCL_HICON));

    SetClassLong(AfxGetApp()->m_pMainWnd->m_hWnd,
     GCL_HICON,
     (long)AfxGetApp()->LoadIcon(IDR_MAINFRAME));

    // Is DND normally enabled? If so, reenable it.
    // DragAcceptFiles(TRUE);

    // Restore ourself
    PostMessage(WM_SYSCOMMAND,SC_RESTORE,0);
  }
}
```

Another stub function in LOCK is RetrieveLockedState(). This function is called at startup to determine if the program was still in its locked persona when it was last shut down, and to retrieve the password. This is the key to making your program remain locked across executions.

In an actual program, RetrieveLockedState() would query some form of persistent storage, such as an INI file, the Windows registry, or the application's own custom format data file. Whatever method you prefer to employ, make sure that you follow the pseudocode in the sample program. If the persistent storage with the password information is missing or otherwise inaccessible, this function must return FALSE, indicating that the program is not locked. Remember, there's no telling what your user or another program will do to the system when you're not looking, or even when you are. Normally you don't want your program to default to the locked state.

*Depending on what your program does and the environment in which it will run, you might want it to default to the locked state, after all, even at the cost of locking some users out of their own data in some rare cases. This is an excellent example of a subtle design decision that can only be made in the context of the program's environment.*

Since this demo version doesn't really do anything with passwords, SaveLockedState() is also a stub. Depending on where you choose to store the password, it might make more sense to move this function into the main program, or change SaveLockedState() and RetrieveLockedState() to accept the handle of an open file, where they will write and read the password information. This will allow you to perform very simple, yet workable streaming within your program's custom data format, without your main program having to deal with the details above this black box level. Once again: abstract, abstract, abstract. These are clearly functions that you'll seldom invoke, so abstract them as much as you can; you and your users will pay no measurable performance penalty, and you might reap considerable benefits, come program maintenance time.

All the functions and data for the locking feature are in one compilation unit and header file (LOCK.CPP and LOCK.H), and the password dialogs can be accessed only through gateway functions. The calling program doesn't even have access to the password in the sample program, a characteristic you should strive to preserve in your real world implementations. This creates the highest, most impenetrable wall between the main program and the locking support, which is good software practice in general, of course, and it also simplifies adding this support to an existing program. And speaking of which....

## Adding a Locked Persona to an Existing Program

Assuming that your converted program will follow the general model outlined at the beginning of this chapter, you can retrofit a locked persona onto an existing program in five steps:

1. Add interface facilities so that the user can lock or unlock the program. This can be as simple as the "Lock/Unlock..." system menu item used in LOCKER, to something much more elaborate and graphical, not to mention graphic. (Fans of Monty Python-style chastity belt jokes, in particular, take note.) The point is, the user needs a good, friendly way to operate this feature, especially when the program is locked. This is why LOCKER provides the system menu command, plus it will interpret an attempt to restore or maximize the program, when it's locked, as a request to display the unlocking password prompt.

2. Decide how and where you will store the password, and update RetrieveLockedState() and SaveLockedState() accordingly. This can be anything

from a few minutes work to several hours, depending on your approach and how you divide the work between the main program and the locking support.

3. Make your program intercept the WM_SYSCOMMAND messages with wParams of SC_RESTORE and SC_MAXIMIZE, and handle them accordingly. The WM_SYSCOMMAND handler from LOCKER is in its MAINFRM.CPP compilation unit, shown in Listing 11.2. The message handler isn't much to look at, which is the whole point— it doesn't *have* to do much. (But note the trickery involving the nID parameter. See the sidebar *Stupid MFC Tricks* in Chapter 7 for an explanation.)

4. Add the OnLockUnlock() and DoLockUnlock() functions to your program, and modify DoLockUnlock() to use the proper icon identifiers, play sound effects, change the program's caption, fiddle other interface elements, and perform what other functions you see fit. Remember, all non-trivial functionality of your program should be disabled when it is locked. This includes drag and drop support and everything else except unlocking and shutting down.

   LOCKER's implementation of OnLockUnlock() and DoLockUnlock() are in Listing 11.2, which shows the basic logic flow of calling the password-prompt dialogs and then switching the program's state. It would have been nice to add these functions to LOCK.CPP, and have the main program simply call it and retrieve a BOOL result that indicates if the program was locked or unlocked. But this isn't desirable, since a lot of information would have to be passed to the function, including the resource IDs of the two icons, plus the main program's hInstance and hWnd values and any other information needed for other interface manipulation.

   Remember that if your program uses any modeless dialogs or other onscreen elements, you probably want to close them down or hide them when the program is locked, and recreate or reveal them when the program is unlocked. Code that takes care of such matters goes in DoLockUnlock(), or is called from there.

   The work here is divided between two functions for a reason. When your program starts up, it might need to come up in the locked state, so it needs access to the locking logic without displaying the password prompt. In LOCKER, this snippet of code is in the OnCreate() method in MAINFRM.CPP.

5. Customize the locking and unlocking dialogs, as needed. See the *Security Issues* section later on for a discussion of some things to keep in mind as you perform this step.

*It takes more than these five steps to create a well-rounded implementation, of course, like good help file support. The last thing you want to do is confuse users with the locking feature! You'll also have to plan for the eventuality of users forgetting passwords and then coming to you,*

*all atremble and hair ablaze, begging you to unlock their data. If your program stores its password or locked state in a custom format data file, you'll probably need to write a minimal unlocking program that will reach into that file and twiddle bits appropriately. In that case, I suggest you spend a few minutes upfront and write the unlocker program when you write the application; you don't want to have to do it with a nervous vice president staring over your shoulder.*

The other major variation on this feature is not holding the documents open when the program is locked. This is a design decision you'll have to make for each program, based on how you know (or, more likely, assume) the typical user operates your program, as well as your program's resource requirements. Keeping track of the exact visual state of the program across a lock/unlock operation can be a challenge. Minimally, you'll want to remember which documents were loaded, which one was active, the exact position (for example, the current line number in an editor), and state (such as insert or overwrite mode or text selected) for each document. This can turn into a mess (and a *lot* of user requests for you to do it better if you cut corners), which is why leaving the documents loaded and simply minimizing the program is such an attractive solution.

# Security Issues

At the beginning of this chapter, I said I wasn't going to wallow in security issues, and I won't. Still, it's worth talking about passwords a bit.

Password handling is one area where your program's human factors have to be *extremely* well thought out. It's very easy to accidentally make your program behave in a way that will reduce the usefulness of this feature, or worse, that will drive your users crazy. Frustrated users won't use this feature, which means you'll have effectively wasted your precious development effort and documentation page space (whether paper or online). It's a critical mass issue; x amount of effort results in a poor implementation that virtually no one uses, effectively wasting all x units of effort. A better, smarter implementation requiring 2×x units of work results in a feature that users like; meaning your development effort paid off in exactly the way it is supposed to: a more useful program.

When dealing with passwords for the locked persona of an individual program (note the careful qualification), you should keep the following guidelines in mind:

1. Don't make the password case sensitive. This only leads to typing errors and confusion on the part of the user. You don't want your program to refuse to unlock when the user enters a password of "fred" because it was locked with "Fred".

2. Make the user type the password twice, for verification. Are you a perfect typist? I'm sure as heck not, and neither are your users. Making the user verify the

password is simple, cheap insurance. I learned this the hard way with Stickies!; I forgot this step in the original locking implementation, and several customers locked the program with a password that (unknown to them until they tried to unlock it) contained a typo, and they came to me for help. Their typo was the proximal cause of the situation, but my design error was the root cause.

3. Enforce a minimum password length, not just a maximum. Is it dumb to use a password of a single letter? Of course it is. But some users, in their haste to run off to yet another meeting or a lunch date with that special someone, will fall into the bad habit of using a single-letter password, if you let them. So don't let them. I suggest a minimum length of five characters.

4. Mask the password entry to prevent "peeking over the shoulder" security exposures. Windows has a special attribute for edit controls (ES_PASSWORD) that makes them echo asterisks as the user types. Use it. It's a good, free security measure, and it makes your program look more professional.

5. Encode the password when you store it on disk. Again, we're talking about "storm door" security here, so don't go roaring off into the sunset with encryption algorithms, hidden disk files, and the like. My advice: Choose an 8-bit value and exclusive-or the password with it, byte by byte. This will make the password look like "binary garbage" to a snooper (assuming you pick a good mask value), and you can retranslate it with the same exclusive-or operation. (It's always fun showing this trick to new programmers; if you do it in a bar, you can usually get a free drink out of it.) This is a simple, effective, and appropriate way (given the application) to keep the password from being human readable.

6. Strip leading and trailing blanks from the password. This is a perfect chance to utilize the toolbox of routines in Chapter 3. Few things cause users and programmers alike annoying little problems as do leading and trailing blanks. When you're dealing with passwords, they can be deadly (the blanks, not the users or the passwords). You should document the fact that your program strips blanks from passwords, of course, but in practice it makes little difference. If the user doesn't know your program does this, you're still safe, since a password with intentional leading or trailing blanks will always be stripped the same way. The user won't know this is happening under the covers; the feature will work just as expected, and your user will be impressed that the "trick password" worked.

7. Depending on the situation, you might need to reject passwords that contain certain characters. Normally this isn't a consideration for application locking, but remember that a program's locked state will persist from one session to the next, which means there's a potential for a user to enter a password on one computer and then have to reproduce it from another keyboard. Your users can unwittingly paint themselves into a corner if a password requires a character not readily available on the second keyboard.

8. Make sure you only take action with a proper password. This probably won't apply to your implementation of a locked persona feature, since you'll likely use the password as a key and not as an input to an algorithm, but this is the best place to mention it. While writing this book, I evaluated a lot of development tools. One of them, which shall remain nameless, included both Windows 3.1 and Windows NT versions on the same CD-ROM, and required both a CD serial number and a password to unlock the program. The problem is that the two versions required different sets of codes, and the person who sent me the package swapped them. When I ran the unlocking program and entered what were supposed to be the codes for the Windows version, it dutifully accepted them and cranked away for a couple of minutes as it used the codes to decrypt the program. Since it had the wrong codes, all it did was mangle the files beyond recognition, resulting in a binary monstrosity that made Windows momentarily go to a black screen and then complain that there wasn't enough memory to run the program.

At first, I assumed I had done something wrong, so I redid the installation and unlocking procedure several times, with the same results. It finally occurred to me that the unlocking program might not be smart enough to complain that I had entered the wrong unlocking codes. I tried again with the "wrong" codes, and everything worked fine.

When I talked to someone at the vendor about this and other problems I had with their product (including a demo program that GPFed), I was told that they're a small company, and they were in a rush to get the product out the door. Well, they got it out the door all right, and it had so many problems beyond this silly but annoying password snafu, that I don't consider it a usable product. You should always think in terms of critical mass of both functionality *and* usability; a bridge that spans 90 percent of a chasm is useless (except as a pedagogical device), yet it costs nearly as much as a complete bridge.

# What Do You Want to Lock Today?

Locked personas have more possibilities for creativity than most presented in this book. In this chapter, I've presented the variation that I'm most comfortable with and have used the most. If you experiment with locked personas, let me know what new variations you come up with, what problems you run into, and how you solve them.

# Part 3

## Crossing the
## Great Divide

# Chapter 12

# From Win16 to Win32

# From Win16 to Win32

*"You can port your code to 32 bits with a simple recompile!"*

*The fourth great software lie, as paraphrased from countless advertisements for development tools. The first three great software lies are:*

1. *"It's fixed in the next release of the driver!"*

2. *"Of course it runs in only 4MB of RAM!"*

3. *"It's not a software (hardware) problem, it must be your hardware (software)!"*

How many times have you seen an ad for some compiler package or application framework that claimed porting your programs from Win16 to Win32 was just a mouse click away? A lot, I bet. I know I've probably seen hundreds of such ads in the last year. These claims always make me shake my head in disbelief, because I know that porting is almost never that simple.

Sure, if you want to write a "Hello, world!" program in MFC or OWL or some other framework, and then port it unchanged to another version of Windows, you can do it; under such artificial and tightly controlled conditions, it does indeed work. Single-click porting is probably the ultimate example of a hothouse feature, which means that in the real world it proves nothing. Out here, where we and our programs have to endure the vagaries of user demands, and we have to deal with endless architectural differences and "minor" incompatibilities between Win16 and the various incarnations of Win32, the theory almost never holds up. (Having said that, I'm sure that someone will write to tell me about how a recent

301

500,000-line-of-code project was ported from Windows 3.1 to Windows NT without touching the source code. In the real world, such things do happen, but they're almost always aberrations or the result of extensive planning and a lot of plain old hard work that was done far in advance, which makes the porting process anything but a one-click step.)

With the arrival of Windows 95, the porting issue became far more important. In the recent past many Windows programmers simplified their lives by the most obvious and direct means possible: They simply targeted 16-bit Windows, and ignored Windows NT, OS/2, and all porting issues. The biggest porting question most Windows programmers faced in the last few years was deciding whether to support Windows 3.0 explicitly and bother with shipping redistributable files, such as COMMDLG.DLL and SHELL.DLL with their programs. Now, we have to wrestle with many more questions, including which platforms to support and which operating system features to exploit.

But I'm getting ahead of myself. In this chapter I'll talk about porting existing Win16 programs to Win32, and some of the issues you'll have to deal with and surprises you might run into along the way. Chapter 14 will focus on the differences between the Win32 platforms.

# An Application Programmer's View of Windows 95

I'm not going to present a detailed architectural view of Windows 95, complete with memory maps and boxes with arrows that show which parts of the system communicate with which others, etc. While I always find such material interesting (the surest symptom that one is afflicted with incurable computer nerdity, I suppose), I've decided not to include it for two reasons:

- This material is widely available in other books and magazines, and if I included it here I would be merely quoting other sources. Instead, let me recommend some sources that (as far as I know) are reliable:

  Matt Pietrek's article "Understanding Windows 95 Memory Management: Paging, Address Spaces, and Contexts," *Microsoft Systems Journal*, April, 1995, also on the *Microsoft Developer Network* CD ROM

  Matt's "Stepping Up to 32 bits: Chicago's Process, Thread, and Memory Management," *Microsoft Systems Journal*, August, 1994, also on the *MSDN* CD ROM

  Andrew Schulman's *Unauthorized Windows 95*, IDG Books, which has more detail about Windows 95's innards than most programmers will ever need or even want to know.

  (There are numerous other articles in *MSJ/MSDN* about Windows 95, but be careful what you believe from these sources or others; the most recent MSDN

CD ROM I have still includes Adrian King's article that says, "The big difference in Chicago's relationship with MS-DOS from that of Windows 3.1 is that if you only run Windows-based applications, you'll never execute any MS-DOS code." This is an assertion that Andrew Schulman refutes in excruciating detail.)

- My primary goal in this book is to address application programming for various Windows platforms, most notably Windows 95. While knowledge of the operating system's internals is indeed still relevant to application programming (sad to say), I think it's clearly far less important than exploring the new features and facilities that Windows 95 presents to the programmer. (Of course, the programming facilities available to us are an emergent property of the underlying support and architecture, but it doesn't matter why the facilities are the way they are, just that they are. Put another way, when I buy a new car, I'm quite interested in its handling, acceleration, and braking characteristics, but I don't much care about the suspension geometry, how many valves per cylinder it uses, or the exact diameter of the disc rotors.)

OK, so what should you care about? In moving from Windows 3.1 to Windows 95 application programming, there are numerous features and differences you should be aware of. The most important five features, in my opinion, are:

- Long file names. This is the big one, and the one that is likely to cause more bugs and usability hassles than any other single change in Windows 95. At first blush, handling long file names seems like a no-brainer: You remember that they can have embedded blanks and they're much longer than the old 8.3 format we're used to, and you use the new APIs to translate between the two name formats, and so on. What could be simpler? Well, it's not that simple, of course (when is it ever?), since Windows 95 throws you several curves in its handling of long file names. See Chapter 13 for much more detail on these surprises.

- Multiple threads per program. Like long file names, this is another great feature that has to be treated with respect. There are the obvious issues concerning thread creation and deletion, and dividing up your program's work among threads in a way that will benefit you and your users. (Even though I think this is an obvious point, I fear that we'll soon start seeing programs that do some very odd and not entirely helpful things with threads, simply so their authors can claim to have used them.) In particular, the more experienced Windows programmers will have to unlearn some old behavior when they start using threads. We're all used to writing single-threaded programs that blithely ignore any synchronization issues; Windows taps our program on the shoulder and says, "Hey! Something happened! You want to do something about this?" and we make the program respond to the event. Simple stuff.

But think for a moment how we make the program react to events—the code almost never checks anything else about its internal state. It typically assumes, for example, that all variables and files are in a known and coherent state, and that there's nothing else "going on" in the program that the code has to worry about. And nor should it worry, since in a single threaded program the executing code is literally in charge of the show. This can lead to unwanted adventures in a multi-threaded program. To pick a trivial example, consider background printing, the most often cited example of a Good Use For Threading. (In this sense, background printing is to threading as complex numbers are to objects, since you can hardly pick up a book that talks about objects without running into yet another treatment of writing your own complex number class.) It can be a great convenience if your program's users can tell it to start printing some document and then continue to edit that document or another one with the same application without having to wait for the print job to be sent to the spooler.

But what would happen if the application accepted the printing request, spun off a new thread to handle it, and then immediately returned control to the main editing thread without taking any other precautions? Chaos would ensue, and the user would quite possibly get a printed copy of the document that included a few (or few dozen) keystrokes of changes made while the print job was still running. The user might even manage to crash the program, depending on how it stores the in-memory representation of the document. (Imagine that the user starts editing some text at the same instant that the printing thread reaches that same part of the data structure. Suddenly you have one piece of code reading the data while another is changing it, and the threads aren't synchronized. Can you say "This program has performed an illegal operation?" I knew you could.) The solution is conceptually simple, of course, and the program merely takes a snapshot of the document at the instant that the printing command is given, and lets the new thread work from that copy and then delete it.

The problem is often that the implementation is more complex, and can even preclude the effective use of background printing. Perhaps the application's document includes data drawn from several remote sources, or a large enough amount of data that creating the snapshot will take nearly as long as will printing the document. In that case, there's no sense in using a printing thread, since it only adds to the complexity of the program, and the user gets no appreciable benefit. Have I talked about cost/benefit ratios recently? Here's another excellent example, and a gentle reminder that you shouldn't use an operating system feature just so you can get another check mark in the features list.

(And notice that you don't need real operating system support for threading to perform background printing; Word for Windows 6.0 does it very nicely under Windows 3.1, as do other programs.)

- 32-bit architecture. I bet you were wondering when I'd get to this one. Yes, our collective arrival at the legendary Land of Thirty Two Bits was long overdue, and I, for one, am very glad that we finally made it. (Windows NT and OS/2 mavens will no doubt howl in protest at that last statement, and with at least some justification. Please understand that I'm talking largely in terms of mainstream Windows programming, which eliminates both OS/2, and, until very recently, Windows NT.) Just getting rid of all that "near" and "far" pointer idiocy, and no longer having to worry constantly about whether numbers/sizes/ whatever are over or under 65,536 is reason enough to celebrate. Add to that the potential for performance improvements, and we all should be dancing in the aisles.

Well, not so fast, light foot. As I point out in this chapter and in Chapter 14, converting to 32-bits is anything but a free lunch, even if we're all more than willing to pay the price. Minimally, there are the changes in data type sizes that we'll all have to deal with. Depending on the nature of your application and the versions of Windows under which you want it to run, a more important issue is that Windows 95 is not entirely 32-bit. This probably isn't news to most people reading this book, but that doesn't make it any less important. The GDI and USER components of Windows 95 are still 16-bit code. That means that Windows 95 programs are still stuck with a 16-bit graphics subsystem that will only use 16-bit integers for graphics coordinates. (Notice that I said "use" and not "accept." This is a subtle hint that there's much more coming on this topic, and it's not good news.)

- New shell. The most obvious change in moving from Windows 3.1 to Windows 95 for a user is the new shell. As you would expect, this change isn't just a facade, but includes new programming APIs relating to folders, property sheets, and links. It's possible to write a full-featured Windows program that doesn't use any of these new facilities, of course, but in many cases you'll want to exploit some of the new Windows 95 (and, presumably, Windows NT 4.0) features to enhance your program's usability.

- New emphasis on the registry. The registry is one of those parts of Windows, like OLE, that many programmers considered too much trouble. And in many cases, we could make our programs do what we wanted just fine without going near the registry, so nothing was lost. As in other areas, Windows 95 changed the rules, and it now provides some very useful features that can be accessed only via the registry. One example that I talked about earlier is the App Paths registry setting, which allows your program to specify its own, unique directory which is pre-pended to its PATH setting, thereby allowing your program to have a private directory for its DLLs, VBXs, and other dynamically located executables. This feature can make your program more configuration friendly, but it also exacts a price—by being tied to the registry and the new Windows 95 support, it forces you to make some hard decisions about running under Win32s and Windows NT (at least until the new support for this feature finds its way onto that platform). Do you support more than one configuration and installation procedure, or do you make your program refuse to install and run under any version of Windows NT before 4.0? In the short run, I suspect a lot of programmers will simplify their lives and use a generic configuration that shuns the new Windows 95 features.

## Win16lock

One Windows 95 issue that I honestly can't assess at this time is the infamous Win16lock. The Win16lock is a solution to a problem that was created by another design decision Microsoft made, namely to keep some components of Windows 95 16-bit, most notably USER and GDI. This decision also means that these components are not re-entrant, which poses an interesting problem, to say the least, for an operating system that now provides pre-emptive multitasking and multithreading.

This was a classic tough design decision, in that Microsoft could have attacked this problem in several ways, none of them perfect. They chose the solution that was probably the best compromise in terms of robustness and size of the eventual implementation. That solution involved creating something called the Win16lock or Win16mutex. ("Mutex" being, perhaps, the ultimate computer geek word; it means "mutual exclusion semaphore," a.k.a. a "busy flag.") In essence, the Win16lock is used by Windows 95 to prevent more than one 16-bit thread from trying to execute non-reentrant code at the same time. This flag is set by Windows whenever a 16-bit thread is dispatched by the scheduler, and whenever a Win32 thread thunks down to 16-bit support. Since GDI and USER are still 16-bit, all Win32 programs do a fair amount of thunking, and therefore frequently acquire and release the Win16lock. Whenever any thread has the Win16lock it blocks any other thread from acquiring the lock and entering the 16-bit system components. In this way, it's possible for a very ill-behaved 16-bit program to tie up all the applications in your system; if a 16-bit program never gives control back to the system, then it will never release the Win16lock. Eventually all the Win32 programs will go into a holding pattern as they try to thunk to 16-bit support and they wind up waiting for the Win16lock to become available. (For a detailed discussion of the Win16lock situation and why Microsoft used it, see Adrian King's article "Memory Management, the Win32 Subsystem, and Internal Synchronization in Chicago" in the May, 1994 issue of *Microsoft Systems Journal.* This article is also on the *Microsoft Developer Network* CD-ROM.)

Long before Windows 95 was released, word about the Win16lock got out, of course, and it triggered quite an uproar. Some people threw such a fit, you'd have thought Microsoft had decided to implement Windows 95 entirely in 8-bit code or make the user interface monochrome-only. (I admit that when I first learned of the Win16lock and the 16-bit system components I was a little disappointed, since I had hoped that Windows 95 would be an all-32-bit OS. Still, some people took the news quite hard.)

The important question, of course, is how does this design decision affect you and your program's users. If you're writing 32-bit programs, or well behaved 16-bit programs ("well behaved" meaning ones that yield control to Windows frequently enough), then there's not much else you can do. It's not like you can decide not to use USER or GDI. (I take that back; there are extreme cases in which you can avoid USER and GDI, by writing a Windows program that doesn't even have a window or dialog box for an interface. But that's such an extreme measure and of such limited usefulness that we can safely ignore it.) About all you can do is be aware of the problem and be prepared for the odd instance of a user complaining about your program not being responsive, when the fault might lie with some other application that's hogging the system.

*I really don't want to get into the eternal "OS war" that keeps the Windows and OS/2 zealots occupied for weeks and months at a time, but I do want to point out one interesting detail that's probably relevant to the Win16lock issue, namely how well OS/2 multitasks. I routinely run 16- and 32-bit programs under Windows for Workgroups 3.11, Windows 95, Win32s 1.30, Windows NT 3.51, and OS/2 Warp 3.0, and every one of my computers has at least three of those operating environments installed.*

*As I run these various systems, I'm always impressed by how smoothly OS/2 multitasks. For example, I have Windows 95, Windows NT 3.51, and OS/2 Warp 3.0 on one computer, a 75MHz Pentium with 24MB of RAM. Windows 95 runs fine, as it should with that amount of horsepower and RAM, particularly when it's executing 32-bit programs. But OS/2 always feels much faster on this box, and is conspicuously smoother once I start to load the system. I've noticed that if I start a large Visual C++ 2.2 build under Windows 95 and then display the task bar, switch to other programs, edit text, etc., that nearly all operations are noticeably slower and far jerkier than they should be. I've heard Windows 95's multitasking described as "chunky", which is pretty accurate, in my experience. OS/2, on the other hand, just keeps on rolling as you start more programs, and seems not to notice "earth mover" tasks running in the background, even though they're executing at a quite respectable clip. Every time I see this, I wish Windows 95 were as graceful under fire.*

## Datatype Changes...

Windows 95 is (for the most part) a 32-bit operating system, which means we'll be writing 32-bit application programs for it. (See the section "Porting 16-bit Code to Windows 95" for more detail on the 16- vs. 32-bit decision.) What does this mean, aside from the fact that we'll have to buy new development tools, or learn to use new facilities in our existing tools?

Being a data-centric guy, I tend to focus on issues like changes in the sizes of datatypes. And in moving from 16-bit Windows development to 32-bit Windows development, there's plenty to focus on.

First of all, it's important to distinguish between the changes in how your compiler implements various datatypes and changes to the basic Windows architecture, since these are quite different issues.

You're probably aware that when you move from a 16-bit C/C++ compiler to a 32-bit C/C++ compiler, some of your existing datatypes change size. This has nothing to do with DOS, Windows, OS/2 or any other operating system. The C/C++ language could have very well left int's as 16-bit, and told people to use the already present "long" for 32-bit integers and avoided the problem entirely. The point is, these changes are due solely to how the language is implemented. See Table 12.1 for a summary of 16- and 32-bit C/C++ datatypes.

*Notice in Table 12.1 that the last three rows are non-standard Microsoft language extensions. Microsoft's documentation says that __int8 is a synonym for char, __int16 is a synonym for short, and __int32 is really an int in this implementation. These size-specific integers provide a way to write code that is insulated from changes in integer size (presumably because future implementations will respect these current sizes and not re-size __int32 to whatever an int becomes). In my opinion, this is how the basic types in C/C++, Pascal, and all programming languages should behave. When you're porting code from one platform to another, you're usually moving from a smaller to a larger word size, so you're not likely to run into problems with calculations, since your variables are getting larger. But you're much more likely to have problems with structures changing size (and possibly alignment).*

*Visual C++ 2.x also supports, in a sort-of-kind-of way, an __int64 type, which gives you signed integers with a range of approximately +/- 9E18, or 0 to 1.8E19 for the unsigned variety. See Mike Potter's article "64-bit Ints for Huge Files and Volumes" in the October, 1995, Windows/DOS Developer's Journal for more on this and some routines that convert 64-bit signed and unsigned integers to ASCII representations, something the compiler doesn't provide on its own.*

The other side to this coin is the changes in the artificial Windows datatypes. As Table 12.2 shows, there are just enough changes here to make life interesting. While I'm glad that the WORD, BYTE, DWORD, and LPARAM types remained

## Table 12.1    C/C++ Datatypes in 16 and 32 bits

| C/C++ Datatype | 16-bit Size (bits) | 16-bit Range | 32-bit Size (bits) | 32-bit Range |
|---|---|---|---|---|
| char | 8 | –128 to 127 | same as 16-bit | same as 16-bit |
| unsigned char | 8 | 0 to 255 | same as 16-bit | same as 16-bit |
| int | 16 | –32768 to 32767 | 32 | –2,147,483,648 to 2,147,483,647 |
| unsigned int | 16 | 0 to 65,535 | 32 | 0 to 4,294,967,295 |
| short | 16 | –32,768 to 32,767 | same as 16-bit | same as 16-bit |
| unsigned short | 16 | 0 to 65,535 | same as 16-bit | same as 16-bit |
| long | 32 | –2,147,483,648 to 2,147,483,647 | same as 16-bit | same as 16-bit |
| unsigned long | 32 | 0 to 4,294,967,295 | same as 16-bit | same as 16-bit |
| enum | 16 | –32,768 to 32,767 | same as 16-bit | same as 16-bit |
| float | 32 | 3.4E ± 38 | same as 16-bit | same as 16-bit |
| double | 64 | 1.7E ± 308 | same as 16-bit | same as 16-bit |
| long double | 80 | 1.2E ± 4932 | same as 16-bit | same as 16-bit |
| __int8 * | N/A | N/A | 8 | –128 to 127 |
| __in16 * | N/A | N/A | 16 | –32,768 to 32,767 |
| __int32 * | N/A | N/A | 32 | –2,147,483,648 to 2,147,483,647 |

\* = Microsoft non-standard extension in Visual C++ 2.x

## Table 12.2    Windows Datatypes in 16 and 32 bits

| Windows Datatype | 16-bit Size (bits) | 16-bit Range | 32-bit Size (bits) | 32-bit Range |
|---|---|---|---|---|
| All handles (HWND, HPEN, etc.) | 16 | 0 to 65,535 | 32 | 0 to 4,294,967,295 |
| UINT | 16 | 0 to 65,535 | 32 | 0 to 4,294,967,295 |
| BOOL | 16 | –32,768 to 32,767 (only 0 and 1 valid) | 32 | –2,147,483,648 to 2,147,483,647 (only 0 and 1 valid) |
| WORD | 16 | 0 to 65,535 | same as 16-bit | same as 16-bit |
| BYTE | 8 | 0 to 255 | same as 16-bit | same as 16-bit |
| DWORD | 32 | 0 to 4,294,967,295 | same as 16-bit | same as 16-bit |
| WPARAM (== UINT) | 16 | 0 to 65,535 | 32 | 0 to 4,294,967,295 |
| LPARAM (== long) | 32 | –2,147,483,648 to 2,147,483,647 | same as 16-bit | same as 16-bit |

the same, I find it painfully counterintuitive when moving between 16- and 32-bit Windows development that ints, UINTs, and even BOOLs did change size.

And please keep in mind that these types are all Microsoft's fabrications; there's no such thing as a built-in BOOL type, for example (although the emerging C/C++ standard (finally!) includes a native boolean type, and as I understand it, one that is supposed to restrict variables of that type to only the values 0 and 1). Likewise, WPARAM and LPARAM are artifacts of the Windows universe.

## ..and the Consequences for Windows Programming

The fallout from these changes in the size of datatypes varies greatly with the nature of your program, of course. Some applications that don't create or store custom format data files and aren't particularly sensitive, can be ported from 16 to 32 bits with very little attention paid to this resizing issue. In many cases, some of your variables get larger, most stay the same size, and you recompile and go about your merry way. (This is not to imply that there aren't a raft of other porting issues, just that this one isn't always a problem.)

Notice in Table 12.2 that one of the datatypes that does change size is WPARAM, which means that both pieces of data in a standard Windows message are now four bytes. Technically WPARAM is still unsigned and LPARAM is still signed, as I've indicated in the table, but these values are really just "bit buckets" that can be used however we please. (I've even passed four-byte-long packed structures in LPARAMS, for example.)

The change in the size of handles, from two bytes to four would seem to be the least interesting detail in Table 12.2. After all, we never put handles in persistent storage (at least we shouldn't be doing such things), and we never do anything with them except hand them back to the system as a "magic key" for certain API calls. (Some people who like to dissect Windows will use handles for other purposes, since under Windows 3.1 they're really pointers. But that's far from mainstream usage and not something we need to be concerned about.) So who cares if they're two or four or 17 bytes?

As it turns out, we do, since there are times when Windows passes a handle in a message, and increasing the handle size to four bytes forced Microsoft to change the packing of the message WM_CTLCOLOR. This message is sent by message boxes, combo boxes, edit controls, list boxes, buttons, static controls, and scroll bars to their parent, to give the parent a chance to override the control's colors. This message is also sent to a dialog (not its parent) to give it a chance to control its own colors.

In Windows 3.1, the interface of the WM_CTLCOLOR message is defined as:

```
hdcChild = (HDC) wParam;            /* child-window display context */
hwndChild = (HWND) LOWORD(lParam);  /* handle of child window       */
nCtlType = (int) HIWORD(lParam);    /* type of control              */
```

If the parent is to make heads or tails out of any given WM_CTLCOLOR message, it needs all three pieces of information shown above, which, in a 16-bit world, just barely fit into a WPARAM and an LPARAM. But in a 32-bit world, the two handles (hdcChild and hwndChild) alone will fill the four-byte WPARAM and four-byte LPARAM. Where do we put the nCtlType parameter? The answer is, we don't, and neither does Microsoft. They had to take the somewhat drastic step of doing away with the WM_CTLCOLOR message and creating several new messages in its place:

- WM_CTLCOLORBTN
- WMCTLCOLORDLG
- WM_CTLCOLOREDIT
- WM_CTLCOLORLISTBOX
- WM_CTLCOLORMSGBOX
- WM_CTLCOLORSCROLLBAR
- WM_CTLCOLORSTATIC.

Each of these new messages uses the same message layout:

```
hdcObject = (HDC) wParam;     // handle of object's display context
hwndObject = (HWND) lParam;   // handle of object
```

Since nCtlType is no longer needed, we once again have room for all the important information. Of course, any 16-bit code that looks for WM_CTLCOLOR messages must be updated to reflect these changes when it's ported to 32-bits. This is one time when using a framework might have saved you some porting effort—in its 16-bit incarnation, MFC "cracked" WM_CTLCOLOR into the CWnd::OnCtlColor() method, and passed the original three pieces of information (the two handles and nCtlType) as separate parameters. In the 32-bit version, the application still sees just that one method with the same three parameters, and the programmer might not even know that the original message has been fragmented into seven new messages in the underlying API.

*MFC's CWnd::OnCtlColor() method is an excellent example of how frameworks can be a blessing when you have to port code from one Windows implementation to another. This is precisely the kind of thing I talked about in Chapter 10 when I stressed that abstraction can be used to create a higher, more amenable platform on which to build programs.*

*The problem is that MFC, OWL, and all the other frameworks I've looked at don't go nearly as far in this area as they should. They pave over some of the lesser architectural differences, such as the WM_CTLCOLOR changes, but they do nothing about differences in the behavior of the individual APIs as you move between Win32 platforms. This is a far more serious issue, since the same Win32 program binary must run on all three Win32 platforms, whereas a program that uses WM_CTLCOLOR must be recompiled before it can be run as a Win32 program. See Chapter 14 for much more on this.*

Another subtle issue regarding the new datatype sizes has to do with the relationship between sizes. Notice that in 16-bit Windows/C programs WORDs, WPARAMs, shorts, UINTs, and ints are all the same size (two bytes), while in 32-bit Windows/C, WORDs and shorts are still two bytes, but WPARAMs, UINTs, and ints are now four bytes. Depending on how you're casting variables between these types, you can be in for some nasty surprises, and some frustrating debugging sessions. The only advice I can give you on this front is to use the highest warning level your compiler supports, and read through all your ported code for this sort of unintentional mixing of variable sizes.

# Porting 16-Bit Code to Windows 95

First, let me be clear about one thing: When I talk about "porting 16-bit code to Windows 95," I'm using the phrase in about the loosest, broadest possible sense. To me, this issue starts with a running Win16 program, and proceeds to the question, "What, if any, changes should I make to this program to accommodate Windows 95?" That sounds like a biased way of presenting the issue, but I think it's a fair one. The majority of Win16 programs will run unaltered under Windows 95 (or with only minor cosmetic problems), so I think it's entirely fair to view the "to port or not to port" question in terms of "what do I get in return for accommodating the operating system." In some cases, possibly because of completely non-technical reasons, the answer is quite a lot, and undertaking a large-scale porting effort is a no-brainer. In other cases, it's nowhere near that cut-and-dried.

I've stressed throughout this book that I think we should all strive to take the long view when facing all the endless little design and implementation decisions that make up the fabric of Windows programming. In my opinion, porting issues are the area of Windows programming most susceptible to knee-jerk, and therefore bad, design decisions. That's why I'll present a spectrum of porting options and talk about some of the factors you should take into account when making this decision for an individual program.

## Select a Porting Strategy

Following the lead of the previous section, let's say you have a fully functional, 16-bit, public Windows program, and like most Windows programmers, you've ignored Win32 until now. But now Windows 95 is upon us, and it's time for you to select a porting strategy. What do you do?

First, you should realize that one of the biggest mistakes you can make is lapsing into bi-polar thinking and assuming that there are only two possibilities—wimpy little Win16 programs and full-blown, hairy-chested Windows 95 programs. This is a gross oversimplification that can get you and your program into deep trouble in a hurry. Because there are significant variations in the shipping Win32 platforms, as well as degrees of Windows 95 awareness and exploitation your program can have, you must make quite a few decisions.

As a start, you should address the following list of questions and issues about your application as honestly and as completely as possible. In all cases, you should determine how important each factor is over time, not just how important it is right now. For example, you might find that for your program and your users, supporting the newer Windows 95-only features isn't that important in the short run, and might even be a hindrance since some of your users are running Windows NT 3.51 or Win32s. But after six or twelve months, you know that this situation will change and it will become much more desirable to provide this kind of support.

1. Which Win32 platforms to support? For someone used to officially supporting only Windows 3.1, this can be a tricky question. The natural response is to try to support all the platforms, to maximize the usefulness of the program. Unfortunately, that requires quite a testing effort, thanks to all the differences between the Win32 platforms, a topic I'll take up in Chapter 14.

2. Will the program handle long file names? This can be a surprisingly tough question. Perhaps your program is relatively insulated from file names, so there's little or no reason to support them. But I suspect that use of long file names will quickly be seen by many mainstream users as the most obvious way of differentiating between "new"/"good" and "old"/"bad" programs, so there still might be a compelling reason for your program to support long file names. This is particularly interesting when you're dealing with 16-bit programs, as I mention in the sidebar "Using LFNs from Win16 Programs: Better Living through Alchemy."

3. Will the program use multithreading? If so, then you're immediately limited to a 32-bit program running under Windows 95 and Windows NT, since only 32-bit programs can use threads, and Win32s does not support multithreading.

4. Does the program care about the 16-bit limitations of Windows 95? GDI and USER are still 16-bit under Windows, which means that all graphics coordinates

and list box indexes are truncated from 32 to 16 bits. In most applications this isn't a problem, especially when you're porting a 16-bit program, which is already living with these 16-bit limitations. Still, it's best to be aware of this situation up front; if you're planning to add new, extensive graphics features to your program that exploit a 32-bit coordinate space, you'll have to choose between limiting your program to Windows NT and not using 32-bit coordinates, after all. (There are other differences in Windows 95's GDI support, as well, such as very limited support for paths. Again, see Chapter 14 for details.)

5. How extensively will the program exploit the new Windows 95 features? Currently, features such as the Explorer context menu, the App Paths registry setting and support, and property sheet extensions are available only under Windows 95. Windows NT will likely gain these features in version 4.0, but Win32s will apparently never get them.

6. Marketing issues. If you're writing a program for internal use at your company, or for casual distribution among a few friends, then clearly you can ignore this category. But if you or your company will be marketing your program, whether it's a shareware program, a mass-market shrink-wrap title, or a high-priced vertical-market application, then you or your company need to do as much analysis as possible in this area. As I mentioned in question two (about long file names), non-technical issues often become critical when you're dealing with the paying public and their perception of what's important.

7. Other misc. non-technical issues. This is one of those areas that programmers hate to deal with but can't escape. Perhaps your program doesn't really need to be ported to Win32 in the short run, but your boss is smitten by Microsoft's new wonderchild. Next thing you know, the edict comes down from on high that everyone will switch to Windows 95, all new in-house development will henceforth be native Windows 95 programs, and all old in-house programs will be converted to Win32/Windows 95 programs as soon as possible. This is a fabricated example, of course, but I've seen site-wide technical decisions made for much flimsier reasons than this.

When something like this comes up, you have to make the call whether to roll with the punches and do a needless conversion, or tell management that it's a waste of resources to convert programs X, Y, and Z. About all you can do is try to identify such issues as early as possible, to minimize the number of surprises you and your development team have to field.

Once you've assessed these questions and issues, you can then select a porting strategy for your program. This might be as simple as a one-stage port, or it might be multiple stages stretched across a year or two. Again, there's no way I or Microsoft or anyone else can tell you what's right for your program and users; it's a decision only you can make, and only in the proper context.

You could invent endless porting taxonomies, but I believe there are four main choices, which I've presented here in order of least to most change to the program (assuming a Windows 3.1/Win16 program is the starting point):

• Stay Win16, and don't change anything. Are you surprised that I've even listed this as an option in this book? You shouldn't be. Microsoft fervently wants to see vendors and customers convert every Windows program in existence to Win32 immediately, if not sooner. I suspect this is largely because such a mass migration to Win32 would strangle OS/2. IBM has said publicly that they have no immediate plans to support native Win32 programs under OS/2 (and it would be quite a daunting task, even if they wanted to).

Why do you care about this stuff? Aren't the technical issues the important ones? As much as we all wish we could make technical decisions based solely on technical merits, this Microsoft vs. IBM nonsense is very important because these companies are such large and powerful entities in the business, and their actions greatly influence everyone, particularly developers. The point is that when Microsoft pushes as hard as it has been to get developers to write Win32 apps, you should understand why. It's not out of an altruistic desire to see users get better applications; it's directly attributable to their own best interest. If Microsoft was somehow convinced that it could maximize its bottom line by convincing people to convert to 1MHz Z80 systems with 16K of RAM, you can bet that the airwaves would be saturated with commercials that made such systems seem oh-so hip for being so small and inexpensive and retro. This doesn't make Microsoft evil. Such behavior is to be expected; it's the nature of capitalism, and IBM or any other company would do the same thing in a heartbeat and with a clear conscience.

Your obligation as a developer is to be aware of such factors and respond to them accordingly. And that means you shouldn't be a lemming and go diving off the porting cliff just because it seems like the thing to do. Nor should you join the "Microsoft is the Evil Empire" bunch and refuse to port your program as a way of "getting" Microsoft. Fanaticism of any stripe is the surest, shortest road to bad decisions any of us can take.

As tempted as you might be to leave a public program in its current Win16 form and do nothing, you should still test it under Windows 95 and Windows NT. Why? While the odds are pretty good that you won't get any nasty surprises, it's not a sure thing. Not too long before Windows 95 was released, Microsoft made public the results of their in-house compatibility testing, and they found numerous application programs that stubbed their toes under Windows 95. Note that these were not just the low-level utilities that you might expect to trip when running under a new operating system. In fact, I ran into some surprises with Stickies!. See the sidebar "Stickies! and Windows 95: A Case Study in Porting" for more details.

- Stay Win16, but add minimal Windows 95 awareness, such as long file name support, and accommodate Windows 95 quirks and enforced changes. This is an option that no one in this business seems to be talking about. I don't know if it's the result of Microsoft's (considerable) public relations prowess, or if it's merely typical American obsession with size (in the sense of 32 bit vs. 16) in action, but everyone seems to have ignored the fact that you can make a Win16 program reasonably Windows 95-like without converting it to 32-bits. It can use long file names, display proportional scroll bar thumbs, use the inherent 3D look, use application-specific paths for DLL placement, etc.

  But note that as soon as you begin to embrace Windows 95-specific features, you either must take great pains to make your program run under other platforms, or restrict your program to running under Windows 95. See the sidebar "Using LFNs from Win16 Programs: Better Living through Alchemy" for more on writing "16/4.0" programs.

- Port to Win32, but make no Windows 95-specific changes. In essence, the goal here is to create a program that will run under Windows 95 and Windows NT 3.51. Depending on your situation, this option might not be viable for long—as I write this it's widely expected that Windows NT 4.0, which is supposedly due in early 1996, will erase nearly all of the feature-set differences between Windows NT and Windows 95. (At least that's the theory; after researching the chapters in this part of the book, I'll remain skeptical until the product ships.)

  I consider the new Windows 95 common controls (image lists, treeviews, richedit controls, tabbed dialogs, etc.) to be Windows 95-specific, even though they can be used under Windows NT 3.51 with the aid of a redistributable DLL (COMCTRL32.DLL). I would consider any use of these controls to place the program into the next category.

  It's useful to distinguish between the operating system features that your program uses, and those required by its default configuration. For example, let's say you write a program that operates equally well under Windows NT 3.51 and Windows 95, and your program uses one or more custom DLLs. You can still use an application-specific directory for the DLLs under Windows 95, via an App Paths registry entry, even though this feature isn't supported by Windows NT. Whether it's worth the effort to create different installation procedures or programs for these two operating systems is another program-specific question, of course, but it is an option.

- Port to Win32 and use Windows 95-specific features. At this stage, your program is restricted to running under Windows 95 and Windows NT 4.0 or later (3.51 and later if the only such feature is the new common controls). Depending on how fully you choose to exploit Windows 95 features, and what, exactly, Microsoft includes in Windows NT 4.0, you could wind up with a Windows 95-only program.

Clearly, this category is a continuum-within-a-continuum, and there are numerous minor decisions you will have to make about exploiting new shell features, for example. I'm grouping all these together in one category, since your program is restricted to Windows 95 and Windows NT 4.0 once you cross this line.

Did I forget something? Win32s, perhaps? No, I didn't forget it, I intentionally didn't mention it. Win32s is definitely the odd duck in this flock. Survey Microsoft's literature on their *Developer Network* CD ROM, for example, and you'll see that between bugs and various limitations, Win32s presents quite a stunning obstacle course for developers. I don't consider Win32s a viable option for non-trivial programs except under extreme circumstances, such as an overwhelming economic incentive. And when you're in the grip of such a situation, all the questions and answers about and analysis of your situation are just about meaningless, since you already know what you're going to do.

*If you think I'm being overly hard on poor little Win32s, see the following Microsoft articles on their Developer Network CD ROM:*

*Q121906 "Win32s 1.2 Bug List (at the Time of its Release)"*

*Q130139 "Win32s 1.25 Fix List"*

*Q130138 "Win32s1.25 Bug List"*

*Q133027 "Win32s 1.3 Fix List"*

*Q133026 "Win32s 1.3 Bug List"*

*and you'll find a truly amazing list of bugs, dozens in each case. The most recent bug list, Q133026, has over 50 bugs, including C runtime library routines getdcwd() and getcwd() not working (no details given), GetFullPathName() returning the root directory when used with any disk that's not the current drive, "biSizeImage field of BITMAPINFOHEADER is zero", "CreateFile() on certain invalid long filenames [sic] closes Windows", "FindText() leaks memory", "[s]tubbed API FindFirstFileW() does not return -1 to indicate failure", and my favorite: "GetShortPathName() doesn't fail with a bad path, as it does on Windows NT." (I talk about the numerous Win32 weirdnesses regarding GetShortPathName() in detail in Chapter 14; this minor admission from Microsoft about Win32s' handling of this API barely scratches the surface.)*

*Win32s 1.30a is supposed to be available as a redistributable very soon (as I write this in mid-October, 1995), and it will no doubt fix many of the problems in 1.30 as listed in Q133026. Microsoft has already released this update on CompuServe, but has not yet released the list of fixed bugs.*

Probably the most important single piece of porting advice I can give you (aside from "test 'til you drop") is: If you're going to port to Win32, do it in stages if at all possible. It's far better to shoot off three toes one at a time with a small-caliber pistol than to take off your entire leg with a single bazooka shot. In less colorful and more politically correct terms, porting, more so than almost any other task in programming, is an exercise in exploring and overcoming the unknown. And because the risk of project failure increases non-linearly with its degree of uncertainty, you're better off, whenever possible, building a bridge and crossing that divide in small steps instead of trying to cover it a single flying leap.

## Using LFNs from Win16 Programs: Better Living through Alchemy

I find it interesting how focused programmers seem to be on 32-bit programs, and how unaware they are that one of the most visible (and likely popular) features of Windows 95, long file names, is not restricted to 32-bit programs. In fact, Microsoft went out of its way to provide a complete set of long-file-name-capable functions that can be accessed from Win16 programs via the interrupt 21h interface. (They even included six functions, among them the very useful GetLongPathName(), which are available *only* via an int 21h call, and have no Win32 API equivalent.) Since no one likes to write assembly language wrappers for these things, I've provided a set of wrappers for most of the functions. They're in the file LFNRTNS.CPP, which is part of the LFNSTUFF program for this chapter. Just to give you a sample, though, here's the lfnDeleteFile() routine from LFNRTNS.CPP:

```
///////////////////////////////////////////////////////////////////////////
// lfnDeleteFile(): LFN-capable file delete function, using the new W95/int
// 21h file support.
///////////////////////////////////////////////////////////////////////////

BOOL lfnDeleteFile(char far *fn)
{
  if(!lfnHasLFNSupport())
    return FALSE;

  _asm push ds
  _asm push di
  _asm push si

  _asm mov ax,7141h
  _asm mov ch,FILE_ATTRIBUTE_NORMAL
  _asm mov cl,FILE_ATTRIBUTE_ANY_FILE
  _asm lds dx,dword ptr fn
  _asm mov si,0
  _asm int 21h

  _asm pop si
```

```
_asm pop di
_asm pop ds
_asm jc error

return TRUE;

error:
  return FALSE;
}
```

These wrapper functions are very easy to use. You can open a file with a long file name, for example, and then use the _fdopen() routine to associate the file handle with a stream, or you can follow the lead of the lfnCreateTextFileStream() function in LFNRTNS.CPP and do the open and _fdopen() in one step. However you choose to do this, you can perform all the normal buffered, text or binary mode file I/O with long file names just as you would with aliases. Even though the LFNSTUFF sample program uses the new functions to create and open a file, you don't really need to use them. I haven't found it documented anywhere, but those old standbys, _lcreat() and _lopen() will accept long file names under Windows 95, even when called from a Win16/3.x program. (Under Windows NT 3.51, though, they don't quite seem to have the hang of things, and they truncate long names to eight characters, etc.) I've also included a minimal sample, LFNDEMO, that shows this.

## Building the Samples: LFNSTUFF and LFNDEMO

**CD Location:** ZEN\CHAP12\LFNSTUFF and ZEN\CHAP12\LFNDEMO

**Platform:** Win16

**Build instructions:** Use the provided .MAK files with Visual C++ 1.52 and compile normally.

Note that LFNDEMO does not have a traditional user interface (or any at all, for that matter) and will simply create a plain text file on your system called "c:\really really long file name.txt" and terminate.

One thing to keep in mind is that these new int 21h functions are not limited to working with long file names; they will handle aliases as well, so you can easily use them all the time (assuming your program will run under only Windows 95; there is no Windows NT support for these services yet).

If you're going to use long file names in your Win16 program, possibly for the sake of appearance, a natural question arises: How do you use the new, Explorer-style common dialogs? I experimented with this a bit using generic thunks, and I couldn't get it to work—my test program worked properly, except for the fact that it always got the old-style common dialogs. I thought I was doing something wrong until I spotted the following in the article "Thunking Benefits and Drawbacks" in the Win32 SDK:

> 16-bit processes cannot create new threads. Certain Win32 API elements, such as the functions supporting the new common dialog boxes or those supporting console applications, create threads on behalf of the calling application. These functions cannot be used in a 16-bit process.

I haven't had a chance to investigate this issue further, but it seems that Microsoft's code is smart enough to check for a Win16 program that tries to do exactly what mine does, and calls the old style common dialogs, as needed. (Which nicely demonstrates the kind of Byzantine issues Microsoft had to address in Windows 95.) If you've found a way around this (aside from the obvious and wholly inelegant tactic of using a Win32 program as a proxy to call the common dialogs), please let me know.

While not needed to use long file names, there is another interesting technique that falls into the same general category of making your Win16 programs more Windows 95-aware: Marking them with an expected Windows version of 4.0. Marking your program this way is very easy; you just use the version of RC.EXE that comes with the Win32 SDK (it's in \WIN32SDK\MSTOOLS\BINW16), which will accept a command-line parameter of "-40" to specify the version number of the target executable.

Why would you want to do this? For one thing, it means that your program, which presumably expects things like the new int 21h functions to work, doesn't have to check to make sure it isn't running under Windows 3.1. Unfortunately, marking your program this way will also prevent Windows NT 3.51 from running it. This seems odd—after all, Windows NT 3.51 will happily run a Win32/4.0 program. But since Windows NT doesn't (yet) support the new int 21h functions, this makes at least some sense.

It's also true that marking your Win16 program with a 4.0 version will cause Windows 95 to treat it differently in a number of not so obvious ways. Some of the more interesting examples that Microsoft documents include:

- Your program can no longer use the SetWindowLong() API to set or clear the WS_EX_TOPMOST window style. It will have to use the SetWindowsPos() API.

- All dialog boxes automatically get the DS_3DLOOK style. This treatment includes 3D borders around all child controls and a non-bold default dialog font. A 3.x program can get this same appearance by explicitly using the DS_3DLOOK style on dialogs.

- Windows 95 will refuse to create a dialog box that has an invalid DS_* style. A 3.x program will still be able to create the dialog box with the same invalid style, though.

- The program will receive WM_CTLCOLORSTATIC messages when buttons are about to be drawn, not the WM_CTLCOLORBTN messages that 3.x programs receive.

- The program will receive WM_CTLCOLOREDIT or WM_CTLCOLORSTATIC messages when an edit control is about to be drawn. The WM_CTLCOLORSTATIC message is sent when the edit control is disabled or read-only, while WM_CTLCOLOREDIT is sent for "normal" edit controls.

- Similarly, the program will receive WM_CTLCOLORSTATIC and WM_CTLCOLOREDIT messages for combo boxes (in the disabled and active states, respectively), while 3.x programs get WM_CTLCOLORLISTBOX messages.

- Multiline edit controls get proportional thumbs in scroll bars.

- A RegisterClass() API call will be rejected if either the cbWndExtra or cbClassExtra field in the provided WNDCLASS structure is greater than 40. (See the WNDEXT16 sample, detailed in the "Horror Stories" section.)

There's one more detail about 16/4.0 programs that I should mention, and it's by far the most interesting, in my opinion. If you have the Windows 95 Device Driver Kit, scan the file \DDK\INC16\WINDOWS.H for the numerous conditional sections that check for a WINVER setting greater than or equal to 4.0. These sections include dozens of Windows 95 constants, structures and APIs that cover areas such as registry access, .INI file access, file system services, and extended error code management (e.g. GetLastError() and SetLastError()). In a way it's even more interesting that not only has Microsoft made these new APIs available to Win16 programs, they aren't supported under Windows NT (at least as of version 3.51). Strangest of all, these new APIs don't appear to be documented anywhere except in this header file, and they work with version 3.x programs. (At least the very few that I tested worked.) Hmm. Just what we needed—undocumented Windows APIs. Someone should write a book about those.

If you want to use these new APIs, you have to use this version of WINDOWS.H, of course (or duplicate portions of it in your program), and you have to link with the LIBW.LIB that's on the DDK\LIB directory on the Windows 95 Device Driver Kit CD ROM. Also be aware that if you use these new Win16 APIs you have to be very careful about making sure your program will run under only those versions of Windows that support the APIs. You can do this by explicitly checking, or better yet, marking your program with an expected Windows version of 4.0. If your program runs on a platform that doesn't support the new APIs, such as Windows 3.1 or Windows NT 3.51, then it will not fail to load; it will load and run fine until it tries to call one of the missing APIs, then it will crash and Windows will display a dialog box saying that your program made a "call to [an] undefined dynalink". Presumably (hopefully?) support for these new Win16 APIs will be added to Windows NT 4.0, but that's still an unknown as I write this.

## Things That Go Thunk in the Night

Thunking refers to the process of making a routine call across a bitness boundary, e.g. a 16-bit application program calls a routine in a 32-bit DLL. (And no, I don't know where the name came from. I've heard at least three different theories about who invented it and when.)

In the various Windows incarnations, there are three different versions of thunking (generic, universal, and flat), no one of which is available across all three Win32 platforms. Microsoft's PSS article Q125710 "Types of Thunking Available in Win32 Platforms" sums up this state of affairs with a table (which I've edited slightly):

| Type of Thunk | Win32s | Windows 95 | Windows NT |
|---|---|---|---|
| Generic | | supported | supported |
| Universal | supported | supported * | |
| Flat | | supported | |

\* = Windows 95 supports universal thunks, "but only for applications marked version 3.1," according to Microsoft. When someone asked about this limitation on CompuServe, a Developer Support representative from Microsoft said, "Universal Thunks are not supported under Windows 95. The capability to do this was added for one particular software company as an interim measure but was never meant to be a permanent feature." (And no, I don't know which company is being alluded to in this passage. If you know, drop me a line.)

Generic thunks allow a 16-bit program to call routines in a 32-bit Windows DLL. Generic thunking is probably the most straightforward and simplest form of thunking, since it merely requires you to use four specific APIs (LoadLibraryEx32W(), FreeLibrary32W(), GetProcAddress32W(), and CallProc32W()), and explicitly load the 32-bit DLL just as you would explicitly handle any other DLL. Well, not quite, since you have to pay special attention to pointers, which are a combination of a 16-bit segment and a 16-bit offset in Win16, but a 32-bit linear pointer in Win32. In some cases you might have to translate a 16:16 pointer to a 0:32 pointer, which you can do with the GetVDMPointer32W(), WOWGetVDMPointer(), or WOWGetVDMPointerFix() APIs.

Universal thunks are restricted to Win32s, and are meant to allow your Win32 program to call routines in a Win16 DLL. Microsoft's PSS article

Q125710 says that universal thunks can also be used to allow a 16-bit program to call 32-bit DLL routines, "but this isn't officially supported." (Why mention it and then not "officially" support it? More mysteries for the Redmondologists to chew on, I suppose.)

Flat thunks allow you to call from 16- to 32-bit code or vice versa, but only under Windows 95. (This leaves Windows NT with no way for 32-bit programs to call routines in 16-bit DLLs, a curious omission.) This thunking method is also more work, in that it requires you to use the thunk compiler and ship an additional "glue" DLL with your application.

For more information on thunking and some sample programs, search the Microsoft *Developer Network* CD ROM or the Win 32 SDK using the keyword "thunk".

If you look at these thunking options carefully, you'll see that the only way you can call a 16-bit routine from a 32-bit program under Windows 95 is via flat thunks, a less than optimally elegant or convenient solution. But wait a minute—doesn't Windows 95 itself do an awful lot of thunking between 32- and 16-bit code, as when GDI32.DLL and USER32.DLL have to call the underlying support in GDI.EXE and USER.EXE? Seems like Microsoft would have given its programmers a simpler and higher performing way to do this, don't you think? It turns out they did, although it's undocumented. Matt Pietrek mentioned this in an article in the September 26, 1995 *PC Magazine.* He pointed out that you, too can make these "thunkless thunk" calls under Windows 95 by using the undocumented APIs LoadLibrary16(), FreeLibrary16(), GetProcAddress16(), and QT_Thunk(), all of which reside in KERNEL32.DLL. In effect, this is nothing more than the complement to generic thunks, with the added thrill of using undocumented features. (See Matt's article and his upcoming book *Windows 95 System Programming Secrets* for more about QT_Thunk().)

I won't rehash the guideline about not resorting to unnatural acts, and why using undocumented features is an unnatural act of the highest order. But I will say that I find it curiouser and curiouser that Microsoft would include such a useful, general purpose mechanism in the system, but leave it undocumented.

# The Great Unknowns

It's worth remembering that the entire Windows world can't possibly cross all these divides in a single, unified step. Between creating Windows 95 and adding numerous APIs and facilities to Windows NT and Win32s, it's a minor project management miracle that the Win32 family hangs together as well as it does. As I write this, the Windows community is "two-thirds converted", if you will: Windows 95 and Win32s have had major updates, but the one that will bring Windows NT into line is still at least three or four months off. In early 1996 Microsoft is expected to release Windows NT 4.0, which will include the Windows 95 shell, and, presumably some quite significant API changes.

This is all still guess work, though, and there are some significant questions that I couldn't get answers to in time for this book:

- Will NT support the new int 21h APIs for Win16 programs?
- Will NT 4.0 support the entire set of new shell APIs?
- Will NT 4.0 allow 16/4.0 programs to run?
- Will NT 4.0 support long file name usage with _lcreat() and _lopen()?
- Will Windows NT and Windows 95 really remain separate product lines for the next few releases? As I've mentioned elsewhere in this book, Jim Allchin of Microsoft was quoted in *InfoWorld* in September 1995 as saying that Windows 95 and Windows NT would not converge, as had been everyone's understanding of Microsoft's plans for some time. This item is very important to developers, since either outcome will have significant ramifications. If these two products remain separate, then I'm quite sure that the differences in their implementations of the Win32 API will persist; after all, each development group within Microsoft will want to avoid making changes that will hurt "their" third-party developers. But if Microsoft forced the Windows 95 and Windows NT groups to converge their products, then we'd see one stupendous train wreck as all these differences are resolved, one way or the other. Some choice (not that I expect we'll get a vote in the matter).

## Stickies! and Windows 95: A Case Study in Porting

When I started beta testing Windows 95, one of the first things I tested, of course, was my own code. Given all the slightly non-standard mucking about that Stickies! does, I expected it to break into roughly a bazillion pieces. I was pleasantly surprised to see that it didn't. Instead, it broke into just a few pieces which were fairly easily reassembled. In this sidebar I'll present the solutions I had to use to get around these problems, and the general decision-making process I went through regarding updating Stickies! for its next two releases.

### The Problems
The first problem I noticed (after a particular update of the beta) was that I could no longer drag and drop files onto the main Stickies! program icon (now a button on the task bar). Windows 95 would refuse and display the "You cannot drag an item onto a button on the Taskbar" dialog box I talked about in Chapter 7. Since Stickies! never opens as a conventional window, the "hovering mouse maneuver" Microsoft wants us to use in such cases wouldn't work, ei-

ther. This wasn't a major problem, since Stickies! gives the user other ways to import files. Still, it bothered me that a mechanism this simple, useful, and (if I may be allowed to use a dirty word amongst programmers) *elegant*, was broken by the operating system.

Another problem involved the task bar and a large number of notes. Stickies! restores the user's notes to the same screen position and size, and the same "show state" (minimized or normal). Under Windows 95, all windows normally get a button on the task bar, which includes all those sticky notes. This didn't seem to be a problem (although it did suggest that perhaps I should look for a way to keep notes off the task bar as individual buttons, as a future user option). It turned out that when Stickies! started up with a large number of notes, over about 25, then not all the notes would get a button on the task bar, and neither would the main program. This was far more serious than the drag and drop surprise, since it prevented users from accessing all of the Stickies! options, some of which are on only the main Stickies! system menu. If the user doesn't have a button for the main program (which in this case never has a window), there's no way to get to the system menu.

In addition to handling these surprises, I also had to make some tough decisions about when to convert Stickies! to 32-bits, when to support long file names, etc., which I'll get to shortly.

### The Solutions

The drag and drop issue was solved pretty easily—I decided to convert Stickies! to a type III minimized program (one that is normally minimized, but presents a window or dialog interface as a drop target, as needed). In fact, most of my development time on this fix was spent drawing a decent bull's eye bitmap for the drop target.

The missing task bar button problem was a lot tougher. When I asked Microsoft about this problem, one of the beta support personnel made it quite clear that this limitation (which only affects 16-bit programs) was not going to be fixed. The core problem, as it turns out, was that Stickies! was overloading the system by creating so many windows in such a short amount of time that some of the backed-up processing for creating new task bar buttons was not being done. (Whether this work was simply never processed or the system intentionally tossed it away is irrelevant; the point is it wasn't being handled.) After some thought it occurred to me that perhaps the solution was as simple as slowing down the process of loading and displaying notes. A quick prototype showed that this guess was correct. All I had to do was run a timer and load a few notes at a time. (The implementation was quite a bit trickier than that, of course, since I had to maintain some state flags, make sure the timer was killed when the notes were all loaded, etc., but you get the idea.) Once I did that, all the notes got task bar buttons, as did the main program, and everything was back to normal in Stickies!Land.

I think this task bar/note loading problem is a good example of the kind of oddball approach you sometimes have to take when porting programs from one Windows platform to another, or just working around some of Windows' quirks. I really didn't like making this change, even though it didn't affect the user's view of the program (the notes still load and display quickly enough that the vast majority of users won't notice the slight delay). This solution is about one bit shy of being a full fledged hack, something that makes my skin crawl. But since Windows left me no choice, I decided to go ahead with this solution, and to test it extensively to determine how quickly I could load the notes and still avoid the problem.

### Other Issues

Once I had decided to make these changes to Stickies! 4.0, I then addressed some less urgent but still important issues: When to convert it to 32-bits, and when to support long file names.

Converting Stickies! to 32-bits will be quite a chore. It's currently written in Borland Pascal for Windows, which means its 43,000+ lines of code are stranded in 16-bit OWL. (There will be no 32-bit OWL for Pascal, and Delphi provides no easy migration path for 16-bit OWL code either to 16- or 32-bit VCL.) Stickies! is interesting in that it won't benefit much from the conversion to 32-bits, at least in terms of how it performs its basic functions. As a result, I made the decision to put off that huge amount of work until at least version 5.0. This delay will give me a chance to assess the 32-bit version of Delphi and the next wave of C++ compilers, and plot out that part of the porting strategy more intelligently. (Also, I know that many of my customers use Stickies! in a business environment where they won't be running Windows 95 for quite some time. I refuse to make Stickies! a Win32s program, so staying 16-bits is the only way to allow the majority of my users to run the next version.)

The decision to support long file names is another area where Stickies! is somewhat atypical, in that its users don't often deal with file names from within the program. (True, users see file names when importing and exporting notes, but in just the normal "note noodling" that occupies most users' time in Stickies!, no filenames are visible.) Since I had already decided that Stickies! 4.0 would not be 32-bit (and, therefore, long file name-enabled), I decided not to add long file name support to version 4.0. This was a close call, since I know that at least some customers will start asking about this feature any day now (I've already received some inquiries about a 32-bit version). Avoiding long file names in the 16-bit version of Stickies! will also insulate my program and my users from one of the bugs I discovered in Symantec's Norton Navigator 1.0 (see the section "Norton Navigator 1.0 and You").

Out of a desire to make Stickies! more Windows 95-like and more usable, I decided to add context menus that the user could open with the right-mouse button or the new "application" key on the Microsoft keyboard. This was very simple, conceptually—just look for and respond to the new WM_CONTEXTMENU message that Windows sends to all windows (even those owned by Win16 programs with version numbers less than 4.0) in response to a right mouse button click or the new keystroke. The problem is, that won't make the menus work for the customers who are still running Windows 3.1. Again, the solution was easy—I simply had to make Stickies! look for the right mouse button click or the WM_CONTEXTMENU message, and perform the context menu function in response to either.

I also had to react to a really silly bug in Symantec's Norton Navigator 1.0 that can make other programs appear to malfunction. As I mention in the section on this topic, the first version of Norton Navigator will sometimes disable the "Close" item on your program's system menu if your program changes the menu. Since this problem affected Stickies! (in fact, I discovered the bug by running Stickies!), I used the most obvious and direct solution—I made Stickies! look for and respond to a custom system menu command code instead of SC_CLOSE. Not exactly rocket science, but it solved the problem in a robust and highly maintainable way. (See the sidebar in this chapter on Norton Navigator 1.0 for more detail on this fix.)

There are other, minor issues that I still have to decide about Stickies! 4.0, such as whether to use the DS_3DLOOK style on dialog boxes, when to start providing a second help file in version 4.0 format, when to start using the new Windows 95 common controls, etc. My current plan is to wait until after Stickies! 4.0 is released, and then see how quickly my customers are migrating to Windows 95, and what features and changes they request.

# Horror Stories

"Horror Stories?" Isn't that a bit sensationalistic? I don't think so, and here's why: Most of the items in this section are exactly the kind of thing that you can avoid for months out of pure, dumb luck, but then suddenly hit at 1AM when you're running 100MPH on adrenaline and caffeine. I've been there, and it ain't pretty. Worse yet, these oddities always seem to find you when you can least afford to burn an hour tracking down some idiot-syncrasy of the system. In my book, that's a Horror Story.

To be clear, I've included anything in this section that I was able to verify independently and that I thought was sufficiently non-obvious to justify inclusion. I didn't bother to mention minor things like new header files you have to include when porting your code from Win16 to Win32, since I know you don't need help on such matters. Less obvious, perhaps, is that I'm not including merely bugs in this section. Like any other 1.0 release, Windows 95 does have its share of peculiarities, in the form of bugs and odd design decisions that will likely be ironed out in the next release, if not sooner. It's not my goal to provide you with a list of these bugs, but to point out some specific problems you might run into that also have value as examples of real world porting problems. The way I see it, if not one item in this section is directly relevant to your work, but reading these entries makes you more alert to potential problems, I've done my job.

I should stress that my raw list of unconfirmed problems was much larger than what I've covered here. Some potential items, like IsGDIObject(), which are in the Win16 API but not the Win32 API, fell out of contention because they're neither a significant hassle nor a quality risk in the real world. (IsGDIObject(), for example, isn't even in the headers—try to use it and you get a compile-time error.) Unfortunately, I couldn't verify and report all the items I wanted to, so I had to resort to triage and only include the ones that I expected to be of interest to most readers. Obviously, that's a judgment call, since it requires me to make numerous assumptions about what kind of programming you'll be doing and which parts of the API you'll be using most. Inevitably these assumptions will be wildly wrong for at least some readers, which will no doubt leave some of you wondering how I could possibly assemble such a list without including problem X. To be perfectly clear, there are three reasons why a non-trivial X didn't make the list:

- I didn't know about X. Researching incompatibilities between various Windows platforms is a huge undertaking, and I'm sure I missed dozens of worthwhile cases. Heck, I'm sure someone with enough energy and persistence could write an entire book on just this topic.

- I knew about X but couldn't reproduce it. Some problems are much trickier to reproduce than others, and if I couldn't explore a problem well enough to present it in this book, I didn't use it. (I know some readers will object to this approach, and will wish that I had simply lumped all the non-verified things into a section labeled "Here be Dragons" and covered them with caveats. That would have been irresponsible and very misleading.)

- I knew about X, but I never tried to verify it because I thought it wasn't a sufficiently "mainstream" issue. Perhaps some of these X's will make the next edition of this book.

One last thing: Please don't be shy about sharing your Win16-to-Win32 porting discoveries with me! My e-mail and street addresses are in the introduction.

## Version Checking Got More Interesting

OK, I admit, this one isn't a full-fledged "horror story." But it is something you should know about, and I would be remiss if I didn't include it somewhere in this book. Since this seemed like the best place for it, here it is.

Windows 95 is really Windows 4.0, of course. So when a 32-bit program asks Windows what version it is, Windows 95 says "4.0", to no one's surprise. But a 16-bit program that asks this question gets a major version of 3 and a minor version of 95. Why the odd behavior? This one we can blame squarely on ourselves. Incredibly, it seems that some programmers were checking the version number incorrectly in their Win16 code. They wanted their program to refuse to run on any version of Windows before 3.1, so they coded something along the lines of:

```
if((major_version < 3) || (minor_version < 10))
  {
  /* Complain to user about wrong version number */
  /* and terminate the program */
  }
```

The problem with this code snippet, of course, is that it will fail whenever the minor version code is less than 10, which it is for version 4.0. Microsoft had little choice in this matter but to accommodate the (supposedly numerous) incorrect programs that were already in use. The solution was to make the system tell a little white lie to 16-bit programs via a doctored version code that will pass the above test but will still allow a program to determine unambiguously that it's running on Windows 95. (Notice that a 16-bit Windows program that has an expected Windows version of 4.0, and is therefore presumably aware of version 4.0 issues, will still see a Windows 95 version of 3.95.)

Of slightly more interest is the fact that a Win16 program running under Windows NT 3.51 will see a version number of 3.10, since that reflects the level of support that platform provides for 16-bit programs.

## GDI Clips Coordinates

Even though this is arguably a topic better suited for Chapter 14 (where I take it up in much more detail), I wanted to mention it here, since I know from talking to other programmers that it's not yet universally understood. The bottom line is that the GDI component of Windows 95 is still 16-bits, even though its API has been widened to 32-bits. This means that when you call the Rectangle() API, for example, you pass it expansive, luxurious, 32-bit-wide signed integers for the co-ordinates. Unfortunately, GDI unceremoniously clips them to 16-bits by tossing out the high-order word of each coordinate and then uses whatever's left without warning the calling program. As if this weren't amazing enough, no attention is paid to the sign of the original value. If your 32-bit integer is positive, but the clipping process happens to leave it as a 16-bit value with its high-order bit on, then your coordinate will not only change value, it will even change sign.

I think this is a 16/32 issue as well as a 32/32 issue simply because some graphics programmers who are anxious to be free of their 16-bit shackles will rush into

Windows 95 development, unaware that they're still not working with 32-bit coordinates. They'll find out about this state of affairs soon enough, since the fact that GDI is still 16-bit is hardly a secret, but it might not be until they've wasted a couple of days rewriting a program or planning ways to exploit a 32-bit coordinate space.

See Appendix C for the Win32u library and one way to attack this problem with a wrapper library.

## cbWndExtra and cbClsExtra Limits

As I mentioned elsewhere in this chapter, Microsoft made a lot of changes to how 16-bit programs are treated under Windows 95 if their expected Windows version is 4.0, although they did a less than satisfactory job of documenting these changes so far. (See the sidebar "Using LFNs from Win16 Programs: Better Living through Alchemy" for some more detail on this topic.) For the most part these changes are welcome, and they allow a Win16 program to be more Windows 95-aware, without requiring that it be converted to 32 bits.

Probably the strangest change these 16/4.0 applications and all 32/4.0 programs see involves the cbWndExtra and cbClassExtra fields in the WNDCLASS structure, which is passed to Windows as part of a RegisterClass() API call. These fields tell Windows how many bytes of window- and class-specific storage, respectively, to reserve for the program's use. The data in these bytes is accessed via the GetWindowLong(), SetWindowLong(), GetClassLong(), and SetClassLong() API functions.

If either cbWndExtra or cbClsExtra is more than 40, the RegisterClass() call will fail and return NULL to the caller. All version 4.0 Win32 programs are subject to the same limitation under Windows 95, but not under Windows NT 3.51. See the Horror Story of this same name under Chapter 14.

Forty bytes isn't a huge amount of memory, and it gets even cozier when you're registering a dialog box class, in which case the first DLGWINDOWEXTRA (30) bytes of cbWndExtra are used by Windows for dialog management, leaving you at most only ten bytes. Microsoft's PSS article Q131288 suggests that if you need more than 40 bytes (or ten, in some cases) you should set cbWndExtra or cbClsExtra to four and use it to store a pointer to a block of dynamically allocated memory.

I tried to find out why Microsoft would impose what seems like such an arbitrary and small limit, and the only explanation I heard was that they found that some programs were failing to initialize cbWndExtra and cbClsExtra, which resulted in the programs passing garbage values in these fields on a RegisterClass() call and causing Windows to allocate large, unneeded blocks of memory. I can understand why Microsoft would want to correct that situation, but why draw a line in the silicon at a paltry 40 bytes? Unless there was a very good reason for choosing such a small limit (and there very well might have been), I would have preferred something a bit roomier that would have satisfied nearly all legitimate requests, say 256 bytes.

## Building the Samples: WNDEXT16

**CD Location:** ZEN\CHAP12\WNDEXT16
**Platform:** Win16
**Build instructions:** See the comments in WNDEXT16.C for notes on the various ways to build the program. Then build the program normally with the provided .MAK file and Visual C++ 1.52.

### *GetOpenFileName() Result Format*

Remember when Windows 3.1 was about to burst on the scene, and one of the biggest improvements it delivered, at least for programmers, was the set of new common dialogs? I certainly considered it good news, and I'm sure that just about all Windows programmers have become quite used to relying on these components.

The common dialogs are still in Windows 95, of course, but there's one small detail about the Open File common dialog that you should be aware of: The GetOpenFileName() API can (but doesn't always) return multiple file names to a Win32 program in a slightly different format than it does Win16 programs. This change was needed to accommodate long file names and their ability to contain embedded blanks. Any Win16 program, even one that uses the new OFN_LONGFILENAMES flag with a GetOpenFileName() call, will see multiple file names selected by the user in the old, Win16 format that uses blanks to separate names. For example, if your program calls GetOpenFileName(), and the user selects the files MARCH.DOC and APRIL.DOC from the directory C:\REPORTS, then your program will receive a string from the API equal to "C:\REPORTS MARCH.DOC APRIL.DOC" (without the quotes, of course). Your program must then parse this string, using a blank as a delimiter, and assemble the two fully qualified file names, C:\REPORTS\MARCH.DOC and C:\REPORTS\APRIL.DOC, from the components. (I've always found this need to parse and assemble the file names manually to be a pain in the low-order bits, and I've often wished that Microsoft had provided a flag that told the common dialogs to provide all filenames in fully-qualified form.)

Notice that even when your Win16 program explicitly requests long file names, it will still get them in this blank-delimited format. How can this be? Simple: The dialog will only return a long file name component in the string if it does not contain embedded blanks. If that component of the name contains an embedded blank, then the alias form of that name is used. (See the section on Norton Navigator 1.0 for more on this issue and how it was broken by a third party program.)

If your Win16 program is marked with a version number of 4.0, then Microsoft still obeys the letter of the law regarding this format. They're probably being a little conservative in this case, since the application did explicitly request long file names and it should know how to handle them, even in the new format. But Microsoft's approach in this area is very solid, and provides excellent backwards compatibility.

If your program is 32-bit, though, and it uses the new Explorer-style file open dialog, then the string will be in a new format. Since this format will return embedded blanks in long file names, it obviously can't use a blank to separate the file name components. Instead, it uses null characters as delimiters, with a double null at the end of the string, which would result in the above example returning:

```
"C:\REPORTS~MARCH.DOC~APRIL.DOC~~"
```

(I've used a tilde to indicate each place where a null character (a '\0' in C-speak) would go.)

One other detail you should be aware of relates to something I said above. Notice I didn't say that your program gets the new file format whenever it is a Win32 program, but when it's Win32 and it uses the Explorer-style dialog. This is a more interesting detail than it might appear. In my testing, I found that if I called GetOpenFileName() with neither the OFN_ALLOWMULTISELECT nor the OFN_EXPLORER flags set, then my program got the Explorer-style dialog, as expected. If I enabled just multiple selections, though, it got the old style dialog, and the old-style return string. If I enabled multiple selections and then used the OFN_EXPLORER flag, the program got the Explorer-style dialog and new string format.

Clearly, this situation could trip you up if you assumed that a Win32 program always got the new style of dialog box and returned string under Windows 95. Even more likely is that you change a particular usage of the open file dialog in an existing program from single selection to multiple selection without realizing that this innicent change will trigger a change to the old style dialogs, and that your program will get the old style return string. The solution, as ever, is to test thoroughly, and make sure that your program's assumptions and Windows' actions are in sync.

## Associations Moved

Most of the time you won't give a flying floppy about the format of file associations, those little bits of information in the system that map file extensions to applications and let users double click on a document to open it. You certainly care that this mechanism exists, of course, but its exact representation in the system data usually isn't of interest.

If you're writing a program that will have to access (not use) file associations, this situation gets interesting in a New York minute. As it turns out, there's no direct, cross-platform way to look up file associations. There is the FindExecutable() API, but that's not quite what we want—it simulates a command execution and takes into account the current directory (which you specify), and you must provide the name of an existing document, i.e. you can't just tell it to go look up the file association for "*.TXT" files, you have to give it something like "c:\mydocs\summary.txt" where that file actually exists. In order to do a "pure" association lookup, you apparently have to go registry diving. (I say "apparently" because I've asked other developers and Microsoft if there's a simple (or even not so simple) way to have the system do association lookups, and no one seems able to find one. I've gone through the API numerous times, and haven't found anything that does this, even as a dreaded side effect.)

OK, so we roll up our sleeves and stick one hand deep into the registry and pull out the file association. What's the big deal? We're all consenting programmers here. The big deal is that file associations have been represented on Windows systems in more than one format, and even in more than one place, so we'll have to do a lot of groping around to find it, depending on the state of the user's machine and the version of Windows being run.

On older Windows systems, file associations are often stored in WIN.INI, in the [Extensions] section. One of my Windows for Workgroups 3.11 installations includes the following entries in its WIN.INI file:

```
[Extensions]
crd=cardfile.exe ^.crd
pcx=pbrush.exe ^.pcx
rec=recorder.exe ^.rec
hlp=WINHELP.EXE ^.hlp
DOC=C:\WINWORD6\WINWORD.EXE ^.doc
LET=C:\WINWORD6\WINWORD.EXE ^.LET
dot=C:\WINWORD6\WINWORD.EXE ^.dot
[ etc., etc., etc. ...]
```

Retrieving a file association from WIN.INI is merely a matter of using GetProfileString() and doing a little parsing to turn the retrieved string into a usable file specification.

But on newer systems (and even many Windows 3.1 systems), file extensions are in the registry. And that means we have to deal with the old and new file association format. The old format is used primarily on Windows 3.11 and some Windows NT systems, but it still shows up on Windows 95 installations, as the following entry from one of my systems shows:

```
HKEY_CLASSES_ROOT\.1st\shell\open\command = "C:\MSDN\PPTVIEW.EXE %1"
```

The new format for file associations consists of two entries. The first maps a file extension to an application identifier:

```
HKEY_CLASSES_ROOT\.mak = "VisualC++"
```

and the second maps the application identifier to a set of commands and configuration details (such as the default icon), including the one we want:

```
HKEY_CLASSES_ROOT\VisualC++\shell\open\command = "D:\MSVC20\BIN\Msvc.exe %1"
```

This situation causes considerable grief for programs that will run on a variety of Windows platforms and must look up file associations. In the general case, you have to code all three implementations, and then decide the order in which to look for the association. It's even possible, although unlikely, that the user will have a mangled registry that contains a combination of these two formats:

```
HKEY_CLASSES_ROOT\.mak = "VisualC++"
HKEY_CLASSES_ROOT\.mak\shell\open\command = "C:\MSVC20\BIN\Msvc.exe %1"
```

As I've stressed before, if your program will be in wide distribution, it should expect that it will eventually encounter any situation that's physically possible. In this case, since different versions of Windows apparently use different formats, you should carefully select the search order, and you might even want to make the order dependent on which version of Windows the program is running under.

I've included this item under the 16/32 issues instead of the 32/32 issues since it's somewhat more likely that you'll run into it when porting a Win16 program to Win32, or simply running an existing Win16 program under Windows 95, and see that it suddenly can't find file associations that your users know are there.

## Awkward Drag and Drop Behavior

You're running Windows 3.1. You grab some files in File Manager with your mouse, and you drag them over to the exposed corner of some program whose window is beneath File Manager's, and you drop them. What happens? The target window gets the focus, pops to the top of the Z-order (meaning it's now on top of all other windows on your virtual desktop), and the program processes the files. Big deal.

Unfortunately, it is a big deal if you expect Windows 95 programs to be handled this gracefully by the system. For some reason unknown to me, when you drag files from Explorer and drop them on either Win16 or Win32 programs that are mostly covered by Explorer, the target program often becomes active, but it remains beneath Explorer in the Z-order. The result is often a program that displays a dialog box or message box in response to the dropped files, yet the user can't see it because it's completely obscured by Explorer. This is a very counterintuitive and very inconvenient detail, albeit one that you can fix pretty easily.

For Win32 programs, the best solution I've found is simply to make your program call the SetForeGroundWindow() API, and specify its own window handle. Place the call at the very beginning of your program's code that fields a WM_DROPFILES message, and the problem will go away.

For Win16 programs, you have to be about 1% more creative, since SetForeGroundWindow() isn't in the Win16 API. (It's not even among the new 16/4.0 APIs listed in the Windows 95 DDK.) The best solution I know of in this case, as I mentioned earlier, is to resort to the truly ugly "double SetWindowPos() hack":

```
::SetWindowPos(m_hWnd,SWP_TOPMOST,0,0,0,0,SWP_NOSIZE | SWP_NOMOVE);
::SetWindowPos(m_hWnd,SWP_NOTOPMOST,0,0,0,0,SWP_NOSIZE | SWP_NOMOVE);
```

This two-liner should also be placed at the very beginning of your program's WM_DROPFILES handling. (And you should also include a block comment that explains what the heck this is doing there, and also apologizes for committing such a heinous affront to all of programmerdom.)

I'm not sure if this Z-ordering behavior is part of Windows 95's intentional design, or if it's just a bug. Whatever the case, I don't like it, since it makes programs that work just fine under Windows 3.1 and Windows NT look broken.

I've noticed that Windows 95 in general does some odd things with the focus and Z-ordering. For example, I have my task bar set to "autohide" itself. After using the task bar and letting it go away, I often wind up with my screen filled with a maximized program that doesn't have the focus. This happens to me about a half-dozen times a day, and I find it very annoying, since I often return to the maximized application and type a few keystrokes, expecting them to be processed by Word, for example, only to have them be handed off to some program I can't see. (I've even hit the Delete key in this state, only to have Windows 95 ask me to confirm that I really want to delete some desktop shortcut, which was presumably the window that really had the focus.) As soon as I click the mouse anywhere on the maximized application, it gets the focus and all is right again. I consider this odd behavior a hole in the user interface design, and I hope Microsoft patches it soon.

## App Paths Feature Semi-Works for Win16 Programs

This is a really odd one. You can create a registry entry under Windows 95 that will allow your application to specify its own private directory for DLLs, VBXs, and other executables. When your program is run, Windows 95 appends this directory to the beginning of its copy of the PATH statement. Since the directories in the PATH statement are part of the DLL search order, your program can squirrel away DLLs anywhere on the system and still use them, without polluting the user's Windows or Windows system directories. (I still think that in most cases the program and the user are better off if the program-specific DLLs are simply stored in the same directory as the program's main executable, but I won't get into that here.)

The difficulty is that this feature works beautifully with Win32 programs, but it only works with Win16 programs when they explicitly load a DLL via LoadLibrary() and GetProcAddress(). Implicitly linking to a DLL results in the DLL not being found at program load time (assuming the DLL is in the App Paths directory and won't be found via the rest of the DLL search order), and the user getting a message from Windows saying as much.

I was quite surprised when I discovered this problem, since it seems like such a simple mechanism—stick the App Paths directory for the application on the front of the program's copy of the PATH statement and away you go—the standard processing should handle everything just fine. At least I was surprised until I went back and re-read Matt Pietrek's description in his book *Windows Internals* of how DLL loading is handled in 16-bit Windows. After reading that, nothing about DLLs surprises me.

I even wrote a Win16 test program that does nothing but display its PATH statement, and sure enough, the App Paths addition is there in all cases. Either the PATH statement is being modified after the implicit loading of DLLs, or the DLL loading process is not using the modified version of the PATH statement. Whatever the case, it's broken, and the best way around it is to explicitly load and manage your DLLs.

## GetFreeSystemResources() Went Away in Win32

One of the silliest problems you run into when porting a program from Win16 to Win32 is the disappearance of GetFreeSystemResources(). I like this Win16 API because it provides a relatively easy way for a program to provide some useful information, typically on its About box. But it is no more in Win32, even though these numbers are still of interest in Windows 95. (To be clear, I consider this change silly because these resource usage numbers are still quite relevant to Windows 95. Heck, Microsoft even supplies a Resource Meter applet with Windows 95 that does nothing but monitor these numbers. Windows NT boosters will no doubt protest that it doesn't make sense to support this API on that platform. No problem. Support it under Windows 95 and Win32s, and make it return a failure condition under Windows NT. This is one instance when that form of API stubbing would be quite effective and safe.)

The Win32 SDK says that this API has been "replaced" by GlobalMemoryStatus(), which retrieves a structure full of memory usage statistics, including the value dwMemoryLoad. This field is described in the Win32 SDK as follows:

> Specifies a number between 0 and 100 that gives a general idea of current memory utilization, in which 0 indicates no memory use and 100 indicates full memory use.

I don't know if this value refers to virtual memory usage, real memory usage, a combined average of the resource values, or what. (In one of the more interesting lapses in the Win32 SDK, the "QuickInfo" popup for the MEMORYSTATUS structure (which is used by GlobalMemoryStatus()) has the names for the various fields ("Windows NT" "Win95", etc.), but no values.)

The Win16 version of the GetFreeSystemResources() API is still part of Windows 95, of course, and Win16 programs can still call it. But it's not directly available to Win32 programs. If you're stubborn, and you really want to call this function, you have the following choices, none of which wins any prizes for elegance:

1. Use the undocumented functions QT_Thunk(), LoadLibrary16(), etc., which I mentioned in the sidebar "Things that Go Thunk in the Night". This is an awful lot of bother just to retrieve some system statistics, and there's always the nasty issue of whether to use undocumented APIs. Plus, this method isn't portable to Windows NT 3.51, and it's anyone's guess if it will work with Windows NT 4.0.

2. Use the thunk compiler and flat thunks. Again, this is a lot of bother, and it's not portable to either Windows NT or Win32s, since neither of those platforms support flat thunks. (In fact, this is the approach someone in Microsoft's Developer Support group suggested on CompuServe when asked how to call this particular API from a Win32 program.)

3. Use a separate Win16 program to act as a proxy. You can write a very small and simple standalone Win16 program that merely retrieves these numbers and tosses them over the wall to your Win32 program via messages or packed into its exit code. This "solution" (to sully an innocent word's reputation) will work across all three Win32 platforms, but it requires a separate Win16 program for a quite limited function. Talk about Medusa code.

In most cases, of course, you won't spend a lot of time on this issue when porting a program to Win32, since you'll likely just throw in the towel and report different, more readily available system statistics. Still, you do have options.

*I'm almost ashamed to admit it, but I did provide a sample program that implements the proxy solution mentioned above. I don't really expect anyone to use this in a shipping program (and if you do, please don't tell anyone you got the idea from me!), but I just had to prove to myself that it would really work. Unfortunately, it does. See the \ZEN\ATTIC\PROXY directory for all the gory details, not to mention the source code.*

## *Icon, Icon, Who's Got My Icon?*

There are numerous icon oddities you can run into when porting your Win16 program to Win32, or even just running your old Win16 program under Windows 95, if it uses a dialog box for its main interface. See the topic with this same name in Chapter 14 for a complete discussion of the situation.

## *Version 4.0 Dialogs Scale Differently*

As I mentioned in the sidebar "Using LFNs from Win16 Programs: Better Living through Alchemy", dialog boxes belonging to 16/4.0 programs get a different treatment under Win32. In fact, this new look is used for any version 4.0 program, Win16 or Win32. This means that you can run into this issue when you port a Win16 program to Win32, or even if you merely make a minor change to a Win32 program and recompile it (and its version number is changed from 3.1 to 4.0 by the latest version of the linker that comes with Visual C++).

This change can alter how text is formatted on your dialogs, and cause you and your users other forms of visual grief. See the Horror Story in Chapter 14 with the same name as this one for more details and some suggestions about how to deal with this situation.

## *INI File Access*

Remember our old friends, .INI files? The ones we used before the new sheriff, the Windows registry, rode into town? Despite all the talk you'll hear from some quarters about the splendor of the registry and how .INI files are passé, they still serve a purpose. I'm no great fan of .INI files, but I do know that they can be a good choice for storing application-specific data. In fact, they're often a better choice than the registry, depending on how portable you want your program to be across Windows platforms.

Well, there's a bit of good news for fans of .INI files: One of the nastiest, most inconvenient problems of .INI files under Win16, the infamous 64K limit, is gone under Windows NT. The bad news, of course, is that I just said "under Windows NT", and not "under Win32". You guessed it—the 64K limit is still in effect for Win32 programs running under Windows 95 and Win32s. It would be bad enough if these two platforms reported failure when a program tried to access an .INI file that's more than 64K bytes long, but they can actually return bad data and give the calling program no clue that something's amiss.

You can reproduce this phenomenon by running the INITEST sample program. This program uses GetPrivateProfileString() to retrieve a string from INITEST.INI, and then it displays the string and checks the return value against the size of the returned buffer and reports whether the API claimed it worked. If you run this program with the provided INITEST.INI, you'll see that under Windows 95 and Win32s, GetPrivateProfileString() retrieves only part of the string ("This is some sample text from" instead of "This is some sample text from the file INITEST.INI."), but it still reports success. Depending on the exact size of the .INI file, this API could report a failure and return nothing, which at least has the dignity and utility of accuracy. As it stands, you can't be 100% sure that a read from an .INI file has worked on Windows 95 or Win32s, even when the API says it has.

## Building the Samples: INITEST

**CD Location:** ZEN\CHAP12\INITEST

**Platform:** Win32

**Build instructions:** Build the program normally with the provided .MAK file and Visual C++ 2.2. Make sure you copy the INITEST.INI file to the main directory of your Windows installation (e.g. C:\WINDOWS) before running the program.

# Norton Navigator 1.0 and You

You know all those jokes and cynical comments we make about how no one should run version 1.0 (or even x.0) of any program? When Symantec's Norton Navigator 1.0 was released, I got yet another reminder of why we say things like that.

Around the time that Windows 95 was released, I installed the shipping version of Norton Navigator 1.0 onto one of my test systems, and I quickly found two ways in which it broke other programs. Since then, I've reported the problems to Symantec, investigated the problems some more, written some demonstration programs, and asked Symantec when a fix would become available.

The bugs I found were:

- If your Win16 or Win32 program modifies its system menu, the Norton Taskbar component of Norton Navigator 1.0 can disable one or more items on your program's menu, including the "Close" entry.
- If your Win16 program uses either the OFN_LONGNAMES and OFN_ALLOWMULTISELECT flags with the GetOpenFileName() API, then Norton Navigator can cause your program to receive indecipherable text in response to the user's file selection.
- If your Win16 program uses the OFN_ALLOWMULTISELECT flag to enable multiple selections with the GetOpenFileName() API, then Norton Navigator can refuse to let your user type in multiple file names. (I found the first two problems immediately, as I said above; I stumbled upon this one a couple of weeks later.)

The "close" problem is very straightforward. If your program deletes some entries from its system menu and adds some others, then it might trigger a condition in which the Norton Taskbar component of Norton Navigator will disable some of your program's system menu entries, including the "close" entry. I haven't bothered to experiment with this bug long enough to define completely its trigger conditions, but I have found a case where I can make the problem appear and disappear at will, merely by adding or deleting one extra entry on a test program's system menu. This program is included as the CLOSE sample. See the comments in the MAINFRM.CPP file in this project for details on how to toggle the problem. All you have to do is build this sample exactly as provided, and run it with the Norton Taskbar component of Norton Navigator 1.0 active, and you'll see disabled entries on the program's system menu.

## Building the Samples: CLOSE

**CD Location:** ZEN\CHAP12\CLOSE

**Platform:** Win32

**Build instructions:** See the comments in the file MAINFRM.CPP for instructions on how to make the program exhibit the Norton Navigator 1.0 problem. Build the program normally with the provided .MAK file and Visual C++ 2.2.

The solution to the "close" problem is simple, but it requires a change to your program, not a pleasant prospect if your program is widely distributed. (Because I originally discovered this problem with Stickies!, I hope you'll forgive me if I seem less than jovial about the whole issue. Once customers start complaining about this, it will be very hard for me not to sound like I'm blaming my bugs on someone else, when in fact they really aren't my bugs. But I digress.) I found that if you change the "close" entry on your program's system menu so that it has the same appearance but uses a custom command code and not SC_CLOSE, the problem disappears. Apparently when Norton Navigator does whatever it's doing to your program's system menu, it's homing in on the entry with the SC_CLOSE code (and making some less-than-perfect assumptions about the layout of the menu, in the process). Once you change your program's menu, you then have to make it look for a WM_SYSCOMMAND with a wParam that matches your new custom code and trigger the normal SC_CLOSE processing.

You could also rearrange your program's system menu, but I don't consider that an acceptable solution; why should my users see even a minor change in my program's appearance because of someone else's bug? (Also, there's no telling what will happen once Symantec fixes this problem or brings out new releases; avoiding the SC_CLOSE command entirely seems like the best way to prevent a recurrence of the problem.)

Based on my testing, I believe that this custom command code solution works in all cases. If you experiment with the CLOSE sample and find something to the contrary, please let me know.

The first "LFN enabler" problem is trickier, and as far as I can see, there isn't a good solution. Windows 95 lets Win16 programs specify that they can accept long file names from the Open File common dialog. A program does this simply by using the OFN_LONGNAMES flag when it calls the GetOpenFileName() API. This is a nice Windows 95 feature, in that it allows long file name-aware 16-bit programs to use them, albeit with the older style common dialogs.

The difficulty, of course, lies in handling those pesky embedded blanks in long file names. Microsoft deserves full credit for getting this detail exactly right in their implementation. Under bare Windows 95, if the user selects multiple files, Windows will still adhere to the documented format for returning the file names: one string with the initial directory and ensuing file names separated by blanks. If a directory or file name contains blanks, Windows will substitute the alias (8.3 name) for that component. If the component is longer than eight characters, but doesn't contain blanks, then Windows will still provide the long version. Clearly, Windows goes out of its way to comply with both the specific API request and the documented format for the returned string. Give Microsoft a big gold star for their attention to detail in this area.

The culprit is Norton Navigator's "LFN enabler" feature, which lets the user work with long file names on the common dialogs, even though it provides aliases to Win16 programs. Symantec clearly knew about the OFN_LONGNAMES flag, since Navigator will return short file names to the program if it doesn't use this flag. But when it does use the flag, a program can be in trouble: Navigator will provide file name components without embedded blanks, as expected, but it will still provide the long file name version of the directory name, even if it has embedded blanks. In other words, if I have the LFN enabler feature of Norton Navigator running, and I select the files c.txt and d.txt from the directory "c:\temp a.txt b.txt", then the program will receive the following string from the File Open common dialog:

```
c:\temp a.txt b.txt c.txt d.txt
```

Without the LFN Enabler active, the program would see:

```
c:\tempa~1 c.txt d.txt
```

(This example assumes that the alias for the directory "c:\temp a.txt b.txt" is c:\tempa~1.) Since the program has no way to parse this string except by using a blank as a delimiter (the method defined in the API), it can't correctly decipher the Norton Navigator version of the returned string. The program will understandably look for four files, a.txt, b.txt, c.txt, and d.txt, all in the directory c:\temp, which might not even exist on the system. Even assuming that the program is smart enough to detect gracefully that the files are missing and not crash, it still won't be able to function properly, leading the user to conclude that it's seriously flawed. (After all, the user selected files that really exist on the system, and the program complained that a different set of files doesn't exist. I don't know about you, but that would certainly lead me to believe that the application was far too buggy to use.)

This is only a problem when your program enables multiple file selections via the OFN_ALLOWMULTISELECT flag. When this flag is not used, your program will know to expect only one file name in the returned string, so no parsing is required and it doesn't matter if the string contains embedded blanks; your program explicitly requested long file names, so it presumably knows how to handle them.

The second "LFN enabler" bug involves any Win16 program that uses the OFN_ALLOWMULTISELECT flag, and it likewise has no good solution. If the user chooses to type in two or more file names, the common dialog (which is clearly no longer quite so common) will interpret the names as a single filename with embedded blanks, convert it to an alias, and return a single file name to the program. If the calling program also used the OFN_FILEMUSTEXIST flag to force the dialog to verify that the chosen file or files really exist, then the user sees a bogus dialog box that says a file doesn't exist—but the user can see from the message that the common dialog clearly checked for a different file name than what was entered. If the program doesn't use the OFN_FILEMUSTEXIST flag the program will get the name of a single non-existent file that the user never entered.

This bug affects all Win16 programs that allow multiple file selections from the common dialogs, and is not restricted to programs that explicitly request long file names.

*This merging conversion of the two typed-in names into a single one is interesting in its own right. In one test I typed in two names of existing files as "d.txt e.txt" (without the quotes, of course). Norton Navigator reported that the file "dtxte~1.txt" could not be found in the directory. Where did this name come from? Either Norton Navigator asked Windows for the alias for the file name "d.txt e.txt" and Windows conjured up "dtxte~1.txt", or Norton Navigator did the conjuring itself, an even more frightening prospect. In either case, someone is doing something funny in the system, since you can't translate a long file name to an alias unless the file exists, which it clearly doesn't in this case. Honest errors in software are one thing, but when programs start taking guesses I get really nervous.*

## Building the Samples: LFNCD

**CD Location:** ZEN\CHAP12\LFNCD

**Platform:** Win16

**Build instructions:** See the comments in the file MAINFRM.CPP for notes on the various ways to build the program. Then build the program normally with the provided .MAK file and Visual C++ 1.52.

The main LFNCD directory already contains all four variations of the program:

LFN_M.EXE: Requests long file names, allows multiple selections

LFN_S.EXE: Requests long file names, does not allow multiple selections

SFN_M.EXE: Does not request long file names, allows multiple selections

SFN_S.EXE: Does not request long file names, does not allow multiple selections

You can experiment with these flag settings with the LFNCD sample program. Make sure that you have the LFN enabler function from Norton Navigator 1.0 running. In my tests Windows 95 performs as it should in all cases if Norton Navigator's LFN enabler feature is not active.

I find this all very bothersome, because Symantec's errors have created conditions in which other, wholly correct programs will appear to be flawed. It's bad enough when programmers cause their users grief through their own errors, but when their errors spill over into someone else's product, it quickly becomes a matter of professional disgrace.

The larger issue, as ever, is what we can learn from this. It's tempting to jump to some unkind conclusions about how well Norton Navigator 1.0 was tested since it was shipped with these problems. I'm not going to do that, however, since it's not my purpose here to beat up Symantec or any other company. (For the record: I've seen companies do far worse than this, and if I was solely interested in throwing rocks I could have come up with a much larger and more inviting target than Norton Navigator.) In fact, I mention these bugs for two very specific reasons. First, this situation, and particularly the fact that other programs are affected, serves as an excellent cautionary tale for all of us about exercising due care when we start performing unnatural acts, such as fiddling with the menus and dialogs of unknown programs. Second, because some of these problems remain unfixed (as I write this in late October 1995), every public Windows 95 program with certain characteristics is still exposed. I thought you should be aware of that.

Late update: Early in October, Symantec released a patch on CompuServe that upgraded Norton Navigator from version 1.0 to version 95.0.a. When I applied this patch, I found that it did indeed fix the "close" bug, but it didn't fix the other two bugs. I asked someone at Symantec about this, a man I'd been talking to in e-mail about these bugs, and he said:

> We have found that the "LFN Enabler" is not compatible with all products. Attached I have provided a program that allows you to configure File Assist and LFN on individual programs. This file is also available on the online services. As to when this problem will be further addressed, I do not know. In the mean time you can use this program to disable/configure the "LFN Enabler" for the programs in question.

The attached file was FACFG.EXE, a utility that lets you tell Norton Navigator not to provide LFN enabler and other services to specific programs. I experimented with it, and it does work as advertised; tell Norton Navigator not to provide LFN enabler support for a given program, and it will obey your wishes, ignore the specified program, and avoid the bugs.

As you can probably guess, I don't consider this much of a solution. Instead of fixing the bugs (and the ones I've presented here should be quite easy to fix), Symantec provided a way to disable the flawed functionality, which leaves the burden on the user to make things work properly. I honestly hope that by the time this book is published version 95.1 (or 95.0.b or whatever they call it) of Norton Navigator is released. Of course, thanks to the very strong initial sales of this product, there will be a sizable number of people running Norton Navigator 1.0 for a long time, so this problem will be with us, and our programs' users, for some time to come.

# A Not-So-Short Discourse on Long File Names

# A Not-So-Short Discourse on Long File Names

*What's in a name? that which we call a rose*
*By any other name would smell as sweet.*

Shakespeare

*When you notice a cat in profound meditation,*
*The reason I tell you is always the same;*
*His mind is engaged in a rapt contemplation*
*Of the thought, of the thought, of the thought of his name:*
*His ineffable effable*
*Effanineffable*
*Deep and inscrutable singular Name.*

T. S. Eliot

I'm convinced that LFNs, even if not "deep and inscrutable" or even "singular," will prove to be one of the most popular features of Windows 95. Finally free of the shackles of 8.3 filenames, users will rejoice and give files names like "Recipe for really really great chili from Aunt Jane.doc." That's nothing short of wonderful; after all, software is here to serve us, not the other way around, so it should accommodate more reasonable, intelligent, human-friendly naming conventions.

Unfortunately, Microsoft's implementation of LFNs has some shortcomings and surprises you should be aware of, and I even found some bugs in how they use them. But I'll get to those shortly.

The first things most users notice about LFNs, as in the chili recipe example above, are their length and the fact that they preserve lowercase characters—finally, no more of the barely legible MYRECORDS.XLS nonsense we all know so well.

The first thing most experienced Windows programmers (who don't have prior NT experience) notice is those pesky embedded blanks. They squirm (the programmers, not the blanks), they furrow their brows, and then they start asking questions in an uneasy voice. "Um, how do I parse these things, anyway? How do they appear on the command line? What about drag and drop?" And those questions, in a nutshell, are the justification for this chapter.

I should confess that I came "cold" to LFNs in Windows 95, meaning I had done very little work with NT, and had almost completely ignored LFNs. My computers all use the infamous FAT file system without disk compression, since I need maximum flexibility in sharing disk space between DOS, various flavors of Windows, and OS/2, sometimes all on the same box; as a result, LFNs were more of a nuisance to me than a benefit, at least until I started running Windows 95.

# Overview of LFNs and Aliases...

Enough of Aunt Jane's chili recipe and ancient history. Let's get specific:

1. LFNs are the ones that show up in Explorer and just about everywhere else in Windows 95, at least in Win32 programs. (This is not strictly truth, as shown in the sidebar, "Using LFNs from Win16 Programs: Better Living through Alchemy," in Chapter 12.) Our old friends, 8.3 filenames are still around, of course, but Microsoft now calls them "aliases," a not-so-subtle demotion via terminology. In the documentation for the WIN32_FIND_DATA structure, Microsoft demotes an 8.3 name even further and refers to it as merely an "alternate name for the file expressed in 8.3 (filename.ext) format." After all 8.3 names have done for Microsoft and its customers, you'd think they would treat them with a bit more respect than that.

2. The filename portion of LFNs (excluding the path component) can be up to 256 characters long, including the terminating null. The path portion can be up to 246 characters, including the drive letter, colon, and the first backslash. 246, plus the 14 characters needed for an 8.3 filename (including the terminating null and, presumably, the trailing backslash on the path) gives us the maximum length of a fully qualified path, 260. This number is enshrined in STDLIB.H as the constant MAX_PATH. (Notice that 246 does not agree with the MAX_DIR constant of 256 in STDLIB.H, though. One wonders if this disagreement is the root cause of the bugs I found in Windows 95, detailed later in this chapter. It's also worth mentioning that when I asked Microsoft about this, I was told that there was no specific limit for the non-filename portion of a path, since such a limit didn't "make sense," and that it was effectively

MAX_PATH minus the length of the filename. Assuming a minimal file name of a single character, plus one byte for the terminating null, this gives us a maximum path component of 258 characters. It's amazing how much conflicting detail can be found in such simple questions.)

3. Windows 95 will automatically create an alias for a file when one is needed, as well as several times when one isn't. If the LFN used to create a file is syntactically acceptable as an alias, Windows 95 will use it as the alias, otherwise it will generate a unique name that usually has at least one tilde in it, for example BARNEY~1.DOC. (This use of tildes and numbers to create "file tails" is an interesting practice which is important, as I'll explain shortly.)

4. The characters acceptable in an LFN are the same as those acceptable in an alias, plus:

    + , ; = [ ] and <space>

5. LFNs can have more than one dot, and can even have a leading dot. If an LFN has more than one dot, then only the part of the name to the right of the rightmost dot is considered the extension; the rest is simply part of the file name.

6. Extensions can now be more than three characters long. The WIN32 SDK (article "Filename Aliases") states that only the first three characters of the extension are used in file associations, but this does not appear to be the case. As a test, I created files with extensions .text and .text2, and was able to associate these extensions with different programs and make them run by double clicking on their document files in Explorer.

7. Aliases and LFNs share the same name space, meaning you can't have two files in the same directory if one file's LFN matches the other's alias. This is another detail with interesting ramifications.

(These details are all taken from Microsoft's WIN32 SDK, particularly the article "Long Filenames and the Protected-Mode FAT File System.")

## ...and What It Means

I won't go into the low-level details of how Windows 95 creates and manages LFNs and aliases on a FAT file system (I'll leave that to some of the hardcore bit bender authors; see Robert Hummel's article *Short Shrift on Windows 95 Long File Names* in the June/July 1995 issue of *PC Techniques* for a good description), but there are some subtleties about LFNs that you and your users should be aware of:

1. Windows 95 preserves the lowercase letters in file names, but always compares names without case sensitivity. This is a very good thing, since it allows everyone to refer to a file without worrying about the exact case of every letter, and it also

prevents your program (and its users) from accidentally littering a directory with files whose names differ only in the case of one or more letters.

2. A side effect of the shared name space is that Windows 95 will change the alias of another file, as needed, to prevent a name space collision after a rename, copy, or move operation. For example, if you try to rename "My January report.DOC" in Explorer to something more mundane, like "REPORT.DOC," it's possible that there's already a file in the directory with an alias of "REPORT.DOC" but an LFN of "My December report.DOC." Microsoft had only two realistic options in this case: Reject the rename attempt and tell the user that there is already a file in the directory with an alias that matches the new name, or they could have done what they did, and silently changed the alias of the other file behind the scenes. This is a classic no-win situation, since either decision will make a significant portion of users unhappy or confused. (On the confusion front, the fact that such a rename operation makes one of the files in Explorer seem to disappear, at least until the view of that directory is refreshed, certainly doesn't help matters. The file is still there, of course. This is just another of the many reasons for serious users to ditch the Explorer in favor of a third-party substitute.)

In fact, Microsoft's chosen solution still requires the other one as a fall-back position; if some program has the other file open when you attempt the rename operation, for example, you'll get a dialog box from Explorer saying, "Cannot rename <filename>. A file with the name you specified already exists. Specify a different filename." This way of explaining the situation to the user is clearly inadequate, since it doesn't say anything about aliases, leaving the user to wonder how the heck there can be another file with that name when there clearly isn't any such file visible in the Explorer.

Notice that if you change a file's LFN Windows 95 will also change the alias even when there's no name collision. If you have a file with the LFN "January summary.XLS" and an alias of JANUAR~1.XLS, and you then change the file's LFN to JANUARY.XLS, Windows 95 will change the alias to JANUARY.XLS. Similarly, if you instead change the file name to "February summary.XLS," Windows 95 will give the file an alias along the lines of FEBRUA~1.XLS.

Similarly, when you move a directory in a way that would create an alias conflict, Windows 95 will resort to this hidden realiasing, but this time it will change the directory that's being moved, not the one that was already in place. This is the right approach, since of the two directories, the one that's already in place and the one that's being moved, only the former can possibly be named in a stored, valid path somewhere, while the latter is being moved, so any stored reference to it is already being broken by the move.

## Storing LFNs

It's possible that this aggressive approach to realiasing might cause problems with programs that remember file aliases from one execution to the next. In the SDK article *Storing Filenames*, Microsoft tells developers to store LFNs instead of aliases, because aliases are so prone to unexpected changes, and not just when someone explicitly changes a file's LFN, as shown above. This advice provides little comfort for the many thousands of Win16 programs that were written and distributed before LFNs became a major factor in the Windows world. It also creates an interesting exposure regarding the maximum path size, since it doesn't take much in the way of long directory names on the front of a really long file name to exceed the 260-character path limit. This is another area I fully expect a lot of Win32 programs will get wrong, sometimes with disastrous results.

Even more interesting, this same SDK article also tells programmers to use the output of the GetShortPathName() API to retrieve the "canonical form of a path," and that this form should be stored if an absolute path is needed. This is interesting, since GetShortPathName() returns aliases for all components, including the file name, which violates the first instruction, to always store LFNs and not aliases.

Perhaps this is hindsight talking, but I would have left the old aliases intact whenever possible, just to be 1 percent safer. (This is another example of cost/benefit analysis in action: The benefit of leaving the old alias in place is likely small, but the cost to leave it unchanged is even smaller, and might even be free, depending on how the code is structured, for example they might have been able simply to skip that realiasing step. And lest I forgo a chance to mention abstraction again, let me point out that this is another example where breaking the code down into small, logical pieces could have made life easier, if a change were to be made in this area. Presumably, the code could have been structured so that the realiasing was a neat, self-contained function that could be called with a one-line invocation, passing some sort of reference to the file in question. Then not doing the realiasing would have been as easy as removing the one-line invocation or making it conditional. I have no idea how Microsoft really implemented this code, of course, but it's a good example of how modularizing support routines can pay off down the road.)

I'm very uneasy about this business of renaming other files without getting the user's permission or even serving notice. True, Microsoft's penchant for using tildes in the generated aliases will somewhat reduce the need for secret realiasing, since few users create oddly decorated names that are likely to cause name space collisions with Microsoft's generated aliases. But collisions will happen, most likely on file copy and move operations involving files with LFNs. For example, if you create files with long and similar LFNs (such as "Report from Dave.DOC" or "Report from Susan.DOC") in two different directories, it's likely that they will have identical aliases (REPOR~1.DOC), since the generated aliases generally include the first few characters of the LFN plus a tilde and a number that makes the alias unique in its directory. Now put those files in the same directory, and Windows 95 will have to change one of the aliases. If you move one of the files to the other's directory, then move it back, the underlying alias will likely be different, even though the visible LFN never changed.

And finally, as if all this weren't enough, here's a sobering quote from the *Filename Aliases* SDK article:

> When an application makes a system call to delete or rename an alias, the system first gathers and saves a packet of information about the file and then performs the delete or rename operation. The information saved includes the long filename as well as the creation date and time, the last modification date and time, and the last access date of the original file. After the system performs the delete or rename operation, the system watches for a short period of time (the default is 15 seconds) to see if a call is made to create or rename a file with the same name. If the system detects a create or rename operation of a recently deleted alias, it applies the packet of information that it had saved to the new file, thus preserving the long filename.

The next time someone implies that backward compatibility is cheap and easily accomplished, show them this gem.

## "Long File Names as Command Line Parameters.EXE"

There are numerous ways a user can tell Windows, "Open this document with the right application." Depending on which method the user employs, your program can see surprisingly different things.

There are two ways to retrieve the command line in C/C++ Win32 programs, not counting additional methods provided by frameworks. The first involves our old friends argc and argv (parameters passed to every program's main function, which contain the count of command line parameters and pointers to the parameters themselves), which date back to the Cretaceous Age of programming, relatively speaking. The other is a Win32 API, GetCommandLine(). GetCommandLine() retrieves a pointer to the entire unparsed, unprocessed, unmolested command line in one gulp—warts, multiple blanks between tokens, and all. Consider it a do-it-yourself parameter kit. At arm's length, it appears that a program has more than enough information to make sense out of any command line. After all, it has access to the original command line plus a parsed version. As we'll see, this is a far more interesting problem than it seems. In fact, this is the best example of a tar pit design that I've yet to find in Windows 95, which is why it's worth exploring with a microscope.

Let's start with a mindlessly simple Win32 console application. Our entire program, CMDLINE.CPP, is:

```
#include <windows.h>
#include <stdio.h>

int main(int argc, char *argv[], char *envp[])
{
    int i;

    for(i = 0; i < argc; i++)
        printf("Parameter %d: [%s]\n",i,argv[i]);

    printf("\nGCL(): [%s]\n\n",GetCommandLine());

    printf("(Press ENTER) ");
    getchar();
    return 0;
}
```

Build this program as CMDLINE.EXE, then create a file named "LFN test file.zzz". This file's contents are irrelevant; it's merely a place holder in the file system's name space. From here on, I'll refer to this file as the document. (There is a Win16 version of CMDLINE on the CD in ZEN\CHAP13\CLINE16. I won't be directly using that program for any of the tests in this chapter, but since I had it sitting around, I figured I'd include it anyway.)

## Building the Samples: CMDLINE and CLINE16

**CD Location:** ZEN\CHAP13\CMDLINE and ZEN\CHAP13\CLINE16

**Platform:** Win32 console application (CMDLINE) and Win16 application (CLINE16)

**Build instructions:** Use the provided .MAK files, CMDLINE.MAK and CLINE16.MAK, with Visual C++ 2.2 and VC++ 1.5, respectively, and build normally.

Note that in the examples that follow, I cut and pasted the output of CMDLINE.EXE directly into this chapter's file in my word processor, so what you see is what I got.

1. To establish a "baseline," double click on CMDLINE.EXE in the Explorer. This results in:

```
Parameter 0: [C:\ZEN\CHAP13\cmdline\WinRel\cmdline.exe]

GCL(): ["C:\ZEN\CHAP13\cmdline\WinRel\cmdline.exe" ]
```

Notice the oddball trailing blank on the GetCommandLine() result that's not in argv[0]. This is yet another situation where those blank-stripping routines from the toolbox in Chapter 2 could be exercised on data that comes from an unreliable source—in this case, Windows itself. Running CMDLINE.EXE from a desktop shortcut produces the same results.

Move the executable into a directory with an embedded blank in the name, and whether you run the program by double clicking on it in Explorer or on its desktop shortcut, you get:

```
Parameter 0: [C:\temp dir\cmdline.exe]

GCL(): ["C:\temp dir\cmdline.exe" ]
```

2. Place CMDLINE.EXE and "LFN test file.ZZZ" in "C:\temp dir," then create an association via the Explorer that maps the extension .ZZZ to CMDLINE.EXE. Make sure the file association looks exactly like this:

```
[assoc.bmp, screen shot of Explorer dialog with CMDLINE association]
```

You must enclose the application's file name in quotes, or Windows 95 won't accept it, thanks to the embedded blanks.

Double click on the document in Explorer. CMDLINE.EXE thinks it has five parameters instead of the expected/desired two:

```
Parameter 0: [c:\temp dir\cmdline.exe]
Parameter 1: [C:\temp]
Parameter 2: [dir\LFN]
Parameter 3: [test]
Parameter 4: [file.ZZZ]

GCL(): ["c:\temp dir\cmdline.exe" C:\temp dir\LFN test file.ZZZ]
```

Notice that the document's path gets broken at embedded blanks while the application's path doesn't, and that GetCommandLine() provides you with quotes around the application name, but not around the document name. This makes picking the document's file name out of the command line extremely difficult; a program can't tell which tokens are supposed to contribute to the file name and which might be other parameters, such as a second file name. Also note that our friend, the mysterious trailing blank in GetCommandLine()'s result, is now gone, and sometimes the drive letter is in upper case and sometimes it's in lower case.

3. Drag the document and drop it on the desktop shortcut for CMDLINE.EXE, and we have our first major surprise:

```
Parameter 0: [C:\temp dir\cmdline.exe]
Parameter 1: [C:\TEMPDI~1\LFNTES~1.ZZZ]
```

```
GCL(): ["C:\temp dir\cmdline.exe" C:\TEMPDI~1\LFNTES~1.ZZZ]
```

Suddenly we're seeing an alias instead of an LFN for the document, which makes parsing a snap; we no longer have to wrestle with embedded blanks, at least in this mode of invocation. But the application is still passed as an LFN, and we can't assume we'll get this format of command line, of course.

4. Now, change the association for .ZZZ and CMDLINE.EXE to:

```
"c:\temp dir\cline1.exe" "%1"
```

using the quotes exactly as shown around the %1.

Double click on the document; it seems that our program's IQ has improved dramatically, since it now knows how to parse a document name with embedded blanks:

```
Parameter 0: [c:\temp dir\cmdline.exe]
Parameter 1: [C:\temp dir\LFN test file.ZZZ]

GCL(): ["c:\temp dir\cmdline.exe" "C:\temp dir\LFN test file.ZZZ"]
```

The secret is not the %1, of course, but the quotes. If you remove the quotes but leave the %1 in place, we're right back to the result in step 1.

This is not just a sterile laboratory experiment; you can trip up real programs with this information. For example, edit the association that links .BMPs to MSPAINT.EXE and remove the "%1" (or just remove the quotes). Then double click on "Carved stone.BMP," one of the bitmaps that comes with Windows 95, and MSPAINT.EXE will complain that it can't find "Carved.BMP." (Shut it down and run it again, and MSPAINT will get it right the second time. Apparently it re-registers its associations, but only for its "normal" types. If you associate the extension .BBB with MSPAINT, it will open a BMP file that has this extension and no embedded blanks in its path, but it won't add the "%1" to the .BBB association.)

Another example involves Word for Windows 6.0. Associate the file extension ZIG with Word, using the "%1" format, and it won't open a file. It will instead complain that "The document name or path is not valid," and reproduce the filename complete with quotes. Looks like Word is parsing the string returned by GetCommandLine(). Remove the "%1" from the association, and everything works fine, even with documents that have LFNs with embedded blanks, since Word 6.0 is, of course, still a Win16 program, and always sees aliases on the command line. The fact that the "proper" way to pass filenames to Word is via DDE, is moot. The vast majority of users won't realize this, and will set up new, non-DDE-style associations manually. If users believe from prior experience that you must use the "%1" format to make a program see an LFN file name that has blanks (as in the MSPAINT example), then they're in for more trouble and confusion when they try to apply this knowledge to other programs, like Word.

*This is a very disturbing situation, since a non-trivial detail of how your program communicates with the system is dictated by an external setting that's freely accessible to the user and other programs. Even worse, as users legitimately set up new associations between your Win32 program and other file extensions, as they routinely have to with some programs, such as text editors, they have to choose between three formats (non-%1, %1, and DDE), with no helpful information available when they're asked to make the choice.*

*Most perverse of all, if the user either forgets or doesn't know which format to use with your program, Windows 95 will still run it when the user double clicks on an associated file, as it does in these examples, and your program ends up looking flawed when in fact it's working as well as it can, under the circumstances.*

5. Create a shortcut on the desktop for the document and then double click on it, and you get the same result as in step 3 (two LFNs, GetCommandLine() passes two LFNs, each surrounded with quotes).

6. Go to Explorer and drag the document and drop it directly on CMDLINE.EXE (not on the desktop shortcut), and you get the result from step 2 (LFN for the application, alias for the document name, GetCommandLine() surrounds the application name with quotes, but not the document name).

7. Open a command line window, switch to "C:\temp dir", and enter the command "cmdline LFN test file.ZZZ". (Remember, one of the long-overdue features of Windows 95 is the ability to run Windows programs from a command line.) As expected, we're back to multiple tokens:

```
Parameter 0: [C:\TEMPDI~1\CMDLINE.EXE]
Parameter 1: [LFN]
Parameter 2: [test]
Parameter 3: [file.ZZZ]

GCL(): [C:\TEMPDI~1\CMDLINE.EXE LFN test file.ZZZ]
```

With the command line window still open, try:

```
cmdline "LFN test file.zzz"
```

and CMDLINE.EXE is once again among the intelligent:

```
Parameter 0: [C:\TEMPDI~1\CMDLINE.EXE]
Parameter 1: [LFN test file.ZZZ]

GCL(): [C:\TEMPDI~1\CMDLINE.EXE "LFN test file.ZZZ"]
```

This handling of the document name makes sense, since users must use quotes to tell the system what's an LFN with embedded blanks, and what are separate tokens. But notice that we finally have a case where the application's name is passed as an alias, and GetCommandLine() doesn't delimit the application's name with quotes. This last detail is arguably bad design, since even though the program only sees quotes when they're needed (a move that should appeal to the minimalist in us all), it means that a program that looks at GetCommandLine()'s output has to be prepared for either case and can't simply look for the character string between the first pair of quotes. Sometimes simpler is more complex.

8. Still at our command line window, enter the following commands exactly as typed (I'm showing blanks as underscores in some places; you should use blanks):

```
cmdline ""_hello,_world"

Parameter 0: [C:\TEMPDI~1\CMDLINE.EXE]
Parameter 1: []
Parameter 2: [hello,]
Parameter 3: [world]

GCL(): [C:\TEMPDI~1\CMDLINE.EXE "" hello, world]

cmdline "__"_hello,_world"

Parameter 0: [C:\TEMPDI~1\CMDLINE.EXE]
Parameter 1: [  ]
Parameter 2: [hello,]
Parameter 3: [world]

GCL(): [C:\TEMPDI~1\CMDLINE.EXE "  " hello, world]
```

Argv[1] is a zero-length string or all blanks? How many existing programs do you think will handle this situation intelligently? And yes, Win16 programs behave the same way. Run this test with the 16-bit version of CMDLINE, CLINE16, and you'll see the same results.

Pass a similar command line to Word, and it tries to use each quote as a filename, or a pair of them as a single file name if they aren't separated by at least one blank. Argue all you want about what a program is and isn't obligated to do when presented with invalid input—this still looks silly, and is easily overcome. All a program has to do is strip surrounding quotes from parameters and ignore all-blank or zero-length parameters.

Had enough? There's more. Put your ZZZ file on a networked disk that isn't mapped to a drive letter. Then double click on the file in Explorer, and an embedded blank in the file's UNC name will wreck havoc in all the expected places above where embedded blanks in the document's file name did. This one even afflicts Win16 programs. Thanks to Don Elder for pointing out this one.

## It Just Keeps Getting Worse and Worse

Based on this testing, there's precious little you can count on in a command line. You can assume that your program's own fully qualified name can be retrieved with argv[0], and it will appear as the first thing in the GetCommandLine() output, possibly delimited with quotes. But it could be an alias or an LFN, so you should also convert an alias to an LFN before you display it to the user in a message. See the AliasToLFN() function in Chapter 3.

As for the document name on the command line, lots of luck. You have to be ready for just about anything: alias or LFN, quoted or not quoted, completely blank or zero length. Since you have no guarantee that the user has set up the association properly (as in step three), or hasn't invoked your program from the command line without quotes around the document name but with other parameters, you're cooked.

Even a very plain command line that includes just the filename of a document and no other text, presents a surprisingly subtle identification problem, if triggered by a minimal, non-"%1" file association, as in step two. Let's say you really need your program to be highly usable, and you want it to be intelligent enough to find the document name in the command line, no matter what. How to proceed? Obviously, the first thing would be to attempt to use whatever argv[1] points to as a document. If the name looks right (well-formed and it has an acceptable, or at least not obviously unacceptable, extension), then you're home free and you've unambiguously identified your intended document, right? No, you're not and you haven't, and here's the killer detail: Go to Explorer and try to rename our trusty testing companion, "LFN test file.ZZZ" to "LFN test file 2.holy cow!.ZZZ". Remember at the beginning of this chapter when I said that your filename can have multiple dots? Well, that design decision, plus support for embedded blanks, have a really nasty bit of synergy. Using the minimal file association from step two, double clicking on this file name gives us the following CMDLINE.EXE output:

```
Parameter 0: [c:\temp dir\cmdline.exe]
Parameter 1: [C:\temp]
Parameter 2: [dir\LFN]
Parameter 3: [test]
Parameter 4: [file]
Parameter 5: [2.holy]
Parameter 6: [cow!.ZZZ]

GCL(): ["c:\temp dir\cmdline.exe" C:\temp dir\LFN test file 2.holy cow!.ZZZ]
```

"No problem," I can imagine the more persistent of you thinking; you can progressively combine tokens from the **GetCommandLine**() output and check for the existence of the file, and when you get a hit, you're home free, right? No, you're not. Go back to Explorer, copy any file, then rename it "file 2.holy". Remember that bit about extensions now being more than three characters? Well, that makes for even more nasty synergy. (Just be glad Microsoft didn't get truly perverse and allow backslashes and colons in file names.) Create some more files in this same directory, say, "cow!.ZZZ", "file 2.holy", and "test file 2.holy". Now look at these filenames and consider the command line data your program can receive. Obviously, this kind of "progressive file existence check" is prone to false positives, so it's unable to disambiguate the command line in all cases. Them's the breaks. Or, as we New Yawkers say—deal with it.

If you want a concrete example of this, go back to the MSPAINT file association. Make sure it's in the non-"%1" state, then create two copies of a bitmap file. Name one "a.BMP" and the other "a.bmp Not!". Then double click on the second file, and MSPAINT will open the first.

## What To Do about This

As a developer, you can't prevent this from happening; about all you can do is make sure your file associations are properly set up at installation time. Barring extreme measures (see below, if you have a strong stomach), you must use the "%1" format for a file association, since your users will love LFNs, embedded blanks and all, and will wield them with all the gusto of a five-year-old boy at the dinner table armed with a full bottle of catsup.

*You should be very careful about re-registering your application's file associations, however. To see why, associate the extension BMP with some other program, and then run MSPAINT.EXE. Congratulations, you just changed your association for BMP files to point to MSPAINT.EXE. That's right; no matter what your current association is, MSPAINT hijacks it, and it isn't the only program I've seen do this. This is about as arrogant as software gets, and it shows a flagrant disregard for the user's configuration. I don't know about you, but this is exactly the kind of thing that makes me delete a program after about one minute of use.*

You should make sure your Win16 and Win32 programs check for all-blank and zero-length parameters. This is a rare situation, but it can lead to some bizarre results, as shown above, which are easily avoided.

Your Win32 program can and should do a bit more when it can't find a file whose name is passed on the command line. It should display a dialog box, as MSPAINT does, but provide a reasonable amount of help, as MSPAINT doesn't. Minimally, your program should suggest that if the user is sure that the file it couldn't locate really does exist, the problem might be in the file association. This dialog should also provide a button that will display a topic in the help file that discusses this contingency. (Richard Alverson, a friend of mine, loves to point out how often he gets a dialog box from Windows or a Windows application that tells him something unpleasant, and the only button on the dialog is "OK." Rich says such dialogs should have a button that says "Not OK," because it isn't. I wouldn't go quite that far in a public program, but I do know that if you give your users ready access to meaningful help in such cases, they'll be at least marginally less annoyed when such things happen.)

## Extreme Measures

I keep harping on taking a cost/benefit view of your technical problems and solutions. The solution I'm about to present is a classic example of one that can only be justified by a fairly unusual set of circumstances. I'm going to present it anyway, because I think it's a good example of what you can do when your back is up against the wall.

In exploring LFNs, I thought that there might be an escape hatch via a Win16 front end for Win32 programs. In other words, you could place your main, Win32 executable in MyProg.PRG, and ship along with it a Win16 program called MYPROG.EXE that does nothing but invoke MyProg.PRG with a WinExec() call, bucket brigading the command line parameters (with just a little bit of pre-processing), and then ending. This would neatly circumvent the file association/ LFN confusion, since all file names would be passed to MYPROG.EXE (and, ultimately, to MyProg.PRG) as aliases or as identifiable LFNs, except for manually entered commands that are syntactically incorrect.

The key to this solution is in the fact that a Win16 program always sees the alias for a file, no matter which of the many methods shown above is used to invoke it. (This is another fact that isn't always a fact. If your Win16 program's header contains an "expected Windows version" of 4.0, then Windows 95 will give it the same command line data we've seen in this chapter for Win32 programs, LFNs and all, even though it's a 16-bit program.) If a user types in the command:

```
myprog "c:\long dir name\my data file.txt"
```

then the front end will see the document name as a single, LFN-style argv[] parameter, thanks to the user's quotes. The front end simply checks each parameter for an embedded blank, and if it finds one, it wraps that parameter in quotes, ensuring that the real application will also see it as a single argv[] entry. The only time this scheme doesn't work is when the user enters an ill-formed command like:

```
myprog c:\long dir name\my data file.txt
```

In that case, the front end will see five parameters instead of two ("<path>\myprog", "c:\long", "dir", "name\my", "data file.txt"), and all it can do is pass them along to the real application, since we're right back at the identification problem again. But at least a well-formed command line will be handled properly. FRONTEND will also, thanks to its use of blank-stripping, eliminate the problem of all-blank parameters. Zero-length parameters automatically drop out in the filtering process.

A simple implementation of such a front end is in ZEN\CHAP13\FRONTEND as FRONTEND.CPP, a WIN16, VC++ 1.5 project. Also included in that directory is another copy of CMDLINE.EXE, named CMDLINE.PRG. To experiment with these programs, simply copy them to your hard disk and re-run tests 1 through 7, using FRONTEND.EXE instead of CMDLINE.EXE.

I consider this kind of front end processing an extreme measure, and I personally would not ship a program that uses this approach unless I had good reason to believe that it was needed. I mean, shipping a separate, easily lost executable that does nothing but pre-digest the command line? If that doesn't score a big, fat, zero on the design elegance scale, I don't know what will.

As I've repeatedly stressed in this book, you should never make such judgments in abstract terms, but only in the context of your program's expected use. Perhaps you know in advance that your program's intended audience is very fond of committing all sorts of configuration mayhem, including creating and editing associations, and for other political or financial reasons, you want your program to do what its users intend (which is not necessarily what they tell it) as close to 100 percent of the time as possible. In that case, front ending your application makes sense.

You may not want to use the non-executable file extension on the main program as I did in this example, because that increases the chance that an adventuresome user will delete the file and then complain to you that your program "won't runany more, and I didn't change anything." Using the extension EXE opens the possibility that users will discover that they can directly run the main application, and they'll set up their associations and desktop shortcuts accordingly. You can counter this eventually, too, by making your main application look for an undocumented "password" as the first parameter. The front end knows to pass this to the main application, of course. If the main application doesn't find that parameter, then it can refuse to run, dispatching a polite message telling the user to run the front end to start the program.

# The Good News

You finally get a break when you're reading the names of dragged and dropped files, since they come through one per call, not all mushed together in one text string, as do filenames on the command line. (There had to be a pony somewhere in here....)

## A Plea for Human Factors

Given all of the above, I just know that one of the small but all-too-persistent annoyances of Windows 95 userhood will be Win32 programs that report aliases in messages without translating them to LFNs. Imagine: You create a desktop shortcut to a program, drag and drop a file on it that has a nice, long, user-friendly filename. But you've made an error—you've tried to open a plain text file with a graphics editor, perhaps. The program sees the document as an alias, tries to open it and can't, then tells you via a message box that the file "C:\TEMPDI~1\LFNTES~1.ZZZ" is not a recognizable graphic format. I can imagine the internal monologue now: "Huh? Why the heck is the program trying to open *that* file? That's not the one I dropped on the icon. That's not even one of my files in that directory, according to Explorer!"

So, please take a minute to add to your public programs code that will translate aliases to LFNs before showing them to the user. See Chapter 3 for an implementation of AliasToLFN() and LFNToAlias(). But note that these functions will return only the filename portion of a file; if you need to translate the entire path, including all directories and the file name LFNs, then you have to resort to either calling AliasToLFN() iteratively, to build the translated name one component at time, or using inline assembly language.

*Incredibly, there are six new documented file system calls in Windows 95 that are only available through int 21h and assembly language, not the Win32 API. The one that's most conspicuous by its absence is Get Long Path Name, which translates an entire path and file name to LFNs. (Don't confuse this function with the GetFullPathName API, which merely combines the supplied filename with the current drive and directory, without checking that the result names an existing file or is even a valid name.)*

*The other five missing APIs are Generate Short Name, Server Create or Open File, Create Subst, Terminate Subst, and Query Subst.*

## Here Be Bugs

I promised myself and my publisher that I wouldn't go ballistic in this book and hammer anyone over bugs. Well, I'll keep those promises, but I do want to talk about some rather dramatic problems in how Explorer and Windows 95 deals with LFNs. I'm guessing, but these problems appear to be external to the actual LFN implementation, and are therefore exactly the kind of errors you and I might make while using LFNs in our own programs.

I can't stress two points enough: First, I've verified these problems in the generally available original August 24, 1995 version of Windows 95, but it's entirely possible that they've been fixed in Windows 95.Winter or Windows 96.Spring by the time you read this. At least, I hope they've been fixed. Second, if you want to try to recreate these bugs, *please* use appropriate caution, save your data, make sure its securely backed up, shut down all applications, check under the bed for monsters or Mac users, and other necessary precautions.

Once again, we can use CMDLINE.EXE, which shows how much functionality you can get out of less than two dozen lines of code. This time around, create a directory under "c:\temp dir" that has a really long file name, something like "really really really long directory filename used for testing." Then create another directory under that one, also with a gratuitously long filename. Finally, move or copy one of your ZZZ files into the bottom directory in this verbose directory tree.

Now, keep renaming one of the long-named directories, increasing its name by a character or two each time. After each renaming, go to the bottom directory and double click on the ZZZ file. Eventually, either Explorer or Windows 95 will refuse to run CMDLINE.EXE and will instead display a dialog box that says the file C:\WINDOWS\SYSTEM\CONAGENT.EXE could not be found. (Couldn't be found? It's right where it's supposed to be. Really.) Once this happens, you can shorten one of the directory names by a character or two, and get the Explorer to invoke CMDLINE.EXE, but without passing the document name on the command line at all. Sometimes it will include an erroneous path (such as, the path names won't reflect a rename operation you just performed on one of the directories). Usually, if you keep this up long enough, whatever part of the system is confused straightens up and flies right. But in the meantime, your poor application might be getting data that doesn't even describe a path that exists on your system, which can only make it look buggy in the eyes of an innocent user.

Try to rename your ZZZ file under similar conditions, and you can also get Windows 95 to tell you that your filename contains illegal characters, when it doesn't. This is not the dual-purpose message I mentioned above, but a different, single-purpose one, that's flat out wrong.

I've even seen Windows 95 change a file's very long LFN when I copy it from one directory to another, and revert the LFN to the file's alias. (In this case, I was moving a file to a directory higher up in the same directory tree (to a location where the file's fully qualified path would be shorter), so it seems clear that this use of an alias was not due to a need to keep the destination file's path under a limit, but a way of overcoming the long path on the source file.)

Microsoft does deserve some credit, I think, for at least trying to prevent such problems. If you have a file named JOE.TXT that is several LFN-style directories deep, and you try to rename it to something longer that would result in the file's fully qualified name exceeding the path limit, then Explorer will stop you. This is a great example of intelligent programming; give Microsoft a gold star for getting it right. The bad news, however, is that it displays one of those vague dual-purpose message boxes without online help. The message says that the file name you're attempting to use is either "too long," or "invalid," and there's no online help available. (Depending on my mood, this kind of thing has been known to make me yell at my screen, "Give me a hint, guys! Which one is it?" It also makes me wish for one of Rich's infamous "Not OK" buttons. After all, somewhere in the program's heart of hearts, it knows which problem triggered the message—so why can't it give me a little help in figuring out what's wrong?) It's also clear that this measure can't possibly catch all ways of creating a too-long fully-qualified path. You can always lengthen an intermediate path, or move or copy a file with an LFN into an LFN directory, for example. Trying to make Explorer catch all such occurrences would have been foolhardy and extremely impractical, if only because it would have had a severe performance impact. Simple file management tasks, such as renaming a directory, that users expect to happen instantly would potentially take a long time while Explorer scans through nested directories in search of newly too-long file names. No amount of advance planning and smart coding could completely defuse such problems.

If the ancestor directory names are sufficiently long, Explorer won't even let you display the files in the lower directories; it complains that the path is too long. (At least that message has the dignity of accuracy, unlike the CONAGENT.EXE head fake it throws you.)

I can't prove it, not having access to the source code for Explorer or Windows 95, of course, but it sure looks like some part of the system isn't checking for buffer overruns when it builds the command line or the document's path. (As mentioned earlier, the path limit is still the paltry 260 characters that it was under Windows 3.1, and there's that disturbing disagreement between the documentation and the code on the maximum length of the directory component of a path.) There's also the persistent problem in C/C++ programming in general that I mentioned in Chapter 3, involving confusion over string lengths and the deadly side effects of unterminated strings. For all we know, it could be that the checks are being made for buffer overruns, but they're buggy, and some string length calculation is off by one. That's all it takes to unwittingly concatenate valid string data with whatever binary garbage happens to be lying about.

Even more interesting, in a sense, this basic test case (attempting to open a document with a too-long path name) will crash NT 3.51's version of File Manager with an illegal memory write error. I'd make the same guess as to the ultimate cause.

## OK, Smart Guy, So How Should Microsoft Have Implemented LFNs?

This is a natural question at this point in this chapter, and I think that trying to answer it shows just what kind of corner Microsoft was painted into, largely by their own brush. It's also an interesting Gedanken design exercise.

I don't view Microsoft (or any other large company) as a temporally monolithic entity. The individuals responsible for Windows 95 probably have little (but surely not zero) overlap with the people at Microsoft who designed their LFN support. In one sense, the Windows 95 crew did the best they could, given the hand they were dealt.

To start with, Microsoft surely couldn't have released Windows 95 without LFN support. This support is in Windows NT, not to mention that operating system from the Big Blue Evil Empire (OS/2), so they had little choice. Had they released without LFN support, the howls of outrage from users, writers, and reviewers would have been thunderous. And because they needed to remain compatible with Windows NT, they were stuck with embedded blanks. But because they couldn't very well remove the command line function from Windows 95, they also had to live with cases where they merely took whatever the user typed in and bucket brigaded it to the program, hoping for the best. (I really wish there had been a way for Microsoft to ditch the current command line model completely and move to a new model of passing parameters to a program, one in which the caller (or the system) filled in members in a structure that was passed to the application, thereby removing all ambiguity and leaving command lines for the history books. There I go again, dreaming of elegance. In fact, there was no practical way they could have done this without causing far too much upheaval. Developers don't often riot, but when they do, it's ugly, and this would have caused just that.)

Given all that, what could Microsoft have done differently? They could have been more consistent in how they pass command lines to programs, for one thing, and always passed aliases, even to Win32 programs. As I've shown above, there's currently no way for a program to predict what form of file reference it will see on a command line, so it always has to be prepared to accept aliases and translate them to LFNs for public display, anyway. Alternatively, they could have always wrapped LFNs that have embedded blanks in quotes, guaranteeing that they would survive the rigors of argv[] parsing as atomic units. I also would have issued a decree saying that there shall not be all-blank or zero-length parameters, and doctored command lines before programs saw them, as needed. Sometimes you have to lay down the law, and this is one time I wish Microsoft had done so.

In an ideal world, Microsoft would have been able to design around this problem. But that would have required an incredible degree of prescience on their part in the early 80s (even though they didn't really write the first version of MS-DOS, as we all know), or a willingness to cause a major upheaval somewhere along the line. Now, it's too late, and we're all stuck with LFNs and command lines as they are.

Lest I end this chapter on a sour note, let me remind you of that old chestnut about making lemonade when life hands you lemons. There are solutions and opportunities here among the pitfalls and quirks of LFNs. So keep an open mind, keep looking for a better way, and if you're careful, this can become one area in which your program distinguishes itself from the pack.

# Chapter 14

# Flavors of Win32

# Flavors
# of Win32

Chapter 14

*The Win32 functions, messages, and structures form a consistent and uniform API for all of Microsoft's 32-bit platforms: Windows 95, Microsoft Windows NT, and Windows version 3.1 with Win32s.*

> Microsoft Corporation,
> *Programmer's Guide to*
> *Microsoft Windows 95,*
> page 14

*Remember, there's just one Win32 API.*

> Matt Pietrek

Only one of these speakers is intentionally being ironic. Unfortunately for all Windows developers, it's Matt, which means that Microsoft wants us to believe something that I believe can be fairly characterized as a factually challenged statement. In other words, it just ain't so.

Andrew Schulman, David Maxey, and Matt Pietrek titled the first chapter of their book *Undocumented Windows* "This Was Not Supposed to Happen" ("this" referring to the large body of either very poorly documented or completely undocumented Windows programming information, a situation that made life quite difficult for many programmers). They spent the chapter telling the world how it did happen and what it meant. As I was working on this chapter and Chapter 12, I kept thinking about their chapter, because the situation I'm writing about also wasn't supposed to happen. The Win32 API was and is completely under the control of one company, Microsoft, so they should have been able to manage this transition from 16 to 32 bits, and from one Win32 variation to another, with

369

minimal fuss and bother. There was no committee to please, no ANSI standards group to drag their feet for months or years and impose their will on Microsoft. It was their sandbox, and they could have made the brand new Win32 implementation, Windows 95, far more compatible with the major existing one, Windows NT, than they did. In this chapter, I'll take an all-too-short look at the issue of these Win32 differences.

Before I get into that, I want to make two points about versions. First, even more so than most other chapters in this book, this one is highly dependent on the versions of Windows that I'm talking about. Unless I indicate otherwise in this chapter, "Windows 95" means the "gold" version of Windows 95 that shipped on August 24, 1995, "Win32s" means Win32s version 1.30 build 159, the "gold" version that was released very shortly after Windows 95 became generally available, and "Windows NT" means version 3.51. Second, I report a lot of problems here with Win32s 1.30. At least some of these were fixed in version 1.30a, which was made available too close to my deadline for me to respond to it. I can tell you that at the end of September, Microsoft made what was highly likely the final, retail version of Win32s 1.30a available on CompuServe, but since the list of bugs it fixed wasn't to be made available until the end of October, I couldn't quote it.

# Who's on 4.0?, or Why Win32 != Win32 != Win32

Normally, when you're faced with multiple operating systems you can target, you proceed in a pretty obvious way: You examine the platforms, the expected costs and benefits of supporting each one, weigh that against your resources, pick one or more, and away you go. When you get down to the actual business of building the executable, it's normally a matter of setting a few compiler and/or linker switches the right way to make sure you use the proper libraries and such and that your program will be properly "tagged" so that it can't be run in a hostile environment, such as the wrong version of the operating system, and you're done. Voilà! One perfectly targeted program.

Welcome to Windows programming in the 90's.

That's right, the process that was oh-so-easy in the Windows 3.0 and 3.1 time frame, when about the hardest decision you had to make was whether you still needed to ship COMMDLG.DLL with your program for the benefit of the users who were still running Windows 3.0, isn't. I'll talk about this issue in considerably more detail later in this chapter, but the bottom line is that Microsoft's design for getting the Windows world to 32 bits is packed with surprises, and they've provided programmers with far less help than I would have preferred. As a sneak preview, think about this: Windows NT 3.5 and 3.51, as well as Win32s (the subsystem designed to let you run 32-bit programs under 16-bit Windows 3.1) will run programs that have a version stamp saying they're expecting Windows 4.0, even though they don't support all the features of Windows 95 (the real Windows 4.0). But notice that Windows NT 3.51 will refuse to run a 16-bit program tagged as version 4.0, even though Windows 95 will run it and treat it as a Windows 95-aware application. (See the sidebar "Using LFNs from Win16 Programs: Better Living through Alchemy" in Chapter 12 for more on 16/4.0 programs.)

If you're wondering if there are significant differences between the Win32 implementations, see Table 14.1 for the "30,000-foot view", and 14.2 for the "10,000-foot view". The first table is merely a summary, showing what I think are the most important features that most programmers will be concerned with, but I think it gives you a feel for the architectural differences between the three platforms. The second table presents a statistical summary of the information Microsoft provides in the file WIN32API.CSV, which I think nicely shows to what extent Win32 is implemented on various platforms. This file shows which elements of the Win32 API (functions, messages, constants, etc.) are supported by each Win32 implementation.

Table 14.2 requires a bit of explanation. I loaded WIN32API.CSV into a database and then ran queries that showed how many items fell into each category. Of the 5,167 items in the table, only 3,882 have a "Yes" or "No" in all three platform categories. Rather than make a hard and fast call about how to count those 1,285 items that were less than completely categorized, I ignored them. (I did spot-check a dozen or so, and I found that nearly all the blanks would have clearly been "No" entries, which would have pushed up the counts and percentages for categories other than Yes/Yes/Yes (supported on all three Win32 platforms). Less than 40 of the entries have a "Yes", a "No", and a blank in some combination. Counting them would slightly increase the size of the population and would decrease the Yes/Yes/Yes percentage, but by less than a percentage point.) I also threw out the

**Table 14.1  The 30,000-foot view of Win32**

| Feature | Windows 95 | Windows NT 3.51 | Win32s 1.30 |
|---|---|---|---|
| Basic 32-bit arch. | Yes | Yes | Yes |
| Multithreading | Yes | Yes | No |
| Console API | Yes | Yes | No |
| Windows 95 shell | Yes | No | No |
| 32-bit USER | No | Yes | No |
| 32-bit GDI | No | Yes | No |
| Named pipes | Yes (client side only) | Yes | No |
| Memory-mapped files | Yes | Yes | Yes |
| Unicode | No | Yes | No |
| OpenGL | No | Yes | No |
| New common controls | Yes | Yes | Yes |
| Security features | No | Yes | No |
| Struct. except. handling | Yes | Yes | Yes |

**Table 14.2    The 10,000-foot view of Win32, according to WIN32API.CSV**

| Windows NT | Windows 95 | Win32s | Number of items | % of total |
|---|---|---|---|---|
| Yes | Yes | Yes | 1779 | 47.7 |
| Yes | No | No | 847 | 22.7 |
| Yes | Yes | No | 692 | 18.6 |
| No | Yes | No | 391 | 10.5 |
| Yes | No | Yes | 15 | 0.4 |
| No | Yes | Yes | 2 | 0.05 |
| No | No | Yes | 1 | 0.02 |

155 No/No/No entries, since these are items that were dropped in going from Win16 to Win32, so there was little point in including them in the analysis. This left me with 3,727 items that were fully categorized and supported by at least one of the three Win32 implementations.

What does this exercise show? Less than 48 percent of the items are Yes/Yes/Yes values, meaning they're on all three platforms (and I'm sure that categorizing all those blank entries would have pushed this number much lower, as low as 35.5 percent if all the blanks are in fact "No" values, the most likely outcome). This is surprisingly low. I should point out that these are unweighted numbers, which means they don't take into account how often individual APIs are used. An obscure API that's used in one in a thousand Windows programs is counted the same as the ubiquitous RegisterClass() or WM_CREATE. But on the other hand, neither does this analysis take into account the differences in implementation of APIs across platforms, such as the way GDI APIs truncate coordinates under Windows 95 and Win32s, making them worse than useless for 32-bit graphics work. If your program requires 32-bit graphics coordinates, then the degree to which the Win32 API is implemented by all three platforms effectively drops from about 48 percent to zero percent.

## The Documentation, Always the Documentation

If you've read much else of this book before you got to this point, it's probably no surprise whatsoever that documentation is a Very Big Deal to me. Well it is, and I hope that if you're involved in any way with serious Windows development that it's a VBD to you, too.

Sadly, the Win32 documentation leaves a lot to be desired. In a discussion about the various Win32 platforms, the most natural thing you would likely want to ask is which functions are available under each of the Win32 platforms. The best single source for that information from Microsoft is the file WIN32API.CSV I used as the basis for Table 14.2. WIN32API.CSV is a comma-delimited plain-text file that's in the directory WIN32SDK\MSTOOLS\LIB\I386 on the Win32

SDK CD ROM. As I said above, this file lists over 5,100 API structures, constants, and functions, and tells you which Win32 platforms, subsystem, header, and import library each one is associated with. Sounds like a great summary, right? It is, and I'm certainly glad it's available. But in the real world it's only helpful up to a very limited point. When I look at this file (which is far more usable once it's loaded into a database), I'm struck by how many things aren't there, like Win16 support (especially in light of the new APIs that are listed only in the DDK version of WINDOWS.H), and which version of each platform first supported each item.

Nearly all APIs, messages, structures, etc., are also documented in the SDK and in API32.HLP (the help file that comes with Visual C++ 2.x). In these sources, they include a "QuickInfo" popup window that covers things like the relevant header and which Win32 platforms support the item. But like WIN32API.CSV, there is no information here about Win16 or when each item gained support under each Win32 platform.

Even more annoying, the information in the QuickInfo popups has quite a few errors, and there are topics where it disagrees with the main text (for example, the topic says a message is new for Windows NT, but the popup says it isn't supported under Windows NT).

Most serious of all, in my opinion, is the way Microsoft has shunned the entire issue of error return codes and the GetLastError() mechanism. This grossly underdocuments the API and makes it much more difficult for programmers to write intelligent, accommodating code, a topic I'll come back to later in this chapter.

Overall, the Win32 documentation shows the classic sign of having been written and reviewed by people who don't actually use it: It's far less detailed than it should be. (I honestly don't know, nor do I care, if this is the true cause of the problems with the Win32 documentation, but speaking as someone who's been on the inside of that particular problem, it sure feels that way.) This is a bit indistinct for my taste; let me give you a specific example of what I mean. When I was working on one of the "Horror Stories" presented later in this chapter, I ran into the quirks of LB_DIR. LB_DIR is a message you can send to a list box to tell it to add the names of files that match a set of file attributes and a specification to its contents. Seems simple enough. API32.HLP and the Win32 SDK document the file specification as:

**lpszFileSpec**

> Value of *lParam*. Points to the null-terminated string that specifies the filename to add to the list. If the filename contains wildcards (for example, *.*), all files that match the wildcards and have the attributes specified by the *uAttrs* parameter are added to the list.

So what file specification should you use if you want the list box to display all the files in the directory C:\MYDOCS? As it turns out, if you send it

"C:\MYDOCS" or even "C:\MYDOCS\", the list box will reject the string and not display the files. You must send it "C:\MYDOCS\*.*". This contradicts normal practice regarding disambiguating between directory and file names—open a Windows 95 command window and type in "dir mydocs", and you'll get a directory listing of the files in the directory MYDOCS (assuming there's a subdirectory of the current directory with that name). If there's a file in the directory named MYDOCS, then you get information on that file. For some reason, list boxes processing LB_DIR messages are much fussier, and act in what I consider a very counterintuitive way. More to the point, the documentation gives the programmer no hint about exactly how the file specification is used, which means that we have to waste yet more time testing something this simple that could have been documented with just a couple more sentences.

To be sure, any API is a moving target, simply because it grows and changes over time. This is nothing more than a side effect of the normal evolution of a successful product. In other words, progress has a price, and we should expect the API to change, as well as inconsistencies in interface design and naming convention to creep in. (And the Win32 API surely has more than its share of such minor annoyances.) That's not in dispute here, and frankly I don't much care about such issues, as long as the overall API is still usable. The fact is that the Win32 API is far harder to track than it should be because not only is it evolving over time, but there are three implementations of it (soon to be four, thanks to IBM), no two of which completely agree. Faced with this state of incomplete documentation, how do you determine the exact behavior of an API function across platforms, or even on a single platform? You have no choice but to experiment.

## Even Microsoft Sings the Blues

Want to see some real world examples of Win32 compatibility problems? I can give you three good ones straight from Microsoft's own code samples on the Visual C++ 2.2 CD ROM.

The first example is MAZELORD, the maze-oriented game that Microsoft has been shipping as a sample for some time, which is in the directory \MSVC20\SAMPLES\WIN32\MAZELORD. Build this program and run it under Windows NT 3.51, and it works as expected. Run the same executable under Windows 95, and you get a somewhat less than optimal result thanks to blanked-out graphics. (See Figure 14.1 for a side-by-side comparison.)

What's going on here? It turns out that the PolyDraw() API isn't supported under Windows 95, and MAZELORD uses it to draw its graphics. Even more interesting, as of the Visual C++ 2.2 online help (the most recent one I saw), Microsoft was still telling the world that PolyDraw() was supported under Windows 95. (But the WIN32API.CSV file got it right.)

The second example is the non-MFC version of MultiPad, the one in the directory \MSVC20\SAMPLES\WIN32\MULTIPAD, not the one in \MSVC20\

**Windows 95 version**

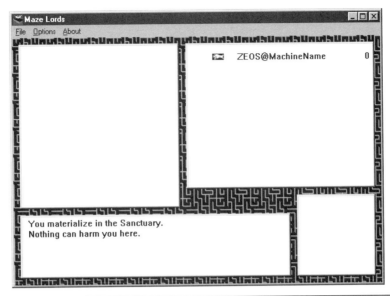

**Windows NT version**

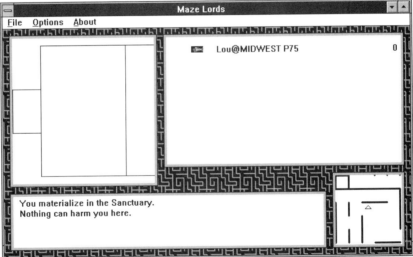

**Figure 14.1   MAZELORD Works, Kind Of.**

SAMPLES\MFC\MULTIPAD. This program also has problems under Windows 95, as you can see from Figure 14.2, which shows what happens when you try to load a small, plain-text file.

Finally, if you build WordPad using the provided source in MSVC20\SAMPLES\MFC\WORDPAD, it won't run under Win32s 1.30. It complains that it can't load RICHED32.DLL because it "may be missing or invalid."

I know what will happen when certain (hopefully small and wholly nonrepresentative) groups of people see these examples. The Microsoft Haters will tear out the pages, have them bronzed, and build small shrines around them on their front

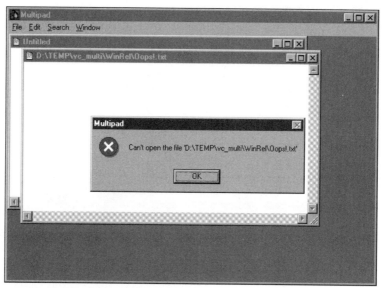

**Figure 14.2    Multipad under Windows 95.**

yards. (Hey, I live in the 'burbs; it's what we do.) The Microsoft Lovers will dismiss them as stupid examples since the programs are only samples, and are therefore not meant to prove anything. To both groups I say: You're wrong. These examples certainly don't prove that Microsoft's programmers are stupid or evil or anything remotely similar, but they do show quite succinctly that something as simple as getting a Win32 program to run on more than one platform can be quite an adventure. After all, one program blithely ran with a completely useless interface, one refused to load a document and merely said it failed to load, and the third produced a bogus error message that would most likely lead a user to conclude that a system DLL was either "missing or invalid," when it was actually present and quite valid.

The obvious retort (and I can hear people warming up their word processors now) is, "This is ridiculous! You can avoid all this nonsense by making your program check which version of Windows it's running under." To which I say, "Bingo! That's precisely the problem! (And thanks for providing a great segue into the next section...)"

*This is a minor issue, but I thought I should mention it somewhere along the line: It's been common knowledge for some time that the file RICHED32.DLL, which provides richedit controls under Win32, would be rolled into COMCTL32.DLL. (See Dave Edson's article, "Chicago's Interface Gadgets, Part II: Toolbars, Status Bars, and the RichEdit Control" in the August 1994 issue of Microsoft Systems Journal, for example.) It turns out now that the plan has*

*changed, and RICHED32.DLL will remain a separate file, according to someone I spoke to at Microsoft.*

# Version and Platform Checking

So one half of the equation is these differences in the Win32 implementations. The other half is the mechanisms available to the system and your program to keep you from inadvertently using them.

Version checking is about as simple and reliable as operating system features get: You mark your program with an expected Windows version of 4.0, say, and only Windows platforms with a version number greater than or equal to 4.0 will run the program. Well, not really. Unfortunately, Microsoft made Windows NT 3.5 and 3.51 accept and run version 4.0 applications, which means that we can't always count on this mechanism.

Also, since there are in effect three different Win32 APIs, and they are not distinguished by version number, there's no centralized, automatic way to detect a platform difference. I wish Microsoft had provided a way for the system to do this, with a matching mechanism for developers. For example, the PE file format used for Win32 executables could have added a field of bit flags that indicates which platforms should run the program. Individual bitfields could for assigned to Windows NT, Windows 95, and Win32s, and these bits could have been set in any combination via the linker. Then, if you tried to run a program marked "Windows NT only" under Windows 95, the system would refuse to run the program with a (hopefully) clear and helpful message. (There's a field in the PE file format called Subsystem, but it's used to indicate whether the program uses the Windows GUI, OS/2 character mode, etc., and doesn't do what I'm talking about.)

All we're left with in the way of operating system support is what I call "ballpark level checking," that is, the system will let your program run if it's in the right ballpark. (Win32s 1.30, which will allow version 4.1 and 5.0 programs to run, appears to be even less discerning in this regard.)

## *Dave's Not Here, Man*

What happens when a program tries to link implicitly to a function in a DLL that isn't there? Under Win16, the linkage is resolved to a routine in KRNL386.EXE (UNDEFDYNLINK), which will shut down your program and display a dialog box, when your program calls what it thinks is the DLL routine. All things considered, this is about the worst possible way to handle this situation.

If Win32 can't find a function in an implicitly linked DLL it refuses to load the program. Win32s reports this condition as an "Error 21", Windows NT tells the user that "The ordinal <number> could not be located in the dynamic link library <name>" and "The application failed to initialize properly (0xc0000138)", and Windows 95, not to be outdone in the Obfuscation Derby, displays the two dialog boxes shown in Figure 14.3. (What is it with Windows 95 and this "device attached to the system is not functioning" stuff, anyway? I've seen this message a number of times, and it never makes sense in the context of the error. For all its relevance it may as well say "Oops!".) Despite the rather deranged nature of these error messages, I much prefer the Win32 approach over that used in Win16, since it prevents a program from even getting control if a DLL routine it clearly intends to call isn't present.

Why is all this relevant to the issue of Win32 platform differences? Simple: The APIs you call all live in DLLs. Since not all these APIs are supported under every 32-bit version of Windows, this left Microsoft with a non-trivial design decision: How do you handle a Win32 program that intends to call an API that's not supported on the current system? There are two approaches, which I'll present in what I consider to be the most to least desirable ordering:

- Conditional compilation. In this approach, the developer is forced to decide up front which versions of the operating system will be supported. The developer then uses switches, library selections, etc., to build a program for just those versions, and is not even allowed to refer to any API element that is not in a version that is explicitly targeted.

In the realm of 32-bit Windows programming, this approach requires considerable support from Microsoft, since developers need headers that are festooned with conditional compilation sections, such as (the fictitious):

```
#ifdef WINNT
BOOL PolyDraw(HDC hdc,CONST POINT *lppt,CONST BYTE *lpbTypes,int cCount);
#endif
```

(Of course, Microsoft could also supply separate headers and libraries for the different platforms.) For Win32, this sort of "header file instrumentation" would be a huge undertaking, and it would create a maintenance nightmare for Microsoft. I think it's safe to say that we won't see anything like this from them in the near future. But it's still worth mentioning, because it's a legitimate approach, and combined with the "fail to load" DLL model mentioned above, it would have provided a very secure and reliable infrastructure. Even if a program

**Figure 14.3    How Windows 95 reports an undefined DLL routine.**

was marked with an incorrect version, and even if it attempted to call unsupported APIs, it would still fail relatively gracefully, since the system would prevent it from running.

The support we had in the Windows 3.0 and 3.1 time frame was a variation of conditional compilation. The DLL loading in that environment is the "runtime fail" mode, but the version checking performed by the system was good enough to cover most needs, at least when dealing with calls to system DLLs. We even had the option of marking a program as version 3.0 and including redistributable files, such as COMMDLG.DLL, so that the program could support either Windows 3.0 or 3.1 with equal ease.

- Conditional execution. This is the model Microsoft chose, and combined with the "3.51 == 4.0" version checking model, it places the entire burden of accounting for the differences in the Win32 platforms on the programmer.

In this approach, the headers simply include everything, with no conditional compilation sections relevant to the numerous API differences. (The W32 headers do include numerous such sections for the Unicode APIs, but that's an exception.) The missing API functions are all "stubbed" on various platforms. If you try to call PolyDraw() on Windows 95, as Microsoft's MAZELORD sample will, then it does nothing and returns FALSE. (Most stubbed APIs will indicate failure and set an extended error code of 120 (ERROR_CALL_NOT_IMPLEMENTED).)

When you think about it, this really is a curious way to handle not-present APIs. Look through WIN32API.CSV and the Win32 online help, API32.HLP, and you'll see numerous stubbed routines. There are only two ways to avoid problems in your programs regarding these APIs. First, avoid the APIs completely. Again, since there is no header file support to trigger errors at build time, it's completely up to you to know which elements of the API to shun. Second, you could, theoretically, exploit the behavior of the stubbed APIs by coding something like this:

```
if(!SomeAPIThatMightBeNTOnlyI(/* parameters */))
  {
    if(GetLastError() == ERROR_CALL_NOT_IMPLEMENTED)
      {
        /* re-try function using Windows 95 and/or Win32s friendly methods */
      }
    else
      ErrorHandler(/* parameters */);
  }
```

I've never seen anyone do this, I know that I'll never code such an abomination in a real program, and I sure hope I never run across anything of this ilk in a public program. It seems ludicrous to suggest that programmers should do this, and I'm quite sure this wasn't Microsoft's intention. So why bother to have the stubbed APIs set the extended error code in the first place? The only reason I can see is to provide a way to debug your program. If it's not doing what it should and you can't find the problem anywhere else, you can resort to checking all your API calls in the relevant section of code to see if you've accidentally stumbled across one that's not really supported on a particular platform. I haven't personally been bitten by this snake yet, but I'm sure I will. (And thanks to documentation errors like the QuickInfo popup that says PolyDraw() is supported under Windows 95, it seems inevitable.)

Clearly, the conditional execution model forces the programmer to do manually what the conditional compilation model would have the compiler do for us automatically. That's not a good tradeoff, in my opinion, and I consider it a huge step backwards. (After all, isn't the idea supposed to be that computers take care of all the nit-picky bookkeeping details like this, and people do the creative work?)

I think the most disturbing aspect of this situation is just how difficult it could be to find the errant API call in a program. Many programs use entire sets or families of APIs, and if one fails in the middle of a sequence, it could be hideously difficult to track down. This is only magnified by the fact that no one checks every single API call for success. I sure don't, and I'm about as paranoid as programmers get. Check the file DRAW.C in the MAZELORD sample, and you'll see that it never checks the return value from PolyDraw(). This isn't a surprise, because PolyDraw() calls are at the end of a drawing procedure. If your code checked for and detected failure at that point, what would it do? Tell the user that it can't continue and then shut down? This would be better than what MAZELORD does today, which is soldier on in complete ignorance of its own failing, but not nearly as good as checking for the proper platform at startup and giving the user a more intelligent response.

So. What do we do about this? Unfortunately, there isn't a really good answer. Unlike some of the differences in API implementation, which can be paved over with simple wrapper functions, stubbed APIs are a much more difficult nut to crack. You could instrument the Windows header files, and require all your own programs to define symbols such as WINNT, WIN95, and WIN32S to make sure you get only the right API elements in each program, but that would be such an enormous amount of work and so prone to error that it's probably not worth it, except under very unusual circumstances.

If desperate enough, you could also resort to a version-checking wrapper, and write functions similar to:

```
BOOL platformSomeAPI(/* parameters */)
{
#ifdef _DEBUG
  if(!((WINNT | WIN95) & current_platform))
```

```
      MessageBox(0,"Attempted call to SomeAPI()!!!","Platform violation!",
        MB_ICONEXCLAMATION | MB_SYSTEMMODAL);
#endif
   return SomeAPI(/* parameters */);
}
```

where the platforms that support this API are represented by flags (WINNT and WIN95 in this example), and current_platform is a variable that uses the same flag definitions and is set at application startup. Besides being a lot of work, this type of wrapper would also require you to be quite careful that you understood exactly which APIs are supported where. (Come to think of it, that's what the current situation does, and this type of wrapper would allow you to force the current_platform variable to be anything you want, allowing you to test for Win32s API compliance under Windows 95 or Windows NT. And you could easily extend it to do version checking as well as platform checking. Hmm.)

It appears that you can't count on the debug version of Windows 95 for help, either. I certainly haven't tested this exhaustively, but the Windows NT-only APIs that I've run under Windows 95 don't produce debug messages from the system.

One solution is to use Bounds Checker Pro, by Nu-Mega Technologies, Inc. Bounds Checker Pro is a very impressive package (see my recommendation in Chapter 15 for more detail), and in particular, it will monitor the APIs your system calls and categorize them according to platform. This is easy to do and quite helpful, but it still doesn't do anything about version support. (If you think this talk about versions is premature, then consider what will happen once Nashville and Memphis, the next two versions of Windows 95, are available, and Windows NT 4.0 and Cairo appear, not to mention at least a couple of new Win32s releases. Writing an application compatible with an "old" release, like our current Windows 95 or even (horrors!) Windows NT 3.5, could become quite an adventure.)

*I'd be remiss if I didn't mentioned Win32c. Remember Win32c, Microsoft's name for the Windows 95 subset of the Win32 API? (Presumably the "c" stood for "Chicago," Windows 95's code name while it was in development.) This was mentioned in several places, and it was an implicit admission that there were three versions of the Win32 API: Win32 (Windows NT), Win32c (Windows 95), and Win32s (Win32-on-Win16). You can still find a few references to Win32c in the current edition of the Microsoft Developer Network CD ROM. It's been quite some time since anyone from Microsoft has used the term, and they've apparently long ago adopted the "uniform API" viewpoint.*

## Don't Touch That Disk!

If you've already given your Visual C++ 2.0 CD ROM to your dog for a chew toy, or you've consigned it to coaster or mobile duty (the CD, not your dog), put this book down *now* and go retrieve the disk. Trust me, it's important.

You'll want your old 2.0 disk, thanks to how intriguing Microsoft has made building your 32-bit Windows executables and tagging them for various OS versions. (Forgive my naiveté, but this one actually surprised me.) The copy of LINK.EXE that comes with Visual C++ 2.1 and 2.2 are bit-for-bit identical, and they use a default Windows subsystem value of 4.0. The LINK.EXE that came with Visual C++ 2.0 uses a default subsystem version of 3.1. Why do you care? Believe it or not, the 2.1 and 2.2 LINK.EXE won't accept a Windows subsystem setting below 4.0. If you try to use 3.0, 3.1, or 3.5, as in a linker option in the Visual C++ IDE of "/subsystem:windows,3.5", it rejects the setting and uses the default value 4.0. This means you must have the old LINK.EXE available if you want to build a program with a subsystem number lower than 4.0. Hence, the loss of Fido's pretty new toy.

You can use the linker from Visual C++ 2.0 to create your program, and it will happily create your program and tag it for 3.1 (but if you explicitly tell it to use version 3.1, then it complains about the "invalid" setting and tells you that it's using the default, which is, uh, 3.1).

Stranger yet, all three linkers will accept a subsystem version of 4.1, 5.0, etc. Why is this odd? Isn't Microsoft just planning for the future, something I keep harping about in this book? I think it is odd, because if you try to run a 4.1-tagged program under Windows 95, you get the spectacle shown in Figure 14.4. (Notice the return of the infamous "device attached to the system is not functioning" dialog.) Windows NT 3.51 isn't immune to this silliness, either. Figure 14.4 also shows the dialog box the same test program generates on that platform, which once again prompted my "Give me a hint!" reaction. Win32s 1.30, ever the unfettered spirit, provides the best entertainment of all. It simply runs the program, which begs an interesting question about what happens once Win32 programs start using a subsystem number greater than 4.0, and people with Win32s 1.30 try to run them. Just another thing for developers to verify manually, since the system won't do it for us, I suppose.

If you want to run your own tests with this phenomenon, I've included the 4.1 and 5.0 tagged versions of one of the sample programs on the CD. (See ZEN\CHAP14\WIN32VER\WINREL for the files WV41.EXE and WV50.EXE.)

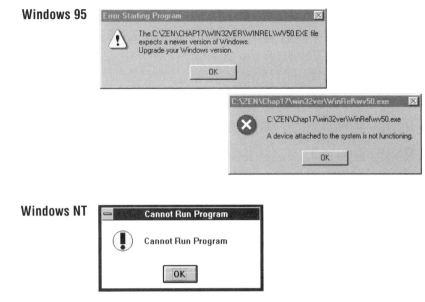

**Windows 95**

**Windows NT**

**Figure 14.4    Trying to run a Version 5.0 Win32 program.**

# Horror Stories

OK, here's where I brain dump every Win32 compatibility problem that I thought was important and that I was able to verify independently. I've collected these items from my own experiences and those of my friends, as well as Microsoft's documentation, CompuServe conversations, and scrawlings on the men's room wall in programmer bars.

As for calling these items "horror stories," and my selection criteria, I would point you to the explanation I gave in the "Horror Stories" section in Chapter 12. Briefly, if you run into one of these quirks of Windows programming, which usually happens at a phenomenally inconvenient time, it *is* a horror story.

Also, please note that in judging an item's information value to you, I concentrated on Windows 95 and Windows NT 3.51. I wanted to include extensive coverage of Windows NT 3.1 and 3.5, since I think they're still relevant to this discussion, but I simply didn't have the time. Similarly, I don't completely discount the importance of Win32s, but I do think it's less important than Windows NT for the purpose of this chapter, so I've only included a few such items about it, and restricted my testing to version 1.30, the one that shipped shortly after Windows 95.

Having said all that about what's not here, let me take a few sentences to soapbox about what is here. Despite Microsoft's assertion that Win32 is a "uniform and consistent" API for all three Win32 platforms, it's pretty clear from this list and Microsoft's admitted incompatibilities and quirks that such claims should be viewed with a quite skeptical eye. There are APIs and system features that only exist in one place or the other, APIs that differ subtly in how they work on both platforms, and even manifest constants that are only defined for one platform, but are accepted by and return bad data from API functions on another.

In other words, it's quite a mess, and thanks to Microsoft's design decisions regarding versioning of executables, which portions of Windows 95 would remain 16 bit, and that not implemented APIs would be stubbed, it's up to us to keep all this stuff straight, since we sure won't get much help, if any, from Microsoft.

Note that I haven't categorized these issues according to compatibility problems versus bugs. On one level, it doesn't really matter. If a given API doesn't work quite as expected under Windows 95 but it does under Windows NT, that's just as big a problem as if it works correctly in one place but isn't available in the other or is buggy.

I want to take a second or three to stress once again something I said way back in Chapter 4, that it really pays to take the time to test even mundane API details to make sure they work as you think they do, or even as documented. For example, I talk about how GetShortPathName() differs subtly between Windows 95, Windows NT, and Win32s. You could conceivably try to use this function as a quick way to verify that a fully qualified file name (one that includes a drive, directory, and/or file name) names an existing file. (That would be questionable practice at best, since you'd be relying on an undocumented side effect, which is never a good idea.) Under the various Win32 platforms and conditions, this usage will fail, and the system will tell you that a non-existent file is really there.

And once again, let me remind you not to be shy about sending me your Win32 porting discoveries. I'm sure there are dozens of additional items that never made it onto my preliminary list, yet should be made common knowledge among Windows programmers.

## GDI Clips Coordinates

"Everyone" knows by now that Windows 95 is not a 100 percent 32-bit operating system. There's a fair amount of 16-bit code floating around in the belly of the beast, a fact that was thrashed about in the press and online discussions endlessly when it first became public knowledge. It's old news, and given Windows 95's well recognized appetite for RAM, it's painfully ironic that one of the primary reasons Microsoft supposedly kept the 16-bit code in-place was the desire to keep the working set of the system small. (See the May, 1994 *Microsoft Systems Journal* article "Memory Management, the Win32 Subsystem, and Internal Synchronization in Chicago" by Adrian King, which says, "Given the goal of running Chicago well on 4 to 8MB systems, this increase [in working set size caused by converting USER and GDI to 32 bits] wasn't acceptable.")

But I digress.

The biggest single side effect of this design decision is that all GDI calls that take coordinates will accept 32-bit signed values, according to the Win32 API definition, but will throw away the high-order word under Windows 95. The MFC documentation for the GDI functions in question doesn't cover this situation, and it's only mentioned in API32.HLP, the Win32 SDK API help file.

By far the worst part of this bizarre situation is that the program calling the API isn't notified that anything is amiss. The GDI call produces a return value that indicates the function completed normally, when in fact it either did nothing (if the clipping produced an unusable value), or it did something bizarre (if the clipping produced a corrupt but legal value).

Because Win16 GDI coordinates are 16-bit signed values and the most significant 16 bits are discarded under Windows 95, the result is that any value with a one in the 15th bit (the 16th one from the right of the coordinate as you would normally write it out in binary) will be interpreted as a negative value, and any number with a zero in this position will be interpreted as a positive one. Your coordinates can change signs, radically change magnitude, and, depending on the nature of your application, literally move all over the map.

See Figure 14.5 for how the sample program GDICLIP appears under Windows 95 and Windows NT 3.51. The Windows 95 version looks fine, until you

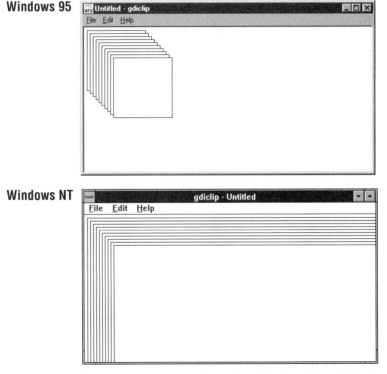

**Figure 14.5   GDICLIP program running under Windows 95 and Windows NT.**

realize that the right and bottom coordinates passed to the Rectangle() API are both just over 65,536. The correct version of the output is shown in the Windows NT version, where the rectangles run very far off the edge of the screen.

There's nothing special about the drawing code in GDICLIP, but the code does present one interesting detail, as shown in Listing 14.1: The program will display a message box if the Rectangle() function fails. Run this program under Windows NT and Windows 95, and it never utters a peep.

## Listing 14.1   GDICLIP's Drawing Code

```
//////////////////////////////////////////////////////////////////////////
// CGdiclipView drawing

void CGdiclipView::OnDraw(CDC* pDC)
{
     CGdiclipDoc* pDoc = GetDocument();
     ASSERT_VALID(pDoc);

   // With such huge coords, the lower-right corner of our rectangles
   // should be far off the edge of our window.  Under NT, they are.
   // But under Windows 95, they're clipped, and we get an entirely
   // different result, and no indication from Windows that anything
   // is amiss.
   for(int i = 1; i < 11; i++)
     if(!pDC->Rectangle(i * 5,i * 5,65636 + i * 5,65636 + i * 5))
       MessageBox("Rectangle call failed!","GDIClip",MB_OK);;
}
```

## Building the Samples: GDICLIP

**CD Location:** ZEN\CHAP14\GDICLIP

**Platform:** Win32

**Build instructions:** Use the provided .MAK file with Visual C++ 2.2 and compile normally. Run the resulting executable under Windows 95 and Windows NT and you'll see the different behavior.

If you have the luxury of knowing that you'll always work with sufficiently small coordinates, then this isn't much of a problem. Go ahead and use your 16-bit values, but try to remember that disaster awaits in the 15th bit.

What if you wrote a program that uses the 32-bit coordinate space of Windows NT? Then you're out of luck because it can't possibly run right under Windows 95 without (probably extensive) modification.

In keeping with the philosophy that there's only one way a program should run, namely correctly, and that it should detect and reject conditions that will prevent it from doing so, what can you do about this? One solution is to create and use your own wrappers for the affected GDI calls. I've presented one possible approach to this task in Appendix C, in the form of the Win32u library.

One last time: Windows 95's handling of GDI coordinates is stupen-
dously bad form. Not only does it do the worst possible thing (that
is, accept but not use 32-bit coordinates), it mangles them and
uses what's left without giving the calling program the barest hint
about what happened. In fact, it's so bad that this behavior, plus
the similar clipping of list box string indexes (see the next item)
wins Microsoft the first ever Null Pointer Award for Bad Design.

## List Boxes Clip String Indexes

A first cousin to the GDI coordinate situation, and one with the same heritage,
involves the string indexes programs pass to list boxes. As you probably know,
there are several LB_* messages which all take one or two 32-bit numbers under
Win32 that indicate which entries in the list box are to be operated on. You
guessed it—Windows 95 quietly tosses out the most significant 16 bits of your
32-bit string index, and only indicates failure if the operation couldn't proceed
with whatever is left. In altering the data like this, the system can easily turn an
invalid parameter into a valid one (such as clipping 65537 to 1), and then use
data the programmer never intended to (and, in fact, didn't) pass, instead of reporting an error.

If Windows 95 list boxes were smart enough to return LB_ERR instead of
clipping the index number, then a program would at least have a fighting chance
of operating properly. Better yet would be the creation and use of a new return
value, say, LB_PARMERR, that would allow Windows 95 to flag indexes outside
the normal 16-bit range.

API32.HLP says in numerous places when describing these LB_* messages:

> Windows 95 only: The wParam parameter is limited to 16-bit
> values. This means list boxes cannot contain more than 32,767
> items. Although the number of items is restricted, the total size
> in bytes of the items in a list box is limited only by available
> memory.

This statement is correct about the limitation on the number of items in a list
box. Run the LBCLIP example and keep adding new strings with the "Add" button, and eventually you'll get the "out of memory" dialog box from the program
at just under 32,767 strings. But this statement is very misleading when it says
"the wParam parameter is limited to 16-bit values." If the list boxes rejected calls
with string indexes not in the range -32,768 to 32,767, then this would be a
meaningful way to state the case; however, as things stand, the list box mangles
the caller's data and uses it, which might come as quite a surprise to someone
reading the above description.

## Building the Samples: LBCLIP

**CD Location:** ZEN\CHAP14\LBCLIP

**Platform:** Win32

**Build instructions:** Use the provided .MAK file with Visual C++ 2.2 and compile normally. Run the resulting executable under Windows 95 and Windows NT, experiment with the buttons, and you'll see the different list box behavior.

It's tempting to say that with the 32K string limit Microsoft got this situation partially right, since they won't let you put strings into a Windows 95 list box that you can't address. I suspect that this limitation is due to list boxes being implemented in Windows 95 in the 16-bit USER code, so this wasn't a good design decision, but merely another side effect of a more basic element of the design, albeit a fortunate one.

I have a hard time understanding Microsoft's approach to this problem, largely because the fix is so simple and so cheap. All they had to do with the LB_* functions is make each one use the following logic on the 32-bit side of the call:

```
if((wParam > 32767) || (wParam < -32768))
  return LB_PARMERR;
else
  {
  /* Call 16-bit implementation */
  }
```

Some people will protest that the added overhead of performing this check on every LB_* message is too great. I disagree. Compared to the system overhead of floating a message to a child control, the few instructions needed to do this quick test (probably less than ten, in fact) are truly insignificant. (And besides, Windows already does this much parameter checking and much more on almost every API call.)

Unfortunately, these are messages and not functions, which means that employing wrappers for them is more problematic than for the GDI functions. It's just as easy to write the wrapper functions, of course, but it takes slightly more effort to use them. The GDI wrappers can be used by merely changing the name of the GDI API called to that of the wrapper, where the LB_* message must be changed from (typically) a SendMessage() API call to a wrapper call. Even that little bit of extra typing can be enough of an excuse for some people not to use a wrapper library.

Ever the optimist, I've included a set of LB_* wrappers in the Win32u library in Appendix C.

*This is a philosophical point that I think bears repeating: What are the only acceptable, intelligent responses to an API or function call? In my opinion they are 1) perform the requested operation as documented, or 2) refuse and indicate to the caller why the request couldn't be carried out. Clearly, error conditions fall into the second category, and this clipping behavior by Windows 95 list boxes violates this contract with the caller.*

*I know that some programmers don't see this sort of issue as a big deal—"Call an API with bad data, and you deserve what you get," they say. I think this attitude is incredibly naive and lazy, and it leads to all manner of bugs in shipping code, because these programmers so often use this fable as an excuse not to write rigorous code or documentation. I've even heard programmers claim that all APIs and function libraries are, by definition, to be used only by "people who know what they're doing", since these are programming interfaces, not end-user interfaces, so any response to a call with invalid input, including crashing the whole system, is perfectly acceptable. I sincerely hope that these people haven't written any of the code I depend on to make my living.*

## List Boxes Can't Handle Long File Names under Windows 95

What? More long file name stuff? Incredibly, and sadly, yes. Just when you thought you'd slain (or at least discovered) the last long file name dragon, another one rears its ugly head. And in this case, it's a doozy.

This time the culprit is the LB_DIR message you send to a list box to tell it to fill itself with a list of the files that meet certain specifications. As it turns out, this support is still in the 16-bit portion of USER under Windows 95, which means it can't handle long file names, even when called from a Win32 program. The good news is that while this one is a pain in the neck, since you have to remember to translate the directory name to an all-alias format, at least the list box will return LB_ERR when it sees a long file name, which is no doubt detected as an invalid file specification and not recognized as a long file name per se. Or at least that's what I thought. Whatever the cause, this API's behavior usually gives you a fighting chance to figure out what went wrong (unlike the list box and GDI clipping problems, which mangle your parameters and never toss you a clue.)

One simple and obvious solution is to add a small routine to your toolbox similar to DoLBDir():

```
int DoLBDir(HWND lb, UINT attrs, char *dir)
{
  char buffer[MAX_PATH];
```

```
if(!GetShortPathName(dir,buffer,sizeof(buffer)))
  return LB_ERR;

return SendMessage(lb,LB_DIR,attrs,(LPARAM)dir);
}
```

and then always use it, even if you think you're sure that your program will run only under Windows NT.

Too bad this doesn't quite work. The LB_DIR message expects the directory specification to include a file name and extension, which can include wildcards (and most often will, in fact). This means that you can't translate the original name to one that has only alias-style components in a sufficiently robust way. (GetShortPathName() won't accept wildcards, for example.) I experimented with this, as I had originally planned to present a wrapper that was smart enough to do this translation for the caller, when needed. Unfortunately, after playing with the _fsplitpath() function and various legal and illegal directory formations, I came to the conclusion that this was a good example of a "tar pit" problem, and a wrapper that shouldn't be written. Every time I thought I had finally covered all the common pathological cases, I found another counter example where the routine would misinterpret the caller's parameters.

While I'm on the topic of LB_DIR, I should mention that even when you pass the list box an all-alias form directory name, Windows 95 will show the user nothing but aliases, while Windows NT will display long file names. There's nothing you can do about this detail, except avoid it completely by rolling your own support to retrieve the long file names and stuff them into the list box by hand. Whether a uniform appearance between Windows 95 and Windows NT is that important to you and your users is a judgment call, of course, but it's a shame you have to make it at all.

Microsoft documents this LB_DIR situation in its PSS article Q131286, which unfortunately includes a code sample in its June 10, 1995 version that was apparently mangled in production:

```
char  szLong [256], szShort [256];
DWORD dwResult;
LONG  lResult;

lstrcpy (szLong, "C:\\This Is A Test Subdirectory");
dwResult = GetShortPathName (szLong, szShort, 256);
if (!dwResult)
  dwResult = GetLastError ();

lstrcat (szShort, "\lResult = SendDlgItemMessage (hdlg,
                          IDC_LIST1,
                          LB_DIR,
                          (WPARAM)(DDL_READWRITE),
      (LPARAM)(LPSTR)szShort);
if (LB_ERR == lResult)
  // an error occurred
```

I had planned to end this "horror story" here, but on one of the very last days I was working on this book, a not so funny thing happened: I found out just how broken LB_DIR really is. I was doing some last-minute testing, and I (briefly) thought I had found a case where Microsoft was claiming that something was broken when, in fact, it was working properly. I wrote a simple test program that sends an LB_DIR message to a list box with the file specification "c:\temp dir\*.*". When it worked, I uttered a few non-deleted expletives, and wondered what was going on. Wasn't this exactly the kind of thing that LB_DIR wasn't supposed to be able to handle? Well, if you look carefully at that file specification, you'll notice that even with the embedded blank, the directory name, "temp dir", is still only eight characters. When I changed the file specification to "c:\temp dir with a really long name" (and renamed the actual directory to match), I was somewhat relieved to see that it failed, since at least that part of the API's behavior was in accordance with Microsoft's and my expectations.

But wait a second—think about what happened here. The file specification "c:\temp dir\*.*" matched with the directory "c:\temp dir", which clearly means that the LB_DIR implementation is searching the entire file system name space, including long file names, not just aliases. This directory's alias was TEMPDI~1, which clearly should not have matched "temp dir".

On a hunch, I set up a directory on my system named "c:\temp dir\temp dir", and placed a couple of dummy files into it. I then ran the LB_DIR test program with a file specification of "c:\temp dir with a really long name\temp dir with another really long name\*.*", and it worked. I next tried the same trick with a file name, and that worked, also. I changed the "*.*" part of the file specification in the previous test to "holy cow really long file name.txt" and it matched and displayed a file named "holy cow.txt". (The alias form of the name was displayed, as mentioned above, but the file had clearly been located via its long file name.) Curiously enough, when I used a file specification that included an extension of ".*" instead of ".TXT", LB_DIR failed to find the same file.

This is a very disturbing situation, since LB_DIR will accept a syntactically correct file specification that contains long file names and match it to the wrong set of files under Windows 95. If LB_DIR always failed to use a long file name, that would be somewhat inconvenient but not much of a quality risk, since it would very likely be caught in testing. But this business of (mis)matching part of a directory name component with a different directory is downright scary.

I described this incident and my investigation in detail because I think it provides a valuable lesson for all of us about working with and testing the Win32 API. It would be very easy for someone to run a test similar to my original "temp dir" program, conclude that LB_DIR must be smart enough to handle long file names, and then not bother with the GetShortPathName() translation that Microsoft (correctly) recommends. In fact, I'm sure I would have jumped to exactly that conclusion had I not already known for a fact that LB_DIR couldn't

392 ⚡ *Chapter 14*

handle long file names. As it turns out, LB_DIR's behavior is even stranger than Microsoft documents, and it includes at least one outright bug. Caveat programmer.

## GetLastError() Returns Unusable Values

This is another tar pit problem, and one that doesn't seem too terribly bad until you start to think about its ramifications. Then you want to scream. (And in cyberspace, no one can hear you scream.)

In *Programmer's Guide to Microsoft Windows 95*, Microsoft says:

> The extended error codes generated by the GetLastError function are not guaranteed to be the same in Windows 95 and Windows NT. This difference applies to extended error codes generated by calls to GDI, window management, and system services functions.

What they're saying in this crystalline example of understatement is that the same Win32 API will interpret the same set of conditions differently, depending on the platform the program is running under, and these different interpretations will be reflected in the exact choice of error codes. For example, the GetShortPathName() API translates a long file name path into an alias-only form. If the long file name you provide to the API doesn't exist, then how should it interpret the situation? Windows 95 leans toward ERROR_PATH_NOT_FOUND, while Windows NT 3.51 prefers ERROR_FILE_NOT_FOUND. (See below for much more on the idiosyncrasies of this API.)

This difference of opinion between Win32 platforms regarding extended error codes means that you can't do anything with the result of GetLastError() except check to see if it's non-zero, or if it's equal to ERROR_CALL_NOT_IMPLEMENTED. You can pass its returned value to the FormatMessage() API, which will translate the number into a text string that your program can then display to the user, but the difference in error codes means your program will display different diagnostic messages for the same inputs and context, depending on which flavor of Windows the user is running. (Notice also that the copy of Microsoft's PSS article Q83520, which is included with the gold Win32 SDK, refers to this constant as ERROR_NOT_IMPLEMENTED, when the name is actually ERROR_CALL_NOT_IMPLEMENTED.)

The worst part of this situation is how Microsoft has documented each API's use of extended error codes: Not at all. Search through the SDK, and you'll find numerous references to the fact that an API, upon failure, will indicate that it didn't complete properly via its return value, and will also set an error code that the calling program can retrieve with GetLastError(). There is no list of the error codes returned by any given API, which reduces GetLastError() to a debugging tool, not a run-time facility. The bottom line is that when something goes wrong, at exactly the time you most need help from the system, you get the least help. If you write a piece of code along the lines of:

```
if(!SomeWin32API(/* parameters */))
{
switch(GetLastError())
  {
  case ERROR_PATH_NOT_FOUND:
    /* Handle path not found case */
    break;

  default:
  /* Report generic/unknown error and terminate program */
  }
}
```

then you're running the risk of making your program terminate when in fact it encountered an easily handled error condition or possibly even one that could safely be ignored. For example, you think that the only "file not there" error you'll get from a given API is ERROR_PATH_NOT_FOUND, based on your testing under Windows 95, so you look for and gracefully handle that case by copying the input file name to the output buffer and ignoring the error value. But you didn't know that your program might also receive an ERROR_FILE_NOT_FOUND code under the same circumstances, which means that under Windows NT an equally trivial and harmless case winds up in your default processing, which terminates your program under the assumption that it encountered some unforeseen and intractable error. How do you know exactly how to handle this situation? You can't. Microsoft took a very simple and useful error reporting mechanism, grossly underdocumented it, implemented it inconsistently, and turned it into a bug generator.

You may scream now.

You have only two choices: 1) Don't do anything with the result of GetLastError(), except when you should look for ERROR_CALL_NOT_IMPLEMENTED; or 2) wrap your API calls and force the extended error information to a known state. Some choice. The first results in code that doesn't bother to check if API calls succeeded, or does and bails out whenever anything is amiss; while the second is a lot of system-level work that we application programmers shouldn't have to do.

What should Microsoft have done in this area? For starters, they should have forced the Windows NT and Windows 95 developers to make all their APIs produce the same error codes under the same conditions. Period. Anything else is chaos. Then they should have documented unambiguously in the API online help exactly which error codes were used and under which circumstances by every API function (and this should have been right on the main topic for each function, not even on a popup). For example, here's how I'd like to see GetShortPathName() behave, and how I think it should be documented in the online help:

| Condition | Extended Error Code |
|---|---|
| Invalid file specification, including NULL ptr and 0-length string | ERROR_BAD_PATHNAME |
| File specification indicates a drive, directory, or file that does not exist | ERROR_PATH_NOT_FOUND |

(This is, in fact, how I made uGetShortPathName(), my GetShortPathName() wrapper in the Win32u library, behave.)

By now, Microsoft has painted themselves, and us, into a very tight corner. If they try to unify the use of extended error codes, they'll no doubt break a lot of existing applications. The current situation is so ill-defined that if they tried to document all the error codes used (for example, imagine the table above with additional columns for various Win32 platforms), they would no doubt get some of them wrong, and cause even more grief. (This sounds like I have very little faith in Microsoft's ability to write usable documentation. To be clear, I think they do a better job in this area than most software vendors, especially development tools vendors, but the Win32 documentation has so many errors and omissions that I'm not optimistic that Microsoft could pull off something like this with an acceptable level of accuracy. I would *love* to be proved wrong, however.) There's also the issue of what happens when new releases of Windows 95 and Windows NT appear. Any guesses as to whether we'll see a few undocumented changes in the undocumented use of extended error codes? I can't read the future any better than you can, but let's just say that some "minor" unannounced changes in this area wouldn't be a shock.

## Windows 95: SUBST/GetShortPathName() Bug

Our old friend from DOS, the SUBST command, is still available under Windows 95 and Windows NT, of course. The problem is that under Windows 95, it can trip up the GetShortPathName() API. (In case you're not familiar with it (and many Windows users and programmers today aren't), the SUBST command allows you to substitute a new drive letter for an existing drive and path. For example, if you don't have a Q: drive on your system, you can use the SUBST command to tell DOS and/or Windows to treat all references to your Q: drive as references to C:\MYDOCS\SUMMARY. Then, you can refer to Q:\JANUARY.DOC instead of C:\MYDOCS\SUMMARY\JANUARY.DOC.)

To see this bug in action, open a command window under Windows 95, and enter the command:

```
SUBST G: C:\TEMP
```

which tells Windows 95 to treat all G: drive references as references to C:\TEMP.

Then run the sample program SUBSTBUG, which is located in \ZEN\CHAP14\SUBSTBUG. This program will call GetShortPathName() a number of times and show you the results. Whenever this program passes a path to GetShortPathName() that refers to the C: drive, the call works. The calls it makes using a drive letter of G: don't fare quite so well: "g:" is translated to "g:TEMP", and "g:\" is translated to "g:\TEMP", both non-existent paths on my system. GetShortPathName() does correctly handle "g:fred.txt" (which indirectly refers to the file "c:\temp\fred.txt"), and translates it to "g:FRED.TXT". These tests all run properly under Windows NT 3.51.

I wouldn't be surprised if there are other, more colorful ways to trip up the GetShortPathName() and SUBST combination, but I haven't found any. My concern here, of course, is that you have no way of knowing if your program's users are employing the SUBST command. If they are, and you're using GetShortPathName() with directory names, then everyone involved could be in for some nasty surprises when your program tries to use the phantom directory names it gets from this API and starts reporting strange errors to the user. (See the "GetShortPathName() Oddities" item in this section for much detail about this particular API.)

## Building the Samples: SUBSTBUG

**CD Location:** ZEN\CHAP14\SUBSTBUG

**Platform:** Win32

**Build instructions:** Use the provided .MAK file with Visual C++ 2.2 and compile normally. Follow the instructions above to run the test.

## GetShortPathName() Oddities

GetShortPathName() is about as simple as an API can get. You give it a path name that might or might not contain long file names, it returns the alias-only version of the path, plus a return code, and it uses SetLastError() to set the extended error code, if any. Not exactly rocket science, but a very useful and seemingly well-documented API.

Hmm. What should this API do if you give it a path with a drive that doesn't exist on your system? Say, "z:\autoexec.bat", when you don't have a z: drive? Should it report an error? I think it should. After all, the purpose of this API is to perform a translation that requires the file to exist—GetShortPathName() isn't using some algorithm to generate a short path name, it's simply running out to the file system and doing a lookup. If the named file doesn't exist, then the only logical response is to return an error.

Unfortunately, between Win32s 1.30, Windows 95, and Windows NT 3.51, you can get quite a variety of answers from GetShortPathName() in this and similar cases. (For the record, the documentation for GetShortPathName(), both in API32.HLP and in the Win32 SDK, is mute on this issue, as it so often is regarding CPC's (common pathological cases).)

Table 14.3 summarizes my test results, which you can duplicate via the GSPN sample in this chapter. Notice that GetShortPathName() shows wildly different behavior across platforms, and it even seems to distinguish between paths that contain one or two file components. In other words, if your C: drive doesn't have a directory in its root called "temp dir", GetShortPathName() will treat the input strings "c:\temp dir" and "c:\temp dir\file.txt" differently. The first string fails on Windows 95 and succeeds under Windows NT 3.51, while the second fails on both platforms, albeit with different extended errors.

Win32s 1.30 is a different animal altogether, which shouldn't be a surprise. It always succeeds, except for that nasty NULL pointer case which makes it throw an exception. (It should return either ERROR_CALL_NOT_IMPLEMENTED or ERROR_NOT_SUPPORTED, in my opinion, since by definition it can't do anything meaningful with a long file name.)

Another interesting point is that GetShortPathName() doesn't always call GetLastError() when it fails. For example, change the SetLastError(0) in the sample

## Table 14.3 The Tale of GetShortPathName()

| Test Case | Win32s 1.30 | Windows 95 | Windows NT |
|---|---|---|---|
| NULL pointer | Unhandled exception in W32SCOMB.DLL | Fails, error code 87 | Fails, error code 87 |
| Zero-length string | Succeeds, leaves output blank | Fails, error code 161 | Fails, doesn't set error code |
| Non-existent drive | Succeeds, copies string to output | Fails, error code 3 | Succeeds, copies string to output |
| Existing drive, non-existing dir., no file name | Succeeds, copies string to output | Succeeds, copies string to output | Fails, error code 2 |
| Existing drive, non-existing dir., file name | Succeeds, copies string to output | Fails, error code 3 | Fails, error code 2 |
| Existing drive and dir., non-existing file | Succeeds, copies string to output | Fails, error code 3 | Fails, error code 2 |

Note: error codes (from WINERROR.H):

   2 = ERROR_FILE_NOT_FOUND
   3 = ERROR_PATH_NOT_FOUND
  87 = ERROR_INVALID_PARAMETER
 161 = ERROR_BAD_PATHNAME

program to SetLastError(300) (or any other value not documented as used in WINERROR.H) and then rebuild and run the program. You'll see that Windows NT 3.51 will report an error for the zero-length input string test, as it should, but it doesn't update the extended error value (not to be confused with incorrectly setting it to 0).

The sample program for this problem is in ZEN\CHAP14\GSPN. The main program merely calls GetShortPathName() with a variety of file specifications, including some common pathological cases, and displays the results. If you experiment with this program, you'll no doubt want to change some of the strings it passes to the DoGSPN() function, to account for differences between my directory and file setup and yours. (See listing 14.2 for the complete source to GSPN.CPP.)

## Listing 14.2   GSPN.CPP

```cpp
#include <windows.h>
#include <stdio.h>

//#define do_wrapped 1

BOOL  DirExists(const char *dn);
BOOL  FileExists(const char *fn);
DWORD uGetShortPathName(LPCTSTR long_path,LPTSTR buffer,DWORD buffer_len);
void  DoGSPN(char *old_path);

int main()
{
  DoGSPN("c:\\temp dir\\test.txt");            // Dir and file exist
  DoGSPN("c:\\temp dir\\file not there.txt");  // Dir exists, file doesn't
  DoGSPN("c:\\temp dir2");                      // Dir doesn't exist
  DoGSPN("c:\\temp dir2\\file not there.txt"); // Dir doesn't exist
  DoGSPN("z:\\readme.txt");                     // Drive doesn't exist
  DoGSPN("z:\\");                               // Drive doesn't exist
  DoGSPN("");                                   // Null input
  DoGSPN(NULL);                                 // Pathological case

  printf("\nPress Enter... ");
  getchar();
  return 0;
}

/////////////////////////////////////////////////////////////////////////

void DoGSPN(char *old_path)
{
  char buffer[MAX_PATH] = "";
  DWORD rc = 0;
  DWORD gle = 0;;

  SetLastError(0);

#ifdef do_wrapped
  rc = uGetShortPathName(old_path,buffer,sizeof(buffer));
```

```
#else
  rc = GetShortPathName(old_path,buffer,sizeof(buffer));
#endif

  gle = GetLastError();

#ifdef do_wrapped
  printf("uGetShortPathName(");
#else
  printf("GetShortPathName(");
#endif

  if(old_path == NULL)
    printf("NULL");
  else
    printf("\"%s\"",old_path);

  printf(") says it ");

  if(rc != 0)
    printf("succeeded\n");
  else
    printf("failed\n");

  printf("  output buffer = \"%s\", rc = %d, GLE() = %d\n",buffer,rc,gle);
}

/////////////////////////////////////////////////////////////////////////////

DWORD uGetShortPathName(LPCTSTR long_path,LPTSTR buffer,DWORD buffer_len)
{
#ifdef _DEBUG
  if((long_path == NULL) || (buffer == NULL))
    {
      OutputDebugString("\nuGetShortPathName: Detected bad parameter!\n\n");
      return TRUE;
    }
#endif

  // This also catches the zero-length and NULL ptr cases
  if(FileExists(long_path) || DirExists(long_path))
    {
      SetLastError(0);
      return GetShortPathName(long_path,buffer,buffer_len);
    }
  else
    {
      if((long_path == NULL) || (strlen(long_path) == 0))
        SetLastError(ERROR_BAD_PATHNAME);
      else
        SetLastError(ERROR_PATH_NOT_FOUND);

      return 0;
    }
}

/////////////////////////////////////////////////////////////////////////////

BOOL FileExists(const char *fn)
{
```

```
  if(fn == NULL || (strlen(fn)) == 0)
    return FALSE;

  DWORD dwFA = GetFileAttributes(fn);

  if(dwFA == 0xFFFFFFFF)
    return FALSE;
  else
    return ((dwFA & FILE_ATTRIBUTE_DIRECTORY) != FILE_ATTRIBUTE_DIRECTORY);
}

/////////////////////////////////////////////////////////////////////////

BOOL DirExists(const char *dn)
{
  if(dn == NULL || (strlen(dn)) == 0)
    return FALSE;

  DWORD dwFA = GetFileAttributes(dn);

  if(dwFA == 0xFFFFFFFF)
    return FALSE;
  else
    return ((dwFA & FILE_ATTRIBUTE_DIRECTORY) == FILE_ATTRIBUTE_DIRECTORY);
}
```

As always, there's the question of what to do about this situation. And once again, I think the best answer, assuming there's even a slim chance that your public program will be run on both Windows 95 and Windows NT (or Win32s), is to resort to a wrapper function that smoothes over the cracks between the variations, such as uGetShortPathName(), as shown in listing 14.2.

## Building the Samples: GSPN

**CD Location:** ZEN\CHAP14\GSPN

**Platform:** Win32

**Build instructions:** See the comments in the main() function in GSPN.CPP about changing the strings passed to DoGSPN(), and using the do_gspn symbol to control the program's execution. Build the program normally with the provided .MAK file and Visual C++ 2.2.

This sort of "unifying wrapper function" can be tricky to write, because its primary goal is to eliminate all the differences in the Win32 platforms. (In effect, you want to hold it to the same standard of uniformity that we all wish Win32 met in the first place.) In uGetShortPathName(), I've taken the following approach:

- Make sure all obviously bad input is detected and treated in a rational way. uGetShortPathName() checks for a long path name pointer that's NULL or points to a zero-length string, and returns a value of zero and an extended error of ERROR_BAD_PATHNAME in those cases.

- If the path name indicates either an existing directory or an existing file name, then let the real GetShortPathName() do its thing, and bucket-brigade the return value to the caller. For the sake of completeness, I did a SetLastError(0) just before calling the real API, although it's probably not needed.

- If the long path name is non-NULL and it points to a non-zero-length string, then return zero and set the extended error value to ERROR_PATH_NOT_FOUND. This is a generalization, since the real problem could be a file that's not found (for example, the caller passes in "c:\long dir\my stuff.doc", and the directory "c:\long dir" exists but it doesn't contain a file or directory named "my stuff.doc"). There's no easy answer here, since there's no way to tell what the caller was trying to accomplish and what the long path name was meant to hold. Notice that Windows 95 and Windows NT disagree on whether this case is a not-found path or a not-found file. Even if you can't tell which one it is, picking one answer and sticking with it is better than using different answers for no valid reason.

## Registry Datatypes

If you look into the SharedDLLs feature in the Windows 95 registry, you'll find that it's supposed to be a place to keep usage counts for system-wide shared DLLs. The idea is that an installation program is supposed to increment the count for a given DLL at application installation time, and decrement the count at uninstall time. (Whether this is a good idea or not is another issue entirely, and one that I've discussed elsewhere in this book. See the sidebar "Standards are for Wimps" in Chapter 6.)

Unfortunately, you have to be prepared for SharedDLLs entries that are the wrong datatype. The really nasty detail is how RegQueryValueEx() works. It will read any datatype, and it returns the data, plus a datatype field that your program should consult. If the registry has a SharedDLLs (or other entry) in string format, and you're expecting a REG_DWORD, for example, then this API will still read the value (it can't read your mind, of course, and there's no way for you to tell it what datatype you're expecting). It's very easy to get careless when calling this API and not check the returned datatype on a successful read. And it's even legal to pass a NULL for the lpdwType parameter, which tells RegQueryValueEx() not to return the datatype. However it happens, you (and your users) can be in for quite a surprise and some long debugging sessions if you treat the first four bytes of a returned string as a DWORD, increment them, and then write them back to the registry.

Lest you think I'm being paranoid, look at the code below and ask yourself if you'd question anything about it if you saw it in some real world application. (Notice that this code snippet isn't on the CD ROM for a very good reason: I don't want you to run it; I'm presenting it solely as a negative example.) This code runs fine, and it's diligent about checking return values, so it looks just peachy, right? Well, it isn't, since it assumes the registry value is the expected datatype and naively reuses the field the_type, since it's sitting around with the (presumed) proper value. Use this code on a string registry value, and you'll find out that it does a simply wonderful job of mangling your data.

Admittedly, this item isn't in the same category as most of the others in this chapter, since it's clearly not a compatibility issue or a bug in any version of Windows. But it's just as clearly something to be concerned about whenever your program is reading or writing a registry entry that it didn't create in its current execution.

```c
// Negative example!!! Do not use!!!

BOOL IncSharedDLLsCounter(char *name)
{
  char *key = "Software\\Microsoft\\Windows\\CurrentVersion\\SharedDLLs";
  HKEY the_key;
  DWORD the_type;
  DWORD buffer;
  BOOL return_value = FALSE;

  if(RegOpenKeyEx(HKEY_LOCAL_MACHINE,key,0,KEY_ALL_ACCESS,&the_key) == _
     ERROR_SUCCESS)
    {
    unsigned long buffer_len = sizeof(buffer);
    if(RegQueryValueEx(the_key,name,0,&the_type,
      (unsigned char *)buffer,&buffer_len) == ERROR_SUCCESS)
       {
         buffer++;
       if(RegSetValueEx(the_key,name,0,the_type,(unsigned char *)buffer,
           sizeof(DWORD)) == ERROR_SUCCESS)
         return_value = TRUE;
        else
         Complain("Set value failed!");
       }
     else
      Complain("Query value failed!");

    RegCloseKey(the_key);
    }
  else
   Complain("Couldn't open key!");

  return return_value;
}
```

## *WNetGetUniversalName() Fails under Windows 95*

Universal names are drive-letter-independent names for files and other system devices, and they're of the general form:

```
\\server\sharename\path\file
```

where server is the server name, share name is typically a name for a disk, and path and file are normal directory and file specifiers. For example, the universal name for a file on the C: drive of one of my test computers is:

```
\\Midwest p75\mwp75_c\temp\barney.txt
```

where "\\Midwest p75" is the computer's server name, "mwp75_c" is the share name for the root of that computer's C: drive, and "temp\barney.txt" is simply a directory and file name.

Before the arrival of Windows 95, many users seldom saw universal names, since they always mapped networked drives to letters, so they saw the above file name as H:\temp\barney.txt, for example. But now that you can directly access networked files through Explorer without first mapping them to drive letters, we'll all see quite a bit more of them. Still, simple stuff.

As you would expect, Windows 95 provides a way for you to translate the drive-mapped version of a file name to the unmapped, universal version. That method is the API WNetGetUniversalName(). Unfortunately, it never works under Windows 95. It always fails with both a return value and an extended error code of 1200 (ERROR_BAD_DEVICE).

Microsoft has acknowledged this bug in their PSS article Q131416, and they provide a way to mimic the function of this API. Their solution is the GetUniversalName() function shown below. Notice that this function is not quite ready for production use, since it assumes that the supplied output buffer is large enough to hold the returned universal name, but it's close enough to give you an idea of what's needed to work around this bug until it's fixed. (Of course, even after it's fixed your public programs will still have to be prepared for this situation; there will certainly be people running the August 24, 1995 version of Windows 95 well into the 21st century.)

I've provided a minimal sample program, GETUNC, that uses Microsoft's GetUniversalName() function and the WNetGetUniversalName() API to demonstrate this problem.

## Building the Samples: GETUNC

**CD Location:** ZEN\CHAP14\GETUNC

**Platform:** Win32

**Build instructions:** See the comments in GETUNC.CPP about changing the variable "fn" to something more appropriate for your system. Build the program normally with the provided .MAK file and Visual C++ 2.2.

```
// Function Name: GetUniversalName
//
// Parameters:     szUniv  - contains the UNC equivalent of szDrive
//                             upon completion
//
//                 szDrive - contains a drive based path
//
// Return value:   TRUE if successful, otherwise FALSE
//
// Comments:       This function assumes that szDrive contains a
//                 valid drive based path.
//
//                 For simplicity, this code assumes szUniv points
//                 to a buffer large enough to accomodate the UNC
//                 equivalent of szDrive.

BOOL GetUniversalName( char szUniv[], char szDrive[] )
{
  // get the local drive letter
  char chLocal = toupper( szDrive[0] );

  // cursory validation
  if ( chLocal < 'A' || chLocal > 'Z' )
    return FALSE;

  if ( szDrive[1] != ':' || szDrive[2] != '\\' )
    return FALSE;

  HANDLE hEnum;
  DWORD dwResult = WNetOpenEnum( RESOURCE_CONNECTED, RESOURCETYPE_DISK,
                                 0, NULL, &hEnum );

  if ( dwResult != NO_ERROR )
    return FALSE;

  // request all available entries
  const int    c_cEntries   = 0xFFFFFFFF;
  // start with a reasonable buffer size
  DWORD        cbBuffer      = 50 * sizeof( NETRESOURCE );
  NETRESOURCE *pNetResource = (NETRESOURCE*) malloc( cbBuffer );

  BOOL fResult = FALSE;

  while ( TRUE )
   {
     DWORD dwSize   = cbBuffer,
           cEntries = c_cEntries;

     dwResult = WNetEnumResource( hEnum, &cEntries, pNetResource,
                                  &dwSize );

     if ( dwResult == ERROR_MORE_DATA )
      {
        // the buffer was too small, enlarge
        cbBuffer = dwSize;
        pNetResource = (NETRESOURCE*) realloc( pNetResource, cbBuffer );
        continue;
      }

     if ( dwResult != NO_ERROR )
       goto done;
```

```
            // search for the specified drive letter
            for ( int i = 0; i < (int) cEntries; i++ )
              if ( pNetResource[i].lpLocalName &&
                   chLocal == toupper(pNetResource[i].lpLocalName[0]) )
                {
                  // match
                  fResult = TRUE;

                  // build a UNC name
                  strcpy( szUniv, pNetResource[i].lpRemoteName );
                  strcat( szUniv, szDrive + 2 );
                  _strupr( szUniv );
                  goto done;
                }
          }

done:
    // cleanup
    WNetCloseEnum( hEnum );
    free( pNetResource );

    return fResult;

}
```

## cbWndExtra and cbClsExtra Limits

No, you're not experiencing *deja vu*, this is basically the same item from Chapter 12. I mention it again here, because it's also an issue with various Win32 platforms. Windows 95 rejects a RegisterClass() API call that specifies either a cbWndExtra or cbClassExtra setting of more than 40 bytes, but Windows NT 3.51 and Win32s 1.30 will accept and process the call normally. (That's right—this is one of the relatively few cases where Win32s sides with Windows NT instead of Windows 95.) See Microsoft's PSS article Q131288 for more details.

I've provided a Win32 version of the WNDEXT16 program, which you can use to experiment with this phenomenon.

## Building the Samples: WNDEXT32

**CD Location:** ZEN\CHAP14\WNDEXT32

**Platform:** Win32

**Build instructions:** See the comments in WNDEXT32.C for notes on the various ways to build the program. Then build the program normally with the provided .MAK file and Visual C++ 2.2.

## Version 4.0 Dialogs Scale Differently

This item isn't just a difference between Win32 platforms, but a difference in how the current Win32 platforms treat applications with different versions, as well.

Create a Win32 application with a subsystem version number of 3.1, and its dialogs will have the familiar, Windows 3.1-style: no 3D effect, white background by default, and a bold default font. Change the subsystem version of that same application to 4.0, however, and under Windows 95 it gets the new Windows 95-style dialogs: 3D effect controls, default gray background, and a non-bold font. Windows NT 3.51 now gives the program a gray background and the non-bold font, and Win32s treats the program as it would a version 3.1 program, at least in this respect.

Issues of esthetics aside, why do you care? Simple: The Windows 95-style non-bold font is a bit smaller than the bold font it replaces, which means the same dialog box will be different sizes (measured in pixels) depending on the application's version number.

For example, I wrote a trivial Win32 program, dlg32, that uses a dialog box for its main interface, and made it display the physical size of its client window upon startup (as reported by GetClientRect()). Built as a version 3.1 program, this program produced a 278 by 150 pixel client area. As a version 4.0 program, its client area was 324 by 150 pixels.

Since Windows 95 allows the user to change the appearance of just about every visual element, it's more important than ever that your program make no assumptions whatsoever about things like the height of a window's caption bar, the width of scroll bars, etc., nor should it use hard-wired locations for dynamically creating or placing controls and drawing bitmaps. Such assumptions have always been extremely bad practice in Windows programming, now they're virtually guaranteed to cause havoc in a public program.

When your program crosses the "version 4.0 line," it could also encounter some unexpected text formatting changes in static controls, as shown in Figure 14.6. The only way to be sure that you won't stumble into such problems is to display every single dialog box in your application on every platform and version that it will allow itself to run under, which changes the appearance of programs. Since it could be quite a chore to reproduce the conditions necessary to cause a large application to display all its dialog boxes, you might want to consider writing a test program that uses the same resource files as your main application and does

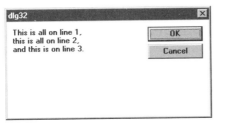
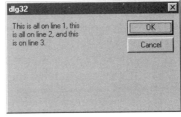

**Figure 14.6  The Shape of Things that Came: Version 3.1 and 4.0 dialog treatments.**

nothing but display all the dialog boxes one at a time. This would allow you to check for formatting errors, but not logic errors (such as dialog box code that draws a bitmap at a fixed location without scaling the coordinates). Depending on the application, it might even make sense to write a test program that exercises each dialog and its supporting code, just as they are used in the original program.

## Icon, Icon, Who's Got My Icon?

This is yet another of the many small mysteries of Windows 95 programming. Use Visual C++ 2.2 to create a brand new Win32 MFC program that uses a dialog box as its main interface. Use AppWizard, and let Visual C++ create and set up everything for you, without the slightest bit of customization. (In other words, build a new, do-nothing application exactly the way that tools vendors love to demo their development environments.) Then build the program and run it under Windows 95, and you'll see that it doesn't have an icon on its task bar button or its caption bar. Run the same program under Windows NT 3.51, and it has the normal, default "AFX" icon when minimized. You can run the DROP2 sample program from Chapter 7 to see this effect, or you can experiment with this chapter's NOICON sample.

There was some discussion about this situation before Windows 95 shipped, but, as I mentioned in Chapter 7, it seemed to boil down to whether a program has the WS_CAPTION and WS_SYSMENU styles. If it does, it gets the icon on its task bar button. If it doesn't, it doesn't. Or at least that's what someone in Microsoft's Developer Support group said. As it turns out, it's not quite that simple.

If your dialog has the "thin" border style, then it will get task bar and caption bar icons if it also has the WS_CAPTION and WS_SYSMENU styles. The dialog will get a dialog-style system menu in this case, that has just the "Move" and "Close" entries. (This is the state I left the NOICON sample program in, by the way.)

If your dialog has a "resizing" border, WS_THICKFRAME style, plus the other two styles, WS_CAPTION and WS_SYSMENU, it will get a task bar icon, and it will have a window style system menu with the "Restore," "Move," "Size," "Minimize," "Maximize," and "Close" entries.

If your dialog has a "Dialog Frame" border, DS_MODALFRAME style, which is the Visual C++ 2.2 default, then it won't get the task bar icon, even if it uses the WS_CAPTION and WS_SYSMENU styles.

Everything I've just said about styles and icons applies to all applications under Windows 95, even Win16 programs, and those with version numbers less than 4.0.

If your program has the right style and its version number is less than 4.0, then it will display the expected icon from its embedded resources. If its version number is 4.0, then by default it will get the familiar Windows icon (the four-color flag trimmed in black). In this case, your program can use the new-for-Windows 95 message WM_SETICON to tap Windows 95 on the shoulder and tell it which icon to use. The OnInitDialog() method for the main dialog interface in NOICON does this with a one-liner:

```
BOOL CNoiconDlg::OnInitDialog()
{
    CDialog::OnInitDialog();
    CenterWindow();

    // TODO: Add extra initialization here
    PostMessage(WM_SETICON,(WPARAM)TRUE,(LPARAM)m_hIcon);

    return TRUE;  // return TRUE  unless you set the focus to a control
}
```

All this missing-icon and which-icon-do-I-get silliness is a minor issue, but it sure can make your program look odd, and for no valid reason. For all the convoluted things that Windows 95 does with version checking, this is one time when you would expect it to make an exception—that is, programs tagged 4.0 would be subject to all the new icon rules, including the one about when a program's task bar button and caption bar get an icon, while pre-4.0 programs would still play by the old rules. (In fact, Microsoft got halfway there—Win32/3.1 programs will get the proper icon, assuming they get one at all.) Most interesting, I think, is the fact that if you played by all the official compatibility rules, generated your Win32 application with Microsoft's compiler and Wizards, and didn't get within a hundred miles of an undocumented feature or even customized the generated code, your program can *still* require a change to look right under Windows 95. Not to mention the fact that pre-existing Win16 programs can be affected, as well. Kinda makes one question the value of living a good, clean life.

## Building the Samples: NOICON

**CD Location:** ZEN\CHAP14\NOICON

**Platform:** Win32

**Build instructions:** Use the provided .MAK file with Visual C++ 2.2 and compile normally. You can experiment with various dialog styles and version numbers to reproduce various effects. (You'll need a copy of LINK.EXE from Visual C++ version 2.0 to set a version number lower than 4.0, however.) The WM_SETICON message is used in the OnInitDialog() method in the file NOICODLG.CPP.

I've included several pre-built versions of NOICON in the directory ZEN\CHAP14\NOICON:

NOCION0.EXE: Version 3.1, uses "dialog frame" style interface

NOICON1.EXE: Version 3.1, uses "thin" style interface

NOICON2.EXE: Version 4.0, uses "dialog frame" style interface

NOICON3.EXE: Version 4.0, uses "thin" style interface, without WM_SETICON message

NOICON4.EXE: Version 4.0, uses "thin" style interface, with WM_SETICON message

## Graphics Paths Are Defunctionalized under Windows 95

Graphics paths are a useful, if somewhat arcane, GDI feature set that allows you to stack up several drawing commands before actually making them display on a device context or doing other things with them, such as converting them to regions. I won't try to explain all the ins and outs of paths here; if you have access to the *Microsoft Developer Network* CD ROM (and you should, if you're developing Windows programs), I suggest you check out some of its articles on paths (search on the keyword "beginpath").

For our purposes, the point is that a path remembers the GDI drawing calls you make after you call the BeginPath() API and until you call EndPath(). At least it will under Windows NT. Under Windows 95, it will only remember calls to the following eleven functions: ExtTextOut(), LineTo(), MoveToEx(), PolyBezier(), PolyBezierTo(), Polygon(), Polyline(), PolylineTo(), PolyPolygon(), PolyPolyline(), and TextOut(). Put another way, the following GDI calls are excluded from a path under Windows 95 (but they're included under Windows NT): Arc(), Chord(), Ellipse(), Pie(), Rectangle(), and RoundRect(). These lists were taken directly from Microsoft's PSS document Q125697; I didn't test every GDI call to see if it was pathable or not. (Other GDI calls, including AngleArc() and PolyDraw(), are pathable under Windows NT, but aren't supported at all under Windows 95.)

If your application uses paths, then you have to be extremely careful, since there's no way that your program can tell that it's tried to use a non-pathable GDI call in a path. Your compiler can't possibly warn you, and you get no indication from the GDI call itself. This can result in some very subtle bugs, or, as Figure 14.7 shows, some not so subtle ones. That figure shows the PATHS sample that Microsoft ships on their *Developer Network* CD. I commented out the few lines in the program that check on startup to see if it's running under Windows NT and bails out if it isn't. As you can see, there's a darn good reason for it to perform the check.

This particular problem is just about impossible to catch since there doesn't seem to be a way to check if a given GDI call is being made between a BeginPath() and an EndPath() pair of calls. (I tried the obvious—making a second BeginPath() call, but it blithely returns TRUE, indicating success.) There's probably some truly hideous and undocumented way of detecting this condition, but I haven't found it yet. If you know of one, please drop me a line.

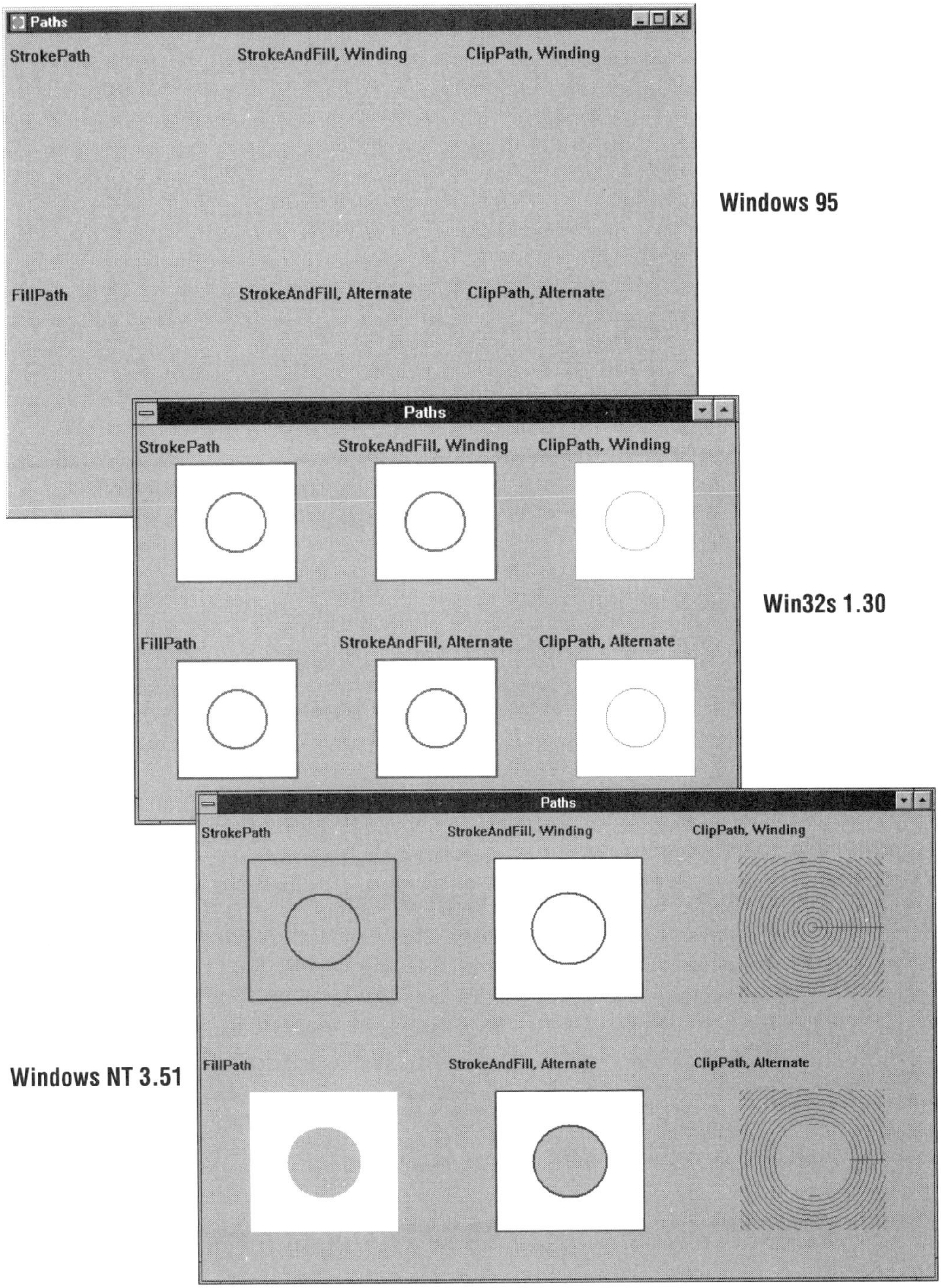

Figure 14.7   Paths under Win32.

As is so often the case in programming, your last line of defense in this area, your own diligence, is your only line of defense. That's not my favorite advice to give any programmer, since I know that we all have off days and forget minutiae, like exactly which GDI calls are pathable on which platforms, but this is the best we have to work with. Better would be some debugging tool that would always catch this error (the Windows 95 debugging kernel doesn't flag this situation). Best of all would be for the path support to work under Windows 95 and Win32s as it does under Windows NT, of course.

*Actually, I lied, and there is one other way to attack this problem: Use a wrapper library. The BeginPath() wrapper could set a "we're in a path" flag that's local to the wrapper library, and the wrappers for all GDI functions that are pathable only under Windows NT could report failure if the flag is set and the program isn't running under Windows NT. Of course, the EndPath() wrapper would clear the flag. The problem is that this arrangement would create the possibility of a "false positive" error report, since a program could start a path by calling the BeginPath() wrapper, and then (accidentally) directly call the bare EndPath() API. That would leave the flag set and trigger a false alarm when the program next called any GDI function that is pathable only under Windows NT. This isn't a fatal drawback to using wrappers to patch this particular hole, though, and depending on your project's needs, you might want to consider it, at least during testing.*

## GetSysColor() Can't Fail (or Can It?)

I won't rehash the whole GetSysColor() saga, but let me remind you that because of its interface definition, this function has no unambiguous way to indicate a failure or that an invalid parameter was passed to it. As a result, your Win32 program can pass this function one of its Windows 95-only constants under Win32s, and get back a value of 0, which is apparently GetSysColor()'s failure mode. The problem is that this mode of failure is indistinguishable from the return value for black, which could lead to your program using some interesting, not to mention wildly inaccurate, colors. (See Chapter 10 for a complete description of GetSysColor() and this situation.)

## Win32s Gets Lost in too Much Virtual Memory

You've probably heard the old programmer's adage that you can never be too rich, too thin, or have too much RAM, hard disk space, or processing power. Well,

Win32s 1.30 proved us wrong on at least one count, virtual memory. The shipping version of Win32s 1.30 has a problem with too much virtual memory, and it can refuse to run a program and report an error code of 21.

The workaround offered by Microsoft is to make sure that the PageOverCommit value in the user's SYSTEM.INI file isn't too large. Specifically, Microsoft says that the setting for this value should be such that the expression:

```
(PageOverCommit + 1) * megabytes of RAM < 256
```

is true. They also said that if the left side of this calculation is exactly 256, then an application "may or may not load, depending on the app."

The default value for PageOverCommit is four, which means you have to have a *lot* of RAM before you'll run into this problem. (Yes, this will probably date this book horribly in a few years, but as of this writing, 64MB of RAM is still quite a handful of chips. Probably makes those of you reading this from your lofty perch of the year 2003 wonder how the heck we ever got anything done on these pathetic, wimpy, underpowered doorstops we called computers.) But this also leads to an interesting situation—if a user has a PageOverCommit value of eight, say, which will trigger the problem with 32MB of RAM (the amount or RAM in my main system, in fact), then there's probably a reason why the user or some other program has set that value, and changing it to accommodate Win32s 1.30 will likely trigger other problems, which makes this situation an excellent example of how programs can compete for control of some detail of the user's configuration.

Microsoft also said that users with more than 128MB of RAM will not be able to use this PageOverCommit workaround, and will have to wait for the official fix, which will be in Win32s 1.30a.

I haven't provided a sample program for this item, since you can demonstrate it with any Win32 program. Just make sure you have Win32s 1.30 installed on a Windows 3.1(1) system, and then change the PageOverCommit setting in the [386enh] section of your SYSTEM.INI file, restart Windows, and try to run a Win32 program. If you attempt to run the program from Program Manager, you'll get a dialog box telling you that the program failed with the error code 21; Central Point's File Manager simply tells you that the program couldn't be run, and it doesn't even give you the error code. (I mention this because it's an interesting example of how the Windows infrastructure can let you down. Win32s incorrectly refuses to run your program, and a third-party file manager provides insufficient information about the situation, leaving you, or possibly one of your users, wondering what happened, and reasonably concluding that there's something wrong with the application when it's perfectly innocent.)

The bottom line is obvious: If you're distributing a Win32s program to unknown computers, you can't include Win32s 1.30 with your package. If you do, your program will eventually find its way onto computers that didn't already have the Win32s support installed, but have the "right" configuration to trigger this problem. And that means problems for your users and support headaches for you.

## Win32s + Richedit Controls = Train Wreck

Besides the normal editing tasks, one of the most basic and necessary functions that a multi-line edit control has to support is telling the world if the text in the control has been modified. The new richedit common control is supported under Win32s 1.30, but its support for the EM_GETMODIFY message is broken. This means there's no supported way for the richedit control's owner to query the control to find out if its contents should be saved.

In normal practice, an application sends the EM_GETMODIFY message to the richedit control, and receives a return value of TRUE if the text buffer has been modified, FALSE if not:

```
if(SendMessage(IDC_RICHEDIT,EM_GETMODIFY,0,0))
  {
  /* Do "buffer modified" processing */
  }
```

Under Win32s 1.30 this call always returns FALSE.

The RICHED sample shows this behavior. Run it, type some text into the edit box, and experiment with the "Modified?," "Clear Modified," and "Set Modified" buttons and see what happens. Under Windows 95 and Windows NT 3.51, you'll get the expected results—type some text and the "Modified?" button says that things changed, the "Clear Modified" button will reset the modified state of the control, and "Set Modified" will set it, even if you haven't made any new changes to the text. Not very exciting, but then it's not supposed to be. Run this program under Win32s 1.30, and it never knows when the text buffer is modified, even when you've sent it an explicit message with the "Set Modified" button that tells it to set the flag for the buffer.

I didn't test the support (or lack thereof) that richedit controls provide for every single EM_* message. But after hearing some comments from other programmers on CompuServe that "none" of these messages were supported under Win32s 1.30, I decided to check a few, and found that:

- EM_SETBKGNDCOLOR, which the shipping Win32 SDK documents as "New - Windows NT" but then says in the QuickInfo popup is not supported under Windows NT or Win32s, does indeed work on these platforms as well as on Windows 95.

- EM_SETLIMITTEXT is documented in the SDK as working under Windows 95 and Windows NT, but not Win32s. This is correct, according to my tests with Win32s 1.30 and Windows NT 3.51. EM_EXLIMITTEXT, which, like EM_SETBKGNDCOLOR, the SDK says is new for Windows NT but not supported in Windows NT or Win32s, works under all three Win32 platforms.

- EM_UNDO, the message used to undo the last editing change, doesn't work under Win32s, even though the SDK says it does. At least we get a minimal break on this one, in that EM_CANUNDO, the message used to ask if the control can perform an undo, always returns FALSE under Win32s. This means that a well-behaved application program can set options appropriately and not promise the user an undo operation that it can't deliver.

- EM_SETREADONLY and EM_GETLINECOUNT, which the SDK documents as working on all three Win32 platforms, don't work under Win32s 1.30. (Not only won't a richedit control under Win32s tell you if its text buffer has been modified via the most obvious and convenient method (EM_GETMODIFY), but it won't even tell you how many lines of text it contains; the return value is always 0. This discovery was what prompted me to characterize richedit controls under Win32s as a train wreck.)

I left all the code in place to experiment with these messages. See the comments in the file RICHEDLG.CPP in the RICHED sample for details.

Microsoft does document some edit control messages that are not supported for rich edit controls, but they don't include any of the messages I mentioned above. See the Win32 SDK topic titled "Unsupported Edit Control Functionality" (search on "EM_SETBKGNDCOLOR").

## Building the Samples: RICHED

**CD Location:** ZEN\CHAP14\RICHED

**Platform:** Win32

**Build instructions:** Use the provided .MAK file with Visual C++ 2.2 and compile normally. Run the program under Win32 1.30, Windows 95, and Windows NT 3.51 and play with the buttons.

See the commented-out code in the OnCreate() method in RICHEDLG.CPP for some other messages you can experiment with.

### Richedit Controls Don't Send EN_CHANGE by Default

This one isn't a bug, but it's just counterintuitive enough that you could lose a couple of hours trying to unravel it, especially in light of the EM_GETMODIFY problem mentioned in the previous item.

As we all know, child controls sometimes send their parents messages triggered by various events. One of the most familiar notification message is EN_CHANGE, which edit controls send to indicate that their text buffer has been changed. Since richedit controls won't handle EM_GETMODIFY properly under Win32s, your only recourse in a Win32 program that will run on that platform is to look for EN_CHANGE messages and set a BOOL every time one comes through, then clear the flag when you save or delete the edit control's contents. (In other words, you have to do manually what the edit control should be doing for you.) Not exactly elegant, but it will get the job done.

Once you set up the plumbing to field the EN_CHANGE messages, you're likely to trip over a little surprise: The messages won't show up unless you explicitly tell the richedit control to send them. That's right, unlike their less capable siblings, richedit controls by default do not send EN_CHANGE messages.

The fix is a one-liner:

```
SendMessage(hWnd_RTF,EM_SETEVENTMASK,0,ENM_CHANGE);
```

You can find this line in the RICHED sample, in the OnCreate() method in the file RICHEDLG.CPP. Notice that the flag used in the EM_SETEVENTMASK message is ENM_CHANGE, *not* EN_CHANGE, which is a message code. The RICHED sample sends this message to the richedit control, and then fields EN_CHANGE messages and beeps on each one, just to show that they're really getting through. If you comment out the SendMessage() line that enables the EN_CHANGE messages and rebuild RICHED, the beeps will go away.

Note that the Win32 SDK is incorrect in its documentation of this API—the QuickInfo popup says that this message is not supported under Windows NT and Win32s, when it is in fact supported under Windows NT 3.51 and Win32s 1.30.

## Windows 95 Doesn't Do MoveFileEx()

MoveFileEx() is documented as not being supported under Windows 95, and based on my testing, this is correct. Try to call it, and it returns FALSE, and sets an extended error code of 120 (ERROR_CALL_NOT_IMPLEMENTED), as is normal practice for stubbed APIs.

This situation deserves a little special attention and explanation, because MoveFileEx() is also the Windows NT mechanism for deleting or replacing a file, such as a DLL, that's currently in use by the system. The process is simple—your program issues a MoveFileEx() call with the source and destination file names, and specifies the MOVEFILE_DELAY_UNTIL_REBOOT flag. When the system reboots, the rename operation (which could really be a file deletion, if the destination filename was passed as a NULL pointer) is performed. This is why some installation and uninstallation procedures require you to reboot your system, even though they don't change your system files.

Since Windows 95 doesn't support MoveFileEx(), you need another mechanism to rename, replace, or delete an in-use file. That mechanism is the

WININIT.INI file. Your program adds entries to this file that describe the actions to be taken, and then at reboot time your wishes are granted. Microsoft documents this in their PSS article Q129532. (I really wish they had also documented this facility in the same help topic with MoveFileEx(), but that's another issue.) The examples Microsoft shows in Q129532 are:

```
[rename]
NUL=C:\TEMP.TXT
C:\NEW_DIR\EXISTING.TXT=C:\EXISTING.TXT
C:\NEW_DIR\NEWNAME.TXT=C:\OLDNAME.TXT
C:\EXISTING.TXT=C:\TEMP\NEWFILE.TXT
```

The first line causes TEMP.TXT to be deleted. The second line causes EXISTING.TXT to be moved to a new directory. The third line causes OLDNAME.TXT to be moved and renamed. The fourth line causes an existing file to be overwritten by NEWFILE.TXT.

It shouldn't surprise any of us that Windows NT doesn't support the WININIT.INI mechanism, so you can't resort to the obvious ploy and always use WININIT.INI and ignore the MoveFileEx() option. (That would have been far too easy.)

Note that because WININIT.EXE, which is the program that processes WININIT.INI at boot time, executes before the protected mode file system is loaded, you can only use aliases in WININIT.INI and not long file names.

# Recommendations

There's a lot of detail here, even though I'm sure that to date my Win32 research has only managed to uncover the tip of the tip of the iceberg. I think the most obvious and relevant question at this point is: What does this all mean for our programming projects? As a way of answering that question, let me provide a set of general recommendations that should help you shoot the Win32 rapids and emerge in one piece (or in as many pieces as you started).

1. Don't trust anything, not previous API behavior, not common sense, and not even the API documentation. If your public program will run under multiple Win32 platforms, you have to test all critical APIs under all versions of the operating system that your program will allow itself to be run on. Period. You don't have a choice. If you think this isn't necessary, look over some of the problems and documentation errors I reported in this chapter and Chapter 12 and honestly tell me (and yourself) how many of these problems you would have expected.

In particular, don't assume anything about GetLastError() return values. As you've seen, they vary from one platform to the next for the same API and context, and I've even found a case where an API won't even use SetLastError() on one platform when it will on the other.

Also, don't make any assumptions about any side effects, return values, or features that aren't clearly documented and committed to by Microsoft, unless you literally have no choice. Depending on any undocumented behavior (even if not a Big, Bad Undocumented API) has always been a very bad idea in any type of programming; in the brave new world of 32-bit Windows programming, it's like making your program play Russian Roulette with half the chambers loaded.

2. Seriously consider making your program refuse to run under Windows NT and Win32s. I know this sounds like a drastic step, and it is. But considering all the problems I was able to document, plus all the ones that I didn't know about or weren't able to verify in time for this book, creating one Win32 program that runs correctly under Windows 95 and Windows NT can be a nightmare. Even if you can do it, you have to squeeze under the lowest-common-denominator limbo bar.

In particular, Win32s is such a persistent mess that I think it should be used only under extreme circumstances, such as an overwhelming economic incentive. (And to be clear, being under the influence of an economic incentive is like being in love: If you have to ask if this applies to you, the answer is no, and if the answer is yes, no one is going to change your mind.) If you think this is an extreme stance, read over some of the Win32s issues I described in this chapter and review Microsoft's PSS articles about Win32s bugs and limitations, and then remind yourself that this is very likely only part of the problem. I shudder to think what else is lurking under the covers of Win32s that none of us have discovered yet.

Checking for Win32s as the operating system and bailing out is very simple, if you use my WIN32VER sample code. In fact, all you need is a carefully placed two-liner:

```
if(ComplainIfNot(WV_W95 | WV_AnyNY,"Sample program"))
  return FALSE;
```

and many of your problems will go away.

## Building the Samples: WIN32VER

**CD Location:** ZEN\CHAP14\WIN32VER

**Platform:** Win32

**Build instructions:** Use the provided .MAK file with Visual C++ 2.2 and compile normally. See the InitInstance() method in the file WVTEST.CPP for an example of how to call the provided support. (As written, the sample program will display several bogus dialog boxes no matter which Win32 platform it is run on, since it uses several calls to the WIN32VER support for demonstration purposes.)

If you find that you must support Win32s in a public program, then your only hope for retaining your sanity is to do the following:

- Check all available Microsoft documentation for news of Win32s issues throughout your development cycle, right up to your ship date. This includes their *Developer Network* CD and the Win32 SDK. As I wrote this chapter, Win32s 1.30.159 was the latest version that was available as a redistributable package and with full documentation, and it was decidedly dysfunctional.

- Decide on a single, exact version of Win32s that your program will run under, and make sure that it will run under only that version.

- Perform *all* testing under the chosen version of Win32s. It's extremely important that you exercise any public program as thoroughly as possible under Win32s if you're going to support it. If you beta test the program, find testers who are running the selected version of Win32s, and send them a version that will run under only that version (that is, not under Windows 95 or Windows NT or any other version of Win32s).

This last point deserves a little elaboration. No matter which operating systems you will officially support, you must take appropriate precautions to ensure that your program will run properly in those environments. Normally this isn't a difficult exercise, but Win32s makes it much trickier, thanks to its quirks. I honestly think that you must choose between performing a very rigorous test cycle under Win32s and making your program refuse to run under it.

3. If your program must run under more than one Win32 platform, then I strongly suggest you wrap any API function that has even a slim chance of causing you problems. Again, test everything, and be very skeptical. On second thought, leapfrog skeptical and go all the way to full-blown paranoid. Think in terms of CPCs (common pathological cases), and never forget that much of the data you hand over to API calls is directly or indirectly derived from unreliable sources including the user, other programs, .INI files, and Windows itself.

*Just in case you missed it, let me hammer the point home one last time: test, test, test, test (that's one "test" for each of the Win32 platforms, plus one for Win16, when appropriate). This applies whenever you're writing a Win32 application or using Windows 95 features, such as long file names, from a Win16 program. And one more thing: Don't forget to test.*

4. Avoid thunking like the plague. I've heard numerous complaints from programmers about the hassles of thunking. So many, in fact, that I have no significant personal experience in this area because I've managed to take my own advice and avoid it to date. If nothing else, remember that thunking is typically a short-term solution, and that a future version of your program will very likely not require thunking at all. If that appears to be where your project is headed in the long run, then make every attempt to avoid thunking and convert every relevant component to 32-bits now, and avoid the hassle and work that will only be thrown away.

Unfortunately this piece of advice is like telling people to avoid Win32s. Those that have to use this facility, *really* have to, usually for compelling economic reasons. And that means advice from me or anyone else to do otherwise will be ignored. Still, if you have a choice, I strongly urge you to avoid thunking.

I found it painful to write this set of recommendations. I had expected that by the end of 1995 Windows programming would have advanced to the point where such concerns no longer cast a doubt over our efforts. I never believed Microsoft's lofty claims, as expressed in the quote that opened this chapter (having been around the block a few too many times with Microsoft, IBM, and other companies of all sizes), but I sure expected them to come at least a little bit closer than they did.

# Windows NT 4.0 and Beyond: The Light at the End of the Tunnel?

I wrote this book in the gap between Windows 95 and Windows NT 4.0. In fact, when I started this book, the industry was still speculating about whether the "version of NT with the Windows 95 user interface" (a.k.a. VONTWTW95UI) would be version 3.52, 3.6, or 4.0.

For some time it was publicly known that Windows 95 and Windows NT would converge into a single product one or two releases after Windows 95. Given all the differences between Win32 variations, that would have given new, pyrotechnic meaning to the word "convergence." [Imagine a grainy, black-and-white film clip of two steam locomotives in a head-on collision.] Then, the September 11, 1995, issue of *InfoWorld* reported on page one that Jim Allchin, vice president of Microsoft's Business Systems division (which is responsible for Windows NT) said, "There will be no convergence, because there's no single product that can meet the needs of every kind of customer." They also quoted him as saying, "We expect to see Win95 and its successors broaden in the consumer market. Long term we want NT to be the standard for corporations on the desktop and server."

Why do we, as developers, care about all this marketing stuff? Simple: If Microsoft isn't going to converge the products, I think it's clear that there's just about zero probability that they'll converge the Win32 implementations to a single behavior. In other words, if Microsoft sticks with this plan as expressed by Allchin, we're very likely stuck with the differing interpretations of Win32 for a very long time.

Frankly, as soon as Microsoft decided to use two different development teams to create parallel versions of Windows, we all should have known what was coming. (I'm reminded of that old seamen's aphorism about never going to sea with two watches, because if you do you'll never be sure what time it is.) I fully expect that Windows NT 4.0 will closely mimic Windows NT 3.51 where it disagrees with Windows 95 and Win32s. I also expect that as Microsoft adds the currently Windows 95-only features, like the new shell, to Windows NT we'll only see the list of incompatibilities and quirks grow.

As for what will happen with the next two versions of Windows 95, code-named Nashville and Memphis, I won't even try to guess, except to observe that it will surely result in yet more adventures for developers.

For now, our best strategy is to bide our time, write wrapper functions and other workarounds as needed, and be diligent.

## And Then There Were Four

I bet that by now your head is spinning with all this talk of Win32 differences and quirks, not to mention wrappers. Unfortunately that's *still* not the end of the story, because IBM has decided to jump into the Win32 API business.

IBM has announced that they're adding something called the Developer API Extensions (DAPIE, formerly called DAX) to OS/2. This is *not* an emulation layer that will allow you to run Win32 programs under OS/2. In IBM's words (from *The Developer Connection News*, (their analog to the *Microsoft Developer Network News*), August 1995, page 5):

> Put simply, the Developer API Extensions for OS/2 are new APIs added to the operating system to provide, as the name implies, new programming interfaces. These interfaces are identical in interface to Win32 APIs. Over 700 APIs and 300 messages that correspond to those in the Win32 definition are being supported initially.

The article also says that the APIs will support common dialogs, GDI, window management, and "other system services, including Date and Time, Environment, File Input/Output, Memory Management, Module Management, Printing, Processes and Threads, Registry, and Resource Management." IBM says that the list of APIs was chosen after analyzing over 9 million lines of source code and receiving input from ISVs (independent software vendors).

IBM's goal is to make it much easier for someone to create one code base that can be used to build both native OS/2 and native Windows versions of a program, albeit after overcoming "some challenges in source code management." (I'm glad to see my old employer hasn't lost its knack for breathtaking understatement.)

You're probably wondering which version of Win32 DAPIE will mimic. I don't know the answer to that (as of this writing I doubt anyone outside IBM knows), but I fear and strongly suspect that the answer will be "a little of all three," creating a de facto fourth Win32 variation. (If Microsoft hasn't even documented the extended error codes and exact behavior of APIs that differ across the Win32 platforms, then how can IBM even figure out what the APIs are supposed to do?) There are also numerous questions about supporting the new features of Windows 95 (and soon, Windows NT 4.0). I'd be very surprised if IBM didn't create an OS/2 version of COMCTL32.DLL, for example. If they don't support these new features, then the Developer API Extensions will effectively be a small subset, and possibly a not very interesting one.

My point is not to take a cheap shot at my old employer, but to alert you to the existence of this porting tool and to point out how easily a good idea can turn into a tar pit. For example, there is no MFC on OS/2, to no one's surprise. (If you were Microsoft, would you license MFC to IBM so they could use it to make porting Windows applications to OS/2 easier? I sure wouldn't, at any price.) Without a common framework between the platforms, DAPIE is almost useless for porting newer Windows projects, since frameworks, and in particular MFC, are dominating Windows development.

But putting the framework issue aside, it's still quite likely that DAPIE will be a hybrid of Win32 behaviors, which makes it yet another reason to consider using a unifying wrapper library.

# Part 4

# *Resources*

# Chapter 15

# Lou's Top Tool Picks

# Lou's Top Tool Picks

Chapter 15

*Give us the tools, and we will finish the job.*

Winston Churchill

*Man is a tool-making animal.*

Benjamin Franklin

Recommending programming tools is a precarious activity, at best; it's the technical writer's equivalent of working without a net. Things change with such blinding speed in this market that the well considered, insightful, possibly even brilliant recommendations you make on Monday can look like the ravings of a drunk fool by the middle of Wednesday afternoon. Them's the breaks.

Despite this risk, I think it's worthwhile to make such recommendations as long as we all keep the following points in mind:

1. I've used all these tools first-hand and found them to be worth recommending. The somewhat more interesting flip side of this mundane point is that I can't possibly use all the development tools available today; there are no doubt items in this chapter that will make you wonder how in the world I could have recommended product X, when "everyone" knows that product Y is better. The answer is very likely that I never used product Y (possibly because the vendor failed to supply a review copy, which has happened more times on this project than you would believe), or maybe I did use Y and I found enough drawbacks or specific problems with it that I felt it didn't deserve a recommendation, or maybe not "everyone" agrees that Y is better than X. In case you missed the distinction, let me stress that selecting a tool for my own use is one thing, selecting one for recommendation is a whole other issue, and I hold products to a much higher standard in that regard.

2. I won't tell you about the products I've evaluated and rejected. I have mixed feelings about this; the militant consumer advocate in me *really* wants to tell you about some of the phenomenally bad products I wrestled with while writing this book, as well as some of the brain-dead customer (non-)service departments out there that won't even answer e-mail or reply to CompuServe messages. I could tell you dozens of horror stories about non-existent or dreadful support, and I'm sure it would feel oh so good to tell those stories in print. But I also realize that once such comments are in print, especially in a book, they're in print forever, which means there's a distinct chance that a product or customer (non-)service department that gave me fits will get their act together. And I really don't like the thought of my book and their new and improved version 2.0 (or support department) being on the shelf at the same time, with my book apparently warning readers to stay away from a genuinely good product. No matter how careful I am in identifying version numbers, this danger is still real, and it's a risk I don't care to take.

It's often enlightening to consider life as a series of impromptu IQ tests, especially when people, companies, or institutions fail them miserably. In this light, one aspect of working on this book was both fascinating and frustrating. I ran into numerous software vendors who couldn't even answer the simplest technical support or marketing question, even though they realized I was working on a book and considering their product for possible recommendation. ("Will there be a Windows 95 version of this product?" turned out to be quite a stumper.) A few wouldn't even reply to repeated e-mail requests, including one company that provides technical support only through e-mail. (I'll give you three guesses if their product got a recommendation, and the first two guesses don't count.)

No, I won't tell you which companies were this far out in left field. I addressed their products in the way I thought most appropriate: I ignored them. As I see it, if they're not even smart enough to reply to a reviewer's e-mail, they sure don't deserve your business.

3. I will make it clear which version I'm talking about. Good products seldom go bad in ensuing releases, but it's still worth your effort to sample more recent opinions, where possible, to ensure that version N+1 of a product I liked isn't loaded with new quality or compatibility problems, and that their support is still acceptable.

4. I won't make recommendations for two classes of products. The first is compilers. Your choice of compiler is far too intimately tied to other project issues,

such as developer skills base and development and target platforms, for me to make a blanket recommendation. Check out some of the forums on CompuServe, and you'll find endless arguments about compilers and frameworks and languages (oh my!) that make you wonder if these eternal combatants have any time left to write code. In fact, you can pick a product at random in these categories and then easily find people who adore it as well as those who think it's the worst piece of binary garbage ever foisted on the paying public.

The other category is text editors, which are problematic for another reason: the infamous "baby duck syndrome." This term refers to the fact (urban myth?) that baby ducks will "imprint" on the first large animal they're around for any significant period of time after hatching and consider that animal their mother. Similarly, programmers and most other computer users often become wedded to the features and "idiot-syncrasies" of the first text editor they use extensively, and then never want to change for the rest of their lives. Just look at all the effort editor vendors expend to make their products emulate each other's keystrokes.

# Recommendations

The (disk) envelopes, please...

## *ABC FlowCharter 4.0 by Micrografx*

Being a gizmonaut of the first order, I hesitate to say that *any* program has too many features. But this one sure comes close. ABC FlowCharter does standard flow charts and includes a basic business graphics package, a viewer program for your charts that you can freely distribute, a spreadsheet-based charting tool, and a CD ROM with over 200 TrueType fonts. None of this would mean a thing if the program were difficult to use or buggy. Well, it's not, and it's not. I got up to speed very quickly and had no troubles with the package at all. Highly recommended.

## *allCLEAR Version III by Clear Software, Inc.*

Like most other charting programs, allCLEAR does flow charts, organizational charts, fishbone diagrams, decision trees, etc., plus it has the bazillion-and-one other graphics and drawing features you expect to find in this type of program. (But please don't read that as a claim that it has every feature that's in any competing product; I didn't compare charting programs as a group that closely.)

I'm recommending allCLEAR for three reasons: First, I found it extremely usable, thanks in no small part to its excellent, task-oriented manuals. Second, I found it did everything I would want a charting package to do (but remember that my needs might be quite different from yours). And most important of all, it will accept plain-text scripts that describe the chart you want to create. As I described earlier in the book, this seemingly minor feature can be a tremendous help to programmers, since it allows you to write a program that will read some custom data source and produce a charting script that you can then feed to allCLEAR. This makes the lowly plain-text script a convenient stepping stone between your raw data (your company's phone directory, the outline for a presentation, the class hierarchy in a library, etc.), and a finished, high-quality view of the same material. Highly recommended.

## Bounds Checker Professional 3.0 by Nu-Mega Technologies, Inc.

Bounds Checker Professional is one of those programs you have to see in action to appreciate fully. BCPro makes it extremely easy to check your program for invalid API usage, memory leaks, invalid memory reads and writes (such as reading from uninitialized memory or overwriting the heap), and invalid pointer manipulations. In addition, BCPro now does compile-time instrumentation, which lets it catch numerous errors you might not expect.

One drawback to BCPro is that the most useful feature, the compile-time instrumentation, produces long build times—up to several times longer, depending on the instrumentation options used. Nu-Mega suggests doing builds overnight for large projects, which is probably a sensible solution for most development teams. Even though this sounds like quite an inconvenience, I think BCPro belongs on every public C/C++ development project possible, and that it should be used extensively during testing. Very highly recommended.

## Drag and File 1.0 for Windows 95 and Windows NT by Canyon Software

In my opinion, the Windows 95 Explorer is not fit for serious work. (And I assume that anyone reading this book does not use their computer casually, probably the safest assumption I've made in these pages.) As a result, you need a decent File Manager-like program, something that fills in all of Explorer's gaps, but is still long file name aware, does drag and drop to the Windows 95 desktop, etc. That's where Drag and File enters the picture.

Drag and File is just that—a 32-bit, fully Windows 95-aware File Manager/ Explorer replacement. If you've used the Windows File Manager so much that you have F8 burned into your DNA as the *only* way to initiate a file copy operation, then you'll probably love Drag and File, and you should feel right at home with it.

Drag and File is shareware, and is available through all the usual shareware outlets, including the WINUTIL forum on CompuServe.

## ISYS for Windows 4.0 by Odyssey Development

Text indexing and retrieval software is like your television's remote control: You don't think you need it until you get used to it, then you wonder how you ever got along without it. As I mentioned earlier in the book, this type of software can be incredibly useful to programmers, since you can use it to find any and all references to keywords, variable names, routine names, etc., in any body of source code (including your own) almost instantly.

I like ISYS for several reasons, most notably because it handles ZIP archives so gracefully; thanks to the FAT cluster size debacle (and the fact that there's no such thing as enough hard disk space, even in an age of 25 cents/MB storage), I strongly prefer to keep my sizable collection of scavenged source code ZIPped. ISYS treats archives like subdirectories, which allows me to have the best of both worlds: compact storage and painless retrieval. I also like the fact that ISYS is configurable and flexible enough in its searching options that I can often fire it up and get a useful answer in about a minute.

Please keep in mind that ISYS has a few rough edges and exhibits some quirks, like the fact that its installation program dumps a lot of files into your Windows system directory. But of the text indexing and retrieval packages that I've used, it's still my favorite, and the one I use to go source file spelunking almost daily.

## Microsoft Developer Network CD ROM by Microsoft

I must have mentioned this product 100 times throughout the book, and there's a reason: It's the best single source of information for Windows developers. There are several levels of subscription available, and the most useful one for the money I think is Level II. This includes the quarterly Development Library CD ROM (a.k.a. Level I), which includes an incredible number of Microsoft technical articles (such as all those PSS articles I mentioned in this book), articles from *Microsoft Systems Journal*, and *Dr. Dobb's Journal*, "backgrounders and white papers", specifications, and entire books. Level II also gets you the U.S., international, and DDK "packs", which include all the current SDKs and operating system releases, also on a quarterly basis.

Be prepared for sticker shock, though, as this subscription costs quite a bit more than pocket change. By coincidence my MSDN renewal notice was delivered while I was writing this recommendation (and I don't even want to think about how Microsoft managed that). It will cost me $554.04, including tax and shipping, for another year of MSDN membership (base price: $495). I still consider that a bargain, all things considered, and I won't hesitate to renew. Highly recommended.

## Multimedia ToolBook 3.0 by Asymetrix

Asymetrix refers to this product as a "multimedia authoring system," which sounds a lot like fancy marketing-speak for "compiler package." In fact, Multimedia ToolBook is more than just another compiler, and in my opinion it really does earn the "multimedia authoring system" tag.

ToolBook arranges your program into visual layers or "pages," and it uses its own vaguely BASIC-like language called OpenScript. This isn't a product you can pick up instantly, but if you're an experienced Windows programmer, you won't have too long or steep a learning curve.

The multimedia version of ToolBook supports Video for Windows, QuickTime, wave audio, MIDI sound, and Macromedia Director and Autodesk animations, as well as numerous image formats including Kodak Photo CD. It's a very powerful package that can save you a great deal of time when creating multimedia applications. Highly recommended.

## Orpheus 1.00 by TurboPower Software Company

The TurboPower people have long had a strong reputation among the Pascalites for producing first-rate products. Orpheus is not about to change that fact one iota.

Orpheus is a library of user interface gadgets for Borland's Delphi, including validated input fields, a text editor (capable of storing up to 16MB of text), spinbutton controls, and a virtual list box that lets you exceed the standard Windows limitation on the number of items in a listbox. As is the norm for TurboPower products, the package provides excellent documentation (the best I've seen for any third-party development tool, in fact) and full source code.

If you're working with Delphi and your goal is to create robust, usable programs without reinventing a lot of wheels along the way, then Orpheus belongs in your toolbox. Highly recommended for all Delphi coders.

(Orpheus is a figure from Greek mythology, of course. He was the son of the Muse Calliope, and played one mean lyre. He also sailed on the *Argo* and saved the crew from the lure of the Sirens with his music. Let's see, if *this* Orpheus is *that* Orpheus, and we're all the crew of the *Argo*, then that makes the Sirens...)

## Partition Magic 1.02.177 by PowerQuest Corporation

Do you hate cutesy product names that have words like "magic" in them? I sure do. It drives me bananas. This is one product that (nearly) justifies the practice, though. Partition Magic does one thing, and it does it exceptionally well: It makes managing your hard disk partitions far easier. Using Partition Magic you can resize and move partitions without having to reformat them and then restore their contents. It will even convert a FAT partition to an HPFS partition for you OS/2 users. (In fact, my only complaint about this product is a purely cosmetic one—the DOS version looks just like an OS/2 session, which I found a little unnerving.)

Don't let the "for OS/2" on the Partition Magic packaging fool you—it includes both 32-bit OS/2 and plain old DOS versions in the same package. PowerQuest tells me that a Windows 95 version is in the works, and that it should be out right after this book is published.

I talked a lot in this book about intelligent, accommodating software. In my opinion, Partition Magic is a great example of just that. Very highly recommended. (See the description of System Commander for another excellent, and complimentary product.)

## SourceSafe 3.1 by Microsoft

I've long had a love-hate relationship with version control programs, which was only reinforced when I was working on this book. I looked at practically every version control program on the market and found one example after another of horrible documentation, incredible product limitations, and enough minor problems to fill a chapter.

The only product I evaluated that I could live with day-in and day-out in the real world is SourceSafe. It's not a perfect product by any means, but it has the best overall cost-benefit ratio, while still providing a critical mass of functionality, including project branching and merging. I was a little disappointed in the manuals, which are skimpy for such a product, but at least they're free of the jargon overload that seems to be a bane of this entire product category. Recommended.

## System Commander 2.11 by V Communications

Another cutesy product name. I really hope this isn't a trend. (I know, I know—strong words from the guy who created Stickies!.) Like Partition Magic, this product does one thing, and does it so well that it's a joy to use: It simplifies the process of managing multiple operating systems on a single computer. This is particularly relevant to Windows programmers, thanks to all the testing we'll have to do on our public programs using various Windows versions and platforms. System Commander lets you set up just about any operating system you can name: DOS, Windows 3.1, Windows 95, Windows NT, OS/2, and various flavors of Unix including Linux. It also lets you set up multiple configurations for the same operating system, another great aid to testing. As if all this weren't enough, the manual is extremely detailed and well written.

System Commander and Partition Magic make an outstanding configuration management team. Very highly recommended.

## Windows 95 Device Driver Kit

If you're not writing device drivers (and very few of us are), why in the world should you care about the DDK? Simple, there are things in the DDK that can be found nowhere else, like the new, otherwise undocumented 16-bit APIs that Windows 95 added. The best way to get the Windows 95 DDK is via the *Microsoft Developer Network* Level II subscription.

## Windows NT 3.51

If you're developing Windows programs, especially public programs written in C++, the chances are pretty good that you're running a system that's somewhere between the middle of the road, performance-wise, up to a BelchFire 5000 Wonderbox. And that means you probably have the MIPS and megs to run Windows NT. If so, you should.

If nothing else, you'll need Windows NT around for testing purposes; your public Windows 95 programs must either run properly under it or correctly detect it and gracefully refuse to run. Also, remember that soon after this book hits the shelves Windows NT 4.0 is supposed to be available. This is the version that includes the Windows 95 user interface, and presumably, many new APIs that currently are unique to Windows 95.

## YAHU: Yet Another Header Utility

Here's a simple little tool you probably have access to, or even have a copy of, and might not even know it. This utility, which is on the *Microsoft Developer Network* Level I CD ROM in both executable and source form, displays all sorts of information from the headers on executable files, including the list of functions programs import from various DLLs. YAHU can be a great help when you're fiddling with various versions of Win16 and Win32 programs (as I did endlessly for this book, and as we'll all likely be doing for some time to come).

# Mixed Media Guide

# Mixed Media Guide

Chapter **16**

*Life without music would be a mistake.*

Friedrich Nietzsche,
Überhacker

So would programming, driving, and other things too numerous or intensely personal to mention. I find that whenever I'm writing or programming, I always have a CD in the player. If, for whatever reason, I'm forced to work sans tunes, I feel as if I'm laboring in a sterile, boring environment, no matter where I am. I suspect a lot of you enjoy and employ "work music" as much as I do. So here's an annotated list of my favorites. My e-mail address is in the introduction; tell me what you listen to.

But since this is the Mixed Media Guide, I've also placed the book recommendations here. I know this might seem like an odd way to do things, but I wanted to stress once more that our tools lie on a continuum, and that even the music we listen to while working are part of that spectrum, albeit at one end.

Abrash, Michael, *Zen of Graphics Programming*, The Coriolis Group, ISBN 1-883577-08-X, 1995

This book is a treasure trove of graphics programming information. Michael covers VGA hardware, split screens, palette manipulation, algorithms for drawing lines, circles, ellipses, and polygons, and animation techniques. And he does it all with a colorful, inviting writing style.

Don't make the mistake of ignoring this book just because you won't be writing low-level graphics code in the near future, or you plan on using the GDI routines for circles, arcs, rectangles and such. I mentioned earlier that we should all read about other areas of programming as a way of broadening our knowledge and picking up new techniques. Michael's book is a great example of the kind of material I had in mind. Very highly recommended.

Abrash, Michael, *Zen of Code Optimization*, The Coriolis Group, ISBN 1-883577-03-9, 1994

I say in *my* Zen book that you usually know in advance when you need to squeeze every last cycle and byte out of your code. When you find yourself in that situation, you need *Michael's* Zen book. He covers just about every aspect of wringing additional performance out of code in general, with copious examples in Intel 80x86 assembly. Very highly recommended.

Aitken, Peter, and Scott Jarol, *Visual C++ Multimedia Adventure Set*, The Coriolis Group, ISBN 1-883577-19-5, 1995

Everyone knows what multimedia is, in general terms, but there are very few genuinely good books on writing multimedia applications. Aitken and Jarol cover numerous multimedia topics for Windows 95 programmers working in C++, including hypermedia, the Windows MCI, palette manipulation, visual effects, animation, and sound programming. Highly recommended.

Badalamenti, Angelo, *Soundtrack from Twin Peaks*, Warner Brothers, 9 26316-2

About as haunting and soothing as music can be at the same time. Goes great with a cup of good coffee and a slice of cherry pie.

Bayless, John, *Bach on Abbey Road*, ProArte, CDD 346
Bayless, John, *John, Bach, Bayless, Beatles*, ProArte, CDD 413

John Bayless plays his own solo piano arrangements of Beatles songs, in the style of J. S. Bach. Great debugging or programming music, especially when you're struggling with a frustrating problem and a calming influence is in order.

Brooks, Frederick P., Jr., *The Mythical Man-Month*, Addison-Wesley, ISBN 0-210-00650-2, 1975

If the young and precocious field of computer science can be said to have classic works, this is surely one of them. Beautifully written and insightful, this book should be required reading on a yearly basis for everyone involved in software development in any capacity, including (especially?) management. Highest possible recommendation.

Byrne, David, *David Byrne*, Warner Brothers, 9 45558-2
Byrne, David, *Rei Momo*, Sire, 9 25990-2

Yep, that David Byrne (the one from *The Talking Heads*). Great stuff, but I find that Byrne's lyrics make it a bit hard to concentrate on programming, simply because they're so hard to ignore.

Calvert, Charles, *Delphi Unleashed*, SAMS Publishing, 1995, ISBN 0-672-30499-6
If you're considering adding Borland's Delphi to your toolbox, but you don't know Pascal (perhaps you're looking for an alternative to C/C++, but that's the only language you've used to any significant extent), you should read this book. Charlie takes you through the architecture of Delphi and Object Pascal, step by step, starting with basic data types and the Delphi IDE, and continuing through OOP, writing data base applications, and creating reusable components. Highly recommended.

Canadian Brass, *Bach: The Art of the Fugue*, CBS Records, MK 44501
A beautiful recording performed by the five-man Canadian Brass. I highly recommend everything this group has released, but this is their best programming music to date.

Canadian Brass, *High, Bright, Light and Clear—The Glory of Baroque Brass*, RCA, RCD14574

Canadian Brass, *Vivaldi: The Four Seasons*, CBS Records, MK 42095

*The Carl Stalling Project: Music from Warner Bros. Cartoons 1936-1958*, Warner Bros., 26027-2
Possibly the ultimate programmer's background music, this CD contains exactly what the title says, all in the form of the original recording sessions. Just don't expect to get too much work done the first dozen times you listen to it.

Carlos, Wendy, *Switched-On Bach*, CBS, MK 7194
Carlos, Wendy, *Switched-On Bach 2000*, Telarc CD-80323
The original SOB, and the 25th anniversary edition. Great, great stuff.

Constantine, Larry, *Constantine on Peopleware*, Prentice Hall/Yourdon Press, ISBN 0-13-331976-8, 1995
This is a collection of Larry Constantine's collection of Peopleware columns from *Computer Language Magazine* and *Software Development*. Throughout these columns Larry shows such a refreshing and conspicuous, almost stunning, amount of common sense that one can only wonder if he's really a computer guy. Highly recommended.

Coplien, Jim, *Advanced C++: Programming Styles and Idioms*, Addison-Wesley, ISBN 0-201-54855-0, 1992
Talk about truth in advertising; this book will leave *very* few readers wondering "where's the beef." Highly recommended for heavy-duty C++ coders.

Crawford, Sharon and Charlie Russel, *OS/2 for Windows Users*, Sybex, ISBN 0-7821-1528-4, 1994

You're a Windows programmer extraordinaire; you can recite the Windows API in reverse alphabetical order; you knew the difference between modal and modeless dialog boxes when you were still in your crib. You're the ruler of all you survey. Then your boss tells you that you've been picked as the technical lead on a project to port one of your company's most profitable products to OS/2, an operating system you've seen maybe once in a magazine screen shot. After you extinguish your hair and climb down off the office furniture, *this* is the book you should read to get up to speed on OS/2 as a user. Crawford and Russel take a refreshing, no-nonsense approach to numerous topics, and nicely flatten the OS/2 learning curve for Windows users.

Dolby, Thomas, *Aliens Ate my Buick*, Capitol, EMI CDP-7-48075-2
Dolby, Thomas, *Astronauts and Heretics*, Giant, 9 24478-2
Dolby, Thomas, *The Flat Earth*, Capitol, CDP 7 46028 2
Dolby, Thomas, *The Gate to the Mind's Eye*, Giant, 9 24586-2
Dolby, Thomas, *The Golden Age of Wireless*, Capitol, CDP 7 46009 2

Thomas Dolby (who brought us "She Blinded Me with Science"), creates music that's not quite like anything else you've heard, and also happens to be great background music for programming.

Dorsey, Don, *Bachbusters*, Telarc, CD-80123
Great electronic renditions of several of J. S. Bach's compositions.

Dorsey, Don, *Beethoven or Bust*, Telarc, CD-80123
Dorsey also gives Ludwig the electronic treatment.

Duntemann, Jeff, and Ron Pronk, *Inside the PowerPC Revolution*, The Coriolis Group, ISBN 1-883577-04-7, 1995
This is by far the most complete book on the PowerPC I've found. It covers the history of this and other chips, the PowerPC architecture, and relates it all to coming products and the market.

Duntemann, Jeff, Jim Mischel, and Don Taylor, *Delphi Programming Explorer*, The Coriolis Group, 1995, ISBN 1-883577-25-X, 1995
Jeff says in this book's introduction, "The idea was to put together a presentation of Delphi that would get a new user up and running in as little time as possible—and make it a wild good time." I like this book for several reasons, not least of which is how well it meets Jeff's goals. This book is a great introduction to Delphi, and it's helped several people I know get up to speed with the product in short order.

Glass, Philip, *Koyaanisqatsi Soundtrack*, Antilles 90626-2

Glass, Philip, *Powaqqatsi Soundtrack*, Elektra 79192-2

Glass, Philip, *Solo Piano*, CBS Records, MK 45576

Fifty one minutes of about the most haunting, evocative piano music you can imagine. Great for prolonged debugging sessions and other frustrating activities.

Harrel, Lynn and Vladimir Ashkenazy, *Beethoven: Cello Sonatas*, London, 417 628-2

Katsaris, Cyprien, Beethoven/Liszt, *Ninth Symphony*, Teldec

Incredibly, Franz Liszt wrote transcriptions of Beethoven's symphonies for solo piano. If you're at all familiar with Beethoven's Ninth, you probably can't imagine how even a genius like Liszt could have pulled this off, but it works.

Lennox, Annie, *Diva*, Arista, 07822-18704-2

Lennox, Annie, *Medusa*, Arista, 74321-25717-2

If we all could program the way Ms. Lennox sings in these recordings, software would be whole lot more interesting.

Maisky, Mischa, *J. S. Bach: Six Cello Suites*, Deutsche Grammophon, 415 416-2

Beautiful, soothing music that's perfect for debugging sessions, particularly the ones in which you've convinced yourself that your computer is executing some instruction sequence wrong, since that's the only possible remaining explanation.

Mehta, Zubin/Israeli Philharmonic Orchestra, *Liszt: Hungarian Rhapsodies*, CBS, MK 44926

If you don't think classical music can be fun, try this recording, particularly the second rhapsody, which will be instantly familiar to everyone who ever spent a Saturday morning with Bugs Bunny.

Meyers, Scott, *Effective C++: 50 Specific Ways to Improve Your Programs and Designs*, Addison-Wesley, ISBN 0-201-56364-9, 1992

Scott presents an astounding amount of practical advice for C++ coders in under 200 pages, and does it all with a gentle sense of humor and a casual yet precise writing style. Highly recommended for C++ programmers of all skill levels, particularly those who are convinced they no longer need such books.

Microsoft Corporation, *Programmer's Guide to Microsoft Windows 95*, Microsoft Press, ISBN 1-55615-834-3, 1995

This book is loaded with details about Windows 95 programming that either aren't available from other sources or aren't nearly as well organized. Highly recommended.

Also serves as an effective one-volume proof that the lives of Windows programmers have been changed forever with the arrival of Windows 95 (as if there were any doubt).

Midori, *Paganini: 24 Caprices*, CBS MK 44944

An astonishing set of 24 exercises written by one of the true characters of classical music, Niccolo Paganini. If you're inspired by flamboyant displays of excellence, you'll love this recording. (See also Perlman's recording of these works.)

Murray, James D. and William vanRyper, *Encyclopedia of Graphics File Formats*, O'Reilly & Associates, Inc., ISBN 1-56592-058-9, 1994

At nearly 900 pages and detailing dozens of graphics file formats, this book truly is encyclopedic. But this title is just as useful as a collection of design case studies. Strongly recommended.

*Mystery Science Theater 3000*, a.k.a. *MST3K*

If you aren't familiar with this show, check your cable TV listings for the Comedy Central channel, and watch an installment or three. It's something of an acquired taste, but well worth the effort. (I could swear Tom Servo (the short, sarcastic, red 'bot) moderated several of my code inspections at IBM, but I can't prove it.)

Perlman, Itzhak, *Paganini: 24 Caprices*, EMI CDC 7 47171 2

Perlman's take on Paganini's torture test for violinists (and violins). (See also Midori's recording of these works.)

Pietrek, Matt, *Windows Internals*, Addison-Wesley, ISBN 0-201-62217-3, 1993

Why should you care about a book that describes the internals of Windows 3.1, when Windows 95 and Windows NT are The Present and The Future? Simple: Much of what Matt had to say then is still relevant now, such as his description of the limitations of how Windows loads DLLs. Highly recommended.

Queen, *Classic Queen*, Hollywood Records, HR-61311-2
Queen, *Greatest Hits*, Hollywood Records, HR-61265-2

Everything Queen did is worth your time, but if you can only add two of their titles to your collection, these are the ones.

Raitt, Bonnie, *Luck of the Draw*, Capitol C2-96111
Raitt, Bonnie, *Nick of Time*, Capitol CDP 7 91268 2

If you like being surrounded by excellence when you work, then you could do a whole lot worse than playing these Bonnie Raitt CDs. Very great stuff.

Schulman, Andrew, *Unauthorized Windows 95*, IDG Books, ISBN 1-56884-305-4, 1994

Remember all the, ahem, misconceptions we had before Windows 95 was released? In particular, the ones about how DOS wasn't even part of the product, or wasn't used by 32-bit Windows programs, got a lot of attention. Andrew examines these issues and many more technical aspects of Windows 95 in excruciating detail, and reveals a great deal about the Windows 95 architecture. Not for the casual programmer, but still highly recommended.

Special EFX, *Slice of Life*, GRP Records, GRP-D-9534

OK, *everyone* likes this title. It's still great programming and debugging music.

Stroustrup, Bjarne, *The Design and Evolution of C++*, Addison-Wesley, ISBN 0-201-54330-3, 1994

Whether you love C++ or hate it, use it casually or professionally, you should read this book. Written by the "father" of C++, it explains in considerable detail why a lot of things were done as they were in the language, as well as why some features, including some that Stroustrup himself favored, were never included. Highly recommended.

Wakeman, Rick, *The Myths and Legends of King Arthur and the Knights of the Round Table*, A&M, CD 3230

Wakeman, Rick, *The Six Wives of Henry VIII*, A&M, 393 229-2

Wakeman's compositions and performances make for outstanding background music for programming, but I find some of his work a little too intense for debugging sessions.

Walnut Creek CD ROMs

Including *The C Users' Group Library, Turbo User Group CD ROM, Perl, CICA Shareware for Windows, Hobbes Archived OS/2*, and *Source Code CD ROM*.

Great resources, as they provide source code, design examples, and some genuinely useful utilities. Highly recommended, especially when you pair them up with a text indexing and retrieval package.

*Windows 95 Resource Kit*, Microsoft Press, 1995

Now here's a fascinating book-and-disks set: Over 1,300 pages of information on Windows 95, including installation and setup, networking, system management, e-mail, the registry, and basic architecture. Whether you're using Windows 95 in a corporate environment or as a standalone system, if you're simply running it or developing for it, you probably want a copy of this book handy. Highly recommended.

# Bonus Section: Three Head Reshapers

Do you like books that alter your world view? I do. Here's a short list that I think most people, especially programmers, will enjoy.

Weidenfeld and Nicolson, *The Mezzanine*, Weidenfeld & Nicolson , ISBN 1-55584-258-5
A 135-page novel that takes place entirely on a 30-second escalator ride? If this doesn't appeal to a programmer's love of minutiae, I don't know what will. Also recommended is Baker's *Room Temperature*, another novel-in-a-moment.

Carse, James P., *Finite and Infinite Games*, The Free Press, ISBN 0-02-905980-1
Carse looks at the nature of games and how they fit into society in 101 short, numbered sections.

Searle, John R., *The Construction of Social Reality*, The Free Press, ISBN 0-02-928045-1
This book is exactly what the title suggests. Deep, intriguing stuff, and highly recommended.

# Appendices

**Megazero, the World's Most Complete Do-Nothing Windows Program**

**A Compendium of Programmer Fables**

**The Win32u Library**

# MegaZero, The World's Most Complete Do-Nothing Windows Program

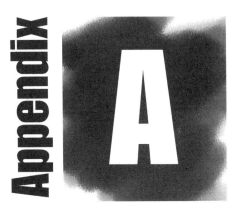

*Example is always more efficacious than precept.*

Samuel Johnson

*Example is the school of mankind, and they will learn at no other.*

Edmund Burke

Throughout this book I've talked about a lot of programming practices and techniques and provided a number of individual example programs. I'm a big believer in such examples, since I think they can often take the place a of a *lot* of prose and communicate programming concepts quickly and clearly. Still, the artificiality of narrow, single-purpose examples sometimes reduces their usefulness; no matter how well chosen and crafted, isolated snippets of code often seem like hothouse orchids that only claim to be able to survive the rigors of the real world. That's why I wanted to use several of the techniques in one more example, to provide you with a somewhat more meaningful program that you can play with and modify to gain a better feeling for these features in a real program. Hence MegaZero.

MegaZero uses the following techniques from the book:

- Self-checking against tampering
- Forcing a dialog-based program to have a Windows 95 icon
- Smart data file usage (including a separate file dumper utility)
- Drag and drop processing

- Explicit DLL management
- Locked persona

To be perfectly honest, the title of this appendix is just a bit misleading. MegaZero does do something—it maintains a list of the last ten file names that have been dropped on it, as well as the date it was last run. But since it doesn't do anything with these file names or the date except display them, that's close enough to nothing that I doubt anyone will object too strenuously.

I should also confess that I didn't completely follow my own advice when I wrote MegaZero. For example, one of the points I stress in this book is that all dialog boxes should have a "Help" button or provide a Yes/No choice of receiving help. I made MegaZero display such a dialog box when it renames an existing file that conflicts with its own data file, or when it can't load its DLL, but I didn't bother writing a Windows help file.

A more serious violation of my own rules involves the two minor routines, FileExists() and AppendSlash(), that I placed in MegaZero's DLL, TOOLBOX.DLL. Lest anyone reading this book think that I've suddenly lost my zeal for avoiding DLLs, let me say that in a real program, particularly a public one, I would most definitely *not* use a DLL this way, since these routines clearly should not be dynamically linked. Also, notice that FileExists() is a particularly tricky routine to store in a DLL and access via a gateway function, as this approach forces you to choose a return value for the case where the DLL isn't available. In this case, I chose FALSE, since that seemed like the safest option. FALSE isn't a perfect choice, of course, since the main program can accidentally call FileExists() without checking that the DLL is loaded (or without even trying to load it), and get a return value of FALSE, when the file name the program provided does indeed name an existing file. This can lead to your program acting strangely, such as telling the user that an existing file isn't there. Clearly, placing routines into a DLL that is explicitly managed requires some careful thought. As this case shows, that sometimes involves restructuring the routine's interface to accomodate an explicit "it's not here" case.

## Building the Samples: MegaZero

**CD Location:** ZEN\APP_A\MEGAZERO, ZEN\APP_A\TOOLBOX, and ZEN\APP_A\PATCHER, ZEN\APP_A\DUMPER

**Platform:** Win32

**Build instructions:** Use the provided .MAK files with Visual C++ 2.2 and compile normally.

These projects contain relative paths for include files, so you must copy the entire ZEN\APP_A directory tree to your hard disk, or edit some #include statements.

Once PATCHER.EXE is built, move it into the directory that contains MEGAZERO.EXE and run PATCHER.EXE. This will enable MegaZero to perform its self-check.

You must copy the MEGAZERO.DAT file created by the program into the directory that contains DUMPER.EXE for that utility to work.

## Listing A.1  ZEN\APP_A\MEGAZERO\CONFIG.H

```
#ifndef __CONFIG_H__
#define __CONFIG_H__

#include <pshpack1.h>        // Byte packing, please

void LoadConfigData(void);
void SaveConfigData(void);

// The following do not include the terminating null
#define MIN_PW_LEN 4
#define MAX_PW_LEN 12

struct config_type
  {
   char fn1[MAX_PATH];
   char fn2[MAX_PATH];
   char fn3[MAX_PATH];
   char fn4[MAX_PATH];
   char fn5[MAX_PATH];
   char fn6[MAX_PATH];
   char fn7[MAX_PATH];
   char fn8[MAX_PATH];
   char fn9[MAX_PATH];
   char fn10[MAX_PATH];

   int last_run_month;
   int last_run_day;
   int last_run_year;

   BOOL locked;
   char password[MAX_PW_LEN + 1];

   int  reserved[10];
  };

// Our globally accessible array of configuration data

extern config_type config;

// Our header, which normally isn't referred to by code outside of this
// compilation unit.

#define eye_catcher_len 9

struct config_header_type
  {
   char eye_catcher[eye_catcher_len];
   WORD major_version;
```

```
    WORD minor_version;
  };

#include <poppack.h>        // Back to whatever was in effect

#endif
```

## Listing A.2    ZEN\APP_A\MEGAZERO\CONFIG.CPP

```
/* Copyright Lou Grinzo 1995
   Zen of Windows 95 Programming */

#include "stdafx.h"
#include "config.h"
#include "io.h"
#include "tb_int.h"
#include "toolbox.h"

// Our global configuration data array, which will be overlaid with
// data from the file, assuming it exists.

config_type config =
  {
  "[no setting]",   // fn1
  "[no setting]",   // fn2
  "[no setting]",   // fn3
  "[no setting]",   // fn4
  "[no setting]",   // fn5
  "[no setting]",   // fn6
  "[no setting]",   // fn7
  "[no setting]",   // fn8
  "[no setting]",   // fn9
  "[no setting]",   // fn10

  0,                // last_run_month
  0,                // last_run_day
  0,                // last_run_year

  FALSE,            // locked
  "",               // password

  { 0, 0, 0, 0, 0,  // reserved
    0, 0, 0, 0, 0 }
  };

static char data_fn[] = "megazero.dat";

config_header_type config_header =
  {
  "megazero",   // eyecatcher (9 chars, incl. term. null)
  1,            // major_version
  0             // minor_version
  };

//////////////////////////////////////////////////////////////////////
// Headers for Local Routines
//////////////////////////////////////////////////////////////////////

static BOOL BuildFN(char *fn, size_t max_len);
static BOOL CreateNewFile(void);
```

```
static UINT GetBaseDirectory(LPTSTR lpBuffer,UINT uSize);
static BOOL IsOurFile(FILE *f);
static BOOL RenameImpostor(void);
static void SetUpData(void);
static BOOL StoreData(FILE *f);

////////////////////////////////////////////////////////////////////////
// Exported routines
////////////////////////////////////////////////////////////////////////


////////////////////////////////////////////////////////////////////////
// LoadConfigData(): Load the in-memory copy of the config array from our
// custom format file.  This function handles all the pathological cases:
// File not found, file found but not really our file, etc.  If a usable data
// file doesn't exist, then the default settings in config_header and config
// are not changed, and they can be used as-is.
////////////////////////////////////////////////////////////////////////

void LoadConfigData(void)
{
  char fn[MAX_PATH];
  FILE *f;

  if(!BuildFN(fn,sizeof(fn)))
      {
#ifdef _DEBUG
      OutputDebugString("*** LoadConfigData: Unable to build data fn.\n");
#endif
      return;
      }

  // Handle the special case and get it out of the way.

  if(!FileExists(fn))
      {
#ifdef _DEBUG
      OutputDebugString("*** LoadConfigData: Data file didn't exist; creating
new one.\n");
#endif
      CreateNewFile();
      return;
      }

  if((f = fopen(fn,"rb")) == NULL)
      {
#ifdef _DEBUG
      OutputDebugString("*** LoadConfigData: Unable to open data file\n");
#endif
      return;
      }

  if(IsOurFile(f))
      {
#ifdef _DEBUG
      OutputDebugString("*** LoadConfigData: IsOurFile() == TRUE\n");
#endif

      // Step over the header, which has already been read in
      fseek(f,sizeof(config_header),SEEK_SET);

      if(fread(&config,sizeof(config),1,f) == 0)
          {
```

```
#ifdef _DEBUG
        OutputDebugString("*** LoadConfigData: Unable to read data file\n");
#endif
        }

    // If we were handling more than one version of the data file, then this
    // is where we'd conditionally read the extensions to the data format,
    // based on the version number

    fclose(f);
  }
 else
    {
#ifdef _DEBUG
    OutputDebugString("*** LoadConfigData: IsOurFile() == FALSE\n");
#endif
    fclose(f);

    if(RenameImpostor())
      CreateNewFile();
    }
}

////////////////////////////////////////////////////////////////////////////
// SaveConfigData(): Save the in-memory copy of the config array in a file
// that has our custom header.  This function handles all the pathological
// cases: File not found, file found but not really our file, etc.
////////////////////////////////////////////////////////////////////////////

void SaveConfigData(void)
{
  char fn[MAX_PATH];
  FILE *f;

  if(!BuildFN(fn,sizeof(fn)))
    {
#ifdef _DEBUG
    OutputDebugString("*** SaveConfigData: Unable to build data fn.\n");
#endif
    return;
    }

  // How could this happen?  Perhaps the user or some other program deleted
  // our data file while we were running?  Whatever the case, it's easily
  // covered.
  if(!FileExists(fn))
    {
#ifdef _DEBUG
    OutputDebugString
      ("*** SaveConfigData: Data file didn't exist; creating new one.\n");
#endif
    CreateNewFile();
    return;
    }

  // Open the file...
  if((f = fopen(fn,"rb+")) == NULL)
    {
#ifdef _DEBUG
    OutputDebugString("*** SaveConfigData: Unable to open data file.\n");
```

```
#endif
      return;
    }

  // ..if it's ours...
  if(IsOurFile(f))
    {
#ifdef _DEBUG
    OutputDebugString("*** SaveConfigData: IsOurFile() == TRUE\n");
#endif
    // ...write the header and data...
    StoreData(f);

    // ...and we're done.
    fclose(f);
    }
  else
    {
#ifdef _DEBUG
    OutputDebugString("*** SaveConfigData: IsOurFile() == FALSE\n");
#endif
    // ...if it's not ours, then we close the old file, whatever it was,
    // rename it, and then create a new file with our in-memory data.
    fclose(f);

    if(RenameImpostor())
      CreateNewFile();
    }
}

/////////////////////////////////////////////////////////////////////////
// Local routines
/////////////////////////////////////////////////////////////////////////

/////////////////////////////////////////////////////////////////////////
// BuildFN(): Build a fully-qualified file name for our data file.  The
// string is built right into the caller's provided buffer.
//
// Return TRUE if the string was built properly, FALSE otherwise.
//
// max_len includes the term. null
/////////////////////////////////////////////////////////////////////////

static BOOL BuildFN(char *fn, size_t max_len)
{
  UINT rc = GetBaseDirectory(fn,max_len);

  if((rc == 0) || (rc > max_len))
    {
#ifdef _DEBUG
    OutputDebugString("*** BuildFN: Unable to retrieve base dir\n");
#endif
    return FALSE;
    }

  // We don't have to verify that AppendSlash did anything or had room for
  // a slash, if one is needed.  strlcatAtomic() will handle the out-of-
  // space problem for us.

  AppendSlash(fn,max_len - 1);
```

```
  return strlcatAtomic(fn,data_fn,max_len);
  }


///////////////////////////////////////////////////////////////////////////
// CreateNewFile(): Create a new copy of our custom data file from the in-
// memory data structures.  Notice that we DON'T check to see if the file
// exists-- we just hammer whatever is there.  Any and all steps to preserve
// the contents of a file with the same name as the one we're about to create
// must be taken before we're called!
//
// Return TRUE if the file was successfully created, FALSE otherwise.
//
///////////////////////////////////////////////////////////////////////////

static BOOL CreateNewFile(void)
{
  char fn[MAX_PATH];
  FILE *f;

  if(!BuildFN(fn,sizeof(fn)))
    {
#ifdef _DEBUG
    OutputDebugString("*** CreateNewFile: Unable to build data file\n");
#endif
    return FALSE;
    }

  if((f = fopen(fn,"wb")) != NULL)
    {
    BOOL rc = StoreData(f);

    fclose(f);

    return rc;
    }
  else
    {
#ifdef _DEBUG
    OutputDebugString("*** CreateNewFile: Unable to open data file\n");
#endif
    return FALSE;
    }
}


///////////////////////////////////////////////////////////////////////////
// GetBaseDirectory(): Retrieve the directory used for our data file.
// Currently, this is always the user's Windows directory, which is why
// this function mimics the GetWindowsDirectory() interface.
///////////////////////////////////////////////////////////////////////////

UINT GetBaseDirectory(LPTSTR lpBuffer,UINT uSize)
{
  if(lpBuffer == NULL)
    {
#ifdef _DEBUG
    OutputDebugString("*** GetBaseDirectory: Null pointer detected\n");
#endif
    return 0;
    }
```

```
  return GetWindowsDirectory(lpBuffer,uSize);
}


////////////////////////////////////////////////////////////////////////////
// IsOurFile(): Examine the specified open file, and determine if
// it is our custom data file format.
//
// If the file is our custom format, then we return TRUE, FALSE otherwise.
// The file is always left positioned at its beginning (offset 0), when we
// exit, regardless of its contents.
////////////////////////////////////////////////////////////////////////////

static BOOL IsOurFile(FILE *f)
{
  // Check the file length.  Anything shorter than this and it isn't our file

  if(_filelength(_fileno(f)) < sizeof(config_header_type) + sizeof(config_type))
    return FALSE;

  // Check the header contents

  config_header_type test_header;

  if(fread(&test_header,sizeof(test_header),1,f) < 1)
    return FALSE;

  // Back to the beginning of the file we go.
  fseek(f,0,SEEK_SET);

  // If it's not our eye-catcher, then it's not our file.
  if(memcmp(&test_header.eye_catcher,&config_header.eye_catcher,
    sizeof(test_header.eye_catcher)) != 0)
    return FALSE;

  // We'll only accept version 1.0 for now
  if((test_header.major_version > 1) || (test_header.minor_version > 0))
    {
     // Possibly issue a version-specific warning to the user here
      return FALSE;
    }

  // Do this copy so that other parts of the program can correctly
  // refer to the header information, including the version codes.
  memcpy(&config_header,&test_header,sizeof(test_header));
  return TRUE;
}


////////////////////////////////////////////////////////////////////////////
// RenameImpostor(): Someone else has determined that there is a file with
// the exact same fully qualified name as the one we want to use, but it
// isn't our file.  Since we don't know what it is, we can't very well
// delete it.  But we need to save our data, so we must first rename the
// the blocking file to something else.
//
// We do NOT verify that the blocking file exists, nor do we check its format!
//
// Return TRUE if the rename operation succeeded, FALSE otherwise.
////////////////////////////////////////////////////////////////////////////

static BOOL RenameImpostor(void)
{
```

```
    char blocking_fn[MAX_PATH], new_fn[MAX_PATH], win_dir[MAX_PATH];

    if(!BuildFN(blocking_fn,sizeof(blocking_fn)))
        {
#ifdef _DEBUG
        OutputDebugString("*** RenameImpostor: Unable to build blocking_fn\n");
#endif
        return FALSE;
        }

    UINT rc = GetBaseDirectory(win_dir,sizeof(win_dir));

    if((rc == 0) || (rc > sizeof(win_dir)))
        {
#ifdef _DEBUG
        OutputDebugString("*** RenameImpostor: Unable to retrieve base dir\n");
#endif
        return FALSE;
        }

    if(GetTempFileName(win_dir,"OLD",0,new_fn) == 0)
        {
#ifdef _DEBUG
        OutputDebugString("*** RenameImpostor: Unable to retrieve temp file
            name.\n");
#endif
        return FALSE;
        }

#ifdef _DEBUG
        OutputDebugString("*** RenameImpostor: blocking_fn: ");
        OutputDebugString(blocking_fn);
        OutputDebugString("\n*** RenameImpostor: new_fn: ");
        OutputDebugString(new_fn);
        OutputDebugString("\n");
#endif

    if(CopyFile(blocking_fn,new_fn,FALSE))
        {
        char buffer[1024];

        wsprintf(buffer,"Your existing file: \n  \"%s\"\nhas been renamed:\n
            \"%s\".  \n\nDo you want help?",blocking_fn,new_fn);

        if(MessageBox(0,buffer,"Please note!",MB_YESNO | MB_ICONEXCLAMATION |
          MB_TASKMODAL) == IDYES)
          MessageBox(0,"Imagine brilliant, insightful, context sensitive help
              here.","Help",MB_OK | MB_ICONINFORMATION | MB_TASKMODAL);
        return TRUE;
        }
    else
        {
#ifdef _DEBUG
        OutputDebugString("*** RenameImpostor: FAILED.\n");
#endif
        return FALSE;
        }
}


///////////////////////////////////////////////////////////////////////
// SetUpData(): Set our date fields in the config array for the current
```

```
// date, and make sure that all filename strings are terminated.
/////////////////////////////////////////////////////////////////////

static void SetUpData(void)
{
  // Set our header fields with today's date

  time_t now;
  tm now2;

  time(&now);
  now2 = *localtime(&now);

  config.last_run_month = now2.tm_mon + 1;  // month is zero-based(!?)
  config.last_run_day   = now2.tm_mday;
  config.last_run_year  = now2.tm_year;

  // If we're going to convert the data file to a newer version, this is the place
  // update the major and minor version numbers, as needed.

  // This is probably the height of paranoia, but at least it ensures that
  // no matter what is in the filename variables, they're still terminated.

  config.fn1[sizeof(config.fn1) - 1]  = '\0';
  config.fn2[sizeof(config.fn2) - 1]  = '\0';
  config.fn3[sizeof(config.fn3) - 1]  = '\0';
  config.fn4[sizeof(config.fn4) - 1]  = '\0';
  config.fn5[sizeof(config.fn5) - 1]  = '\0';
  config.fn6[sizeof(config.fn6) - 1]  = '\0';
  config.fn7[sizeof(config.fn7) - 1]  = '\0';
  config.fn8[sizeof(config.fn8) - 1]  = '\0';
  config.fn9[sizeof(config.fn9) - 1]  = '\0';
  config.fn10[sizeof(config.fn10) - 1] = '\0';

  return;
}


/////////////////////////////////////////////////////////////////////
// StoreDataFile(): Save the header and data for the file using the open
// file handle provided by our caller, which we assume is opened for binary
// writes.
//
// Return TRUE if the writes are successful, FALSE otherwise.
/////////////////////////////////////////////////////////////////////

static BOOL StoreData(FILE *f)
{
  // Clean up data, update the version number, etc. as needed
  SetUpData();

  if(fwrite(&config_header,sizeof(config_header),1,f) < 1)
    {
#ifdef _DEBUG
      OutputDebugString("*** StoreData: Unable to write data file\n");
#endif
      return FALSE;
    }

  // If there are version-specific extensions to the file's header, they
  // would be written to the file here.
```

```
   if(fwrite(&config,sizeof(config),1,f) < 1)
      {
#ifdef _DEBUG
      OutputDebugString("*** StoreData: Unable to write data file\n");
#endif
      return FALSE;
      }

   // If there are version-specific extensions to the file's data, they
   // would be written to the file here.

   fclose(f);

   // If we got here, everything went according to plan...
   return TRUE;
}
```

## Listing A.3   ZEN\APP_A\MEGAZERO\MEGAZDLG.H

```
// megazdlg.h : header file
//

/////////////////////////////////////////////////////////////////////////
// CMegazeroDlg dialog

class CMegazeroDlg : public CDialog
{
// Construction
public:
      CMegazeroDlg(CWnd* pParent = NULL);        // standard constructor

// Dialog Data
      //{{AFX_DATA(CMegazeroDlg)
      enum { IDD = IDD_MEGAZERO_DIALOG };
            // NOTE: the ClassWizard will add data members here
      //}}AFX_DATA

      // ClassWizard generated virtual function overrides
      //{{AFX_VIRTUAL(CMegazeroDlg)
      protected:
      virtual void DoDataExchange(CDataExchange* pDX);        // DDX/DDV support
      //}}AFX_VIRTUAL

// Implementation
protected:
      HICON m_hIcon;

   void DoLockUnlock(void);
   void DoSelfCheck(void);
   void OnLockUnlock(void);
   void ProcessDroppedFile(char * fn);
   void UpdateFileNames(void);

      // Generated message map functions
      //{{AFX_MSG(CMegazeroDlg)
      virtual BOOL OnInitDialog();
      afx_msg void OnSysCommand(UINT nID, LPARAM lParam);
      afx_msg void OnPaint();
      afx_msg HCURSOR OnQueryDragIcon();
      afx_msg void OnDestroy();
```

```
        afx_msg void OnDropFiles(HDROP hDropInfo);
        //}}AFX_MSG
        DECLARE_MESSAGE_MAP()
};
```

## Listing A.4    ZEN\APP_A\MEGAZERO\MEGAZDLG.CPP

```
/* Copyright Lou Grinzo 1995
   Zen of Windows 95 Programming */

// megazdlg.cpp : implementation file
//

#include "stdafx.h"
#include "megazero.h"
#include "megazdlg.h"
#include "..\\patcher\\checker.h"
#include "config.h"
#include "lock.h"

#ifdef _DEBUG
#undef THIS_FILE
static char BASED_CODE THIS_FILE[] = __FILE__;
#endif

/////////////////////////////////////////////////////////////////////////////
// CAboutDlg dialog used for App About

class CAboutDlg : public CDialog
{
public:
        CAboutDlg();

// Dialog Data
        //{{AFX_DATA(CAboutDlg)
        enum { IDD = IDD_ABOUTBOX };
        //}}AFX_DATA

// Implementation
protected:
        virtual void DoDataExchange(CDataExchange* pDX);        // DDX/DDV support
        //{{AFX_MSG(CAboutDlg)
        virtual BOOL OnInitDialog();
        afx_msg void OnDestroy();
        //}}AFX_MSG
        DECLARE_MESSAGE_MAP()
};

CAboutDlg::CAboutDlg() : CDialog(CAboutDlg::IDD)
{
        //{{AFX_DATA_INIT(CAboutDlg)
        //}}AFX_DATA_INIT
}

void CAboutDlg::DoDataExchange(CDataExchange* pDX)
{
        CDialog::DoDataExchange(pDX);
        //{{AFX_DATA_MAP(CAboutDlg)
        //}}AFX_DATA_MAP
}
```

```
BEGIN_MESSAGE_MAP(CAboutDlg, CDialog)
     //{{AFX_MSG_MAP(CAboutDlg)
     //}}AFX_MSG_MAP
END_MESSAGE_MAP()

/////////////////////////////////////////////////////////////////////////
// CAboutDlg message handlers

BOOL CAboutDlg::OnInitDialog()
{
     CDialog::OnInitDialog();
     CenterWindow();

     // TODO: Add extra about dlg initialization here

     return TRUE;  // return TRUE  unless you set the focus to a control
}

/////////////////////////////////////////////////////////////////////////
// CMegazeroDlg dialog

CMegazeroDlg::CMegazeroDlg(CWnd* pParent /*=NULL*/)
     : CDialog(CMegazeroDlg::IDD, pParent)
{
     //{{AFX_DATA_INIT(CMegazeroDlg)
          // NOTE: the ClassWizard will add member initialization here
     //}}AFX_DATA_INIT
     // Note that LoadIcon does not require a subsequent DestroyIcon in Win32
     m_hIcon = AfxGetApp()->LoadIcon(IDR_MAINFRAME);
}

void CMegazeroDlg::DoDataExchange(CDataExchange* pDX)
{
     CDialog::DoDataExchange(pDX);
     //{{AFX_DATA_MAP(CMegazeroDlg)
          // NOTE: the ClassWizard will add DDX and DDV calls here
     //}}AFX_DATA_MAP
}

BEGIN_MESSAGE_MAP(CMegazeroDlg, CDialog)
     //{{AFX_MSG_MAP(CMegazeroDlg)
     ON_WM_SYSCOMMAND()
     ON_WM_PAINT()
     ON_WM_QUERYDRAGICON()
     ON_WM_DESTROY()
     ON_WM_DROPFILES()
     //}}AFX_MSG_MAP
END_MESSAGE_MAP()

/////////////////////////////////////////////////////////////////////////
// CMegazeroDlg message handlers

BOOL CMegazeroDlg::OnInitDialog()
{
     CDialog::OnInitDialog();
     CenterWindow();

     // Add "About..." menu item to system menu.

     // IDM_ABOUTBOX must be in the system command range.
     ASSERT((IDM_ABOUTBOX & 0xFFF0) == IDM_ABOUTBOX);
```

```
        ASSERT(IDM_ABOUTBOX < 0xF000);

        // IDM_SELFCHECK, too.
        ASSERT((IDM_SELFCHECK & 0xFFF0) == IDM_SELFCHECK);
        ASSERT(IDM_SELFCHECK < 0xF000);

        // IDM_LOCKUNLOCK, too.
        ASSERT((IDM_LOCKUNLOCK & 0xFFF0) == IDM_LOCKUNLOCK);
        ASSERT(IDM_LOCKUNLOCK < 0xF000);

        CMenu* pSysMenu = GetSystemMenu(FALSE);
        CString strAboutMenu;
        strAboutMenu.LoadString(IDS_ABOUTBOX);
        if (!strAboutMenu.IsEmpty())
        {
            pSysMenu->AppendMenu(MF_SEPARATOR);
            p SysMenu->AppendMenu(MF_STRING, IDM_SELFCHECK, "&Perform self-check...");
            pSysMenu->AppendMenu(MF_STRING, IDM_LOCKUNLOCK,"&Lock/unlock...");
            pSysMenu->AppendMenu(MF_SEPARATOR);
            pSysMenu->AppendMenu(MF_STRING, IDM_ABOUTBOX, strAboutMenu);
        }

    // Read the configuration file into the config array

    LoadConfigData();

    // Set our "last run" date from the config array

    if(config.last_run_year == 0)
      SetWindowText("MegaZero [first execution]");
     else
        {
         char buffer[100];

         wsprintf(buffer,"MegaZero [last run %d/%d/%d]",
          config.last_run_month,config.last_run_day,config.last_run_year);

         SetWindowText(buffer);
        }

    // Set our file name fields

    UpdateFileNames();

    // Ensure we get our own icon, and not the generic one

    PostMessage(WM_SETICON,(WPARAM)TRUE,(LPARAM)m_hIcon);

    // Tell Windows we'll accept dargged and dropped files

    DragAcceptFiles(TRUE);

    if(config.locked)  // Only call DoLockUnlock() if we are locked
      DoLockUnlock();

        return TRUE;  // return TRUE  unless you set the focus to a control
}

void CMegazeroDlg::OnSysCommand(UINT nID, LPARAM lParam)
{
    UINT the_real_nID = nID & 0xFFF0;
```

```
        CAboutDlg dlgAbout;

    switch (the_real_nID)
       {
       case SC_RESTORE:      // If we're unlocked, we process these normally
       case SC_MAXIMIZE:     // If locked, we display the unlock PW prompt
          if(config.locked)
            OnLockUnlock();
          else
           CDialog::OnSysCommand(nID, lParam);
        break;

       case IDM_ABOUTBOX:
         dlgAbout.DoModal();
          break;

       case IDM_SELFCHECK:
         DoSelfCheck();
          break;

       case IDM_LOCKUNLOCK:
         OnLockUnlock();
          break;

      default:
         CDialog::OnSysCommand(nID, lParam);
      }
}

// If you add a minimize button to your dialog, you will need the code below
// to draw the icon.  For MFC applications using the document/view model,
// this is automatically done for you by the framework.

void CMegazeroDlg::OnPaint()
{
    if (IsIconic())
    {
        CPaintDC dc(this); // device context for painting

        SendMessage(WM_ICONERASEBKGND, (WPARAM) dc.GetSafeHdc(), 0);

        // Center icon in client rectangle
        int cxIcon = GetSystemMetrics(SM_CXICON);
        int cyIcon = GetSystemMetrics(SM_CYICON);
        CRect rect;
        GetClientRect(&rect);
        int x = (rect.Width() - cxIcon + 1) / 2;
        int y = (rect.Height() - cyIcon + 1) / 2;

        // Draw the icon
        dc.DrawIcon(x, y, m_hIcon);
    }
    else
    {
        CDialog::OnPaint();
    }
}

// The system calls this to obtain the cursor to display while the user drags
//  the minimized window.
HCURSOR CMegazeroDlg::OnQueryDragIcon()
{
```

```
        return (HCURSOR) m_hIcon;
}

// Do the self-check by calling the GoodCRC() function in CHECKER.CPP

void CMegazeroDlg::DoSelfCheck()
{
  if(GoodCRC())
    MessageBox("Self-Check Passes!","MegaZero",MB_OK | MB_ICONINFORMATION);
  else
    if(MessageBox("Self-Check Fails!\n\nDo you want help?","MegaZero",MB_YESNO
            | MB_ICONQUESTION) == IDYES)
      MessageBox("Imagine brilliant, insightful, context sensitive help here.",
        "Help",MB_OK | MB_ICONINFORMATION);
}

void CMegazeroDlg::OnDestroy()
{
        CDialog::OnDestroy();

        SaveConfigData();
}

/////////////////////////////////////////////////////////////////////////////
// OnDropFiles(): Handle one or more dragged and dropped files.
/////////////////////////////////////////////////////////////////////////////

void CMegazeroDlg::OnDropFiles(HDROP hDropInfo)
{
    char file_buffer[MAX_PATH];
        UINT num_files, i;

    // Make sure we're really on top, since W95 has a funny idea of what to do
    // with the target window after a DND operation.
    SetForegroundWindow();

    // Get the number of dropped files from Windows
        num_files =
            DragQueryFile(hDropInfo,0xffffffff,file_buffer,sizeof(file_buffer));

    // Now retrieve names and process each one
        for(i = 0; i < num_files; i++)
          {
            DragQueryFile(hDropInfo,i,file_buffer,sizeof(file_buffer));
                ProcessDroppedFile(file_buffer);
          }

    // Tell Windows we're done with the DND operation
    DragFinish(hDropInfo);
}

/////////////////////////////////////////////////////////////////////////////
// ProcessDroppedFile(): Add a filename to our in-memory config array.
/////////////////////////////////////////////////////////////////////////////

void CMegazeroDlg::ProcessDroppedFile(char *fn)
{
  if(fn == NULL)
     {
#ifdef _DEBUG
     OutputDebugString("*** ProcessDroppedFile: Null pointer detected!!!\n");
```

```
#endif
    return;
    }

  size_t fn_len = strlen(fn);

  // Note that thanks to this check, we don't have to worry about exceeding the
  // the length of config.fn1 below when we copy fn into it.

  if((fn_len == 0) || (fn_len > sizeof(config.fn1) - 1))
    {
#ifdef _DEBUG
    OutputDebugString("*** ProcessDroppedFile: Invalid fn detected!!!\n");
#endif
    return;
    }

  // Ripple the old entries down one slot...
  strcpy(config.fn10,config.fn9);
  strcpy(config.fn9,config.fn8);
  strcpy(config.fn8,config.fn7);
  strcpy(config.fn7,config.fn6);
  strcpy(config.fn6,config.fn5);
  strcpy(config.fn5,config.fn4);
  strcpy(config.fn4,config.fn3);
  strcpy(config.fn3,config.fn2);
  strcpy(config.fn2,config.fn1);

  // ...and insert the new one at the head of the list.
  strcpy(config.fn1,fn);

<Cod  // Update our interface to reflect the change
  UpdateFileNames();
}

///////////////////////////////////////////////////////////////////////////
// UpdateFileNames(): Update our main interface with the in-memory file names.
///////////////////////////////////////////////////////////////////////////

void CMegazeroDlg::UpdateFileNames(void)
{
   SetDlgItemText(IDC_FN1,config.fn1);
   SetDlgItemText(IDC_FN2,config.fn2);
   SetDlgItemText(IDC_FN3,config.fn3);
   SetDlgItemText(IDC_FN4,config.fn4);
   SetDlgItemText(IDC_FN5,config.fn5);
   SetDlgItemText(IDC_FN6,config.fn6);
   SetDlgItemText(IDC_FN7,config.fn7);
   SetDlgItemText(IDC_FN8,config.fn8);
   SetDlgItemText(IDC_FN9,config.fn9);
   SetDlgItemText(IDC_FN10,config.fn10);
}

///////////////////////////////////////////////////////////////////////////
// OnLockUnlock():
//
// We only call DoLockUnlock() on a verified state change.

void CMegazeroDlg::OnLockUnlock(void)
{
  if(config.locked)
     {
```

```
      TRACE("OnLockUnlock: IsLocked() == TRUE\n");
      if(!UnlockPWDlg())        // FALSE: We're now unlocked
        DoLockUnlock();
      }
  else
      {
      TRACE("OnLockUnlock: IsLocked() == TRUE\n");
      if(LockPWDlg())           // TRUE: We're now locked
        DoLockUnlock();
      }
}


///////////////////////////////////////////////////////////////////////////
// DoLockUnlock():
//
// This code assumes that it is only called when needed, i.e. when the
// program's locked status has actually changed.

void CMegazeroDlg::DoLockUnlock(void)
{
  CMenu* pSysMenu = GetSystemMenu(FALSE);

  if(config.locked)
      {
        // Change to the locked icon
        DestroyIcon(m_hIcon);
        m_hIcon = AfxGetApp()->LoadIcon(IDR_LOCKEDMAINFRAME);
        SetClassLong(AfxGetApp()->m_pMainWnd->m_hWnd,GCL_HICON,(long)m_hIcon);
        PostMessage(WM_SETICON,(WPARAM)TRUE,(LPARAM)m_hIcon);

        // Is DND normally enabled?  If so, disable it.
        DragAcceptFiles(FALSE);

        // Disable our menu items
        pSysMenu->EnableMenuItem(IDM_SELFCHECK,MF_BYCOMMAND | MF_GRAYED);
        pSysMenu->EnableMenuItem(IDM_ABOUTBOX,MF_BYCOMMAND | MF_GRAYED);

        // Minimize ourself
        PostMessage(WM_SYSCOMMAND,SC_MINIMIZE,0);
      }
  else
      {
        // Change to the normal icon
        DestroyIcon(m_hIcon);
        m_hIcon = AfxGetApp()->LoadIcon(IDR_MAINFRAME);
        SetClassLong(AfxGetApp()->m_pMainWnd->m_hWnd,GCL_HICON,(long)m_hIcon);
        PostMessage(WM_SETICON,(WPARAM)TRUE,(LPARAM)m_hIcon);

        // Is DND normally enabled?  If so, re-enable it.
        DragAcceptFiles(TRUE);

        // Enable our menu items
        pSysMenu->EnableMenuItem(IDM_SELFCHECK,MF_BYCOMMAND | MF_ENABLED);
        pSysMenu->EnableMenuItem(IDM_ABOUTBOX,MF_BYCOMMAND | MF_ENABLED);

        // Restore ourself
        PostMessage(WM_SYSCOMMAND,SC_RESTORE,0);
      }
}
```

## Listing A.5    ZEN\APP_A\MEGAZERO\MEGAZERO.H

```
// megazero.h : main header file for the MEGAZERO application
//

#ifndef __AFXWIN_H__
     #error include 'stdafx.h' before including this file for PCH
#endif

#include "resource.h"          // main symbols

/////////////////////////////////////////////////////////////////////////////
// CMegazeroApp:
// See megazero.cpp for the implementation of this class
//

class CMegazeroApp : public CWinApp
{
public:
     CMegazeroApp();

// Overrides
     // ClassWizard generated virtual function overrides
     //{{AFX_VIRTUAL(CMegazeroApp)
     public:
     virtual BOOL InitInstance();
     //}}AFX_VIRTUAL

// Implementation

     //{{AFX_MSG(CMegazeroApp)
          // NOTE - the ClassWizard will add and remove member functions here.
          //    DO NOT EDIT what you see in these blocks of generated code !
     //}}AFX_MSG
     DECLARE_MESSAGE_MAP()
};


/////////////////////////////////////////////////////////////////////////////
```

## Listing A.6    ZEN\APP_A\MEGAZERO\MEGAZERO.CPP

```
// megazero.cpp : Defines the class behaviors for the application.
//

#include "stdafx.h"
#include "megazero.h"
#include "megazdlg.h"
#include "win32ver.h"
#include "tb_int.h"

#ifdef _DEBUG
#undef THIS_FILE
static char BASED_CODE THIS_FILE[] = __FILE__;
#endif


/////////////////////////////////////////////////////////////////////////////
// CMegazeroApp
```

```
BEGIN_MESSAGE_MAP(CMegazeroApp, CWinApp)
    //{{AFX_MSG_MAP(CMegazeroApp)
        // NOTE - the ClassWizard will add and remove mapping macros here.
        //    DO NOT EDIT what you see in these blocks of generated code!
    //}}AFX_MSG
    ON_COMMAND(ID_HELP, CWinApp::OnHelp)
END_MESSAGE_MAP()

/////////////////////////////////////////////////////////////////////////
// CMegazeroApp construction

CMegazeroApp::CMegazeroApp()
{
    // TODO: add construction code here,
    // Place all significant initialization in InitInstance
}

/////////////////////////////////////////////////////////////////////////
// The one and only CMegazeroApp object

CMegazeroApp theApp;

/////////////////////////////////////////////////////////////////////////
// CMegazeroApp initialization

BOOL CMegazeroApp::InitInstance()
{
    if(!LoadTB())
        {
         if(::MessageBox(0,
          "Unable to load TOOLBOX.DLL.\n\nDo you want help?","MegaZero",
          MB_YESNO | MB_ICONQUESTION | MB_TASKMODAL) == IDYES)
          ::MessageBox(0,
          "Imagine brilliant, insightful, context sensitive help here.",
          "Help",MB_OK | MB_ICONINFORMATION | MB_TASKMODAL);

         return FALSE;
        }

    if(ComplainIfNot(WV_AnyNT | WV_W95,"MegaZero"))
        {
         UnloadTB();
         return FALSE;
        }

        // Standard initialization
        // If you are not using these features and wish to reduce the size
        //  of your final executable, you should remove from the following
        //  the specific initialization routines you do not need.

        LoadStdProfileSettings(); // Load standard INI file options (including MRU)

        CMegazeroDlg dlg;
        m_pMainWnd = &dlg;
        int nResponse = dlg.DoModal();
        if (nResponse == IDOK)
        {
            // TODO: Place code here to handle when the dialog is
            //  dismissed with OK
```

```
        }
        else if (nResponse == IDCANCEL)
        {
                // TODO: Place code here to handle when the dialog is
                // dismissed with Cancel
        }

    // Unload our DLL.  Good hygiene is important.
    UnloadTB();

        // Since the dialog has been closed, return FALSE so that we exit the
        // application, rather than start the application's message pump.
        return FALSE;
}
```

## Listing A.7    ZEN\APP_A\MEGAZERO\TB_INT.H

```
#ifndef __tb_int_h__
#define __tb_int_h__

// Load TOOLBOX.DLL and set it up for usage.  The return value indicates
// whether the DLL is loaded and ready for use, not whether it was loaded
// on this particular call.
extern BOOL LoadTB(void);

extern void UnloadTB(void);
extern BOOL GotTB(void);

extern void AppendSlash(char *dest, size_t max_len);
extern BOOL FileExists(const char *fn);

#endif
```

## Listing A.8    ZEN\APP_A\MEGAZERO\TB_INT.CPP

```
/* Copyright Lou Grinzo 1995
   Zen of Windows 95 Programming */

#include <stdafx.h>
#include "tb_int.h"

typedef void (*pfnAppendSlash)(char *dest, size_t max_len);
typedef BOOL (*pfnFileExists)(const char *fn);

// Anchors for the DLL-resident rtns.
static pfnAppendSlash   AppendSlashAnchor   = NULL;
static pfnFileExists    FileExistsAnchor    = NULL;

// Anchor for the DLL itself
static HINSTANCE hTB = NULL;

// Load the DLL and establish links to the needed rtns.
BOOL LoadTB(void)
  {
    if(hTB != NULL)
      {
```

```
#ifdef _DEBUG
        OutputDebugString("*** LoadTB() invocation with DLL present\n");
#endif
        return TRUE;
        }

    if((hTB = LoadLibrary("toolbox.dll")) != NULL)
        {
            if (((AppendSlashAnchor = (pfnAppendSlash)
                GetProcAddress(hTB,"AppendSlash")) == NULL) ||
                ((FileExistsAnchor = (pfnFileExists)
                GetProcAddress(hTB,"FileExists")) == NUL    L))
            {
#ifdef _DEBUG
            OutputDebugString("*** LoadTB() failed to find DLL rtns\n");
#endif
                UnloadTB();
            return FALSE;
            }
        }
    else
        {
#ifdef _DEBUG
            OutputDebugString("*** LoadTB() failed to load DLL\n");
#endif
        UnloadTB();
        return FALSE;
        }

    return TRUE;
    }

// Unload the DLL and set all anchors accordingly.
void UnloadTB(void)
    {
    if(GotTB())
        FreeLibrary(hTB);

        hTB = NULL;
        AppendSlashAnchor = NULL;
        FileExistsAnchor  = NULL;
    }

void AppendSlash(char *dest, size_t max_len)
{
  if(GotTB())
    AppendSlashAnchor(dest,max_len);
#ifdef _DEBUG
  else
    OutputDebugString("*** AppendSlash() invocation without DLL present!\n");
#endif
}

BOOL FileExists(const char *fn)
{
  if(GotTB())
    return FileExistsAnchor(fn);
  else
    {
#ifdef _DEBUG
      OutputDebugString("*** FileExists() invocation without DLL present!\n");
```

```
#endif
    return FALSE;
    }
}


// Is the DLL and its required fns loaded?
BOOL GotTB(void)
{
  return (hTB != NULL);
}
```

## Listing A.9    ZEN\APP_A\MEGAZERO\WIN32VER.H

```
#ifndef __win32ver_h__
#define __win32ver_h__


// If more platforms are added, change the DoIt() method implementation
#define WV_UNKNOWN     0
#define WV_WIN32S      1
#define WV_W95         2
#define WV_NTWS        4
#define WV_NTSERVER    8
#define WV_NTAS        16


#define WV_AnyNT    (WV_NTWS | WV_NTSERVER | WV_NTAS)


// Retrieve just the WV_* OS code
DWORD GetOS(void);


// Retrieve the WV_* code and all version information
void  GetOSVersion(DWORD *os, DWORD *major, DWORD *minor, DWORD *build);


// Are we running under Windows 95?
BOOL IsW95(void);


// Are we running under any variation of Windows NT?
BOOL IsNT(void);


// Are we running under NT 4.0 or later (presumably the version that will
// have the W95 shell)?
BOOL IsNT40rLater(void);


// Are we running under a version of Windows that has the W95 shell (W95
// or NT >= 4.0)?
BOOL IsW95Shell(void);


// Issue a MessageBox telling the user that this program requires one of
// the Windows versions specified by needed_OS.  Title is used as the title
// of the MessageBox.
//
// Returns TRUE if the MessageBox was displayed, meaning that the program is
// NOT running under one of the specified Windows variations, and the program
// should therefore shut down.
//
// Returns FALSE if the program is running under one of the specified Windows
// versions.
BOOL ComplainIfNot(DWORD needed_OS, char *title);


#endif
```

## Listing A.10    ZEN\APP_A\MEGAZERO\WIN32VER.CPP

```
// WIN32 Version Services
// Copyright 1995 Lou Grinzo
// Zen of Windows 95 Programming

#include "stdafx.h"
#include "win32ver.h"

static BOOL have_version_info = FALSE;

static DWORD Windows_version = WV_UNKNOWN;
static DWORD major_version = 0;
static DWORD minor_version = 0;
static DWORD build_number  = 0;

// Local Function Idiom.  See book for explanation.
class pckComplainIfNot
  {
    public:
     pckComplainIfNot(void);
     BOOL DoIt(DWORD Aneeded_OS, char *Atitle);

    private:
     int platforms_needed, platforms_remaining;
      char *title;
      char msg_text[500];
      DWORD needed_OS;

      int  CountOneBits(DWORD x);
      void AddPlatform(DWORD platform, char *platform_name);
      pckComplainIfNot& operator=(const pckComplainIfNot& x);
      pckComplainIfNot(const pckComplainIfNot& x);
  };

static void GetVersionInfo(void);

DWORD GetOS(void)
{
  if(!have_version_info)
    GetVersionInfo();

  return Windows_version;
}

void GetOSVersion(DWORD *os, DWORD *major, DWORD *minor, DWORD *build)
{
  if(!have_version_info)
    GetVersionInfo();

  *os = Windows_version;
  *major = major_version;
  *minor = minor_version;
  *build = build_number;

  return;
}

BOOL IsNT(void)
{
```

```
      if(!have_version_info)
        GetVersionInfo();

      return (Windows_version == WV_NTWS) ||
            (Windows_version == WV_NTAS) ||
            (Windows_version == WV_NTSERVER);
    }

BOOL IsW95(void)
{
  if(!have_version_info)
    GetVersionInfo();

  return (Windows_version == WV_W95);
}

BOOL IsNT40OrLater(void)
{
  if(!have_version_info)
    GetVersionInfo();

  return (IsNT() && major_version >= 4);
}

BOOL IsW95Shell(void)
{
  if(!have_version_info)
    GetVersionInfo();

  return (Windows_version == WV_W95) || IsNT40OrLater();
}

pckComplainIfNot::pckComplainIfNot(void) { }

pckComplainIfNot::DoIt(DWORD Aneeded_OS, char *Atitle)
{
  if(!have_version_info)
    GetVersionInfo();

  // We have what the caller says is needed, so bail out
  if(Aneeded_OS & Windows_version)
    return FALSE;

  // Modify the following as needed if more platforms are defined.  This
  // merely restricts needed_OS to valid bit flags.
  needed_OS = Aneeded_OS & (WV_WIN32S | WV_W95 | WV_AnyNT);

  platforms_remaining = platforms_needed = CountOneBits(needed_OS);

  title = Atitle;

  strcpy(msg_text,"Sorry, this program requires ");

  AddPlatform(WV_WIN32S,"Win32s");
  AddPlatform(WV_W95,"Windows 95");
  AddPlatform(WV_NTWS,"Windows NT Workstation");
  AddPlatform(WV_NTSERVER,"Windows NT Server");
  AddPlatform(WV_NTAS,"Windows NT Advanced Server");

  MessageBox(0,msg_text,title,MB_OK | MB_ICONEXCLAMATION);
```

```
   return TRUE;
}

int pckComplainIfNot::CountOneBits(DWORD x)
{
  int count = 0;

  for(int i = 0; i < sizeof(x) * 8; i++)
    {
      if(x & (DWORD)1)
        count++;

      x = x >> 1;
    }

  return count;
}

void pckComplainIfNot::AddPlatform(DWORD platform, char *platform_name)
{
  if(needed_OS & platform)
    {
      strcat(msg_text,platform_name);

      platforms_remaining--;

      switch(platforms_remaining)
        {
          case 0:
           strcat(msg_text,".");
            break;

          case 1:
           if(platforms_needed > 2)
             strcat(msg_text,", or ");
           else
             strcat(msg_text," or ");
            break;

          default:
           strcat(msg_text,", ");
        }
    }
}

// Simple wrapper/gateway function
BOOL ComplainIfNot(DWORD needed_OS, char *title)
{
  pckComplainIfNot worker;

  return worker.DoIt(needed_OS,title);
}

static void GetVersionInfo(void)
{
  OSVERSIONINFO osvi;

  have_version_info = TRUE;

  memset(&osvi, 0, sizeof(OSVERSIONINFO));
  osvi.dwOSVersionInfoSize = sizeof (OSVERSIONINFO);
  GetVersionEx(&osvi);
```

```
      major_version = osvi.dwMajorVersion;
      minor_version = osvi.dwMinorVersion;
      build_number = osvi.dwBuildNumber & 0xFFFF;

   Windows_version = WV_UNKNOWN;

   if(osvi.dwPlatformId == VER_PLATFORM_WIN32s)
     Windows_version = WV_WIN32S;
   else
    if(osvi.dwPlatformId == VER_PLATFORM_WIN32_WINDOWS)
      Windows_version = WV_W95;
    else
     if(osvi.dwPlatformId == VER_PLATFORM_WIN32_NT)
        {
        Windows_version = WV_NTWS;  // Default, until we know better

         HKEY  the_key;
         BYTE  nt_type[100];
         DWORD type_size = sizeof(nt_type);

        if(RegOpenKeyEx(HKEY_LOCAL_MACHINE,
           "SYSTEM\\CurrentControlSet\\Control\\ProductOptions",
           0,KEY_READ,&the_key) == ERROR_SUCCESS)
           {
           if(RegQueryValueEx(the_key,
             "ProductType",0,NULL,nt_type,&type_size) == ERROR_SUCCESS)
              {
              if(stricmp((char *)nt_type,"SERVERNT") == 0)
                Windows_version = WV_NTSERVER;
                else
                if(stricmp((char *)nt_type,"LANMANNT") == 0)
                  Windows_version = WV_NTAS;
                  else
                  Windows_version = WV_NTWS;
              }

           RegCloseKey(the_key);
           }
        }
     }
}
```

## Listing A.11    ZEN\APP_A\MEGAZERO\LOCKPW.H

```
// lockpw.h : header file
//


/////////////////////////////////////////////////////////////////////////
// LockPW dialog

class LockPW : public CDialog
{
// Construction
public:
     LockPW(CWnd* pParent = NULL);   // standard constructor

// Dialog Data
     //{{AFX_DATA(LockPW)
     enum { IDD = IDD_LOCKPW };
          // NOTE: the ClassWizard will add data members here
     //}}AFX_DATA
```

```
// Overrides
    // ClassWizard generated virtual function overrides
    //{{AFX_VIRTUAL(LockPW)
    protected:
    virtual void DoDataExchange(CDataExchange* pDX);    // DDX/DDV support
    //}}AFX_VIRTUAL

// Implementation
protected:

    // Generated message map functions
    //{{AFX_MSG(LockPW)
    virtual void OnOK();
    virtual BOOL OnInitDialog();
    //}}AFX_MSG
    DECLARE_MESSAGE_MAP()
};
```

## Listing A.12  ZEN\APP_A\MEGAZERO\LOCKPW.CPP

```
// Copyright 1995 Lou Grinzo
// Zen of Windows 95 Programming

// lockpw.cpp : implementation file
//

#include "stdafx.h"
#include "megazero.h"
#include "lockpw.h"
#include "config.h"
#include "toolbox.h"

#ifdef _DEBUG
#undef THIS_FILE
static char BASED_CODE THIS_FILE[] = __FILE__;
#endif

/////////////////////////////////////////////////////////////////////////////
// LockPW dialog


LockPW::LockPW(CWnd* pParent /*=NULL*/)
    : CDialog(LockPW::IDD, pParent)
{
    //{{AFX_DATA_INIT(LockPW)
        // NOTE: the ClassWizard will add member initialization here
    //}}AFX_DATA_INIT
}

void LockPW::DoDataExchange(CDataExchange* pDX)
{
    CDialog::DoDataExchange(pDX);
    //{{AFX_DATA_MAP(LockPW)
        // NOTE: the ClassWizard will add DDX and DDV calls here
    //}}AFX_DATA_MAP
}

BEGIN_MESSAGE_MAP(LockPW, CDialog)
    //{{AFX_MSG_MAP(LockPW)
    //}}AFX_MSG_MAP
END_MESSAGE_MAP()
```

```
///////////////////////////////////////////////////////////////////////////
// LockPW message handlers

void LockPW::OnOK()
{
    char pw1[MAX_PW_LEN + 1] = "";
    char pw2[MAX_PW_LEN + 1] = "";

    ::GetWindowText(::GetDlgItem(m_hWnd,IDC_PW1),pw1,sizeof(pw1));
    ::GetWindowText(::GetDlgItem(m_hWnd,IDC_PW2),pw2,sizeof(pw2));

    // Get rid of those nasty leading and trailing blanks
    stripLT(pw1);
    stripLT(pw2);

    if(strcmp(pw1,pw2) != 0)
       {
        ::MessageBox(m_hWnd,
        "The passwords you entered were not the same.\n\nPlease try again.",
        "MegaZero",MB_OK | MB_ICONEXCLAMATION);
        return;
       }

    if(strlen(pw1) < MIN_PW_LEN)
       {
        if(::MessageBox(m_hWnd,
          "Your password is too short.\n\nDo you want help?",
         "MegaZero",MB_YESNO | MB_ICONQUESTION) == IDYES)
         ::MessageBox(m_hWnd,
           "Imagine brilliant, insightful, context sensitive help here.",
           "Help",MB_OK | MB_ICONINFORMATION);
        return;
       }

    // If we got here, all must be OK, so we go ahead and set the lock
    config.locked = TRUE;
    strcpy(config.password,pw1);

    CDialog::OnOK();
}

BOOL LockPW::OnInitDialog()
{
    CDialog::OnInitDialog();
    CenterWindow();

    // TODO: Add extra initialization here

    SendDlgItemMessage(IDC_PW1,EM_LIMITTEXT,MAX_PW_LEN,0);
    SendDlgItemMessage(IDC_PW2,EM_LIMITTEXT,MAX_PW_LEN,0);

    return TRUE;  // return TRUE unless you set the focus to a control
                  // EXCEPTION: OCX Property Pages should return FALSE
}
```

## Listing A.13    ZEN\APP_A\MEGAZERO\UNLOCKPW.H

```
// unlockpw.h : header file
//
```

```
/////////////////////////////////////////////////////////////////////////
// UnlockPW dialog

class UnlockPW : public CDialog
{
// Construction
public:
     UnlockPW(CWnd* pParent = NULL);   // standard constructor

// Dialog Data
     //{{AFX_DATA(UnlockPW)
     enum { IDD = IDD_UNLOCKPW };
          // NOTE: the ClassWizard will add data members here
     //}}AFX_DATA


// Overrides
     // ClassWizard generated virtual function overrides
     //{{AFX_VIRTUAL(UnlockPW)
     protected:
     virtual void DoDataExchange(CDataExchange* pDX);   // DDX/DDV support
     //}}AFX_VIRTUAL

// Implementation
protected:

     // Generated message map functions
     //{{AFX_MSG(UnlockPW)
     virtual void OnOK();
     virtual BOOL OnInitDialog();
     //}}AFX_MSG
     DECLARE_MESSAGE_MAP()
};
```

## Listing A.14  ZEN\APP_A\MEGAZERO\UNLOCKPW.CPP

```
// Copyright 1995 Lou Grinzo
// Zen of Windows 95 Programming

// unlockpw.cpp : implementation file
//

#include "stdafx.h"
#include "megazero.h"
#include "unlockpw.h"
#include "config.h"
#include "toolbox.h"

#ifdef _DEBUG
#undef THIS_FILE
static char BASED_CODE THIS_FILE[] = __FILE__;
#endif


/////////////////////////////////////////////////////////////////////////
// UnlockPW dialog


UnlockPW::UnlockPW(CWnd* pParent /*=NULL*/)
     : CDialog(UnlockPW::IDD, pParent)
{
```

```
        //{{AFX_DATA_INIT(UnlockPW)
              // NOTE: the ClassWizard will add member initialization here
        //}}AFX_DATA_INIT
    }

    void UnlockPW::DoDataExchange(CDataExchange* pDX)
    {
        CDialog::DoDataExchange(pDX);
        //{{AFX_DATA_MAP(UnlockPW)
              // NOTE: the ClassWizard will add DDX and DDV calls here
        //}}AFX_DATA_MAP
    }

    BEGIN_MESSAGE_MAP(UnlockPW, CDialog)
        //{{AFX_MSG_MAP(UnlockPW)
        //}}AFX_MSG_MAP
    END_MESSAGE_MAP()

    /////////////////////////////////////////////////////////////////////////
    // UnlockPW message handlers

    void UnlockPW::OnOK()
    {
        char pw[MAX_PW_LEN + 1] = "";

      ::GetWindowText(::GetDlgItem(m_hWnd,IDC_PW),pw,sizeof(pw));

      // Get rid of those nasty leading and trailing blanks
      stripLT(pw);

      if(strcmp(pw,config.password) != 0)
        {
         MessageBox("Incorrect password!","MegaZero",MB_OK | MB_ICONEXCLAMATION);
          return;
        }

      // If we got here, everything must be OK, so we unlock the program
       config.locked     = FALSE;
      config.password[0] = '\0';

        CDialog::OnOK();
    }

    BOOL UnlockPW::OnInitDialog()
    {
        CDialog::OnInitDialog();
        CenterWindow();

      SendDlgItemMessage(IDC_PW,EM_LIMITTEXT,MAX_PW_LEN,0);

        return TRUE;  // return TRUE unless you set the focus to a control
                   // EXCEPTION: OCX Property Pages should return FALSE
    }
```

# Listing A.15   ZEN\APP_A\MEGAZERO\TOOLBOX.H

```
#ifndef __TOOLBOX_H__
#define __TOOLBOX_H__

void stripLeading(char *s);
void stripLT(char *s);
```

```
void stripTrailing(char *s);

BOOL strlcat(char *dest, const char *src, size_t max_len);
BOOL strlcatAtomic(char *dest, const char *src, size_t max_len);

#endif // __TOOLBOX_H__
```

## Listing A.16  ZEN\APP_A\MEGAZERO\TOOLBOX.CPP

```cpp
// Copyright 1995 Lou Grinzo
// Zen of Windows 95 Programming

#include "stdafx.h"
#include "toolbox.h"

////////////////////////////////////////////////////////////////////////////
// stripLeading: Strip the leading blanks and tabs from a character string.
//
// Parameter is validated:
//   NULL or zero-length string is rejected
//
////////////////////////////////////////////////////////////////////////////

void stripLeading(char *s)
{
#ifdef _DEBUG
  if((s == NULL) || (*s == '\0'))
    OutputDebugString("stripLeading: Invalid parameter detected!\n");
#endif

  if((s == NULL) || (*s == '\0'))
    return;

  char *z = s;

  while(*z && ((*z == ' ') || (*z == '\t')))
    z++;

  if(s != z)
    memmove(s,z,strlen(z) + 1); // Safe-- can't possibly overflow
}

////////////////////////////////////////////////////////////////////////////
// stripLT: Strip leading and trailing blanks and tabs from a char. string.
//
// Parameter is validated:
//   NULL or zero-length string is rejected
//
////////////////////////////////////////////////////////////////////////////

void stripLT(char *s)
{
#ifdef _DEBUG
  if((s == NULL) || (*s == '\0'))
    OutputDebugString("stripLT: Invalid parameter detected!\n");
#endif

  if((s == NULL) || (*s == '\0'))
    return;
```

```
  stripLeading(s);
  stripTrailing(s);
}


///////////////////////////////////////////////////////////////////////////
// stripTrailing: Strip trailing blanks and tabs from a character string.
//
// Parameter is validated:
//   NULL or zero-length string is rejected
//
///////////////////////////////////////////////////////////////////////////

void stripTrailing(char *s)
{
#ifdef _DEBUG
  if((s == NULL) || (*s == '\0'))
    OutputDebugString("stripTrailing: Invalid parameter detected!\n");
#endif

  if((s == NULL) || (*s == '\0'))
    return;

  int z = strlen(s);

  while((z >= 0) && ((s[z] == ' ') || (s[z] == '\t') || (s[z] == '\0')))
    z--;

  s[z + 1] = 0;
}


///////////////////////////////////////////////////////////////////////////
// strlcatAtomic: Concatenate characters from src onto dest, with a maximum
// length for dest of max_len, and always ensure proper termination.  This
// function will only concatenate characters from src onto dest if all the
// characters in src will fit.
//
// max_len includes the term. null
//
// Returns TRUE if concatenation was performed, FALSE if it wasn't.
//
// Parameters are validated:
//   NULL or zero-length strings are rejected
//   max_len of 0 or smaller than dest's initial length is rejected
//
///////////////////////////////////////////////////////////////////////////

BOOL strlcatAtomic(char *dest, const char *src, size_t max_len)
{
#ifdef _DEBUG
  if((dest == NULL) || (src == NULL) || (max_len == 0) || (strlen(dest) >=
       max_len - 1))
    OutputDebugString("strlcatAtomic: Invalid parameter detected!\n");
#endif

  if((dest == NULL) ||
     (src == NULL) ||
     (max_len == 0))
    return FALSE;

  UINT d_len = strlen(dest);
```

```
  if(d_len + strlen(src) >= max_len - 1)   // Ensure all chars will fit
    return FALSE;

  strncat(dest,src,max_len - d_len - 1);
  return TRUE;
}


//////////////////////////////////////////////////////////////////////////
// strlcat: Concatenate characters from src onto dest, with a maximum length
// for dest of max_len, and always ensure proper termination.  This function
// will concatenate as many characters from src onto dest as will fit.
//
// max_len includes the term. null
//
// Returns TRUE if concatenation was performed, FALSE if it wasn't.
//
// Parameters are validated:
//   NULL or zero-length strings are rejected
//   max_len of 0 or smaller than dest's initial length is rejected
//
//////////////////////////////////////////////////////////////////////////

BOOL strlcat(char *dest, const char *src, size_t max_len)
{
#ifdef _DEBUG
  if((dest == NULL) || (src == NULL) || (max_len == 0) || (strlen(dest) >=
max_len - 1))
    OutputDebugString("strlcat: Invalid parameter detected!\n");
#endif

  if((dest == NULL) || (src == NULL) || (max_len == 0))
    return FALSE;

  UINT d_len = strlen(dest);

  if(d_len >= max_len - 1)
    return FALSE;

  strncat(dest,src,max_len - d_len - 1);
  return TRUE;
}
```

## Listing A.17   ZEN\APP_A\TOOLBOX\TOOLBOX.CPP

```
/* Copyright Lou Grinzo 1995
   Zen of Windows 95 Programming */

#include <windows.h>


//////////////////////////////////////////////////////////////////////////
// AppendSlash: Append a backslash to the provided string only if there is
// room for one and the string does not already end in a backslash.
//
// dest: string to be modified
// max_len: Maximum allowable length of dest, including a term. NULL
//
// Parameters are validated:
//   NULL or zero-length dest parameter is rejected
//   max_len less than 3 is rejected
//////////////////////////////////////////////////////////////////////////
```

```
void AppendSlash(char *dest, size_t max_len)
{
#ifdef _DEBUG
  if((dest == NULL) || (*dest == '\0') || (max_len < 3))
    OutputDebugString("AppendSlash: Invalid parameter detected!\n");
#endif

  if((dest == NULL) || (*dest == '\0')|| (max_len < 3))
    return;

  if((strlen(dest) + 1 < max_len) &&
    (dest[strlen(dest) - 1] != '\\'))
      strcat(dest,"\\");
}


/////////////////////////////////////////////////////////////////////////
// FileExists: Checks to see if the specified file exists and is NOT a
// directory.
//
// Returns TRUE if the file exists, FALSE if it doesn't or is a directory.
//
// Parameter is validated:
//   NULL or zero-length string is rejected
//
/////////////////////////////////////////////////////////////////////////

BOOL FileExists(const char *fn)
{
#ifdef _DEBUG
  if(fn == NULL || (strlen(fn)) == 0)
    OutputDebugString("FileExists: Invalid parameter detected!\n");
#endif

  if(fn == NULL || (strlen(fn)) == 0)
    return FALSE;

  DWORD dwFA = GetFileAttributes(fn);

  if(dwFA == 0xFFFFFFFF)
    return FALSE;
  else
    return ((dwFA & FILE_ATTRIBUTE_DIRECTORY) != FILE_ATTRIBUTE_DIRECTORY);
}
```

## Listing A.18    ZEN\APP_A\DUMPER\DUMPER.CPP

```
/////////////////////////////////////////////////////////////////////////
// Dumper: Read and display the contents of a MEGAZERO.DAT custom data file.
// This program also performs some minimal validation.
//
// Copyright Lou Grinzo 1995, Zen of Windows 95 Programming
/////////////////////////////////////////////////////////////////////////

#include <windows.h>
#include <stdio.h>
#include "..\\megazero\\config.h"

void DumpHeader(const config_header_type *ch);
void DumpData(const config_type *c);
void Pause(void);
```

```
int main()
{
 char fn[] = "megazero.dat";
 FILE *f;
 config_header_type config_header;
 config_type        config;

 if((f = fopen(fn,"rb")) == NULL)
    {
     printf("Unable to open input file \"%s\".\n",fn);
     Pause();
     return 0;
    }

 if(fread(&config_header,sizeof(config_header),1,f) != 1)
    {
     fclose(f);
     printf("Unable to read header from input file \"%s\".\n",fn);
     Pause();
     return 0;
    }

 DumpHeader(&config_header);
 Pause();

 if(fread(&config,sizeof(config),1,f) != 1)
    {
     fclose(f);
     printf("Unable to read data from input file \"%s\".\n",fn);
     Pause();
     return 0;
    }

 DumpData(&config);
 printf("Finished!  ");
 Pause();

 fclose(f);

 return 0;
}

/////////////////////////////////////////////////////////////////////////
// PrintChar(): Print a character, substituting an underscore for a 0x00,
// and a question mark for all control characters
/////////////////////////////////////////////////////////////////////////

void PrintChar(char c)
{
  if(c == '\0')
    printf("_");
  else
    if(!iscntrl(c))
      printf("%c",c);
    else
      printf("?");
}

/////////////////////////////////////////////////////////////////////////
// DumpHeader(): Display the file header's fields
/////////////////////////////////////////////////////////////////////////
```

```
void DumpHeader(const config_header_type *ch)
{
  printf("Fingerprint: ");

  for(int i = 0; i < eye_catcher_len; i++)
    PrintChar(ch->eye_catcher[i]);

  printf("\n\n");

  if(strncmp(ch->eye_catcher,"megazero",eye_catcher_len) == 0)
    printf("Fingerprint is correct.\n\n");
  else
    printf("Fingerprint is not correct.\n\n");

  printf("File version: %hu.%hu\n\n",ch->major_version,ch->minor_version);
}


/////////////////////////////////////////////////////////////////////////
// DumpFN(): Display one of the fn fields from the file's data portion
/////////////////////////////////////////////////////////////////////////

void DumpFN(const char *fn,int fn_num)
{
  printf("FN%d : ",fn_num);

  for(int i = 0; i < MAX_PATH; i++)
    PrintChar(fn[i]);
  printf("\n");
}


/////////////////////////////////////////////////////////////////////////
// DumpData(): Display the fields from the data portion of the file, and
// validate the reserved/must-be-zero fields.
/////////////////////////////////////////////////////////////////////////

void DumpData(const config_type *c)
{
  int i;

  DumpFN(c->fn1,1);
  DumpFN(c->fn2,2);
  DumpFN(c->fn3,3);
  Pause();

  DumpFN(c->fn4,4);
  DumpFN(c->fn5,5);
  DumpFN(c->fn6,6);
  Pause();

  DumpFN(c->fn7,7);
  DumpFN(c->fn8,8);
  DumpFN(c->fn9,9);
  DumpFN(c->fn10,10);
  Pause();

  printf("Last-run date (M/D/Y): %d/%d/%d\n\n",
    c->last_run_month,c->last_run_day,c->last_run_year);

  if(c->locked)
    printf("Application is locked.\n\n");
```

```
  else
    printf("Application is not locked.\n\n");

  printf("Password: ");
  for(i = 0; i < sizeof(c->password); i++)
    PrintChar(c->password[i]);
  printf("\n\n");

  printf("Reserved/must be zero fields: ");
  for(i = 0; i < sizeof(c->reserved) / sizeof(int); i++)
    printf("%d ",c->reserved[i]);
  printf("\n\n");

  for(i = 0; i < sizeof(c->reserved) / sizeof(int); i++)
    if(c->reserved[i] != 0)
      {
        printf("*** Reserved fields are not all zero!!!\n\n");
        return;
      }
}


//////////////////////////////////////////////////////////////////////////

void Pause(void)
{
  printf("Press ENTER... \n\n");
  getchar();
}
```

## Listing A.19   ZEN\APP_A\PATCHER\PATCHER.CPP

```
//////////////////////////////////////////////////////////////////////////
// PATCHER.CPP: File patching utility in the form of a WIN32 console app
//
// Copyright 1995 Lou Grinzo
// Zen of Windows 95 Programming

#include "stdafx.h"
#include <stdio.h>
#include <io.h>
#include "checker.h"

FILE* f;
const buffer_size = 16384;
unsigned long i, crc_start, file_pos;
eye_catcher_type pattern;
unsigned short the_crc;
BYTE the_byte;
char buffer[buffer_size];
long buffer_pos, data_size;
char NextByte(void);
void ReadNextCatcher(eye_catcher_type & c);

int main()
  {
    // Change the following to match the name of the file to be patched!
    char * file_name = "megazero.exe";   // !!!!!!!!!!!!!!!!!!!!!!!!!!!!!!!!!!!

    printf("About to patch file \"%s\"...\n\n",file_name);
```

```
  if(!(f = fopen(file_name,"rb")))
   printf("Unable to open file.\n\n\n");
  else
     {
      buffer_pos = buffer_size;
      data_size = 0;
      file_pos = 0;

     printf("Searching for the start of the CRC data...\n");

     // Seed the pattern with the initial bytes of the file

     for(i = 0; i < sizeof(pattern); i++)
       pattern[i] = NextByte();

     crc_start = 0;    // Init to "not found" value

     // Scan through the rest of the file, looking for the eye catcher.
     // Note that we DON'T stop at the first occurrence!  We must scan
     // the entire file, so that we're completely sure there isn't a
     // second copy of the eye catcher floating about.

     unsigned long limit = _filelength(fileno(f)) - sizeof(pattern);

      for(i = 0; i < limit; i++)
        {
         if(!memcmp(crc_data.eye_catcher,pattern,sizeof(pattern)))
            if(crc_start > 0)
               {
                printf("File contains more than one instance of the eye
                        catcher!\n\n");
                 fclose(f);
                 getchar();
                 return 0;
               }
            else
            crc_start = file_pos - sizeof(pattern);

         ReadNextCatcher(pattern);
        }

     fclose(f);

     if(crc_start == 0)
        {
        printf("Couldn't find the eye catcher!\n\n");
         getchar();
         return 0;
        }

     // Could check here to see if the file is already patched, and bail
     // out with a msg if it is.  But patching is non-destructive and
     // resonably quick, so it's probably not worth the effort in a
     // development tool.

     printf("Found eye catcher.  Doing CRC calculation...\n\n");

     // CalcCRC trusts us to supply the one, true offset of the crc_data

     if(!FindCRC(file_name,crc_start,&the_crc))
        {
```

```
              printf("Couldn't calculate the file's CRC!\n\n");
                getchar();
                return 0;
                }

       if(!(f = fopen(file_name,"rb+")))
            {
            printf("Couldn't re-open file!\n\n");
              getchar();
              return 0;
              }

       // We have our data, so it's time to patch the crc_data struct in
        // the file.

       // Position to the start of the data we're about to write, which is
       // NOT the beginning of crc-data, but the crc_start field within it.
        //
       // This assumes a specific layout of the crc_data_type structure!
       fseek(f,crc_start + sizeof(pattern),SEEK_SET);

        // Write out our data
       fwrite(&crc_start,1,sizeof(crc_start),f);
       fwrite(&the_crc,1,sizeof(the_crc),f);

        // Take 'er home
        fclose(f);

       printf("\"%s\" has been updated with the following values:\n",file_name);
       printf("  CRC offset: %d\n",crc_start);
       printf("  CRC value:  %d\n",the_crc);

       printf("\nDone!!!\n\n");
       }

   printf("(Press ENTER) ");
   getchar();

   return 0;
   }

///////////////////////////////////////////////////////////////////////////
// NextByte(): Return the next buffered byte of the input file

char NextByte(void)
  {
   if(buffer_pos >= data_size)
      {
      data_size = fread(buffer,1,buffer_size,f);
       buffer_pos = 0;
      }

   buffer_pos++;
   file_pos++;
   return buffer[buffer_pos - 1];
  }

///////////////////////////////////////////////////////////////////////////
// ReadNextCatcher(): Read a new character, and roll it into our current eye-
// catcher candidate.
```

```
void ReadNextCatcher(eye_catcher_type & c)
  {
  memmove(&c[0],&c[1],sizeof(c) - 1);
  c[sizeof(c) - 1] = NextByte();
  }
```

## Listing A.20    ZEN\APP_A\PATCHER\CHECKER.CPP

```
////////////////////////////////////////////////////////////////////////
// CHECKER.CPP: Core CRC calculation code and data
//
// Copyright 1995 Lou Grinzo
// Zen of Windows 95 Programming

#include "stdafx.h"
#include "checker.h"
#include <stdlib.h>
#include <stdio.h>
#include <io.h>
#include <malloc.h>
#include <assert.h>

static long buffer_pos, data_size;
static BYTE *buffer;
static const alloc_buffer_size = 4096;
static FILE *f;

// Local functions
static unsigned short UpdateCRC(BYTE new_byte, unsigned short crc);
static char NextByte(void);

// This instance of a crc_data_type must be here.  This is the one that
// will ultimately wind up in the application and contain its calculated
// CRC value.
crc_data_type crc_data =
  {
  'M', 'E', 'G', 'A', 'Z', 'E', 'R', 'O',   // eye_catcher
  0,                                         // start
  0                                          // crc_value
  };

////////////////////////////////////////////////////////////////////////
// The data table used by the UpdateCRC() function to calculate a CRC
static unsigned short crctab[256] =
  {
  0x0000, 0x1021, 0x2042, 0x3063, 0x4084, 0x50a5, 0x60c6, 0x70e7,
  0x8108, 0x9129, 0xa14a, 0xb16b, 0xc18c, 0xd1ad, 0xe1ce, 0xf1ef,
  0x1231, 0x0210, 0x3273, 0x2252, 0x52b5, 0x4294, 0x72f7, 0x62d6,
  0x9339, 0x8318, 0xb37b, 0xa35a, 0xd3bd, 0xc39c, 0xf3ff, 0xe3de,
  0x2462, 0x3443, 0x0420, 0x1401, 0x64e6, 0x74c7, 0x44a4, 0x5485,
  0xa56a, 0xb54b, 0x8528, 0x9509, 0xe5ee, 0xf5cf, 0xc5ac, 0xd58d,
  0x3653, 0x2672, 0x1611, 0x0630, 0x76d7, 0x66f6, 0x5695, 0x46b4,
  0xb75b, 0xa77a, 0x9719, 0x8738, 0xf7df, 0xe7fe, 0xd79d, 0xc7bc,
  0x48c4, 0x58e5, 0x6886, 0x78a7, 0x0840, 0x1861, 0x2802, 0x3823,
  0xc9cc, 0xd9ed, 0xe98e, 0xf9af, 0x8948, 0x9969, 0xa90a, 0xb92b,
  0x5af5, 0x4ad4, 0x7ab7, 0x6a96, 0x1a71, 0x0a50, 0x3a33, 0x2a12,
  0xdbfd, 0xcbdc, 0xfbbf, 0xeb9e, 0x9b79, 0x8b58, 0xbb3b, 0xab1a,
  0x6ca6, 0x7c87, 0x4ce4, 0x5cc5, 0x2c22, 0x3c03, 0x0c60, 0x1c41,
  0xedae, 0xfd8f, 0xcdec, 0xddcd, 0xad2a, 0xbd0b, 0x8d68, 0x9d49,
```

```
  0x7e97,  0x6eb6,  0x5ed5,  0x4ef4,  0x3e13,  0x2e32,  0x1e51,  0x0e70,
  0xff9f,  0xefbe,  0xdfdd,  0xcffc,  0xbf1b,  0xaf3a,  0x9f59,  0x8f78,
  0x9188,  0x81a9,  0xb1ca,  0xa1eb,  0xd10c,  0xc12d,  0xf14e,  0xe16f,
  0x1080,  0x00a1,  0x30c2,  0x20e3,  0x5004,  0x4025,  0x7046,  0x6067,
  0x83b9,  0x9398,  0xa3fb,  0xb3da,  0xc33d,  0xd31c,  0xe37f,  0xf35e,
  0x02b1,  0x1290,  0x22f3,  0x32d2,  0x4235,  0x5214,  0x6277,  0x7256,
  0xb5ea,  0xa5cb,  0x95a8,  0x8589,  0xf56e,  0xe54f,  0xd52c,  0xc50d,
  0x34e2,  0x24c3,  0x14a0,  0x0481,  0x7466,  0x6447,  0x5424,  0x4405,
  0xa7db,  0xb7fa,  0x8799,  0x97b8,  0xe75f,  0xf77e,  0xc71d,  0xd73c,
  0x26d3,  0x36f2,  0x0691,  0x16b0,  0x6657,  0x7676,  0x4615,  0x5634,
  0xd94c,  0xc96d,  0xf90e,  0xe92f,  0x99c8,  0x89e9,  0xb98a,  0xa9ab,
  0x5844,  0x4865,  0x7806,  0x6827,  0x18c0,  0x08e1,  0x3882,  0x28a3,
  0xcb7d,  0xdb5c,  0xeb3f,  0xfb1e,  0x8bf9,  0x9bd8,  0xabbb,  0xbb9a,
  0x4a75,  0x5a54,  0x6a37,  0x7a16,  0x0af1,  0x1ad0,  0x2ab3,  0x3a92,
  0xfd2e,  0xed0f,  0xdd6c,  0xcd4d,  0xbdaa,  0xad8b,  0x9de8,  0x8dc9,
  0x7c26,  0x6c07,  0x5c64,  0x4c45,  0x3ca2,  0x2c83,  0x1ce0,  0x0cc1,
  0xef1f,  0xff3e,  0xcf5d,  0xdf7c,  0xaf9b,  0xbfba,  0x8fd9,  0x9ff8,
  0x6e17,  0x7e36,  0x4e55,  0x5e74,  0x2e93,  0x3eb2,  0x0ed1,  0x1ef0
};

////////////////////////////////////////////////////////////////////////
// UpdateCRC(): Update the current CRC for the data stream by taking into
// account the next byte in the stream, new_byte.

static unsigned short UpdateCRC(BYTE new_byte, unsigned short crc)
  { return crctab[(crc & 0x00ff) ^ new_byte] ^ (crc >> 8); }

////////////////////////////////////////////////////////////////////////

BOOL FindCRC(char *fn, unsigned long crc_start, unsigned short * the_crc)
  {
    assert(fn != NULL);
    assert(fn[0] != '\0');
    assert(crc_start != 0);

    if(fn == NULL)
      return FALSE;

    if(fn[0] == '\0')
      return FALSE;

    *the_crc = 0;
    unsigned long i;

    if((buffer = (BYTE *)malloc(alloc_buffer_size)) == NULL)
      return FALSE;

    if(!(f = fopen(fn,"rb")))
      return FALSE;

    // Grab the file size here, and not in a loop!
    unsigned long limit = _filelength(fileno(f));

    // Make sure crc_start points to a valid position in the file
    if(limit - sizeof(crc_data_type) < crc_start)
      {
        fclose(f);
        return FALSE;
      }
```

```
      buffer_pos = alloc_buffer_size;
      data_size = 0;

      // Calculate the CRC for the file before the CRC data structure...
      for(i = 0; i < crc_start; i++)
       *the_crc = UpdateCRC(NextByte(),*the_crc);

      // ...then step over the entire structure...
      for(i = 0; i < sizeof(crc_data_type); i++)
        NextByte();

      // ...and finish up with what follows the structure.
      for(i = crc_start + sizeof(crc_data_type); i < limit; i++)
       *the_crc = UpdateCRC(NextByte(),*the_crc);

      free(buffer);

      fclose(f);

      return TRUE;
    }

//////////////////////////////////////////////////////////////////////////

BOOL GoodCRC(void)
  {
    char fn[MAX_PATH];
    unsigned short the_crc;

    if(crc_data.start != 0)
       {
       GetModuleFileName(NULL,fn,sizeof(fn));

        // If something was amiss, we return false
       if(!FindCRC(fn,crc_data.start,&the_crc))
          return FALSE;
        else
         return the_crc == crc_data.crc_value;
       }
     else
      return FALSE;       // No data, no sense in performing calculation
  }

//////////////////////////////////////////////////////////////////////////
// NextByte(): Return the next buffered byte of the input file.

char NextByte(void)
  {
    if(buffer_pos >= data_size)
       {
       data_size = fread(buffer,1,alloc_buffer_size,f);
        buffer_pos = 0;
       }

    buffer_pos++;
    return buffer[buffer_pos - 1];
  }
```

# A Compendium of Programmer's Fables

*The foul sluggard's comfort: "It will last my time."*
Thomas Carlyle

Now that I've set the mood with Mr. Carlyle's sneering quotation, let me assure you that I've committed every sin I'm about to talk about, some of them more times than I care to admit before I learned my lesson. If nothing else, through experience and hubris I've earned the right to talk about such things.

I also want to make clear why I decided to include this appendix. I'm not doing it because I want to beat up programmers; there's no profit in that (in any sense of the word), and besides, I like programmers. Still, I felt it was a good idea to make one last pass at these fables, even though I've already mentioned most of them in the book. Here, in isolation, I can give them a somewhat fuller treatment and remind you (and myself) why these seemingly harmless excuses can be so dangerous to our programs and our users. If nothing else, I hope this will help us all to stay on the lookout for these fables, and to be prepared to counteract them, no matter who the speaker is.

## "All software has bugs."

This is the Big Kahuna, the most often used and most damaging programmer fable. I've heard this one hundreds of times from programmers, and it's always used with the same implication: Other people's software sure isn't perfect, so why the heck should *I* strive for an abnormally high quality level? This mindset is the steepest, slipperiest slope in all of programming, and it very quickly leads to shortcuts in design, coding, and packaging, and a cavalier attitude about quality and usability issues in general. Like all programmer fables, this one is particularly inviting because it's so obviously true, at least in part; no one who's used a computer with commercially available software for more than about an hour would dispute that.

Let's turn the issue around: The next time you pay good money for a Windows application or development tool, and it's so buggy and poorly documented that you wind up muttering all sorts of crude things under your breath, think of this fable. There's an excellent chance that it's been used as an excuse a few too many times by the programmers and managers responsible for the binary atrocity that's just consumed your time and money.

**"You can't check for everything."/"I don't want to waste cycles."**

These are the Vice Big Kahunas. The second one, in particular, leads to some rather amazing coding decisions. Notice that I didn't say design decisions, because they aren't. These fables come into play at the micro level, when programmers are in the trenches and deciding on the fly whether to validate parameters or otherwise ensure that everything is as it should be.

The problem with this fable is that it leads to the creation of software that's grossly lacking in firewalls and filters that catch or correct the spread of bad data within an application. Many programmers have learned that swearing blind allegiance to performance pleases management and is therefore a great way to avoid doing some unpleasant things that they *should* do. The result is hollow, fragile programs that can be a nightmare to debug when the inevitable bugs crop up.

**"I had to use tool X, management made me/it was the only one available/I didn't have time to learn the right one."**

This one is nothing more than classic shirking of responsibility. As I mentioned earlier in this book, there are indeed times when programmers have no choice; economic realities and management decrees can be quite inflexible and cold-hearted task masters. But just as often this fable is simply an excuse to take the easy way out, or a revelation of someone's misunderstanding, e.g. "Why didn't you package those icons in the main executable?" "I couldn't—Windows won't let you use any icon except the first one in the file." (This isn't true, of course.)

This fable also ties in to one of the most pervasive and troubling tendencies that programmers exhibit: The desire to play. Face it—programmers, as a group, like to play with their tools more than people in just about any other profession. I speak from experience; I practically invented this programming sin. Combine this tendency with this fable, and you have a formula for programmers using the wrong tool for a job, simply because it has greater entertainment value. Mix in the tendency for programmers and managers to play office politics and indulge in "empire building," and it's a miracle that anyone in a business setting ever finishes a programming project.

**"I'll know what this means when I see it again."**

No, you probably won't. It's that simple. Remember the guideline you(now) != you(later)? This fable is yet another excuse to cut corners, particularly in writing commentary and documentation, which no one likes to do. I don't like to do it, that's for sure, yet I write extensive commentary in my code. Why? Because every minute I spend writing it probably saves me three minutes in the long run. That commentary also greatly reduces the chance that I'll accidentally misunderstand my own code and introduce a very expensive bug at a later date. Sounds like the bargain of the century to me.

**"Why should I comment this? This is self-documenting code!"**

This one always makes me laugh, because when it's wrong (about half the time), it's typically about 50 percent excuse and 50 percent dare. The speaker is not only looking for an excuse not to write some commentary, of course, but is also hoping that someone will protest that the code in question isn't clear enough to stand on its own. Anyone naive enough to walk into the trap is told in no uncertain terms that the speaker found the code crystal clear, the implication being that the protester isn't quite as skilled as a programmer as the original speaker.

This sort of behavior is nothing but childishness in the workplace, something I normally wouldn't concern myself with in this book. But the bottom line is that this nonsense winds up affecting the maintainability of the code, which means more bugs we all have to contend with in future releases. From that standpoint it is an important issue for this book, and it's something we all have to worry about as programmers.

**"If I document this, then it just becomes another maintenance hassle."**

Yep, another excuse not to document code. I think of this one almost every time I open the online documentation for the Win32 API and see how many details it leaves to my fertile imagination. (I'll spare you the tirade about extended error codes and all the other sins of the Win32 API; see practically the entire book for more detail on these issues.)

Typically, we hear this fable when the speaker doesn't want to be locked in to the program's current behavior, and doesn't want to be forced to document all the quirks of the current system. In many cases, the speaker doesn't know all the things that should be documented (a situation that I strongly suspect applies to the Win32 API), and would have to spend a great deal of time testing the code and reading the source code before the documentation could be completed. And yes, that does become a maintenance hassle. Even worse (from the speaker's viewpoint), complete documentation severely limits a programmer's "creativity" in future releases, since there's now an official statement of what the code is supposed to do, and changing that behavior would be viewed as a bug. I have no sympathy whatsoever for people who try to shirk their responsibilities like this; such requirements are the price we pay for calling programming a profession (and a very well paid one, at that). Or as we say in New York, deal with it.

### "If you call an API or function with bad data, you deserve what you get."

This one is particularly reprehensible, in that it's normally used by one programmer in reference to other programmers in the same company who want to use the speaker's code. The other programmers have found that if they accidentally pass bad data (and it's often the case that they can't validate the data themselves before making the call, for some obscure reason or another), the program crashes or corrupts user data, or even takes down the whole system. It's quite obvious to them that the code in question should be smart enough to detect and react to bad parameters gracefully, and it's equally obvious to the code's author that the documentation (if any) doesn't even mention parameter validation, so all bets are off. In no time this situation turns into Egos in Collision, and management gets dragged into the picture, which almost never makes things better. (An example: A compromise is cooked up by management in which the documentation is changed to say explicitly that no parameter validation is done, and the speaker promises to "seriously investigate" adding the validation in the next release, which, of course, never happens. The manager feels good for having defused a technical debate, and both parties in the conflict get something and give something. The real loser is the program's users, since the needed validation never gets into the code, and remains a quality exposure.)

The solution is to avoid the situation entirely by determining as early in the project as possible (i.e., before people start writing code that's loaded with assumptions, and before they become too entrenched in their positions) what individual functions will and won't do in terms of parameter validation, and detecting and reporting various error conditions. This is particularly important if code will be passing data that it literally can't validate to another routine (e.g., the caller doesn't have access to the customer records to verify an account number), so the called routine must do the validation. Whatever the details, once you identify the cases where one party needs another to provide some extra functionality, the issue can often be settled much quicker and with far less head-butting.

### "If the user can't figure this out, he or she shouldn't be using the program."

Sure, blame the user. What better way to improve the usability and quality of your program? All this wrestling with human factors issues and other wimpy, warm and fuzzy stuff is no fun. After all, we're *real programmers*! Let's just write new code and grunt like Tim Allen on *Home Improvement!* Damn the bugs, full speed ahead!

OK, I'm calm now. I apologize for standing on the table and yelling, but it drives me crazy that so many software vendors and programmers forget the most basic fact of our profession: Without users we're nothing. And as bad as poor user interface design is (and we all sure see a lot of it), even worse is a program that provides useless online help. In many cases we run into some incomprehensible aspect of a program, only to find that the online help will tell us everything in the world about the program except what happens when we select a particular configuration option.

### "See, it works!"/"It works for me!"

What's the only part of software development that's even less popular than writing documentation? It has to be testing. That's why this particular fable is so interesting, in a driving-past-the-accident sort of way: Programmers will sometimes use minimal, laughably insufficient testing to "prove" to themselves and others that their code is correct and no further work on it, including testing, is needed.

As with all other programmer fables, this one is attractive because of its plausibility in the abstract—just as there really is such a thing as self-documenting code, there really is such a thing as a routine or program fragment so small and simple that it only requires minimal testing, or even none at all. In those cases, "See, it works!" is not a programmer fable, but merely a statement of the obvious.

This fable can be very difficult to argue against, since the discussion invariably turns into a test of wills. The author of the software in question claims that the minimal testing "proves" the code's correctness, while another person is, in effect, claiming to know the code better. When the outsider asks about a particular case, the author typically trots out another programmer fable to deflect it, or (rarely) acknowledges the problem, fixes it, and then proclaims anew that the code is demonstrably correct. (The speaker will even proclaim that the code "did have one problem, but I fixed it," as yet further proof that no further testing is needed.) Programmers being programmers, this can peg the needle on the Ugly Scale in a hurry. At that point the situation is one of office politics and interpersonal relationships and not technical matters. Your goal should be to recognize and defuse such situations before they escalate to that point.

### "I'll just put the tricky code into a DLL, so it will be easier to update if anything goes wrong."

This is bone-headedness at its worst, for two reasons. First, you're making a product packaging decision for a completely irrelevant reason. Second, as soon as you identify some code as "tricky," you're really admitting that you don't know enough about it to handle it with complete confidence. (I'm not blaming you or any other programmer for this; I've been in this same situation more times than I care to think about, thanks to managers and clients with last-minute, surprise requirements. When will the non-programmers of the world learn that programming is nearly as specialized and fragmented an occupation as medicine or engineering?)

And once you make that admission, it's a short step to stuffing the code into a DLL so that you can (hopefully) provide a quick fix when something goes wrong. If you're honest with yourself, you'll know when you're covering your hind quarters instead of making a design or packaging decision for the right reason. Best of all, you don't have to admit it to anyone else—tell your management that you need a little more time to investigate some aspect of the API or third-party library or whatever the area of difficulty is, so you can do a proper job, and then do the right thing and leave DLLs out of it. In many cases this will work, and everyone involved will be happier in the long run.

# The Win32u Library

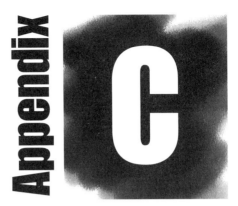

Appendix C

This appendix contains the beginning of what I expect will be a long and quite interesting experiment that I hope you'll participate in. The Win32u library presented below is the first primordial form of a wrapper library whose primary goal is to unify the behavior of the three Win32 platforms (Win32s, Windows 95, and Windows NT). There are some additional functions in the library that are meant to address other, lesser issues, as well.

My plans for the Win32u library are wide open. I most certainly intend to continue researching Win32 compatibility issues, and I will update this library as appropriate. If nothing else, I should be able to update the library in the next edition of this book and provide source listings online.

Eventually I would like to provide Object Pascal, MFC, and VCL versions of Win32u (e.g. create a uCDC class in MFC descended from CDC, and make its methods call the wrapped GDI functions in Win32u). For now, I'm starting with vanilla C++, since that will have the widest applicability.

Any such effort begs many questions. Which Win32 issues should the library address? How aggressively should it try to conceal Win32 platform differences? How closely should the wrappers mimic the underlying API functions? Should the wrappers be used only during debugging, or should they become a permanent part of the application? And that's just for starters. My gut feeling is that there's no way to address all these questions with one library; minimally, there would have to be several variations, and the coverage of the Win32 API possibly should be broken up into sub-libraries, allowing programmers to pick and choose which portions of it to monitor or attempt to unify. I could imagine someone who's writing a heavily graphics-oriented program wanting to use just the wrappers that catch 16/32-bit coordinate problems, for example, and not caring much about other issues.

# Where You Fit In

I really do want to hear from you on this project. Please send me your comments, and by all means share your experiences in finding Win32 incompatibilities. (My e-mail and paper addresses are in the introduction.) But please note that I'll need at least a minimum of detail if you report a Win32 issue. Don't just send me a one-line e-mail that says, "The Fred() API doesn't work." Tell me which Win32 platforms you've tested on and which ones exhibit the problem, and tell me what Microsoft told you, if you've contacted them already. You don't have to write *War and Peace*, just a few sentences will do nicely in most cases. If you prefer, you can send me the source code for an example program in C/C++ or Object Pascal, and tell me how it runs differently under different platforms. That will be more than enough to put me on the trail.

# What's in Win32u

Please keep in mind that this is really version 0.01 of the Win32u library, and that at this stage it's meant to be a demonstration of the concept and a starting point for further work, not something you should be building public programs around. I've talked with numerous people in e-mail about Win32 issues, but I haven't yet had a chance to get large scale feedback on this effort. (I'm almost afraid to think about how many pieces of e-mail I'll get once this book hits the shelves and readers start sending me their Win32 horror stories and suggestions for changes to Win32u...)

As for which items I covered in this first public release, I concentrated on those that Microsoft acknowledged were problems, plus the more important ones that I became aware of through my own testing or the help of others. (Plus one or two that were personal peeves of mine that I just had to fix right away.)

## *General Philosophy and Versioning*

As I've said numerous times throughout this book, one of the keys to software engineering is balance. In keeping with that concept, I haven't tried to catch every single error in calls to the wrapped APIs in Win32u, but I have tried to catch the most common pathological cases. For example, this version looks for things like NULL pointers, but doesn't verify that every handle or DC passed to an API function is valid.

The most precarious issue in creating this sort of wrapper, is, of course, ensuring compatibility with various versions of Windows, including those that don't yet exist. To that end, I've taken great pains to make sure these functions contain the fewest possible assumptions about the underlying system.

## Listbox Message Wrappers

Since list box support is still 16-bit in Windows 95 and Win32s, this creates numerous problems, the most significant of which is the fact that on these platforms list box string indexes are truncated from four to two bytes. I've provided a set of wrappers for the LB_* messages, all of which verify that the provided string indexes are within the range of a 16-bit value (meaning they will not be changed when the API truncates them), and return an error result if they aren't.

## GDI Function Wrappers

Similar to the list box wrappers, there are wrappers for the GDI functions that verify that the provided coordinates are within the range of a signed 16-bit number, so that they, too, will survive truncation intact, and report an error when they aren't. I haven't provided wrappers for APIs that are not supported under Windows 95 or don't accept coordinates, of course.

## Misc. Wrappers and Functions

I've also included a handful of other items, such as a wrapper for GetShortPathName() that unifies its behavior and use of extended error codes, a reformulated GetDlgItemInt() that returns its success/failure indication as the result of the function, not a parameter, and a pair of wrappers for the LB_SELITEMRANGEEX that eliminates that message's silly parameter ordering convention.

## Platform Checking and Debug Mode

There are two aspects to how the list box and GDI APIs are checked that I want to point out. The first is that the parameter validation can be done either with or without respect to the Win32 platform the code is running on. This feature is controlled by the flag DoPlatformCheck, which is accessed via the GetPlatformCheck() and SetPlatformCheck() functions. If this flag is TRUE, then the parameters are only checked when the program is running under Windows 95 or Win32s; when it's FALSE, the checks are always done. Your program can change the setting of this flag during execution. To be honest, I'm not sure why you'd want to do this, but it was such a simple and cheap feature, not to mention one that could be easily removed, that I added it.

The other issue is how the wrappers behave in debug mode. In that mode, the routines that actually perform the parameter validation will use OutputDebugString() to let you know that something is amiss. You could change this behavior to writes to a log file, MessageBox() calls, etc., as needed.

## Listing C.1    WIN32U.H

```
#ifndef __win32u_h__
#define __win32u_h__

BOOL GetPlatformCheck(void);
BOOL SetPlatformCheck(BOOL new_platform_check);

// The LB_* message wrappers, which check for illegal string indexes

LRESULT LBDeleteString(HWND lb_handle,WPARAM index);

LRESULT LBFindString(HWND lb_handle,WPARAM index,LPCTSTR string);

LRESULT LBFindStringExact(HWND lb_handle,WPARAM index,LPCTSTR string);

LRESULT LBGetItemData(HWND lb_handle,WPARAM index);

LRESULT LBGetItemHeight(HWND lb_handle,WPARAM index);

LRESULT LBGetItemRect(HWND lb_handle,WPARAM index,LPRECT rect);

LRESULT LBGetSel(HWND lb_handle,WPARAM index);

LRESULT LBGetSelItems(HWND lb_handle,WPARAM index,LPINT buffer);

LRESULT LBGetText(HWND lb_handle,WPARAM index,LPCTSTR buffer);

LRESULT LBGetTextLen(HWND lb_handle,WPARAM index);

LRESULT LBInsertString(HWND lb_handle,WPARAM index,LPCTSTR buffer);

LRESULT LBSelectString(HWND lb_handle,WPARAM index,LPCTSTR buffer);

LRESULT LBSelItemRangeEx(HWND lb_handle,WPARAM wFirst,LPARAM wLast);

LRESULT LBSetCaretIndex(HWND lb_handle,WPARAM index);

LRESULT LBSetCurSel(HWND lb_handle,WPARAM index);

LRESULT LBSetItemData(HWND lb_handle,WPARAM index,LPARAM dwData);

LRESULT LBSetItemHeight(HWND lb_handle,WPARAM index,LPARAM cyItem);

LRESULT LBSetTopIndex(HWND lb_handle,WPARAM index);

// The GDI API wrappers, which check for illegal coordinates

BOOL uArc(HDC hdc,int nLeftRect,int nTopRect,int nRightRect,int nBottomRect,
  int nXStartArc,int nYStartArc,int nXEndArc,int nYEndArc);

BOOL uBitBlt(HDC hdcDest,int nXDest,int nYDest,int nWidth,int nHeight,
  HDC hdcSrc,int nXSrc,int nYSrc,DWORD dwRop);

BOOL uChord(HDC hdc,int nLeftRect,int nTopRect,int nRightRect,int nBottomRect,
  int nXRadial1,int nYRadial1,int nXRadial2,int nYRadial2);

HRGN uCreateEllipticRgn(int nLeftRect,int nTopRect,int nRightRect,
  int nBottomRect);
```

```
HRGN uCreateEllipticRgnIndirect(CONST RECT *lprc);

HRGN uCreatePolygonRgn(CONST POINT *lppt,int cPoints,int fnPolyFillMode);

HRGN uCreatePolyPolygonRgn(CONST POINT *lppt,CONST INT *lpPolyCounts,
  int nCount,int fnPolyFillMode);

HRGN uCreateRectRgn(int nLeftRect,int nTopRect,int nRightRect,int nBottomRect);

HRGN uCreateRectRgnIndirect(CONST RECT *lprc);

HRGN uCreateRoundRectRgn(int nLeft,int nTop,int nRight,int nBottom,
  int nWidth, int nHeight);

BOOL uDPtoLP(HDC hdc,LPPOINT lpPoints,int nCount);

BOOL uEllipse(HDC hdc,int nLeftRect,int nTopRect,int nRightRect,int nBottomRect);

int uExcludeClipRect(HDC hdc,int nLeftRect,int nTopRect,int nRightRect,
  int nBottomRect);

BOOL uExtFloodFill(HDC hdc,int nXStart,int nYStart,COLORREF crColor,
  UINT fuFillType);

BOOL uExtTextOut(HDC hdc,int X,int Y,UINT fuOptions,CONST RECT *lprc,
  LPCTSTR lpString,UINT cbCount,CONST INT * lpDx);

BOOL uFloodFill(HDC hdc,int nXStart,int nYStart,COLORREF crFill);

BOOL uFrameRgn(HDC hdc,HRGN hrgn,HBRUSH hbr,int nWidth,int nHeight);

COLORREF uGetPixel(HDC hdc,int nXPos,int nYPos);

int uIntersectClipRect(HDC hdc,int nLeftRect,int nTopRect,int nRightRect,
  int nBottomRect);

BOOL uLineTo(HDC hdc,int nXEnd,int nYEnd);

BOOL uLPtoDP(HDC hdc,LPPOINT lpPoints,int nCount);

BOOL uMaskBlt(HDC hdcDest,int nXDest,int nYDest,int nWidth,int nHeight,
  HDC hdcSrc,int nXSrc,int nYSrc,HBITMAP hbmMask,int xMask,int yMask,
  DWORD dwRop);

BOOL uMoveToEx(HDC hdc,int X,int Y,LPPOINT lpPoint);

int uOffsetClipRgn(HDC hdc,int nXOffset,int nYOffset);

int uOffsetRgn(HRGN hrgn,int nXOffset,int nYOffset);

BOOL uOffsetViewportOrgEx(HDC hdc,int nXOffset,int nYOffset,LPPOINT lpPoint);

BOOL uOffsetWindowOrgEx(HDC hdc,int nXOffset,int nYOffset,LPPOINT lpPoint);

BOOL uPatBlt(HDC hdc,int nXLeft,int nYLeft,int nWidth,int nHeight,DWORD dwRop);

BOOL uPie(HDC hdc,int nLeftRect,int nTopRect,int nRightRect,int nBottomRect,
  int nXRadial1,int nYRadial1,int nXRadial2,int nYRadial2);

BOOL uPolyBezier(HDC hdc,CONST POINT *lppt,DWORD cPoints);
```

```
BOOL uPolyBezierTo(HDC hdc,CONST POINT *lppt,DWORD cCount);

BOOL uPolygon(HDC hdc,CONST POINT *lpPoints,int nCount);

BOOL uPolyline(HDC hdc,CONST POINT *lppt,int cPoints);

BOOL uPolylineTo(HDC hdc,CONST POINT *lppt,DWORD cCount);

BOOL uPolyPolygon(HDC hdc,CONST POINT *lpPoints,LPINT lpPolyCounts,int nCount);

BOOL uPolyPolyline(HDC hdc,CONST POINT *lppt,CONST DWORD *lpdwPolyPoints,
  DWORD  cCount);

BOOL uPtInRegion(HRGN hrgn,int X,int Y);

BOOL uPtVisible(HDC hdc,int X,int Y);

BOOL uRectangle(HDC hdc,int nLeftRect,int nTopRect,int nRightRect,int nBottomRect);

BOOL uRectInRegion(HRGN hrgn,CONST RECT *lprc);

BOOL uRectVisible(HDC hdc,CONST RECT *lprc);

BOOL uRoundRect(HDC hdc,int nLeftRect,int nTopRect,int nRightRect,
  int nBottomRect,int nWidth,int nHeight);

BOOL uScaleViewportExtEx(HDC hdc,int Xnum,int Xdenom,int Ynum,int Ydenom,
  LPSIZE lpSize);

BOOL uScaleWindowExtEx(HDC hdc,int Xnum,int Xdenom,int Ynum,int Ydenom,
  LPSIZE lpSize);

UINT uSetBoundsRect(HDC hdc,CONST RECT *lprcBounds,UINT flags);

BOOL uSetBrushOrgEx(HDC hdc,int nXOrg,int nYOrg,LPPOINT lppt);

BOOL uSetPixelV(HDC hdc,int X,int Y,COLORREF crColor);

BOOL uSetRectRgn(HRGN hrgn,int nLeftRect,int nTopRect,int nRightRect,
  int nBottomRect);

BOOL uSetViewportExtEx(HDC hdc,int nXExtent,int nYExtent,LPSIZE lpSize);

BOOL uSetViewportOrgEx(HDC hdc,int X,int Y,LPPOINT lpPoint);

BOOL uSetWindowExtEx(HDC hdc,int nXExtent,int nYExtent,LPSIZE lpSize);

BOOL uSetWindowOrgEx(HDC hdc,int X,int Y,LPPOINT lpPoint);

BOOL uStretchBlt(HDC hdcDest,int nXOriginDest,int nYOriginDest,int nWidthDest,
  int nHeightDest,HDC hdcSrc,int nXOriginSrc,int nYOriginSrc,int nWidthSrc,
  int nHeightSrc,DWORD dwRop);

BOOL uTextOut(HDC hdc,int nXStart,int nYStart,LPCTSTR lpString,int cbString);

// Misc. wrappers and functions

DWORD uEMGetLineCount(HWND edit_handle);

BOOL uDirExists(const char *dn);
```

```
BOOL uFileExists(const char *fn);

BOOL uGetDlgItemInt(HWND hDlg,int nIDDlgItem,UINT* lpValue,BOOL bSigned);

BOOL uGetPrivateProfileString(LPCTSTR lpAppName,LPCTSTR lpKeyName,
  LPCTSTR lpDefault,LPTSTR lpReturnedString,DWORD nSize,LPCTSTR lpFileName);

DWORD uGetShortPathName(LPCTSTR long_path,LPTSTR buffer,DWORD buffer_len);

BOOL uGetSysColor(int nIndex,DWORD *color);

BOOL uLBDeselItemRange(HWND lb, int start, int end);

BOOL uLBSelItemRange(HWND lb, int start, int end);

#endif
```

## Listing C.2   WIN32U.CPP

```cpp
/* Copyright Lou Grinzo 1995
   Zen of Windows 95 Programming */

#include <windows.h>
#include "win32u.h"

////////////////////////////////////////////////////////////////////////////
// The following flag controls whether the listbox index and GDI coord. checks
// are sensitive to the platform the program is running under.  If this flag
// is false, then the index is always checked.  If it is true, then the checks
// are made only if we're running under Windows 95 or Win32s.
////////////////////////////////////////////////////////////////////////////

static BOOL DoPlatformCheck = FALSE;

static DWORD Windows_version;
static DWORD major_version;
static DWORD minor_version;
static DWORD build_number;

static BOOL have_version_info = FALSE;

////////////////////////////////////////////////////////////////////////////
// Retrieve the current platform check setting.
////////////////////////////////////////////////////////////////////////////

BOOL GetPlatformCheck(void)
{
  return DoPlatformCheck;
}

////////////////////////////////////////////////////////////////////////////
// Allow the caller to set our platform checking flag.  Returns the old
// setting.
////////////////////////////////////////////////////////////////////////////

BOOL SetPlatformCheck(BOOL new_platform_check)
{
  BOOL temp = DoPlatformCheck;
  DoPlatformCheck = (new_platform_check != FALSE);  // Force TRUE or FALSE
```

```
  return temp;
}


///////////////////////////////////////////////////////////////////////
// Retrieve the platform version code from Windows.
///////////////////////////////////////////////////////////////////////

static void GetVersionInfo(void)
{
  OSVERSIONINFO osvi;

  memset(&osvi, 0, sizeof(OSVERSIONINFO));
  osvi.dwOSVersionInfoSize = sizeof (OSVERSIONINFO);
  GetVersionEx(&osvi);

  Windows_version = osvi.dwPlatformId;

  major_version = osvi.dwMajorVersion;
  minor_version = osvi.dwMinorVersion;
  build_number  = osvi.dwBuildNumber & 0xFFFF;
}


///////////////////////////////////////////////////////////////////////
// Return TRUE if we're running under Windows NT, FALSE if we're not (i.e.
// we're running under Windows 95 or Win32s).
///////////////////////////////////////////////////////////////////////

BOOL IsWinNT(void)
{
  if(!have_version_info)
    GetVersionInfo();

  return (Windows_version == VER_PLATFORM_WIN32_NT);
}


///////////////////////////////////////////////////////////////////////
// Return TRUE if we're running under Windows NT, FALSE if we're not (i.e.
// we're running under Windows 95 or Win32s).
///////////////////////////////////////////////////////////////////////

BOOL IsVer351OrLater(void)
{
  if(!have_version_info)
    GetVersionInfo();

  return ((major_version > 3) ||
         ((major_version == 3) && (minor_version >= 51)));
}


///////////////////////////////////////////////////////////////////////
// BadLBIndex: Return TRUE if the provided listbox index is an unusable
// value, FALSE if it is usable.  See the comment above near the
// DoPlatformCheck variable definition for more details.
///////////////////////////////////////////////////////////////////////

BOOL BadLBIndex(WPARAM index)
{
  if(DoPlatformCheck && IsWinNT())
    return FALSE;
  else
    {
```

```
#ifdef _DEBUG
    if(index > 32767)
        {
        OutputDebugString("\n*** BadLBIndex: Rejecting index value! ***\n\n");
         return TRUE;
        }
#endif
    return (index > 32767);
    }
}


//////////////////////////////////////////////////////////////////////////
// IsBadGDICoord: Return TRUE if the supplied coordinate won't fit into a
// 16-bit signed integer.
//////////////////////////////////////////////////////////////////////////

BOOL IsBadGDICoord(int c)
{
  return ((c > 32767) || (c < -32768));
}


//////////////////////////////////////////////////////////////////////////
// BadGDICoords: Return TRUE if any of the provided GDI coords are unusable,
// FALSE if all are usable.  See the comment above near the DoPlatformCheck
// variable definition for more details.
//////////////////////////////////////////////////////////////////////////

BOOL BadGDICoords(int c1, int c2, int c3 = 0, int c4 = 0, int c5 = 0, int c6 = 0)
{
  if(DoPlatformCheck && IsWinNT())
    return FALSE;
  else
    {
#ifdef _DEBUG
    if(IsBadGDICoord(c1) || IsBadGDICoord(c2) || IsBadGDICoord(c3) ||)
       IsBadGDICoord(c4) || IsBadGDICoord(c5) || IsBadGDICoord(c6))
        {
        OutputDebugString("\nBadGDICoords: Rejecting coord. value(s)!\n\n");
         return TRUE;
        }
#endif
    return (IsBadGDICoord(c1) || IsBadGDICoord(c2) || IsBadGDICoord(c3) ||
            IsBadGDICoord(c4) || IsBadGDICoord(c5) || IsBadGDICoord(c6));
    }
}


//////////////////////////////////////////////////////////////////////////
//////////////////////////////////////////////////////////////////////////
// LB_* Wrappers
//////////////////////////////////////////////////////////////////////////
//////////////////////////////////////////////////////////////////////////


//////////////////////////////////////////////////////////////////////////
// LBDeleteString: Wrapper for the LB_DELETESTRING message
//////////////////////////////////////////////////////////////////////////

LRESULT LBDeleteString(HWND lb_handle,WPARAM index)
{
  if(BadLBIndex(index))
    return LB_ERR;
```

```
    return SendMessage(lb_handle,LB_DELETESTRING,index,0);
}


//////////////////////////////////////////////////////////////////////
// LBFindString: Wrapper for the LB_FINDSTRING message
//////////////////////////////////////////////////////////////////////

LRESULT LBFindString(HWND lb_handle,WPARAM index,LPCTSTR string)
{
  if(BadLBIndex(index))
    return LB_ERR;

  return SendMessage(lb_handle,LB_FINDSTRING,index,(LPARAM)string);
}


//////////////////////////////////////////////////////////////////////
// LBFindStringExact: Wrapper for the LB_FINDSTRINGEXACT message
//////////////////////////////////////////////////////////////////////

LRESULT LBFindStringExact(HWND lb_handle,WPARAM index,LPCTSTR string)
{
  if(BadLBIndex(index))
    return LB_ERR;

  return SendMessage(lb_handle,LB_FINDSTRINGEXACT,index,(LPARAM)string);
}


//////////////////////////////////////////////////////////////////////
// LBGetItemData: Wrapper for the LB_GETITEMDATA message
//////////////////////////////////////////////////////////////////////

LRESULT LBGetItemData(HWND lb_handle,WPARAM index)
{
  if(BadLBIndex(index))
    return LB_ERR;

  return SendMessage(lb_handle,LB_GETITEMDATA,index,0);
}


//////////////////////////////////////////////////////////////////////
// LBGetItemHeight: Wrapper for the LB_GETITEMHEIGHT message
//////////////////////////////////////////////////////////////////////

LRESULT LBGetItemHeight(HWND lb_handle,WPARAM index)
{
  if(BadLBIndex(index))
    return LB_ERR;

  return SendMessage(lb_handle,LB_GETITEMHEIGHT,index,0);
}


//////////////////////////////////////////////////////////////////////
// LBGetItemRect: Wrapper for the LB_GETITEMRECT message
//////////////////////////////////////////////////////////////////////

LRESULT LBGetItemRect(HWND lb_handle,WPARAM index,LPRECT rect)
{
  if(BadLBIndex(index))
    return LB_ERR;

  return SendMessage(lb_handle,LB_GETITEMRECT,index,(LPARAM)rect);
}
```

```
//////////////////////////////////////////////////////////////////////
// LBGetSel: Wrapper for the LB_GETSEL message
//////////////////////////////////////////////////////////////////////

LRESULT LBGetSel(HWND lb_handle,WPARAM index)
{
  if(BadLBIndex(index))
    return LB_ERR;

  return SendMessage(lb_handle,LB_GETSEL,index,0);
}

//////////////////////////////////////////////////////////////////////
// LBGetSelItems: Wrapper for the LB_GETSELITEMS message
//////////////////////////////////////////////////////////////////////

LRESULT LBGetSelItems(HWND lb_handle,WPARAM index,LPINT buffer)
{
  if(BadLBIndex(index))
    return LB_ERR;

  return SendMessage(lb_handle,LB_GETSELITEMS,index,(LPARAM)buffer);
}

//////////////////////////////////////////////////////////////////////
// LBGetText: Wrapper for the LB_GETTEXT message
//////////////////////////////////////////////////////////////////////

LRESULT LBGetText(HWND lb_handle,WPARAM index,LPCTSTR buffer)
{
  if(BadLBIndex(index))
    return LB_ERR;

  return SendMessage(lb_handle,LB_GETTEXT,index,(LPARAM)buffer);
}

//////////////////////////////////////////////////////////////////////
// LBGetTextLen: Wrapper for the LB_GETTEXTLEN message
//////////////////////////////////////////////////////////////////////

LRESULT LBGetTextLen(HWND lb_handle,WPARAM index)
{
  if(BadLBIndex(index))
    return LB_ERR;

  return SendMessage(lb_handle,LB_GETTEXTLEN,index,0);
}

//////////////////////////////////////////////////////////////////////
// LBInsertString: Wrapper for the LB_INSERTSTRING message
//////////////////////////////////////////////////////////////////////

LRESULT LBInsertString(HWND lb_handle,WPARAM index,LPCTSTR buffer)
{
  // We have to explicitly allow for an index of -1!
  if((index != (DWORD)-1) && BadLBIndex(index))
    return LB_ERR;

  return SendMessage(lb_handle,LB_INSERTSTRING,index,(LPARAM)buffer);
}
```

```
//////////////////////////////////////////////////////////////////////////
// LBSelectString: Wrapper for the LB_SELECTSTRING message
//////////////////////////////////////////////////////////////////////////

LRESULT LBSelectString(HWND lb_handle,WPARAM index,LPCTSTR buffer)
{
  if(BadLBIndex(index))
    return LB_ERR;

  return SendMessage(lb_handle,LB_SELECTSTRING,index,(LPARAM)buffer);
}


//////////////////////////////////////////////////////////////////////////
// LBSelItemRangeEx: Wrapper for the LB_SELITEMRANGEEX message
//////////////////////////////////////////////////////////////////////////

LRESULT LBSelItemRangeEx(HWND lb_handle,WPARAM wFirst,LPARAM wLast)
{
  if(BadLBIndex(wFirst) || BadLBIndex(wLast))
    return LB_ERR;

  return SendMessage(lb_handle,LB_SELITEMRANGEEX,wFirst,wLast);
}


//////////////////////////////////////////////////////////////////////////
// LBSetCaretIndex: Wrapper for the LB_SETCARETINDEX message
//////////////////////////////////////////////////////////////////////////

LRESULT LBSetCaretIndex(HWND lb_handle,WPARAM index)
{
  if(BadLBIndex(index))
    return LB_ERR;

  return SendMessage(lb_handle,LB_SETCARETINDEX,index,0);
}


//////////////////////////////////////////////////////////////////////////
// LBSetCurSel: Wrapper for the LB_GETCURSEL message
//////////////////////////////////////////////////////////////////////////

LRESULT LBSetCurSel(HWND lb_handle,WPARAM index)
{
  // We have to explicitly allow for an index of -1!
  if((index != (DWORD)-1) && BadLBIndex(index))
    return LB_ERR;

  return SendMessage(lb_handle,LB_SETCURSEL,index,0);
}


//////////////////////////////////////////////////////////////////////////
// LBSetItemData: Wrapper for the LB_SETITEMDATA message
//////////////////////////////////////////////////////////////////////////

LRESULT LBSetItemData(HWND lb_handle,WPARAM index,LPARAM dwData)
{
  if(BadLBIndex(index))
    return LB_ERR;

  return SendMessage(lb_handle,LB_SETITEMDATA,index,dwData);
}
```

```
///////////////////////////////////////////////////////////////////////////
// LBSetItemHeight: Wrapper for the LB_SETITEMHEIGHT message
///////////////////////////////////////////////////////////////////////////

LRESULT LBSetItemHeight(HWND lb_handle,WPARAM index,LPARAM cyItem)
{
  if(BadLBIndex(index))
    return LB_ERR;

  return SendMessage(lb_handle,LB_SETITEMHEIGHT,index,cyItem);
}


///////////////////////////////////////////////////////////////////////////
// LBSetTopIndex: Wrapper for the LB_SETCTOPINDEX message
///////////////////////////////////////////////////////////////////////////

LRESULT LBSetTopIndex(HWND lb_handle,WPARAM index)
{
  if(BadLBIndex(index))
    return LB_ERR;

  return SendMessage(lb_handle,LB_SETTOPINDEX,index,0);
}


///////////////////////////////////////////////////////////////////////////
///////////////////////////////////////////////////////////////////////////
// GDI Wrappers
///////////////////////////////////////////////////////////////////////////
///////////////////////////////////////////////////////////////////////////


///////////////////////////////////////////////////////////////////////////
// uArc: Wrapper for the Arc API
///////////////////////////////////////////////////////////////////////////

BOOL uArc(HDC hdc,int nLeftRect,int nTopRect,int nRightRect,int nBottomRect,
       int nXStartArc,int nYStartArc,int nXEndArc,int nYEndArc)
{
  if(BadGDICoords(nLeftRect,nTopRect,nRightRect,nBottomRect) ||
    BadGDICoords(nXStartArc,nYStartArc,nXEndArc,nYEndArc) ||
    (nLeftRect + nRightRect > 32767) || (nTopRect + nBottomRect > 32767))
    return FALSE;

  return Arc(hdc,nLeftRect,nTopRect,nRightRect,nBottomRect,nXStartArc,
        nYStartArc,nXEndArc,nYEndArc);
}


///////////////////////////////////////////////////////////////////////////
// uBitBlt: Coord-safe wrapper for the BitBlt API
///////////////////////////////////////////////////////////////////////////

BOOL uBitBlt(HDC hdcDest,int nXDest,int nYDest,int nWidth,int nHeight,
  HDC hdcSrc,int nXSrc,int nYSrc,DWORD dwRop)
{
  if(BadGDICoords(nXDest,nYDest,nWidth,nHeight,nXSrc,nYSrc))
    {
     SetLastError(ERROR_INVALID_PARAMETER);
      return NULL;
    }

  return BitBlt(hdcDest,nXDest,nYDest,nWidth,nHeight,hdcSrc,nXSrc,nYSrc,dwRop);
}
```

```
/////////////////////////////////////////////////////////////////////////
// uChord: Coord-safe wrapper for the Chord API
/////////////////////////////////////////////////////////////////////////

BOOL uChord(HDC hdc,int nLeftRect,int nTopRect,int nRightRect,int nBottomRect,
  int nXRadial1,int nYRadial1,int nXRadial2,int nYRadial2)
{
  if(BadGDICoords(nLeftRect,nTopRect,nRightRect,nBottomRect) ||
    BadGDICoords(nXRadial1,nYRadial1,nXRadial2,nYRadial2) ||
    (nLeftRect + nTopRect + nRightRect + nBottomRect > 32767) ||
    (nLeftRect + nRightRect > 32767) ||
    (nTopRect  + nBottomRect > 32767))
    {
     SetLastError(ERROR_INVALID_PARAMETER);
      return FALSE;
     }

  return Chord(hdc,nLeftRect,nTopRect,nRightRect,nBottomRect,nXRadial1,
    nYRadial1,nXRadial2,nYRadial2);
}


/////////////////////////////////////////////////////////////////////////
// uCreateEllipticRgn: Coord-safe wrapper for the CreateEllipticRgn API
/////////////////////////////////////////////////////////////////////////

HRGN uCreateEllipticRgn(int nLeftRect,int nTopRect,int nRightRect,int nBottomRect)
{
  if(BadGDICoords(nLeftRect,nTopRect,nRightRect,nBottomRect))
    return NULL;

  return CreateEllipticRgn(nLeftRect,nTopRect,nRightRect,nBottomRect);
}


/////////////////////////////////////////////////////////////////////////
// uCreateEllipticRgnIndirect: Coord-safe wrapper for the
// CreateEllipticRgnIndirect API
/////////////////////////////////////////////////////////////////////////

HRGN uCreateEllipticRgnIndirect(CONST RECT *lprc)
{
  if((lprc != NULL) &&
     BadGDICoords(lprc->left,lprc->top,lprc->right,lprc->bottom))
     return NULL;

  // Note: If lprc is NULL we pass it along anyway!

  return CreateEllipticRgnIndirect(lprc);
}


/////////////////////////////////////////////////////////////////////////
// uCreatePolygonRgn: Coord-safe wrapper for the CreatePolygonRgn API
/////////////////////////////////////////////////////////////////////////

HRGN uCreatePolygonRgn(CONST POINT *lppt,int cPoints,int fnPolyFillMode)
{
  if(lppt != NULL)
    for(int i = 0; i < cPoints; i++)
    if(BadGDICoords(lppt[i].x,lppt[i].y))
      return NULL;
```

```
    // Note: If lppt is NULL we pass it along anyway!

    return CreatePolygonRgn(lppt,cPoints,fnPolyFillMode);
}

///////////////////////////////////////////////////////////////////////////
// uCreatePolyPolygonRgn: Coord-safe wrapper for the CreatePolyPolygonRgn API
///////////////////////////////////////////////////////////////////////////

HRGN uCreatePolyPolygonRgn(CONST POINT *lppt,CONST INT *lpPolyCounts,
  int nCount,int fnPolyFillMode)
{
  // Count the total number of POINT structure in the polylines, as needed,
  // then check each pair via BadGDICoords()
  if(lppt != NULL)
    {
      int total_points = 0, i;

      for(i = 0; i < nCount; i++)
       total_points += lpPolyCounts[i];

      for(i = 0; i < total_points; i++)
       if(BadGDICoords(lppt[i].x,lppt[i].y))
           return FALSE;
      }

  // Note: If lppt is NULL we pass it along anyway!

   return CreatePolyPolygonRgn(lppt,lpPolyCounts,nCount,fnPolyFillMode);
}

///////////////////////////////////////////////////////////////////////////
// uCreateRectRgn: Coord-safe wrapper for the CreateRectRgn API
///////////////////////////////////////////////////////////////////////////

HRGN uCreateRectRgn(int nLeftRect,int nTopRect,int nRightRect,int  nBottomRect)
{
  if(BadGDICoords(nLeftRect,nTopRect,nRightRect,nBottomRect))
    return ERROR;

  return CreateRectRgn(nLeftRect,nTopRect,nRightRect,nBottomRect);
}

///////////////////////////////////////////////////////////////////////////
// uCreateRectRgnIndirect: Coord-safe wrapper for the CreateRectRgnIndirect API
///////////////////////////////////////////////////////////////////////////

HRGN uCreateRectRgnIndirect(CONST RECT *lprc)
{
  if((lprc != NULL) &&
     BadGDICoords(lprc->left,lprc->top,lprc->right,lprc->bottom))
     return NULL;

  // Note: If lprc is NULL we pass it along anyway!

  return CreateRectRgnIndirect(lprc);
}
```

```
/////////////////////////////////////////////////////////////////////////
// uCreateRoundRectRgn: Coord-safe wrapper for the CreateRoundRectRgn API
/////////////////////////////////////////////////////////////////////////

HRGN uCreateRoundRectRgn(int nLeft,int nTop,int nRight,int nBottom,
 int nWidth, int nHeight)
{
  if(BadGDICoords(nLeft,nTop,nRight,nBottom,nWidth,nHeight))
    return NULL;

  return CreateRoundRectRgn(nLeft,nTop,nRight,nBottom,nWidth,nHeight);
}


/////////////////////////////////////////////////////////////////////////
// uDPtoLP: Coord-safe wrapper for the DPtoLP API
/////////////////////////////////////////////////////////////////////////

BOOL uDPtoLP(HDC hdc,LPPOINT lpPoints,int nCount)
{
  if(lpPoints != NULL)
    for(int i = 0; i < nCount; i++)
     if(BadGDICoords(lpPoints[i].x,lpPoints[i].y))
        return FALSE;
<C
  // Note: If lpPoints is NULL we pass it along anyway!

  return DPtoLP(hdc,lpPoints,nCount);
}


/////////////////////////////////////////////////////////////////////////
// uEllipse: Coord-safe wrapper for the Ellipse API
/////////////////////////////////////////////////////////////////////////

BOOL uEllipse(HDC hdc,int nLeftRect,int nTopRect,int nRightRect,int nBottomRect)
{
  if(BadGDICoords(nLeftRect,nTopRect,nRightRect,nBottomRect) ||
    (nLeftRect + nTopRect + nRightRect + nBottomRect > 32767) ||
    (nLeftRect + nRightRect > 32767) ||
    (nTopRect  + nBottomRect > 32767))
    {
    SetLastError(ERROR_INVALID_PARAMETER);
     return FALSE;
    }

  return Ellipse(hdc,nLeftRect,nTopRect,nRightRect,nBottomRect);
}


/////////////////////////////////////////////////////////////////////////
// uExcludeClipRect: Coord-safe wrapper for the ExcludeClipRect API
/////////////////////////////////////////////////////////////////////////

int uExcludeClipRect(HDC hdc,int nLeftRect,int nTopRect,int nRightRect,
 int nBottomRect)
{
 if(BadGDICoords(nLeftRect,nTopRect,nRightRect,nBottomRect))
    return ERROR;

 return ExcludeClipRect(hdc,nLeftRect,nTopRect,nRightRect,nBottomRect);
}
```

```
/////////////////////////////////////////////////////////////////////////
// uExtFloodFill: Coord-safe wrapper for the ExtFloodFill API
/////////////////////////////////////////////////////////////////////////

BOOL uExtFloodFill(HDC hdc,int nXStart,int nYStart,COLORREF crColor,UINT
fuFillType)
{
  if(BadGDICoords(nXStart,nYStart))
    {
     SetLastError(ERROR_INVALID_PARAMETER);
      return FALSE;
    }

  return ExtFloodFill(hdc,nXStart,nYStart,crColor,fuFillType);
}

/////////////////////////////////////////////////////////////////////////
// uExtTextOut: Coord-safe wrapper for the ExtTextOut API
/////////////////////////////////////////////////////////////////////////

BOOL uExtTextOut(HDC hdc,int X,int Y,UINT fuOptions,CONST RECT *lprc,
  LPCTSTR lpString,UINT cbCount,CONST INT * lpDx)
{
  if(BadGDICoords(X,Y) ||
     ((lprc != NULL) &&
      BadGDICoords(lprc->left,lprc->top,lprc->right,lprc->bottom)))
    {
     SetLastError(ERROR_INVALID_PARAMETER);
      return FALSE;
    }

  // Note: If lprc is NULL we pass it along anyway!

  return ExtTextOut(hdc,X,Y,fuOptions,lprc,lpString,cbCount,lpDx);
}

/////////////////////////////////////////////////////////////////////////
// uFloodFill: Coord-safe wrapper for the FloodFill API
/////////////////////////////////////////////////////////////////////////

BOOL uFloodFill(HDC hdc,int nXStart,int nYStart,COLORREF crFill)
{
  if(BadGDICoords(nXStart,nYStart))
    {
     SetLastError(ERROR_INVALID_PARAMETER);
      return FALSE;
    }

  return FloodFill(hdc,nXStart,nYStart,crFill);
}

/////////////////////////////////////////////////////////////////////////
// uFrameRgn: Coord-safe wrapper for the FrameRgn API
/////////////////////////////////////////////////////////////////////////

BOOL uFrameRgn(HDC hdc,HRGN hrgn,HBRUSH hbr,int nWidth,int nHeight)
{
  if(BadGDICoords(nWidth,nHeight))
    return FALSE;

  return FrameRgn(hdc,hrgn,hbr,nWidth,nHeight);
}
```

```
////////////////////////////////////////////////////////////////////////////
// uGetPixel: Coord-safe wrapper for the GetPixel API
////////////////////////////////////////////////////////////////////////////

COLORREF uGetPixel(HDC hdc,int nXPos,int nYPos)
{
  if(BadGDICoords(nXPos,nYPos))
    return CLR_INVALID;

  return GetPixel(hdc,nXPos,nYPos);
}


////////////////////////////////////////////////////////////////////////////
// uIntersectClipRect: Coord-safe wrapper for the IntersectClipRect API
////////////////////////////////////////////////////////////////////////////

int uIntersectClipRect(HDC hdc,int nLeftRect,int nTopRect,int nRightRect,
  int nBottomRect)
{
  if(BadGDICoords(nLeftRect,nTopRect,nRightRect,nBottomRect))
    return ERROR;

  return IntersectClipRect(hdc,nLeftRect,nTopRect,nRightRect,nBottomRect);
}


////////////////////////////////////////////////////////////////////////////
// uLineTo: Coord-safe wrapper for the LineTo API
////////////////////////////////////////////////////////////////////////////

BOOL uLineTo(HDC hdc,int nXEnd,int nYEnd)
{
  if(BadGDICoords(nXEnd,nYEnd))
    return FALSE;

  return LineTo(hdc,nXEnd,nYEnd);
}


////////////////////////////////////////////////////////////////////////////
// uLPtoDP: Coord-safe wrapper for the LPtoDP API
////////////////////////////////////////////////////////////////////////////

BOOL uLPtoDP(HDC hdc,LPPOINT lpPoints,int nCount)
{
  if(lpPoints != NULL)
    for(int i = 0; i < nCount; i++)
      if(BadGDICoords(lpPoints[i].x,lpPoints[i].y))
        return FALSE;

  // Note: If lpPoints is NULL we pass it along anyway!

  return LPtoDP(hdc,lpPoints,nCount);
}


////////////////////////////////////////////////////////////////////////////
// uMaskBlt: Coord-safe wrapper for the MaskBlt API
////////////////////////////////////////////////////////////////////////////

BOOL uMaskBlt(HDC hdcDest,int nXDest,int nYDest,int nWidth,int nHeight,
  HDC hdcSrc,int nXSrc,int nYSrc,HBITMAP hbmMask,int xMask,int yMask,
  DWORD dwRop)
```

```
{
  if(BadGDICoords(nXDest,nYDest,nWidth,nHeight,nXSrc,nYSrc) ||
    BadGDICoords(xMask,yMask))
    {
      SetLastError(ERROR_INVALID_PARAMETER);
      return FALSE;
    }

  return MaskBlt(hdcDest,nXDest,nYDest,nWidth,nHeight,hdcSrc,nXSrc,nYSrc,
    hbmMask,xMask,yMask,dwRop);
}

/////////////////////////////////////////////////////////////////////////////
// uMoveToEx: Coord-safe wrapper for the MoveToEx API
/////////////////////////////////////////////////////////////////////////////

BOOL uMoveToEx(HDC hdc,int X,int Y,LPPOINT lpPoint)
{
  if(BadGDICoords(X,Y))
    return FALSE;

  return MoveToEx(hdc,X,Y,lpPoint);
}

/////////////////////////////////////////////////////////////////////////////
// uOffsetClipRgn: Coord-safe wrapper for the OffsetClipRgn API
/////////////////////////////////////////////////////////////////////////////

int uOffsetClipRgn(HDC hdc,int nXOffset,int nYOffset)
{
  if(BadGDICoords(nXOffset,nYOffset))
    return ERROR;

  return OffsetClipRgn(hdc,nXOffset,nYOffset);
}

/////////////////////////////////////////////////////////////////////////////
// uOffsetRgn: Coord-safe wrapper for the OffsetRgn API
/////////////////////////////////////////////////////////////////////////////

int uOffsetRgn(HRGN hrgn,int nXOffset,int nYOffset)
{
  if(BadGDICoords(nXOffset,nYOffset))
    return ERROR;

  return OffsetRgn(hrgn,nXOffset,nYOffset);
}

/////////////////////////////////////////////////////////////////////////////
// uOffsetViewportOrgEx: Coord-safe wrapper for the OffsetViewportOrgEx API
/////////////////////////////////////////////////////////////////////////////

BOOL uOffsetViewportOrgEx(HDC hdc,int nXOffset,int nYOffset,LPPOINT lpPoint)
{
  if(BadGDICoords(nXOffset,nYOffset))
    return FALSE;

  return OffsetViewportOrgEx(hdc,nXOffset,nYOffset,lpPoint);
}
```

```
///////////////////////////////////////////////////////////////////////////
// uOffsetWindowOrgEx: Coord-safe wrapper for the OffsetWindowOrgEx API
///////////////////////////////////////////////////////////////////////////

BOOL uOffsetWindowOrgEx(HDC hdc,int nXOffset,int nYOffset,LPPOINT lpPoint)
{
  if(BadGDICoords(nXOffset,nYOffset))
    return FALSE;

  return OffsetWindowOrgEx(hdc,nXOffset,nYOffset,lpPoint);
}

///////////////////////////////////////////////////////////////////////////
// uPatBlt: Coord-safe wrapper for the PatBlt API
///////////////////////////////////////////////////////////////////////////

BOOL uPatBlt(HDC hdc,int nXLeft,int nYLeft,int nWidth,int nHeight,DWORD dwRop)
{
  if(BadGDICoords(nXLeft,nYLeft,nWidth,nHeight))
    {
     SetLastError(ERROR_INVALID_PARAMETER);
      return FALSE;
    }

  return PatBlt(hdc,nXLeft,nYLeft,nWidth,nHeight,dwRop);
}

///////////////////////////////////////////////////////////////////////////
// uPie: Coord-safe wrapper for the Pie API
///////////////////////////////////////////////////////////////////////////

BOOL uPie(HDC hdc,int nLeftRect,int nTopRect,int nRightRect,int nBottomRect,
 int nXRadial1,int nYRadial1,int nXRadial2,int nYRadial2)
{
  if(BadGDICoords(nLeftRect,nTopRect,nRightRect,nBottomRect) ||
    BadGDICoords(nXRadial1,nYRadial1,nXRadial2,nYRadial2) ||
    (nLeftRect + nTopRect + nRightRect + nBottomRect > 32767))
        {
         SetLastError(ERROR_INVALID_PARAMETER);
          return FALSE;
        }

  return Pie(hdc,nLeftRect,nTopRect,nRightRect,nBottomRect,
    nXRadial1,nYRadial1,nXRadial2,nYRadial2);
}

///////////////////////////////////////////////////////////////////////////
// uPolyBezier: Coord-safe wrapper for the PolyBezier API
///////////////////////////////////////////////////////////////////////////

BOOL uPolyBezier(HDC hdc,CONST POINT *lppt,DWORD cPoints)
{
  if(lppt != NULL)
    for(DWORD i = 0; i < cPoints; i++)
     if(BadGDICoords(lppt[i].x,lppt[i].y))
        return FALSE;

  // Note: If lppt is NULL we pass it along anyway!

  return PolyBezier(hdc,lppt,cPoints);
}
```

```
//////////////////////////////////////////////////////////////////////
// uPolyBezierTo: Coord-safe wrapper for the PolyBezierTo API
//////////////////////////////////////////////////////////////////////

BOOL uPolyBezierTo(HDC hdc,CONST POINT *lppt,DWORD cCount)
{
  if(lppt != NULL)
    for(DWORD i = 0; i < cCount; i++)
      if(BadGDICoords(lppt[i].x,lppt[i].y))
        return FALSE;

  // Note: If lppt is NULL we pass it along anyway!

  return PolyBezierTo(hdc,lppt,cCount);
}

//////////////////////////////////////////////////////////////////////
// uPolygon: Coord-safe wrapper for the Polygon API
//////////////////////////////////////////////////////////////////////

BOOL uPolygon(HDC hdc,CONST POINT *lpPoints,int nCount)
{
  if(lpPoints != NULL)
    for(int i = 0; i < nCount; i++)
      if(BadGDICoords(lpPoints[i].x,lpPoints[i].y))
        {
        SetLastError(ERROR_INVALID_PARAMETER);
         return FALSE;
        }

  // Note: If lpPoints is NULL we pass it along anyway!

  return Polygon(hdc,lpPoints,nCount);
}

//////////////////////////////////////////////////////////////////////
// uPolyline: Coord-safe wrapper for the Polyline API
//////////////////////////////////////////////////////////////////////

BOOL uPolyline(HDC hdc,CONST POINT *lppt,int cPoints)
{
  if(lppt != NULL)
    for(int i = 0; i < cPoints; i++)
      if(BadGDICoords(lppt[i].x,lppt[i].y))
        return NULL;

  // Note: If lppt is NULL we pass it along anyway!

  return Polyline(hdc,lppt,cPoints);
}

//////////////////////////////////////////////////////////////////////
// uPolylineTo: Coord-safe wrapper for the PolylineTo API
//////////////////////////////////////////////////////////////////////

BOOL uPolylineTo(HDC hdc,CONST POINT *lppt,DWORD cCount)
{
  if(lppt != NULL)
    for(DWORD i = 0; i < cCount; i++)
      if(BadGDICoords(lppt[i].x,lppt[i].y))
        return NULL;
```

```
    // Note: If lppt is NULL we pass it along anyway!

    return PolylineTo(hdc,lppt,cCount);
}

/////////////////////////////////////////////////////////////////////////////
// uPolyPolygon: Coord-safe wrapper for the PolyPolygon API
/////////////////////////////////////////////////////////////////////////////

BOOL uPolyPolygon(HDC hdc,CONST POINT *lpPoints,LPINT lpPolyCounts,int nCount)
{
  // Count the total number of POINT structure in the polylines, as needed,
  // then check each pair via BadGDICoords()
  if(lpPoints != NULL)
    {
      int total_points = 0, i;

      for(i = 0; i < nCount; i++)
       total_points += lpPolyCounts[i];

      for(i = 0; i < total_points; i++)
       if(BadGDICoords(lpPoints[i].x,lpPoints[i].y))
           return FALSE;
      }

  // Note: If lpPoints is NULL we pass it along anyway!

  return PolyPolygon(hdc,lpPoints,lpPolyCounts,nCount);
}

/////////////////////////////////////////////////////////////////////////////
// uPolyPolyline: Coord-safe wrapper for the PolyPolyline API
/////////////////////////////////////////////////////////////////////////////

BOOL uPolyPolyline(HDC hdc,CONST POINT *lppt,CONST DWORD *lpdwPolyPoints,
  DWORD  cCount)
{
  // Count the total number of POINT structure in the polylines, as needed,
  // then check each pair via BadGDICoords()
  if(lppt != NULL)
    {
      DWORD total_points = 0, i;

      for(i = 0; i < cCount; i++)
       total_points += lpdwPolyPoints[i];

      for(i = 0; i < total_points; i++)
       if(BadGDICoords(lppt[i].x,lppt[i].y))
           return FALSE;
      }

  // Note: If lppt is NULL we pass it along anyway!

  return PolyPolyline(hdc,lppt,lpdwPolyPoints,cCount);
}

/////////////////////////////////////////////////////////////////////////////
// uPtInRegion: Coord-safe wrapper for the PtInRegion API
/////////////////////////////////////////////////////////////////////////////
```

```
BOOL uPtInRegion(HRGN hrgn,int X,int Y)
{
  if(BadGDICoords(X,Y))
    return FALSE;

  return PtInRegion(hrgn,X,Y);
}

//////////////////////////////////////////////////////////////////////////
// uPtVisible: Coord-safe wrapper for the PtVisible API
//////////////////////////////////////////////////////////////////////////

BOOL uPtVisible(HDC hdc,int X,int Y)
{
  if(BadGDICoords(X,Y))
    return FALSE;

  return PtVisible(hdc,X,Y);
}

//////////////////////////////////////////////////////////////////////////
// uRectangle: Coord-safe wrapper for the Rectangle API
//////////////////////////////////////////////////////////////////////////

BOOL uRectangle(HDC hdc,int nLeftRect,int nTopRect,int nRightRect,int nBottomRect)
{
  if(BadGDICoords(nLeftRect,nTopRect,nRightRect,nBottomRect))
    {
     SetLastError(ERROR_INVALID_PARAMETER);
      return FALSE;
    }

  return Rectangle(hdc,nLeftRect,nTopRect,nRightRect,nBottomRect);
}

//////////////////////////////////////////////////////////////////////////
// uRectInRegion: Coord-safe wrapper for the RectInRegion API
//////////////////////////////////////////////////////////////////////////

BOOL uRectInRegion(HRGN hrgn,CONST RECT *lprc)
{
  if((lprc != NULL) &&
     BadGDICoords(lprc->left,lprc->top,lprc->right,lprc->bottom))
     return NULL;

  // Note: If lprc is NULL we pass it along anyway!

  return RectInRegion(hrgn,lprc);
}

//////////////////////////////////////////////////////////////////////////
// uRectVisible: Coord-safe wrapper for the RectVisible API
//////////////////////////////////////////////////////////////////////////

BOOL uRectVisible(HDC hdc,CONST RECT *lprc)
{
  if((lprc != NULL) &&
     BadGDICoords(lprc->left,lprc->top,lprc->right,lprc->bottom))
     return NULL;

  // Note: If lprc is NULL we pass it along anyway!
```

```
     return RectVisible(hdc,lprc);
   }


   //////////////////////////////////////////////////////////////////////////
   // uRoundRect: Coord-safe wrapper for the RoundRect API
   //////////////////////////////////////////////////////////////////////////

   BOOL uRoundRect(HDC hdc,int nLeftRect,int nTopRect,int nRightRect,
     int nBottomRect,int nWidth,int nHeight)
   {
     if(BadGDICoords(nLeftRect,nTopRect,nRightRect,nBottomRect,nWidth,nHeight))
       {
        SetLastError(ERROR_INVALID_PARAMETER);
        return FALSE;
       }

     return RoundRect(hdc,nLeftRect,nTopRect,nRightRect,nBottomRect,nWidth,
       nHeight);
   }


   //////////////////////////////////////////////////////////////////////////
   // uScaleWindowExtEx: Coord-safe wrapper for the ScaleWIndowExtEx API
   //////////////////////////////////////////////////////////////////////////

   BOOL uScaleWindowExtEx(HDC hdc,int Xnum,int Xdenom,int Ynum,int Ydenom,
     LPSIZE lpSize)
   {
     if(BadGDICoords(Xnum,Xdenom,Ynum,Ydenom))
       return FALSE;

     return ScaleWindowExtEx(hdc,Xnum,Xdenom,Ynum,Ydenom,lpSize);
   }


   //////////////////////////////////////////////////////////////////////////
   // uScaleViewportExtEx: Coord-safe wrapper for the ScaleViewportExtEx API
   //////////////////////////////////////////////////////////////////////////

   BOOL uScaleViewportExtEx(HDC hdc,int Xnum,int Xdenom,int Ynum,int Ydenom,
     LPSIZE lpSize)
   {
     if(BadGDICoords(Xnum,Xdenom,Ynum,Ydenom))
       return FALSE;

     return ScaleViewportExtEx(hdc,Xnum,Xdenom,Ynum,Ydenom,lpSize);
   }


   //////////////////////////////////////////////////////////////////////////
   // uSetBoundsRect: Coord-safe wrapper for the SetBoundsRect API
   //////////////////////////////////////////////////////////////////////////

   UINT uSetBoundsRect(HDC hdc,CONST RECT *lprcBounds,UINT flags)
   {
     if((lprcBounds != NULL) &&
       BadGDICoords(lprcBounds->left,lprcBounds->top,lprcBounds->right,
       lprcBounds->bottom))
         return 0;

     return SetBoundsRect(hdc,lprcBounds,flags);
   }


   //////////////////////////////////////////////////////////////////////////
   // uSetBrushOrgEx: Coord-safe wrapper for the SetBrushOrgEx API
```

```
///////////////////////////////////////////////////////////////////////////

BOOL uSetBrushOrgEx(HDC hdc,int nXOrg,int nYOrg,LPPOINT lppt)
{
  if(BadGDICoords(nXOrg,nYOrg))
     {
      SetLastError(ERROR_INVALID_PARAMETER);
       return FALSE;
      }

  return SetBrushOrgEx(hdc,nXOrg,nYOrg,lppt);
}

///////////////////////////////////////////////////////////////////////////
// uSetPixelV: Coord-safe wrapper for the SetPixelV API
///////////////////////////////////////////////////////////////////////////

BOOL uSetPixelV(HDC hdc,int X,int Y,COLORREF crColor)
{
  if(BadGDICoords(X,Y))
     {
      SetLastError(ERROR_INVALID_PARAMETER);
       return FALSE;
      }

  return SetPixelV(hdc,X,Y,crColor);
}

///////////////////////////////////////////////////////////////////////////
// uSetRectRgn: Coord-safe wrapper for the SetRectRgn API
///////////////////////////////////////////////////////////////////////////

BOOL uSetRectRgn(HRGN hrgn,int nLeftRect,int nTopRect,int nRightRect,
  int nBottomRect)
{
  if(BadGDICoords(nLeftRect,nTopRect,nRightRect,nBottomRect))
    return FALSE;

  return SetRectRgn(hrgn,nLeftRect,nTopRect,nRightRect,nBottomRect);
}

///////////////////////////////////////////////////////////////////////////
// uSetViewportExtEx: Coord-safe wrapper for the SetViewportExtEx API
///////////////////////////////////////////////////////////////////////////

BOOL uSetViewportExtEx(HDC hdc,int nXExtent,int nYExtent,LPSIZE lpSize)
{
  if(BadGDICoords(nXExtent,nYExtent))
    return FALSE;

  return SetViewportExtEx(hdc,nXExtent,nYExtent,lpSize);
}

///////////////////////////////////////////////////////////////////////////
// uSetViewportOrgEx: Coord-safe wrapper for the SetViewportOrgEx API
///////////////////////////////////////////////////////////////////////////

BOOL uSetViewportOrgEx(HDC hdc,int X,int Y,LPPOINT lpPoint)
{
  if(BadGDICoords(X,Y))
    return FALSE;
```

```
    return SetViewportOrgEx(hdc,X,Y,lpPoint);
}


//////////////////////////////////////////////////////////////////////////////
// uSetWindowExtEx: Coord-safe wrapper for the SetWindowExtEx API
//////////////////////////////////////////////////////////////////////////////

BOOL uSetWindowExtEx(HDC hdc,int nXExtent,int nYExtent,LPSIZE lpSize)
{
  if(BadGDICoords(nXExtent,nYExtent))
    return FALSE;

  return SetWindowExtEx(hdc,nXExtent,nYExtent,lpSize);
}


//////////////////////////////////////////////////////////////////////////////
// uSetWindowOrgEx: Coord-safe wrapper for the SetWindowOrgEx API
//////////////////////////////////////////////////////////////////////////////

BOOL uSetWindowOrgEx(HDC hdc,int X,int Y,LPPOINT lpPoint)
{
  if(BadGDICoords(X,Y))
    return FALSE;

  return SetWindowOrgEx(hdc,X,Y,lpPoint);
}


//////////////////////////////////////////////////////////////////////////////
// uStretchBlt: Coord-safe wrapper for the StretchBlt API
//////////////////////////////////////////////////////////////////////////////

BOOL uStretchBlt(HDC hdcDest,int nXOriginDest,int nYOriginDest,int nWidthDest,
  int nHeightDest,HDC hdcSrc,int nXOriginSrc,int nYOriginSrc,int nWidthSrc,
  int nHeightSrc,DWORD dwRop)
{
  if(BadGDICoords(nXOriginDest,nYOriginDest,nWidthDest,nHeightDest) ||
    BadGDICoords(nXOriginSrc,nYOriginSrc,nWidthSrc,nHeightSrc))
      {
      SetLastError(ERROR_INVALID_PARAMETER);
       return FALSE;
      }

  return StretchBlt(hdcDest,nXOriginDest,nYOriginDest,nWidthDest,nHeightDest,
    hdcSrc,nXOriginSrc,nYOriginSrc,nWidthSrc,nHeightSrc,dwRop);
}


//////////////////////////////////////////////////////////////////////////////
// uTextOut: Coord-safe wrapper for the TextOut API
//////////////////////////////////////////////////////////////////////////////

BOOL uTextOut(HDC hdc,int nXStart,int nYStart,LPCTSTR lpString,int cbString)
{
  if(BadGDICoords(nXStart,nYStart))
      {
      SetLastError(ERROR_INVALID_PARAMETER);
       return FALSE;
      }

  return TextOut(hdc,nXStart,nYStart,lpString,cbString);
}


//////////////////////////////////////////////////////////////////////////////
```

```
//////////////////////////////////////////////////////////////////////
// Misc. Wrappers and Minro Functional Abstractions
//////////////////////////////////////////////////////////////////////
//////////////////////////////////////////////////////////////////////


//////////////////////////////////////////////////////////////////////
// uEMGetLineCount(): Return the number of lines in a multi-line edit ctrl,
// and specially handle the case where the EM_GETLINECOUNT message considers
// a completely empty edit control to have one line of text.
//
// Returns the number of lines in the edit control.
//
// Parameter is not verified
//////////////////////////////////////////////////////////////////////

    DWORD uEMGetLineCount(HWND edit_handle)
    {
      if((lines = SendMessage(edit_handle,EM_GETLINECOUNT,
        0,0)) > 1)
        return lines;
      else
        {
         int start_char = SendMessage)edit_handle,
           EM_LINEINDEX,0,0);
         if(SendMessage(edit_handle,EM_LINELENGTH,
           start_char,0) == 0)
             return 0;
          else
             return 1;
        }
    }


//////////////////////////////////////////////////////////////////////
// Unifying wrapper for the GetShortPathName() API.  Returns 0 with an
// appropriate extended error if the provided string does not name an
// existing file or directory.  Otherwise, the result from calling
// GetShortPathName() is returned to the caller.
//
// Pointer parameters are validated
//////////////////////////////////////////////////////////////////////

DWORD uGetShortPathName(LPCTSTR long_path,LPTSTR buffer,DWORD buffer_len)
{
#ifdef _DEBUG
  if((long_path == NULL) || (buffer == NULL))
    OutputDebugString("\n*** uGetShortPathName: Detected bad parameter! ***\n\n");
#endif

  // This also catches the zero-length and NULL ptr cases
  if(uFileExists(long_path) || uDirExists(long_path))
    {
     SetLastError(0);
     return GetShortPathName(long_path,buffer,buffer_len);
    }
  else
    {
     if((long_path == NULL) || (strlen(long_path) == 0))
       SetLastError(ERROR_BAD_PATHNAME);
      else
       SetLastError(ERROR_PATH_NOT_FOUND);
```

```
        return 0;
    }
}


///////////////////////////////////////////////////////////////////////////
// Return TRUE if the provided string names an existing file (not a
// directory), FALSE otherwise.
//
// Parameter is validated
///////////////////////////////////////////////////////////////////////////

BOOL uFileExists(const char *fn)
{
#ifdef _DEBUG
  if((fn == NULL) || (strlen(fn) == 0))
    OutputDebugString("\n*** uFileExists: Detected bad parameter! ***\n\n");
#endif

  if(fn == NULL || (strlen(fn)) == 0)
    return FALSE;

  DWORD dwFA = GetFileAttributes(fn);

  if(dwFA == 0xFFFFFFFF)
    return FALSE;
  else
    return ((dwFA & FILE_ATTRIBUTE_DIRECTORY) != FILE_ATTRIBUTE_DIRECTORY);
}


///////////////////////////////////////////////////////////////////////////
// Return TRUE if the provided string names an existing directory, FALSE
// otherwise.
//
// Parameter is validated
///////////////////////////////////////////////////////////////////////////

BOOL uDirExists(const char *dn)
{
#ifdef _DEBUG
  if((dn == NULL) || (strlen(dn) == 0))
    OutputDebugString("\n*** DirExists: Detected bad parameter! ***\n\n");
#endif

  if(dn == NULL || (strlen(dn)) == 0)
    return FALSE;

  DWORD dwFA = GetFileAttributes(dn);

  if(dwFA == 0xFFFFFFFF)
    return FALSE;
  else
    return ((dwFA & FILE_ATTRIBUTE_DIRECTORY) == FILE_ATTRIBUTE_DIRECTORY);
}


///////////////////////////////////////////////////////////////////////////
// uLBDeselItemRange(): Partial wrapper for the LB_SELITEMRANGEEX message
// that checks for listbox index clipping and removes the need for correct
// index ordering.
//
// Index parameters are validated for clipping
///////////////////////////////////////////////////////////////////////////
```

```
BOOL uLBDeselItemRange(HWND lb, int start, int end)
{
  if(BadLBIndex(start) || BadLBIndex(end))
    return LB_ERR;

  // Ensure the indexes are properly ordered.  For LB_SELITEMRANGEEX to perform
  // a deselection, the indexes we pass it must be in descending order.
  if(start < end)
    {
      int temp = start;
      start = end;
      end = temp;
    }

  return (SendMessage(lb,LB_SELITEMRANGEEX,start,end) != LB_ERR);
}

///////////////////////////////////////////////////////////////////////////
// uLBDeselItemRange(): Partial wrapper for the LB_SELITEMRANGEEX message
// that checks for listbox index clipping and removes the need for correct
// index ordering.
//
// Index parameters are validated for clipping
///////////////////////////////////////////////////////////////////////////

BOOL uLBSelItemRange(HWND lb, int start, int end)
{
  if(BadLBIndex(start) || BadLBIndex(end))
    return LB_ERR;

  // Ensure the indexes are properly ordered.  For LB_SELITEMRANGEEX to perform
  // a selection, the indexes we pass it must be in ascending order.
  if(start > end)
    {
      int temp = start;
      start = end;
      end = temp;
    }

  return (SendMessage(lb,LB_SELITEMRANGEEX,start,end) != LB_ERR);
}

///////////////////////////////////////////////////////////////////////////
// uGetDlgItemInt(): A minimal wrapper for the GetDlgItemInt() API that
// provides a more accommodating interface for normal Windows usage.
///////////////////////////////////////////////////////////////////////////

BOOL uGetDlgItemInt(HWND hDlg,int nIDDlgItem,UINT* lpValue,BOOL bSigned)
{
  BOOL rc;
  DWORD value;

  value = GetDlgItemInt(hDlg,nIDDlgItem,&rc,bSigned);

  if(rc)
    {
      *lpValue = value;
      return TRUE;
    }
  else
    return FALSE;
}
```

```
///////////////////////////////////////////////////////////////////////////
// uGetSysColor(): A minimal wrapper for the GetDlgItemInt() API that
// screens out color index values that are not supported under Win32s.
//
// Returns TRUE if the index was valid and a color was returned, FALSE
// otherwise.
//
// Note the version dependencies!  This function assumes that Win32s will not
// have a version number greater than 3.51 before it knows about the new new
// Windows 95-only color indexes.  It also assumes that the highest color
// index value (in WINUSER.H) is COLOR_INFOBK (24) for Windows 95, and
// COLOR_BTNHIGHLIGHT (20) pre-Windows 95.
///////////////////////////////////////////////////////////////////////////

BOOL uGetSysColor(int nIndex,DWORD *color)
{
  if((((IsVer351OrLater()) && ((nIndex < 0) || (nIndex > COLOR_INFOBK)) ) ||
    (!IsVer351OrLater()) && ((nIndex < 0) || (nIndex > COLOR_BTNHIGHLIGHT)))
    return FALSE;
  else
    {
     *color = GetSysColor(nIndex);
      return TRUE;
    }
}


///////////////////////////////////////////////////////////////////////////
// uGetPrivateProfileString(): A wrapper for the GetPrivateProfileString()
// API that removes the potential for ambiguity in its indication of
// success or failure.  See the
//
// Returns TRUE if the entire request was completed, FALSE otherwise.
///////////////////////////////////////////////////////////////////////////

BOOL uGetPrivateProfileString(LPCTSTR lpAppName,LPCTSTR lpKeyName,
 LPCTSTR lpDefault,LPTSTR lpReturnedString,DWORD nSize,LPCTSTR lpFileName)
{
  // First, try the underlying API with the caller's parameters...
  DWORD result1 = GetPrivateProfileString(lpAppName,lpKeyName,lpDefault,
   lpReturnedString,nSize,lpFileName);

  // If we hit one of the ambiguous conditions, then we have to try again
  // with a local buffer to see if we really got the whole result.  See the
  // API documentation for details on the nSize -1 and nSize - 2 conditions.
  if((((lpAppName == NULL) || (lpKeyName == NULL)) && (result1 == nSize - 2)) ||
   (((lpAppName != NULL) && (lpKeyName != NULL)) && (result1 == nSize - 1)))
    {
     char *local_buffer = (char *)malloc(nSize + 1);
     if(local_buffer == NULL)
       return FALSE;

     // Retry, using our own buffer but the caller's other parameters.
     DWORD result2 = GetPrivateProfileString(lpAppName,lpKeyName,lpDefault,
      local_buffer,nSize + 1,lpFileName);

     free(local_buffer);  // Whatever happened, we're done with this

     // If we got the same result both times it was a false alarm
     if(result2 == result1)
       return TRUE;
     else
```

```
         // If we didn't, then the caller's buffer was too small
          return FALSE;
      }
   else
     // The caller got lucky on the first try, so we just return TRUE
     return TRUE;
}
```

# *Epilog*

*Youth, what man's age is like to doth show,*
*We may our ends by our beginnings know.*

Sir John Denham

*I have seen the future, and it works.*

Lincoln Steffens

In the Introduction, I gave you a snapshot of the state of the Windows world when I started writing this book. Now it's time to close that circle and recount some of the things that happened while this book was in development.

I do this for two reasons. First and simplest, I know that some people will find amusement in this list years from now, as we all hurtle into the future at 133MHz, and today's breaking news turns into painfully quaint remembrances. Second, this gives me one last chance to remind you that this book is still a work in progress, and that I want to hear from you. As I write this in late October of 1995, I'm already making plans for the second edition of this book and other projects, so don't be a stranger, OK?

On to the soon-to-be-quaint details:

- IBM buys Lotus in a $3.6 billion deal, and later announces that their desktop software offerings will be sold largely under the Lotus name.

- Sales of Borland's Delphi, as well as general interest in the product, are very strong. I receive numerous e-mails asking for advice on which language to use. Many are from people who want to switch from C++ to something else, Delphi being the primary candidate.

- July 14, 1995: Windows 95 "goes gold" and is released to manufacturing to begin the creation of the millions of floppies and CDs that will be on store shelves August 24th. On this date, the U.S. Department of Justice is supposedly still investigating the legality of bundling The Microsoft Network access software with Windows 95. The general perception is that Microsoft is gambling by going into production before this matter is settled; if the DOJ says that Microsoft can't bundle the MSN access software, then Redmond will be stuck with millions of tiny Frisbees and coasters.

- July 26, 1995, Borland surprises the investment community by posting a $2.8 million profit, in part thanks to having sold 125,000 copies of Delphi in its first full quarter of availability.

- Tiger Software issues a catalog (Volume V, Issue 10) before Windows 95 is released that says: "Unlike any other operating system, Windows 95 actually enables you to accomplish many varied tasks at once—without waiting for them to be completed individually." This is a stunning revelation to the millions of people (including your faithful correspondent) who have multitasked programs under Windows 3.1, Windows NT, OS/2, Unix, and mainframe operating systems for years. I guess until Windows 95 came along we were all breaking the laws of physics and doing the impossible. Go figure.

- August 24, 1995: Windows 95 becomes generally available.

- Intel announces that its successor to the Pentium chip, which had previously been known by its James Bondian code name P6, will be known as the Pentium Pro. Presumably those of us running plain old Pentiums had really purchased Pentium Amateurs.

- It becomes generally known that the P6, er, Pentium Pro, will not run 16-bit code nearly as fast as it runs 32-bit code. The reason is related to the segment reloads and partial register operations that are common in 16-bit code, which greatly hinder the heavily pipelined architecture of the Pentium Pro.

- In its September 11, 1995 issue, *InfoWorld* quotes Jim Allchin, senior vice president of Microsoft's Business Systems Division as saying, "There will be no product convergence [the products in question being Windows 95 and Windows NT], because there's no single product that can meet the needs of every kind of customer." (The comment in brackets is mine, not *InfoWorld*'s.) According to this article, he also said, "We expect to see Win95 and its successors broaden in the consumer market. Long term, we want NT to be the standard for corporations on the desktop and server." Before this announcement, Microsoft's plan (supposedly) was to converge Windows 95 and Windows NT into a single product one or two releases after Windows 95. Assuming Microsoft sticks to this new plan, the Windows world just changed around us, yet again.

- In late September, 1995, the United States Supreme Court agrees to hear the Lotus/Borland look and feel copyright case. Whatever the outcome, this decision will likely have significant repercussions across the software industry.

# *Index*

# M

Magic car duster, 102

Maintenance cost, 40

Maisky, Mischa, 9

Major functional abstraction, 260

Mandelbrot set, 282

MAPI.DLL, 93, 169, 170

Maria, 48

Mathematicians and cabinetmakers
  (programmers as), 20

Maxey, David, 369

Maximize button, 191

MAX_DIR, 347

MAX_PATH, 347-348

MAZELORD, 374, 379-380

MegaZero, 15, 214, 237, 286

MEGAZERO.DAT, 237

Mehta, Zubin, 9

memset(), 24

Message boxes, 309

MessageBox(), 239, 67

Meyers, Scott, 9

MFC, 59, 161, 170, 176, 181, 189-190, 195,
  197-198, 285-286, 300, 310, 420, 65
    as a thin layer, 253, 261

MFC30.DLL, 161, 176

Micrografx, 427

Microsoft Developer Network, 36, 72,
  277, 429
    CD, 111-112

Microsoft Haters, 375

Microsoft Lovers, 376

*Microsoft Systems Journal*, 160

Microsoft Word, 180

Microsoft's Developer Network
  CD, 127, 131

Midori, 10

Minimize button, 191

Minimized programs, 282, 286

Minor functional abstraction, 259

Mischel, Jim, 8

Modeless dialogs, 292

Monsters and/or Mac users, 362

Monty Python, 291

MoveFileEx(), 414

MOVEFILE_DELAY_UNTIL_REBOOT, 414

MoveToEx(), 408

MS Write, 232

MSDOS.SYS, 226

MSPAINT.EXE, 354, 358

Multimedia ToolBook, 430

MultiPad, 374

Multiple dots, 348

Multiple inheritance, 117

Multiple Windows installations, 48

Multithreading, 302

Murray, James D., 10

Mystery Science Theater 3000, 10

m_nCmdShow, 181, 195

# N

Naming conventions, 265

Nannyisms, 13

Neanderthal, 108

Nelson, Mark, 131

Neo-Luddite, 101

Nested classes, 147

New Yawkers, 358

New York programmers, 21

Nietzsche, Friedrich, 435

NIH syndrome, 109

NOICON, 406

Non-TRUE TRUEs, 274

NORMAL.DOT, 223

Norton Navigator, 56, 174, 228, 326, 338

Norton Taskbar, 338

Norton Utilities, 163

Notepad, 283

Not OK button, 359, 363

Novell, 129

NTFS, 222

Null Pointer Award for Bad Design, 387

Null-terminated strings, 120

Nu-Mega Technologies, Inc., 125, 428, 381

# CORIOLIS GROUP BOOKS
# Order Form

Name _____

Company _____

Address _____

City/State/ZIP _____

Phone _____

VISA/MC # _____  Expires: _____

Signature for charge orders: _____

| Quantity | Description | Unit Price | Extension |
|----------|-------------|------------|-----------|
|          |             |            |           |
|          |             |            |           |
|          |             |            |           |
|          |             |            |           |
|          |             |            |           |
|          |             |            |           |
|          |             | **TOTAL**  |           |

**FAX, Phone, or
send this order form to:**

**The Coriolis Group
7339 E. Acoma Drive, Suite 7
Scottsdale, AZ 85260**

FAX us your order at (602) 483-0193
Phone us your order at (800) 410-0192
Check out our online site at http://www.coriolis.com

Form: 58-6

# What's on the CD-ROM?

The companion CD-ROM for this book contains all the source code from the book as well as some shareware and freeware programs that may help you in your programming endeavors. If you like them, contact the manufacturers for details on purchasing the full packages.

Here is a breakdown of the directory structure of the CD:

\SOURCE      All the source code from the book

\TOOLS       This directory contains helpful applications and tools that may make you more productive

Here are brief descriptions of a few of the tools you'll find on the companion CD-ROM:

**Application:** Paint Shop Pro V3.11

**Where on CD-ROM:** \TOOLS\PSP3

**Where Online:** http://www.winternet.com/~jasc/index.html

**Description:** The complete windows graphics program for image creation, viewing, and manipulation. Features include painting, photo retouching, image enhancement and editing, color enhancement, image browser, batch conversion, and TWAIN scanner support. Also included are 20 standard image-processing filters and 12 deformations. The program supports Adobe style image processing plug-in filters. Also, over 30 file formats are supported, including JPEG, Kodak Photo-CD, PBM, and GIF. This is one graphics package you won't want to be without. It has many of the features of much more expensive graphics programs at a fraction of the cost.

**Application:** WinZip V5.6

**Where on CD-ROM:** \TOOLS\WINZIP

**Where Online:** http://www.winzip.com/winzip/

**Description:** WinZip brings the convenience of Windows to the task of compressing and uncompressing ZIP files—without requiring PKZIP and PKUNZIP. It features an intuitive point-and-click drag-and-drop interface for viewing, running, extracting, adding, deleting, and testing files in archives. ARJ, LZH, and ARC files are supported via external programs. WinZip also interfaces to most virus scanners so that you can check your compressed files before you run them. New in WinZip 5.6 is built-in support for popular Internet file formats: TAR, gzip, and Unix compress. Now you can use WinZip to access most of the compressed files you download from the Internet.

**Application:** InstallShield Express

**Where on CD-ROM:** \TOOLS\INSTSHLD

**Where Online:** http://www.installshield.com/

**Description:** InstallShield Express is a beta version of Sterling's latest installation mechanism. Their software is probably some of the most popular for doing custom installation routines. This is a beta version, so don't try to use this version to create any commercial setup programs. This beta does, however, give you a good demonstration of both the power and features of InstallShield.

**Where on CD-ROM:** \TOOLS\DRAGNZIP\WIN31
\TOOLS\DRAGNZIP\WIN95

**Where Online:** http://www.canyonsw.com/

**Description:** Drag And Zip lets you quickly and easily compress and decompress files. To compress files, you select files, and then click the right mouse button to select Drag And Zip from a shortcut menu or drag the files you want zipped to a zipper icon. Next, you provide a destination path and a name for the compressed, ZIP file, which Drag And Zip then creates. This is all done from within Windows with Drag And Zip's built-in compression program—andwithout the need for PKZIP. Extracting files from a ZIP file is accomplished by double clicking on the file or by dragging it to the zipper icon. A viewer window will appear, showing the contents of the ZIP file. From this viewer window, users can select files for extracting, deleting, launching, or viewing. Drag And Zip can also be used as an interface to PKZIP, LHA, GnuZip, and tar programs. Drag And Zip works in conjunction with World Wide Web browsers and includes a built-in virus scanner.

**Where on CD-ROM:** \TOOLS\DRGNFILE\WIN31
\TOOLS\DRGNFILE\WIN95

**Where Online:** http://www.canyonsw.com/

**Description:** Drag And File is one of the most powerful file manager available. In addition to the standard copy, move, view, and delete functions, Drag And File gives you other file management options that no other file manager provides. In Drag And File, you can select directories, even across drives, and list the files in those directories; list the files on selected drives; list duplicate files; and copy, move, view, and drag and drop files from multiple Drag And File windows in one operation. The multi-associate feature lets you specify more than one application to be associated with a data file. For example, you can launch a bitmap (BMP) file and choose any of a number of application programs—such as Paintbrush, Word Art and Paint Shop Pro—to edit the file.

**Where on CD-ROM:** \TOOLS\DRAGNVEW\WIN31
\TOOLS\DRAGNVEW\WIN95

**Where Online:** http://www.canyonsw.com/

**Description:** Drag And View allows you to view the contents of your files in a format similar to the way they will appear in the application with which they were created. Drag And View also can display numerous word processing documents, spreadsheets, databases, archives, and bitmapped and vector graphics. Viewing files is as easy as selecting the files, clicking the right mouse button, and selecting Drag And View from the shortcut menu or dragging them to the Drag And View icon. Up to 100 files can be dragged to the Drag And View icon and you can use Drag And View's tool bar to scroll through the files. Selections of any view can be copied to the Windows Clipboard or printed. All viewers have Search and Go To functions. You can open up as many Drag And View windows as you want to for viewing and comparing files.

## Stickies! Special Discount for Readers of

## *"Zen of Windows 95 Programming"*

Return this coupon with your order to Lou Grinzo, P. O. Box 8636, Endwell, NY 13762-8636, and you can license Stickies! for only $19.95 per copy. That's one-third off the normal price. This price includes the registered disk (with extensive online help and a user's manual in the form of an MS Write file), plus a lifetime 50% discount on disk upgrades to Stickies! releases after version 4.0.

If you place your order before Stickies! 4.0 is available (in early 1996), you will receive a *free* upgrade to the new version.

See the order form included with the evaluation copy of Stickies! for complete pricing details, plus information on sales tax and shipping costs to locations outside the U.S. *To qualify for this discount, your order must include this original coupon. No copies will be accepted.*